Lecture Notes in Computer Science 13306

More information about this series at https://link.springer.com/bookseries/558

Sakae Yamamoto · Hirohiko Mori (Eds.)

Human Interface and the Management of Information

Applications in Complex Technological Environments

Thematic Area, HIMI 2022
Held as Part of the 24th HCI International Conference, HCII 2022
Virtual Event, June 26 – July 1, 2022
Proceedings, Part II

 Springer

Editors
Sakae Yamamoto
Tokyo University of Science
Tokyo, Saitama, Japan

Hirohiko Mori
Tokyo City University
Tokyo, Japan

ISSN 0302-9743   ISSN 1611-3349 (electronic)
Lecture Notes in Computer Science
ISBN 978-3-031-06508-8   ISBN 978-3-031-06509-5 (eBook)
https://doi.org/10.1007/978-3-031-06509-5

This Springer imprint is published by the registered company Springer Nature Switzerland AG
The registered company address is: Gewerbestrasse 11, 6330 Cham, Switzerland

Foreword

Human-computer interaction (HCI) is acquiring an ever-increasing scientific and industrial importance, as well as having more impact on people's everyday life, as an ever-growing number of human activities are progressively moving from the physical to the digital world. This process, which has been ongoing for some time now, has been dramatically accelerated by the COVID-19 pandemic. The HCI International (HCII) conference series, held yearly, aims to respond to the compelling need to advance the exchange of knowledge and research and development efforts on the human aspects of design and use of computing systems.

The 24th International Conference on Human-Computer Interaction, HCI International 2022 (HCII 2022), was planned to be held at the Gothia Towers Hotel and Swedish Exhibition & Congress Centre, Göteborg, Sweden, during June 26 to July 1, 2022. Due to the COVID-19 pandemic and with everyone's health and safety in mind, HCII 2022 was organized and run as a virtual conference. It incorporated the 21 thematic areas and affiliated conferences listed on the following page.

A total of 5583 individuals from academia, research institutes, industry, and governmental agencies from 88 countries submitted contributions, and 1276 papers and 275 posters were included in the proceedings to appear just before the start of the conference. The contributions thoroughly cover the entire field of human-computer interaction, addressing major advances in knowledge and effective use of computers in a variety of application areas. These papers provide academics, researchers, engineers, scientists, practitioners, and students with state-of-the-art information on the most recent advances in HCI. The volumes constituting the set of proceedings to appear before the start of the conference are listed in the following pages.

The HCI International (HCII) conference also offers the option of 'Late Breaking Work' which applies both for papers and posters, and the corresponding volume(s) of the proceedings will appear after the conference. Full papers will be included in the 'HCII 2022 - Late Breaking Papers' volumes of the proceedings to be published in the Springer LNCS series, while 'Poster Extended Abstracts' will be included as short research papers in the 'HCII 2022 - Late Breaking Posters' volumes to be published in the Springer CCIS series.

I would like to thank the Program Board Chairs and the members of the Program Boards of all thematic areas and affiliated conferences for their contribution and support towards the highest scientific quality and overall success of the HCI International 2022 conference; they have helped in so many ways, including session organization, paper reviewing (single-blind review process, with a minimum of two reviews per submission) and, more generally, acting as goodwill ambassadors for the HCII conference.

This conference would not have been possible without the continuous and unwavering support and advice of Gavriel Salvendy, founder, General Chair Emeritus, and Scientific Advisor. For his outstanding efforts, I would like to express my appreciation to Abbas Moallem, Communications Chair and Editor of HCI International News.

June 2022   Constantine Stephanidis

HCI International 2022 Thematic Areas
and Affiliated Conferences

Thematic Areas

- HCI: Human-Computer Interaction
- HIMI: Human Interface and the Management of Information

Affiliated Conferences

- EPCE: 19th International Conference on Engineering Psychology and Cognitive Ergonomics
- AC: 16th International Conference on Augmented Cognition
- UAHCI: 16th International Conference on Universal Access in Human-Computer Interaction
- CCD: 14th International Conference on Cross-Cultural Design
- SCSM: 14th International Conference on Social Computing and Social Media
- VAMR: 14th International Conference on Virtual, Augmented and Mixed Reality
- DHM: 13th International Conference on Digital Human Modeling and Applications in Health, Safety, Ergonomics and Risk Management
- DUXU: 11th International Conference on Design, User Experience and Usability
- C&C: 10th International Conference on Culture and Computing
- DAPI: 10th International Conference on Distributed, Ambient and Pervasive Interactions
- HCIBGO: 9th International Conference on HCI in Business, Government and Organizations
- LCT: 9th International Conference on Learning and Collaboration Technologies
- ITAP: 8th International Conference on Human Aspects of IT for the Aged Population
- AIS: 4th International Conference on Adaptive Instructional Systems
- HCI-CPT: 4th International Conference on HCI for Cybersecurity, Privacy and Trust
- HCI-Games: 4th International Conference on HCI in Games
- MobiTAS: 4th International Conference on HCI in Mobility, Transport and Automotive Systems
- AI-HCI: 3rd International Conference on Artificial Intelligence in HCI
- MOBILE: 3rd International Conference on Design, Operation and Evaluation of Mobile Communications

List of Conference Proceedings Volumes Appearing Before the Conference

1. LNCS 13302, Human-Computer Interaction: Theoretical Approaches and Design Methods (Part I), edited by Masaaki Kurosu
2. LNCS 13303, Human-Computer Interaction: Technological Innovation (Part II), edited by Masaaki Kurosu
3. LNCS 13304, Human-Computer Interaction: User Experience and Behavior (Part III), edited by Masaaki Kurosu
4. LNCS 13305, Human Interface and the Management of Information: Visual and Information Design (Part I), edited by Sakae Yamamoto and Hirohiko Mori
5. LNCS 13306, Human Interface and the Management of Information: Applications in Complex Technological Environments (Part II), edited by Sakae Yamamoto and Hirohiko Mori
6. LNAI 13307, Engineering Psychology and Cognitive Ergonomics, edited by Don Harris and Wen-Chin Li
7. LNCS 13308, Universal Access in Human-Computer Interaction: Novel Design Approaches and Technologies (Part I), edited by Margherita Antona and Constantine Stephanidis
8. LNCS 13309, Universal Access in Human-Computer Interaction: User and Context Diversity (Part II), edited by Margherita Antona and Constantine Stephanidis
9. LNAI 13310, Augmented Cognition, edited by Dylan D. Schmorrow and Cali M. Fidopiastis
10. LNCS 13311, Cross-Cultural Design: Interaction Design Across Cultures (Part I), edited by Pei-Luen Patrick Rau
11. LNCS 13312, Cross-Cultural Design: Applications in Learning, Arts, Cultural Heritage, Creative Industries, and Virtual Reality (Part II), edited by Pei-Luen Patrick Rau
12. LNCS 13313, Cross-Cultural Design: Applications in Business, Communication, Health, Well-being, and Inclusiveness (Part III), edited by Pei-Luen Patrick Rau
13. LNCS 13314, Cross-Cultural Design: Product and Service Design, Mobility and Automotive Design, Cities, Urban Areas, and Intelligent Environments Design (Part IV), edited by Pei-Luen Patrick Rau
14. LNCS 13315, Social Computing and Social Media: Design, User Experience and Impact (Part I), edited by Gabriele Meiselwitz
15. LNCS 13316, Social Computing and Social Media: Applications in Education and Commerce (Part II), edited by Gabriele Meiselwitz
16. LNCS 13317, Virtual, Augmented and Mixed Reality: Design and Development (Part I), edited by Jessie Y. C. Chen and Gino Fragomeni
17. LNCS 13318, Virtual, Augmented and Mixed Reality: Applications in Education, Aviation and Industry (Part II), edited by Jessie Y. C. Chen and Gino Fragomeni

39. CCIS 1582, HCI International 2022 Posters - Part III, edited by Constantine Stephanidis, Margherita Antona and Stavroula Ntoa
40. CCIS 1583, HCI International 2022 Posters - Part IV, edited by Constantine Stephanidis, Margherita Antona and Stavroula Ntoa

http://2022.hci.international/proceedings

Preface

Human Interface and the Management of Information (HIMI) is a Thematic Area of the International Conference on Human-Computer Interaction (HCII), addressing topics related to information and data design, retrieval, presentation and visualization, management, and evaluation in human computer interaction in a variety of application domains, such as, for example, learning, work, decision, collaboration, medical support, and service engineering. This area of research is acquiring rapidly increasing importance towards developing new and more effective types of human interfaces addressing the new emerging challenges, and evaluating their effectiveness. The ultimate goal is for information to be provided in such a way as to satisfy human needs and enhance quality of life.

The related topics include, but are not limited to the following:

- Service Engineering: Business Integration, Community Computing, E-commerce, E-learning and e-education, Harmonized Work, IoT and Human Behavior, Knowledge Management, Organizational Design and Management, Service Applications, Service Design, Sustainable Design, and User Experience Design.
- New HI (Human Interface) and Human of QOL (Quality of Life): Electric Instrumentation, Evaluating Information, Health Promotion, E-health and its Application, Human Centered Organization, Legal Issues in IT, Mobile Networking, and Disasters and HCI.
- Information in VR, AR, and MR: Application of VR, AR, and MR in Human Activity, Art with New Technology, Digital Museum, Gesture/movement Studies, New Haptic and Tactile Interaction, Information of Presentation, Multimodal Interaction, and Sense of Embodiment (SoE) in VR and HCI.
- AI, Human Performance, and Collaboration: Automatic Driving Vehicles, Collaborative Work, Data Visualization and Big Data, Decision Support Systems, Human AI Collaboration, Human Robot Interaction, Humanization of Work, Intellectual Property, Intelligent System, Medical Information System and Its Application, and Participatory Design.

Two volumes of the HCII 2022 proceedings are dedicated to this year's edition of the HIMI Thematic Area, entitled Human Interface and the Management of Information: Visual and Information Design (Part I) and Human Interface and the Management of Information: Applications in Complex Technological Environments (Part II). The first focuses on topics related to human-centred design approaches, information design and quality, visual design, visualization and big data, and information, cognition and learning, while the second focuses on topics related to the appearance and embodiment of robots and avatars, information in virtual and augmented reality, and information in complex technological environments.

Papers of these volumes are included for publication after a minimum of two single-blind reviews from the members of the HIMI Program Board or, in some cases, from members of the Program Boards of other affiliated conferences. We would like to thank all of them for their invaluable contribution, support, and efforts.

June 2022   Sakae Yamamoto
                                                               Hirohiko Mori

Human Interface and the Management of Information Thematic Area (HIMI 2022)

Program Board Chairs: **Sakae Yamamoto,** Tokyo University of Science, Tokyo, Japan, and **Hirohiko Mori,** Tokyo City University, Tokyo, Japan

- Yumi Asahi, Tokyo University of Science, Japan
- Michitaka Hirose, University of Tokyo, Japan
- Yasushi Ikei, University of Tokyo, Japan
- Keiko Kasamatsu, Tokyo Metropolitan University, Japan
- Daiji Kobayashi, Chitose Institute of Science and Technology, Japan
- Kentaro Kotani, Kansai University, Japan
- Hiroyuki Miki, Oki Consulting Solutions, Japan
- Miwa Nakanishi, Keio University, Japan
- Ryosuke Saga, Osaka Prefecture University, Japan
- Katsunori Shimohara, Doshisha University, Japan
- Yoshinobu Tamura, Yamaguchi University, Japan
- Takahito Tomoto, Tokyo Polytechnic University, Japan
- Kim-Phuong L. Vu, California State University, USA
- Tomio Watanabe, Okayama Prefectural University, Japan
- Takehiko Yamaguchi, Suwa University of Science, Japan

The full list with the Program Board Chairs and the members of the Program Boards of all thematic areas and affiliated conferences is available online at

http://www.hci.international/board-members-2022.php

HCI International 2023

The 25th International Conference on Human-Computer Interaction, HCI International 2023, will be held jointly with the affiliated conferences at the AC Bella Sky Hotel and Bella Center, Copenhagen, Denmark, 23–28 July 2023. It will cover a broad spectrum of themes related to human-computer interaction, including theoretical issues, methods, tools, processes, and case studies in HCI design, as well as novel interaction techniques, interfaces, and applications. The proceedings will be published by Springer. More information will be available on the conference website: http://2023.hci.international/.

General Chair
Constantine Stephanidis
University of Crete and ICS-FORTH
Heraklion, Crete, Greece
Email: general_chair@hcii2023.org

http://2023.hci.international/

Contents – Part II

Information in Virtual and Augmented Reality

Information in Complex Technological Environments

Contents – Part I

Visual Design

Visualization and Big Data

Information, Cognition and Learning

Recommender Systems

Research on Household Product Design Based on Design Knowledge Hierarchy and Text Mining—Taking Aroma Diffuser as an Example

Zinan Chen, Xingguo Zhang, Xinyu Zhu, and Zhenyu Gu[✉]

Shanghai Jiao Tong University, Shanghai, China
zygu@sjtu.edu.cn

Abstract. Online review data on e-commerce websites is one of the most important channels that reflect user demands and preferences. This work takes household aroma diffusers products as the study object, conducts text mining based on design knowledge hierarchy (DKH) to explore a user demand acquisition and analysis method to obtain the structural relationship among multiple demands then evaluate the importance, so as to help develop product improvement strategies and product design positions. Applying the method in this work, three design positions of household aroma diffusers are defined with the typical part option clusters, and a specific design is proposed.

Keywords: Online reviews · Text mining · Design knowledge hierarchy · Product design · Aroma diffusers

1 Introduction

More than 70% of the total cost of product development lies in product design. In the product design process, especially in the early stage of product conceptualization, it is important to understand user demand to determine the design position and specific features of products [1]. For demand acquisition, traditional methods, such as questionnaires and interviews, are time-consuming, labor-intensive, and highly subjective [2]. At present, online e-commerce platforms have become the main channel for users to purchase consumer products. Researches have shown that the product features and their corresponding emotional responses can be extracted through text mining of online reviews [3], which is an effective and objective method to collect user demand information [4]. However, the features extracted by text mining based on the existing lexicon are still un-structured data, so further analysis methods are required to clarify the structural relationship of demands and evaluate them, so as to transform user demand into available design knowledge and product guidelines.

This work introduces a method to obtain structured user demand from text mining of online reviews for product conceptual design based on DKH (Design Knowledge Hierarchy). Taking the design of household aroma diffusers as a case, the DKH is introduced to establish the lexicon for text mining and emotion analysis, with a set of

4,200 reviews on JD.com (the biggest online retailer in China). The features in the reviews can be efficiently identified according to the lexicon, and the structural relationship between their corresponding demands can be explored according to the inheritance logic of DKH. KANO Model is used to evaluate the importance of demands. Thus, the demands corresponding to the features can be transformed into a structured expression. The results effectively reflect the user demands of household aroma diffusers, from which we summarize the key points for design into five improvement strategies: appearance, function, experience, quality, and sales service. Furthermore, after evaluating the part options of DKH, three feasible product design clusters are generated: the efficiency-oriented, the economy-oriented, and the aesthetics-oriented. Finally, according to our proposed method, a specific design of household aroma diffusers is proposed.

2 Related Works

2.1 Text Mining

The purpose of data mining is to find useful information from a large amount of data, among which text mining is a big topic. For the previous studies on the text mining of user reviews, analysis methods usually include text content analysis, sentiment analysis, and text link analysis [5, 6], through which user's thoughts, attitudes, and emotional tendencies, and the hidden association between relevant keywords can be explored. Now text mining has been proved to be of great significance in many fields and has high commercial potential value [7].

Wang et al. combined the text mining of online reviews with explanatory econometric modeling to effectively evaluate the impact of washing machine product features on user satisfaction [8]. Hu et al. applied content analysis with repertory grid analysis (RGA) to obtain a comprehensive insight into hotel brand positioning [3, 9]. Wang et al. developed an unsupervised perceptual text mining method combined with Kansei Engineering to classify emotional opinions so as to effectively identify the product features and emotional attributes and visualize their relationships [3].

The review text is natural language so word segmentation and information encoding must be carried out to translate it into computer language for subsequent mining and analysis. Typical preprocessing methods include tokenization, stop word removal, word stemming tag replacement, etc. [10]. Unlike English texts, which are easy to segment words according to spaces, for Chinese texts, it is necessary to segment words according to standard corpora based on statistics [11]. Jieba, the open-source Chinese word segmentation application of Python language, is one of the most commonly used Chinese word segmentation systems, so we choose Jieba as our segmentation tool.

2.2 Design Knowledge Hierarchy

DKH is derived from Kelly's personal construct theory [12]. In general, DKH is a four-layer top-down architecture for presenting product design concepts. The DKH consists of four layers: category, component, part, and part option, with the logical relationship of decomposition and inheritance. The parent layer can be further decomposed into multiple child layers until decomposed into multiple part options to provide design alternatives. Previous studies have shown that DKH is a simplified and effective design knowledge structure, which can help the design team to coordinate and visualize the concept [12], facilitate the evaluation of the structural consistency of the concepts [13], and moreover, effectively improve the product competitiveness with the user participation in customization of DKH [1]. The typical process of product conceptual design using DKH includes the following steps: 1. Obtain the terms of product knowledge through design experts, literature retrieval, or other sources; 2. Sort the terms to form a hierarchical structure; 3. generate clusters from different combinations of options to form conceptual design schemes through further evaluation of each design option.

This work aims to obtain structured user demands from the text mining of online reviews for product conceptual design. Applying DKH's advantage of the clear hierarchy of product knowledge, the DKH of aroma diffusers and structured lexicon of product features are established according to the method described above. Text mining is conducted based on this hierarchy to ensure the relative independence of various types of features after extraction and classification, so as to transform user demand into a low-coupling and orderly structured expression, which guides the subsequent conceptual design.

3   Research Process

The whole process of this study consists of five stages (Fig. 1): data preparation, data processing, demand mining, design positioning, and design practice.

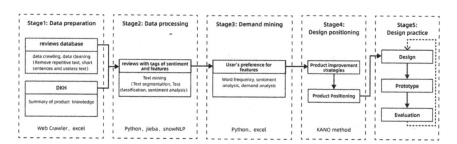

Fig. 1. Research framework

3.1   Data Preparation

The work in the stage of data preparation includes the establishment of a review database and design knowledge hierarchy of certain household products.

In this paper, the database of users' reviews on household aroma diffusers was created through data crawling and data cleaning. It consists of 4,200 reviews of 30 high-selling household aroma diffusers from JD.com. These reviews were collected through the web crawler platform Octopus. The 30 products selected have different diffusing principles, styles, and functions. Users are allowed to post additional reviews about their feelings after purchasing and using the product for a long time on e-commerce websites. Since these additional reviews have indispensable emotional and semantic information, they were combined with the original reviews of the user to obtain complete data when establishing the review database. Besides, the data crawled by the web crawler may contain invalid information and the quality of online reviews is uneven, therefore data cleaning is a necessity. In this paper, we adopted the cleaning rules of removing repetitive text, short sentences, and useless text to reduce noise interference during text mining. Specifically, useless reviews lack specific evaluations on products based on user experience and are only generalized by adjectives. For example, "I have not used it yet but it looks good". This kind of review was excluded since the lack of actual reference value for user demand mining. The removal of repetitive text and short sentences was automatically conducted through excel, and the selection and removal of useless text were conducted by the three authors of this paper manually. According to the rules of data cleaning mentioned above, a total of 3,763 valid reviews remained for subsequent research.

The design knowledge hierarchy for household aroma diffusers (Fig. 2) is established based on the features of existing products and the experience of four expert designers.

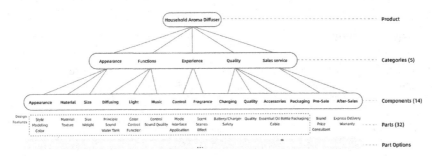

Fig. 2. DKH of household aroma diffusers

3.2 Data Processing

In the stage of data processing, we use Python and related toolkits to carry out text segmentation, text classification, and sentiment analysis.

Text segmentation is the basis of text mining, which refers to splitting a complete sentence into single words in order to analyze the sentimental and semantic information. In this paper, Jieba is used for segmentation. Since the reviews from e-commerce websites contain many colloquial words, we loaded a customized dictionary based on review contents and popular words into the prefix dictionary of Jieba to improve the accuracy of text segmentation.

Text classification is a typical task of natural language processing that classifies original text into specified categories according to a corpus. It helps to quickly locate the features mentioned in the reviews, contributing to demand mining. In this study, the 14 features from the third layer of DKH (components) were used as the classification labels considering the review contents and the difficulty of demand mining. Three authors of this paper extended the lexicon for the 14 product features based on the list of the manufacturer's specifications and high-frequency words from the user reviews. The lexicon was used to classify the review database. For example, if a user review contains words such as "lavender", it will be automatically labeled as "fragrance".

Sentiment analysis refers to extracting subjective sentiments from natural language. In this study, SnowNLP, a strong text processing toolkit for Chinese, is applied for sentiment analysis. The sentiment module of SnowNLP uses a shopping-related training set and performs well in sentiment analysis of online reviews from e-commerce websites, thus it is suitable for this study. By calling its sentiments function, we obtained the sentimental tendency of each user review, which was presented with a score of [0,1]. A score of 0 refers to extremely negative emotions, and 1 refers to positive emotions. In order to further explore user preferences for certain features of the product, we divided the reviews labeled as 14 features into three groups. Reviews with sentiment scores of [0,0.3), [0.3, 0.8] and (0.8, 1] were classified as negative, neutral, and positive respectively.

Table 1. Sentiment analysis of user reviews

Components	Positive emotions	Neutral emotion	Negative emotions	Total reviews
Music	100.00%	0.00%	0.00%	11
Appearance	88.58%	8.03%	3.39%	1445
Packaging	82.50%	8.33%	9.17%	360
Size	78.86%	11.54%	9.60%	823
Light	78.56%	13.07%	8.38%	597
Pre-sale	75.59%	12.62%	11.79%	721
Material	75.42%	5.08%	19.49%	118
Fragrance	74.12%	15.01%	10.86%	1399
Control	73.05%	16.47%	10.49%	1087
After-sales	72.25%	11.69%	16.06%	573
Quality	71.64%	11.19%	17.16%	536
Diffusing	67.88%	18.16%	13.96%	1834
Charging	66.06%	12.73%	21.21%	165
Accessories	49.06%	22.64%	28.30%	53

As shown in Table 1 the feedback focuses on "fragrance", "appearance" and "control", indicating that users pay great attention to the appearance and core functions of household aroma diffusers. More than 80% of the reviews labeled as "music", "appearance", and "packaging" expressed positive emotion while more than 20% of those labeled as "charging" and "accessories" expressed negative emotions. However, it should be acknowledged that the statistical reliability of the reviews of "music" and "accessories" is not high because of the small sample size. That may be partly explained by the fact that the household aroma diffusers with music function account for a relatively small proportion of all the existing products.

3.3 Demand Mining

In the stage of demand mining, we obtained user demands by counting the high-frequency words of the classified reviews. As mentioned in the previous section, the reviews have been labeled with corresponding features based on the "components" layer of DKH and been classified with sentimental tendencies. For each of the 14 components, we extracted words from the reviews involved and sorted them in descending order according to their proportion in positive, neutral, and negative reviews. Then we generated a table of these top words, from which we summarized user demands.

Table 2. The top15 words of the reviews labeled as "Diffusing" (translated from Chinese)

No.	Words in positive reviews	Words in neutral reviews	Words in negative reviews
1	Even	Steam	Mist
2	Pervade	Fragrance	Heavy on oil
3	Ultrasound wave	Wet	Spray
4	Moist	Molecule	Water outlet
5	Rapid	No-fire	Block up
6	Pure dew	Area	Cotton swab
7	Humidify	Mist outlet	Air outlet
8	Full	Fast	Dry
9	Nebulizing	Evaporate	Mist outlet
10	Compatible	Deodorize	Water-soluble
11	Speedy	Heavy on oil	Mist amount
12	Purify	Material	Unpleasant smell
13	Range	Moisturize	Flavoring essence
14	Diffusing	Mist	Wet
15	Delicate	Moist	Diffusing

Taking the data of "Diffusing" as an example, the top 15 words from positive, neutral, and negative reviews labeled as "diffusing" are shown in Table 2. Combined with the analysis of the original reviews, it can be found that users are more concerned about the diffusing speed and effect. The delicate, and even mist, and the rapid and comprehensive diffusing effect have been well received. Regarding the aroma diffusers with humidification function, many users place them in air-conditioned rooms and are satisfied with moisturizing effects. Most of the negative reviews mentioned that (i) the mist amount is uneven, (ii) the essential oil consumption is large, (iii) the diffusing range is small, and

(iv) the diffusing effect is not significant. Other negative feedback also mentioned that the mist outlet is easy to be blocked by droplets and impurities, and the mist may wet the fabrics and furniture, which seriously reduce the user experience and satisfaction. Applying this analysis method, we explored the specific user preferences for 14 product features. Table 3 shows some of the results of demand mining.

Table 3. Partial results of demand analysis

Components	Positive	Negative
Appearance & size	The appearance is suitable for home decoration style (modern & simple, vintage & elegant, etc.) The appearance is unique and innovative The size is compact and does not take up too much space	The product is too large and bulky in size
Material	The material leaves users a good impression in terms of visual and tactile The material is of good quality and has no unpleasant smell	The surface of the product is rough, burr, and thin The material is of poor quality and production process and has a heavy odor
...	...	...

3.4 Design Positioning

Product Improvement Strategies. Kano Model can effectively extract hidden user demands from the sentimental tendency of online reviews and guide the product development and iteration. In this process, the features of user demand can be identified into their varying importance of at-tributes. According to the PR-kano (a kind of Kano analysis based on the review data) [14], must-be attributes determine the minimum product standards, which will lead to dissatisfaction when not fulfilled while do not increase satisfaction when fulfilled. They are the primary problems to be solved in product upgrading, which often appear in negative reviews. User satisfaction is directly proportional to the satisfaction of one-dimensional attributes, which almost equally appear in various reviews. Attractive attributes can sharply generate high user satisfaction when met, which are mostly reflected in positive reviews. one-dimensional attributes and attractive attributes suggest the direction of product evolution, as the competitiveness and reputation of products will be improved when meeting these attributes. In This section, we summarize the product improvement strategies from the following five aspects based on kano theory and the results of demand mining mentioned in the previous section.

(1) Appearance

Generally speaking, the appearance of the product belongs to the one-dimensional attributes and attractive attributes. The household aroma diffusers are placed in the home environment to help improve the quality of life and spiritual pleasure, so users expect them to match the overall home style or show the owner's aesthetic taste. Therefore, the appearance style can usually be simple, elegant, or vintage. High-standard surface treatment and material arrangement can improve visual beauty and tactile feeling. Therefore, manufacturers can choose high-quality materials such as metal, glass, and wood, or add some simple texture. The product size should be as small as possible without taking up too much space on the premise of meeting its basic functions. In addition, manufacturers can further study the subjective preferences of target users according to user persona and fashion trends to launch creative and stylized appearance designs.

(2) Function

The core function of aroma diffusion belongs to the must-be attributes, which should be focused on. Aroma diffusers with ultrasonic atomization can diffuse aroma and meanwhile adjust humidity, but users may be unsatisfied with the water storage. Considering the use scenario, it is recommended to set a water tank with a larger capacity (more than 500 ml) in the product iteration to ensure the running time. Meanwhile, the manufacturers need to adjust the components and structure of the atomization parts to ensure that the mist is uniform and the nozzle is not easy to be blocked. The aroma diffusers are mostly used in office and sleep scenes, where the mute effect is highly required. Manufacturers need to reduce the noise of water flow and the motor during operation by setting sound insulation materials.

Other additional functions such as music and lighting are the one-dimensional or attractive attributes, which can be flexibly set by the manufacturer according to its own product positioning. The addition of lighting and music functions can increase the sense of quality and atmosphere, and expand the use scenarios, thus perhaps increase user satisfaction. Manufacturers need to pay attention to their operation convenience and independent adjustability. For example, in the lighting function, users expect to independently adjust the color, brightness, operation duration, and other parameters of the light.

(3) Experience

Interactive experience belongs to the must-be attributes and one-dimensional attributes. Due to the great differences in users' preferences for aromas, the adjustability of aroma diffusion mode is important. It is recommended to provide parameter adjustments such as operating power and operating duration to support users to control aroma concentration according to the environment and personal preferences. In product iteration and development, attentions need to be paid to the simplicity and consistency of the user interface and the convenience of manipulation. The manufacturers shall select the most maneuverable position according to the product form when setting the physical interface, and prompt the functions through clear diagrams, lights, etc. In addition, the diffuser can be connected to the smart home ecosystem, and inter-active methods such as app control and voice control can be used to simplify the control, so as to improve the user experience. Meanwhile, the multi-scene use of the product is one of the attractive attributes, so the storage of a variety of essential oils and the aroma switching of multiple scenes can better meet the diversified demand of heavy users.

(4) Quality
Product quality is a must-be attribute. Features such as product workmanship, material selection, surface treatment, and electrical safety greatly affect users' perception of product quality. The aroma diffusers with rough workmanship, thin materials, heavy peculiar smell, surface burrs, and functional defects cannot meet the basic product standards and user expectations. Therefore, the manufacturers should normalize the production standards, improve the overall quality of the products and pay attention to quality control. Although the electrical safety is often mentioned in the positive reviews, the design of safety ensurance is indispensable. The manufacturers should provide circuit protection measures against dry burning, overturning, and power failure through sensor monitoring on the basis of meeting the national standards. Further considering the use scenario, split structure, waterproof and anti-skid accessories, and fireproof materials can be used to reduce the potential safety hazards. Moreover, the quality of product packaging and accessories will also affect users' perception of product quality.

(5) Sales Service
Although the sales service does not belong to product design features, it also affects user satisfaction to a great extent. Users are more concerned about the merchant's service attitude and service quality. Before sale, it is necessary to provide users with detailed consulting services, such as recommending product models, confirming product functions and accessories, etc. For aroma diffusers, the products with great subjective preference differences, the introduction, and recommendation of essential oils with different smells and efficacy are helpful for users, so relevant services can be provided before sales. In the after-sales stage, the sellers need to timely and properly deal with the problems fed back by users, so as to minimize the dissatisfaction of users caused by product problems.

Product Positioning. According to the improvement strategies for the existing household aroma diffusers products summarized above, we extract 27 product design features (excluding sales services) from the fourth layer of DKH, and match them with part options to generate a design option table, partly shown in Fig. 3.

Based on the results of user demand mining, the experts and designers have discussed and formulated three product positioning for household aroma diffusers: the efficiency-oriented, the economy-oriented, and the aesthetics-oriented. The three types of positioning focus on different aspects and can meet the demand of different user groups. Designers can select different clusters from the design options table for specific design objectives and quickly generate design concepts. Table 4 shows three typical part option clusters.

(1) Efficiency-oriented
The efficiency-oriented cluster focuses on the upgrading of core functions to meet the demand of heavy users, emphasizing the diffusion effect and interaction mode. This kind of product adopts a more effective nebulizing mode and high-capacity battery power supply, which is convenient for users to move and use. According to the demand

- PARTS -		- PART OPTIONS -		
①	Style ▲▲	Modern&Simple	Vintage&Elegant	Innovative&Novel
②	Material ▲▲	Plastic	Metal	Others
③	Size ▲	Big	Medium	Small
④	Interface ▲▲	Physical	Virtual	Physical+Virtual
⑤	Diffusing principle ▲▲▲	Nebulizing	Ultrasonic	
⑥	Water tank ▲▲	Big	Medium	Not included
⑦	Charging ▲▲	Battery	Charger	
⑧	Light function ▲	Indictation	Illumination	Atmosphere creation
⋮				
㉗	Music ▲	Included	Not included	

Fig. 3. Table of design options for home aroma diffusers

for functional fragrance in different scenarios, the product can set multiple essential oil tanks, and provide both basic presets and custom modes to support users to switch fragrance and operation modes. The modes and specific parameters can be adjusted on the virtual interface, and the equipment status information is presented on the product with indicative lights, so as to simplify the product appearance and meet the usage habits of target users. The appearance is mainly simple with high-quality materials and surface treatment technology to enhance physical texture.

(2) Economy-Oriented
The economy-oriented cluster focuses on the dual demand of aroma diffusion and humidification, emphasizing upgrading products and improving user experience. This kind of product adopts ultrasonic atomization to diffuse aroma and is equipped with a large-capacity water tank and power adapter to ensure that the product can work stably for a long time. Considering the relatively simple function, the switching of preset modes can be controlled through the physical interface on the product, and the adjustment of user-defined modes is carried out in the virtual interface. Special attention should be paid to the safety of power for such products. A split structure can be adopted to enable users to disassemble and wash the water tank more conveniently. Functions such as water level monitoring and circuit protection are recommended so as to reduce potential safety hazards. The appearance is suggested to be simple and generous with a good material texture.

Table 4. List of typical design options

Design parts	Efficiency -oriented	Economy -oriented	Aesthetics -oriented
Style	Modern & simple	Modern & simple	Vintage & elegant, innovative & novel
Material	Plastic	Plastic	Others besides plastic
Surface	Frosted	Glossy	Glossy
Size	Medium	Big	Medium
Interface	Virtual	Physical + virtual	Virtual
Mode	Preset + customization	Preset	Preset + customization
Diffusing	Nebulizing	Ultrasonic	Ultrasonic
Essential oil tank	2 +	1	2 +
Water tank	Not included	Big	Medium
Charging	Battery	Charger	Charger
Light function	Indication	Illumination	Atmosphere creation
Music	Not included	Included	Included
Safety	Circuit protection	Water level monitoring + circuit protection	Water level monitoring + circuit protection

(3) Aesthetics-Oriented

The aesthetic-oriented cluster focuses on the multi-sensory experience and integrates the functions of aroma diffusion, humidification, atmosphere lighting, and music playing, which can be applied to yoga, meditation, reading, and other scenes to create an immersive atmosphere. It is recommended to improve the product structure to support the storage and release of a variety of essential oils. In addition to the basic preset modes, users can also customize and control parameters such as flavor aroma type, flavor concentration, and working duration through the virtual interface. This kind of product is suggested to be powered by a wired power supply and provide water level monitoring and circuit protection functions to ensure safe use. More creative shapes, materials, and surface treatments can be appropriately selected for such products to increase the characteristics and texture.

4   Design Practice

In the design practice stage, we select the efficient-orientated cluster as an example and carry out the conceptual design based on the design options sorted out in the previous section.

The product appearance is modern and simple. The modeling shape is transformed from basic geometric elements and the color is mainly white embellished with a small amount of secondary color. As shown in Fig. 4 there are three typical design concepts, and concept 3 is selected for further refinement.

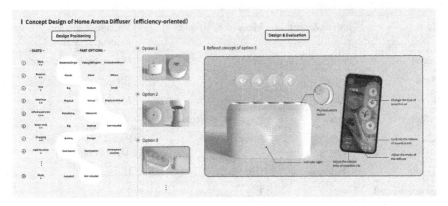

Fig. 4. The concept design of efficiency-oriented home aroma diffusers

In order to simplify the interaction mode and improve the user experience, only one physical button is set as the on-off switch. Other functions including adjusting the release time and oil type can be set in the mobile app. This product supports the storage of up to 4 different essential oils, and RFID readers are set in the device. Therefore, the types of oils are automatically identified after installation and the information is synchronized with the app without other operations. Users can select the corresponding type of essential oil to release according to the needs of specific scenes. Both the preset modes and user-defined modes can be chosen to adjust the intensity and duration of the release of aroma. When the diffuser receives commands from the app, the aroma diffusion module starts to work. The pixel LED light on the front of the device serving as an indicator dynamically shows the operation status and the type of aroma being released.

After the conceptual design, we develop an interactive prototype for experience. As shown in Fig. 5, the shell and internal structure of the prototype are 3D printed. The inner hardware part mainly includes esp8266 module, motor drive module, LED pixel screen, and air pump. The background control program is written by Arduino. The prototype is used to test and evaluate the usability and experience of the concept, verify the feasibility of the scheme, and find problems for iterative optimizations.

The design case shows the simple steps from demand mining to design output. In actual projects, designers often need to put forward multiple design concepts according to different product feature clusters, and then get the final scheme after scheme selection, scheme refinement, comprehensive evaluation, and multiple iterative optimizations according to their own brand positioning and target population.

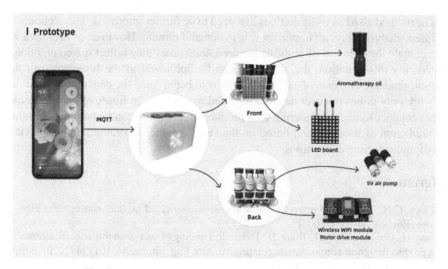

Fig. 5. The structure of the prototype of the refined concept

5 Discussion

Nowadays, online reviews data is an important channel for manufacturers and designers to obtain user feedback, which has attracted increasing research attention. However, the result of text mining from online reviews with traditional methods is an unstructured demand data, which cannot be directly transformed into product design guidelines. Generally, this paper introduces a design method based on design knowledge hierarchy and text mining on online user reviews, by which feature preferences and user demands can be obtained and the mapping relationship between features and demands is established to guide the conceptual design.

In order to illustrate how the proposed method is carried out and prove the effectiveness, we take the design of household aroma diffusers as a case and use this method to mine a set of 4,200 review data. Based on the conclusions of user demand mining, four expert designers conclude five improvement strategies for appearance, function, experience, quality, and sales service. Furthermore, we position three types of household aroma diffusers: efficiency-oriented, economy-oriented, and aesthetics-oriented, and select typical features from the table of design options (Fig. 3) to generate clusters of design options. In this paper, we take efficiency-oriented aroma diffusers as an example and carry out a conceptual design. Based on the option cluster, we create several concepts, select one for refinement through discussion and develop an interactive prototype for experience, evaluation, and subsequent iterations.

The advantages of this method can be highlighted in two aspects: (i) Compared with the traditional methods of demand acquisition, the research cycle is shorter, saving much time and cost, and is not limited by time and space (ii) Structured and detailed user demands can be efficiently extracted to create effective design improvement strategies, and provide more intuitive and reliable guidance for design practice.

The method also has its limitations that need to be further improved. The accuracy of sentiment analysis plays an important role in demand mining. However, as user reviews often contain the opinions of multiple features, sometimes they reflect mixed emotions. Considering this situation, the algorithm can be optimized in the future to split the different semantic contents of each review, so as to better mine the demand. In addition, this work only mines the user demand reflected by reviews. In future research, we can further conduct Kansei engineering with product pictures, and conduct dynamic mining and prediction of user demand based on the sales volume, favorable rate, and review data of multiple time dimensions.

References

1. Chen, C.-H.: Trends and research issues in customer-oriented product conceptualization. J. Des. Environ. 87–106 (2006)
2. Sun, H., Guo, W., Shao, H., Rong, B.: Dynamical mining of ever-changing user requirements: a product design and improvement perspective. Adv. Eng. Inform. **46**, 101174 (2020). https://doi.org/10.1016/j.aei.2020.101174
3. Wang, W.M., Li, Z., Tian, Z.G., Wang, J.W., Cheng, M.N.: Extracting and summarizing affective features and responses from online product descriptions and reviews: a kansei text mining approach. Eng. Appl. Artif. Intell. **73**, 149–162 (2018). https://doi.org/10.1016/j.eng appai.2018.05.005
4. Zheng, L.: The classification of online consumer reviews: A systematic literature review and integrative framework. J. Bus. Res. **135**, 226–251 (2021). https://doi.org/10.1016/j.jbusres. 2021.06.038
5. Villeneuve, H., O'Brien, W.: Listen to the guests: text-mining Airbnb reviews to explore indoor environmental quality. Build. Environ. **169**, 106555 (2020). https://doi.org/10.1016/j. buildenv.2019.106555
6. Zhou, J., Zhou, M.: Sentiment analysis of elderly wearable device users based on text mining. In: International Conference on Applied Human Factors and Ergonomics, pp. 360-5 (2021)
7. Gupta, V., Lehal, G.S.: A survey of text mining techniques and applications. J. Emer. Technol. Web Intel. **1**, 60–76 (2009)
8. Wang, Y., Lu, X., Tan, Y.: Impact of product attributes on customer satisfaction: An analysis of online reviews for washing machines. Electron. Commer. Res. Appl. **29**, 1–11 (2018). https://doi.org/10.1016/j.elerap.2018.03.003
9. Hu, F., Trivedi, R.H.: Mapping hotel brand positioning and competitive landscapes by text-mining user-generated content. Int. J. Hosp. Manag. **84**, 102317 (2020). https://doi.org/10. 1016/j.ijhm.2019.102317
10. Weiss, S.M.I.N., Zhang, T., Damerau, F.J.: Overview of Text Mining. Text Mining. Springer, New York, NY (2005)
11. Day, M., Lee, C.: Deep learning for financial sentiment analysis on finance news providers. In: 2016 IEEE/ACM International Conference on Advances in Social Networks Analysis and Mining (ASONAM), pp. 1127–34 (2016). https://doi.org/10.1109/ASONAM.2016.7752381
12. Yan, W., Chen, C.-H., Chang, W.: An investigation into sustainable product conceptualization using a design knowledge hierarchy and Hopfield network. Comput. Ind. Eng. **56**, 1617–1626 (2009). https://doi.org/10.1016/j.cie.2008.10.015
13. Yan, W., Khoo, L.P., Chen, C.-H.: A QFD-enabled product conceptualisation approach via design knowledge hierarchy and RCE neural network. Knowl.-Based Syst. **18**, 279–293 (2005). https://doi.org/10.1016/j.knosys.2004.09.001
14. Zhang, W.: Review data driven customer need model research based on product performance lexicon. China Mecha. Eng. **31**, 1866–1876 (2020)

Mitigating Position Bias in Review Search Results with Aspect Indicator for Loss Aversion

Hiroki Ihoriya[✉], Masaki Suzuki, and Yusuke Yamamoto[✉]

Shizuoka University, Hamamatsu, Japan
{ihoriya,suzuki,yamamoto}@design.inf.shizuoka.ac.jp

Abstract. Conventional review websites display a list of item search results with average rating scores (i.e., star ratings). We propose a method of designing snippets that encourage users to search items on review websites more carefully. The proposed snippets include aspect indicators that identify negative aspects if the item has a good star rating and vice versa. We expect the aspect indicators will help mitigate biases due to ranking position and star ratings by making users feel a "loss" if they do not carefully examine items. Our user study showed that the proposed method of including aspect indicators for loss aversion made participants spend more time searching a list of search results and checking items with worse star ratings, especially when searching hospitals. In contrast, showing aspect indicators that conformed to star ratings caused shortsighted review searches.

Keywords: Information retrieval · Cognitive bias · Human factor · Search user interaction

1 Introduction

Many people use review websites to purchase products and services, which we refer to as *items* in this paper. Similar to conventional web search engines such as Google, review websites provide users with a function to rank and list items. A typical search engine results page (SERP) lists items with their average customer ratings (i.e., *star ratings*) as well as a *snippet* including their name and description. Although star ratings are helpful for quickly understanding other customers' satisfaction with items, the ratings themselves and ranking lists based on them often cause a cognitive bias in users. This leads to shortsighted decision-making on review websites; users often choose items only because they have good star ratings or high-ranking positions in review searches.

Researchers have confirmed various cognitive biases that occur during web searches and have reported that these biases often negatively influence information seeking and outcomes [3]. One of the most famous cognitive biases is the *position bias*, in which people often preferentially click higher-ranked items on a list of search results [4]. As another example of bias, White [18] reported that users

© The Author(s), under exclusive license to Springer Nature Switzerland AG 2022
S. Yamamoto and H. Mori (Eds.): HCII 2022, LNCS 13306, pp. 17–32, 2022.
https://doi.org/10.1007/978-3-031-06509-5_2

HOTEL RELIEF

⭐⭐⭐⭐⭐ 5.0

Bad Points: toilet cleanness   parking lot

HOTEL RELIEF offers ultimate comfort and luxury. It is conveniently located near the
Sapporo city's tourist attractions. Decorated & furnished in a modern style. Indoor pool
and a fitness center. We provide you with a comfortable and relaxing time.

THE GLORY HOTEL

⭐⭐⭐ 3.2

Good Points: restaurant   Wi-Fi

THE GLORY HOTEL is located in beautiful nature. The hotel serves a buffet
breakfast daily, and room service is also available. Each room has a microwave,
a private bathroom with a bathtub, and a hairdryer. High-speed Wi-Fi is available
in all rooms.

Fig. 1. Overview of snippets with aspect indicators for loss aversion in hotel review
search.

prefer positive information to negative information. As noted above, most review
websites rank and list items along with star ratings on SERPs. Therefore, good
star ratings can promote the effect of position bias, which can cause users to prior-
itize higher-ranked items and make shortsighted decisions without detailed exploration, even though such items may have flaws that are unacceptable to the user.
For example, a user may be searching a hotel review website, and toilet cleanliness is a critical consideration for them. Some hotels may gain good star ratings
from other customers and be ranked high, even though their toilets are not clean.
However, conventional SERPs do not display such negative information. Therefore, the user may be biased by the ranking position and star rating and select a
high-ranked hotel with unclean toilets.

In this paper, we propose a method of designing snippets that mitigate the
biases of the ranking position and star rating to encourage users to search items
on review websites more carefully. Our method is inspired by the *loss aversion
rule*, which explains the tendency of people to prefer avoiding the pain of losing
more to acquiring an equivalent gain. In our proposed method, the snippets
display *aspect indicators* that identify negative aspects of items with good star
ratings and vice versa as Fig. 1 shows. Such snippets should help make users feel
a "loss" if they do not carefully examine items and mitigate the position bias
when searching the review website.

Our contributions can be summarized as follows:

– We designed snippets with aspect indicators for loss aversion to mitigate the
  position and star rating biases of review searches.
– We performed a user study to confirm the effectiveness of presenting snippets
  with aspect indicators relative to snippets without aspect indicators.
– We demonstrated the negative effects of aspect indicators that conform to
  star ratings rather than display contrasting information.

2   Related Work

2.1   Cognitive Bias in Information Retrieval

Many studies have focused on cognitive biases in information retrieval. White [18] investigated the influence of users' prior beliefs on their web search behavior and showed that users prefer to view information that supports their prior beliefs and are reluctant to view information that supports the opposite belief. Baeza-Yates [4] demonstrated a position bias in user searches where higher rankings on SERPs tend to result in higher click rates. Craswell et al. [7] developed a probabilistic model of how position bias occurs in the real world. Yue et al. [21] reported on the influences of the attractiveness of the title, URL, summary, and other aspects of items on SERPs on users' clicking behavior. Their results revealed that items with attractive titles can bias users' clicking behavior. Ieong et al. [10] demonstrated the existence of a domain bias, where users tended to trust webpages published in a specific domain. Lindgaard et al. [12] found that people are more likely to trust a webpage that looks attractive.

2.2   Changing Behaviors and Attitudes During Web Searches

Several studies have investigated interactions that change the behaviors and attitudes of web search users. Agapie et al. [1] proposed a search user interface (UI) that places a halo around a query box if a user inputs long queries. They reported that their proposed interface encourages users to input longer queries for better search results. Harvey et al. [9] demonstrated that providing examples of high-quality queries can help users formulate queries more effectively. Scott et al. [5] proposed the Search Dashboard system to visualize the search and browsing behaviors of web search users. Their experimental results showed that their system improves the search behavior of users.

Some researchers have studied methods of promoting careful information seeking. Munson et al. [15] proposed a web browser extension that indicates whether the user's browsing history is politically balanced. Hamborg et al. [8] developed NewsBird, which aggregates international news from various perspectives. Liao et al. [11] showed that indicating the opinion stance and expertise of the information sender could mitigate the echo chamber effect. Yamamoto et al. [19] proposed the `Query Priming` system, which inserts queries that evoke critical thinking during query completion/recommendation in a search system. They showed that this system helps make web search users more likely to correct their queries and visit websites that provide relevant data and evidence-based information. Yamamoto et al. [20] also proposed the `Personalization Finder` web browser extension, which reveals the effects of web search personalization and promotes careful web searching.

2.3   Product Search

With the proliferation of e-commerce and review sites, product search is a branch of information retrieval that has gained increasing attention. Ai et al. [2]

proposed an explanatory search model that focuses on the gap between the search system and the customer's perception of product relevance. Empirical experiments showed that their proposed model could produce reasonable explanations for search results. To predict the overall rating on review websites more accurately, Cheng et al. [6] presented a novel aspect-aware latent factor model that estimates the importance of an aspect of an item for a user. Qiu et al. [16] used online experimental data from Airbnb users to investigate whether the average star rating or number of reviews was more important for indicating users' trustworthiness. Their results showed that the relative effectiveness of ratings and reviews varies greatly depending on the strength of the differentiating power of reputation. To measure the actual quality of a product, McGlohon et al. [14] analyzed 8 million product reviews collected from multiple review sites.

The approaches presented in these studies are helpful for users who proactively search for products and services on review websites. However, if users have low motivation to scrutinize products, they tend to make shortsighted decisions based on superficial information such as ranking positions and star ratings. Therefore, promoting a more careful approach to information seeking on review websites is necessary.

3   Proposed Method: Aspect Indicators for Loss Aversion

3.1   Overview

Our proposed method mitigates the bias of ranking position and star ratings on SERPs in review websites by extending snippets to display aspect indicators (i.e., positive/negative aspects of items). The intent is to make users feel a "loss" if they do not scrutinize items more carefully.

Figure 1 illustrates an example where the proposed method is applied to search results in a hotel review website. Aspect indicators are presented along with the snippet of each item based on an analysis of review comments about each item. For example, Hotel Relief has an excellent star rating, but the aspect indicator suggests that some users have complained about its toilet cleanliness. The proposed method determines the polarity of aspect indicators according to the degree of the star rating for an item. If an item has a better star rating than the average rating of items in the search result list, negative aspect indicators are displayed with its snippet to make the user aware of disadvantages. In contrast, when an item has a worse star rating than average, positive aspect indicators are displayed to make the user aware of advantages. For example, the Glory Hotel has a star rating of 3.2, which is lower than average. Thus, the proposed method displays a positive aspect indicator suggesting that the hotel serves an excellent dinner. In this case, we expect that users looking for gourmet food will check the hotel's information in more detail because they do not want to miss the possibility of a good dinner.

3.2   Algorithm to Find Aspect Indicators

Once a review website returns a list of items to a query, the following procedure is adopted to display aspect indicators along with snippets of the items:

1. Analyze the sentiment expressed about entities within review comments about items matching a given query.
2. Determine characteristic entities for each item as aspect indicator candidates considering their frequency in review comments.
3. Calculate the sentiment score of the characteristic entities obtained in Step 2, and classify the entities as positive or negative aspect indicators.
4. Display some of the selected aspect indicators along with each snippet considering the star rating of the item.

In Step 1, the system extracts entities from review comments about searched items and analyzes the sentiment score for each entity. Although various methods have been proposed for entity sentiment analysis [13], we adopted Google Natural Language API[1] to review comments about items listed for a given query. The API then returns a list of entities with sentiment scores ranging from -1.0 to 1.0. For example, an entity sentiment analysis on the comment "This hotel's breakfast was good" would extract "breakfast" as an entity with a sentiment value of 0.75. In Step 2, the system determines characteristic entities for each item as aspect indicator candidates. We used term frequency–inverse document frequency (TF-IDF) weighting to calculate the feature scores of entities extracted in Step 1. Let N be the number of items in a search result list for a query, i_k be the k-th item in the list, and c_{i_k} be a set of review comments about item i_k. Then, the system calculates the TF-IDF score $tfidf(e, i_k)$ of the entity e for item i_k as follows:

$$tfidf(e, i_k) = tf(e, i_k) \times idf(e) \tag{1}$$

$$idf(e) = log\frac{N}{df(e)} \tag{2}$$

where $tf(e, i_k)$ is the frequency of e in review comments about i_k and $df(e)$ is the number of items for which e appears in review comments. For each item, we calculate the TF-IDF values of all entities appearing in its review comments, and we use the top 10 entities as aspect indicator candidates.

In Step 3, we further refine the indicator candidates. Our aim is to present negative or positive aspects of items so that users will feel loss if they do not check them. Therefore, the indicator candidates are classified based on the sentiment intensity in the review comments. The system calculates the average sentiment scores of each indicator candidate appearing in the review comments for each item. When the average sentiment score of an aspect indicator is greater or less than 0.0, the indicator is considered as positive and negative, respectively.

---

[1] Google Cloud Natural Language API: https://cloud.google.com/natural-language/docs/analyzing-entity-sentiment.

In Step 4, the system determines whether to display positive or negative aspect indicators for each item by considering the average rating score (i.e., star rating). If an item has a better star rating than the average star rating for all items returned to a query, then negative aspect indicators are presented along with the snippet. Similarly, positive aspect indicators are presented if the star rating is worse than average.

3.3 Hypothesis

We expect our proposed method mitigates the bias induced by the ranking position and star rating by making users feel a "loss" if they do not scrutinize items more carefully on review websites. We built the following hypotheses:

H1. Aspect indicators for loss aversion encourage users to spend more time reviewing searches more carefully and to compare more items.

H2. Aspect indicators for loss aversion encourage users to check items with low rankings or bad star ratings.

We speculated that the effect of aspect indicators for loss aversion would vary depending on search topics. We expected the aspect indicators to be more effective for critical topics such as health than casual topics such as travel. Therefore, we built an additional hypothesis:

H3. The presentation of aspect indicators for loss aversion is more effective for searches of hospitals than searches of hotels.

4   User Study

We performed an online user study to evaluate the effectiveness of the proposed method of aspect indicators for loss aversion in review searches. The user study was conducted in Japanese on June 22 and 23, 2021.

4.1 Participants

We recruited 560 participants via Lancers.jp, which is a Japanese crowdsourcing service.[2] Before the user study, we also explained our data collection policy, and participants proceeded only if they agreed that we could use the data collected during the search tasks. We excluded 95 participants from the analysis as outliers because they did not complete the tasks or spent an unusually long time performing the tasks.[3] Finally, we analyzed 465 participant responses. All participants who completed the tasks received 150 JPY (approximately 1.50 USD). On average, the participants finished all tasks within 9.18 min.

---

[2] https://lancers.jp/.
[3] We used the 1.5x interquartile range rule to identify outlier participants.

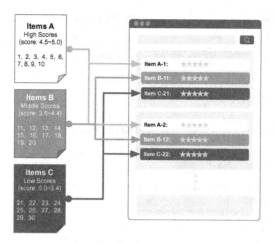

Fig. 2. Manipulation of the search result list.

4.2   Search Tasks

We prepared two topics for the search tasks: hospitals and hotels. According to Hypothesis **H3**, the effectiveness of the aspect indicators varies depending on the importance of the topic. Therefore, we set hospitals as a critical topic and hotels as a non-critical topic.

For each topic, we prepared three search tasks, including a practice task. For the hospital topic, we asked the participants to search for the best hospital where they would want to go for respiratory medicine and cardiology. For the hotel topic, we asked the participants to search for the best hotel to stay in Hokkaido and Tokyo.[4] Each participant performed either the hospital or hotel search task in the user study.

4.3   Search System

We developed a search system to monitor participant behavior during the user study. The system displayed two types of pages: SERPs and detailed pages each linked to an item on the SERP. The SERPs presented a list of 30 items matching a query. Each search result comprised three components common to review search results: the title (item name), star rating (average score of customer ratings), and item description (i.e., snippet). To collect the information displayed in the search results, we crawled two popular review websites[5] before the user study. Then, we collected information on hotels and hospitals relevant to search tasks.

For the user study, we disabled the search system to prevent participants from changing the query for each search task so that a fixed list of 30 items would be

---

[4] Hokkaido and Tokyo are popular travel destinations in Japan.
[5] caloo.com for hospitals and jalan.net for hotels (both websites are in Japanese).

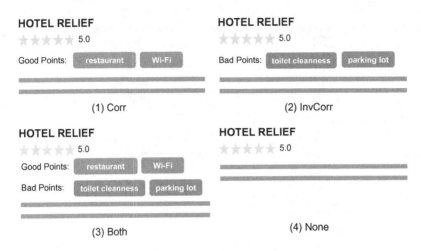

Fig. 3. Four SERP UIs for user study.

displayed. We manipulated the ranking order of the list in the following steps. First, we ordered the collected items by star rating and divided the items into three groups: top 10, middle 10, and bottom 10. Then, we created a list of the items by alternately allocating items from the three groups as described in Fig. 2. One purpose of the user study was to examine whether aspect indicators can mitigate the tendency of users to ignore search results with bad star ratings and prefer high-ranked items with good star ratings. We expected that this ranking manipulation would give participants more opportunities to see items with average or bad star ratings on the list.

The participants could view detailed information on items by clicking each search result in the SERPs. The system displayed a copy of the webpages that we crawled before the study as detailed information on items. We disabled hyperlinks in the detailed pages to prevent the participants from leaving the website of the user study.

Figure 3 illustrates the four SERP UIs that we developed for the user study: Both, Corr, InvCorr, and None. The Both, Corr, and InvCorr UIs are extensions of the None UI. The None UI was the baseline and displayed only titles, star ratings, and item descriptions. The Corr UI displayed positive aspect indicators along with item descriptions for items with good star ratings (better than average) and negative aspect indicators for items with bad star ratings (worse than average). In contrast, the InvCorr UI displayed positive aspect indicators along with item descriptions for items with bad star ratings and negative aspect indicators for items with good star ratings. Finally, the Both UI displayed both positive and negative aspect indicators for each item regardless of the star rating.

Table 1. Participant allocation.

Search topic	Search UI			
	Corr	InvCorr	Both	None
Hotel	61	59	58	60
Hospital	56	61	53	57

4.4 Design and Procedure

We adopted a 2×4 factorial design to examine the effects of two factors: the search topic and search UI condition. The search topic factor had two levels: hospital and hotel. The search UI condition had four levels: Both, Corr, InvCorr, and None.

After the participants agreed to a consent form on Lancers.jp, they moved to our website for the user study. Then, we randomly allocated a search UI condition and search topic to each participant. Table 1 presents the allocation.

First, the participants read a description of the task flow and search system. We also explained our data collection policy. The participants proceeded with the user study only if they agreed that we could use the data collected during the search task. Next, we asked the participants to perform a practice task to familiarize them with the search system. Then, each participant performed two main search tasks with either the hospital or hotel topic. The task order was randomized for each participant. Before each main search task, each participant was presented with the task scenario. An example task scenario for the hospital topic is presented below:

Please assume the following case. One day, you are told that your mother has lung cancer. To help her, you visit a review website to find a hospital offering good treatment regarding respiratory medicine. Check the displayed hospital search results and check several reviews about hospitals. When you come to a satisfactory decision, stop the search, and report your decision.

Then, each participant clicked a "start search" button to display the list of search results. The participants browsed the list to formulate their answers. Once the participants reached their decision, they reported their best choice on our study website. Then, we asked the participants to explain the reason for their decision.

5 Results

We analyzed 465 participant responses to examine the effect of aspect indicators for loss aversion. We employed a non-parametric one-way analysis of variance (ANOVA) (Kruskal-Wallis test) for the UI factor separate from the search topics because the collected data did not follow a normal distribution. We used the Benjamini-Hochaberg FDR test [17] for multiple comparison tests in the post hoc analysis. Effects were considered significant at the significance level $\alpha = 0.05$.

Table 2. Statistics on the search behavior for the hotel search task. The mean and standard deviation (SD) of each response are shown (significance level at ***: 0.001, **: 0.01, and *: 0.05).

Metric	UI condition				p-value
	Corr	InvCorr	Both	None	
Session time (s)	252.9 (156.0)	264.1 (150.0)	289.7 (195.9)	251.2 (163.4)	0.71
SERP dwell Time (s)	55.8 (56.6)	68.8 (59.1)	80.8 (74.1)	63.3 (94.2)	*
Average page dwell time (s)	83.6 (66.1)	94.5 (66.6)	104.8 (67.0)	83.6 (59.0)	0.37
Page view count	4.03 (3.13)	3.91 (4.04)	3.52(2.75)	3.75(3.15)	0.80
Minimum click depth	2.85 (3.34)	5.91 (5.89)	5.41 (5.91)	4.66 (4.32)	***
Average score of clicked items	4.31 (0.18)	4.06 (0.33)	4.16 (0.21)	4.20 (0.21)	***
Score of decided item	4.35 (0.17)	4.11 (0.35)	4.17 (0.24)	4.23 (0.25)	***

Table 3. Statistics on search behavior for the hospital search task. The mean and standard deviation (SD) of each response are shown (significance level at ***: 0.001, **: 0.01, and *: 0.05).

Metric	UI condition				p-value
	Corr	InvCorr	Both	None	
Session time (s)	292.6 (159.2)	276.8 (159.2)	344.6 (196.3)	238.9 (133.3)	*
SERP dwell time (s)	67.5 (52.8)	74.5 (83.5)	91.5 (80.6)	46.4 (44.8)	***
Average page dwell time (s)	82.2 (77.2)	86.4 (59.7)	93.7 (65.2)	77.9 (50.5)	0.37
Page view count	4.56 (3.74)	4.15 (3.65)	4.73 (3.47)	4.48 (3.56)	0.53
Minimum click depth	2.79 (3.67)	3.67 (4.31)	3.93 (4.57)	2.34 (2.84)	0.11
Average score of clicked items	4.06 (0.15)	3.92 (0.32)	3.95 (0.23)	4.08 (0.17)	***
Score of decided item	4.04 (0.23)	3.93 (0.32)	3.9 (0.35)	4.04 (0.26)	*

5.1   Session Time

To investigate the effort that participants put into the tasks, we first analyzed how long participants spent on search tasks (i.e., session time). As indicated in Table 2, we did not observe significant differences between the four UIs for the hotel search tasks ($p = 0.71$). On the other hand, Table 3 indicates statistically significant differences between the four UIs for the hospital search tasks ($p < 0.05$). The post hoc analysis indicated that the mean session times of participants using the Both UI was statistically longer than the times of participants using the None UI for the hospital search tasks (mean: 344.6 vs 238.9; $p < 0.05$).

In summary, these results demonstrate that showing both positive and negative aspects along with each search result encouraged participants to spend more time on the hospital search tasks than the plain SERPs.

5.2   Dwell Times on SERPs and Detailed Pages

Next, to investigate how much time participants spent examining a list of item search results, we analyzed the dwell times on SERPs. As indicated in Tables 2 and 3, we observed significant differences between the four UIs for both the hotel ($p < 0.05$) and hospital ($p < 0.001$) search tasks. The post hoc analysis showed that the UIs did not have a significant effect on the hotel search tasks. In contrast, the mean SERP dwell times of the Corr UI (67.5 s), InvCorr UI (74.5 s), and Both UI (91.5 s) were statistically longer than that of the None UI (46.4 s) for the hospital search tasks (Corr-None: $p < 0.05$; InvCorr-None: $p < 0.05$; Both-None: $p < 0.001$).

We also analyzed the average dwell times on detail pages to investigate how carefully participants read them. We did not observe significant differences between the four UIs for both the hotel ($p = 0.37$) and hospital ($p = 0.37$) search tasks.

In summary, these results indicate that SERPs with any aspect indicators made participants spend more time viewing the search results than SERPs without aspect indicators for hospital search tasks. However, the indicators did not affect the time spent viewing detailed pages.

5.3   Page Views

To investigate whether participants checked multiple information sources, we analyzed how many detailed pages participants viewed (i.e., clicked) during the search tasks (i.e., page views). As indicated in Tables 2 and 3, we observed no significant differences between the four UIs in the hotel ($p = 0.80$) and hospital ($p = 0.53$) search tasks.

5.4   Minimum Click Depth

To investigate whether the participants had a position bias, we examined the ranks of the search results that the participants clicked on to analyze the minimum search result rank (i.e., minimum click depth). We interpreted a greater minimum click depth to mean that the participant checked search results lower on the list.

As presented in Tables 2 and 3, the ANOVA results indicated significant differences between the four UIs in the hotel search tasks ($p < 0.001$). The post hoc analysis revealed that the Corr UI had a smaller mean minimum click depth (2.85) than the InvCorr UI (5.91), Both UI (5.41), and None UI (4.66) (Corr-InvCorr: $p < 0.001$; Corr-Both: $p < 0.01$; Corr-None: $p < 0.01$). However, we observed no significant differences between the four UIs in hospital search tasks ($p = 0.11$).

These results indicate that, when the displayed aspect indicators conformed to the star ratings of the items (i.e., the Corr UI), the participants tended to click shallower search results than for the other UIs in hotel search tasks.

5.5   Rating Scores of Clicked Items

We investigated how aspect indicators affected the star ratings of clicked items (i.e., average score of clicked items). Tables 2 and 3 indicate significant differences between the four UIs in the hotel ($p < 0.001$) and hospital ($p < 0.01$) search tasks.

The post hoc analysis of the hotel search tasks revealed that the `Corr` UI had a statistically greater average score of clicked items (4.31) than the `InvCorr` UI (4.06), `Both` UI (4.16), and `None` UI (4.20) (`Corr`-`InvCorr`: $p < 0.001$; `Corr`-`Both`: $p < 0.001$; `Corr`-`None`: $p < 0.01$). Meanwhile, the post hoc analysis of the hospital search tasks revealed that the `InvCorr` UI and `Both` UI had statistically smaller average scores of clicked items (3.92 and 3.95, respectively) than the `None` UI (4.08) (`InvCorr`-`None`: $p < 0.05$; `Both`-`None`: $p < 0.01$). Furthermore, the `Corr` UI had a statistically larger average score of clicked items (4.06) than the `Both` UI (3.95) ($p < 0.05$).

These results suggest that, when the participants performed hotel search tasks by using the `Corr` UI, they tended to click items with better star ratings than with other UIs. In contrast, when the aspect indicators contrasted with the star ratings of items for hospital search tasks, the participants tended to view items with worse star ratings than when no aspects were displayed on the SERPs.

We also examined the star ratings of items that the participants selected for each task (i.e., decided item score). Tables 2 and 3 indicate significant differences between the four UIs for the hotel ($p < 0.001$) and hospital ($p < 0.05$) search tasks. The post hoc analysis of the hotel search tasks revealed that the `Corr` UI had a statistically larger decided item score (4.35) than the `InvCorr` UI (4.11), `Both` UI (4.17), and `None` UI (4.23) (`Corr`-`InvCorr`: $p < 0.001$; `Corr`-`Both`: $p < 0.001$; `Corr`-`None`: $p < 0.01$). Meanwhile, the post hoc analysis of the hospital search tasks revealed that the `Both` UI had a statistically smaller decided item score (3.90) than the `None` UI (4.04) ($p < 0.05$).

These results show that the `Corr` UI made participants select items with better star ratings as their final answer than other UIs for the hotel search tasks. Furthermore, displaying aspect indicators that contrasted with the star ratings (i.e., the `InvCorr` and `Both` UIs) encouraged participants to select items with worse star ratings for the hospital search tasks.

6   Discussion

The results of the user study revealed that the participants tended to spend more time examining the list of item search results with the `InvCorr` UI and `Both` UI than with the `None` UI for hospital search tasks (Sect. 5.2). In addition, the `InvCorr` UI and `Both` UI did not encourage participants to check more items than the `None` UI for both the hotel and hospital search tasks (in Sect. 5.3). The click-through analysis revealed that the `InvCorr` UI and `Both` UI promoted viewing detailed pages about items with worse star ratings than `None` UI for hospital search tasks (in Sect. 5.5). In particular, the participants using the `Both` UI in hospital search tasks tended to select items with worse star ratings as their final decision than those using the `None` UI.

The InvCorr UI and Both UI displayed aspect indicators that contrasted with the star ratings of items to make users feel loss aversion. The results of the user study led to the following interpretations of their effectiveness:

1. For hospital search tasks, participants using the InvCorr UI and Both UI felt "the loss of not viewing hospital pages with low scores and positive aspects" and "the loss of viewing hospital pages with high scores and negative aspects."
2. Participants spent a longer time viewing the hospital list to think carefully about which hospital to check.
3. They considered hospitals with bad star ratings as candidates if presented with positive aspects.

On the other hand, although participants tended to spend more time on SERPs in the hospital search tasks when using the Corr UI rather than the None UI, the participants also clicked items with better star ratings when using the Corr UI rather than the Both UI.

The Corr UI displayed aspect indicators conforming to the star ratings of items (i.e., positive aspects for items with above-average star ratings and negative aspects for items with below-average star ratings). The results of the user study led to the following interpretations:

1. The Corr UI provided information that reinforced the star ratings of items.
2. Consequently, the participants using the Corr UI spent less time viewing the item lists and jumped to items with higher-ranking positions.

Unlike the InvCorr UI and Corr UI, the Both UI displayed both positive and negative aspects for items regardless of the star rating. We think that the Both UI provided the participants with useful information for decision-making while mitigating the biases caused by the ranking position and star rating. Thus, we concluded that the Both UI could promote more careful information seeking than the InvCorr UI.

The analytical results suggest that the InvCorr UI and Both UI were more effective for the hospital search tasks than for the hotel search tasks. One possible reason for this result may be the degree of risk of the decision. Obviously, hospital selection would have a more significant impact than hotel selection. Thus, the InvCorr UI and Both UI would make the participants feel a greater loss from shortsighted information seeking for hospitals than for hotels.

In summary, displaying aspect indicators that contrast with star ratings could mitigate biases caused by position ranking and star ratings. Consequently, users would spend more time viewing a list of hospital search results and checking hospitals with lower ranking or worse star ratings, although the aspect indicators did not seem to encourage them to compare detailed pages more often. Thus, we concluded that **H1**, **H2**, and **H3** were partially supported.

6.1   Limitations

One limitation of our study concerns the statistical analysis. We adopted a 2×4 factorial design to examine two factors: search topics and search UIs.

We employed a non-parametric one-way ANOVA for search topics because we assumed that hospital search tasks would be considered more crucial than hotel search tasks. However, we needed to statistically analyze the difference between the search topics for a more rigorous discussion. In future studies, we plan to apply statistical models such as generalized linear mixture modeling to analyze the effect of search topics.

Another limitation was our approach to finding aspect indicators for loss aversion. We used TF-IDF weighting to determine aspect indicator candidates for items (i.e., hotels and hospitals). In addition, we used the Google Natural Language API to determine whether the extracted aspect candidates are positive or negative. We think that this approach can be improved to find better aspect indicators.

7 Conclusion

We proposed a method of mitigating the biases of the ranking position and star rating to encourage users to search items on review websites more carefully. Our proposed method extends snippets to display negative aspects of items with good star ratings and vice versa. Thus, the snippets provide information that users could miss if they only looked at star ratings.

The results of an online user study indicated that aspect indicators contrasting with star ratings could encourage users to spend more time viewing a list of hospital search results and to check hospitals with lower rankings or worse star ratings. On the other hand, we found that aspect indicators conforming to star ratings could cause shortsighted information seeking, especially for hotel search tasks. These results imply that snippets should display both positive and negative aspects of items to mitigate biases and let users know additional features of items.

This study had several issues that should be improved upon. We need to examine for which search topics the proposed method would be effective more rigorously. Furthermore, we should improve the method of extracting aspect indicators for loss aversion.

Acknowledgements. This work was supported in part by Grants-in-Aid for Scientific Research (18H03244, 21H03554, 21H03775) from MEXT of Japan.

References

1. Agapie, E., Golovchinsky, G., Qvarfordt, P.: Leading people to longer queries. In: Proceedings of the SIGCHI Conference on Human Factors in Computing Systems. CHI 2013, pp. 3019–3022, ACM, New York (2013)
2. Ai, Q., Zhang, Y., Bi, K., Croft, W.B.: Explainable product search with a dynamic relation embedding model. ACM Trans. Inf. Syst. (TOIS) **38**(1), 1–29 (2019)
3. Azzopardi, L.: Cognitive biases in search: a review and reflection of cognitive biases in information retrieval. In: Proceedings of the 2021 Conference on Human Information Interaction and Retrieval (CHIIR 2021), p. 27–37 (2021)

4. Baeza-Yates, R.: Bias on the web. Commun. ACM **61**(6), 54–61 (2018)
5. Bateman, S., Teevan, J., White, R.W.: The search dashboard: how reflection and comparison impact search behavior, pp. 1785–1794. Association for Computing Machinery, New York (2012). https://doi.org/10.1145/2207676.2208311
6. Cheng, Z., Chang, X., Zhu, L., Kanjirathinkal, R.C., Kankanhalli, M.: MMALFM: explainable recommendation by leveraging reviews and images. ACM Trans. Inf. Syst. (TOIS) **37**(2), 1–28 (2019)
7. Craswell, N., Zoeter, O., Taylor, M., Ramsey, B.: An experimental comparison of click position-bias models. In: Proceedings of the 2008 International Conference on Web Search and Data Mining, pp. 87–94 (2008)
8. Hamborg, F., Meuschke, N., Gipp, B.: Matrix-based news aggregation: Exploring different news perspectives. In: Proceedings of the 17th ACM/IEEE Joint Conference on Digital Libraries. JCDL 2017, pp. 69–78 (2017)
9. Harvey, M., Hauff, C., Elsweiler, D.: Learning by example: training users with high-quality query suggestions. In: Proceedings of the 38th International ACM SIGIR Conference on Research and Development in Information Retrieval. SIGIR 2015, pp. 133–142. ACM (2015)
10. Ieong, S., Mishra, N., Sadikov, E., Zhang, L.: Domain bias in web search. In: Proceedings of the Fifth ACM International Conference on Web Search and Data Mining. WSDM 2012, pp. 413–422. Association for Computing Machinery, New York (2012). https://doi.org/10.1145/2124295.2124345
11. Liao, Q., Fu, W.: Expert voices in echo chambers: effects of source expertise indicators on exposure to diverse opinions. In: Proceedings of the 32nd SIGCHI Conference on Human Factors in Computing Systems. CHI 2014, pp. 2745–2754. ACM (2014)
12. Lindgaard, G., Dudek, C., Sen, D., Sumegi, L., Noonan, P.: An exploration of relations between visual appeal, trustworthiness and perceived usability of homepages. ACM Trans. Comput.-Hum. Interact. **18**(1) (2011). https://doi.org/10.1145/1959022.1959023
13. Liu, Q., Zhang, H., Zeng, Y., Huang, Z., Wu, Z.: Content attention model for aspect based sentiment analysis. In: Proceedings of the 2018 World Wide Web Conference (WWW 2018), pp. 1023–1032 (2018)
14. McGlohon, M., Glance, N., Reiter, Z.: Star quality: aggregating reviews to rank products and merchants. In: Fourth International AAAI Conference on Weblogs and Social Media (2010)
15. Munson, S., Lee, S., Resnick, P.: Encouraging reading of diverse political viewpoints with a browser widget. In: Proceedings of the Seventh International AAAI Conference on Weblogs and Social Media. ICWSM 2013, pp. 419–428 (2013)
16. Qiu, W., Parigi, P., Abrahao, B.: More stars or more reviews? In: Proceedings of the 2018 CHI Conference on Human Factors in Computing Systems, pp. 1–11 (2018)
17. Thissen, D., Steinberg, L., Kuang, D.: Quick and easy implementation of the Benjamini-Hochberg procedure for controlling the false positive rate in multiple comparisons. J. Educ. Behav. Stat. **27**(1), 77–83 (2002)
18. White, R.: Beliefs and biases in web search. In: Proceedings of the 36th International ACM SIGIR Conference on Research and Development in Information Retrieval, pp. 3–12 (2013)
19. Yamamoto, Y., Yamamoto, T.: Query priming for promoting critical thinking in web search. In: Proceedings of the 2018 Conference on Human Information Interaction and Retrieval. CHIIR 2018, pp. 12–21. Association for Computing Machinery, New York (2018). https://doi.org/10.1145/3176349.3176377

20. Yamamoto, Y., Yamamoto, T.: Personalization finder: a search interface for identifying and self-controlling web search personalization. In: Proceedings of the ACM/IEEE Joint Conference on Digital Libraries in 2020. JCDL 2020, pp. 37–46. Association for Computing Machinery, New York (2020). https://doi.org/10.1145/3383583.3398519
21. Yue, Y., Patel, R., Roehrig, H.: Beyond position bias: examining result attractiveness as a source of presentation bias in clickthrough data. In: Proceedings of the 19th International Conference on World Wide Web, pp. 1011–1018 (2010)

Comic Contents Retrieval Support Interface Using Speech Frequencies of Characters

Kaifeng Lei[1]($\boxtimes$), Yoko Nishihara[1], and Ryosuke Yamanishi[2]

[1] College of Information Science and Engineering, Ritsumeikan University, Shiga 5258577, Japan
is0439sp@ed.ritsumei.ac.jp, nisihara@fc.ritsumei.ac.jp
[2] Faculty of Informatics, Kansai University, Osaka 5691095, Japan
ryama@kansai-u.ac.jp

Abstract. Over the past few decades, reading comics has become a globally accepted and appreciated form of entertainment. Although certain comics are easy to be found at bookstores and search engines, it is not guaranteed that readers can find the exact chapter and episode they desire. If the reader happens to find some unread chapters or episodes, It can end up being a spoiler. In this study, the authors do something by hypothesizing that readers can recall the content of comics by looking at the characters' speech frequencies in the already read part. This paper proposes an interface to support the retrieval of comic content by visualizing the speech frequencies of characters in each volume using a stacked area graph. Through experiments, the authors confirmed that the proposed interface could support the retrieval of comic content.

Keywords: Comic computing · Retrieval of comic content · Timeline visualization

1 Introduction

Comics is a form of entertainment that is enjoyed around the world. In the past, comics were mainly published in paper forms in the past but have been currently enjoyed in electronic forms as well with the spread of digital devices. While some people enjoy only one title of a comic at a time, many others read several titles in parallel. For most comics, new episodes and volumes are released at different intervals. Therefore, it is not always clear for the readers to remember how many episodes or volumes he/she has already read. In order to clarify whether or not an episode/volume corresponds to the part he/she has already read, people need to read the story again or search it on the Internet. However, when the reader reads the story and looks it up with a search engine, he/she may get a summary of the story and speeches of the characters. Although there is no problem if the reader has read the part already, but the reader may encounter spoilers if he/she has not read this part. At present, very few systems enable readers to search for certain contents of comics without being exposed to spoilers.

In this study, the authors hypothesize that readers who have read the comic can recall the contents of a comic by checking the characters' speech frequencies in each episode/volume. Based on this hypothesis, the authors propose an interface that supports the retrieval of the contents of a comic by visualizing the time-series changes of the characters' speech frequencies using a stacked area graph. Since the frequency information does not correspond to the story directly, it should have the advantage of preventing spoilers to a certain extent. However, even without the use of text messages, the appearance and exit of comic characters can lead to the spoiler of the plot. When people watch a novel or a movie, they are likely to begin imagining what will happen afterwards [5]. The advent and departure of a character are one of the significant events in a story. If it is spoiled before the designed moment, the enjoyment may be reduced [1]. For example, for a user who likes a character very much, knowing that the character will not appear in the future may cause her to lose interest in the comic. In this paper, The authors propose a method to support the retrieval of comic content with fewer spoilers.

2   Related Work

On a search engine, it is possible to search for comics using bibliographic information such as the title and author name. However, it is difficult to find desired contents of comic books with such searching methods. To improve the retrieval of comic content, there is research on a question-answering system for comic [7]. Moriyama et al. developed the question-answering system for automatically answering questions that correspond to specific elements (such as secret props in the Japanese comic "Doraemon") and contents in a comic. The datasets of the elements and contents of the comic, which are the answers to the questions, are constructed manually. Then, their study uses a Japanese analysis engine to analyze the text of the questions to identify their types and contents. Finally, the extracted keywords are used to retrieve the answers by referring to the dataset. The objective of the study is to develop a system that does not distinguish between information about reading and unread parts of a comic but returns a suitable answer to the question. In this study, the authors propose a system that supports the retrieval of comic content while preventing spoilers of unread parts.

Studies on spoiler prevention include preventing spoilers from spoiling the results of sports games by Nakamura et al. [4] and preventing posts about soccer games with spoiler information from being posted on SNS by Shiratori et al. [6]. They found that just a few words can cause a serious spoiler by text messages and analyzed how to prevent the spoiler of text messages in their studies. Therefore, our research avoids using textual information that could easily lead to spoilers to describe the content of a comic and instead statistical information, i.e., characters' speech frequencies to prevent spoilers.

Nakamura et al. proposed four methods for disambiguating spoiler-like information and compared their effectiveness [4]. Hiding spoiler-equivalent information, blacking out the information, including reverse, similar results, and reversing the results. In another study by Nakamura et al. [3], they proposed a method that automatically hides content that the user has not yet seen, depending on the user's chronological behavior. Their system analyzes the web content requested by the user and uses filters to prevent the display of parts that would spoil the user's enjoyment. From the study, it seems that hiding spoiler-prone parts from view is an effective way to prevent spoilers. Our research adopts the same idea and uses a blacking-out technique to hide and display spoiler information that is known from characters' speech frequencies.

Maki et al. have proposed a method for constructing comic spoiler datasets and analyzed spoiler trends [2]. The dataset is constructed by asking subjects to judge whether or not a certain page of a comic is spoiled and the degree of spoiling in multiple levels. To determine whether a page is spoiled or not, our research assumes that a person who has read up to n episodes of a comic is disgusted when presented with p pages from $n + 1$ episodes. The study by Maki et al. deals with spoilers in unread parts, which is consistent with the present study. In their research, the frequency of spoilers in the unread part of the story is measured. In our research, the characters' speech frequencies were presented, so the story's ending and its related scenes could not be visualized clearly. Instead, the characters' appearances and exits are clearly visualized, which may lead to new spoilers. Therefore, the authors assess the spoilers due to entry and leave of characters and prevent them using visualization.

3   Case Study for Designing Functions of the Proposed Interface

We consider possible cases of comic content retrieval and propose the necessary functions for the proposed interface.

3.1   User Settings

John, a university student who loves comics and reads comics every day in magazines and offprints. He reads several titles of comics simultaneously and the interval between the release of each new episode is different. He can recall the contents of frequently updated comics. However, it is difficult for him to remember the contents of the ones that have not been updated for a period of time.

3.2   Case Study in Comic Content Retrieval

Case 1: Failing to Find a Specific Scene. While waiting for his meal at a restaurant, John decides to read a comic book provided by a restaurant. John remembers that there has a scene in the comic in which a character plays an active role. He starts to search for it. However, he forgets in which episode the scene is included. He cannot find it from the comics he picked. In the meantime, the meal comes out and John fails to find the comics that contain the scene he is looking for.

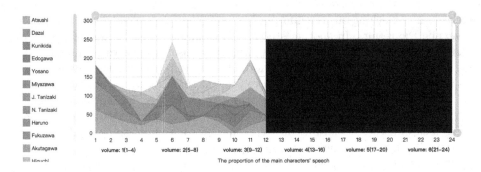

Fig. 1. Overview of the proposed interface.

Case 2: Encountering a Spoiler in Unread Part of Comic. Later, when John is eating at a restaurant, James and Robert start talking about a certain comic at the table behind him. John also read the comic but the contents of the conversation between Mr. James and Mr. Robert don't match with his memory. John gets curious and searches for the contents of the conversation on his smartphone, which shows the contents of the unread part of the comic. He finds out that his favorite characters have disappeared and new characters have shown up. John gets spoiled and feels very disappointed.

3.3   Required Functions Obtained from the Cases

The reason why John cannot read the comic containing the intended content in Case 1 is that he cannot find out in which episodes the character appears. In this case, if the appearance information of the characters in each story of the comic is presented, the story in which the characters are active and the desired content can be found at a glance. The appearance information will be presented by the speech frequencies of characters.

The reason why John encounters spoilers is that contents related to the spoilers in unread parts are shown. The information about speech frequencies of characters is less to be spoilers in the proposed method. However, the appearance and the exit of characters in unread parts would be spoilers. In this case, hiding the information related to the appearance and exit of the characters in the unread part should help to avoid spoilers. Therefore, this research adds a function to the proposed interface that hides information related to the appearance and exit of characters in unread parts.

4   Proposed Interface

The overview of the proposed interface is shown in Fig. 1. The proposed interface uses three types of data: the characters' speech frequencies, the unread parts, and the appearance and leaving of the characters in the unread parts. The unread

Fig. 2. Example of speech lines counted-up ("Arisa2" (c) Ken Yagami from Manga109)

part is given by the user. The characters' speech frequencies designed to cover Case 1, and the judgment of the potential spoiler parts designed to cover Case 2. Using the data, a graph visualizing the time series of characters' speech frequencies is presented, and black curtains are added to hide the potential spoiler parts. A stacked area graph is used to present the frequencies. A list of characters is displayed on the left of the interface. The characters can be selected, and only the characters' speech frequencies are visible. By moving the scrollbar in the upper part of the interface, the user can adjust the range of episodes the user wants to search from.

4.1   Data Preparation of Speech Frequencies of Characters

Figure 2 shows an example of a comic book page and explains how to count up the characters' speech frequencies. In the figure, there are two characters, and the speeches uttered by the characters are surrounded by borders. All the speeches that are judged to have been uttered by the characters are used, even if they are not included in the speech balloons[1]. In the figure, there are six speeches for the male character and seven speeches for the female character.

---

[1] This work is currently done manually.

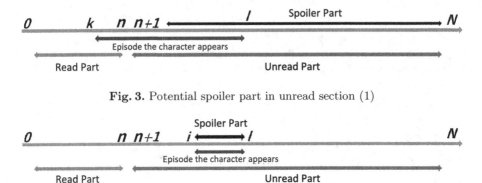

Fig. 3. Potential spoiler part in unread section (1)

Fig. 4. Potential spoiler part in unread section (2)

4.2   Data Preparation of Potential Spoiler Parts

By showing the characters' speech frequencies, the user can know when a new character appears and when a character leaves, which may become a spoiler. Therefore, the authors propose a new interface that detects possible spoilers using changes in characters' speech frequencies. In our proposed interface, the authors consider two cases of spoilers related to the appearances and leaves of characters.

Suppose a comic book has episodes 1 to N. The user has read from episode 1 to M, and has not read from $M + 1$ to N. In the unread part of the story $M + 1$ to N, a character appears in story i and leaves in story j, i.e., $M + 1 <= i < j <= N$. Figure 3 shows the position relation of these important points. In a comic, the story is character-driven, and the set of active characters changes as the story goes on, so if there is appearances or leaves of characters in the range of i to j episodes in the unread portion of the story, then there has been a major development in the story. The major development of the story in the unread part may become a spoiler.

Another case is considered. The user has read from episode 1 to episode M, and has not read from episode $M + 1$ to episode N. A character appears in the read part of k episodes, but leaves in the unread part of l episodes, i.e., $1 <= k <= M$ and $M + 1 <= l <= N$. Figure 4 shows the position relation of these important points. In this case, there is also a major development in the unread part of the story, and the range from $n + 1$ to N episodes is considered to be potential a spoiler part.

4.3   Visualization of Characters' Frequencies and Hiding Potential Spoiler Parts

The proposed interface visualizes the characters' speech frequencies and hides the potential spoiler parts. Figure 1 shows an example of hiding the potential spoiler part. The figure shows an example of the interface display that the user has read from episode 1 to 13 and has not read episode 14 and more yet.

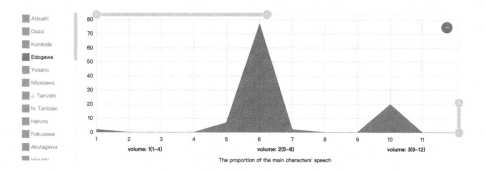

Fig. 5. Usage example 1 of the proposed interface (corresponding to Case 1)

4.4   How to Use the Proposed Interface

This section describes the instructions for searching the contents of comic books using the proposed interface through the case study in Sect. 3.

In this paper, the proposed interface is designed to run in an HTML browser. Suppose the user John, likes "Edogawa Rampo," a character in the manga "Bungo Stray Dogs (Kafka Asagiri)." John has already read episodes 1 to 12. One day, John Sits in a restaurant and wants to read again the story in which "Rampo" is active to pass the time while waiting for the meal. John can select only "Edogawa Rampo" in the list on the left side of the interface shown in Fig. 1. Then, John can move the scrollbar at the top of the interface to make the graphs of episodes 1 to 12 display. Then, Fig. 5 will be displayed, and John can see that "Edogawa Rampo" appears mostly in episodes 6 and 10 so that John can quickly find the episode John want to read. This allows John to avoid the problem happened in Case 1.

While John eats the meal, he/she hears someone at the next table talking about "Kenji Miyazawa". Another character in the comic "Bungo Stray Dogs." John is not sure whether he had read the story about "Kenji Miyazawa's" story or not. In this case, in the proposed interface shown in Fig. 1, John can move the top scrollbar so that the graphs of episodes 1 through 12, which are the parts already read, are displayed. Then, Fig. 6 will be displayed, and John can look back at the stories in which "Kenji Miyazawa" appeared. As a result of looking back, John found that "Kenji Miyazawa" appeared only in the 1 to 10 episodes, and only five times in the speech. Because of the small number of speeches, John is able to reconfirm his/her memory that the story of the different abilities had not yet appeared, and John did not end up knowing the contents of the different abilities. This avoids problem happened in Case 2.

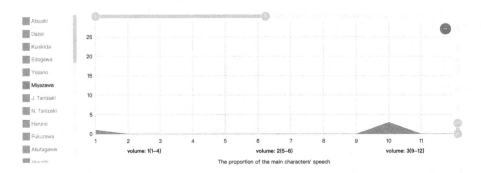

Fig. 6. Usage example 2 of the proposed interface (corresponding to Case 2)

5   Evaluation Experiments

The authors conducted experiments to evaluate whether or not the proposed interface can help users to find the desired content. The authors conducted two types of experiments. In Experiment 1, the authors conducted an experiment on the assistance of the retrieval of comic book contents and evaluated the results corresponding to Case 1. In Experiment 2, the authors conducted an experiment to the judgment of whether the contents of a comic had been read or unread and evaluated the results corresponding to Case 2.

5.1   Experiment 1: Comic Content Retrieval

The experiment was carried out as the following procedure;

1. The subject reads a comic designated by the experimenter from volume 1 to volume 5. The duration is 2 h.
2. The subject needs to answer questions about the location of certain contents of the comic. The time for response to all questions is 15 min.

The experimenter was the first author of this paper. The subjects were 18 undergraduate and graduate students of the College of Information Science and Engineering, Ritsumeikan University. The subjects were divided into two groups, Group A and Group B, with nine subjects each. The comics used in experimental procedure 1 are shown in Table 1. These were three types of comics of different genres, which were ranked high in the popularity of "Bilibili Comics," one of the largest comic Websites in China. These comics were selected as comics that none of the subjects had read before.

The questions about comic content retrieval used in experimental procedure 2 were designed by the first author. The questions were to find the number of episodes of a character or to find the characters related to which episodes. Examples of questions are shown in Table 2. A total of 24 questions, 8 for each manga, were designed. When answering the questions, Group A used the proposed interface to search, while Group B did not use anything and answered the questions by relying on their memories.

Table 1. Comic used in the evaluation experiments

Genre	Title (author)
Romance	"Fly Me to the Moon" (Kenjiro Hata)
Mystery	"In/spectre" (Kyo Shirodaira)
Action	"Bungo Stray Dogs" (Kafka Asagiri)

Table 2. Example of questions used in the evaluation experiment 1

Manga and Questions
"Fly Me to the Moon"
In which episode did Nasa and Tsukasa bought rings together?
In which episode did Chitose went to the hot spring for the first time?
"In/spectre"
Which episode was Police Terada's first appearance?
In which volume did Kotoko and Saki meet each other for the first time?
"Bungo Stray Dogs"
In which volume was Dazai kidnapped by the mafia?
In which episode did Higuchi and Black Lizard rescued Akutagawa?

The evaluation method of the proposed interface was based on the percentage of correct answers to the retrieval questions of Group A and Group B. If the correct answers rate of Group A using the proposed interface is high, the visualization of the speech frequencies provided by the proposed interface is effective for content retrieval.

5.2 Results of Experiment 1

Table 3 shows the average correct answers rate for each group. The average correct answers rate for Group A, who searched and answered using the proposed interface, was 0.76, and that for Group B, who answered by memory, was 0.30. This result shown that the visualization of the time series of speech frequencies could support the retrieval of comic contents more.

5.3 Experiment 2: Judgement of Read/unread Part of Comic

The experiment was carried out as the following procedure;

1. The subject reads a comic designated by the experimenter from volume 1 to volume 3. The duration is 1.5 h.
2. The subject judges whether the contents of the manga specified by the experimenter have been read (in volumes 1 to 3) or not (in volumes 4 and 5). The proposed interface is used for judgment. The response time to all questions is set to 15 min.

Table 3. Correct answer rate of judgement questions in evaluation experiment 1

Comic	Group A	Group B
"Fly Me to the Moon"	**0.83**	0.21
"In/spectre"	**0.75**	0.41
"Bungo Stray Dogs"	**0.71**	0.29
Average	**0.76**	0.30

Table 4. Example of judgment questions used in Experiment 2

Comic and Questions
"Fly Me to the Moon"
In which volume did Tsukasa and Nasa's parents meet each other for the first time?
Which volume was the first appearance of Nasa's teacher?
"In/spectre"
In which volume did Police Terada die?
Which volume explained the past of Kuro and Rikka?
"Bungo Stray Dogs"
In which volume did Dazai and Nakahara meet?
Which volume showed Miyazawa's ability?

The experimenter and subjects were the same as in Experiment 1. The comics used in the experiment was also the same as in Experiment 1. The subjects read volumes 1 to 3 and did not read volumes 4 and 5[2]. The judgment questions of the comic content presented in Experimental Procedure 2 were set by the experimenter. The judging questions were to ask the subjects to choose the volume in which the episode of the characters occurred, either read or unread parts. Examples of the judgment questions are shown in Table 4. A total of 24 questions were designed, 8 for each comic. The judging questions ask the readers to identify the volume containing the episodes related to the characters, and the correct answer was the volume numbers. There were 14 questions for which the correct answer was in the read part and 10 questions for which the correct answer was in the unread part.

The evaluation of this experiment was based on the correct answer rate to the judgment questions. If the percentage of correct answers is equal to or larger than 0.5, the proposed interface was proven to be effective to support judging whether the contents of a comic have been read or not.

5.4   Results of Experiment 2

The average correct answers rates are shown in Table 5. The overall average percentage of correct answers rate was 0.61, with the correct answers rate for

---

[2] Actually, Evaluation Experiment 2 was conducted firstly, followed by Evaluation Experiment 1.

Table 5. Correct answer rate of judgement questions in evaluation Experiment 2

Comic	Overall	Read	Unread
"Fly Me to the Moon"	0.69	0.75	0.62
"In/spectre"	0.58	0.55	0.67
"Bungo Stray Dogs"	0.58	0.79	0.37
Average	**0.61**	**0.69**	**0.55**

the read portion being 0.69 and the correct answers rate for the unread portion being 0.55. The correct answers rate for the unread part of "Bungo Stray Dogs" was 0.37, which was lower than that of the other two mangas. The reason for the low Correct answer rate was there had a question whose correct answers rate were zero. All the correct answer rates were 0.5 or higher, indicating that the proposed interface could be used to help judge whether the contents of a comic had been read or not. In the case of the result with a correct answer rate of zero, the question was: "In which volume do most of the members of the Guild (an organization name in this manga) appear?" and the correct answer was volume 4. Since one member of "Guild" appeared at the end of Volume 3 and "Guild" was also written there, the subjects misunderstand the counting. Although the subjects failed to answer the read/unread question, the potential spoiler (Case 2) did not exist.

6   Conclusion and Future Work

In this paper, the authors proposed an interface to support the retrieval of comic book contents using time-series visualization of characters' speech frequencies. The proposed interface visualizes the characters' speech frequencies in a comic book using a stacked area graph. In the visualization, the authors hide the parts of the comic where might be the spoiler, where the characters appear and leave in the unread parts of comics. The authors conducted two experiments: Experiment 1 to evaluate whether the proposed interface supports the retrieval of comic contents, and Experiment 2 to evaluate whether the proposed interface supports the judgment of read and unread comic contents. In both experiments, the subjects were asked to read comic books, and were asked to answer search questions about the contents of the comic books and judgment questions about whether they had read or not the part of the comic books. In Experiment 1, the average correct answers rate was 0.76 for the group using the proposed interface, and 0.30 for the group without the interface. This result indicated that the proposed interface supported the retrieval of comic contents. In Experiment 2, the average correct answer rate of the subjects who used the proposed interface was 0.61. From this result, the authors found that the proposed interface supports the judgment of read and unread contents of comics to some extent. In the future, the authors would like to apply the proposed interface for novel and movie content retrievals.

Acknowledgement. This work was partly supported by JSPS Kakenhi (JP20K12130) and "International Collaborative Research for the Digital Archive of Japanese Cultural Resources," Art Research Center, Ritsumeikan University.

References

1. Alex, S.L.T., Yan, D.: The pleasures of uncertainty: prolonging positive moods in ways people do not anticipate. In: Advances in Consumer Research, vol. 36, pp. 708–709 (2009)
2. Maki, Y., Shiratori, Y., Sato, K., Nakamura, S.: A consideration to estimate spoiling pages in comics. In: Proceedings of the 4th International Symposium on Affective Science and Engineering 2018, and the 29th Modern Artificial Intelligence and Cognitive Science Conference, pp. 1–6 (2018)
3. Satoshi, N., Katsumi, T.: Temporal filtering system to reduce the risk of spoiling a user's enjoyment. In: Proceedings of the 12th International Conference on Intelligent User Interfaces, pp. 345–348 (2007)
4. Satoshi, N., Takanori, K.: Study of information clouding methods to prevent spoilers of sports match. In: Proceedings of the International Working Conference on Advanced Visual Interfaces, pp. 661–664 (2012)
5. Wilson, T.D., Centerbar, D.B., Kermer, D.A., Gilbert, D.T.: The pleasures of uncertainty: prolonging positive moods in ways people do not anticipate. J. Pers. Soc. Psychol. 5–21 (2005)
6. Shiratori, Y., Maki, Y., Nakamura, S., Komatsu, T.: Detection of football spoilers on Twitter. In: Egi, H., Yuizono, T., Baloian, N., Yoshino, T., Ichimura, S., Rodrigues, A. (eds.) CollabTech 2018. LNCS, vol. 11000, pp. 129–141. Springer, Cham (2018). https://doi.org/10.1007/978-3-319-98743-9_11
7. Yukihiro, M., Byeongseon, P., Shinnosuke, I., Mitsunori, M.: A designing a question-answering system for comic contents. In: Proceedings of the 1st International Workshop on coMics ANalysis, Processing and Understanding, pp. 1–6 (2016)

Research on Demand Forecasting Method of Multi-user Group Based on Big Data

Miao Liu$^{(\boxtimes)}$ ⓘ and Liangliang Ben$^{(\boxtimes)}$ ⓘ

East China University of Science and Technology, Shanghai 200237, People's Republic of China
183787975@qq.com, 953811759@qq.com

Abstract. In order to accurately meet the purchasing needs of consumers, this paper proposes a multi-user demand forecasting model based on big data that organically combines sentiment classification and user portraits. The study takes the online reviews of smart watches on an e-commerce website as the data source, the product attributes that users pay attention to are obtained through word frequency analysis and LDA model, and the NLPIR sentiment analysis tool is used to analyze their sentiment tendency to construct a user demand evaluation system; then count the word frequency of perceptual words, classify them with kJ analysis method, so as to mine the perceptual needs of users, and use the Censydiam model to explore the user's purchasing motivation and perform crowd clustering, and finally build user portraits; then count the scores of each user group on the demand evaluation indicators, extract the product design objectives and distinguish their importance according to the functional positioning and application strategy of the indicator type, and establish the demand forecasting model of multi-user groups. The research results show that through data mining and perceptual engineering analysis, we can get the improvement trend of products in the future, make them better meet the needs of users, and provide effective guidance for product design.

Keywords: Big data · Kansei engineering · User group · User needs

1 Introduction

In the increasingly competitive market environment, the external environment changes rapidly. If enterprises want to develop in this dynamic environment, they must speed up the update of product design. Due to time constraints, the traditional research model has low user participation and small research scope, which easily makes the product design direction deviate from user needs, and lacks in-depth analysis of the commonalities and differences of needs among user groups, making it impossible for products to meet the needs of multiple user groups Differentiated requirements [1]. The generation of big data provides new research conditions and opportunities, and methods that rely on small-scale data to discover laws in unknown fields are gradually being replaced by big data analysis [2]. Most of the existing research is on the mining of user reviews of smart phones, and there are also food and hotels as research objects, while the popular smart watches in

© The Author(s), under exclusive license to Springer Nature Switzerland AG 2022
S. Yamamoto and H. Mori (Eds.): HCII 2022, LNCS 13306, pp. 45–64, 2022.
https://doi.org/10.1007/978-3-031-06509-5_4

recent years have not been paid attention to. As an emerging product, smart watches are not a necessity for every user like mobile phones, so it is particularly important to analyze users' needs and consumption motivations for purchasing smart watches [3]. Using big data to extract users' rational and perceptual cognition results of products, transforming them into design information and summarizing product improvement trends can help designers design products that meet user needs under the guidance of these design information, so as to improve the competitiveness of products [4].

2   Problem Analysis and Research Ideas

With the increasing maturity of technologies and concepts in the field of industrial design, enterprises have gradually realized that products oriented by user needs are more likely to win the favor of the market. Kansei engineering, as a research framework that correlates users' perceptual emotions with product design elements, can effectively mine user needs [5]. Kansei engineering is a combination technology that establishes a connection between sensibility and engineering. Its design concept is people-oriented, design from the user's point of view, and avoid designers designing products from their own point of view, only for themselves [6]. Applying Kansei Engineering to user demand forecasting research first requires designers to clarify what users want and need, as well as their perceptual cognition of the product, and then determine the target user group and establish product positioning corresponding to the user group., thus guiding the design of future products [7]. This is an important design strategy, and research around it keeps emerging. Luo et al. [8] proposed a product family shape genetic design method driven by user demand preference; Su et al. [9] proposed a user cluster-oriented product design method to accurately locate target users and meet the perceptual needs and preferences of their groups; Han et al. [10] proposed a modular product configuration method driven by both user perceptual needs and functional requirements; Liu et al. [11] proposed a multi-objective-driven product family modeling design method to meet the various perceptual needs of users; Zuo et al. [12] proposed a subjective product evaluation system based on Kansei engineering and AHP; Xue et al. [13] proposed an integrated decision-making system for product image optimization design based on kansei engineering. Most of the above literatures are developed from the perspective of shaping the perceptual image characteristics of products and satisfying the individual needs and preferences of user groups. Although a few of them involve the characteristics and attributes of user groups, they lack in-depth analysis of the commonality and differences of needs among user groups makes it impossible for products to meet the differentiated needs of multiple user groups. Moreover, these methods rely too much on the subjective cognition of domain experts and there is a certain lag in the research time. It is difficult to do quantitative research under a large number of data samples, making it difficult for user research to conduct fine-grained and comprehensive analysis of user behavior.

Based on this, this paper proposes a demand forecasting model for multi-user groups based on big data, aiming at the compatibility problems of different product design goals among different user groups and the problem of insufficient data volume, which are generally ignored in current research. Taking smart watches as an example, the main research work completed for Chinese comment data is as follows:

1. Obtain the online evaluation text of users of the product. Using Python software to write crawler functions to obtain online user comment information, and to perform data cleaning and word segmentation on the obtained online comments.
2. Establish a user demand evaluation system. Through word frequency analysis and LDA model, the topic extraction of online reviews is performed to obtain product attributes and corresponding attribute words that users pay attention to, and the usefulness of online reviews is judged based on attribute words and sentiment words, so as to remove useless comments. Helpful reviews are then categorized based on product attributes and sentiment words. By calculating the sentiment score of a single comment, the user's attention to each attribute of the product and other indicators, a user needs evaluation system is established.
3. Determine the target user group of the product. The word frequency analysis is carried out on the perceptual words in the user's evaluation, and the KJ analysis method is used to screen out the perceptual words as the user's perceptual preference for the product, and corresponding to the Censydiam user motivation analysis model to analyze the user's intrinsic motivation to buy the product, so as to Cluster the target user groups of the product and build user portraits.
4. Establish a multi-user group demand forecasting model. The scores of each user group on the demand evaluation indicators are counted, and the significance of the difference in demand weight between user groups is verified by the least significant difference method. Then, according to the functional positioning of the index type and its application strategy, the product design goals are extracted and their importance is distinguished, and a multi-user group demand forecasting model is established.
5. Figure 1 shows the framework of the demand forecasting model for multi-user groups based on big data.

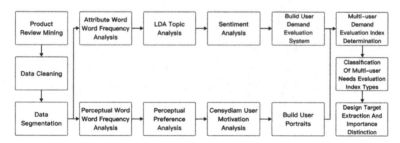

Fig. 1. Multi user group demand forecasting model framework based on big data.

3 Data Acquisition and Preprocessing

3.1 Data Acquisition

The selection of data sources for online reviews is the first step in crawling data. For the smart watches selected in this study, shopping websites are a better choice. JD.com is the main e-commerce company for 3C digital products, and consumers prefer JD.com to purchase consumer electronic products, and the transaction volume is also larger, so the number of online reviews on mobile phones related to the comment area on the product purchase page will be relatively large. Therefore, JD.com is chosen as the online review data source.

Crawling comments from web pages requires the help of crawler technology. Existing crawler tools include Requests library, Scrapy crawler framework and Selenium. Selenium is a powerful browser-based open source automated testing tool. It provides a set of simple and easy-to-use APIs to simulate various operations of the browser, and its behavior is almost the same as that of the user, so it can bypass the anti-crawling strategy of the website [14]. This article uses Python to cooperate with Selenium to capture the web page reviews of smart watches. Selenium simulates user operations to open a smart watch evaluation page of a brand in JD.com, locates the evaluation area of the HTML page, and extracts the corresponding evaluation information according to the page tags,

Table 1. Examples of comment information.

Serial number	Username	Evaluation content	Score	Purchase model	Date
1	少***美	真香, 太好看了, 纠结了很久, 终于买了, 算是给自己的新年礼物吧, 希望明年好好努力, 做一个守时的人。	5	GPS款 44毫米	2021–09–06 20:47
2	超****	很好的一个产品, 一直很期待s6, 蜂窝款更是可以跟手机完全脱离使用。接下来就看看续航是怎么样了。值得推荐	5	GPS + 蜂窝款 44毫米	2021–08–30 07:58
3	j***1	很喜欢, 感觉还不是很独立, 好像很多都是镜像, 能像一块手机一样的手表就好了!	4	GPS + 蜂窝款 44毫米	2021–11–28 10:59
…	…	…	…	…	…
100917	****y	工艺细腻精湛, 整体高端精致, 蓝宝石镜面晶莹剔透极具质感。功能丰富强大, 尤其是心脏和睡眠监测非常适合中年人, 强力推荐!	5	46mm-运动款-幻夜黑	2021–11–19 09:08

including user name, evaluation content, score, purchase model and date, etc. A total of 100918 comments have been crawled. Four of the comments are listed in Table 1.

3.2 Data Cleaning

Considering that the data mined by the crawler technology will contain invalid data, and some comments are completely copied from other comments, the reference value is limited, if not removed, it will affect the subsequent research and analysis. In order to ensure the accuracy of the comment data, data cleaning was performed on the crawled comment data, and repeated comments, comments containing advertisements, and comments with punctuation marks were removed, and finally 95,268 comments were obtained.

3.3 Data Segmentation

Word segmentation is a key step in text mining, which is the process of splitting a sentence into several words. Accurate word segmentation can improve the efficiency and accuracy of subsequent text mining. Considering that a large number of Internet terms are involved in online shopping reviews, in order to improve the accuracy of word segmentation, it is necessary to add a new Internet terminology vocabulary. In this paper, the online vocabulary of Baidu input method, Sogou input method, and QQ input method are combined as a custom dictionary. The most commonly used toolkit for Chinese word segmentation is Jieba. This article uses the Jieba word segmentation package to load a custom network term dictionary and perform word segmentation on the cleaned data.

4 Establish a User Demand Evaluation System

4.1 Obtaining Product Attribute Words

The first step in researching the user needs of a product is to identify the attributes of the product. Identifying product attributes in online reviews can help manufacturers understand the topics consumers care about as well as product features and performance. Attribute words are words that describe the attributes of things (products). Product attribute is a collection of multiple similar attribute words, representing a certain attribute of the product, such as color, shape and other similar attribute words representing the appearance attribute of the product [15]. According to existing research, most of the product attribute words are nouns, such as the appearance, space, power and so on of automobile products. Therefore, this paper firstly uses the ICTCLAS tool to perform part-of-speech tagging and word frequency analysis on the data, and uses frequently occurring nouns or noun phrases as candidate product attribute words. Figure 2 is a word cloud diagram of product attribute words.

Latent Dirichlet Allocation (LDA) model is a Bayesian network model with a clear hierarchical structure "document-topic-word", and it is also a new method for mining text topics [16]. The similarity between the product attributes is calculated by the given number K of product attributes. The smaller the similarity, the smaller the repetition between the product attributes, and the better the corresponding K value. Through calculation, it is found that when K = 13, the similarity between the attributes of each

Fig. 2. The word cloud of product attribute words.

product is the lowest, thus obtaining 13 attribute word sets. By consulting the opinions of professional designers and combining the classification standards of smart watch attributes on the official websites of well-known companies such as Huawei and Apple, the product attributes represented by the 13 attribute word sets were determined. Table 2 is the attribute dictionary of the product.

Table 2. Product attribute dictionary.

Product attributes	Number of attribute words	Set of attribute words
Size and weight	8	大小/重量/小巧/尺寸/厚度/直径/体积/宽度
Package	9	产品包装/包装/包装盒/外包装/盒子/礼品/礼盒/说明书/配件
Battery	24	电量/电池/待机时间/待机/续航力/功率/持续时间/电池容量/时长/损耗/…
Price	13	价位/价格/价格低/价格便宜/价格合理/价钱/售价/小贵/很贵/性价比高/…
Screen	40	亮度/全屏/分辨率/刷新/双屏/圆盘/密度/屏幕/帧数/帧率/方型/方屏/柔性/…
Exterior	68	风格/产品设计/颜色/造型/前卫/后盖/圆形/视觉效果/壁纸/复古/外壳/…
System performance	49	内存/准确率/卡顿/响应速度/固件/处理器/安卓/延迟/性能/灵敏度/…

(continued)

Table 2. (*continued*)

Product attributes	Number of attribute words	Set of attribute words
Exercise and health	32	体温/健康状况/脉搏/血压/体育锻炼/体能/卡路里/徒步/步数/跳绳/...
Function	64	人脸识别/传感器/助理/地图/天气预报/录音/手电/指南针/播放器/日历/...
Material of case	12	不锈钢/合金/塑料/材料/材质/玻璃/金属外壳/金属表/钛金/钛金/铝/铝合金
Data connections	16	wifi/信号/北斗/卫星/插卡/数据/无线网络/生态圈/生态系统/生态链/离线/...
Watch strap	22	刚带/塑胶/尼龙/带子/橡胶/氟橡胶/牛皮/皮/皮带/皮表带/皮质/皮革/真皮/...
Texture	34	不适感/产品品质/人机/割手/压迫感/厚重感/品质/商品质量/工程学/工艺/...

4.2 Review Usefulness Analysis

The review usefulness analysis in this paper mainly focuses on the description of the product, that is, the attribute words that describe the product and the sentiment words that represent the user's emotions. If a comment is a useful comment, it must contain the product attributes that the user is concerned about (expressed by attribute words) and the user's emotional tendencies (expressed by emotional words) about the performance of the product attributes. The attribute word has been obtained in the step of obtaining the product attribute above. The emotional word lexicon in HowNet is also one of the most well-known Chinese emotional word lexicons. Therefore, this paper uses the attribute words obtained above and the emotional words in HowNet emotional lexicon as the basis for judging the usefulness of reviews.

If a comment has both attribute words and sentiment words, it is considered as a useful comment, and the judgment rule is

$$p_i = p_i^o \times p_i^e \qquad (1)$$

In the formula: p_i is the judgment value of whether the i-th comment is a valid comment, and the values are 0 and 1. If $p_i = 1$, the i-th comment is a useful comment, and $p_i = 0$, the i-th comment is a useless comment; p_i^o is the judgment value of whether the i-th comment has a product attribute word, and the values are 0 and 1. If the i-th comment has a product attribute word, $p_i^o = 1$, otherwise $p_i^o = 0$; p_i^e is the judgment value of whether the i-th comment has an emotional word, and the values are 0 and 1. If the i-th comment has an emotional word, $p_i^e = 1$, otherwise, $p_i^e = 0$.

Based on Eq. (1), the usefulness of all comments is analyzed, and 75,746 useful comments are finally obtained.

4.3 Establish a User Demand Evaluation System

After identifying the product attributes, it is also necessary to know whether the user's view of the product is positive or negative, so that the merchant can better understand the quality of the product function and make a decision. Understanding users' opinions is to perform sentiment analysis on product attributes. This study uses the NLPIR sentiment analysis module to perform sentiment analysis on the useful comments obtained above. Its module has an emotional dictionary containing more than 20,000 words. In order to improve the fit and accuracy of the dictionary and the original data, the words with emotional color will be filtered according to the part of speech and imported into its own dictionary. The dictionary is divided into three attributes: type, word, and weight. The types are divided into four types: positive words, negative words, negative words and degree words. The weights represent the emotional strength of words, and the four types of words have their own choices. The value range, within the specified range, the weight of the word can be adjusted as needed. The system will finally calculate the score of the sentence according to the weight of each word, and then judge the corresponding emotional tendency.

Denote the perceptual score of the i-th comment in the N-th product attribute as S_{Ni}, and calculate the mean score P_N for it,

$$P_N = \sum_{i=1}^{t_N} \frac{S_{Ni}}{t_N} \tag{2}$$

In the formula: S_{Ni} is the perceptual score of the i-th review in the N-th product attribute; t_N is the number of reviews describing the N-th product attribute.

The evaluation of the product attribute appears in the review, that is, the user's attention to the product attribute. Denote the user's degree of attention to the N-th product attribute as T_N,

$$T_N = \frac{t_N}{n} \tag{3}$$

In the formula: t_N is the number of reviews of the N-th product attribute; n is the total number of useful reviews. The higher the T_N value, the higher the user's attention. Therefore, the user's total evaluation of the product is H,

$$H = \sum_{i=1}^{N} (P_N \times T_N) \tag{4}$$

In order to maximize H, the evaluation degree $P_N \times T_N$ of a single product attribute needs to reach the maximum value of $1 \times T_N$ (the maximum value of P_N is 1), so the improvement space of the evaluation degree of a single product attribute is $(1 - P_N)?T_N$ The improvement space of the product attribute evaluation degree is regarded as the degree I_N that the product attribute needs to be improved urgently,

$$H = \sum_{i=1}^{N} (P_N \times T_N) \tag{5}$$

Therefore, a user demand evaluation system for smart watches is established, as shown in Table 3.

Table 3. User demand evaluation system.

Product attributes	Perceptual score (P$_N$)	Attention (T$_N$)	Degree of urgent improvement (I$_N$)
Size and weight	0.821	0.045	0.008
Package	0.841	0.074	0.012
Battery	0.666	0.144	0.048
Price	0.750	0.082	0.021
Screen	0.721	0.109	0.030
Exterior	0.746	0.530	0.135
System performance	0.878	0.244	0.029
Exercise and health	0.767	0.250	0.058
Function	0.685	0.567	0.179
Material of case	0.847	0.033	0.005
Data connections	0.752	0.072	0.018
Watch strap	0.775	0.161	0.036
Texture	0.839	0.329	0.053

5 Determine the Target User Group of the Product

5.1 User Perceptual Needs Mining

In Kansei Engineering evaluation, perceptual word or perceptual word pairs are usually used to describe users' psychological feelings about products [17]. Therefore, this paper selects the perceptual words in user comments to mine the perceptual needs of users. The importance of a word is proportional to the number of times it appears in the text. If a word appears repeatedly in the text under study, the word can be used to characterize the mainstream tendency of the text.

First identify and obtain all adjectives in the product review dataset by part-of-speech tagging. The data set constructed above has a total of 4994 adjectives. After manual screening, 163 adjectives expressing positive emotions are selected, and word frequency statistics are carried out to obtain the word cloud of perceptual words as shown in Fig. 3.

Fig. 3. The word cloud of perceptual words.

Afterwards, the KJ analysis method is used in combination with expert opinions to classify the perceptual words with similar meanings, and the total word frequency of the perceptual words contained in each is calculated. The final 14 perceptual words are used as the user's perceptual preference for smart watches, and a product perceptual semantic word database is constructed, as shown in Table 4.

Table 4. Perceptual semantic lexicon of products.

Perceptual words	Word frequency	Perceptual words	Word frequency
Pleasure	1703	Smooth	4526
Stable	481	Dignified	1394
Beautiful	18207	Individuality	690
Comfortable	17820	Quality	4867
Elegant	293	Convenient	7524
Lively	382	Technology	6244
Concise	7650	Delicate	10466

5.2 User Motivation Analysis

The needs of users exist objectively, but the key to determining whether a product can realize its value is whether the product can induce the user's motivation to meet the needs [18]. Demand is the source of motivation, and motivation is the cause of behavior. It can be seen that whether the user's motivation can be accurately grasped when designing a product is directly related to the future performance of the product.

The Censydiam user motivation analysis model is developed from the personality theories of Freud, Jung and Adler. The entire model is an eight-dimensional model consisting of two axes. The horizontal and vertical coordinates are self-belonging, release-rationality, and the model is divided into eight dimensions: enjoyment, vitality, power, recognition, control, security, belonging, and conciciality [19]. The Censydiam model is shown in Fig. 4.

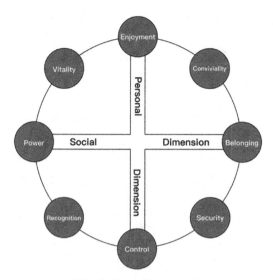

Fig. 4. Censydiam model.

In the field of academic research, this model is mainly combined with other methods to study the type of consumers in a specific market. In practical applications, it is an effective means for companies to study the motivation of target consumers and determine the direction of product design. As one of the electronic consumer goods, smart watches are not necessary for every user, unlike mobile phones. In-depth research on users' purchasing motivation will help designers to accurately locate the target users of the product and provide direction for later design positioning.

5.3 User Portrait Construction

In the increasingly differentiated product groups, by subdividing each product group, helping enterprises to find suitable target customers and their market segments according to their own positioning and existing resources will greatly improve the possibility of enterprise success, so as to effectively take advantage of trends Let enterprises better serve target users [18]. Fill in the product perceptual semantic words extracted above: pleasure, stable, beautiful, comfortable, elegant, lively, concise, smooth, dignified, individuality, quality, convenient, technology, delicate, and the corresponding word frequency into the Censydiam model, Thereby, the target user groups of smart watches are clustered, as shown in Fig. 5.

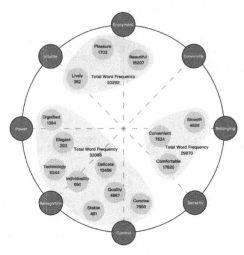

Fig. 5. Positioning of target user groups.

In order to gain valuable and deep insight into users' emotions, taking the three types of user prototypes analyzed by censydiam model as a reference, 18 smart watch users (6 users in each type) were selected to conduct in-depth research on their related life forms, attitudes and purchase factors. Finally, three types of user portraits are obtained, which are refined, hedonic and comfortable, as shown in Table 5. The first type of refined users are mainly those who are rational and pursue cutting-edge technology. They buy smart watches mainly to show their difference, but also pay more attention to the functions and quality of the products; the second type of hedonic users are mainly concentrated on people who are sensual and full of enjoyment, they buy smart watches mainly to decorate themselves, release their desires, and make themselves happy; the third type of comfortable users mainly focus on people who like to follow the trend of the times but do not want to be troubled by trivial matters, they buy smart watches mainly to obtain a convenient and comfortable experience and improve their quality of life.

Table 5. Three types of personas.

User portrait type	Attitude description	Purchase motivation
Refined	Rational and the pursuit of cutting-edge technology, focusing on product function and quality	Show the difference
Hedonic	Sensual and energetic	Decorate themselves, release their desires and make them happy
Comfortable	Likes to follow the trend of the times but does not want to be bothered by trivial matters	Get a convenient and comfortable experience and improve the quality of life

6 Demand Forecast for Multiple User Groups

6.1 Multi-user Group Evaluation Index Determination

In order to obtain the demand evaluation indicators of the above three types of user groups, it is necessary to bring the corresponding positive perceptual words and negative perceptual words into the data set constructed above for retrieval, and calculate the perceptual score (P_N), user attention (T_N) and degree of urgent improvement (I_N). Because I_N can comprehensively reflect users' expectations for product attributes, I_N is taken as the index weight of users' demand for products. Thus, the demand evaluation index of each user group for smart watches is obtained, as shown in Table 6.

Table 6. Multi user group demand evaluation index.

Product attributes	Refined	Hedonic	Comfortable
Size and weight	0.004681	0.005315	0.031268
Package	0.000617	0.007440	0.003074
Battery	0.045038	0.036564	0.046297
Price	0.005529	0.003971	0.010506
Screen	0.026937	0.024080	0.044067
Exterior	0.119784	0.182874	0.135980
System performance	0.021397	0.008718	0.046682
Exercise and health	0.038625	0.026929	0.040278
Function	0.175943	0.140203	0.180871
Material of case	0.002940	0.000503	0.009724
Data connections	0.018280	0.008153	0.015396
Watch strap	0.017614	0.036908	0.062653
Texture	0.041945	0.009298	0.074844

The calculation results of the demand evaluation index weight of each user group member are taken as the sample data and imported into SPSS software for the minimum significant difference method test to verify the significance of the perceptual demand difference between user groups. The results show that there are significant differences among all index groups ($P \leq 0.05$), indicating that there are significant differences in perceptual needs among user groups.

6.2 Differential Positioning of Multi-user Group Design Goals

According to the calculation results of the weights of the needs evaluation indicators of each user group, draw a scatter diagram that aggregates the weight distribution of the needs evaluation indicators of multiple user groups, so as to intuitively reflect the

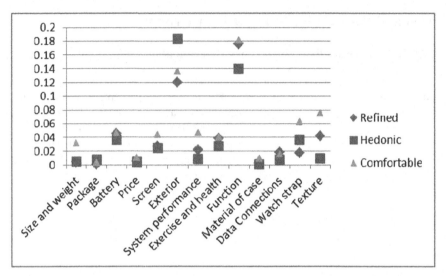

Fig. 6. Weight distribution of multi-user group demand evaluation index.

commonality and difference of the needs of each user group. The results are shown in Fig. 6.

The weight distribution characteristics of the multi-user group demand evaluation indicators include the weight mean and weight standard deviation of the indicators. The former reflects the importance of the indicator to the multi-user group, and the latter reflects the difference in the importance of the indicator among the multi-user groups. The more obvious the level of the standard deviation of the indicator weight is, the more it can reflect the needs of multi-user groups for product commonality or product personality, and it is the design object that should be paid attention to in order to form product commonality or product personality.

Further analysis of the weight distribution characteristics of the above indicators:

1. When an indicator has a high weight mean, if the indicator has a high weight in the same user group, it can usually be used as an important design goal of the product, otherwise it is a secondary design goal (except when it can reflect the commonality of products).
2. When an indicator has a low weight mean, no matter the weight of the indicator in the same user group, the indicator is not important to the user group, so this indicator can usually be used as the secondary design goal of the product. Only when its weight standard deviation is high (can reflect the product's personality) and has a high weight in the same user group, it can be used as a light important design goal of the product.
3. In order to form the product personality, the index with higher weight standard deviation can be taken as the non secondary object of the design (the important object is when the weight mean is high, and the general object is when the weight mean is low), and it can be set to have obvious weight difference in the product design of the same user group. In order to form product commonness, the index with

lower weight standard deviation can be taken as the non secondary object of the design, and it can be set to the same weight in the product design of the same user group.

4. In order to consolidate the product commonness and product individuality, the index with medium weight standard deviation can be taken as the non important object of the design (the general object when the weight mean is high and the secondary object when the weight mean is low), and the weight difference degree can be set freely in the product design of the same user group, but the weight relationship should be considered to meet the needs of multiple user groups at the same time.

The types of multi-user group demand evaluation indicators and their application strategies proposed based on the characteristic analysis of the above-mentioned indicator weight distribution are shown in Table 7. In Table 7, the high and low level distinction of each parameter of the indicator (including weight, weight mean and weight standard deviation) is completed by K-Means clustering algorithm. The K-Means clustering algorithm is used to calculate the level of each parameter of the index, and the calculation results of the level of the index weight are shown in Table 8. Combined with the calculation results of the parameter levels of the indicators and the feature definitions of the indicator types in Table 7, the classification results of the types of evaluation indicators for the needs of smart watch multi-user groups are obtained, as shown in Table 9.

Table 7. Types of multi-user group demand evaluation indicators and their application strategies.

Type	Type name	Type features	Function and orientation of type	Application strategy of type
T1	Important Personality Indicator	High mean value and high standard deviation	It is important for multi-user groups and can reflect product personality. It is an important design object	It should be set with obvious weight difference in the product design of the same user group; When the weight value is high, it should be regarded as an important design goal of the corresponding product, otherwise it should be regarded as a secondary goal

(*continued*)

Table 7. (*continued*)

Type	Type name	Type features	Function and orientation of type	Application strategy of type
T2	General Liberty Indicator	High mean value and medium standard deviation	It is important for multi-user groups, but it can not reflect the individuality and commonness of products. It is a general design object	The weight difference degree can be set freely in the product design of the same user group; When the weight value is high, it can be regarded as the light important design goal of the corresponding product, otherwise it can be regarded as the light secondary goal
T3	Important common indicator	High mean value and low standard deviation	It is important for multi-user groups and can reflect the commonness of products. It is an important design object	The same weight should be set in the product design of the same user group; No matter how high or low the weight of the product is, it should be regarded as an important design goal
T4	General Personality Indicator	Low mean value and high standard deviation	It is not important for multi-user groups, but it can reflect the product personality. It is a general design object	It can be set to have obvious weight difference in the product design of the same user group; When the weight value is high, it can be regarded as the light important design goal of the corresponding product, otherwise it can be regarded as the light secondary goal
T5	Secondary Freedom Indicator	Low mean value and medium standard deviation	It is not important to multi-user groups and cannot reflect the individuality and commonness of products. It is a secondary design object	The weight difference degree can be set freely in the product design of the same user group; Regardless of the weight, it can be used as the secondary design goal of the corresponding product

(*continued*)

Table 7. (*continued*)

Type	Type name	Type features	Function and orientation of type	Application strategy of type
T6	General common indicator	Low mean value and low standard deviation	It is not important for multi-user groups, but it can reflect the commonness of products. It is a general design object	The same weight can be set between product designs of the same user group; Regardless of the weight, it can be used as the light secondary design goal of the corresponding product

Table 8. Weight level of multi-user group demand evaluation index.

Product attributes	Refined	Hedonic	Comfortable
Size and weight	-	-	*
Package	-	-	-
Battery	*	*	*
Price	-	-	-
Screen	*	*	*
Exterior	*	*	*
System performance	*	-	*
Exercise and health	*	*	*
Function	*	*	*
Material of case	-	-	-
Data connections	-	-	-
Watch strap	-	*	*
Texture	*	-	*

Note: High weights are marked as *, and low weights are marked as -

As shown in Table 10, after obtaining the design goal of smart watch multi-user group, the demand trend of users for the product can be summarized. Among them, battery, screen, exterior, exercise and health have the same importance in the three user groups, which can be regarded as important design goals; Package, price, material of case and data connections are of the same importance in the three user groups, which can be used as light important design goals; The function has the same importance in the three user groups and can be used as an important design goal; The size and weight are the light secondary design goals in the refined and hedonic user groups, and the light important design goals in the comfortable user groups; System performance is the light

Table 9. Multi user group demand evaluation index type.

Product attributes	Type	Product attributes	Type
Size and weight	T4	Exercise and health	T3
Package	T6	Function	T2
Battery	T3	Material of case	T6
Price	T6	Data Connections	T6
Screen	T3	Watch strap	T2
Exterior	T1	Texture	T2
System performance	T2		

Table 10. Multi user group design objectives.

Product attributes	Refined	Hedonic	Comfortable
Size and weight	■	■	◇
Package	■	■	■
Battery	○	○	○
Price	■	■	■
Screen	○	○	○
Exterior	○	○	○
System performance	◇	■	◇
Exercise and health	○	○	○
Function	◇	◇	◇
Material of case	■	■	■
Data Connections	■	■	■
Watch strap	■	◇	◇
Texture	◇	■	◇

Note: The important goal is recorded as ○, the light important goal is recorded as ◇, the light secondary goal is recorded as ■, the secondary goal is recorded as □.

important design goal in refined and comfortable user groups, and the light secondary design goal in hedonic user groups; The watch strap is the light important design goal in the hedonic and comfortable user group, and the light secondary design goal in the refined user group; Texture is the less important design goal in refined and comfortable user groups, and the light secondary design goal in hedonic user groups.

7 Conclusion

The increasingly competitive market environment and changing user needs make product design updates faster, and how to quickly find product improvement strategies is now the focus of product design updates. The rapid development of e-commerce has brought together a large amount of data, and the product-related information accumulated in the process has injected a new source of ideas for product design. Among them, online product reviews are an important data asset that can provide valuable user feedback for product designers, but online reviews have big data characteristics such as large data volume, low value density, and high commercial value, which make it difficult to obtain useful information through formalized and organized model descriptions. Kansei Engineering is often used to explore the relationship between human perception and product design parameters. In this paper, based on the analysis of online product review data and the characteristics of Kansei Engineering, we propose a multi-user demand forecasting model that organically combines sentiment classification and user profiling.

Based on the big data of smart watches reviews, this paper firstly combines text mining and sentiment analysis to establish a smart watches user demand evaluation system to obtain user feedback quickly. After that, we summarize users' perceptual preferences of using smart watches through word frequency analysis and KJ analysis of perceptual words, and cluster the target user groups through Censydiam analysis of perceptual preferences to infer their purchase motives, so as to build user portraits, and finally count the ratings of each user group on demand evaluation indexes, extract product design goals and distinguish their importance based on the functional positioning of index types and their application strategies, and establish a multi-user group. Finally, we count the ratings of each user group on demand evaluation indicators, extract the product design objectives and distinguish their importance based on the functional orientation of the indicator types and their application strategies, and establish a multi-user group demand forecasting model. The weight distribution characteristics of the multi-user group demand evaluation indicators determine the functional positioning of the indicator types, which can be used as an important decision basis for product design objectives and enhance the overall satisfaction of the multi-user group with the product. Compared with the traditional design method, the data used has the characteristics of real-time and large data volume, and the acquired perceptual words and perceptual evaluation are more reasonable. The method can collect user perception information more extensively and classify information more precisely to better correlate users' needs, thus forming a more standardized design guide and improving user experience. Since JD.com's online review anti-crawling mechanism limits the number of users' online reviews to be crawled, the review data is still not large enough, and this paper has not comprehensively considered the relationship between mapping product design positioning and various design elements, so follow-up work Further research is needed.

References

1. Huan, Y.: The integration of data and design - a research on the innovation path of big data analysis to derive insight into user needs. Art & Design **05**, 100–103 (2019)
2. Xuanhui, Y., Bingbing, C., Jing, Z.: Research on the mining strategy of users' potential information needs based on computational intelligence analysis under the background of big data. Inf. Rec. Mat. **20**(09), 196–198 (2019)
3. Yang, Y.: Research on the Evaluation Method of Smart Watch User Experience. Jiangnan University (2018)
4. Jiangyong, L., Wei, Z.: Research on product improvement design from the perspective of online review data mining. Pack. Eng. **42**(06), 135–141 (2021)

5. Danping, J., Jian, J., Qian, G., Siyu, D.: Research on user demand mining from the perspective of kansei engineering. J. China Soc. Sci. Tech. Info. **39**(03), 308–316 (2020)

6. Jinliang, C., Feng, Z., Yi, L., Qianyi, Z.: Research on product design method based on kansei engineering. Pack. Eng. **40**(12), 162–167 (2019)

7. Man, D., Yu, C., Xiaoguang, H., Lingying, Z.: Research status and progress of kansei engineering design methods. J. Machi. Desi. **37**(01), 121–127 (2020)

8. Shijian, L., Wenjie, L., Yetao, F.: Gene design of side profile of SUV product family driven by consumer preference. J. Mech. Eng. **52**(02), 173–181 (2016)

9. Jianning, S., Zhaoshan, T., Nan, J., Yanhao, C., Xiong, L.: Research on product design method for user cluster. J. Mach. Desi. **36**(04), 119–123 (2019)

10. Yudong, H., Wei, L., Huiyong, Y.: Product modular configuration method considering customers' perceptual needs. J. Comp.-Aid. Desi. Comp. Grap **27**(07), 1320–1326 and 1340 (2015)

11. Lu, L., Yongnian, Z., Weimin, D., Min, K.: Multi-objective-driven tractor product family shape genetic design. Trans. Chinese Soc. Agri. Eng. **33**(17), 82–90 (2017)

12. Yaxue, Z., Zhenya, W.: Subjective product evaluation system based on kansei engineering and analytic hierarchy process. Symmetry **12**(8) (2020)

13. Lei, X., Xiao, Y., Ye, Z.: Research on optimized product image design integrated decision system based on kansei engineering. Applied Sciences **10**(4), (2020)

14. Linxuan, Y., Yeli, L., Qingtao, Z., Yanxiong, S., Yuning, B., Wei, H.: Summary of web crawler technology research. J. Physics: Conf. Series 1449 (2020)

15. Chang, Y., Kun, T., Chunyang, Y.: Mobile phone product improvement based on review bigdata. Comp. Integra. Manuf. Sys. **26**(11), 3074–3083 (2020)

16. Amjad, O., Jamshid, M., Farhad, G.: Enriched latent dirichlet allocation for sentiment analysis. Expert Systems **37**(4) (2020)

17. Yan, G., Yingrui, J., Yuzhe, S., Xinxiong, L.: User perceptual cognition and product perceptual design method and application. Pack. Eng. **42**(02), 22–27 and 34 (2021)

18. Qing, B., Yuxiang, R.: Analysis of the relationship between product design and consumer behavior. Appreciation **05**, 274 (2015)

19. Yue, Q., Chaoyue, D.: Based on censydiam model and characters in contemporary TV series to create persona. Comp. Sci. Softw. Eng. (2020)

Understanding User Perception and Trust when Results from a Dating Abuse Detection Application Are Displayed

Tania Roy[1]([✉]) [iD], Larry F. Hodges[2] [iD], and Fehmi Neffati[1]

[1] New College of Florida, Sarasota, FL, USA
{troy,fehmi.neffati24}@ncf.edu
[2] North Carolina School of Science and Mathematics, Morganton, NC, USA
larry.hodges@ncssm.edu

Abstract. SecondLook is a mobile phone application that uses machine learning algorithms to detect digital dating abuse from text messages. An online survey was conducted where participants (N = 202) were provided with three different visualizations of the detection screen (labeled *text only*, percentage of abusive text messages only, and labeled and percentage of abusive text messages) to understand a) What is the threshold of abusive text messages that would motivate the user to consider themselves in an abusive relationship? (30%, 50%, or 70% abusive text messages) b) What is the most effective way to visualize the results of the detection classifier that would invoke user trust and encourage them to receive necessary help? c) Which visualizations nudge users to trust machine learning-based classification results? We found the *Text only* condition to show significant differences across all three research questions and will use these results for future iterations of SecondLook.

Keywords: Digital dating abuse · Data visualization · User trust

1 Introduction

SecondLook is a mobile app-based intervention targeted toward individuals who suspect they may be in an abusive relationship. SecondLook includes three main functions: 1) Awareness – which follows a traditional awareness-based abuse intervention campaign. The app includes selected content about relationships from the U.S. Department of Health and Human Services-sponsored online intervention website, loveisrespect.org, as well as resources for self-analyzing a relationship [4, 17] 2) Detection – this allows users to obtain an automated "second look" at text messages exchanged with their partner. Users select a contact to be analyzed, and the application returns a response as to which, if any, of the messages sent by that contact indicates abuse. SecondLook uses a machine-learning algorithm [18] on a remote server to classify individual messages as "abusive" or "non-abusive" in the context of interpersonal relationships 3) Resources – this displays local interpersonal abuse-related resources (shelters, hotlines, counselors,

S. Yamamoto and H. Mori (Eds.): HCII 2022, LNCS 13306, pp. 65–79, 2022.
https://doi.org/10.1007/978-3-031-06509-5_5

etc.) in a consolidated list. If the user declines to provide their location, SecondLook displays resources at the national level [19].

The current iteration of SecondLook utilizes a Linear Support Vector Machine with a tf-idf feature extractor with a unigram input as its detection algorithm. Its accuracy, compared to the other classifiers on the test dataset, was 91%. This accuracy score is in the same range as other mental health-related apps that utilize machine learning algorithms reported in the literature [5, 6, 10]. Due to the sensitive nature of the information that is being presented to the user, it is also essential to be extremely cautious about how the results are displayed. We are interested in understanding how data visualization has an impact on a user's trust in the information reported by the app. The questions driving the exploration of this paradigm are: 1) How can we support the credibility of the detection algorithm to enable the user to trust the results they view? and; 2) Is there a correlation between users' trust in the results presented and their likelihood of seeking help. As the purpose of the phone app is to prevent abuse preemptively in its early stages, user trust plays a huge role in the intervention and success of this app. Interpersonal relationships, what is acceptable in a relationship, and language usage are subjective and unique to every couple. Our training set is a representative sample but does not account for the diversity in language and relationship dynamics.

We all recognize the need to design a user interface that will empower the user to choose whether they want help or not. The purpose of the detection feature and the machine learning classifier is to support the decision-making process around whether the user is in an abusive relationship or not. *This paper focuses on the data visualization of the results from the machine learning algorithms, as the success and acceptance of the detection feature of this application is heavily dependent on the accuracy and ability to gain user trust.* This paper also seeks to explore the social question - what is the threshold value of a user considering themselves in an abusive relationship (i.e.- what are the number of text messages that would enable the user to consider themselves in an abusive relationship)? Finally, we are interested in further understanding which visualizations nudge people into trusting the results generated via machine learning models.

2   Background

The issue of addressing trust in machine learning and artificial intelligence has been explored. These papers investigate how humans develop trust in new technologies and apply that knowledge in enhancing trust. A starting point for all these papers is to define *trust*. Trust is a societal building block that allows humans to make decisions about uncertain or unfamiliar events [2, 8, 9]. Trust is a multi-dimensional paradigm that is difficult to define broadly. According to Patrick et al. [16], trust can be differentiated into three layers: *dispositional trust, learned to trust, and situational trust* [8]. This complexity has led to multiple researchers identifying parts of the trust paradigm to understand how those portions affect trust levels. Interface designs can affect the trust of users, and design guidelines have helped in identifying such issues and resolving them [11]. However, with machine learning algorithms and results being displayed to users the challenge has compounded. Patrick et al. discuss that trust require two parties: "the truster and the trustee". The user, being the *truster,* makes informed decisions based on information from *someone.* There have been mixed results when someone the user is trusting is a machine or an algorithm. Schaefer et al. [20] have identified that equal consideration should be given to the machine, as well as the individual user's character, when considering trust in machines. They argue that paying attention to the user's character and their background could have a strong influence on building trust in a new technology. Pandey et al. identify factors or motivators behind why people struggle to change opinions and are skeptical of the data source and logic. They discussed why people anchor to core beliefs and the complexity of the situation influences these opinions. The results of the paper discuss that the potential factors that can help change opinions are 1) negative thoughts experienced through a boomerang effect, 2) overwhelming evidence, and 3) persuasion [14]. This work also investigates whether the visualization of statistical information leads to increased persuasion when compared with lack of visualizations and found consistent results supporting this hypothesis. Yuki et al. [21] address cultural differences and how people from different cultural settings would approach the same situation differently. The literature discusses how users from Western societies, such as the U.S., are generally willing to build trust faster in newer environments than users from Eastern societies, such as Japan. We observed a commonality in most of the studies when it comes to potential practices that would increase users' trust in the technology. The most common combination is predictability and dependability, with the studies showing [3, 12, 20] that predictable, consistent outcomes increase trust over time. In this paper, we try to consider how all those factors can play a role in a user trusting the results that the models would display. We seek to determine what improvements we can implement that can induce the user to seek help promptly. Building trust in machines can be a complex subject. Existing evidence suggests that several stable human traits can affect how each individual responds to automation. These traits include age, gender, ethnicity, and personality. However, the power and directionality of these various relationships have not been consistent across differing studies. A great way to increase this trust is through having multiple users and reviewers try out the technology and write quality reviews to be published. Seeing that someone else has tried, and vouches for, the app has been found to increase a new user's trust [3]. Moreover, knowing how something works in advance of using it can help build users' trust. If the reasoning process can be made knowledgeable and inspectable, the data rendered understandable, and the path from data to decision made intelligible, then a relationship of trust could be constructed [3]. Evidence of good functioning was one of the factors driving people to develop trust and change their minds about machine-generated intel. On the other hand, Pandey et al. [14] point out that skepticism in the logic behind the machine learning algorithm - or the complexity - can reduce trust and serve as an obstacle to people changing their minds.

3   Methods

The three primary research questions for this paper focus on understanding the impact of data visualization on machine learning results and user trust.

- RQ1: What is the threshold of abusive text messages that would motivate the user to consider themselves in an abusive relationship?

- RQ2: What is the most effective way to visualize the results of the detection classifier that would invoke user trust and encourage them to receive necessary help?
- RQ3: Which visualizations nudge users to trust machine learning-based classification results?

Fig. 1. The home screen, or landing page, of the app (Left).

Fig. 2. The page containing the definition of dating abuse (Right)

To explore our research questions detailed above, we conducted a cross-sectional survey. The survey was a within-subject study where we recruited 202 participants who were randomly assigned to one of the nine conditions (Table 1). In this section, we describe how we developed the survey and recruited participants, including detailing the contents of the survey questionnaires, the study participant selection procedure, and the demographic questionnaire. As the target population of the SecondLook phone app is college-aged women in the United States, we primarily recruited female participants who had a minimum of a U.S. high school education as a representative sample to participate in this study. They were given a demographic questionnaire and a modified dating abuse awareness questionnaire asking about their knowledge or personal experience related to interpersonal violence [13].

3.1 Survey: Conditions and Experiment Design

There were three primary research questions and three conditions to support each of these questions: Presented with a set of text messages which contained both abusive and non-abusive text messages *What is the threshold of abusive text messages (in a percentage value) that will lead a user to conclude they are in an abusive relationship?* Three conditions are:

- 50%–50% (abusive – non-abusive)
- 70%–30% (abusive – non-abusive)

Table 1. The nine conditions of the study: participants were randomly assigned to one of these conditions

Percentage of Abusive – Non-abusive text messages	Visualization 1: Pie chart only (Pie)	Visualization 2: Text Messages with labels (Text)	Visualization 3: Text Messages with labels & pie chart (Pie & Text)
50%–50%	Condition 1	Condition 4	Condition 7
70%–30%	Condition 2	Condition 5	Condition 8
30%–70%	Condition 3	Condition 6	Condition 9

- 30%–70% (abusive – non-abusive)

Does data visualization have an impact on the user's trust when it comes to using the detection application? Three conditions are:

- Pie chart showing a percentage value for abusive and non-abusive text messages
- Text messages that have been labeled as abusive and non-abusive
- Pie chart showing the percentage value of text messages that have been labeled as abusive and non-abusive

The thresholds of the number of text messages were varied to understand whether the percentage of text messages has an impact on how users perceive abusive relationships. The data visualization conditions were designed to understand the type of visualizations and the level of transparency in terms of the machine learning detection algorithm that are needed to gain user trust. For the RQ3 mentioned in Sect. 3, we displayed a visualization to the participants. Based on the visualization and their perception of it, we asked them whether they think that the person receiving the text messages is in an abusive relationship or not. The participants were asked to label 10 text messages according to 3 categories: "Abusive," "Non-Abusive," or "I don't know." The first two categories are aligned with the machine learning classification labels used by our detection program, and we chose to add the category of "I don't know" to account for the fact that human raters are more adept at understanding nuances. In doing so, we hoped to capture the subjective nature of digital dating abuse detection.

3.2 Survey Questions

The survey was developed using Balsamiq's online wireframe tool to create the user-interface mockups and then deployed through Qualtrics.com. The participants were recruited through Mechanical Turk, a crowdsourcing web service that manages the supply and demand of tasks requiring human intelligence to complete [7, 15]. We recruited 202 participants in all, with approximately 21 (Mean = 22.4, SD = 1.13) participants per condition, after eliminating those with incomplete surveys.

The survey tool walked the participants through the mock-ups of the apps where they were shown each screen (Figs. 1 and 2) and provided with a background scenario stating, *"In a hypothetical scenario, imagine you are Jane. To evaluate the text messages Jack has sent you, click on the 'Detecting Abusive Text Messages Button' (To simulate this click, please click on the arrow at the bottom of the page)."* This randomly allocated participants in 1 out of the 9 conditions listed in Table 1 and displayed a screen with the results from the detection application (ex- Fig. 3a, b, or c).

Depending on the condition, a random user-interface mockup of the detection page was displayed, along with the analyzed results. The participants were then asked to answer the following questions using a 5-point Likert scale (Strongly Disagree – Strongly Agree).

- If you were Jane, based on the results presented in the study, would you consider yourself in an abusive dating relationship?

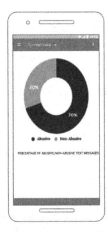

Fig. 3. a, b, c: What the users saw if they were assigned to Condition 5, Condition 8 or Condition 2, respectively.

- Have the results been presented in an effective manner such that you understand the analysis of the text messages clearly?
- If you were Jane, would you trust the information about the abusive text messages that the app has provided to you?
- Based on the definition of digital dating abuse provided earlier, please drag and drop the texts in the three boxes provided and arrange the text messages into one of three categories ("Abusive," "Non-Abusive," or "I don't know").

All the participants were shown in Fig. 4, which provided a mock-up of the resources page and asked the following questions:

- In your opinion, would Jane use the resources feature, as shown above, to get help?
- As a user, would you use the resources feature, as shown above, to get help?
- How would you rank the list of resources in order of preference (1 - most preferred)?

All participants were then shown a screen with unlabeled text messages based on certain conditions. For example, Condition 2 participants were shown 7 abusive and 3 non-abusive text messages and asked to place them into 3 categories based on both their prior knowledge and the information provided during the study. The 3 categories that they could select were "Abusive," "Non-Abusive," and "I don't know."

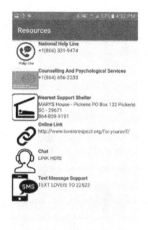

Fig. 4. Resources page displayed to the users

4 Results

4.1 Demographic Questionnaire

We had 202 participants complete the surveys on Mechanical Turk. The mean age of the participants was 36 years (SD = 11.727), they were primarily female (96.53%), Caucasian (57.43%), had a bachelor's degree (42.57%), and were married (48.51%). The participant pool is representative of our target population regarding ethnicity, gender, and education level. 65.5% of the participants selected "Definitely yes" when asked if they or someone they knew had ever been in an unhealthy relationship, and 41.5% responded "Definitely yes" when asked if they were aware of unhealthy dating relationships at school, within the community, or the workplace. Both responses reinforced the necessity of the phone app. In response to the question, "would you want to use technology, such as a phone or web application, to help understand if you are being abused?" 50.50% replied "yes," and 35.64% said "maybe" (Fig. 5).

4.2 Data Analysis

From the survey, we collected Likert Scale responses from all the participants, which were coded as "Strongly Agree," "Somewhat Agree," "Neither Agree nor disagree,"

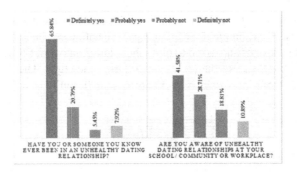

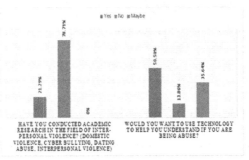

Fig. 5. Results of the demographic questionnaire

"Somewhat Disagree," or "Strongly Disagree." The responses were re-coded to numerical values 1-5, where 1 corresponded to "Strongly Agree" and 5 was coded for "Strongly Disagree." All further analysis was conducted on the re-coded numerical values. We used SPSS to analyze each of the results for the questions mentioned in the previous section. We first conducted a full factorial ANOVA to determine if there is an interaction effect between any of the nine conditions (visualizations - Pie, Text, and Pie & Text and the percentage of abusive text messages - 30–70, 70–30, and 50 -50). As none of the factors had any interaction effect, we conducted a univariate posthoc multiple comparison for observed means with Bonferonni correction [1].

For the question, *"Have the results been presented in an effective manner such that you understand the analysis of the text messages clearly?"* we conducted multiple comparisons across three visualizations (Text, Pie, and Pie & Text). We found a significant mean difference between the conditions Pie vs Text (mean difference = -.67) and Pie vs Pie & Text (mean difference = -.49). However, there was no significant difference between the conditions Pie & Text and Text only (Fig. 6). For the same question, when we looked at the percentage condition, we found a significant difference between the conditions where the users were presented with the conditions 30% abusive vs 50% abusive (mean difference = 0.77), and conditions 70% abusive vs 50% abusive (mean difference = 0.96) (Fig. 7).

Multiple Comparisons

Dependent Variable: Effective
Bonferroni

(I) presentation		Mean Difference (I-J)	Std. Error	Sig.	95% Confidence Interval	
					Lower Bound	Upper Bound
Pie	Text	-.67*	0.179	0.001	-1.10	-0.23
	Pie&Text	-.49*	0.179	0.021	-0.92	-0.06
Text	Pie	.67*	0.179	0.001	0.23	1.10
	Pie&Text	0.18	0.179	0.957	-0.25	0.61
Pie&Text	Pie	.49*	0.179	0.021	0.06	0.92
	Text	-0.18	0.179	0.957	-0.61	0.25

Based on observed means.
The error term is Mean Square(Error) = 1.077.
* The mean difference is significant at the .05 level.

Fig. 6. Comparison of visualizations for the question: have the results been presented in an effective manner such that you understand the analysis of the text messages clearly?

percentageabusive

Multiple Comparisons

Dependent Variable: Effective
Bonferroni

(I) percentageabusive		Mean Difference (I-J)	Std. Error	Sig.	95% Confidence Interval	
					Lower Bound	Upper Bound
30.00	50.00	.77*	0.179	0.000	0.34	1.20
	70.00	-0.19	0.179	0.842	-0.63	0.24
50.00	30.00	-.77*	0.179	0.000	-1.20	-0.34
	70.00	-.96*	0.179	0.000	-1.39	-0.53
70.00	30.00	0.19	0.179	0.842	-0.24	0.63
	50.00	.96*	0.179	0.000	0.53	1.39

Fig. 7. Comparison of percentage abusive text messages for the question: have the results been presented in an effective manner such that you understand the analysis of the text messages clearly?

For the question - *If you were Jane, based on the results, would you consider yourself in an abusive dating relationship?* - we did not find any significant differences when comparing the three different visualizations (Fig. 8). When comparing the percentage of abusive vs non-abusive text messages displayed to the user (Fig. 9), we found significant differences between the conditions 70% vs 50% and 30% vs 70%.

presentation

Multiple Comparisons

Dependent Variable: Abusive
Bonferroni

(I) presentation		Mean Difference (I-J)	Std. Error	Sig.	95% Confidence Interval	
					Lower Bound	Upper Bound
Pie	Text	-0.19	0.183	0.880	-0.64	0.25
	Pie&Text	0.12	0.183	1.000	-0.32	0.56
Text	Pie	0.19	0.183	0.880	-0.25	0.64
	Pie&Text	0.31	0.184	0.269	-0.13	0.76
Pie&Text	Pie	-0.12	0.183	1.000	-0.56	0.32
	Text	-0.31	0.184	0.269	-0.76	0.13

Based on observed means.
The error term is Mean Square(Error) = 1.131.

Fig. 8. Comparison of visualizations for the question - If you were Jane, based on the results, would you consider yourself in an abusive dating relationship?

For the *question- If you were Jane, would you trust the information about the* abusive *text messages that the app has provided to you* - when comparing the three different visualizations (Fig. 10), there was a significant difference between the conditions Pie vs Text only. When comparing the percentage of abusive vs non-abusive text messages

percentageabusive

Multiple Comparisons

Dependent Variable: Abusive
Bonferroni

(I) percentageabusive		Mean Difference (I-J)	Std. Error	Sig.	95% Confidence Interval	
					Lower Bound	Upper Bound
30.00	50.00	0.07	0.183	1.000	-0.37	0.51
	70.00	-.46*	0.184	0.038	-0.91	-0.02
50.00	30.00	-0.07	0.183	1.000	-0.51	0.37
	70.00	-.53*	0.183	0.012	-0.98	-0.09
70.00	30.00	.46*	0.184	0.038	0.02	0.91
	50.00	.53*	0.183	0.012	0.09	0.98

Based on observed means.
The error term is Mean Square(Error) = 1.131.
*. The mean difference is significant at the .05 level.

Fig. 9. Comparison of percentage of abusive text messages for the question - If you were Jane, based on the results, would you consider yourself in an abusive dating relationship?

presentation

Multiple Comparisons

Dependent Variable: Trust
Bonferroni

(I) presentation		Mean Difference (I-J)	Std. Error	Sig.	95% Confidence Interval	
					Lower Bound	Upper Bound
Pie	Text	-.54*	0.178	0.008	-0.97	-0.12
	Pie&Text	-0.37	0.178	0.124	-0.80	0.06
Text	Pie	.54*	0.178	0.008	0.12	0.97
	Pie&Text	0.18	0.179	0.952	-0.25	0.61
Pie&Text	Pie	0.37	0.178	0.124	-0.06	0.80
	Text	-0.18	0.179	0.952	-0.61	0.25

Based on observed means.
The error term is Mean Square(Error) = 1.070.
*. The mean difference is significant at the .05 level.

Fig. 10. Comparison of visualizations for the question - If you were Jane, would you trust the information about the abusive text messages that the app has provided?

percentageabusive

Multiple Comparisons

Dependent Variable: Trust
Bonferroni

(I) percentageabusive		Mean Difference (I-J)	Std. Error	Sig.	95% Confidence Interval	
					Lower Bound	Upper Bound
30.00	50.00	.66*	0.178	0.001	0.23	1.09
	70.00	-0.21	0.179	0.731	-0.64	0.22
50.00	30.00	-.66*	0.178	0.001	-1.09	-0.23
	70.00	-.87*	0.178	0.000	-1.30	-0.44
70.00	30.00	0.21	0.179	0.731	-0.22	0.64
	50.00	.87*	0.178	0.000	0.44	1.30

Based on observed means.
The error term is Mean Square(Error) = 1.070.
*. The mean difference is significant at the .05 level.

Fig. 11. Comparison of percentage of abusive text messages for the question -:If you were Jane, would you trust the information about the abusive text messages that the app has provided?

displayed to the user (Fig. 11), we found significant differences between the conditions 70% vs 50% and 30% vs 50%.

For the questions - In *your opinion, would Jane use the resources feature as shown above to get help? And, comparing percentage abusive text messages, would you use the resources feature shown above to get help?* - none of the conditions had any significant differences.

We then analyzed how the participants labeled the text messages that were presented to them at the end of the study into the three categories: "abusive," "non-abusive," and "I don't know." Appendix: Table 1 contains all the mislabeled sentences across all conditions. To align with our machine learning classification labels, we counted all responses of "I don't know" as a mislabel or the wrong classification. The participants were unaware that the messages being displayed to them in this task were identical to the ones they had observed earlier in Conditions 4–9. However, as participants for Conditions 1–3 did not have access to labeled text messages before completing this task, we ensured that this question appeared in a separate screen and that none of the participants could navigate back to previous screens. When adding all the scores of the mislabeled sentences per condition together, we found that the combination of Pie & Text had the most mislabels, with a difference of 32% of mislabeled sentences from the least mislabeled vitalization, which is the Pie visualization. We found a steady increase of around 17% in the mislabeled sentences as we increased in complexity. The difference between Pie and Text is 17.18%, and the difference between Pie & Text and Text only is 17.94% (Table 2). The sentence that was mislabeled consistently across all conditions was, *"Ok we will text when we leave"* (Mean = 3.77, S. D = 3.08), and the highest number of mislabels were recorded for the participants in Condition 4, with a total of 10 mislabels. The sentence, *"U handing out with Mike and Marvin?'* recorded the 11 mislabels for Condition 3, but other conditions were mislabeled sporadically (Mean = 2, s.d = 3.77).

Table 2. Total number of text messages mislabeled by the user across 3 visualizations.

	Pie & Text	Text	Pie
Total number of mislabeled sentences	78	64	53

5 Discussion

The results from the data analysis clearly indicate that, when presented with a set of text messages with a varying percentage of abusive text messages (30%, 50%, and 70%) for the question – *If you were Jane, would you consider yourself in an abusive relationship?* - there was a significant difference between the conditions 30% vs. 70% abusive text messages and the thresholds 50% vs. 70% abusive text messages. This indicates that, if the percentage of abusive text messages was increased, the perception of another person being in an abusive relationship would increase. We were unable to find any indications for the lower thresholds, suggesting that the higher number of abusive text messages did nudge participants to consider that Jane was in an abusive relationship. For the same questions, we were unable to find any significant difference when comparing across the three visualization conditions. We had initially hypothesized that the Text only condition would outperform Pie& Text and the Pie only conditions. The Pie only condition does not provide any contextual information that could nudge users toward any conclusion. However, the Pie & Text condition provides visualization and labeled text messages. The results from the survey can be interpreted as a lack of personal connection with the scenario presented to the user. As the character Jane was fictional, the participants were unable to see themselves in Jane's scenario and, hence, we found no significant results for the visualizations. For RQ1, we were unable to pinpoint a single threshold that made participants think that Jane was in an abusive relationship. However, we can conclude that the higher the number of abusive text messages, the more likely people are to agree that the relationship is abusive.

When considering RQ2 and RQ3 (data visualization, effectiveness, and trust), we found significant differences between the conditions Pie vs. Text, which was aligned with our initial hypothesis. We hypothesized that, if the user is presented with the labeled text messages, they will tend to trust the results rather than depending on percentage output values presented from an unknown black-box algorithm. We were unable to find any significant differences between the Text only vs. Pie & Text conditions. Although the findings align with the work of Pandey et al. [14], we hope to further explore this paradigm in future studies to understand the connection between data presentations and mental overload. Based on these results, for future iterations of the SecondLook mobile application, we are moving toward a data visualization with labeled text messages to increase data transparency and trust in the results.

For the second part of RQ3 (resources for help), we were unable to find any significant differences across the resource list presented. Although we did not find any significant differences across experimental conditions in terms of using resources for help or help-seeking behavior, participants ranked the list of resources in order of preference. Participants ranked online resources, such as websites and forums, above any other form of support. We will use this observation to restructure the resources feature for SecondLook and add a tiered and customizable approach to resources instead of simply listing them.

For the self-classification of text messages task, the results were not significant. Most participants were able to label text messages in correct categories. However, the text messages that were mislabeled (Appendix: Table 3) provided insights on the subjective nature of digital dating abuse and the complexity of using machine learning algorithms effectively and gaining user trust. We hypothesize that, since the text messages were not shown as a list (Fig. 3a), participants may have considered the list as a conversation thread, hence concluding that the text messages were abusive or were too ambiguous to classify.

6   Limitations and Future Work

Although we were unable to draw concrete conclusions for RQ1, RQ2, and RQ3 from the results, we were able to identify significant factors that will allow us to make informed choices about future design iterations in relation to SecondLook. These results also have broader impacts in terms of the longevity of an application using machine learning applications to detect mental health-related concerns or interpersonal violence-related issues. As the Text only condition outperformed the Pie only condition, we can conclude that providing context to the results of the application (in this case, labels to the text messages) is key to gaining user trust. However, we were unable to determine the balance between information overload and lack of information. For future iterations of the study, we propose using a different visualization and adding more contextual information about the machine learning algorithm to identify whether knowing about the algorithm and its functioning impacts user trust. Digital dating abuse detection and user trust in the detection algorithm are multi-faceted problems that require further investigation. However, we infer from the results that data transparency and clarity about how the data is being analyzed have the potential to nudge users toward trusting the application and thus increase the chances of preventing dating abuse-related violence.

Acknowledgements. We would like to thank Dr. Jerome McClendon and Ms. Adriana Souza for their contributions to the research methodology and data analysis.

Appendix

Table 3. Number of mislabeled text messages, per condition, presented to participants randomly assigned to 9 experimental conditions. In the table below column C9-C1 are experimental conditions. Column labelled Miss refers to total missed classifications or classification errors

Sentences	C9	C8	C7	C6	C5	C4	C3	C2	C1	Miss	Mean	Std.dev
Ok we will text when we leave	0	6	5	2	2	10	3	1	5	35	3.78	3.07
Still at dinner, in a good conversation. Didn't forget about you,	3	8	2	1	4	5	2	4	5	34	3.78	2.11
Had a big pizza earlier, where are ya thinken	4	0	5	0	0	4	3	0	4	20	2.22	2.17
I can't stand this I'm going to find you and then we'll see how much talking you do,	2	4	1	2	2	3	2	3	1	20	2.22	0.97

(continued)

Table 3. (*continued*)

Sentences	C9	C8	C7	C6	C5	C4	C3	C2	C1	Miss	Mean	Std.dev
gimme ur fb pw right now you crazy girl. right now. who r u tslking to you? tell me ASAP	0	4	3	0	2	5	0	2	2	18	2.00	1.80
U handing out with Mike and Marvin?,	5	0	0	2	0	0	11	0	0	18	2.00	3.77
Do this for me. DO it. WTH	0	6	0	0	5	0	0	6	0	17	1.89	2.85
Sorry for not responding, got sidetracked	1	4	1	0	0	6	1	2	1	16	1.78	1.99
If you do not send me nudes then I will slander your name	0	3	3	0	2	3	0	0	1	12	1.33	1.41
WTH.Bitch.Asshole	0	3	0	0	3	0	0	2	0	8	0.89	1.36
Cool will try to make it. hungry,	2	0	0	0	0	0	4	0	0	6	0.67	1.41
Nice we re just leavin lol,	1	0	0	1	0	0	2	0	0	4	0.44	0.73
Who are you always texting? I know that you're cheating? If I catch you & don't send me the passwords, I'll kill you and whoever you are tweeting,	0	2	0	0	0	0	0	0	0	2	0.22	0.67
One of my friends said he saw you walking on campus? I thought you were busy all day today. Shouldn't you be in the library? If you had all this free time,you should've been it at my place,	0	0	0	0	0	0	0	0	0	0	0.00	0.00

References

1. Bland, J.M., Altman, D.G.: Multiple significance tests: the Bonferroni method. BMJ. **170**(310), 6973 (1995)
2. Bok, S.: Lying: Moral choice in public and private life. Vintage. (2011)
3. Chatzimparmpas, A., Martins, R.M., Jusufi, I., Kucher, K., Rossi, F., Kerren, A.: The state of the art in enhancing trust in machine learning models with the use of visualizations. Computer Graphics Forum. 713–756 (2020)
4. Dating Abuse Statistics (2018)
5. De Choudhury, M., Gamon, M., Counts, S., Horvitz, E.: Predicting Depression via Social Media (2013)
6. Dinakar, K., Reichart, R., Lieberman, H.: Modeling the detection of Textual Cyberbullying (2011)
7. Ipeirotis, P.G.: Analyzing the amazon mechanical turk marketplace. XRDS: Crossroads. The ACM Magazine for Students **17**(2), 16–21 (2010)
8. Marsh, S., Dibben, M.R.: The role of trust in information science and technology. Ann. Rev. Inf. Sci. Technol. **37**, 465–498 (2003)
9. Marsh, S., Meech, J.: Trust in design. CHI'00 extended abstracts on Human factors in computing systems 45–46 (2000)
10. McGhee, I., Bayzick, J., Kontostathis, A., Edwards, L., McBride, A., Jakubowski, E.: Learning to identify internet sexual predation. Int. J. Electron. Commer. **15**(3), 103–122 (2011)
11. Nielsen, J.: Trust or bust: communicating trustworthiness in web design. Jacob Nielsen's Alertbox (1999)
12. Oleson, K.E., Billings, D.R., Kocsis, V., Chen, J.Y., Hancock, P.A.: Antecedents of trust in human-robot collaborations. In: IEEE International Multi-Disciplinary Conference on Cognitive Methods in Situation Awareness and Decision Support (CogSIMA), pp. 175–178 (2011)
13. Organizaing a teen dating abuse awareness week (2009)
14. Pandey, A.V., Manivannan, A., Nov, O., Satterthwaite, M., Bertini, E.: The persuasive power of data visualization. IEEE Trans. Visual Comput. Graphics **20**(12), 2211–2220 (2014)
15. Paolacci, G., Chandler, J., Ipeirotis, P.G.: Running experiments on amazon mechanical turk (2010)
16. Patrick, A.S., Briggs, P., Marsh, S.: Designing systems that people will trust. Security and Usability **1**(1), 75–99 (2005)
17. QUIZ: Is My Relationship Healthy? - www.loveisrespect.org: https://www.loveisrespect.org/for-someone-else/is-my-relationship-healthy-quiz/
18. Roy, T., McClendon, J., Hodges, L.: Analyzing abusive text messages to detect digital dating abuse. In: IEEE International Conference on Healthcare Informatics (ICHI), pp. 284–293 (2018)
19. Roy, T., Young, E., Hodges, L.F.: A second look at SecondLook: design iterations and usability of digital dating abuse detection and awareness app. In: IEEE International Conference on Healthcare Informatics (ICHI), pp. 1–11 (Nov. 2020)
20. Schaefer, K.E., et al.: A meta-analysis of factors influencing the development of trust in automation: implications for human-robot interaction. Army Research Lab Aberdeen Proving Ground Md Human Research And Engineering (2014)
21. Yuki, M., Maddux, W.W., Brewer, M.B., Takemura, K.: Cross-cultural differences in relationship-and group-based trust. Pers. Soc. Psychol. Bull. **31**(1), 48–62 (2005)

Recommendation Model for Tourism by Personality Type Using Mass Diffusion Method

Ni Xu[1], Yu-Hsuan Chen[1], Ping-Yu Hsu[1], Ming-Shien Cheng[2(✉)], and Chi-Yen Li[1]

[1] Department of Business Administration, National Central University, No.300, Jhongda Rd., Jhongli City, Taoyuan County 32001, Taiwan (R.O.C.)
984401019@cc.ncu.edu.tw
[2] Department of Industrial Engineering and Management, No.84, Ming Chi University of Technology, Gongzhuan Rd., Taishan Dist., New Taipei City 24301, Taiwan (R.O.C.)
mscheng@mail.mcut.edu.tw

Abstract. Recommendation systems were applied in various fields, such as e-tailing, movies, books,…, and so on. Among them, tourism recommendation systems are also one of the widely research topics. Many tourism recommendation system studies use Collaborative Filtering (CF) method and try to add personality traits to the recommendation system methods to improve the precision. Zhou et al. (2007) suggested that Mass Diffusion (MD) method has more precision than CF method, but this method is mostly applied to recommending movie genres or books, but less often in tourism. Compared to other recommendation systems, fewer studies have considered personality traits such as Big Five Factor (BFF) and Myers-Briggs Type Indicator (MBTI) 16 (personality type). In this study, we used the MD method to establish a model of tourism attraction recommendation, and combined the personality traits commonly used in other recommendation system studies, such as BFF and MBTI 16, to achieve personalized recommendation of tourism attractions. According to the experimental results of this study, compared with the CF method combined with personality traits, the MD method combined with personality traits can recommend attractions to users more accurately.

Keywords: Tourism recommendation · Big Five Factor (BFF) · Myers-Briggs type indicator (MBTI) 16 personality type · Mass diffusion method

1 Introduction

The topics of research on recommendation systems are various, such as online retail, movies, books, etc. Among them, the tourism recommendation system for tourism, the third largest industry in the international economic development, is also one of the topics widely studied [1]. Studies [2] have indicated that about 65% of people often rely on Internet resources, such as travel websites or social media, to choose their tourist attractions initially when arranging their travel itineraries. Since travel is an emotional experience, it is usually difficult for people to know exactly which tourist attractions

S. Yamamoto and H. Mori (Eds.): HCII 2022, LNCS 13306, pp. 80–95, 2022.
https://doi.org/10.1007/978-3-031-06509-5_6

they want to go to when arranging a trip in the early stage [3]. In addition, compared to watching movies or reading books, the composition factors of tourist products are more complex, and there are more items to consider, so more costs, such as energy and time, must be spent to collect relevant information.

Collaborative Filtering (CF) is a method commonly used by recommendation systems and often used for research on tourism-related recommendation systems. In order to be able to recommend products to users more accurately, some studies have tried to add personality traits to the recommendation system method, such as Ishanka and Yukawa (2018) [4] combining the Big Five (BF) personality traits with articles on Twitter to connect users' personality traits and emotion and recommend tourist attractions to them. Hafshejani and Kaedi et al. (2018) [5] used the BF personality test and K-means clustering to improve the collaborative filtering.

Personality traits are believed to affect people's preferences [1, 6, 7], for example, Jani (2014) [8] thought that there is a significant relationship between the BF personality traits and the travel curiosity of travelers, or people with certain personality traits prefer certain trips, such as Tok (2011) [9] showed that people with extroversion and openness to experience are more likely to take adventure trips. Research results [10] have shown that the most commonly used personality measurement methods in the survey of recommendation system are BF personality test and MBTI 16 personality test. Zhou et al. (2007) [11] believed that the mass diffusion method has a higher accuracy rate than the collaborative filtering has been mostly used for recommending movie genres or books, etc. [12, 13], but it is rarely used in tourism-related fields. The studies based on mass diffusion method, compared with other recommendation system methods, have less considered personality traits, such as BF personality traits or MBTI-16 personality.

For this study, the Mass Diffusion (MD) method was used to build a tourist attraction recommendation model, combined with the techniques of assessing personality traits commonly used in other recommendation system research, such as BF personality test and MBTI-16 personality test, to achieve personalized recommendation of tourist attractions.

This paper organized as follow: (1) Introduction: Research background, motivation and purpose. (2) Related work: Review of scholars' researches on the mass diffusion method and personality traits. (3) Research methodology: Content of research process in this study. (4) Result analysis: Experimental results and the discussion of the test results. (5) Conclusion and future research: Contribution of the study, and possible future research direction is discussed.

2 Related Work

2.1 Mass Diffusion Method

MD, in physics, refers to a system in which two groups of substances with different components are transported outwards according to their diffusion coefficients. The higher the diffusion coefficient, the easier it is for the substance to be diffused into another component with a lower diffusion coefficient until the substances in the system are evenly distributed. In the research of recommendation system methods, a bipartite graph is often used to represent the relationship between users and items. Both users and items are regarded as two different categories. When a user touches (likes or buys) an item, there will be a line between the two nodes, which means that there is a relationship between the two. The line is non-directional, and there are no lines between nodes in the same category. Based on the fact that there will be two different categories (components) in a system, MD theory can be adopted as a method for recommendation system.

Zhou et al. (2007) [11] proposed that the resources of a node should be evenly distributed to the nodes in another category that is connected to it. It also means that the resources should be spread out evenly and the node no longer holds any resources. This is not the same as in physics, where the substances diffused into the system are in balance (including the diffusion coefficients of the two components). It is assumed that a bipartite graph is used to represent the relationship between users and items, and the user set is $U = \{u_1, u_2, ..., u_j\}$, while the item set is $I = \{i_1, i_2, ... i_k\}$. Given a target user v (the object of the item to be recommended by the system), the method consists of three steps as follows:

$$\bullet MD_{vi} = \left\{ \begin{array}{c} 1, \; there\ is\ an\ edge\ between\ target\ user\ v\ and\ i \\ 0, \; otherwise \end{array} \right\} \quad (1)$$

$$\bullet MD'_{ui} = \sum_{i \in I} \frac{MD_{vi}}{D(i)}, \quad u \in U, \; i \in I \quad (2)$$

$$\bullet MD''_{ui} = \sum_{u \in U} \frac{MD_{ui}}{D(i)}, \quad u \in U, \; i \in I \quad (3)$$

Among them, D(i) and D(u) in (2) and (3) represent the node degree of the item or the user and refer to the number of nodes connected to the other set. After taking the above steps, the node score of each item will be calculated. The items with high node scores represent that the target user may be interested in them. The system will recommend the items to the target user in descending order of scores according to the recommended item list. The studies [11] have pointed out that this method can recommend items to users more accurately than the standard CF, because the system tends to recommend more popular items (with higher node degree) based on the law of conservation of mass in the mass diffusion theory. There are researches on improving MD methods, such as Zhou, Kuscsik et al. (2010) [13] combining the MD method with another recommendation system method—heat spreading, and using λ to adjust the ratio of the two methods. Zhang and Liu et al. (2017) [12] used the KNN method to treat users who are close to the target user as the target user, and increased the nodes degree of the item to improve the recommendation probability of items that may be of interest to the target user.

2.2 Personality Traits

Everyone has a different personality and behavior pattern. In the same environment, different people will show different behaviors. Even so, there are still some people who perform similar behaviors or make similar decisions. Using personality traits to classify people can easily describe these similar behaviors. Some psychologists believe that personality traits are a characteristic of people, which can be used to explain different people's consistent behaviors or responses to the same environment [14]. Personality traits can be used to explain differences in general behaviors.

The BF personality or Big Five Factor (BFF) model is the most commonly used model to describe personality traits in psychology today. According to the model people's personality are divided into five dimensions, namely Openness to experience, Conscientiousness, Extroversion, Agreeableness and Neuroticism, referred to as OCEAN using the acronyms. The Big Five personality traits are independent of each other [15], which means that a person can have multiple personality traits, such as having a higher degree of openness in experience and a higher degree of conscientiousness at the same time. Some studies [16] pointed out that people's personality will not change much even after a major event. long-term steady personality is the advantage of BFF model.

There are many ways to measure the BF dimensions. Among them, the most commonly used by scholars is the Big Five Inventory (BFI), including forty-four items, of which the feature is that there are multiple descriptors for some BFI items instead of a single one, so as to measure the BF dimensions more accurately. The five-level Likert Scale format (strongly agree, agree, neutral, disagree, and strongly disagree) is used. Later, some scholars designed questionnaires with only five questions and ten questions, called BFI-10 (shorter version of the BFI) and Ten-Item Personality Inventory (TIPI) [17], in response to the reality that it is difficult for some respondents to complete the questionnaire in time. The TIPI(Fig. 1) was used for this study, because some research results [18] have shown that the survey results were not much different from those using BFI, and that the effectiveness of TIPI is slightly better than other shorter version of the BFI.

Disagree strongly	Disagree moderately	Disagree a little	Neither agree nor disagree	Agree a little	Agree moderately	Agree strongly
1	2	3	4	5	6	7

I see myself as:
1. _____ Extraverted, enthusiastic.
2. _____ Critical, quarrelsome.
3. _____ Dependable, self-disciplined.
4. _____ Anxious, easily upset.
5. _____ Open to new experiences, complex.
6. _____ Reserved, quiet.
7. _____ Sympathetic, warm.
8. _____ Disorganized, careless.
9. _____ Calm, emotionally stable.
10. _____ Conventional, uncreative.

TIPI scale scoring ("R" denotes reverse-scored items): Extraversion: 1, 6R; Agreeableness: 2R, 7; Conscientiousness: 3, 8R; Emotional Stability: 4R, 9; Openness to Experiences: 5, 10R]

Fig. 1. TIPI subject

MBTI-16: The 16 personality types, its concept originated from the book "Psychological Types" (or "The Psychology of Individuation") by Swiss psychologist Carl Gustav Jung, whose personality taxonomies originated from the author's subjective observation, not an objective experiment. The 16 personality types are divided into four dimensions and each dimension contains two types, namely Extraversion/Introversion, Sensing/iNtuition, Thinking/Feeling, Judging/ Perceiving. The two personality types in each dimension are opposite to each other. Each person is said to have one preferred quality from each dimension, producing 16 personality types. Unlike the BF model, a person can only have one personality based on MBTI 16. MBTI-16 is widely used for aptitude test [19–21], and some studies [22] have pointed out that MBTI-16has a certain degree of reliability and validity. According to statistics from the Center for Applications of Psychological Type (CAPT), about two million people take the MBTI-16 personality test every year (Table 1).

Table 1. MBTI 16 types personality classification

ISTJ	ISFJ	INFJ	INTJ
ISTP	ISFP	INFP	INTP
ESTP	ESFP	ENFP	ENTP
ESTJ	ESFJ	ENFJ	ENTJ

3 Research Methodology

A new method was created for this study to combine personality trait weight with mass diffusion method. In this study the model is divided into two parts, the first one is the MD method, and the second is the addition of personality trait weight. For example, as shown in Fig. 2, the user is User (u), the tourist attraction is Item (i), and the personality trait is P (p).

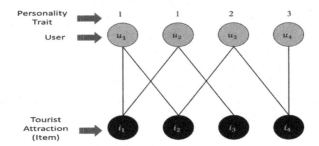

Fig. 2. Structure of research method

3.1 Mass Diffusion Method

The first part of the model is the MD method, which will perform two diffusions. Given the target user u_1, the item linked to u_1 is marked as 1, otherwise it is 0. The first diffusion as Fig. 3 is from the items to the users, and the fractions are evenly distributed. For example, i_1 will distribute 1/2 to u_1 and 1/2 to $u2$. After the diffusion is over, each user's fractions will be added up separately. The second diffusion as Fig. 4 is from the users to the items, and the fractions are also equally distributed. For example, u_1 will distribute 1/2 to $i1$ and 1/2 to i_2, and u_2 will distribute 1/4 to i_1 and 1/4 to i_3.

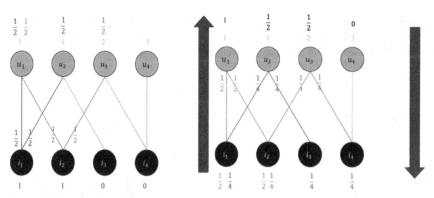

Fig. 3. First diffusion   **Fig. 4.** Second diffusion

3.2 Personality Trait Weight,

The second part of the recommendation system model is to add the personality trait weight. When calculating the weight of personality traits, only the personality types and items are considered, not the users as showed in Fig. 5. Take the first type of personality as an example (the personality type is marked as 1). There are two users who have this personality and like two specific tourist attractions. Therefore, the first type of personality will have four lines connected to the tourist attractions (including the same tourist attractions). The number above the personality node is four, as shown in Fig. 6. By analogy, the number of the second type of personality (the personality type is marked as 2) is two, and the number of the third type of personality (the personality type is marked as 3) is 1, as shown in Fig. 7.

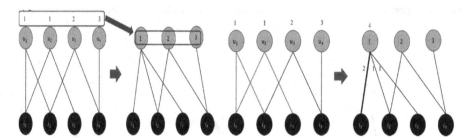

Fig. 5. Replace user with personality trait   **Fig. 6.** Type1 personality trait as example

Assume that the personality trait set is $P = \{p_1, p_2, p_3, ..., p_t\}$ and the item set is $I = \{i_1, i_2, i_3, ..., i_k\}$. The personality weight formula, $wp_t \rightarrow i_k$, represents the proportion of people with the t-th type of personality who like the k-th tourist attraction, calculated as follows:

$$\bullet w_{p_t \rightarrow i_k} = \frac{D_{(p_t \rightarrow i_k)}}{D_{(p_t)}}, \quad p \in P, \ i \in I \qquad (4)$$

$(p_t \rightarrow i_k)$ represents the number of those have the t-th type of personality and like the k-th tourist attraction; (pt) represents the total number of tourist attractions (including the number of tourist attractions repeated calculated) that the people with t-th type of personality like. Taking the first type of personality as an example, $wp_1 \rightarrow i_1$ is 2/4, $wp_1 \rightarrow i_2$ is 1/4, and $wp_1 \rightarrow i_3$ is 1/4 as showed in Fig. 8.

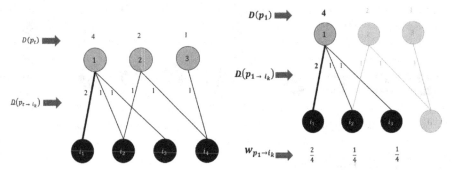

Fig. 7. The volume of each personality trait   **Fig. 8.** Type1 personality trait weights

3.3 Combining Personality Traits and Mass Diffusion Method

Taking Fig. 4 above as an example, the fractions below the tourist attractions are the original ones after two processes of diffusion, and now the personality trait weight is added (Fig. 9). Taking i_1 as an example, it receives the fractions from u_1 and u_2, which are 1/2, and 1/4 respectively. Each fraction is then multiplied by the weight of the tourist attraction corresponding to the user's personality trait ($wp_1 \rightarrow i_1$). Next, taking i_2 as an example, it receives the fractions from u_1 and u_3, which are 1/2, and 1/4 respectively. Each fraction is then multiplied by the weight of the tourist attraction corresponding to the user's personality trait ($wp_1 \rightarrow i_2$ & $wp_2 \rightarrow i_2$), as shown in Fig. 10.

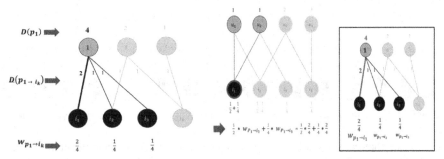

Fig. 9. The volume and personality trait weight of type1

Fig. 10. Combining personality traits weight—i_1 as example

Next, taking i_2 as an example, it receives the fractions from u_1 and u_3, which are 1/2 and 1/4 respectively. Each fraction is then multiplied by the weight of the tourist attraction corresponding to the user's personality trait ($wp_1 \rightarrow i_2$ & $wp_2 \rightarrow i_2$), as shown in Fig. 11. Then, add all the products, and the sum is the final recommendation score

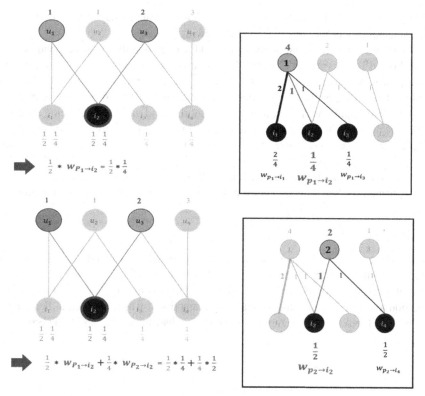

Fig. 11. Combining personality traits weight—i_2 as example

of the item. For example, the recommendation score of i_1 is 3/8(1/2*2/4 + 1/4*2/4), and that of i_2 is 2/8(1/2*1/4 + 1/4* 1/2). The items will be recommended in descending order from the item with highest scores to that with lowest scores.

4 Research Results

4.1 Data Collection

The data of this study has been collected from the online questionnaire survey. Respondents have been asked to take the Big Five personality test, MBTI 16 personality test and choose tourist attractions.

The data on tourist attractions has been collected from the Tourism Bureau, Ministry of Transportation and Communications, including the photos of the top 30 tourist attractions of the quick search options. The number of visitors to each of the top 30 attractions is about 500,000 or more (2020/10). For this study, respondents were asked to browse the photos of these 30 tourist attractions first, and then selected four from them that they had visited and like in no order of priority. The selection of four photos is based on the research of Cowan (2001) [23], indicating that people have four most impressive blocks (images) in their Short-Term Memory (STM), which means that people's most impressive number of pictures is four after viewing pictures.

Data on the Big Five personality and MBTI 16 personality of the respondents has been collected for this study. The MBTI test questions come from the public test website (https://www.16personalities.com/), based on and adapting the research results of Katharine Cook Briggs, the first scholar who studied the MBTI 16 personality trait theory. The questionnaire has a high degree of reliability and validity after being tested by the website author. The Chinese version of the Big Five personality test, containing ten multiple-choice questions, comes from Lu and Liu et al. (2020) [24]. The personality score calculation is performed according to Goslingc and Rentfrow et al. (2014) [25]. The topic is TIPI, which is often used in the Big Five personality research, and it has been confirmed by research [18] that it has a high degree of reliability and validity.

4.2 Data Processing

In this study, a total of 522 questionnaires were collected, of which 42% of the respondents were males and 58% were females, aged from 21 to 25. The aforementioned 30 photos of tourist attractions have been transformed into 01 matrix, of which 1 means that the respondent selected the attraction and 0 means that it was not selected. Personality traits are also labeled in order. Figure 12 shows the distribution of MBTI 16 personality types.

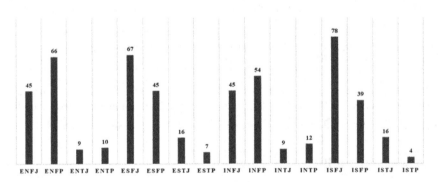

Fig. 12. The distribution of MBTI 16 personality types

Based on Gosling and Rentfrow et al. (2014) [25], in this study, the score of each personality was calculated separately, and showed the range each personality dimension of the user lies in according to the quartile standard. According to the range, four indicators, Low, Medium Low, Medium High and High, can be created and then simplified to 1 (Medium High & High) and 0 (Low) according to the indicators, with Medium Low not counted. In this study, Medium Low is also reduced to 0 to facilitate the subsequent calculation of personality taxonomy.

Because in this study it is assumed that each personality is one type (typological personality) and there will not be multiple types, so the way the personality is expressed in the Big Five personality model needs to be modified. The personality dimension

(OCEAN) marked with 0 or 1 is regarded as binary, and then converted into decimal, which is the so-called binary to decimal conversion. Figure 13 shows the distribution of the number of people who have been divided into thirty-two personality types modified according to the Big Five personality model.

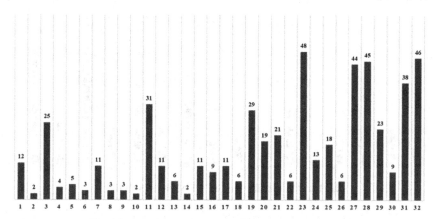

Fig. 13. The distribution of OCEAN with decimal code

Imbalanced classes of data are a common problem encountered in classifier model training, which may cause the model to encounter the "accuracy paradox" problem when carrying out performance evaluation. Although the accuracy of the model is high, it cannot indicate that the model performance is good. Taking the data set of this study as an example, there are 16 types of personality types in MBTI, and the number of people with certain personality is roughly the same with each other. As shown in Fig. 12, there are 78 persons with ISFJ personality, but only 4 persons have ISTP personality, with classes of data imbalanced.

Because the number of datasets in this study is small, the oversampling method is used. Synthetic Minority Over-sampling TEchnique (SMOTE) is an oversampling method commonly used for the related research currently, and is an improved method of random oversampling [26]. The random over-sampling method is to directly copy the data with a small number of types, which is prone to cause the problem of model over-fitting. The SMOTE is designed to artificially synthesize new data for data with a small number of types. The following is the SMOTE formula: xi is one of the data with a small number of categories, xj is one of the data with a small number of adjacent types in xi, and δ is a random number, the value of which is 0–1.

In this study, SMOTE was performed on MBTI-16 personality types and BF personality traits. Because the BF categories are subdivided into thirty-two personality traits, the number of respondents with certain personality traits is too small. When divided into training sets and test sets, in some sets there is only one respondent with certain personality trait, so SMOTE cannot be performed. The big five personality dimensions are all independent, and it is impossible to merge minor categories into other categories. According to Jani (2014) [8], as for the tourism topic, the proportion of neuroticism describing the personality traits of travelers is the lowest among the five personality dimensions.

Therefore, the dimension of neuroticism was omitted from this study, focusing on the other four dimensions (OCEA). Then the code was transformed, personality types were labeled, sixteen personality types were determined, and then SMOTE was performed. Figure 14 shows the distribution of the number of personality types after the neuroticism has been omitted from the Big Five.

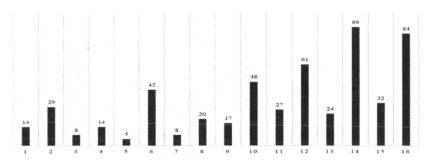

Fig. 14. The distribution of OCEAN after SMOTE

In this study, the data set was divided into training sets and test sets according to the ratio of the number of personality types, and the ratio of training sets to test sets was 8:2. SMOTE was performed on training sets (except for the Big Five personality traits (OCEA) divided into thirty-two personality types), the K of SMOTE was set to 2, and the data items in all categories were oversampled, so as to make the number the same as that of data items in the largest category. Each data item in the training set contains four tourist attractions, representing the four selected by the user from 30. On the other hand, two favorite tourist attractions are randomly hidden in each data item in the test set, that is, assuming that each user has only two favorite tourist attractions, and the other two hidden attractions are used to test whether they can be recommended by the model.

4.3 Experimental Results

In order to ensure the stability of the experimental results, the model has been used to process the data several times, only adding the personality trait weight for the first time, and after that the simple MD method was employed. The results showed as followed (Fig. 15). MD is the mass diffusion method; MD & MBTI is MD combined with the MBTI-16 personality types; MD & BFF is MD combined with the Big Five personality traits; MD & BFF marked with OCEAN is MD combined with all the dimensions of the BF model and divided into 32 types; that marked with OCEAN is MD combined with four dimensions of the BF personality excluding neuroticism and divided into 16 types; that marked with SMOTE is the training set has been synthesized using SMOTE. According to previous studies [27, 28], a model would approach stability after the data items it contains have been diffused about five to ten times. The diffusion has been performed twice for the models used for this study. As shown in Fig. 15, it can be seen that after repeating the process for four times (a total of eight times of diffusion), the value will be consistent.

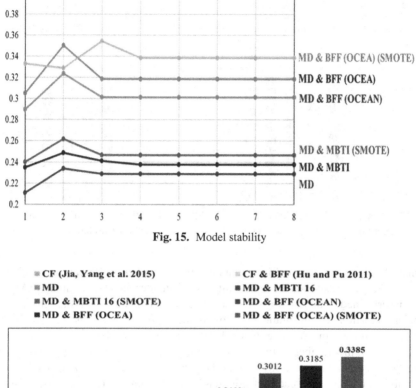

Fig. 15. Model stability

Fig. 16. Comparison of the precision/recall of each model (recommend two attractions) * When two attractions are recommended, the accuracy and recall will be the same

Figure 16 shows the results of all models after eight times of diffusion (except for the CF). In addition, the CF (based on Jia and Yang (2015) [29]) was compared with CF combined with the Big Five factors (CF & BFF) (based on Hu and Pu (2011) [30]).

As shown in Figs. 17 and 18, the accuracy and recall of the model MD & BFF (OCEAN) (SMOTE) are the best among all models. When two tourist attractions are recommended, the accuracy rate and recall rates are both 0.33; when four tourist attractions are recommended, the accuracy rate and recall rate are 0.28 and 0.52.

Next, observe the accuracy rate of each personality category in the two models, MD vs MBTI (SMOTE) and MD vs BFF (OCEA) (SMOTE), of which the training set on

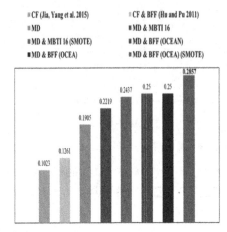

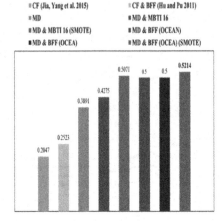

Fig. 17. Comparison of precision of each model (recommended four attractions)

Fig. 18. Recall comparison of each model (recommended four attractions)

which the SMOTE has been performed. In Fig. 19, the numbers of training sets for No. 3, No. 4, No. 8, No. 11, and No. 16 personality are all smaller than ten. Although SMOTE has been performed on the training set, because the number of data items of each category has been oversampled to the number of those of the largest category, the categories with fewer data items are mostly fake data, which cannot improve the individual accuracy rate. In Fig. 20, the number of training sets of No. 3, No. 5 and No. 7 personality are all smaller than ten. Although SMOTE has been performed on the training set, because the number of data items of each category has been oversampled to the number of those of the largest category, the categories with fewer data items are mostly fake data, which cannot improve the individual accuracy rate. As a result, if the correct tourist attractions are not recommended for the category at the beginning (individual accuracy rate is 0), it is still not easy to recommend the correct tourist attractions even if the SMOTE has been performed on the training set and the number of data items has been increased.

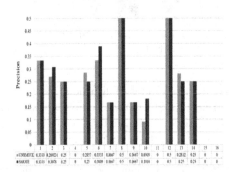

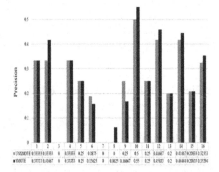

Fig. 19. Each accuracy of MD vs MBTI (SMOTE)

Fig. 20. Each accuracy of MD vs BFF (OCEA) (SMOTE)

The model used for this study needs to select two from 28 tourist attractions and recommend them to the target user (excluding the respondent's favorite two attractions), with a random hit rate of 0.07. According to experiments, the tourist attraction recommendation model built using the mass diffusion method and personality traits (the accuracy rate is 0.33 when two attractions are recommended) has a higher accuracy rate, compared with the tourist attraction recommendation model built using the collaborative filtering method and personality traits (the accuracy rate is 0.12 when two attractions are recommended). On the other hand, among the methods combining MD and personality traits, the BF personality model (the accuracy rate is 0.33 when two attractions are recommended) has higher accuracy rate than the MBTI-16 personality model (the accuracy rate is 0.24 when two attractions are recommended).

5   Conclusion and Future Research

Based on the experiments of this study, the tourist attraction recommendation model built using the MD method (the accuracy rate is 0.22 when two attractions are recommended) can recommend attractions more accurately to target users than the collaborative filtering method (the accuracy rate is 0.12 when two attractions are recommended). On the other hand, the personalized tourist attraction recommendation model built using personality traits and MD method can further improve the accuracy rate of the model (the accuracy rate is 0.33 when two attractions are recommended), helping target users to faster find the tourist attraction that they may have an interested.

The experimental data sets collected for this study, whether it is BF personality traits or MBTI-16 personality types, have a serious imbalance in the number of personality categories, which affects the model's recommendation accuracy. Future research can focus on tourist attractions and distinguish them by types (natural landscapes, historical sites…) instead of specific locations (Jufen, Forbidden City…), making tourist attractions more diverse. In practice, travel arrangements are often planned on the basis of itinerary (package), including accommodation, catering, transportation, etc., rather than a single tourist attraction, so travel itinerary recommendations can also be included in the research. In addition, it is suggested that different research methods can be used to combine personality traits and MD methods to improve the performance of the model.

References

1. Braunhofer, M., Elahi, M., Ricci, F.: User Personality and the New User Problem in a Context-Aware Point of Interest Recommender System. Inf. Comm. Technol. Tour. 537–549 (2015)
2. Crowel, H., Gribben, H., Loo, J.: Travel content takes off on YouTube. Think with Google (2014)
3. Neidhardt, J., Schuster, R., Seyfang, L., Werthner, H.: Eliciting the users' unknown preferences. In: Paper presented at the Proceedings of the 8th ACM Conference on Recommender systems – RecSys '14 (2014)
4. Ishanka, U.P., Yukawa, T.: User Emotion and personality in contextaware travel destination recommendation. In: Paper presented at the 2018 5th International Conference on Advanced Informatics: Concept Theory and Applications (ICAICTA) (2018)

5. Hafshejani, Z.Y., Kaedi, M., Fatemi, A.: Improving sparsity and new user problems in collaborative filtering by clustering the personality factors. Electron. Commer. Res. **18**(4), 813–836 (2018). https://doi.org/10.1007/s10660-018-9287-x

6. Sertkan, M., Neidhardt, J., Werthner, H.: What is the "Personality" of a tourism destination? Inf. Technol. Tour. **21**(1), 105–133 (2018). https://doi.org/10.1007/s40558-018-0135-6

7. Al-Samarraie, H., Eldenfria, A., Dawoud, H.: The impact of personality traits on users' information-seeking behavior. Inf. Process. Manage. **53**(1), 237–247 (2017). https://doi.org/10.1016/j.ipm.2016.08.004

8. Jani, D.: Relating travel personality to Big Five Factors of personality. Tourism: Int. Interdiscip. J. **62**(4), 347–359 (2014)

9. Tok, S.: The big five personality traits and risky sport participation. Soc. Behav. Personal. Int. J. **39**(8), 1105–1111 (2011)

10. Dhelim, S., Aung, N., Bouras, M.A., Ning, H., Cambria, E.: A survey on personality-aware recommendation systems (2021)

11. Zhou, T., Ren, J., Medo, M., Zhang, Y.C.: Bipartite network projection and personal recommendation. Phys. Rev. E Stat. Nonlin. Soft. Matter Phys. **76**(4 Pt 2), 046115 (2007). https://doi.org/10.1103/PhysRevE.76.046115

12. Zhang, F., Liu, Y., Xiong, Q.: A novel preferential diffusion recommendation algorithm based on user's nearest neighbors. Int. J. Digital Multimed. Broadcast. **2017**, 1–7 (2017). https://doi.org/10.1155/2017/1386461

13. Zhou, T., Kuscsik, Z., Liu, J.-G., Medo, M., Wakeling, J.R., Zhang, Y.-C.: Solving the apparent diversity-accuracy dilemma of recommender systems. Proc. Natl. Acad. Sci. **107**(10), 4511–4515 (2010)

14. Pervin, L.A.: Personality: current controversies, issues, and directions. Annu. Rev. Psychol. **36**(1), 83–114 (1985)

15. Costa, P.T., McCrae, R.R.: Normal personality assessment in clinical practice: the NEO personality inventory. Psychol. Assess. **4**(1), 5 (1992)

16. Komarraju, M., Karau, S.J., Schmeck, R.R., Avdic, A.: The Big Five personality traits, learning styles, and academic achievement. Personality Individ. Differ. **51**(4), 472–477 (2011)

17. Gosling, S.D., Rentfrow, P.J., Swann, W.B., Jr.: A very brief measure of the Big-Five personality domains. J. Res. Pers. **37**(6), 504–528 (2003)

18. Furnham, A.: Personality and Intelligence at Work: Exploring and Explaining Individual Differences at Work (2008)

19. Yu, C.: The relationship between MBTI and career success-for chinese example. In: Paper presented at the 2011 International Conference on Management and Service Science (2011)

20. Garden, A.: Relationships between MBTI profiles, motivation profiles, and career paths. J. Psychol. Type **41**, 3–16 (1997)

21. McCaulley, M.H., Martin, C.R.: Career assessment and the Myers-Briggs type indicator. J. Career Assess. **3**(2), 219–239 (1995)

22. Randall, K., Isaacson, M., Ciro, C.: Validity and reliability of the Myers-Briggs personality type indicator: a systematic review and metaanalysis. J. Best Pract. Health Prof. Divers. **10**(1), 1–27 (2017)

23. Cowan, N.: The magical number 4 in short-term memory: a reconsideration of mental storage capacity. Behav. Brain Sci. **24**(1), 87–114 (2001)

24. Lu, J.G., Liu, X.L., Liao, H., Wang, L.: Disentangling stereotypes from social reality: astrological stereotypes and discrimination in China. J. Pers. Soc. Psychol. (2020)

25. Gosling, S., Rentfrow, P., Potter, J.: Norms for the ten item personality inventory (2014). Unpublished data

26. Chawla, N.V., Bowyer, K.W., Hall, L.O., Kegelmeyer, W.P.: SMOTE: synthetic minority over-sampling technique. J. Artif. Intell. Res. **16**, 321–357 (2002)

27. Zeng, W., Zeng, A., Shang, M.-S., Zhang, Y.-C.: Information filtering in sparse online systems: recommendation via semi-local diffusion. PLoS ONE **8**(11), e79354 (2013)
28. Wang, Y., Han, L.: Personalized recommendation via network-based inference with time. Phys. A: Stat. Mech. Appl. **550**, 123917 (2020)
29. Jia, Z., Yang, Y., Gao, W., Chen, X.: User-based collaborative filtering for tourist attraction recommendations. In: Paper Presented at the 2015 IEEE International Conference on Computational Intelligence and Communication Technology (2015)
30. Hu, R., Pu, P.: Enhancing collaborative filtering systems with personality information. In: Paper Presented at the Proceedings of the Fifth ACM Conference on Recommender Systems (2011)

Robots and Avatars Appearance and Embodiment

Effect of Face Appearance of a Teacher Avatar on Active Participation During Online Live Class

Tomohiro Amemiya$^{(\boxtimes)}$ (ID), Kazuma Aoyama, and Kenichiro Ito (ID)

Virtual Reality Educational Research Center, The University of Tokyo,
7-3-1 Hongo, Bunkyo, Tokyo 113-8656, Japan
amemiya@vr.u-tokyo.ac.jp
https://vr.u-tokyo.ac.jp/

Abstract. The worldwide outbreak of the COVID-19 pandemic led to many changes in the methods used to impart education, with nearly all university courses in Japan transitioning to an online format, particularly video conferencing of live lectures. Considering the difficulties students face in remaining engaged during online lectures, we propose methods to maximize student participation by displaying a real-time animated avatar of the teacher's face over the lecture slides. Students were presented with photos of different teachers and asked to select whom they would prefer to take a class with, and whom they would not prefer. An open-source deep fake tool was then used to animate the selected photos by following the facial expressions of a teacher in real-time. These animations were superimposed over the lecture slides in an online class. Our experimental results show that students taught by their preferred teacher's animated avatar posted more comments, which was the form of feedback used, compared to when they were taught by a less preferred teacher's avatar on the slides. We speculate that a change in the teacher's avatar influences active student participation in online learning.

Keywords: Avatar · Deep fake · Online lecture

1 Introduction

The outbreak of the COVID-19 pandemic led approximately 83% of university classes in Japan to transition to an online format in the spring semester of 2020 [13]. Academic institutions worldwide are witnessing a similar transition. Online or remote lectures fall into two categories: asynchronous and synchronous. In an asynchronous class, a pre-recorded video of a lecture that is uploaded on a video streaming site or on a shared drive can be played on demand by students. In a synchronous class, a live-streaming lecture is conducted, wherein the video file is broadcast using remote video conferencing systems, such as Zoom[1] and

---

[1] https://zoom.us/.

S. Yamamoto and H. Mori (Eds.): HCII 2022, LNCS 13306, pp. 99–110, 2022.
https://doi.org/10.1007/978-3-031-06509-5_7

Google Meet[2]. Students participate in these lectures through group discussions, practical sessions, or experiments.

The most common format of remote lectures is delivered as presentation slides with the lecturer's face shown on a webcam. However, some lecturers request all videos to be switched off to reduce bandwidth and protect privacy. Although research focusing on whether displaying an instructor's face is effective in online education have been inconclusive, some researchers claim that students rated a class more positively when a video of the lecturer's face was displayed [8,9,21,23] (but see also [1,6]). Wilson *et al.* found that students had more positive perceptions when the instructor was visually present in videos, compared with when the videos did not show the instructor [23]. Kizilcec *et al.* noted that students preferred their instructors to be visible via video in online lectures, although this did not particularly help them learn more than when an instructor was not visually present [9]. Although significant differences have not been noted in the class results between the presence or absence of the teacher's face in remote lectures, a study reported that improved information recall from video lectures is solely dependent on the difficulty level of the content. However, [22] participants preferred video instructions with the instructor's face displayed [9]. Moreover, displaying pictures of the instructor's face or anthropomorphic faces improves learning performance, compared to when they are not displayed [17]. In contrast to these findings, other studies have found that students perceive the instructor's visual presence as unsatisfactory or distracting [1] and demanding high cognitive load [6].

Lecturer videos have been used to convey accurate information and learning that would otherwise be conducted face-to-face. However, accomplishing this task does not require a webcam, per se. For example, an application that uses virtual camera features can allow users to transform their own appearance (e.g., FaceRig and Snap Camera), and they are widely used in remote video conferencing systems. Another study examined the use of a facial expression transformation system in a teleconference setting and revealed that transforming participants' facial expressions into smiling characters led to more ideas being presented during brainstorming, compared to a typical teleconferencing situation [14]. The positive effects of smiling on interpersonal outcomes in a virtual environment have been reported [15], and nonverbal cues in facial expression have been shown to produce more positive outcomes [10,12,16]. These results indicate that utilizing VR technology to transform one's face or body may evoke a positive effect in a virtual education setting.

Physical appearance plays a role in various aspects of daily life, and evaluating educational merit is no exception. For example, highly attractive people are judged to be more intellectual [20]. Instructors with attractive appearances are rated more highly by their students [24]. This is especially true among male lecturers and female students [2]. Craig *et al.* found that instructors wearing business attire had a higher effect on student performance, compared with those wearing casual attire [3]. Although an individual's appearance can be

---

[2] https://meet.google.com/.

manipulated to a certain extent by, for example, changing one's hairstyle, clothes, and makeup, the avatar of a lecturer's appearance can be further manipulated in a similar manner through image processing. Lecturers whose appearance can be controlled can positively affect students' learning. However, so far, studies have yet to verify the effect of the avatar of a lecturer's appearance on learning in lectures and classes at educational institutions.

This study presents a report wherein a lecturer's face is presented as a real-time animated avatar displayed alongside the lesson slides to increase student participation in live online classes. In the study, students were presented with photos of different teachers and asked to select whom they would prefer to take a class with and whom they would not prefer. An open-source deep fake tool was then used to animate the selected photos by following the facial expressions of the actual teacher in real-time.

2   Approach

2.1   Participants

We examined an online lecture titled "Mixed Reality Systems/Media Informatics" for graduate students at the University of Tokyo. The class was 105 min long and took place via Zoom on July 2, 2020. A preparation class was conducted on June 25 to prepare for the experiment. A total of 105 participants were randomly divided into two groups and each group was given a different URL for the Zoom meeting, and those who were absent during the preparation session were assigned to Group 1. Finally, 51 students were assigned to Group 1, whereas 49 students were assigned to Group 2, and five or more students were absent from the main experiment. This experiment was approved by the Ethics Committee of the University of Tokyo.

2.2   Stimuli

To determine the face images for the avatars in the main experiment, photographs of four faces shown in Fig. 1 (a) were presented in the preparation class. We asked students the following question: "Which teacher would you like to take a class with?" Students were then requested to rank the face images using the entire ranking method.

We asked students the following question: "Which teacher would you like to take a class with?" They were then requested to rank the face images using the entire ranking method. Images A and C were face images generated by StyleGAN [7] and portrayed Asian male faces that do not exist[3]. Images B and D were created based on images of real males (B: first author, D: a professor emeritus of the University of Tokyo). The age-filtering process was applied to images A, B, and C using FaceApp[4] (Wireless Lab; v4.0.12) to control the appearance of age among the four images.

---

[3] https://generated.photos/faces.

[4] https://www.faceapp.com/.

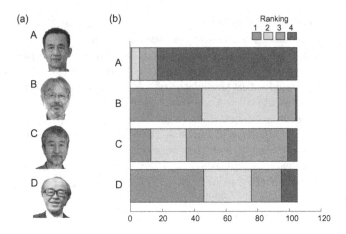

Fig. 1. (a) Candidates whose facial photographs were used to portray a teacher. (b) Band chart of ranking against photos (N = 105). A ranking of 1 indicates the best.

The histogram of rankings obtained from the 105 students in the preparation session is presented in Fig. 1 (b). The Friedman test result revealed a significant difference between the photos ($\chi^2(3) = 163.5$, $p < .0001$). The post-hoc test of the Wilcoxon signed rank test with Bonferroni correction showed no significant difference between B and D ($z = 1.57$, $p = .12$, $PS_{dep} = .53$), whereas other combinations showed significant differences ($zs > 4.00$, $ps < .0001$, PS_{dep} .70). Note that PS_{dep} is the probability of dominance, which represents the effect size.

These results suggest that the order of the photos of the instructors whose classes students wanted to was attend was (B,D) > C > A. Therefore, we selected the photos of A and B as a pair of images with different degrees of agreeableness or preference for the lecturers in the main experiment.

The open-source software Avatarify[5] (v0.2.0; 56e8f6d) was used to generate a video of the lecturer's face. Avatarify uses a generative adversarial network (GAN) to convert the still image of a face into a video based on other reference videos [18]. As shown in Fig. 2, facial motion was transferred from the driving video (from a webcam) to the teacher's photo. We adopted this as our experimental system because it does not necessitate the use of any special hardware other than a webcam, nor a 3D model of the face beforehand. We used OBS Studio[6] (v25.0.8) to display the instructor's face as a Picture-in-Picture mode to prevent students from switching off the webcam view (i.e., lecturer's face view) on Zoom.

---

[5] https://github.com/alievk/avatarify.
[6] https://obsproject.com/.

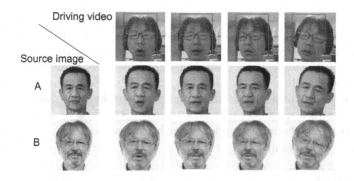

Fig. 2. Examples of face animation driven by webcam.

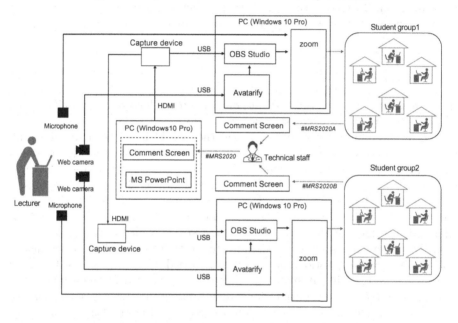

Fig. 3. System configuration.

2.3   System

Figure 3 shows the system configuration wherein the photos of a teacher's face were animated using facial and non-verbal cues extracted from the teacher's real-time video in an online live class. We issued different Zoom meeting IDs to the two randomly selected groups and requested them to access the IDs specified in the main experiment. Although the Zoom meeting IDs were transmitted from different PCs, the lecturer's PC screen output was branched using a capture board (AVerMedia GC550 PLUS) to ensure that the shared documents and comment display described below would be identical. The face of the lecturer was captured using two webcams placed in front of him and processed using different computers. Two laptop computers (Windows 10 Pro; Intel Core i7-8750H, 2.2 GHz; RAM 32 GB) with NVIDIA GeForce GTX 1080 (GeForce Game Ready Driver 451.48) were used to run the Avatarify program.

Unlike face-to-face classes, a student's response is difficult to identify in a remote lecture. Studies on video lectures have utilized questionnaires after the lecture to capture subjective feedback from the students on impacts, mental-effort, perceived learning, and user preferences [4, 8, 9]. In some studies, continuous feedback of the learning experience has been measured with a physical slider [19]. We used the Comment Screen[7] (v1.0.4) service, which allows individuals to anonymously post from a website by specifying a hashtag. The number of comments from students during the class was used as an index of class participation. The comment screen hashtags were prepared both for each group and separately for tabulation. To ensure that identical comments appeared on the screens of both groups, two assistants manually posted comments from one hashtag to the other hashtag.

2.4 Procedure

In the main experiment, the first author presented a lecture as himself. At the beginning of the experiment, students were informed that a test would be conducted at the end of the experiment and they could input their opinions and questions using the comment screen during the class. Students were also informed that their participation in the experiment would not affect their grades and was entirely voluntary. The first half of the lesson content was "Illusionary Interfaces" and the second half was "Telepresence." The students were asked to answer six quizzes—three quizzes from the first half and three quizzes from the second half. The difficulty level of the quizzes was adjusted based on the results of a pilot study by the research staff in our affiliated institution to achieve a correct answer rate of 50%. Some questions on the quiz provided to students were based on questions from the Virtual Reality Society of Japan's certification examinations.

The questions were multiple-choice questions with four answer options to select from. Students were given 10 min to respond after the lecture, and web-browsing was not permitted. In Group 1, face image A (low-rated) was used in the first half and image B (high-rated) was used in the second half. Group 2 used the images throughout the class in reverse order. In addition to the quiz, students were instructed to submit questions and comments about the slide content within one week after the experiment using a Google Form.

2.5 Result

The total number of comments for each group was divided based on the section of the lectures, as shown in Fig. 4 (a). Comments such as "test" were excluded from the analysis. We received more comments in the first half of the lecture, compared with the second half. In the first half, the number of statements from

---

[7] https://commentscreen.com/.

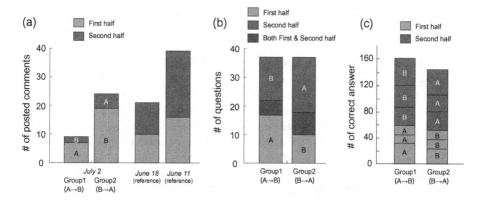

Fig. 4. (a) Histogram of number of comments during the class. (b) Number of impressions and questions after the class. (c) Number of correct answers received for the quiz.

Group 2 was approximately 1.7 times that of Group 1. On the other hand, the number of statements in the second half was approximately 1.25 times more than that of Group 1, although the number of statements in Group 2 remained higher. Posted comments from Group 1 included a test, a comment about the video in the slide content, and a comment about how the face image used Avatarify tracking. In contrast, posted comments from Group 2 included questions about the comment screen and one about the experiment. The two bars on the right in Fig. 4 (a) indicate the total number of comments in the classes on the other days for reference.

We categorized comments and questions posted after the class based on the lesson contents—that is, the first or second half of the class. Figure 4 (b) shows the number of comments and questions.

Figure 4(c) shows the number of correct answers for the quiz in each group. The total number of correct answers is 151 for face image A (i.e., a summation of the first half of Group A and the second half of Group B) and 155 for face image B (i.e., a summation of the first half of Group B and the second half of Group A).

3   Discussion

3.1   Effect on Active Class Participation

To examine the effect of manipulating the appearance of the lecturer's face image in the online lecture, we used an open-source deep fake tool to animate photos of faces by following the facial expressions of a teacher lecturing in real-time. Our experimental results show that students left more comments during the class featuring the lecturer avatars they preferred more. This experimental lecture did not necessarily prompt students to voice their opinions; however, the comments posted during the lecture are considered positive contributions to the class because students shared their interests, opinions, and doubts with each other.

The number of comments and questions posted after the class with image A (the less preferred face) was higher than that of the class with image B. In contrast, the number of comments made during the class was higher for image B. Therefore, the number of comments made during class was negatively correlated with the number of questions after the class. A potential interpretation of this result may be related with the atmosphere created by the spontaneous reactions of students in response to the lecturer's face image. Comments and questions after the class were mandatory, whereas posting comments during the class was voluntary. Therefore, impressions and questions that were noted during the class but could not be submitted may have been submitted after the class. This hypothesis must be tested in ongoing experiments.

3.2   Effect on Learning Outcome

Due to lack of a significant difference in the number of correct quiz answers among both groups, this experiment does not allow us to conclude the impact of agreeableness or preference of an instructor on students' level of understanding of the content. Studies have also reported that the presence or absence of the lecturer's video does not affect student performance on comprehension tests (e.g.,[9]). Therefore, our experimental results are consistent with earlier findings.

3.3   Effect of the Experimental Design

We examined the grades of students and the number of posted comments in a within-subjects design, rather than a between-subjects design. Conducting such experiments in a conventional face-to-face class is impossible because the behavior of the lecturer is different among groups. Therefore, the content of the lecture is likely to change according to the comments. In this study, the lecturer was able to respond to questions or comments of both groups because the content was identical, despite it being a "live" lecture and both groups received the same content, which changed according to the questions of the students. Therefore, the effect of the instructor's face image can be compared using the within-subjects design.

However, this experiment utilized a within-subjects design; therefore, the resulting effects cannot be overruled. For example, the number of comments tended to increase in the first half of the lecture, which can be attributed to students checking the operation of the system. Differences were not noted in the number of test comments between the two groups. The number of comments for the verification is slightly higher than the number of comments for the pre-experimental lecture series, but this may be because the number of tags on the comment screen was only two for the experiment. The comments, with the exception of the system tests, focused on the current content of the class. To offset the sequential effect, we can design an experiment wherein the lecture is divided into four parts, rather than two parts, although doing so may make it difficult for students to focus on the class contents. In the lectures during the preparation session, many comments were posted at the beginning and toward the end of the lecture, which was the reason for using the experimental plan of splitting the lecture into two halves.

3.4   Effect of Animated Photo

The image of the lecturer's face was animated in real-time in conjunction with the video from the webcam; however, some issues occurred wherein the lecturer's face was not displayed correctly due to a tracking error by the webcam. This may have been distracting for the students because some students pointed it out in the comments. The total duration of incorrect images being displayed was about 3% of the lecture duration (approximately 3 min in 95 min, except for short break and quizzes). Images other than faces are displayed on the screen, thus it is necessary to ask the instructor to stay in the tracking area or to develop software that can follow the instructor's gaze.

Moreover, agreeable or preferred ratings of the lecturer's face image may have differed between the still and animated images. Studies have shown that students experience more intimacy from the lecturer's face when the lecturer's video is displayed in a video lecture, compared with when a still picture is displayed [8, 9]. Still images of a face alone can reveal only so much about the individual's mood [5]. To interpret facial expressions depicting emotions, the human visual system resolves the inverse problem of production [11]. Although a comparison of the effects of still and moving images is beyond the scope of this paper, we wish to study these effects on online lectures in the future.

3.5   Limitations and Future Work

The questionnaire responses collected after the lectures show that some students considered gray hair, beard, glasses, and facial expressions when ranking the lecturer's images in the preparation session. Our results do not provide sufficient evidence on the impact of the parameters of face images because they were selected based on a ranking at the preparation session conducted beforehand, wherein students made their selections regarding whose class they wished to take based on the faces presented. Future studies should include quantitative evaluations of the effects of sufficient parameters of facial components.

In addition, the long-term effects of changes in the appearance of instructors have not been clarified in this study. Most students in this experiment had experienced a class with a different instructor's appearance before the main experiment. This may have contributed to a few comments related to the novelty of the system itself in the main experiment. However, comments were posted asking who the instructor was in the photograph that was used. This question was raised after the class. If the same instructor's photo is used over a long period, students would not pay much attention to the photo. The effect of frequent eye movement on the instructor's photo presented on the screen, such as through an analysis of gaze variability due to the presence or absence of the instructor in the video [9], must be examined in future research.

The effect of the gender of the instructors on the students was not clarified in this experiment. Studies have reported significant correlations between agreeableness of instructor appearance and instructor ratings only in the case of male instructors and female students [2]. To test the effects of gender using information technology, not only is speech modulation necessary, but the wording needs to be altered as well. Moreover, determining whether the interaction of such factors should be considered is a necessary task.

4   Conclusion

Studies have reported that remote learning, if conducted appropriately, may have an effect on learning equivalent to that of face-to-face lectures. This finding implies that a remote lecture is a lower-quality version of a face-to-face lecture. On the other hand, for the first time, factors that were once impossible to introduce in face-to-face lectures can now be utilized in distance learning. Although remote learning has both advantages and disadvantages, compared to conventional face-to-face lectures, the usefulness of distance learning is being reconsidered in today's society. Under such circumstances, efforts to incorporate information technology into actual lectures, rather than laboratory experiments and simulated lectures, must be actively implemented and continuously evaluated. In this study, we examined the reactions of two student groups to instructors' live-action avatars and examined the relation between their attractiveness and students' willingness to comment and understand. We found that the agreeableness or preference of a lecturer's face affected the number of comments made in a remote lecture, wherein the lecturer's face was displayed alongside the slide presentation. This study is an example of educational research on distance learning wherein information technology is actively used in education. In the future, we would like to investigate the appearance of the instructor's face and the influence of their voice and whole-body gestures on learning, in distance learning.

References

1. Berner, E.S., Adams, B.: Added value of video compared to audio lectures for distance learning. Int. J. Med. Inform. **73**(2), 189–193 (2004). https://doi.org/10.1016/j.ijmedinf.2003.12.001
2. Bokek-Cohen, Y., Davidowitz, N.: Beauty and teaching evaluation: a comparison between female and male college professors. Probl. Educ. 21st Century **7**, 15–30 (2008)
3. Craig, J.D., Savage, S.J.: Instructor attire and student performance: evidence from an undergraduate industrial organization experiment. Int. Rev. Econ. Educ. **17**, 55–65 (2014). https://doi.org/10.1016/j.iree.2014.07.001

4. Cross, A., Bayyapunedi, M., Cutrell, E., Agarwal, A., Thies, W.: Typerighting: combining the benefits of handwriting and typeface in online educational videos. In: Proceedings of the SIGCHI Conference on Human Factors in Computing Systems, pp. 793—796. Association for Computing Machinery, New York (2013). https://doi.org/10.1145/2470654.2470766

5. Heaven, D.: Why faces don't always tell the truth about feelings. Nature **578**, 502–504 (2020). https://doi.org/10.1038/d41586-020-00507-5

6. Homer, B.D., Plass, J.L., Blake, L.: The effects of video on cognitive load and social presence in multimedia-learning. Comput. Hum. Behav. **24**(3), 786–797 (2008). https://doi.org/10.1016/j.chb.2007.02.009

7. Karras, T., Laine, S., Aila, T.: A style-based generator architecture for generative adversarial networks. In: Proceedings of IEEE/CVF Conference on Computer Vision and Pattern Recognition (CVPR), pp. 4396–4405 (2019). https://doi.org/10.1109/CVPR.2019.00453

8. Kizilcec, R.F., Bailenson, J., Gomez, C.D.: The instructor's face in video instruction: evidence from two large-scale field studies. J. Educ. Psychol. **107**, 724–739 (2015)

9. Kizilcec, R.F., Papadopoulos, K., Sritanyaratana, L.: Showing face in video instruction: effects on information retention, visual attention, and affect. In: Proceedings of the SIGCHI Conference on Human Factors in Computing Systems, pp. 2095–2102. ACM (2014). https://doi.org/10.1145/2556288.2557207

10. Lau, S.: The effect of smiling on person perception. J. Soc. Psychol. **117**(1), 63–67 (1982)

11. Martinez, A.M.: Visual perception of facial expressions of emotion. Curr. Opin. Psychol. **17**, 27–33 (2017). https://doi.org/10.1016/j.copsyc.2017.06.009

12. Mc Ginley, H., Blau, G.L., Takai, M.: Attraction effects of smiling and body position: a cultural comparison. Percept. Mot. Skills **58**(3), 915–922 (1984)

13. Ministry of Education, Culture, Sports, Science and Technology (MEXT), Japan: Education in japan beyond the crisis of Covid-19 (2020). https://www.mext.go.jp/en/content/20200904_mxt_kouhou01-000008961_1.pdf. Accessed 01 Feb 2022

14. Nakazato, N., Yoshida, S., Sakurai, S., Narumi, T., Tanikawa, T., Hirose, M.: Smart face: enhancing creativity during video conferences using real-time facial deformation. In: Proceedings of CSCW, pp. 75–83. Association for Computing Machinery (2014). https://doi.org/10.1145/2531602.2531637

15. Oh, S.Y., Bailenson, J., Krämer, N., Li, B.: Let the avatar brighten your smile: effects of enhancing facial expressions in virtual environments. PLOS ONE **11**(9), 1–18 (2016). https://doi.org/10.1371/journal.pone.0161794

16. Pugh, S.D.: Service with a smile: emotional contagion in the service encounter. Acad. Manag. J. **44**(5), 1018–1027 (2001)

17. Schneider, S., Nebel, S., Beege, M., Rey, G.D.: Anthropomorphism in decorative pictures: benefit or harm for learning? J. Educ. Psychol. **110**(2), 218–232 (2018). https://doi.org/10.1037/edu0000207

18. Siarohin, A., Lathuilière, S., Tulyakov, S., Ricci, E., Sebe, N.: First order motion model for image animation. In: Advances in Neural Information Processing Systems, vol. 32, pp. 7137–7147. Curran Associates, Inc. (2019)

19. Srivastava, N., Velloso, E., Lodge, J.M., Erfani, S., Bailey, J.: Continuous evaluation of video lectures from real-time difficulty self-report. In: Proceedings of the 2019 CHI Conference on Human Factors in Computing Systems, pp. 1—12. Association for Computing Machinery, New York (2019). https://doi.org/10.1145/3290605.3300816

20. Talamas, S.N., Mavor, K.I., Perrett, D.I.: Blinded by beauty: attractiveness bias and accurate perceptions of academic performance. PLoS ONE **11**(2), 1–18 (2016). https://doi.org/10.1371/journal.pone.0148284

21. Wang, J., Antonenko, P., Dawson, K.: Does visual attention to the instructor in online video affect learning and learner perceptions? An eye-tracking analysis. Comput. Educ. **146**, 103779 (2020). https://doi.org/10.1016/j.compedu.2019.103779

22. Wang, J., Antonenko, P.D.: Instructor presence in instructional video: effects on visual attention, recall, and perceived learning. Comput. Hum. Behav. **71**, 79–89 (2017). https://doi.org/10.1016/j.chb.2017.01.049

23. Wilson, K.E., Martinez, M., Mills, C., D'Mello, S., Smilek, D., Risko, E.F.: Instructor presence effect: liking does not always lead to learning. Comput. Educ. **122**, 205–220 (2018). https://doi.org/10.1016/j.compedu.2018.03.011

24. Wolbring, T., Riordan, P.: How beauty works. Theoretical mechanisms and two empirical applications on students' evaluation of teaching. Soc. Sci. Res. **57**, 253–272 (2016). https://doi.org/10.1016/j.ssresearch.2015.12.009

How to Elicit Ownership and Agency for an Avatar Presented in the Third-Person Perspective: The Effect of Visuo-Motor and Tactile Feedback

Ryo Hanashima[1,2] and Junji Ohyama[1,3(✉)]

[1] Human Augmentation Research Center, National Institute of Advanced Industrial Science and Technology, Kashiwa, Japan
{ryo.hanashima,j.ohyama}@aist.go.jp
[2] Graduate School of Comprehensive Human Science, University of Tsukuba, Tsukuba, Japan
[3] Faculty of Human Science, University of Tsukuba, Tsukuba, Japan

Abstract. The realism of experience of using a virtual body in virtual reality (VR) is associated with ownership (one's self-attribution of a body) has been shown. However, whether or not ownership can be elicited for a virtual body presented by the third-person perspective is under debate. This study investigated the effect of multimodal presentations on the ownership of a male virtual body presented in the third-person perspective in three conditions (Visuo-tactile, visuo-motor, visuo-motor-tactile condition) (N = 40). We compared the illusory effect of ownership in the three conditions in male and female participants using a questionnaire and a 2×3 mixed-design ANOVA. Our study revealed that the male participants in the visuo-motor-tactile condition affirmed moderate (+1) of ownership, but the female participants did not. Ownership was significantly higher in the visuo-tactile ($p < .01$) and visuo-motor ($p < .05$) conditions. The results suggest that both visuo-motor synchrony and visuo-tactile feedback are essential factors to induce ownership to the virtual body in a third-person perspective. Moreover, our data suggest that matching the participant's gender identity and the appearance of an avatar's gender might be important for elicited ownership. Additionally, we evaluated the agency on the virtual body in the third-person perspective in the same three feedback conditions and found that only visuo-motor feedback is essential to elicit agency, unlike the causal factors of the ownership.

Keywords: Ownership · Agency · Third-person perspective

1 Introduction

The genuine power of virtual reality (VR) is not necessarily to produce a faithful reproduction of "reality" but that it offers the possibility to step outside of the normal bounds of reality and realize goals in a totally new and unexpected way [1]. One of these use cases of VR would be a third-person perspective experience. In the third-person perspective, the body is presented away from the actual body, enabling a person to look at

© The Author(s), under exclusive license to Springer Nature Switzerland AG 2022
S. Yamamoto and H. Mori (Eds.): HCII 2022, LNCS 13306, pp. 111–130, 2022.
https://doi.org/10.1007/978-3-031-06509-5_9

his/her own full body. Previous studies have reported that the third-person perspective is better than the first-person perspective with regard to motion (e.g., walking, catching a ball) and spatial awareness [2–4]. In fact, some technologies to capture external self-body image have been developed using a head-mounted display (HMD), a drone or augmented reality glasses [5–7]. On other hand, using VR would present the benefits of safety, time, space, equipment, cost efficiency, and ease of documentation for rehabilitation or motor learning [8]. The use of the effective design of the third-person perspective in VR may open up a new path for rehabilitation or training, which reflecting a full body while moving or posing.

In realizing third-person perspective in VR, one of the important factors might be self-cognition for virtual body presented in VR. The sense of ownership (often called body ownership) and agency are fundamental factors for relative self-cognition [9–11]. Ownership refers to one's self-attribution of a body [9, 12]. Agency refers to global motor control, including the subjective experience of action, control, intention, and motor selection and the conscious experience of will [13]. Research has shown that importance of ownership and agency for self-avatar in VR. For example, ownership is associated with physiological responses and cognitive and behavioral changes when using a virtual body [14–17] On the other hand, agency is related motor control [18]. In addition, ownership and agency may be elements that make an avatar feel like one's own biological body, embodiment [19]. In fact, ownership and agency are associated with the effect of VR training on physiological, cognitive, and neural changes, similar to the actual exercise [20].

Previous VR studies have reported that people can feel as if the virtual body is their own body, i.e., experiencing ownership and agency for the virtual body in a first-person perspective [3, 15, 16]. A full-body illusion (FBI) as a known method for eliciting ownership for full body. In the FBI, ownership is elicited by simultaneously and synchronously stroking or touching a mannequin or virtual avatar and actual body with a rod or brush [15, 22]. On other hand, agency is elicited by the synchronized synchronous movement of a virtual body and the actual body in addition of ownership [3, 14, 21]. Visuo-tactile or visuo-motor multimodal feedback is a matter of ownership on a mannequin or virtual avatar presented in a first-person perspective. Contrary to the consistent results in first-person perspective studies, how to elicit ownership and agency for an avatar presented in the third-person perspective remains unclear.

Ownership of a virtual body presented in the third- person perspective was first studied by Lenggenhager et al. [23]. They reported that participants experienced ownership of a virtual body placed 2 m away from their own body in the extraperipersonal space. However, some other studies reported different results in the follow-up studies of Lenggenhager et al. [23], whereby ownership could not be elicited for a mannequin or virtual body presented in a third-person perspective and could be elicited only in the peripersonal space [24–27]. Contrarily, other studies argue that ownership could be elicited in the third-person perspective [3, 14, 29]. These contradictory results may be due to differences in multisensory synchrony (visuo-tactile or visuo-motor synchrony) of a mannequin or virtual body with the actual body in these studies. Most visuo-tactile studies in the third-person perspective, except for Lenggenhager et al. [24], have reported that ownership is not elicited by visuo-tactile synchrony [24–27], whereas most visuo-motor studies have reported that ownership is elicited by visuo-motor synchrony [3, 14, 21, 28]. Thus, whether ownership is elicited for the virtual body or mannequin might depend on differences in multisensory synchrony. In the study by Lenggenhager et al. [24] and some studies under very similar conditions [29, 30], participants saw a video image of their body presented in the third-person perspective through a head-mounted display in real time, as well as a video image of their body being stroked in synchrony with their actual body. In this paradigm, subtle movement of the actual body reflected the video image of their body. This visuo-motor synchrony between the video image of their body and the actual body could affect ownership of one's own body presented in the third-person perspective, in addition to visuo-tactile synchrony induced by stroking synchronously. On the other hand, visuo-motor synchrony between the actual and artificial body used in previous studies constitutes merely visuo-motor synchronization behavior (e.g., moving hand) and visuo-motor synchronization plus tactile synchronization behavior (e.g., walking). Participants get synchronized visuo-motor information while moving their hand and synchronized visuo-motor information plus tactile information when their feet hit the ground while walking. However, previous studies did not directly compare multisensory synchronicity. Therefore, with regard to eliciting ownership, whether synchronized visuo-motor information or visuo-motor plus tactile information is critical in visuo-motor synchrony between actual and artificial body remains unclear.

Unlike ownership, participants experience agency for a virtual body presented in the third-person perspective in visuo-motor synchrony [3, 21]. However, whether "visuo-tactile" or "visuo-motor plus visuo-tactile" information enhances the agency rather than "visuo-motor" synchrony without tactile feedback for an avatar presented in the third-person perspective remains unclear.

To answer this question, our study aimed to investigate the effect of multimodal presentations on ownership and agency for a male avatar presented in the third-person perspective in VR. We modified and applied the FBI paradigm and compared the effect of the modality condition (visuo-tactile, visuo-motor, and visuo-motor-tactile) on ownership and agency. The use of the third-person perspective avatar within ownership and agency in VR will contribute to developing a new rehabilitation and training method, alongside novel VR content.

Several studies exist on the synchronized effect on ownership and agency. In the study of the effect of ownership using first-person perspective, the synchronization and asynchronization of visual and motor stimuli were compared; ownership was not elicited in asynchronization [3, 14, 16, 21]. Another study examined the effect of ownership on an avatar presented in a first-person perspective with the synchronization and asynchronization of visual and tactile stimuli and reported that ownership was not elicited in asynchronization [15, 22]. The fact that ownership was not elicited in asynchronization using a first-person perspective, which is more likely to elicit ownership, suggests that synchronization is a fundamental condition, even in a third-person perspective. Therefore, in this study, we aimed to determine which synchronous presentation condition (visuo-motor, visuo-tactile, or visuo-motor-tactile) would elicit ownership if visual, motor, and tactile stimuli are presented synchronously. On the other hand, agency is elicited by the synchronized multimodal presentation of visuo-motor but not by asynchronized multimodal presentation of visuo-motor stimuli [3, 14, 15, 21, 22]. Therefore, our study did not compare between synchronized and asynchronized multimodal presentation conditions for agency. This study examined the difference between visuo-motor and visuo-motor-tactile synchrony conditions for ownership and agency.

2   Methods

2.1 Participants

A total of 23 men (mean age = 22.39, SD = 1.81) and 20 women (mean age = 22.4, SD = 1.29) participated in this study. Gender is biologically divided (groups were divided according to the gender assigned at birth). All participants had normal or corrected vision. Data obtained from three male participants were excluded from the analysis because two had poor understanding of the experimental procedure and one received no vibration from the haptic device. Thus, 20 men (mean age = 22.2, SD = 1.62) and 20 women (mean age = 22.4, SD = 1.29) were included for sub sequent analysis. All participants were recruited through an advertisement published by the National Institute of Advanced Industrial Science and Technology and were from Tsukuba city, Japan. Written informed consent was obtained from all the participants prior to the experiment, and they were paid for participating (3300 JPY). The experiment was approved by the Ethics Board of the National Institute of Advanced Industrial Science and Technology.

Power analysis of post-hoc test was conducted to confirm that the number of participants was appropriate for this experimental design. A post-hoc power test was per-formed using G power; the power was 0.94. Parameter values as flowing were set (statistical test = ANOVA: repeated-measures, within-between interaction, effect size = .25, alpha = .05, total sample size = 40, number of groups = 2, and number of measurements = 3, correlation among repeated measures = .5, nonsphericity correction $\ni$ = 1).

2.2 Apparatus

HMD, tracker, and haptic device were used for this experiment controlled by Unity 3D on a VR ready PC (Alienware15, Dell, Texas, USA). The HMD (HTC VIVE PRO, HTC, New Taipei, Taiwan; resolution 1440 × 1600 pixels in each screen) was used to display three-dimensional images and head tracking. Five trackers (VIVE Tracker, HTC, New Taipei, Taiwan) were used to track the participant's body movement for real time reflection to virtual body movements. The three-dimensional image was generated and presented by Xperigrapher [31], platform created with Unity 3D (Unity Technologies, San Francisco, USA). The avatar we used was that of a brown-skinned Latin male.

A haptic device (310-113, Precision Microdrives, Brixton Road, England) was used to present vibration to the participant's hand. An analog output device (NI-9264, National Instruments, Texas, USA) was connected to the haptic device and used for transforming digital signals from the computers to an analog signal, transmitted signals to the haptic device. When there was a white ball in contact with an avatar's right hand in the virtual space, participants received vibration to the right hand from the haptic device (not for the visuo-motor condition, as is mentioned later in this section).

The experimental setup is shown in Fig. 1.

2.3 Procedure

Participants wore the HMD and had five trackers attached to both wrists, both feet, and abdomen, one in each place, and a haptic device was attached to the right hand. Before starting the experiment, adjustment of the virtual body to each participant's body, equipped with the HMD, trackers, and haptic device, was conducted. The length and thickness of the arms, foot, and torso and posture of the virtual body were automatically adjusted by Final IK (Unity asset), and the orientation of the trackers was manually adjusted. The participants then looked to the virtual body in a first-person perspective, through the virtual mirror, and checked whether the virtual body matched own body in terms of the length and thickness of body parts and posture. If they were not matched, the virtual body was adjusted again.

At the beginning of the trial, the virtual body was presented 2.0 m in front of the participant. The virtual body moved in synchrony with the participant's body. Two parallel horizontal black lines were presented diagonally forward right of the virtual body; one line (above line) was at a height of 1.3 m and another line (under line) at a height of 1.0 m (Fig. 2). Participants were instructed to look at the virtual body reaching out above the line with their right hand while doing the same.

There were three conditions across the trials. In the visuo-tactile condition, participants were required to look at the virtual body and not move. In this condition, a white ball (60 cm in diameter) was presented on the bottom line and popped up to the upper line. When it reached upper line, the white ball disappeared and vibration was presented to the participant's right hand by the haptic device (Fig. 3). In the visuo-motor condition, participants were required to move the virtual body's right hand once between the bottom line and upper lines back and forth using their right hand every time the white ball was presented (Fig. 4). In the visuo-motor-tactile condition, participants were required to move the virtual body's right hand once between the upper line and bottom line using their own hand every time the white ball was presented. When the virtual body's hand reached on the bottom line, the white ball disappeared and vibration was presented to the participant's right hand by the haptic device (Fig. 5). The phase shows the timing and sequence of the visual, tactile, and motor (participant movements) in Figs. 4, 5, and 6. Participants took part in each of the three multimodal feedback conditions (visuo-tactile, visuo-motor or visuo-motor-tactile condition) once in block design. 10 trials were repeated in each condition block. The order of the condition blocks was also counterbalanced for each participant. At the end of each feedback condition block, participants took off the HMD and verbally responded to the questionnaire. The questionnaire included four categories (ownership, ownership control, agency, agency control) of items. Each category was consisted of three questions. The mean and variance of 40 participants were calculated in 12 conditions [=3 feedback × 4 categories] for the statistical analysis. The total duration of the experiment was approximately 60 min.

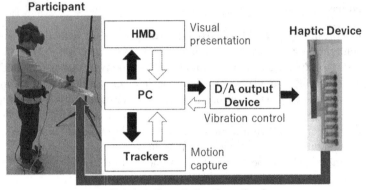

Fig. 1. Illustration of the system architecture

3D image was generated and presented by PC and head-mounted display. The movement of the participant was tracked using five trackers. Vibration was presented by a haptic device.

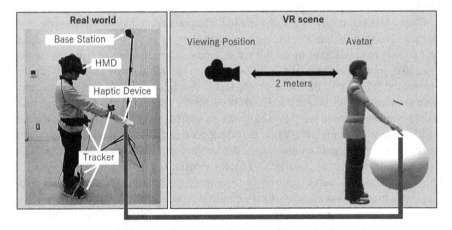

Fig. 2. The participant in real world and the presented avatar in virtual reality

Avatar presented 2 m away from the viewing position. The participant could view the avatar from the viewing position and move it. Avatar touching an object (while ball); vibration is presented to the right hand of the participant through a haptic device in the visuo-tactile and visuo-motor-tactile conditions, but not in the visuo-motor condition.

2.4 Questionnaire

We used 12 items of the questionnaire, adopted from the version statement by Kalckert and Ehrsson (2014) [32] (Table 1).

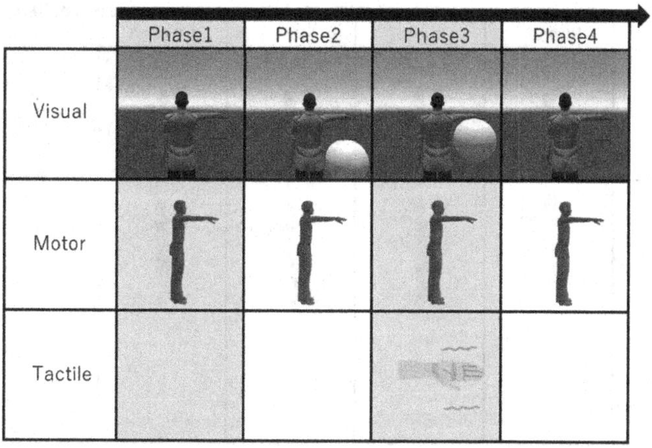

Fig. 3. Visuo-tactile condition. The phase shows the timing and sequence of the visual, tactile, and motor (participant movements). Visual: view through head-mounted display; Motor: participants' posture; Tactile: vibration presentation through the haptic device attached to the participants' right hand. Participants were asked to be still and looking at the virtual body. White ball appears on the bottom black line, pops up until the upper black line, and disappears. Participants received vibration on their right hand through the attached haptic device when the virtual body's right hand touched the ball.

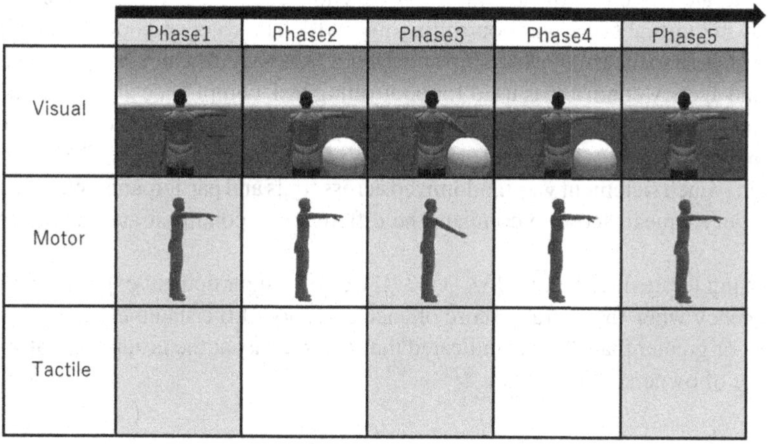

Fig. 4. Visuo-motor condition. Participants manipulate the virtual body's right hand by their own right hand while looking at the virtual body. White ball appears on the bottom black line, and the ball disappears soon after the virtual body's hand returns to the original position. In this condition, participants did not receive vibration on their right hand through the attached haptic device.

The 12 items spanned four categories; ownership, agency, ownership control, and agency control. Each category had three items. The statement for the item categorized as ownership concerned the feeling of ownership (e.g., I felt as if I looked at my body), that for the item categorized as agency concerned agency (e.g., I felt as if I could control the

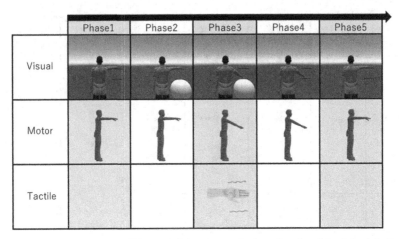

Fig. 5. Visuo-motor-tactile condition. Participants manipulate the virtual body's right hand by their own right hand while looking at the virtual body. Participants received vibration on their right hand through the attached haptic device when the virtual body's right hand touched the ball (the ball disappeared at this moment).

movement of the virtual body), that for the item categorized as ownership control did not concern the feeling of ownership (e.g., It seems as if I had more than one body), and that for the item categorized for ownership control did not concern the feeling of agency (e.g., I felt as if the virtual body was controlling my will). The categories of ownership and agency was used to measure ownership and agency, whereas the categories of ownership control and agency control was used for controlling task compliance and suggestibility. Participants responded to each statement by choosing a number on the 7-point Likert scale, ranging from -3 for "strongly disagree" to 3 for "strongly agree," with 0 indicating "uncertain." Each statement was randomized across trials and participants. We calculated each category's mean score to compare the difference in condition and gender for the FBI.

Referring to previous studies [33, 35–37], we defined participant experience ownership or agency when the average score of each category of the statement in group level was equal or greater than 1. This indicated that participants at the group level affirm the experience of ownership or agency.

2.5 Statistical Analysis

The score questionnaire was calculated for each category (ownership, ownership control, agency, agency control) of three items by averaging each of the three item scores. The average of each category score was used further statistical analysis. Thus, there are (3 feedback conditions) × (4 categories) × (3 questions) per each participant, and the mean and variance of 40 participants were calculated in 12 conditions [=3 feedback × 4 questionnaires (mean of three questions)] for the statistical analysis.

To assess the effect of modality condition and gender, there were used as factors in a mixed-design two-way ANOVA. The condition was the within subject factor, and

Table 1. Ownership and agency questionnaire applied to each condition.

Category	Statement
Ownership	Q1. I felt as if I was looking my own body.
	Q2. I felt as if the hand of the virtual body was part of my body.
	Q3. I felt as if the virtual body was my body.
Ownership control	Q4. It seems as if I had more than one body.
	Q5. It felt as if I had no longer body, as if I had disappeared.
	Q6. I felt as if my real body was resembling virtual body in terms of skin tone or some other visual feature.
Agency	Q7. I felt as if I could cause movements of the virtual body.
	Q8. I felt as if I could control movements of the virtual body.
	Q9. The virtual body was obeying my will and I can make it move just like I want it.
Agency control	Q10. I felt as if the virtual body was controlling my will.
	Q11. It seemed as if the virtual body had a will of its own.
	Q12. I felt as if the virtual body was controlling me.

gender was the between subject factor. All p-values in multiple comparisons were Holm-corrected.

To confirm the order effect, we conducted an analysis of variance with order as a factor. The results showed that the order effect was not significant for any of the categories (ownership: $F (2, 78) = 1.90$, $p = .156$, $\eta2 = .018$; ownership control: $F (2, 78) = .421$, $p = .668$, $\eta2 = .003$; agency: $F (2, 78) = 1.06$, $p = .350$, $\eta2 = .002$; agency control: $F (2, 78) = .34$, $p = .672$, $\eta2 = .004$).

3 Results

3.1 Ownership

Male participants in the visuo-motor-tactile condition affirmed experiencing ownership for the virtual body (the average of category score $= 1.23$) while affirming the score of ownership (the average of category score ≥ 1), but male participants in the visuo-tactile or visuo-motor condition or female participants in all conditions did not (visuo-tactile condition in male participants: mean $= 0.58$, visuo-motor condition in male participants: mean $= 0.75$, visuo-tactile condition in female participants: mean $= -0.33$, visuo-motor condition in female participants: mean $= 0.58$, visuo-motor-tactile condition in female participants: mean $= 0.15$) (Fig. 6).

Repeated-measures ANOVA revealed significant main effects of condition and gender (condition: $F (2, 76) = 7.31$, $p = .008$, $\eta2 = .06$; gender: $F (1, 38) = 7.82$, $p = .001$, $\eta2 = .11$). Therefore, multiple comparisons were conducted for each condition. The ownership scores in the visuo-motor and visuo-motor-tactile conditions were significantly larger than those in the visuo-tactile condition (visuo-motor condition vs visuo-tactile condition; t (19) = 2.67, p = .002, visuo-motor-tactile condition vs visuo-tactile condition; t (19) = 3.30, p = .012), and there was no significant difference between the visuo-motor and visuo-motor-tactile conditions (t (38) = .22, p = .83). An interaction was also revealed (F (2, 76) = 4.25, p = .02, η2 = .03). Post-hoc multiple comparisons on male participants revealed that the visuo-motor-tactile condition score was larger than the visuo-tactile and visuo-motor condition scores (visuo-motor-tactile condition vs visuo-tactile condition: t (19) = 3.82, p = .03; visuo-motor-tactile condition vs visuo-motor condition: t (19) = 3.00, p = .014).

Post-hoc multiple comparisons on female participants revealed that the visuo-motor condition score was larger than the visuo-tactile and visuo-motor-tactile condition scores (visuo-motor condition vs visuo-tactile condition; t (19) = 2.85, p = .031, visuo-motor condition vs visuo-motor-tactile condition; t (19) = 2.67, p = .031).

3.2 Ownership Control

Participants did not affirm ownership control (the average score of ownership control < 1) across the three conditions, irrespective of gender (visuo-tactile condition in male participants: mean = −1.45, visuo-motor condition in male participants: mean = − 1.40, visuo-motor-tactile condition in male participants: mean = −1.10, visuo-tactile condition in female participants: mean = −1.61, visuo-motor condition in female participants: mean = −1.42, visuo-motor-tactile condition in female participants: mean = −1.48) (Fig. 6).

Repeated-measures ANOVA revealed no significant main effects of condition or gender and interaction (condition: F (2, 76) = 1.75, p = .18, η2 = .01; gender: F (1, 38) = 0.52, p = .48, η2 = .01; condition × gender: F (2, 76) = 1.02, p = .37, η2 = .01).

3.3 Agency

Participants in the visuo-motor and visuo-motor-tactile conditions experienced agency (the average score of ownership control > 1) for the virtual body, irrespective of gender (visuo-motor condition in male participants; mean = 1.5, visuo-motor-tactile condition in male participants; mean = 1.78, visuo-motor condition in female participants; mean = 1.42, visuo-motor-tactile condition in female participants; mean = 1.22), but those in the visuo-tactile condition did not, irrespective of gender (visuo-tactile condition in male participants; mean = 0.22, visuo-tactile condition in female participants; mean = −0.20) (Fig. 7).

Repeated-measures ANOVA revealed a significant main effect of condition (F (2, 76) = 26.99, p < .0001, η2 = .29). Therefore, a multiple comparison analysis was conducted. The visuo-motor and visuo-motor-tactile condition scores were significantly larger than the visuo-tactile condition scores (visuo-motor condition vs visuo-tactile condition; t (38) = 5.61, p < .0001; visuo-motor-tactile condition vs visuo-tactile condition; t (38) = 5.27, p < .0001). There was no significant difference between the visuo-motor and visuo-motor-tactile conditions (t (38) = .35, p = .72).

No main effect of gender or interaction was revealed (gender: F (1, 38) = 2.48, p = .12, η2 = .02; condition × gender: F (2, 76) = .57, p = .56, η2 = .01).

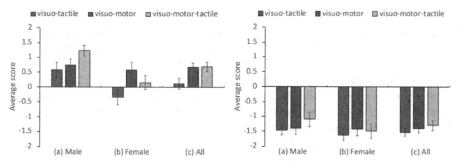

Fig. 6. Questionnaire results of main effect of condition for ownership and ownership control. Error bar shows a standard error. (Left: Ownership; Right: Ownership control)

3.4 Agency Control

Participants did not affirm agency (the average score of agency control < 1) control across the three conditions, irrespective of gender (visuo-tactile condition in male participants: mean = −1.53, visuo-motor condition in male participants: mean = −1.73, visuo-motor-tactile condition in male participants: mean = −1.45, visuo-tactile condition in female participants: mean = −1.35, visuo-motor condition in female participants: mean = −1.48, visuo-motor-tactile condition in female participants: mean = −1.58) (Fig. 7).

Repeated-measures ANOVA revealed no significant main effect of condition or gender and interaction (condition: $F (2, 76) = .46$, $p = .63$, $\eta2 = .004$; gender: $F (1, 38) = .15$, $p = .70$, $\eta2 = .002$; condition × gender: $F (2, 76) = .75$, $p = .45$, $\eta2 = .01$).

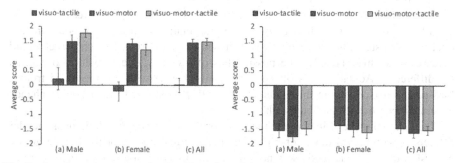

Fig. 7. Questionnaire results of main effect of condition for agency and agency control. Error bar shows a standard error (Left: agency; Right: agency control).

4   Discussion

This study assessed the effect of multimodal presentations (visuo-tactile, visuo-motor, and visuo-motor-tactile) on ownership and agency for a male avatar presented in the third-person perspective in VR. Results showed that ownership was elicited in the visuo-motor-tactile condition only for the male group and agency was elicited in the visuo-motor and visuo-motor-tactile conditions for both groups.

This study only used a synchronized multimodal presentation because previous studies had reported that a synchronized multimodal presentation is a fundamental condition to elicit both ownership and agency. Ownership is elicited by the synchronized multimodal presentation of visuo-tactile or visuo-motor stimuli but not by the asynchronized multimodal presentation of visuo-tactile or visuo-motor stimuli [3, 14, 15, 21, 22]. On the other hand, agency is elicited by the synchronized multimodal presentation of visuo-motor stimuli but not by the asynchronized multimodal presentation of visuo-motor stimuli [3, 14, 15, 33]. In the following section, we will discuss ownership, agency, and the relationship between ownership and agency.

4.1 Ownership

We found that participants affirmed ownership in the visuo-motor-tactile condition in the male group. This finding is inconsistent with reports that ownership was elicited only in the first-person perspective [24–27]. This finding supports the notion that the lack of information could be compensated for by other information, as suggested by Ma and Hommel (2015) [38]. In FBI, ownership could be elicited only by looking at the virtual body or mannequin in the first-person perspective, i.e., in a visuo-proprioceptive feedback condition [25]. On the other hand, the virtual body presented in the third-person perspective does not offer synchronized feedback of visual and proprioceptive feedback of body information. Therefore, for the subjects to assess whether the body is their own body, a variety of additional information, such as multimodal feedback of visual, motor, and tactile information, might be needed to compensate for the lack of visuo-proprioceptive information to the virtual body.

This result is inconsistent with previous two studies showing that availability of synchronous information does not increase ownership [39, 40]. One reason for this could be the difference of the way of tactile presentation (self-touch or goal-directed touch). In this study, tactile feedback was presented goal-directed touch, which could increase ownership [41, 42]. The possibilities of a ceiling effect could also explain this difference. Actual images of the participants themselves were presented from a third-person perspective in those studies [39, 40]. Personalized avatar could enhance ownership over the virtual body [43].

The fact that ownership was elicited only for the male group might indicate gender differences with regard to ownership of the male virtual body. For the female group, ownership of the virtual body was not elicited in any condition (the average score of ownership was < 1) and was negatively affected, which was different from the male group. The results suggest an effect of gender match with the virtual body. This finding seemingly contradicted the fact that gender differences do not affect ownership using a first-person perspective [17, 22]. In contrast, Tacikowski et al. [44] showed that ownership could be elicited for the opposite gender body using a first-person perspective and that eliciting ownership for the opposite gender body could change sense of one's own gender. The difference between that study and ours lies in the fact that theirs was based on a first-person perspective and not VR. In addition, what was implied in their study was quite the opposite of causality with regard to how the emergence of a sense of body ownership for gender-different bodies transforms gender identity (i.e., whether ownership affect gender identity). However, they also showed that the median value of elicited ownership for the opposite gender body was less than that matched for gender body (supporting online material [44]). This result is consistent with the idea that there is an effect of gender match, as noted in this study. The effects seen in this study could be attributed to the following two reasons. First, the resemblance between fake and real body is a top-down factor affecting ownership [43, 45]. The similarity with the male virtual body in the female group was less pronounced than that in the male group. This point might affect ownership in the female group. The use of more realistic avatars in this study than those used in previous studies [17, 22] might have made females more aware of the differences between the avatars and their actual bodies and felt tactile feedback unnatural. Second, there may also be something beyond the simple lack of similarity. Schwind et al. [46] showed that the female group dislike the male hand and felt less presence than the male group while using the male hand in VR. The male virtual body used in this study may appear to be more masculine than the mannequin or avatar used in the previous studies [17, 22]. This point might also affect ownership in the female group.

Another possible influence on the sense of body ownership in this study is the avatar's skin color concerning race. There are no consistent findings on how skin color could affect ownership. Some studies [17, 47, 48] showed that there is no difference of ownership between right-skin and black-skin avatars for white people. However, Farmer et al. [49] showed that showed that ownership of a white hand was stronger for white people. Lire et al. [50] reproduced these results and was faster elicited in synchronous condition with a black hand. In addition to those conflicting results on skin color, previous studies have mainly focused on white people, and the impact of skin color on Asians has not been fully explored. The avatar used in this study has brown skin, which is different to that of most Japanese. This point would weaken ownership irrespective of gender.

4.2 Agency

We found that participants affirmed agency (the average score of ownership was > 1) in the visuo-motor and visuo-motor-tactile conditions in both the male and female groups. These results were consistent with previous studies of agency with a rubber hand from the first-person perspective. Kalckert and Ehrsson [32, 33] showed that agency was elicited for a moving rubber hand according to the actual hidden hand movement but not in the visuo-tactile condition. This is an issue with regard to the validity of discrimination of the visuo-tactile and visuo-motor-tactile conditions. It is suggested that the synchronization of visual stimuli and movement is a sufficient condition for agency.

The comparator model suggests that agency occurs when sensory prediction and actual sensory feedback are matched [51]. In this study, participants were asked explicitly to control the virtual body in the visuo-motor and visuo-motor-tactile conditions. Therefore, the prediction of moving the virtual body and the feedback of the movement of the virtual body could be fully tied together; hence, agency was elicited. In the visuo-tactile condition, the sensory prediction of moving the virtual body and actual sensory feedback of the movement of the virtual body were absent; thus, agency was not elicited. The results show that agency was equally elicited, regardless of whether the gender of the participant is same as that of the avatar.

However, agency was affected by comparison and but also by many other factors, such as goal achievement [52] or emotion [53]. Then, why did not tactile feedback and gender difference affect agency? two-step account of agency, different perspective of comparator model, suggests that agency could be divided by feeling of agency (non-conceptual and sensory motor level) and judgment of agency (conceptual judgment) [54]. The extent to which the feeling and judgement of agency, respectively, contribute to the overall agency depends on the context and task requirements. Sensory prediction is matched with afferent information such as proprioception and visual feedback, and if no particular discrepancy between the information is detected at this stage, agency occurs without no further processing. If there is a discrepancy between the information, further processing is done. At second stage, Intentions, beliefs, and contextual cues are used to judge who is the agent. In visuo-motor and visuo-motor-tactile condition, it is obvious that participants are the agent. Therefore, tactile feedback or gender difference was not used for the process by which agency occur.

4.3 Ownership and Agency

The relationship between ownership and agency is a matter debate. As previously mentioned in the Introduction and Discussion sections above, ownership is elicited from mainly multisensory synchrony and agency from the match between intention and outcome. Each have mostly different independence mechanisms [33, 35, 55] but can affect each other under some circumstances [38, 56]. In this study, we did not directly investigate the relationship between ownership and agency because the aim of this study was to elucidate the independent effect of FBI manner on ownership and agency. Therefore, this relationship is unknown in this study. However, the reason for the score for the visuo-motor-tactile condition in ownership being higher than that for other conditions in the male group might have involved agency.

We speculate that our findings may also have been affected by the peripersonal space. The peripersonal space is the space immediately surrounding one's body; it plays a special role in interaction, where one can perform an action such as grasping [57]. This space may be closely associated with bodily ownership illusion, such as the rubber hand illusion and FBI [58, 59]. Some studies suggested that ownership in the rubber hand illusion or FBI was elicited only in the peripersonal space [24–27]. Lloyd [61] showed that the rubber hand illusion was elicited only in the limits of the peripersonal space. Similarly, Guterstam et al. [62] showed that the magnetic touch illusion was similar to the rubber hand illusion, in that visuo-tactile integration occurred in the peripersonal space. In the same vein as the FBI using visuo-tactile synchrony, most studies showed that ownership could be elicited only in the peripersonal space [24–27]. On the other hand, the peripersonal space is not fixed. Studies have shown that motor behavior could widen the peripersonal space [37, 63, 64] and that this process was modulated by agency [36] and could be occurred for separated body parts in the actual body [37, 64]. In our study, the peripersonal space enlarged by agency might have affected the full-body illusion. Thus, visuo-tactile synchrony in the enlarged peripersonal space toward the virtual body presented in the third-person perspective might have affect ownership in the visuo-motor-tactile condition. Conversely, the peripersonal space may limit the surrounding physical body in the visuo-tactile condition; ownership was not elicited despite visuo-tactile synchrony.

5 Limitation and Future Work

There are a few limitations to this study. First, that the influence of gender difference on avatar ownership may be caused by the biological gender of the user seems clear. In addition of appearance characteristics of shape, face or color of skin, self-concept might be related ownership [65]. Therefore, the gender identity of the participant, rather than just identification with the avatar's appearance, could be related to ownership. Thus, those who perceive themselves as more male would feel a stronger ownership towards a male avatar, and vice versa. Second, the reasons for which ownership and agency could influence training and rehabilitation in embodiment VR using third-person perspective were not investigated. In a task such as learning to use an avatar presented in the third person perspective, it is necessary to examine whether increasing ownership or agency could in turn enhance learning, if the participant feels that the avatar's body feels like their own. Hülsmann et al. [66] demonstrated improved full body motor learning using an avatar presented in the third-person perspective while measuring ownership and agency to the avatar. However, they did not analyze their effects on learning. Third, the visuo-motor-tactile condition in this study was a goal-directed behavior: touching the ball. Similar to the visuo-motor-tactile condition, visuo-tactile and visuo-motor synchrony could be separated. For example, the condition of the virtual body could be moved and touched with the actual body at the same time, as in the setup of Lenggenhager et al. [23]. The effect of this difference in the visuo-motor-tactile condition on ownership should be investigated. It may be also necessary to compare the effect of a goal-directed behavior under the condition of not touching the object and under the condition of touching the object to examine the effect of a goal-directed behavior. These points should be investigated in future research using a third-person perspective in VR. Fourth, the participants, who were all Japanese, found the avatar and task to have low fidelity. The task used in this study is very simple (touching a ball ten 10 times). Thus, higher fidelity could make the task more ecologically valid and meaningful. With the involvement of movement and other more complex interactions with the environment, ownership and agency could be improved. Further research is needed to determine whether similar results could be obtained using a high-fidelity avatar and in more ecologically valid environments. Fifth, while in the pre-experiment questionnaire, twenty-nine participants answered that they had experienced using VR before, none of the volunteers were particularly familiar with it. However, all participants were young adults familiar with cyber communication technologies. Age could influence embodiment [67, 68]. Thus, future research should explore whether similar results could be obtained in different age groups. These points should be investigated in future research using a third-person perspective in VR.

Moreover, there are limitation about the accuracy of the questionnaire. Peck and Gonzalez-Franco (2021) [68] suggested a standardized avatar embodiment questionnaire including categories of Appearance, Response, Ownership, and Multi-Sensory, and subscale of agency. Using the questionnaire by Peck and Gonzalez-Franco (2021) [68] will be more appropriate for future study.

6 Conclusion

The main purpose of this study was to the investigate how to elicit ownership and agency for a virtual body presented in the third-person perspective. Our study revealed that ownership was elicited for the male virtual body presented in a third-person perspective by the synchronized condition of all visual, motor, and tactile multimodal feedback information in the male group. Moreover, our study revealed that agency was elicited for the male virtual body presented in the third-person perspective by the visuo-motor synchronized condition and that tactile feedback is not necessary to elicit agency.

Nevertheless, additional studies are required to explore the effect of gender match, the relationship between agency and ownership, and the use of the virtual body in VR.

Acknowledgments. We would like to thank Seiichi Takamatsu for providing haptic device, and Yuki Harada for his discussion and suggestion.

References

1. Slater, M., Sanchez-Vives, M.V.: Enhancing our lives with immersive virtual reality. Front. Robot. AI. **3**, 1–47 (2016). https://doi.org/10.3389/frobt.2016.00074
2. Salamin, P., Thalmann, D., Vexo, F.: The benefits of third-person perspective in virtual and augmented reality? In: Proceedings of the ACM Symposium on Virtual Reality Software and Technology - VRST 2006, p. 27. ACM Press, New York (2006)
3. Debarba, H.G., Molla, E., Herbelin, B., Boulic, R.: Characterizing embodied interaction in first and third person perspective viewpoints. In: 2015 IEEE Symposium on 3D User Interfaces, 3DUI 2015 – Proceedings, pp. 67–72. Institute of Electrical and Electronics Engineers Inc. (2015)
4. Gorisse, G., Christmann, O., Amato, E.A., Richir, S.: First- and third-person perspectives in immersive virtual environments: presence and performance analysis of embodied users. Front. Robot. AI. **4**, 33 (2017). https://doi.org/10.3389/frobt.2017.00033
5. Higuchi, K., Shimada, T., Rekimoto, J.: Flying sports assistant: external visual imagery representation for sports training. In: ACM International Conference Proceeding Series, pp. 1–4. ACM Press, New York (2011)
6. Ukai, Y., Rekimoto, J.: Swimoid: a swim support system using an underwater buddy robot. In: ACM International Conference Proceeding Series, pp. 170–177. ACM Press, New York (2013)
7. Hamanishi, N., Rekimoto, J.: Body cursor: supporting sports training with the out-of-body sence (2017)
8. Holden, M.K., Todorov, E.: Use of virtual environments in motor learning and rehabilitation. Handb. Virtual Environ. Des. Implement. Appl. **44**, 1–35 (2002)
9. Gallagher, S.: Philosophical conceptions of the self: Implications for cognitive science. Trends Cogn. Sci. **4**, 14–21 (2000). https://doi.org/10.1016/S1364-6613(99)01417-5
10. Jeannerod, M.: The mechanism of self-recognition in humans (2003). https://linkinghub.elsevier.com/retrieve/pii/S0166432802003844
11. Braun, N., et al.: The senses of agency and ownership: a review. Front. Psychol. **9**, 1–17 (2018). https://doi.org/10.3389/fpsyg.2018.00535
12. Tsakiris, M., Prabhu, G., Haggard, P.: Having a body versus moving your body: how agency structures body-ownership. Conscious. Cogn. **15**, 423–432 (2006). https://doi.org/10.1016/j.concog.2005.09.004

13. Blanke, O., Metzinger, T.: Full-body illusions and minimal phenomenal selfhood. Trends Cogn. Sci. **13**, 7–13 (2009). https://doi.org/10.1016/j.tics.2008.10.003

14. González-Franco, M., Pérez-Marcos, D., Spanlang, B., Slater, M.: The contribution of real-time mirror reflections of motor actions on virtual body ownership in an immersive virtual environment (2010)

15. Slater, M., Spanlang, B., Sanchez-Vives, M.V., Blanke, O.: First person experience of body transfer in virtual reality. PLoS ONE **5**, 1–9 (2010). https://doi.org/10.1371/journal.pone.0010564

16. Banakou, D., Groten, R., Slater, M.: Illusory ownership of a virtual child body causes overestimation of object sizes and implicit attitude changes. Proc. Natl. Acad. Sci. **110**, 12846–12851 (2013). https://doi.org/10.1073/pnas.1306779110

17. Kilteni, K., Bergstrom, I., Slater, M.: Drumming in immersive virtual reality: the body shapes the way we play. IEEE Trans. Vis. Comput. Graph. **19**, 597–605 (2013). https://doi.org/10.1109/TVCG.2013.29

18. Matsumiya, K.: Awareness of voluntary action, rather than body ownership, improves motor control. Sci. Rep. **11**, 418 (2021). https://doi.org/10.1038/s41598-020-79910-x

19. Kilteni, K., Groten, R., Slater, M.: The sense of embodiment in virtual reality. Presence Teleoper. Virtual Environ. **21**, 373–387 (2012). https://doi.org/10.1162/PRES_a_00124

20. Burin, D., Liu, Y., Yamaya, N., Kawashima, R.: Virtual training leads to physical, cognitive and neural benefits in healthy adults. Neuroimage **222**, 117297 (2020). https://doi.org/10.1016/j.neuroimage.2020.117297

21. Debarba, H.G., Bovet, S., Salomon, R., Blanke, O., Herbelin, B., Boulic, R.: Characterizing first and third person viewpoints and their alternation for embodied interaction in virtual reality. PLoS ONE **12** (2017). https://doi.org/10.1371/journal.pone.0190109

22. Petkova, V.I., Ehrsson, H.H.: If I were you: perceptual illusion of body swapping. PLoS ONE **3**, e3832 (2008). https://doi.org/10.1371/journal.pone.0003832

23. Lenggenhager, B., Tadi, T., Metzinger, T., Blanke, O.: Video ergo sum: manipulating bodily self-consciousness. Science **317**(80-), 1096–1099 (2007). https://doi.org/10.1126/science.1143439

24. Petkova, V.I., Khoshnevis, M., Ehrsson, H.H., Borghi, A.M., Moseley, G.L.: The perspective matters! Multisensory integration in ego-centric reference frames determines full-body ownership. Article **2** (2011). https://doi.org/10.3389/fpsyg.2011.00035

25. Maselli, A., Slater, M.: The building blocks of the full body ownership illusion. Front. Hum. Neurosci. **7** (2013). https://doi.org/10.3389/fnhum.2013.00083

26. Maselli, A., Slater, M.: Sliding perspectives: dissociating ownership from self-location during full body illusions in virtual reality. Front. Hum. Neurosci. **8** (2014). https://doi.org/10.3389/fnhum.2014.00693

27. Preston, C., Kuper-Smith, B.J., Ehrsson, H.H.: Owning the body in the mirror: the effect of visual perspective and mirror view on the full-body illusion. Sci. Rep. **5**, 1–10 (2015). https://doi.org/10.1038/srep18345

28. Kondo, R., Sugimoto, M., Minamizawa, K., Hoshi, T., Inami, M., Kitazaki, M.: Illusory body ownership of an invisible body interpolated between virtual hands and feet via visual-motor synchronicity /631/378/2649/1723 /631/477/2811 article. Sci. Rep. **8**, 1–8 (2018). https://doi.org/10.1038/s41598-018-25951-2

29. Aspell, J.E., Lenggenhager, B., Blanke, O.: Keeping in touch with one's self: multisensory mechanisms of self-consciousness. PLoS ONE **4**, 25–27 (2009). https://doi.org/10.1371/journal.pone.0006488

30. Lenggenhager, B., Mouthon, M., Blanke, O.: Spatial aspects of bodily self-consciousness. Conscious. Cogn. **18**, 110–117 (2009). https://doi.org/10.1016/j.concog.2008.11.003

31. Ohyama, J. Xperigrapher: Social-Lab Experimental platform to evaluate experience in cyber physical society. Trans. Japan. Soc. Med. Biol. Eng. **59**, 811–813 (2021). https://doi.org/10. 11239/jsmbe.Annual59.811

32. Kalckert, A., Ehrsson, H.H.: Moving a rubber hand that feels like your own: a dissociation of ownership and agency. Front. Hum. Neurosci. **6**, 1–14 (2012). https://doi.org/10.3389/fnhum. 2012.00040

33. Kalckert, A., Ehrsson, H.H.: The moving rubber hand illusion revisited: comparing movements and visuotactile stimulation to induce illusory ownership. Conscious. Cogn. **26**, 117–132 (2014). https://doi.org/10.1016/j.concog.2014.02.003

34. Ehrsson, H.H., Spence, C., Passingham, R.E.: That's my hand! Activity in premotor cortex reflects feeling of ownership of a limb. Science 305(80-), 875–877 (2004). https://doi.org/10. 1126/science.1097011

35. Braun, N., Thorne, J.D., Hildebrandt, H., Debener, S.: Interplay of agency and ownership: the intentional binding and rubber hand illusion Paradigm Combined. PLoS ONE **9** (2014). https://doi.org/10.1371/journal.pone.0111967

36. Braun, N., Emkes, R., Thorne, J.D., Debener, S.: Embodied neurofeedback with an anthropomorphic robotic hand. Sci. Rep. **6**, 1–13 (2016). https://doi.org/10.1038/srep37696

37. D'Angelo, M., di Pellegrino, G., Seriani, S., Gallina, P., Frassinetti, F.: The sense of agency shapes body schema and peripersonal space. Sci. Rep. **8** (2018). https://doi.org/10.1038/s41 598-018-32238-z

38. Ma, K., Hommel, B.: The role of agency for perceived ownership in the virtual hand illusion. Conscious. Cogn. **36**, 277–288 (2015). https://doi.org/10.1016/j.concog.2015.07.008

39. Swinkels, L.M.J., Veling, H., Dijksterhuis, A., van Schie, H.T.: Availability of synchronous information in an additional sensory modality does not enhance the full body illusion. Psychol. Res. **85**(6), 2291–2312 (2020). https://doi.org/10.1007/s00426-020-01396-z

40. Hara, M., Kanayama, N., Blanke, O., Salomon, R.: Modulation of bodily self-consciousness by self and external touch. IEEE Trans. Haptics. **14**, 615–625 (2021). https://doi.org/10.1109/ TOH.2021.3067651

41. Choi, W., Li, L., Satoh, S., Hachimura, K.: Multisensory integration in the virtual hand illusion with active movement. Biomed Res. Int. **2016** (2016). https://doi.org/10.1155/2016/8163098

42. Wen, W., et al.: Goal-directed movement enhances body representation updating. Front. Hum. Neurosci. **10**, 1–10 (2016). https://doi.org/10.3389/fnhum.2016.00329

43. Waltemate, T., Gall, D., Roth, D., Botsch, M., Latoschik, M.E.: The impact of avatar personalization and immersion on virtual body ownership, presence, and emotional response. IEEE Trans. Vis. Comput. Graph. **24**, 1643–1652 (2018). https://doi.org/10.1109/TVCG.2018.279 4629

44. Tacikowski, P., Fust, J., Ehrsson, H.H.: Fluidity of gender identity induced by illusory body-sex change. Sci. Rep. **10**, 14385 (2020). https://doi.org/10.1038/s41598-020-71467-z

45. Costantini, M., Haggard, P.: The rubber hand illusion: sensitivity and reference frame for body ownership. Conscious. Cogn. **16**, 229–240 (2007). https://doi.org/10.1016/j.concog. 2007.01.001

46. Schwind, V., Knierim, P., Tasci, C., Franczak, P., Haas, N., Henze, N.: "These are not my hands!": effect of gender on the perception of avatar hands in virtual reality. In: Conference on Human Factors in Computing Systems – Proceedings, pp. 1577–1582. ACM, New York (2017)

47. Peck, T.C., Seinfeld, S., Aglioti, S.M., Slater, M.: Putting yourself in the skin of a black avatar reduces implicit racial bias. Conscious. Cogn. **22**, 779–787 (2013). https://doi.org/10.1016/j. concog.2013.04.016

48. Banakou, D., Hanumanthu, P.D., Slater, M.: Virtual embodiment of white people in a black virtual body leads to a sustained reduction in their implicit racial bias. Front. Hum. Neurosci. **10**, 1–12 (2016). https://doi.org/10.3389/fnhum.2016.00601

49. Farmer, H., Tajadura-Jiménez, A., Tsakiris, M.: Beyond the colour of my skin: how skin colour affects the sense of body-ownership. Conscious. Cogn. **21**, 1242–1256 (2012). https://doi.org/10.1016/j.concog.2012.04.011

50. Lira, M., Egito, J.H., Dall'Agnol, P.A., Amodio, D.M., Gonçalves, Ó.F., Boggio, P.S.: The influence of skin colour on the experience of ownership in the rubber hand illusion. Sci. Rep. **7**, 1–13 (2017). https://doi.org/10.1038/s41598-017-16137-3

51. Frith, C.D., Blakemore, S.J., Wolpert, D.M.: Abnormalities in the awareness and control of action (2000). https://royalsocietypublishing.org/doi/10.1098/rstb.2000.0734

52. Wen, W., Yamashita, A., Asama, H.: The influence of goals on sense of control. Conscious. Cogn. **37**, 83–90 (2015). https://doi.org/10.1016/j.concog.2015.08.012

53. Gentsch, A., Synofzik, M.: Affective coding: the emotional dimension of agency. Front. Hum. Neurosci. **8**, 1–7 (2014). https://doi.org/10.3389/fnhum.2014.00608

54. Synofzik, M., Vosgerau, G., Newen, A.: Beyond the comparator model: a multifactorial two-step account of agency. Conscious. Cogn. **17**, 219–239 (2008). https://doi.org/10.1016/j.concog.2007.03.010

55. Ishikawa, R., Ayabe-Kanamura, S., Izawa, J.: The role of motor memory dynamics in structuring bodily self-consciousness. iScience **24**, 103511 (2021). https://doi.org/10.1016/j.isci.2021.103511

56. Banakou, D., Slater, M.: Body ownership causes illusory self-attribution of speaking and influences subsequent real speaking. Proc. Natl. Acad. Sci. U.S.A. **111**, 17678–17683 (2014). https://doi.org/10.1073/pnas.1414936111

57. di Pellegrino, G., Làdavas, E.: Peripersonal space in the brain. Neuropsychologia **66**, 126–133 (2015). https://doi.org/10.1016/j.neuropsychologia.2014.11.011

58. Ehrsson, H.H.: The concept of body ownership and its relation to multisensory integration, 775–792 (2011)

59. Blanke, O., Slater, M., Serino, A.: Behavioral, neural, and computational principles of bodily self-consciousness (2015)

60. Makin, T.R., Holmes, N.P., Ehrsson, H.H.: On the other hand: dummy hands and peripersonal space. Behav. Brain Res. **191**, 1–10 (2008). https://doi.org/10.1016/j.bbr.2008.02.041

61. Lloyd, D.M.: Spatial limits on referred touch to an alien limb may reflect boundaries of visuo-tactile peripersonal space surrounding the hand. Brain Cogn. **64**, 104–109 (2007). https://doi.org/10.1016/j.bandc.2006.09.013

62. Guterstam, A., Zeberg, H., Özçiftci, V.M., Ehrsson, H.H.: The magnetic touch illusion: a perceptual correlate of visuo-tactile integration in peripersonal space. Cognition **155**, 44–56 (2016). https://doi.org/10.1016/j.cognition.2016.06.004

63. Noel, J.-P., Grivaz, P., Marmaroli, P., Lissek, H., Blanke, O., Serino, A.: Full body action remapping of peripersonal space: the case of walking. Elsevier (2014). https://doi.org/10.1016/j.neuropsychologia.2014.08.030

64. Mine, D., Yokosawa, K.: Disconnected hand avatar can be integrated into the peripersonal space. Exp. Brain Res. **239**(1), 237–244 (2020). https://doi.org/10.1007/s00221-020-05971-z

65. Krol, S.A., Thériault, R., Olson, J.A., Raz, A., Bartz, J.A.: Self-concept clarity and the bodily self: malleability across modalities. Personal. Soc. Psychol. Bull. **46**, 808–820 (2020). https://doi.org/10.1177/0146167219879126

66. Hülsmann, F., Frank, C., Senna, I., Ernst, M.O., Schack, T., Botsch, M.: Superimposed skilled performance in a virtual mirror improves motor performance and cognitive representation of a full body motor action. Front. Robot. AI. **6**, 1–17 (2019). https://doi.org/10.3389/frobt.2019.00043

67. Graham, K.T., Martin-Iverson, M.T., Holmes, N.P., Waters, F.A.: The projected hand illusion: component structure in a community sample and association with demographics, cognition, and psychotic-like experiences. Atten. Percept. Psychophys. **77**(1), 207–219 (2014). https://doi.org/10.3758/s13414-014-0748-6

68. Peck, T.C., Gonzalez-Franco, M.: Avatar embodiment. A standardized questionnaire. Front. Virtual Real. **1**, 1–12 (2021). https://doi.org/10.3389/frvir.2020.575943

Reality Avatar for Customer Conversation in the Metaverse

Ryoto Kato[1]([⊠])⦿, Yusuke Kikuchi[1]⦿, Vibol Yem[1]⦿, and Yasushi Ikei[2]⦿

[1] Tokyo Metropolitan University, 6-6 Asahigaoka, Hino, Tokyo 191-0065, Japan
{kato-ryoto,kikuchi-yusuke4}@ed.tmu.ac.jp, yemvibol@tmu.ac.jp
[2] The University of Tokyo, 7-3-1 Hongo, Bunkyo, Tokyo 113-8656, Japan
ikei@vr.u-tokyo.ac.jp

Abstract. Much emphasis has been placed on the expansion of the metaverse space, which enables a large number of people to participate concurrently and conduct business or entertainment in their field of interest. A close connection between the metaverse and the real space is expected to significantly increase the availability of the two spaces; however, an effective method for this connection has not yet been presented. In this paper, we propose the XR (cross reality) Telexperience Portal as one method for connecting both remote real space and past space with the metaverse. Furthermore, when people communicate in the metaverse's 3D space, they require avatars to represent themselves, for which a variety of avatar designs are used. However, highly realistic avatars that hold the identity of the participant are not yet used. In this paper, we propose a method for generating natural facial expressions of a high-reality avatar to become a reliable conversation partner.

Keywords: Metaverse · Portal · Reality avatar · Facial animation

1 Introduction

The era of the metaverse is fast approaching where many people can participate in a shared digital space. The metaverse is a massively shared 3D space synthesized on cloud computers, a term coined by Neal Stephenson in his science fiction novel published in 1992 [1]. A discussion of the process of turning the idea into reality was also presented [2], but the unprecedented entry of Meta Platforms (Facebook), Inc. into the metaverse market has resulted in rapid progress in practical applications. In the roadmap, as a long-term prediction, the metaverse is described as including both augmentations of real space and the VR world on the server. It is a continuous extension of the current real world in which the digital world interacts with a similar three-dimensional real space structure, giving it affinity with the real world. The metaverse is expected to grow in the fields of business, education, and entertainment in the future, particularly in commercial

Supported by the MIC/SCOPE #191603003, JSPS KAKENHI Grant Number 18H04118 and 18H03283.

and industrial applications, where spaces that complement real-world activities and create new demands will expand.

However, there are still many problems that need to be solved for future development. Secure and efficient asset management (including privacy protection) in the virtual space is a minimum requirement. Furthermore, the avatar representation of participants as an interface to the VR space, as well as the live reflection of real-world information, are thought to be important for the metaverse's dependability and availability. The latter is a required function for the operation of a digital twin, which is regarded as one of the most useful types of metaverse because it allows not only the simulation of the copy space but also the design planning and management of the real space. It is useful for diagnosis to be able to observe live images of remote real space in a stereoscopic view from within the metaverse, as if one were there, and to be able to share the scene's viewpoint with a large number of people. Furthermore, since the metaverse is intended to be a space where humans can virtually enter, avatars as portraits of the humans participating in the metaverse and AI avatars such as salespersons in the virtual shop are essentially important elements. The avatars' quality must be improved so that they can act freely from an individual's subjective point of view and interact with other avatars in a natural and trustworthy manner.

The shared-space avatars that have been realized so far have been improved from 2D graphics to the recent 3D low polygon models, but the reality that represents the identity of individuals is insufficient. This is primarily due to the limited computing power of end-user terminals. Because the metaverse assumes the participation of many avatars representing human beings, the load on the terminals is typically high. With the recent improvement in the performance of user terminals and the expansion of the capacity of the cloud server that controls the shared space, high-reality avatars are expected to become popular in the future. In this paper, we propose a new method for generating facial expressions, especially around mouth movements, for human communication. Although various factors are involved in human communication, reproducing natural mouth movements during conversations and being able to read facial expressions is the basis for conveying emotional elements. As a result, both AI-powered avatars and avatars that project actual users must generate and display facial changes during speech.

Automatic generation of speech animation of CG avatars has been developed by methodologies from traditional linguistic analysis to current performance capture and machine learning. [3–5]. Face synthesis based on linguistic phonology [6] is distinguished by a high degree of freedom in facial expression modification due to procedural manipulation. Performance capture [7] can generate highly realistic facial expressions by measuring the actor's face with image processing (e.g., faceware, faceshift) and applying it to changes in a CG model's face mesh.

A procedural method based on phonology has been proposed in MikeTalk [8] which maps speech phonemes to visual phonemes (visemes); this is an early example using 2D images. Edwards et al. [4] developed an animator-oriented face animation system (JALI) that creates an expressive speaker avatar from speech and its transcript. Based on English phonemes and their corresponding face shapes, they proposed a combination of jaw rigging and blendshapes (shape interpolation [9]). It took a long time to process and was an offline process at the time. The generation of viseme curves using machine learning models allowed the process to be completed in near real time [10]. There are some Generative Adversarial Network approaches to synthesize a talking head with realistic motions of lips, head poses, and eye blinks from a target audio signal and a single target picture [11,12] or a reference video [13]. Recently, it has become possible to generate audio-driven emotional talking faces using a machine learning approach to address the importance of emotional expression while talking by humans [14].

In this paper, we first show an example of one simple way to connect the metaverse space with the real-world space before describing a real-time method for synthesising natural facial expression for an avatar in the metaverse. It is possible to increase the diversity of the space and enrich the content of people's activities by reflecting information from the real-world space in the metaverse space. There are numerous candidates for inputting data from the real world, but live image information from the real world is one of the most common applications. Not only feature information extracted by specific sensors, but also real-time visual information of arbitrary points in the real space is useful in the case of digital twins, where the metaverse takes events that are linked to the real space. Another application is a 3D space that allows for the telepresence of a remote location in real space or a virtual journey to a past real space. This is the ability to enter the video space of various real-world points, and it can be regarded as a time and space portal.

2   Multiple Real Spaces on the Metaverse

Metaverse is a 3D space, and it is characterized by the fact that many users can experience various spaces. However, having a unified visual experience in the portal to connect the metaverse space and the real space is desirable. The current metaverse is distinguished by its ability to deliver a high level of realism via stereoscopic viewing in all directions of polygon-base space via a Head-Mounted Display (HMD). As an extension of it, we built the XR (cross reality) Telexperience portal (XRT portal), which allows users wearing HMDs to continuously experience spatial understanding via stereoscopic viewing. As the metaverse is a collection of different VR worlds, the XRT portal is one of the subspaces that realize the unique features of a cross-world metaverse.

In this design, to share the video experience of the remote real space in the context of the previous chapter, one member of the group who is working together acts as a viewpoint operator or guide to move the viewpoint in the space, and other participants can view the video in any orientation from that viewpoint position. A VR object made of 3D polygons and an archive of remote-live or full-field video can be found in this space. The portal itself appears as a polygon-base VR space. Figure 1 depicts an overview of the portal and a guide avatar implemented by the method described in the later sections. The group's viewpoint is the virtual fulldome camera's center, and the images seen from this point are distributed to the participants. The virtual fulldome camera is made up of two cameras that work together to create images for the left and right eyes, and it differs from other virtual cameras in that each of them is a fulldome lens. The difference is that each of them is a fulldome lens so that each participant in the group can see a different direction.

Fig. 1. XR Telexperience Portal and a guide avatar.

Figure 2 shows the visual field images of two participants looking from the same viewpoint position at certain points in the viewing direction. The images on the left (a) depict two images with the stereoscopic disparity in the field of view of two full-dome cameras facing the front of the building. The image on the right (b) shows an image of monocular view at the same shared viewpoint in the different direction looking at the road. It is possible to share the perspective of the other stereoscopic camera position by controlling a smooth transition between the two images.

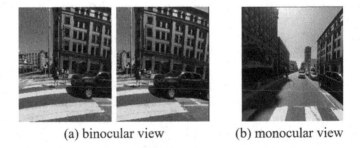

(a) binocular view   (b) monocular view

Fig. 2. Binocular views (a) and monocular view (b) of HMDs.

Figure 3 shows a scene in which a real avatar is entering a conference room in a shared space (metaverse). Because of the high computational load on local clients, high-resolution avatars are not currently widely used, but it is expected that they will be in the future. When using such realistic avatars for dialog interaction that is close to the real world, it is critical to generate not only body skeleton movements but also mouth movements and natural facial expressions associated with conversation. In particular, when some of the economic activities in the real world are conducted in the metaverse using AI avatars in the future, it would be necessary to make the trustworthiness of the agent represented by the avatar closer to that of a real person.

Fig. 3. Real avatars in a meeting room (Hubs).

3   AI Avatar for Customer Service in the Metaverse

In the metaverse space, it is necessary to synthesize natural animations for the facial expressions during the interaction of AI-driven avatars as well as human avatars. Since AI avatars are usually used for specific purposes, it is possible to set up a topic domain to enable some degree of natural interaction. Ideally, an AI avatar should be able to understand not only the language of its interlocutor but also nonverbal information, just like a human, and should be able to express facial expressions in three-dimensional space.

The process of implementing these functions is roughly shown in Fig. 4. We analyze the customer's facial expressions and speech to determine the text and style of speech to be used when responding to the customer. It generates speech for the text and style, as well as animates the face using the face model and style. The avatar's face and body are projected onto the environment and become the subject of the customer's conversation. In such a situation, it is not always easy to generate an interactive and natural response. There are several problems to be solved to synthesize speech and facial expressions with the shortest possible delay, including correct recognition of the human speech and facial expressions, appropriate response content, and nonverbal information such as emotional expressions.

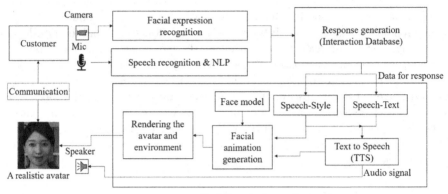

Realistic avatar face synthesis system

Fig. 4. The system architecture of the communication between a customer and a realistic avatar.

In this study, we use a cloud server for preprocessing of animation rendering on a local PC. Microsoft Cognitive Service handles speech recognition and synthesis, Google Dialogflow handles response generation, and Unity Editor handles face synthesis and rendering. The method for generating facial expressions is described in detail in the following chapter. The shortest loop response time is fairly less than one second. This enables a conversation with a human voice to take place.

4   Facial Expressions of a Japanese Reality Avatar

4.1   Feature of Japanese Speech

Previous studies conducted using English as the main target language were able to create convincing facial animations by adding visual representations derived from English speech. However, an audio-driven facial animation approach that is multilingual in nature has yet to be developed. They were not always successful in applying the results to animations of speakers in other languages with different utterance structures, particularly Japanese. This is because the number of phonemes and the structure of phoneme sequences in words and sentences in Japanese differs from those in English. The Japanese language has a very restricted phonological inventory. It is composed of five vowel phonemes (/a e i o u/) and sixteen consonantal phonemes (/p t k b d g s h z r m n w j N Q/) [15]. English, on the other hand, has fourteen to twenty vowels and twenty-four consonants [16]. As a result, the registered or learned face shapes during speech differ from those of Japanese speakers. In English, syllables are used for phonological segmentation, whereas mora is used in Japan [17]. The syllable segmentation of English is not a simple task that leaves considerable discussion, however, the mora segmentation in Japanese is rather easy because a mora is a unit that can be represented by one letter of "kana" (a Japanese pseudo-character used in syllabic writing) [15]. We concluded that using mora-characterized speech segmentation as a criterion of speech analysis is appropriate based on the characteristics of Japanese speech described above. We propose a new method for generating real-time realistic facial animation from face mesh data corresponding to the fifty-six CV (Consonant and Vowel) type morae that comprise Japanese speech shown in Table 1.

Table 1. Fifty-six morae used in this system.

		Consonants										
		/k-/	/s-/	/t-/	/n-/	/h-/	/p-/	/b-/	/m-/	/r-/	/j-/	/w-/
Vowels	/-a/	/ka/	/sa/	/ta/	/na/	/ha/	/pa/	/ba/	/ma/	/ra/	/ja/	/wa/
	/-i/	/ki/	/si/	/ti/	/ni/	/hi/	/pi/	/bi/	/mi/	/ri/		
	/-u/	/ku/	/su/	/tu/	/nu/	/hu/	/pu/	/bu/	/mu/	/ru/	/ju/	
	/-e/	/ke/	/se/	/te/	/ne/	/he/	/pe/	/be/	/me/	/re/		
	/-o/	/ko/	/so/	/to/	/no/	/ho/	/po/	/bo/	/mo/	/ro/	/jo/	/wo/
Syllabic nasal	/N/											

4.2 Modeling of a Realistic Avatar

Using publicly available basic tools, we designed a procedure that can build a realistic model of any person in a short time. In this study, the speech avatar system consists of a 3D mesh of a neutral face, fifty-two 3D meshes for the facial expression synthesis system, which deforms the neutral face, and a TTS (text-to-speech) system. The blendshape method [18] is used to synthesize the time course of facial expressions during a speech by interpolating fifty-three 3D meshes of facial shapes, including a neutral shape. The fifty-two 3D meshes were constructed by using Apple ARkit AR-FaceAnchor (Apple.ARkit.ARFaceAnchor. BlendShapeLocation (AAR) [19]) in which the deformation element (fifty-two coefficients) was set at the maximum point for each particular expression. Apple TrueDepth can easily and cheaply obtain the amount of facial deformation in the CV-type morae utterance, which is represented by fifty-two coefficients.

The modeling procedure is shown in Fig. 5. The first step is to prepare 1.1 million points of photogrammetrically measured head shape data (Fig. 5 (a)) as the face shape (neutral face) of the particular person to be made into a realistic avatar. (Photogrammetry itself is not our process.) The neutral face photogrammetry model is converted to a polygon mesh (Fig. 5 (b)) by Russian3DScanner's Wrap [20]. We also rebuilt AAR's fifty-two sample meshes at the time when the amount of each coefficient in AAR was at its peak using the same polygon mesh. Finally, fifty-three meshes with target identity are modeled (Fig. 5 (c)) by adding the amount of deformation from a neutral to arbitrary expressions obtained from the converted sample of fifty-three face meshes to the target neutral mesh.

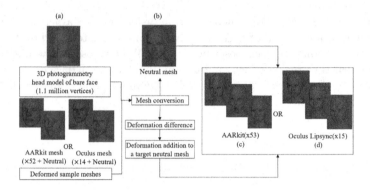

Fig. 5. The procedure of face mesh modeling.

For comparison in the evaluation of the accuracy of mouth shape and naturalness with Oculus Lipsync which is a popular real-time facial generation system, we prepared a head mesh to which we applied fifteen different viseme provided as expression deformation elements in Oculus Lipsync [21], a software that generates facial expressions during speech. It is capable of generating shapes near the mouth that correspond to phonemes in the audio stream. We used the same modeling technique to create a face mesh with fifteen faces that all have the same identity (Fig. 5 (d)).

This modeling method requires only the scanning data of the reference face of the target person, which greatly simplifies the animation process.

4.3   Generation Approaches

Mora-driven Facial Expression. The Mora-driven Facial Expression (MDFE) method was developed for an avatar that speaks Japanese. Figure 6 shows the process of MDFE. A 3D neutral face mesh, fifty-two 3D face meshes for each facial expression, and text-to-speech with an audio processing system is included in this speech animation system. The blendshape method, which interpolates fifty-three 3D face meshes, including a neutral face mesh, is used to generate the face animation while speaking.

The set of the deformation coefficients was obtained from the distance sensor (Apple TrueDepth camera system) and stored as a vector $AAR(52, 1)$ after it was sent to a PC via the user datagram protocol. The CV-mora facial expression matrix was built based on the facial measurements during each of the fifty-six morae utterances performed by a single assistant of the experiment. These fifty-six AARs are different from the neutral face mesh during Japanese mora pronunciation. The shape of the face starts to deform at 120 ms before vocalization, and the deformation reaches the apex at the onset of vocalization [22]. To incorporate this process, we captured two AARs at 120 ms before vocalization onset and at the apex and obtained $BVO_{s,t}$ and $Apex_{s,t}$ ($0 \leq s \leq 51$) for each mora t ($0 \leq t \leq 55$), respectively.

The pronounced sound of a single Japanese kana grapheme that corresponds to one mora was recorded, and its acoustic feature was calculated and stored in twelve-dimensional mel-frequency cepstrum coefficients (MFCCs) 100 Hz. First, we registered the average dimension of the MFCC for each of the fifty-six morae for 1024 ms during kana (mora) pronunciation. The cosine similarity of the input audio to profile t determines the mora intensity vector MIV_t ($0 \leq t \leq 55$, $0 \leq MIV_t \leq 1.0$) 100 Hz. The vectors $BVO_{s,t}$ and $Apex_{s,t}$ for each mora t were added using a linear interpolation function with mora intensity MIV_t as the weight. Finally, the result passes through a cubic interpolation function with previous vector to avoid unnaturalness caused by high-frequency deformation.

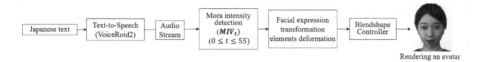

Fig. 6. The generation process of speech facial animation of MDFE.

Vowel-driven Facial Expression. We prepared a simpler method for comparison in the user study to evaluate our proposed method (MDFE). This method detects only five vowels that are always included in the CV-mora of Japanese speech.

Figure 7 shows the process of Vowel-Driven Facial Expression (VDFE). This process is similar to MDFE. It uses the intensity of only the mora corresponding to the five Japanese vowels (/a/, /e/, /i/, /o/, /u/) and their face mesh data. In other words, the mora intensity vector MIV_t ($0 \leq t \leq 4$, $0 \leq MIV_t \leq 1.0$) is detected from the input speech stream. The other procedures for obtaining the expression transformation element are the same as in MDFE.

Two Other Methods for Evaluation. Two methods were prepared in addition to the one described in the previous section: a method that only detects the magnitude of voice sound (Volume) and the Oculus Lipsync [21], a well-known real-time speech expression synthesis method accepting speech audio stream.

In the volume method, the magnitude of an audio signal entering the audio buffer in Unity is reflected only to "jawOpen" deformation which represents the jaw motion dedicated to one of the fifty-two expression deformation elements in the AAR.

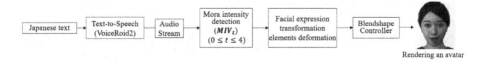

Fig. 7. The generation process of speech facial animation of VDFE.

Oculus Lipsync detects phonemes corresponding to characteristic consonants and vowels in English [23] and displays fifteen viseme (Fig. 8).

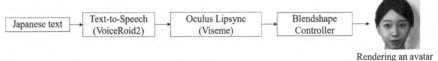

Rendering an avatar

Fig. 8. The generation process of speech facial animation of Oculus Lipsync.

5   User Study

5.1   Objective and Participants

We evaluated our proposed mora-driven facial expression generation (MDFE) in comparison with the three methods (Volume, Oculus Lipsync, and VDFE) described in the previous chapter. The points of evaluation were the accuracy of the lip sync and the naturalness of the facial expression during speech. The experiment included fifteen engineering Japanese students (twelve males and three females), with an average age of 24.1 years.

5.2   Stimulus

The presented stimuli were facial animations in which Japanese sentences were read in four different ways for 21 s. Movements unrelated to speech facial expression such as head and eye movements, body swaying were added randomly to all four avatars. The sum of occurrences of fifty-six morae in the read-out Japanese transcript (Total: 136 morae) is shown in Table 2. The voice was a female voice generated by speech synthesis software (VoiceRoid2: Yukari Yuzuki) and delivered via headphones. The speech expressions of each avatar were recorded into a 4K resolution, 100 FPS video, or generated in real time using four speech expression generation methods using this audio stream as input. Unity 2019 4.9f1 (High Definition Render Pipeline: HDRP) and a GeForce RTX 3090 GPU were used to create the video.

Table 2. The number of CV-mora in the 21 s transcript (arranged in IPA alphabet).

			Consonants										
			/k-/	/s-/	/t-/	/n-/	/h-/	/p-/	/b-/	/m-/	/r-/	/j-/	/w/
	/-a/	6	3	1	3	3	2	0	0	2	4	0	2
	/-i/	11	8	6	1	1	1	0	0	1	9		
Vowels	/-u/	11	4	4	1	0	0	0	0	1	1	0	
	/-e/	4	1	0	5	0	1	0	0	1	1		
	/-o/	10	4	0	1	4	0	0	0	0	2	2	0
Syllabic nasal	/N/	14											

Two environments of image presentation were used: 2D (flat display) and 3D (HMD). To eliminate order effects, the order of presentation was randomized in both environments. If a participant requested it, we presented the stimulus as many times as necessary until the participant completed the evaluation.

2D Viewing. The quality evaluation is performed by displaying the avatar's speech expression on a 2D flat display. The display used was a 4K (3840 × 2160), HDR (High Dynamic Range), 31.5-in. LCD, 144 Hz monitor (JAPANNEXT). We placed four avatar speech videos on the screen with each avatar measuring 190 mm (height) × 220 mm (width) (Fig. 9(a)). We prepared four different arrangements and distributed them randomly among the participants to cancel the positional error (dependence on the presentation position). The participants' points of view were set at 400 mm from the display (Fig. 9(b)).

3D Viewing. An HMD (Vive Pro, HTC) was used to generate and present disparity 3D images of four avatars, one by one, in real time. The resolution of the presentation was 1440 × 1600 (each eye), the update rate 90 Hz, and the viewing angle was 110°C. Figure 9(c) shows the field of view of the HMD as seen by the participants in the experiment. For each visual analog scale (VAS) item, the participants evaluated them with each of four avatars being viewed once for two sets (Fig. 9(d)).

5.3   Evaluation Items and Scales

The evaluation items were (1) correctness of mouth shape to speech voice, (2) congruency of speech and facial expression, and (3) naturalness (a human likeness), and the participants were asked to rank the items on a VAS between methods. The scale was anchored (1) "completely mismatch" to "completely match", (2) "unsynchronized of voice and facial expression" to "synchronized as the avatar itself is speaking", (3) "robot-like and expressionless" to "natural expression of human speech", from left to right end, respectively. Furthermore, the four avatars were ranked by the naturalness of the sussian3dscanner.com/peech expression (degree of human likeness) at the end of the evaluation.

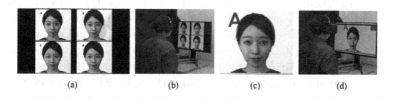

Fig. 9. (a) Arrangement of four avatars in 2D viewing, (b) Display setup in 2D flat display condition, (c) Avatar in HMD 3D viewing, and (d) HMD setup in 3D condition.

6   Results and Discussion

6.1   Results

Figures 10(a) and (b) show the result of the accuracy of mouth shape and the naturalness of facial expression during sentence speech for 2D and 3D viewings. The synchronization evaluation (2nd question) was omitted here because it produced the same graph as the previous two. The two-way ANOVA for 2D/3D viewing and the animation method revealed that 2D/3D viewing and interaction were not statistically significant (p = .66, p = .77), but the animation method was (p < .001). Almost the same observation could be made about the naturalness. The multiple comparisons (Holm's method) indicated highly significant difference between two groups of MDFE/VDFE and Volume/Oculus Lipsync (p < .001) for both accuracy and naturalness. On the other hand, there was no significant difference between MDFE and VDFE, also between Volume and Oculus Lipsync.

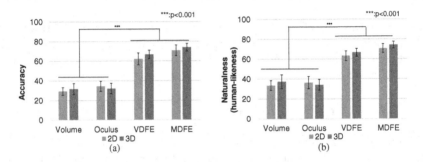

Fig. 10. (a) Accuracy of mouth shape during Japanese speech, and (b) Naturalness of facial expressions during Japanese speech (N = 15).

Table 3(a) and (b) show the result of ranking among methods. The order was MDFE, VDFE, Volume, and Oculus in both 2D and 3D viewings. There was a complete agreement between participants about the ranking in 2D and 3D viewing according to Kendall's coefficient of concordance (2D: W = 0.69, 3D: W = 0.74). The results of a Chi-square test revealed that there is a strong relationship between the rankings by each rater (2D: $\chi^2 = 31.16$, $df = 3$, p < 0.01, 3D: $\chi^2 = 33.48$, $df = 3$, p < 0.01). The results of the ranking were tested with the least significant difference method to reveal if there is a significant difference among the four avatars. There was a significant difference between two groups of Volume/Oculus Lipsync and VDFE/MDFE. So, we marked the groups based on this result of ranking as "a" and "b" because no significant (p < 0.05) difference was observed within the same group.

Table 3. (a) Total and an average of rank for methods in 2D viewing, (b) in 3D viewing.

	Volume	Oculus	VDFE	MDFE			Volume	Oculus	VDFE	MDFE
SUM	48a	54a	28b	20b		SUM	48a	54a	28b	19b
Average	3.20	3.60	1.87	1.33		Average	3.27	3.60	1.87	1.27
Variance	0.69	0.24	0.38	0.22		Variance	0.60	0.24	0.12	0.33
		(a)						(b)		

6.2 Discussion

From the average of the rankings shown in Table 3, the MDFE with fifty-six CV-type morae was evaluated to have more natural facial expressions than the VDFE. It may be easy to predict that MDFE will produce more accurate mouth shapes than VDFE, because bilabial speech sounds that close the mouth in the speech expression is not considered in VDFE. Shutting the lips is easy for the observer to detect, and then the best elements to be aware of the timing synchronization with speech.

The VDFE that uses face shape data corresponding to only five vowels has the advantage that it is easy to construct because the number of data is very small, but the complexity of speech expressions is a little less than that of the facial expression of avatars that use face shape data for fifty-six mora. The VDFE sometimes gives a monotonous impression, which leads the observer to perceive it as robotic at times. However, no significant difference was found between the two in the rank test or the VAS multiple comparisons. As a result, if people do not pay close attention, they may miss the relatively minor difference. This could be because avatars' facial expressions change very quickly, just like real human speech.

Both MDFE and VDFE correspond to the Japanese mora and gained high evaluation, whereas Volume and Oculus Lipsync, which does not, dropped significantly in evaluation. Obviously their facial expressions did not have the exact shape of the face corresponding to the "kana" sequence, which is a basic element of Japanese speech. It is interesting to note that Oculus Lipsync, which detects phonemes, and Volume, which simply opens and closes the jaw, produce almost identical results. In other words, the VAS evaluations of Volume and Oculus Lipsync are close enough that there is no significant difference, but this does not imply that they are far apart from the correct facial expression in the same direction. Therefore, the fact that Volume was rated in the ranking as having more natural speech expressions than Oculus Lipsync should not be taken too meaningful.

6.3 Limitation

In this study, we realized a highly realistic real-time speech animation of avatars based on the segmental structure of mora, which characterizes Japanese speech. However, some limitations remain that will need to be addressed in future research. Currently, the data of the amount of change from the neutral face to make the faces of fifty-six morae was derived from one of the authors. It is necessary to consider individual facial differences when creating natural facial expressions for any particular person. Capturing the face data in fifty-six visemes of the user would be required.

The speaker's style of speech, changes in gaze and head posture, and the emotional component of facial expressions are not currently considered. Since our method is a procedural control, it is possible to divide this information into parts, then include them in the speech information for the synthesis process.

7   Conclusion

We proposed an XR Telexperience portal that bridges the VR space (metaverse) and real spaces via omnidirectional stereo cameras that can provide live images of both spaces to binocular and monocular viewers. We developed a method for animating facial expressions that takes advantage of Japanese characteristics. Our approach is based on the fact that the basic Japanese alphabet, mora, is a simple combination of vowels and consonants and serves as the foundation of speech. This method can produce high-quality animations that have a direct correspondence between these mora and face shapes (viseme) and their temporal transitions. When voice streaming is provided, natural facial expressions can be displayed immediately on a high-reality avatar. We believe that this real-time avatar can be one of important assets that establish the future metaverse fusing the real and VR spaces where we will be immersed on a daily basis.

Acknowledgment. This work was partially supported by the MIC/SCOPE #191603003, JSPS KAKENHI Grant Number 18H04118 and 18H03283.

References

1. Stephenson, N.: Snow Crash. Bantam Books, New York (1993)
2. Smart, J., Cascio, J., Paffendorf, J.: Pathways to the 3d web: A cross-industry public foresight project. Metaverse Roadmap (2007)
3. Bailly, G., Perrier, P., Vatikiotis-Bateson, E. (eds.): Audiovisual Speech Processing. Cambridge University Press, New York (2012). https://doi.org/10.1017/CBO9780511843891
4. Edwards, P., Landreth, C., Fiume, E., Singh, K.: Jali: an animator-centric viseme model for expressive lip synchronization. ACM Trans. Graph. **35**(4) (2016). https://doi.org/10.1145/2897824.2925984
5. Karras, T., Aila, T., Laine, S., Herva, A., Lehtinen, J.: Audio-driven facial animation by joint end-to-end learning of pose and emotion. ACM Trans. Graph. **36**(4) (2017). https://doi.org/10.1145/3072959.3073658
6. Blair, P.: Advanced Animation: Learn How to Draw Animated Cartoons. Walter T, Foster (1947)
7. Williams, L.: Performance-driven facial animation. In: Proceedings of the 17th Annual Conference on Computer Graphics and Interactive Techniques, SIGGRAPH 1990, pp. 235–242. Association for Computing Machinery, New York (1990). https://doi.org/10.1145/97879.97906

8. Ezzat, T., Poggio, T.: Miketalk: a talking facial display based on morphing visemes. In: Proceedings Computer Animation 1998 (Cat. No.98EX169), pp. 96–102 (1998). https://doi.org/10.1109/CA.1998.681913

9. Parke, F.I.: Computer generated animation of faces. In: Proceedings of the ACM Annual Conference - Volume 1. ACM 1972, pp. 451–457. Association for Computing Machinery, New York (1972). https://doi.org/10.1145/800193.569955

10. Zhou, Y., Xu, Z., Landreth, C., Kalogerakis, E., Maji, S., Singh, K.: Visemenet: audio-driven animator-centric speech animation. ACM Trans. Graph. **37**(4) (2018). https://doi.org/10.1145/3197517.3201292

11. Chen, L., Maddox, R.K., Duan, Z., Xu, C.: Hierarchical cross-modal talking face generation with dynamic pixel-wise loss. In: Proceedings of the IEEE/CVF Conference on Computer Vision and Pattern Recognition, pp. 7832–7841 (2019)

12. Zhou, Y., Han, X., Shechtman, E., Echevarria, J., Kalogerakis, E., Li, D.: Makelttalk: Speaker-aware talking-head animation. ACM Trans. Graph. **39**(6) (2020). https://doi.org/10.1145/3414685.3417774

13. Zhang, C., Zhao, Y., Huang, Y., Zeng, M., Ni, S., Budagavi, M., Guo, X.: Facial: Synthesizing dynamic talking face with implicit attribute learning. In: Proceedings of the IEEE/CVF International Conference on Computer Vision, pp. 3867–3876 (2021)

14. Ji, X., Zhou, H., Wang, K., Wu, W., Loy, C.C., Cao, X., Xu, F.: Audio-driven emotional video portraits. In: Proceedings of the IEEE/CVF Conference on Computer Vision and Pattern Recognition, pp. 14080–14089 (2021)

15. Shibatani, M.: Japanese in Concise Encyclopedia of Languages of the World. Elsevier, Tokyo (2006)

16. Shibatani, M.: English in the Present Day in Encyclopedia of Language & Linguistics, pp. 149–156. Elsevier, Tokyo (2006)

17. Otake, T., Hatano, G., Cutler, A., Mehler, J.: Mora or syllable? speech segmentation in Japanese. J. Mem. Lang. **32**(2), 258–278 (1993)

18. Lewis, J.P., Anjyo, K., Rhee, T., Zhang, M., Pighin, F.H., Deng, Z.: Practice and theory of blendshape facial models. Eurographics (State of the Art Reports) **1**(8), 2 (2014)

19. Apple: ARFaceAnchor.BlendShapeLocation - Apple Developer Documentation. https://developer.apple.com/documentation/arkit/arfaceanchor/blendshapelocation. Accessed 13 Feb 2022

20. Russian3dscanner: Wrapping - R3DS Wrap documentation. https://www.russian3dscanner.com/docs/Wrap3/Nodes/Wrapping/Wrapping.html. Accessed 13 Feb 2022

21. Oculus: Tech Note: Enhancing Oculus Lipsync with Deep Learning. https://developer.oculus.com/blog/tech-note-enhancing-oculus-lipsync-with-deep-learning/. Accessed 13 Feb 2022

22. Bailly, G.: Learning to speak. sensori-motor control of speech movements. Speech Commun. **22**(2), 251–267 (1997). https://doi.org/10.1016/S0167-6393(97)00025-3

23. Visage-Technologies: Mpeg-4 face and body animation (mpeg-4 fba). In: An Overview, pp. 37–40 (2012)

Effect of Attractive Appearance of Intelligent Agents on Acceptance of Uncertain Information

Young ah Seong[1]([✉])[iD] and Takuji Narumi[2][iD]

[1] Hosei University, 2-17-1 Fujimi, Chiyoda-ku, Tokyo, Japan
`youngah.seong.54@hosei.ac.jp`
[2] The University of Tokyo, 7-3-1 Hongo, Bunkyo-ku, Tokyo, Japan
`narumi@cyber.t.u-tokyo.ac.jp`

Abstract. The appearance of an intelligent agent, such as a social robot or avatar, affects the trust, expectations, and satisfaction of human users. Despite the variety of information types conveyed by intelligent agents, such as certain and uncertain information, the effect of an attractive appearance on the acceptance of uncertain information has not been sufficiently investigated. To investigate the effect of an attractive appearance of intelligent agents, as preliminary research, we conducted a user study to compare the perceived trust, attractiveness, intelligence, and usefulness of the participants as measured through a questionnaire and behavior using three smart speakers with different appearances. The results show that people tend to feel more trust and less distrust in agents with an attractive appearance than in those with a less attractive appearance. And the attractiveness of an agent's appearance has little effect on user's behavior based on the uncertain information provided. Our study contributes when agent designers consider the appearance of agents in their particular application.

Keywords: Appearance · Attractiveness · Perception · Agent · Social robot

1 Introduction

When communicating with social robots or avatars in virtual space, people model them based on their appearance and communicate based on that model. That is, the appearance of the agent will strongly affect not only the interaction between users and agents, but also the expectations, satisfaction, and trust of the user in the function itself. Therefore, in human-agent interaction research, what appearance an agent should have in order for humans and agents to interact effectively has been studied intensively.

Intelligent agents convey two types of information: certain information with clear correct and incorrect answers, such as timers and arithmetic operations, and uncertain information, such as future predictions and recommendations,

S. Yamamoto and H. Mori (Eds.): HCII 2022, LNCS 13306, pp. 146–161, 2022.
https://doi.org/10.1007/978-3-031-06509-5_11

which can be perceived differently by different recipients. For information that is certain to be correct or incorrect, users can make general judgments, and there are few individual differences in the degree of trust in performance. However, for uncertain information, where the correct answer is unknown or there is no correct answer fundamentally, the level of trust and acceptance may change depending on the impression of the device that conveys the information. Many studies have shown that intelligence inferred from the appearance of the agents affects the acceptance of certain or uncertain information [1–4]. In particular, the effect of manipulating the degree of anthropomorphism in an appearance to imagine a human-like intelligence has been a central area of investigation [1,3]. However, intelligence is not the only factor that changes the way users accept information from agents.

Cheng et al. [5] examined the effect of an attractive (cute) appearance on interactions with agents. Social psychology studies have revealed that attractiveness/cuteness can trigger care-taking behaviors and promote social engagement [10]. In addition, because many products are designed to attract consumers through their attractive appearance, the effect of providing such an appearance to agents should be examined. In a study by Cheng et al., when the participants interacted with two different types of agents with different degrees of cuteness by changing the apparent age of the anthropomorphic avatar, the effect of such differences on the impression of the user during a malfunction of the agent was investigated. The results showed that avatar cuteness can significantly reduce the user's perceived severity of software errors. In this study, the influence of an attractive appearance on the acceptance of certain information was investigated. However, the effect of an attractive appearance on the acceptance of uncertain information has yet to be sufficiently considered.

In the acceptance of uncertain information, it has been confirmed that the user's perceived trust and behavior based on such information are sometimes inconsistent. For example, several studies have shown that when a trusted agent presents low-certainty information, the user's trust in the agent decreases; however, the user's behavior follows low-certainty information [6–9]. In light of these considerations, the influence of an attractive appearance on the acceptance of uncertain information should be investigated from the combined perspectives of impression and behavior.

Therefore, in this study, we investigated whether the apparent attractiveness of intelligent agents can change the way we perceive uncertain information. As a first step, we conducted a preliminary study using smart speakers with different appearances as the simplest and most familiar intelligent agents. The results of this research can contribute to the field of social robots, smart speakers, and avatars that use intelligent agents by providing meaningful knowledge regarding the design of their attractiveness.

2   Research Framework

This study investigates the effects of an attractive appearance of smart speakers on the acceptance of human users toward uncertain information provided thorough them. We developed two main hypotheses for our preliminary research.

– Explicit acceptance: Participants will give positive evaluations of trust, attractiveness, and usability as measured through a questionnaire to a smart speaker that they perceived as attractive.
– Implicit acceptance: Participants will make decisions according to uncertain information (in this case, fortune-telling) given by a smart speaker that they perceived as attractive.

To clarify these hypotheses, we conducted a between-participants study using three experiment design samples with different appearances of attractiveness. We examined whether the trends in the questionnaire results for each group of participants in each sample were different. To examine the internal effects, we designed a situation in which the participants made a choice after hearing uncertain information and observed how they received the uncertain information using behavioral indicators.

2.1 Attractive Appearance

To determine the experimental samples that differed in their apparent attractiveness, a preliminary impression assessment was conducted using nine plush toys and three popular smart speakers. Several smart speakers have an enhanced their visual attractiveness by using character-based forms[1]. Considering this, we decided to use plush toys to control the appearance of the smart speakers. We assumed that by placing a plush toys of various designs on top of the smart speaker, the participants would have different impressions of it. As candidates, we selected the most popular plush toys without any inherent story or context, those that were sold and looked as ugly as possible, smart speakers based on a plush toy concept, and commercial smart speakers that are widely used.

We conducted an online questionnaire survey and asked 30 people to evaluate their impressions of 12 images (9 plush toys and 3 smart speakers). As dependent variables for the impressions, the questionnaire had two 7-point Likert-scale questions ranging from 1 (totally disagree) to 7 (totally agree), which evaluated the attractiveness and intelligence.

Figure 1 and Table 1 show the results of the impression evaluation. The purpose of this study was to investigate the effect of the attractiveness of an agent's appearance on the acceptance of uncertain information. Because prior research has shown that apparent intelligence influences the acceptance of information [3], it was necessary to select samples with similar intelligence ratings and extremely different levels of appearance attractiveness to independently examine the effects of an attractive appearance. Based on the results of the impression evaluation, we decided to use a plush toy of a rabbit and a plush toy with a lemon head as comparison samples for this study. Furthermore, in this preliminary study, we also examined the acceptance of information when using a typical smart speaker as a baseline condition for comparison with attractive/non-attractive

---

[1] LINE Clova: https://clova.line.me/device/
   Kakao mini: https://kakao.ai/product/kakaomini.

smart speakers. We selected an Amazon Echo Dot (2nd Generation), which is in the middle of the attractiveness scale and has the highest intelligence rating.

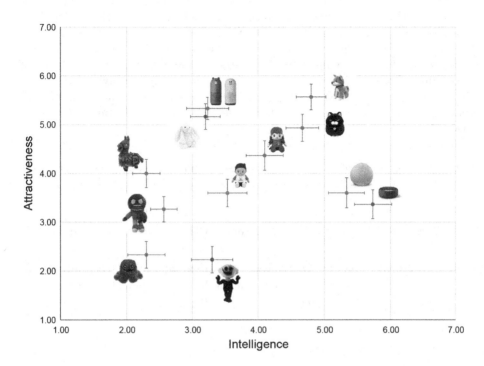

Fig. 1. Results of impression evaluation (red dots indicate the samples selected for this study) (Color figure online)

Table 1. Results of impression evaluation with three samples selected for this study

Name	Sample	Intelligence rate Average (Standard Error)	Attractiveness rate Average (Standard Error)
Rabbit	Attractive	3.20 (0.23)	5.17 (0.26)
Echo Dot	Intelligent	5.73 (028)	3.37 (0.30)
Lemon	Non-attractive	3.30 (0.31)	2.23 (0.27)

2.2 Uncertainty of Information

Three types of information presented by smart speakers to users with different degrees of uncertainty, including certain information, were prepared to investigate how the apparent attractiveness of smart speakers affects the acceptance of information with different degrees of certainty. Among the functions offered by smart speakers, calculations and timers provide certain information that can be easily determined to be accurate. Functions such as weather forecasting and song recommendations are information that is processed based on data and algorithms; therefore, although there is uncertainty regarding the probability of a prediction being correct or the satisfaction of a recommendation, it is not completely unknown information. By contrast, information with unclear evidence, such as fortune-telling, can be regarded as information with the highest uncertainty. Based on these characteristics, in this study, we divided information with uncertainty into three types and designed an experiment to experience timers, song recommendations, and fortune-telling as its representative functions (Table 2).

Table 2. Three types of information provided by functions of smart speakers with uncertainty

Uncertainty level	Functions	Characteristics
No uncertainty	Calculations, timer, clock	Can judge if generally correct or not
Low uncertainty	Weather forecasting, song/item recommendation	Have uncertainty but processed based on data and algorithms
High uncertainty	Fortune telling	Has uncertainty with unclear evidence

3   Methodology

3.1   Participants

To clarify our hypotheses, we conducted a between-participants study using three experiment samples having designs with different levels of attractiveness.

To recruit participants for the experiment, we announced an open call on social media platforms. A total of 29 participants (11 females and 18 males) participated in the experiment, ranging in age from 21 to 46 years (M = 27.69, SD = 6.64). They were randomly assigned to one of the following three experiment conditions with one of three samples selected from the preliminary impression evaluation: rabbit, lemon, or Echo Dot (Fig. 2). The conditions with the rabbit and the lemon had 10 participants and the condition with the Echo Dot had 9 participants (rabbit, 4 females and 6 males; lemon, 3 females and 7 males; and Echo Dot, 4 females and 5 males). We informed the participants that we would pay 2000 Japanese yen (approximately 20 US dollars) and the duration of the experiment would be within 1 h.

3.2   Questionnaire for Impression Assessment

To examine how the explicit acceptance from smart speakers is changed based on its appearance, we developed a questionnaire to examine four categories of

Fig. 2. Experiment environment using three selected samples (left, rabbit; center, Echo Dot; right: lemon)

opinions towards the smart speaker and the information provided by it: trust (Positive), trust (Negative), attractiveness, intelligence, and Usefulness. The questionnaire consisted of questions given on a 7-point Likert-scale questions.

Trust questions ask the user to rate whether the smart speaker is trustworthy. To measure the trust that participants felt toward the smart speakers, we used survey items from a previous study on trust between people and automated systems [12], excluding several items related to perceived risk that were irrelevant to the purpose of this study. These survey items contained both positive items that examined trust and negative items that examined distrust, allowing us to measure trust in an intelligent agent in a stable manner through two sets of questions with different orientations. To assess the perceived attractiveness, intelligence, and usefulness of the smart speakers, the survey items in a previous study that evaluated the likeability of recommendations from robots [11] were used. In addition, three additional questions were asked to confirm their attractiveness and usefulness. The questionnaire used in this experiment is shown in Table 3.

3.3   Procedure

Table 4 presents the entire study procedure. The flow was designed such that the participants experienced three functions with different certainty of information, i.e., timer, recommendation, and fortune-telling.

First, the participants completed a brief demographic questionnaire, followed by an initial impression assessment using the same questions as in the preliminary survey introduced in the previous chapter. This was applied to confirm that there were no differences in the impressions of attractiveness and intelligence given by the appearance of the three smart speakers during the preliminary study, in

Table 3. Questionnaire used for measurements

	Questionnaire
Trust (Positive)	I can trust this smart speaker [12]
	This smart speaker has integrity [12]
	This smart speaker is dependable [12]
Trust (Negative)	This smart speaker is deceptive [12]
	I am suspicious of this smart speakers' intent, action, or outputs [12]
	I am wary of this smart speaker [12]
Attractiveness	This smart speaker is attractive
	This smart speaker is likeable [11]
	This smart speaker is friendly [11]
	This smart speaker is approachable [11]
Intelligence Usefulness	This smart speaker is intelligent [11]
	The information this smart speaker gave is useful
	I would ask this smart speaker for advice [11]
	I want to keep using this smart speaker

Table 4. Study procedure

Action	Tasks with smart speaker	Questionnaire
1		Participant characteristics survey (Age, Gender, Experience with smart speaker, etc.)
2		Impression evaluation (Intelligence, Attractiveness)
3	Set a timer for 5/10/20/30sec (The timer works accurately)	
4		Questionnaire on Table 3 (Evaluation1)
5	Set a timer for 1 h (The timer will go off before 1 h in action 13)	
6	Play the four specified songs (Specified songs will be played)	
7		Questionnaire on Table 3 (Evaluation2)
8	Play the other four specified songs (Recommended song will be played instead)	
9		Questionnaire on Table 3 (Evaluation3)
10	Listen to today's horoscope	
11		Questionnaire on Table 3 (Evaluation4)
12	Select color box	
13	(1 h timer goes off earlier than scheduled)	
14		Questionnaire on Table 3 (Evaluation5)
15		Performance evaluation and User behavior survey
16		Short interview

which the participants were asked to rate their impressions by showing them pictures online, and in the user study, in which they were asked to rate their impressions in person.

Subsequently, they conducted the given tasks by using a smart speaker assigned to the experiment conditions. The first task was to set a short timer and check whether the tasks were completed on time (Task 1). The participants were instructed to set the timers to 5, 10, 20, and 30 s in sequence with oral instructions, and to stop when they sounded. These timers functioned accurately, indicating to the participants that the smart speaker was functioning correctly. After completing this task, the participants evaluated their impressions of the smart speaker by using a questionnaire presented in Table 3 (E1). The second task was to set a timer for 1 h (Task 2). As soon as the timer was set, participants moved on to the next task and did not evaluate their impressions.

The third task was involved playing several specified songs (Task 3). Participants were presented with four song title/singer pairs and were asked to give instructions to the smart speaker to play those songs in order. The participants were instructed that they did not need to listen to the entire song, and that they could stop it if they were satisfied that it was playing correctly. Well-known were selected form Japan's most-watched music program (Red & White Year-end Song Festival, NHK) and world famous songs on YouTube that the local participants were likely to have heard before. In this task, the smart speaker was able to correctly play the indicated song, again giving the participants the impression that it was working correctly. After this task, the participants evaluated their impressions using the same questionnaire (E2).

The fourth task was the same as the third task and involved playing four specified songs (Task 4). However, unlike the third task, however, the smart speaker tells the user that it will play a different recommended song because the specified song does not exist in its library. A different list of songs and singers was used than in Task 3. The songs played as recommendations were those that the experimenter judged to have similar characteristics based on suggestions from YouTube music and Spotify. This task was set up to investigate the impressions of the participants when they were given recommendations as low-uncertainty information. After this task, the participants evaluated their impressions by using the same questionnaire (E3).

The fifth task was to listen to a horoscope (Task 5). The participants were instructed to ask the smart speaker about the horoscope on the day of their zodiac sign. The smart speaker responded with, "Okay, I will tell you today's fortune. Someone is likely to be attracted to the way you enjoy yourself to the fullest. Work is going well! This is when everyone is drawn to your charisma. If you are able to take charge accurately, you will be assured of your position as a leader. Your lucky color today is green, and your lucky item is a handkerchief!" This task was set up to investigate whether the impression of such information given with high uncertainty changes depending on appearance. After this task, the participants evaluated their impressions using the same questionnaire (E4). After Task 5 was completed, the participants were instructed to choose one of the three color boxes (Task 6). Red, green, and blue boxes were placed on a table in the experimental space from the beginning. They were told that the color box contained a reward and that the amount of the reward depended on the box they chose. Once the participants selected one of the boxes, they were instructed to tell the experimenter the color without opening or touching it. In fact, every box contained the same amount of reward. We set up this task to investigate whether the participants consciously or unconsciously accepted the uncertain information conveyed by the smart speaker and changed their behavior by examining whether they behaved in accord with the lucky colors included in the fortune-telling results.

After the participants selected one color box, the experimenter instructed the participant to wait until the experiment ended. At this time, the timer set to 60 min during Task 2 sounded even though only approximately 15 min had elapsed. Up to this point, the participants experienced whether the smart speaker was working properly with respect to the timer, recommendations, and horoscope. However, for the first time, the smart speaker performed an incorrect action. This setting was chosen to investigate the effect of apparent attractiveness on a change of impression, including distrust, in the face of a clearly erroneous behavior. subsequently, the participants were asked to evaluate their impressions using the same questionnaire (E5).

After all tasks were completed, we asked questions to determine whether the experiment designed in this study worked correctly. For example, did the participants think the first alarm was correct, did they think the last alarm was incorrect, did they feel the recommendation function worked well, and so on? Finally, we conducted a brief interview, in which we asked the participants about their reasons for choosing the color boxes and their acceptance of uncertain information.

3.4   System and Experiment Setup

We conducted a Wizard of OZ method in which the participants interacted with a system that they believed was autonomous but was controlled by humans. Because the impression of the smart speaker depends significantly on the success or failure of the task, we did not use an existing speech recognition algorithm to control the same performance in all experiments, and instead used a method in which the experimenter in the same room manually controlled the behavior of the smart speaker.

The system consists of a Mac book pro used to control the speaker's response, an Echo Dot that produces sound as a speaker, a stuffed animal that controls its appearance, and an iPad for entering task descriptions and questionnaires. Figure 3 shows the experiment setup. As shown in Fig. 3(b), the experimenter manually controlled the device a short distance away from the participants.

Fig. 3. Experiment setup

4 Result

4.1 Result of Impression Assessment

Table 5 presents the results of the initial impression assessments of the three samples. The Kruskal-Wallis test revealed significant differences in both attractiveness and intelligence ($p < 0.05$). A post-hoc analysis using the Steel-Dwass test revealed that the attractiveness rating of the rabbit was significantly higher than that of the lemon ($p < 0.05$). The same trend was observed in a preliminary online experiment. This confirms that participants rated the appearance of agent as designed and that this user study can adequately assess the impact of apparent attractiveness on the impression made by agent.

Table 5. Results of impression evaluation with three samples used in the experiment

Name	Sample	Intelligence rate	Attractiveness rate
		Average (standard error)	Average (standard error)
Rabbit	Attractive	2.80 (0.87)	5.00 (1.41)
Echo dot	Intelligent	4.22 (1.31)	3.78 (1.62)
Lemon	Unattractive	2.80 (1.25)	3.20 (1.40)

4.2 Results of Impression Questionnaire

The average ratings for each impression item at the end of each task are shown in Fig. 4. The post-experiment question revealed that three participants did not

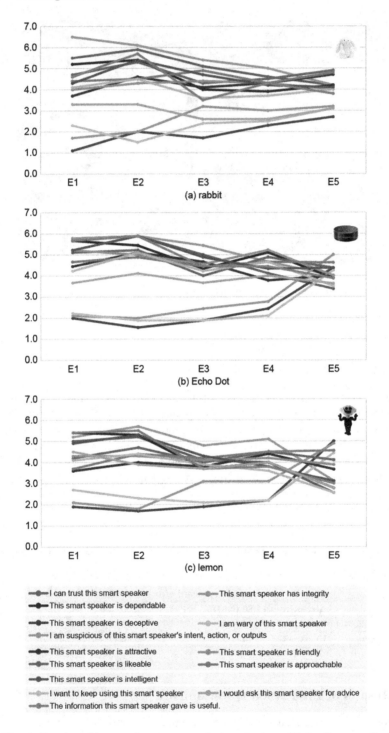

Fig. 4. Results of impression assessment at each stage (Color figure online)

recognize that the 60-min timer had rung at the wrong time. The data of the participants were excluded from the analysis of E5. Therefore, for E5, one person per condition was excluded from the data, and the analysis was conducted with data on the rabbit from 9 participants, Echo Dot from 8 participants, and lemon from 9 participants. Other evaluations were analyzed with data on the rabbit from 10 participants, Echo Dot from 9 participants, and lemon from 10 participants.

We used non-parametric procedures and the Kruskal-Wallis test to analyze whether there were any differences among the three conditions. Table 6 shows the results for any differences among the three conditions. The Kruskal-Wallis tests only showed the marginal trends in integrity for E1, trust for E5, and deception for E5. Therefore, the post-hoc test cannot be used to clearly show the differences between conditions. By interpreting the trend from the averages, the following could be said;

- A smart speaker with a more attractive appearance is more likely to be trusted than speakers with other type of appearance, even when they succeed or fail in a clear task with certain information.
- A smart speaker with a more attractive appearance is less likely to be suspected of deception than speakers with other type of appearance, even when it fails in a clear task with certain information.

Table 6. Results of Kruskal-Wallis tests on impression assessment among three conditions with

Stage	Question	Condition	Mean	SD	p
E1: After the short timer worked well	This smart speaker has integrity (Trust: positive)	rabbit	6.50	0.81	$p < 0.10$
		Echo Dot	5.78	1.13	
		lemon	5.20	1.40	
E5: After the long timer worked incorrectly	I can trust the agent (Trust: positive)	rabbit	3.89	1.45	$p < 0.10$
		Echo Dot	3.38	0.86	
		lemon	2.56	1.17	
E5: After the long timer worked wrong	The agent is deceptive (Trust: negative)	rabbit	2.89	1.79	$p < 0.10$
		Echo Dot	4.38	1.73	
		lemon	5.00	1.76	

4.3   Results of Behavior Analysis

In the task of selecting a colored box, we observed how participants made decisions after hearing their lucky color in the fortune-telling of the smart speaker. In the case of rabbits, 6 out of 10 of the participants selected the green box. In the case of lemons, 4 out of 10 of the participants selected the green box. In the case of Echo Dot, 8 out of 9 of the participants selected the green box. A χ^2 test was used to analyze whether the number of participants who selected the green box differed among the three conditions. The test revealed a significant effect on the participants' behavior based on the appearance of the smart speaker ($\chi^2 =$ 4.84; p <0.05). The results of the analyzed data show that in the case of Echo Dot, the participants are more likely to choose the green box, as mentioned by the fortune-telling.

5   Discussion

The implications obtained from the experiment results for the two hypotheses in this study can be summarized as follows:

- Explicit acceptance: People tend to feel more trust in agents with an attractive appearance than in those with a less attractive appearance. In addition, when an agent behaves erroneously, an agent with an attractive appearance tends to be less distrusted by the user than an agent with an unattractive appearance.
- Implicit acceptance: The attractiveness of an agent's appearance has little effect on the user's behavior based on the uncertain information it provides.

In terms of explicit acceptance, the impression assessment results tended to support these hypotheses. In other words, an attractive appearance tended to have a positive effect on perceived trust. Specifically, the integrity rating under the rabbit condition, with an attractive appearance for E1, was the highest. Although these differences were significant in the early stages of the interaction (E1), they became less pronounced as the interaction progressed (E2 – E4). However, the effect of an attractive appearance seems to be stronger when the agent behaves erroneously, and the results of the ratings on trust and distrust for E5 partially support this. This implication is in line with the findings in the research conducted done by Cheng et al. [5].

However, in terms of explicit acceptance, the attractiveness of an agent's appearance has little effect on the users' behavior in the box selection task (Task 6). Specifically, the results of the box selection task showed that the proportion of participants who chose green, which was presented as a lucky color in the fortune-telling task, did not change under either the rabbit or lemon condition. By contrast, under the Echo Dot condition, almost all participants chose green. This discrepancy between implicit and explicit acceptance does not seem to be explained by apparent attractiveness alone. Past research has shown that trust in agents formed through an interaction has little effect on decisions based on uncertain information that is suddenly presented, and even has a negative effect, such that the more one trusts, the longer it takes to make a decision. In light of this, it can be inferred that the acceptance of uncertain information is not determined by trust, but by other factors. One possible explanation for this difference is that perceived intelligence, and not trust, influences user behaviors based on uncertain information. The participants evaluated Echo Dot as more intelligent than the other samples, and their ratings on the lemon and rabbit were almost the same. It can be inferred from this that the behavior associated with uncertain information may be influenced by the appearance of intelligence.

The implications of this study can contribute to the design of social robots and agents. For example, in the case of a robot that conveys only certain information, a robot with high attractiveness is expected to be more effective in providing users with an impression of trustworthiness. However, if we want to encourage users to take action, an agent that gives an impression of intelligence is more likely to be effective in changing behavior.

In terms of an impression assessment, the lemon was not as non-attractive as in the preliminary online questionnaire. Because there was a sufficient difference in attractiveness between lemon and rabbit, the results of this study may not have been influenced by this difference. However, in controlling and evaluating impressions in the future, the control of such impressions requires more further consideration.

In the post-evaluation interviews, many of the participants said that the rabbit was indeed a lovable figure, but the speech of the speaker was mechanical; therefore, they felt a gap between appearance and speech style. Others expected robot-like movement interactions when a stuffed animal was present. Considering these opinions, it seems that factors such as voice characteristics and expectations of movement may also influence the appearance when interacting realistically over time. Indeed, a previous study suggested that people preferred robots for jobs when the robot's appearance matched the sociability required in those jobs and complied more with a robot whose demeanor matched the seriousness of the task [2]. Appearances not only function on their own, they can also interact with a variety of social cues involved in an interaction, such as speech and gestures. Future research should consider matching apparent attractiveness with other social cues.

One limitation of this study is that the number of participants was considered insufficient for a data analysis. The face-to-face experiment was also limited in the context of the COVID 19; although the statistical analysis seemed to reveal a trend, additional experiments with a larger number of people are needed to find more reliable results/obvious characteristics and to reconfirm the results.

6   Conclusion

To understand the effect of the acceptance of intelligent agents, we investigated whether an attractive and intelligent appearance can change the way we perceive uncertain information. As a preliminary study, we conducted a user study to compare trust, attractiveness, intelligence, and usefulness measured by questionnaires and behavior using three smart speakers with different appearances. The implications can be summarized as follows:

- Explicit acceptance: People tend to feel more trust in agents with an attractive appearance than in those with a less attractive appearance. In addition, when an agent behaves erroneously, an agent with an attractive appearance tends to be less distrusted by the user than an agent with an unattractive appearance.

– Implicit acceptance: The attractiveness of an agent's appearance has little effect on the user's behavior based on the uncertain information it provides.

Thus, our study could provide insight to agent designers indicating that it is important to consider attractive appearances when the agent is expected to provide users with trustworthy information. However, further research is strongly required to clarify the results with significant differences among the various situations.

Acknowledgements. This work was supported by JSPS KAKENHI (Grant Numbers JP20K19904) and JST Moonshot R&D Program Project "Cybernetic being" (Grant number JPMJMS2013). The authors thank Chi-lan Yang for the meaningful advice on the experimental design and measurements.

References

1. Kiesler, S., Sproull, L., Waters, K.: A prisoner's dilemma experiment on cooperation with people and human-like computers. J. Pers. Soc. Psychol. **70**(1), 47 (1996)
2. Goetz, J., Kiesler, S., Powers, A.: Matching robot appearance and behavior to tasks to improve human-robot cooperation. In: The 12th IEEE International Workshop on Robot and Human Interactive Communication, 2003, Proceedings of IEEE ROMAN 2003, pp. 55–60 (2003)
3. de Visser, E., Monfort, S., Mckendrick, R., Smith, M., Mcknight, P., Krueger, F., Parasuraman, R.: Almost human: anthropomorphism increases trust resilience in cognitive agents. J. Exp. Psychol. Appl. **22**(3), 331 (2016). https://doi.org/10.1037/xap0000092
4. T. W. Liew, S. Tan, S. Exploring the effects of specialist versus generalist embodied virtual agents in a multi-product category online store. Telematics Inform. **35**(1), 122–135 (2018)
5. Cheng, Y., Qiu, L., Pang, J.: Effects of avatar cuteness on users' perceptions of system errors in anthropomorphic interfaces. In: Nah, F.F.-H., Siau, K. (eds.) HCII 2020. LNCS, vol. 12204, pp. 322–330. Springer, Cham (2020). https://doi.org/10.1007/978-3-030-50341-3_25
6. Bainbridge, W.A., Hart, J.W., Kim, E.S., Scassellati, B.: The benefits of interactions with physically present robots over video-displayed agents. Int. J. Soc. Robot. **3**(1), 41–52 (2011)
7. Robinette, P., Li, W., Allen, R., Howard, A.M., Wagner, A.R.: Overtrust of robots in emergency evacuation scenarios. In: Proceedings of the Eleventh Annual ACM/IEEE International Conference on Human-Robot Interaction, vol. 2016-April, pp. 101–108 (2016)
8. Salem, M., Lakatos, G., Amirabdollahian, F., Dautenhahn, K.: Would you trust a (faulty) robot?: effects of error, task type and personality on human-robot cooperation and trust. In: Proceedings of the Tenth Annual ACM/IEEE International Conference on Human-Robot Interaction, pp. 141–148 (2015)
9. Tokushige, H., Narumi, T., Ono, S., Fuwamoto, Y., Tanikawa, T., Hirose, M.: Trust lengthens decision time on unexpected recommendations in human-agent interaction. In: Proceedings of the 5th International Conference on Human Agent Interaction 2017, pp. 245–252. Association for Computing Machinery, New York (2017). https://doi.org/10.1145/3125739.3125751

10. Sherman, G.D., Haidt, J.: Cuteness and disgust: the humanizing and dehumanizing effects of emotion. Emot. Rev. **3**(3), 245–251 (2011)
11. Rau, P.L., Li, Y., Li, D.: Effects of communication style and culture on ability to accept recommendations from robots. Comput. Hum. Behav. **25**(5), 587–595 (2009)
12. Jian, J.Y., Bisantz. A.M., Drury, C.G.: Foundations for an empirically determined scale of trust in automated systems. Int. J. Cogn. Ergon. **4**(1), 53–71 (2000)

Effects of Virtual Character's Eye Movements in Reach Motion on Target Prediction

Liheng Yang[1], Yoshihiro Sejima[2(✉)], and Tomio Watanabe[3]

[1] Graduate School of Informatics, Kansai University, 2-1-1 Ryozenji-cho, Takatsuki-shi, Osaka 569-1095, Japan

[2] Faculty of Informatics, Kansai University, 12-1-1 Ryozenji-cho, Takatsuki-shi, Osaka 569-1095, Japan
sejima@kansai-u.ac.jp

[3] Faculty of Computer Science and Systems Engineering, Okayama Prefectural University, 111 Kuboki, Soja-shi, Okayama, Japan

Abstract. In human communication, nonverbal behaviors play an important role in realizing smooth communication. However, it is not clear that the effects of reliability for the information transmission of the motion in each body part such as eye movements and body movements. In this study, we designed and developed a virtual character with movable right arm, head, and eyes to investigate the effects of reliable motion. The virtual character acted simply as reaching a cup on the table, while participants were asked to predict which cup the character would grab. Participants' predictions were highly consistent with where the character gazed, especially when the eye movements were oriented differently from the face. The results suggest that eye movements affect target prediction.

Keywords: Non-verbal communication · Virtual character · Eye movement · Target prediction

1 Introduction

With the development of information technology, the communication media such as robots and agents have rich social features in human daily life. For instance, virtual pets that provide companionship for owners were reported (Chesney and Lawson, 2007), as well as Zhu (2021) suggested that the interaction with virtual agents helps humans escape from the loneliness. It is conceived that with the rapid increment of such communication media, the communication design with reliable relationship between humans and communication media are in expectation. Thus, in order to build a reliable relationship and realize a smooth communication with humans, it is important to investigate how the behaviors by the communication media such as robots and agents affect the reliable relationship with humans.

In human communication, not only verbal messages but also nonverbal behaviors such as facial expressions, eye movements, body movements and paralanguage play an important role in realizing smooth communication (Ruesch and Kees, 1974; Argyle,

S. Yamamoto and H. Mori (Eds.): HCII 2022, LNCS 13306, pp. 162–171, 2022.
https://doi.org/10.1007/978-3-031-06509-5_12

1972). In addition, it is well known that humans use nonverbal behaviors as clues to build relationships of trust with others (Thioux, Gazzola and Keysers, 2008). In the previous study, Mehrabian (1971) reported that visual information is a reliable clue among nonverbal behaviors when the information transmission is non-correspondence in each channel. However, it is not clear that the effects of reliability for the motion of visual information in each body part such as facial directions, eye movements and body movements. Therefore, it is expected that a highly reliable motion for the communication media such as robots and agents can be designed by analyzing the reliability of motion in information transmission as important clues.

In this study, we designed and developed a virtual character to investigate the effects of reliable motion in each body part. The virtual character acted simply as reaching a cup on the table while participants were asked to predict which cup the character would grab. Generally, it is reported that humans move with all parts of body in coordination (Gahéry and Massion, 1981). Especially, when humans reach to something, the human eyes move in cooperation with own hand/arm (Johansson, Westling, Bäckström and Flanagan, 2001; Neggers and Bekkering, 2000). Therefore, the virtual character was of movable right arm, head, and eyes. Participants' predictions were highly consistent with where the character gazed, especially when the eye movements were oriented differently from the face. The results suggest that eye movements affect on target prediction.

2 Motion Design of Virtual Character

2.1 Virtual Character

The virtual character was designed in a 3D model by modeling software called Metasequoia. The designed virtual character, as a lovely bear showed in Fig. 1, seems to look friendly and familiar. The virtual space was generated by Microsoft DirectX 9.0 SDK and a laptop PC (CPU: Core i-7 1.80 GHz, Memory: 8 GB). The development environment was programmed with C++ in Visual Studio 2019.

The virtual character's head, eyes, and right arm are independent for more natural movement. The right arm can rotate around and translate along with x, y, and z axes, while the head and the eyes can rotate around x and y axes.

Fig. 1. The designed virtual character and virtual space.

2.2 Motion Design

In front of the virtual character, there was a table with two cups on it. The yellow cup was on the virtual character's right side while the blue one was on the left. The cups were placed equidistant to the virtual character.

The virtual character would take the one of the cups on the table. The virtual character's right arm, head, and eyes were designed to be controlled independently. When the virtual character started moving, it would take the arm of the virtual character 3 s to reach the cup. For instance, as showed in Fig. 2(a), the virtual character was reaching to the yellow cup while the arm, face, and eyes were all directing to the yellow cup. As showed in Fig. 2(b), the virtual character faced to the yellow cup but looked at the blue cup while reaching to the yellow cup. As showed in Fig. 2(c), at the phase 2, the virtual character's arm shifted direction from the yellow cup to the blue cup, while the direction of face and eyes would not change.

Therefore, the arm's motion was divided into phase 1 and phase 2. Table1 indicated the 16 conditions of the action of the virtual character that combine two matched conditions (No.1 and No.16 condition in Table1 that arm-face-eyes always direct to the same cup) with 14 mismatched conditions (from No.2 to No. 15 conditions in Table1). The color in Table 1 refers to the cup.

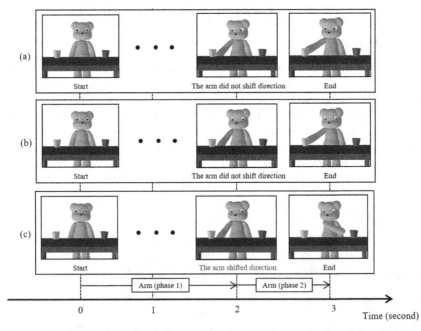

Fig. 2. The conditions of the virtual character's action. (a) The matched condition. (b) The mismatched condition without the arm shifted. (c) The mismatched condition with the arm shifted at the phase 2. (Color figure online)

Table 1. The 16 conditions of the virtual character's action.

Number of condition	Arm (phase 1)	Arm (phase 2)	Face	Eye movement
1	Yellow	Yellow	Yellow	Yellow
2	Yellow	Yellow	Yellow	Blue
3	Yellow	Yellow	Blue	Yellow
4	Yellow	Yellow	Blue	Blue
5	Yellow	Blue	Yellow	Yellow
6	Yellow	Blue	Yellow	Blue
7	Yellow	Blue	Blue	Yellow
8	Yellow	Blue	Blue	Blue
9	Blue	Yellow	Yellow	Yellow
10	Blue	Yellow	Yellow	Blue
11	Blue	Yellow	Blue	Yellow
12	Blue	Yellow	Blue	Blue
13	Blue	Blue	Yellow	Yellow
14	Blue	Blue	Yellow	Blue
15	Blue	Blue	Blue	Yellow
16	Blue	Blue	Blue	Blue

3 Experiment

3.1 Experiment Procedures

The participants were asked to sit on a chair in front of a table with a 23.8-in monitor and a keyboard on it. The distance between the participants and the monitor was about 70 cm while they were not moved in the experiment. The resolution of the monitor was 1920× 1080 pixels. The participants were 16 students (8 females and 8 males).

In the experiment, the participants were asked to make predictions during watching the virtual character acting. They were required to press the correspondent key on the keyboard as soon as they predict which cup the virtual character would take. They watched each condition one time, while the order of the 16 action conditions was random. Before the experiment started, the participants were told a brief introduction as below.

The bear will take one of the cups on the table. Please predict which cup the bear is going to take. If you guess it will be the left cup, press the left key of the keyboard. If you guess it will be the right one, press the right key of the keyboard. Please press the key once you figure it out. The bear will take the cup at 16 times.

After completing all conditions, the participants were asked to answer a questionnaire about the impression of the designed character and its behavior. Specifically, they were asked the questions about whether they were playing the competitive games, and the difficulty of the experiment as well as the preference to the virtual character (both in

5-point Likert scale). They had also required to write down the clues they used to make the predictions.

3.2 Results

In the experiment, due to one participant failed to understand the main idea of this experiment, 15 available experimental data had been collected.

By comparing the recorded key that participants pressed in each condition with the virtual character's actions, the proportions that the participants' prediction consistent with the virtual character's eyes, arm, and face were obtained. Additionally, the response time from the virtual character started moving until the participant pressed the key had been recorded.

Figure 3 shows the result of the ratio in the correct predictions and the average response time regarding to 15 participants. The correct predictions refer to the match that the participants predicted the second phase of the arm which was the true target of the virtual character. Only four participants had correct rates above 80%, with all having a response time longer than 2.3 s. The remaining 11 participants had correct rates above 35% but less than 60%, with response times from 1 s to 2.5 s. Only one participant had a response time of less than 1.5 s.

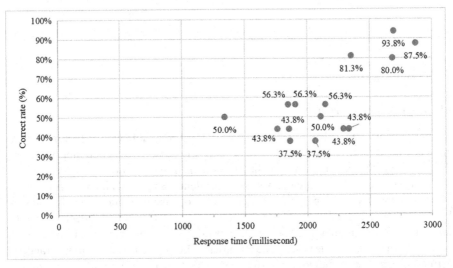

Fig. 3. The correct rate and the average response time regarding to 15 participants.

Figure 4 shows the consistent ratios with the virtual character's face, eyes, and arm (the second phase) regarding to each participant. The consistent ratio is the proportion of participants' predictions for each body part of the virtual character. Ten of fifteen participants had the highest consistent ratio with the virtual character's eyes among the arm, face, and eyes. Five participants had over 80% consistent ratio with the virtual character's eyes, and four participants had over 80% consistent ratio with the virtual character's arm. Meanwhile, there was no participant who had consistent ratio with the face above 80%, and the highest consistent ratio with the face was 56%.

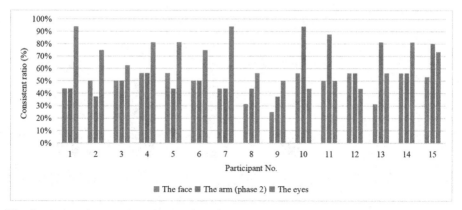

Fig. 4. The consistent ratios with the virtual character's face, eyes, and arm (the second phase) regarding to each participant.

Figure 5 shows the result of the difficulty that the participants felt towards the target prediction. There were only one participant chose *easy* and three chose *fairly easy*, while 8 participants chose *fairly difficult* and two chose *difficult*. Only one participant chose *neither difficult nor easy*.

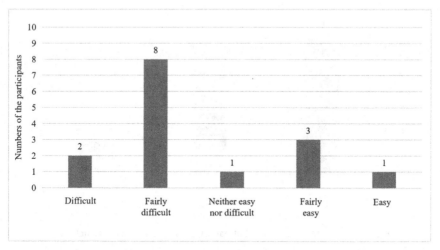

Fig. 5. The result of the difficulty towards the experiments.

Figure 6 shows the result of the participants' preference towards the virtual character. Five participants chose *favorable* and five chose *fairly favorable* while four chose *Neither favorable nor unfavorable*. There was only one participant chose *fairly unfavorable* and none chose *unfavorable*.

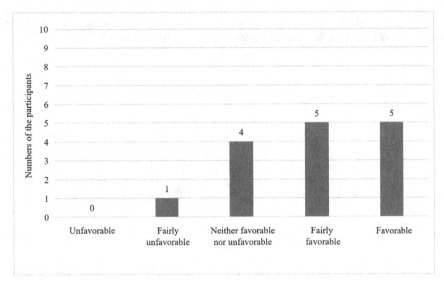

Fig. 6. The result of the participants' preference towards the virtual reality.

As for the cues that participants used in target prediction showed in Fig. 7, 13 participants mentioned eyes movement, while 12 participants mentioned arm and three mentioned body (face).

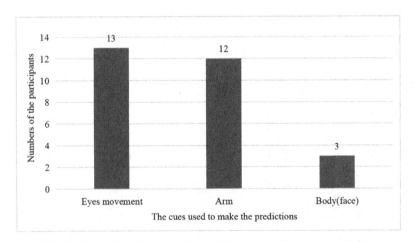

Fig. 7. The result of the cues that participants used in target prediction.

4   Discussion

As suggested in Fig. 4 that 11 participants' predictions are mostly consistent with the eyes as well as 13 participants mentioned using eyes movement as the cue, there is a possibility that the eye movements have stronger effects than arm and face on target prediction. Noticed that, although the character's actions were disordered to participants, for playing 16 times, participants should notice at any time that the virtual character's arm could shift direction midway and the character's eye movements and face had no connection with the actual target. Therefore, the participants should have waited until confirming the action of the arm (check whether the arm shifts direction) and hence should have performed a higher correct rate as well as a higher response time over two seconds. However, only four participants' correct rates were over 80%. It suggests that even human understand eye movements were irrelevant to the true target, the eye movements were still used as a cue and influenced the judgement on prediction.

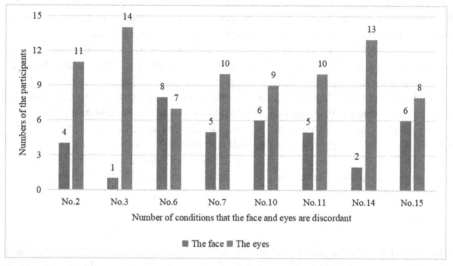

Fig. 8. The consistent ration regarding the eight conditions in which the face and eyes are discordant.

Regarding the effects of the face, it is suggested that the face may make less efforts in target prediction. As can be seen from Fig. 4, the consistent ratio with the face remained low, peaking at less than 60%, which is the lowest consistent ratio among the face, arm, and eyes. Figure 8 shows the ratio that the participants' predictions consistent with the eye movements as well as face, regarding to the eight conditions in which the face and eye movements are discordant. The consistent ratio of the eyes was higher than the face in seven of the eight conditions. It suggests that, when face and eye movements are discordant, human would be likely to use eye movements instead of the face as the clue in target prediction.

Regarding the difficulty perceived by the participants, as showed in Fig. 5, 9 of 15 participants chose *difficult* or *fairly difficult*. This suggests that the discordance of the face, arm, and eyes made it difficult to predict the true target of the virtual character. As for the correlation with the average response time and the correct rates, there is no notable correlation between the difficulty and the response time ($r = 0.2395, p < 0.01$) as well as the correct rates ($r = 0.3258$, $p < 0.01$). This suggests that the participants' self-evaluation of experiment has no notable association with their objective performance in the experiment.

As to the participants' preference towards the virtual character showed in Fig. 6, 10 of 15 participants chose *favorable* or *fairly favorable* while none chose *unfavorable*. This result was not unexpected as the virtual character was designed as a lovely bear. However, it is worth noting that, although the participants tend to feel difficult of the target prediction, which discussed above, the most participants still have positive attitudes towards the virtual character. It suggests that, although the discordance of the face, arm, and eyes made the prediction difficult, such a small unpleasant behavior did not lead to the unfavorable towards the virtual character.

There are several limitations of this study. Firstly, the sample size was small and therefore the statistical result may not be generalized to a large population. Secondly, the effect of participants' personality was not taken into account. Ponari et al. (2013) reported that the differences in personality can affect processing of social signals such as eye gaze. There might be the possibility that the eyes movement of the virtual character influenced introverted personalities and extroverted personalities differently, and this assumption might be addressed in future studies. Another limitation in this study is, although the participants stated that they had used the eye movement as a clue as well as suggested by the consistent ratio, no direct evidence can demonstrate the eyes were actually used as the clue. Future studies will be conducted in using eye-tracking devices that recording the visual information of participants to demonstrate whether participants spend more time looking at the virtual character's eyes instead of the arms or face.

5   Conclusion

This study investigated the effects of the virtual character's eye movements in reach motion on target prediction. The designed virtual character was of the movable arm, head, and eyes. The participants were asked to observe the virtual character's motion in 16 conditions and predict which cup the virtual character would take in each condition. Eleven of fifteen participants had a correct ratio under 60% with response time around two seconds. Ten participants had predictions that were consistent with the eye movements mostly among the arm, head, and eyes. Additionally, the consistent ratio with the face remained low and when face and eye movements are discordant, human are more likely to use eye movements instead of the face as the cue to target prediction. According to the results, eye movements in reach motion may play a significant role in target prediction.

Future work will be conducted in a larger sample size by using eye-tracking devices, and the potential effects of participants' personalities will be considered more carefully.

Acknowledgments. This work was supported by JSPS KAKENHI Grant Numbers 19K12890 and Organization for Research and Development of Innovative Science and Technology of Kansai University.

References

Chesney, T., Lawson, S.: The illusion of love: does a virtual pet provide the same companionship as a real one? Interact. Stud. **8**(2), 337–342 (2007)

Zhu, L.: The psychology behind video games during COVID-19 pandemic: a case study of animal crossing: new horizons. Hum. Behav. Emerg. Technol. **3**(1), 157–159 (2021)

Ruesch, J., Kees, W.: Nonverbal Communication. University of California Press (1974)

Argyle, M.: Non-verbal communication in human social interaction. In: Hinde, R.A. (ed.) Non-Verbal Communication. Cambridge University Press (1972)

Mehrabian, A.: Silent Messages, vol. 8, No. 152, pp. 30. Wadsworth, Belmont, CA (1971)

Thioux, M., Gazzola, V., Keysers, C.: Action understanding: how, what and why. Curr. Biol. **18**(10), R431–R434 (2008)

Gahéry, Y., Massion, J.: Co-ordination between posture and movement. Trends Neurosci. **4**, 199–202 (1981)

Johansson, R.S., Westling, G., Bäckström, A., Flanagan, J.R.: Eye–hand coordination in object manipulation. J. Neurosci. **21**(17), 6917–6932 (2001)

Neggers, S.F., Bekkering, H.: Ocular gaze is anchored to the target of an ongoing pointing movement. J. Neurophysiol. **83**(2), 639–651 (2000)

Ponari, M., Trojano, L., Grossi, D., Conson, M.: "Avoiding or approaching eyes"? Introversion/extraversion affects the gaze-cueing effect. Cogn. Process. **14**(3), 293–299 (2013)

Increasing Motivation of Walking Exercise Using 3D Personalized Avatar in Augmented Reality

Sungjae Yoo(ID) and Jiro Tanaka(✉)(ID)

Waseda University, Kitakyushu, Japan
yoo.sungjae@fuji.wasdeda.jp, jiro@aoni.waseda.jp

Abstract. Walking is an easily accessible and effective exercise, hence it can be easily participated as a part of a person's everyday. However, due to changes in our social environment such as the increase in single-person households, hectic lifestyles and an unprecedented pandemic, the number of people who walk alone is increasing. We found that people lack motivation when they walk alone; to address this, we designed an interactive full-body 3D personalized avatar in augmented reality (AR) as a virtual walking partner. Our research goal is to increase the motivation of walking exercise using an AR 3D avatar. This approach focuses on the social aspects of physical exercise, that is, cooperation and competition with a partner. The proposed system has two types of use cases: (1) walking with an avatar, and (2) walking with a remote user using an avatar. We investigated the effect of designed interactions with a virtual walking partner for both cases. In addition, we designed a method of movement synchronization between a user and an avatar using only a head-mounted display (HMD) without separate sensors. The preliminary evaluation of the system indicated positive response from participants. We believe that our findings support the idea that designed interactions with a virtual walking partner can increase a person's motivation of walking exercise.

Keywords: Augmented reality · 3D personalized avatar · Motivation for walking exercise

1 Introduction

We explore a future in which people spend more time using augmented reality (AR) technology, even during activities of everyday life. We are interested in how AR technology can improve the human experience [1,2] regarding physical activity. Walking is an easily accessible and effective exercise, so it can be easily participated in person's everyday. However, due to the change of social structure and environment, for example, the increasing numbers of single-person households, hectic lifestyles and an unprecedented pandemic, the number of people who are walking exercise alone is increasing [3]. Additionally, we have identified a problem in that people often have lower levels of motivation for walking

S. Yamamoto and H. Mori (Eds.): HCII 2022, LNCS 13306, pp. 172–191, 2022.
https://doi.org/10.1007/978-3-031-06509-5_13

exercise when doing it alone. Therefore, in this paper we propose an AR system to address the lack of the motivation issue in walking exercise. We believe that existing methods, such as devices and applications for walking, have limitations. According to the related studies in physical exercise [3,4], motivation is usually generated when exercising with a partner or group. Thus, in this study, we focus on the social aspect of exercise to increase a person's motivation in terms of walking exercise [5] (i.e., cooperation or competition with a partner). In short, we aim to provide the sense of walking together experience with a virtual walking partner to overcome the limitations of time and place. In our research, AR technology was applied for the realistic interaction with a virtual walking partner.

2   Related Work

Since there have been few related works that have studied the use of an AR 3D avatar as a virtual walking partner, we investigated and analyzed related studies that featured relevant topics and keywords in the following categories: social aspects of physical exercise, AR and mixed reality (MR) for motivation, interactive virtual full-body 3D avatar and walking support in AR.

2.1   Leverage of Social Aspects in Physical Exercise

Previous research has also investigated the social aspect of physical exercise. We designed interactions that the user can walk while cooperating and competing with a virtual walking partner. Hanson and Jones [6] studied the motivation generated by being part of a group, which encouraged healthy behavior in participants and inspired positive physical activity. It has been proven that regular walking exercise can contribute to people's well-being life [7]. Other studies have confirmed results the positive effect of cooperation with walking partners or groups [8]. For example, Futami et al. [9] presented a competition system using the number of steps of a participant and confirmed a positive effect of competition factors on walking motivation. Based on these social effects related to physical exercise, in this study, we attempt to increase walking exercise motivation through interactions with a 3D avatar as a virtual walking partner.

Additionally, in our system, an individual who has access to walk in a long-distance remote location can experience the sense of walking together with a partner in separate location using the avatar. To share the walking experience with remote user and make it more realistic, various methods for recognizing a user's gait have been studied [10,11]. For example, Baldi et al. [3] presented a method of using a wearable device to share a walking experience with a person located in a remote place. The user could experience the walking of the remote user through the vibrations of the wearable device. However, unlike these studies, our study provides visual feedback through an AR 3D avatar which can provide a more intuitive walking exercise experience. Since the positive effects of being with a group or partner during physical activity have been confirmed in previous studies, we utilized the two factors of cooperation and competition using the realistic sense of presence in the avatar.

2.2 Effectiveness of Walking Partner

We designed a virtual walking partner using a 3D avatar. The proposed 3D avatar was implemented in the form of a full-body human shape. Previous studies on the implementation and effect of walking partners can largely be divided into two categories: with physical partner and virtual partner. Karunarathne et al. [5] presented a humanoid robot as a walking partner and conducted a study on the effect. The results suggested that participants rated walking with robot partner higher than walking alone, and the robot as a walking partner was found to alleviate the loneliness of users walking alone or to increase the effectiveness of exercise, and even medical effect [12,13]. These studies confirm the positive feedback on the effects of walking partners.

Virtual reality (VR) and AR technology is the most common method used to realize a virtual partner. In this study, we realized a virtual walking partner using AR technology. Norouzi et al. [14] presented walking with a virtual AR dog as a partner and investigated participants perception and behavior. The findings showed that the experience with the AR dog as a companion changed participants' behavior and social interactions with other people who could not see the dog. We believe this is also confirms the effectiveness of virtual objects as partners. Above all, the research outlined in these sections supports the fact that interactions with virtual objects can affect a user's emotionality. However, we believe that the effectiveness of a virtual partner depends on how realistic it is; this requires not only visual information, but also the sense of being together. Nevertheless, there are still many awkward interactions with the real space that go beyond physical common sense of the human's perception. To overcome these limitations, Kim et al. [15] investigated and designed an effective method for the implementation of visual effects that decreased collisions between AR virtual humans and real objects. Additional studies have also attempted this, with approaches such as applying visual effects and psychological improvement methods to improve a user's AR recognition effect [16,17]. The system proposed in this paper is designed so that the user can interact with the avatar through an intuitive interface, assuming various situations that may occur while walking exercise.

2.3 Interactive Full-body 3D Avatar in Augmented Reality

To create a realistic sense of presence of partner, we designed a full-body for the 3D virtual walking partner, with realistic appearance and physical conditions. Related studies, which use avatars mainly for the purpose of remote collaboration, found that virtual avatars had a positive effect on cooperative work. To create an avatar with an appropriate shape, we considered previous research into the optimal shape of an avatar. The effectiveness of using 3D model in AR has been studied in the domain of education and it applied to physical education and sports. For example, Chang et al. [18] presented the effectiveness of a 3D model in physical education. Unlike the video-assisted instruction method, their system provided interactive feedback to learners using an 3D AR model. Koulouris et al. [19] investigated the effectiveness of three types of avatars in VR exergame system: generic, realistic, and idealized avatar. Praetorius et al. [20] presented the effect of the shape of an avatar according to context. The above studies confirm that an avatar that is of a human shape is preferable in the context of an interpersonal relationship. Thus, we believe the shape of an user-friendly avatar as a walking partner is a significant factor in increasing the effectiveness and motivation of walking exercise.

3   Research Goal and Approach

The goal of this research is to increase an individual's motivation of walking exercise using a 3D avatar. To achieve this, we designed an interactive full-body 3D personalized avatar in AR as a virtual walking partner. We designed the avatar to behave like a real human. In addition, to provide a simultaneous walking experience between two remote users, we designed a method to visually present the movement of a remote user using an avatar. Furthermore, we designed interactions by predicting events that may occur while walking exercising with a physical partner. Therefore, we aim to increase the user's motivation for walking exercise through the designed interactions.

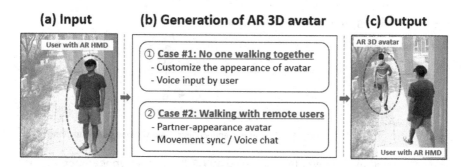

Fig. 1. Approach overview. (a) The input is a real scene, viewed through the AR HMD. (b) The generation of a 3D avatar depending on the case. Each case generates a different avatar appearance and action. (c) The output of the approach is the generated 3D AR avatar.

Figure 1 shows the overview of the approach, which has three parts: (a) Input, (b) Generation of an AR 3D avatar, and (c) Output. Figure 1(a) outlines the input of the model. This is a real scene, seen through the AR HMD. Next, as in Fig. 1(b), an AR 3D avatar is generated. The avatar's appearance and action depends on whether the user is walking alone or with a remotes user. Finally, the user can walk with a full-body 3D avatar as a virtual partner, shown in Fig. 1(c). AR technology is applied to ensure realistic interactions with the virtual avatar. The AR can expand a user's perception not only by simply showing additional digital information but also by engaging their capabilities and emotions. Since an avatar's action can be changed by the user's voice input or by interaction with a physical object, we believe that the designed virtual walking partner can provide the realistic sense of presence as if walking together with the partner.

4 System Design

In our system, the existence of a physical walking partner can depend on whether they are able to share the same space at the same time. Hence, we designed our system based on two possible cases, depending on the presence and absence of a physical walking partner: Case #1, when a user does not have a physical walking partner in the same location; and Case #2, when a user has a physical walking partner who can walk together at the same time, but who is located in long-distance remote location. Both cases have a corresponding 3D personalized avatar. The avatar is expressed on top of the real world by applying AR technology. We believe that AR technology is the key to connect digital information and reality in a realistic manner. We designed interactions to provide the sense of walking together experience with a 3D avatar by providing a real walking experience with a virtual partner, rather than not just digital information in the user's line of vision. (see Fig. 2)

Case #1. Walking with an AR 3D personalized avatar

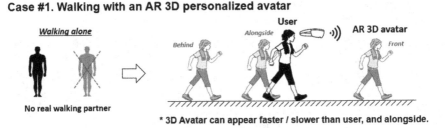

Case #2. Walking with remote user using an AR 3D partner-appearance avatar

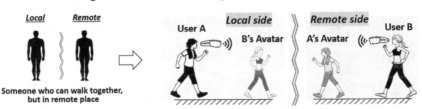

Fig. 2. The two cases of the proposed system: Case #1, in which a user is walking without a real partner; and Case #2, in which a user is walking with a real partner, but in long-distance remote.

In the proposed system, the user can select the interaction depending on the user's purpose, preference, or situation. In both cases, an AR 3D virtual partner is used due to the absence of a physical walking partner in the same physical space. We believe that the effectiveness of a virtual walking partner will be determined by the extent to which it can replace the role of a physical partner. Thus, we analyzed the design of interaction in the two possible cases in advance, to determine the best way to implement the 3D avatar to each situation.

4.1 Case #1. Walking with an AR 3D Avatar

In Case #1, a user can walking exercise with a virtual partner because a physical walking partner is not available. The virtual partner is a full-body 3D personalized avatar in the form of a human, implemented with AR technology for a realistic interaction providing the user with a real sense of presence. We believe that the user's motivation for walking exercise will be increased due to the realistic interaction with the virtual partner.

User can customize the appearance of the avatar, for example, to represent oneself or friends which can provide a better user experience [26]. The user can interact with the AR 3D avatar while walking together. Case #1 is divided into three types of walking interactions depending on user's walking purpose and preference: *Normal*, in which the user can simply walking exercise with the AR 3D avatar; *Pacemaker*, in which the user can engage in comparative walking with the AR 3D avatar, who has the user's previous walking information (to set a pace); and *Competition*, in which the user can compete with the AR 3D avatar with simple a rule, such as the firstcomer reach the goal wins the competition (see Fig. 3).

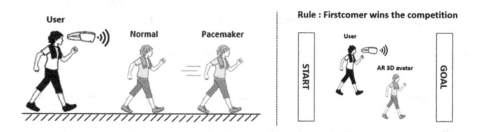

Fig. 3. Case #1 is separated into three types of walking interaction: Normal, Pacemaker, and Competition.

The three types of walking interactions represent situations that can occur during walking exercise with a partner in real life, and all were implemented for the purpose of increasing a user's walking motivation. In our system, the user can select a walking interaction type according to the user's walking purpose and preference. We designed appropriate behaviors and interactions for each situation. In addition, we designed an intuitive interfaces for users so that their walking exercise experience was immersive and so that they could interact with the AR 3D avatar using their voice input, gaze, and movement.

4.2   Case #2. Walking with a Remote User Using an AR 3D Avatar

If a physical walking partner exists, but is in a long-distance remote location, it is difficult to share the sense of walking together experience at the same time. Related studies on the simultaneous walking experience between remote users; for example, a method using auditory and tactile feedback was presented to simulate walking with a remote partner [3,10]. However, the method proposed in this paper enables visual feedback by applying AR technology. Our system provides the walking together experience for local and remote users, using a 3D avatar for each user, which has the appearance of their walking partner. The movement of the avatar is synchronized with the remote user's HMD location data, and real-time voice chat is available between the two users. (see Fig. 4)

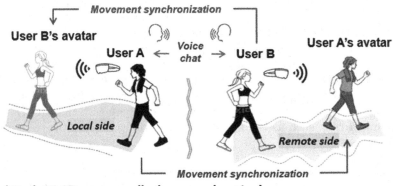

Fig. 4. In Case #2, each avatar's movement is synchronized with their respective user.

We designed a method to synchronize the movement of a remote user with that of an avatar, which can then be viewed by the local user. That is, the local user walks while watching the avatar move according to the movement of the remote user. We expect that the movement of remote users is visually provided through a 3D avatar as a virtual walking partner. It will provide an intuitive sense of mutual presence. In addition, this is supported by real-time voice chat that is available in our system. Through this, the user can recognize the movement of the remote user through the 3D partner-appearance avatar and while having a natural conversation with the remote user. Thus, we expect this interaction to increase both users' motivation for walking exercise.

We designed interactions to provide the sense of mutual presence [21,22] to two users in separate locations. As a consideration, an avatar can only walk along the course of the corresponding user, regardless of the difference in course shape between users. In addition, different individuals' walking abilities, for example depending on gender or age, can be resolved by changing the walking speed of the avatar. Usually, the walking speed is different depending on gender or age. In our system, the avatar's different walking speed can be set by the user. This makes it possible for each user to walk at their own speed, while still viewing and interacting with the unique characteristics of the partner in the form of avatar.

4.3   Social Aspects of Interactions in Walking Scene

One of the effects of having a walking partner is having others pushing oneself to do one's best, that is, motivating oneself. When performing physical exercise, difficulties, such as lack of motivation, can occur. This can be overcome by exploiting its social aspects of exercise [3]. The designed interactions in this study that consider the social aspects of walking exercise are expected to increase user's motivation. In our system, the user and the avatar cooperate or compete to improve the user's experience and increase their motivation of walking exercise.

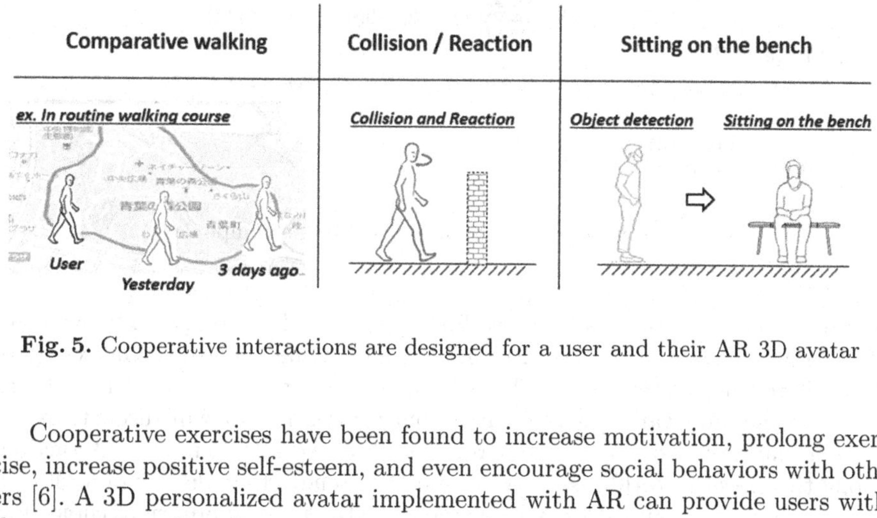

Fig. 5. Cooperative interactions are designed for a user and their AR 3D avatar

Cooperative exercises have been found to increase motivation, prolong exercise, increase positive self-esteem, and even encourage social behaviors with others [6]. A 3D personalized avatar implemented with AR can provide users with the perception that they are doing a specific action, rather than just showing digital information. Through cooperation with an AR 3D avatar, that is, the recognition of walking together, a partner effect can occur during physical activity. The experience of being with someone can increase interest and motivation in users. To make the user aware that they are walking together with a partner, we designed various cooperative interactions (see Fig. 5).

Competition is also an effective way to achieve goals and motivate oneself. It is commonly known that competition has the effect of maximizing human abilities [8]. The scope and form of competition can be diverse; in our system, competition is presented as an intuitive goal and can be performed based on simple rules, during a user's walking exercise. We expect to increase the motivation of a user by encouraging competition with the avatar. To enhance the sense of realism, the emotional expression of the avatar was designed to reflect the competition result. Depending on the competition result, the avatar can express the corresponding emotion through action, such as victory and disappointed.

4.4   System Overview

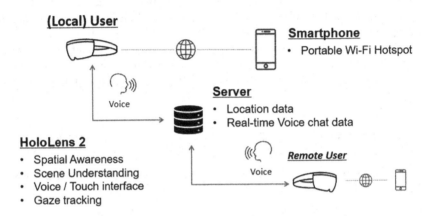

Fig. 6. Overview of the system's structure an components.

Figure 6 shows the overall structure of our system and its components; we used AR HMD (Microsoft HoloLens 2), and a smartphone (Samsung Galaxy S10) for our hardware devices. An HMD can enable a user to experience VR and AR easily by combining various sensors and input devices and allowing users to experience a fully immersive virtual environment [23]. An HMD enables interaction among the physical world, user, and avatar. We believe that the use of an HMD that can provide a hands-free AR experience is the most appropriate choice for the activity of walking exercise. Hence, the system consisted of minimum hardware, to provide a hands-free walking experience. Since the use of smartphones has become common in physical activity environments in recent years, we also utilized the computing ability of smartphones. We used a server to synchronize the movement of the user and the avatar and to enable the real-time voice chat.

The connection between the HMD and server is made in the state in which the network connection is established. For example, HoloLens 2 supports Wi-Fi, and so can user the internet to connect to a network. Therefore, we used a server that can be connected to through a device's internet connection. The interaction between local and remote users was through their respective HMDs. Each HMD connects to the network and sends and receives data between the two users through the server under the network connection. In our system, similar to the concept of a multi player game, two players connect to the same room and control their corresponding character. We designed the method of movement synchronization using only the user's HMD, that is, without separate sensors, devices, or equipment.

We used the built-in features of HoloLens 2, such as spatial awareness, scene understanding, voice and touch interface, and gaze tracking. This enabled our system to provide not only visual feedback, but also auditory feedback. We used a smartphone as a portable Wi-Fi hotspot to provide outdoor internet access. The use of the system was divided into the case of one or two users. A single user wears the HoloLens 2 device, and place their 3D personalized avatar in the physical space. The system provides an interface, for example, voice input, eye tracking, and touch interface, and the user starts walking exercise at the desired time and place, with the suggested interactions. In the case of two users, a local and remote user both wear the HoloLens 2 device. Each users' movement is recognized using the camera position of the HoloLens 2, and the corresponding data are transmitted to the server. Meanwhile, real-time location and voice chat data are also transmitted and received through the server.

5   System Implementation

We designed an AR system to provide immersive interaction with a virtual partner while walking exercise, using off-the-shelf devices such as a smartphone and freeware software development kits. This enabled the simple creation of an avatar with the desired appearance, without being overly time-consuming.

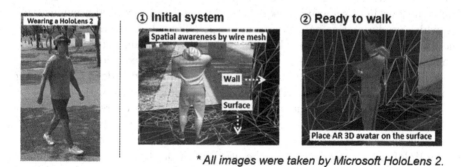

Fig. 7. Demonstration of spatial awareness in our system.

We designed novel interactions for appropriate avatar behavior for the context and situation in walking exercise scenes. Among the many features of the HoloLens 2, our system first utilized the spatial awareness feature. Figure 7 shows that this spatial awareness feature provides real-world environmental awareness in mixed reality applications. A user can place their avatar in the physical space and perceive it using the HoloLens 2. Then, the user can walking exercise with the AR 3D avatar. For an immersive walking exercise experience, we designed various interactions with the AR 3D avatar using an interface that the user can intuitively understand; these are outlined in Fig. 8.

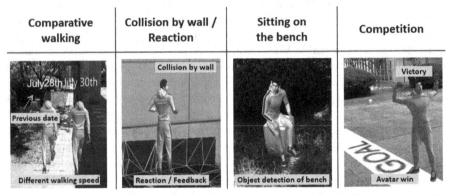

| Comparative walking | Collision by wall / Reaction | Sitting on the bench | Competition |

All images were taken by Microsoft HoloLens 2.

Fig. 8. The proposed system's designed interactions to promote an immersive walking exercise experience.

5.1   Movement Synchronization Between User and Avatar

We designed a novel method to synchronize the movement between the user and the avatar. This method is implemented using the camera position of the HoloLens 2 without separate sensors or equipment, unlike several previous studies, which used a motion capture sensor [24,25]. Thus, both users can experience the mutual presence of each other, through the avatar which the movement is synchronized by remote user, while having hands-free experience. The user's movement state is classified as either idling or walking and is determined by the camera position using the coordinate values of HoloLens 2 (Fig. 9).

Our system recognizes the change in "z" value in the coordinate system of HoloLens 2 as a change in the user's position and implements the corresponding change in the action of the avatar. When the system is initialized, the position of the HoloLens 2 camera, that is, the user's position, has a coordinate value of $(0, 0, 0)$. For example, the current location of the avatar is changed, and is set to $(0, 0, 1)$, so that is differs only in the "z" value, so that the user can see it. For reference, a coordinate value 1 in the HoloLens 2 system represents 1 m in physical space. When the "z" value of the remote user changes from the above coordinates, the system determines that the user's walking exercise has started. The movement of the avatar is controlled by the user changing coordinates in the physical space, according to the movement synchronization. To determine the continuous movement of the user, it is necessary to initialize the current position to the previous position every time. Thus, at the code level, an algorithm (see

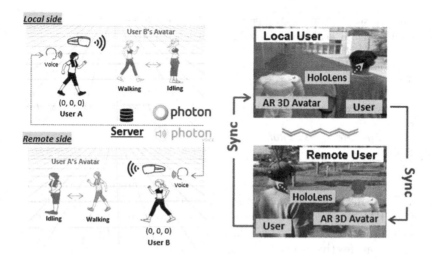

Fig. 9. Movement synchronization method.

Algorithm 1) determines whether the user is moving by inspecting whether the value of the current position is greater that of the previous position. Specifically, a C# code is implemented to initialize the current position to the previous position in every single frame. Hence, aforementioned, if the current position is greater than the previous position, the action state of the avatar changes to start walking by changing the parameters of the animation controller. Otherwise, the action state is changed to stop walking.

We utilized the concept of a multi player game. First, both local and remote users access the same virtual room. Then, the basic structure of server construction is as follows: (1) create network account, (2) connect network and callbacks, (3) matchmaking: lobby/room, and (4) player synchronization. In our implementation, we built the local and remote user applications separately. Each application is applied to the opponent's avatar in the player prefab. After initializing the application, both users connect to the same room, but each user can only see the other user's avatar. Each avatar's movement is synchronized according to the location data of the corresponding user's HoloLens 2 camera. Since the movement of the HMD coincides with the movement of the user, HoloLens 2 is used as a controller to control the movement of the avatar. In this study, we only consider the case of two users. However, we expect to be able to consider the participation of more than two users in the future, depending on the capabilities of the server.

Algorithm 1 Avatar action change depending on HMD camera position

---

Require: Initialization of previous position as a current position

1: $Y \leftarrow$ *PreviousPosition*
2: $X \leftarrow$ *CurrentPosition*
3: **if** $X > Y$ **then**
4:     *SetParameter* $\leftarrow$ **START***walking*   ▷ *Changing animation state*
5:     *PreviousPosition* $\leftarrow$ *CurrentPosition*   ▷ *Update by z value in every single frame*
6: **else**
7:     *SetParameter* $\leftarrow$ **STOP***walking*
8: **end if**

The advantages and disadvantages of the current implementation are as follows. The designed method of movement synchronization uses the camera position of the HMD and does not require separate sensors or equipment to capture the user's motion. In the case of walking exercise, a hands-free user experience is essential for effective exercise. Thus, our method has the advantage of providing a hands-free user experience and minimizing the restrictions on walking exercise location issues. In addition, since the actual walking motion is applied to the avatar's motion, the most frequent user behavior, a walking motion, can be faithfully expressed in this system. However, in the current stage, the system can only implement basic motions such as walking, stopping, and idling. That is, when the user's HMD moves, the avatar starts walking at the same time, and when the HMD stops, the avatar stops and displays an idling motion. Although the study is targeted relatively predictable user's behavioral patterns of walking. However, a useful extension of this study would be by the implementation of additional synchronization of various actions.

5.2   Direction Control of Avatar by Tracking of User's Gaze

The proposed system uses a method of tracking a user's gaze to control the direction of the avatar. Figure 10 shows an editor view, where the yellow line represents the user's gaze. When the user's gaze moves, the avatar follows the yellow line. In this method, HoloLens 2 becomes the controller and controls the direction of the avatar. This is because the recognition of progress direction while walking exercises is most directly and intuitively gained from the user's gaze. The gaze of the user wearing the HoloLens 2 coincides with the direction of the HMD's camera. Thus, the change in the user's gaze coincides with the direction and angle the camera is pointing in. This method is implemented using *Follow* among Mixed Reality Toolkit (MRTK) components, which is a feature in which a digital object tracks the camera position according to the change of the camera.

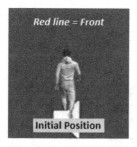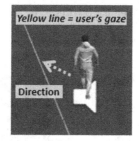

Fig. 10. Tracking of user's gaze for direction control in editor view.

Figure 11 shows a variety of real examples of our direction control method. We implemented the direction control of the avatar with an interface that users can intuitively understand. The results of these examples confirmed that the avatar moved naturally with the user using this method through the test. We also considered a course identification method using artificial intelligence (A.I.) in the development stage; road segmentation and detection, which are mainly used in autonomous vehicle research, were attempted. During the development process, we succeeded in classifying a road based on a line in the 2D video input. However, we identified a disadvantage in that we were not being able to identify places properly in places where the physical line was not clear. In addition, it was also confirmed that powerful computing is required for a more robust implementation.

* All images were taken from HoloLens 2

Fig. 11. Several test examples of direction control method in a variety of location.

5.3 Interactions for Encouraging the User

Our system can recognize the distance between a user and an avatar; if this reaches a certain distance, without a stop command during the walking exercise, the system determines that the pace of the user's walking is slow, which means the walking exercise motivation is insufficient. Accordingly, the avatar stops the walking action, turns to face the user, and then gives encouragement by clapping; visual and auditory feedback is provided (see Fig. 12). Then, when the distance between the avatar and the user is restored, the avatar changes action back to the idling state.

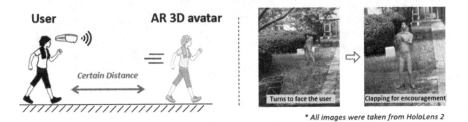

Fig. 12. Clapping action for encouragement.

Our system determines that a user is fatigued based on the duration of the system of use. We designed a high-five interaction between the user and the avatar in order to engage and promote enjoyment in the user. The interaction between the user and avatar is implemented using a touch interface. When a high-five is successfully achieved, visual and auditory feedback is provided (see Fig. 13.)

Fig. 13. High-five interaction between user and avatar.

HoloLens 2's camera has the ability to recognize a user's physical hand, the result of which is displayed with an AR mesh. The touch interface between the user and the digital object (i.e., the avatar and physical hand) uses MRTK's *Near Interaction Touchable* and *Hand Interaction Touch* components. We applied the collider to the part of the avatar's body to be touched. If the touch is successful, the animation state of the animation controller is changed to provide visual feedback, and auditory feedback is implemented by assigning the sound effect to the *Audio Source* component and assigning the corresponding audio source to *On Touch Started* of the *Hand Interaction Touch* component.

6   Preliminary Evaluation

We conducted a preliminary evaluation to evaluate the effectiveness of the proposed system by qualitatively surveying participants regarding their perception and behaviors. A key interest was to obtain feedback from participants. We analyzed the results of the initial user participation and feedback and noted any issues to be addressed in future work.

6.1   Participants and Method

We recruited 8 participants *(6 males, 2 females)* with an age range of 20 to 39: 6 Waseda University graduate students with AR experience and 2 ordinary people with no AR experience. The basic usage of HoloLens 2 was explained before the study for the participants with no AR experience.

The method of preliminary evaluation was a questionnaire, completed by participants after experiencing the system. We conducted the experiment in groups of two people and took about 1 h per group. This timeframe was appropriate for those with previous AR experience, but it was insufficient for those without. We provided a demonstration video (5 min version) to the participants in advance, to give them an approximate understanding of the system. All participants wore a HoloLens 2 and experienced both use cases (walking with an AR 3D avatar or walking with a remote partner) in outdoor setting. We observed and recorded the participants' behaviors and comments during the user study. After the questionnaire was completed, a brief interview was conducted with the participants, and the results of both the questionnaire and short interview were analyzed. Since this preliminary evaluation was a qualitative evaluation, specific measurements of usage time and walking distance were not conducted. This evaluation method aimed to identify the understanding, experience, and interest of the participants in the overall system.

6.2   Results

In this section, we present the analysis of the results from the preliminary evaluation of the proposed system. We analyzed five areas based on the result of the questionnaire and short interviews, and observation of participants behavior: *(1) usability, (2) sense of presence, (3) novelty, (4) effectiveness,* and *(5) continued use of system.* Figure 14 outlines these results. We can see that most of the participants responded positively in the questionnaire, suggesting that designed interactions with a virtual walking partner can increase a person's motivation or walking exercise. All the results in this preliminary evaluation are qualitative, thus a quantitative evaluation will be conducted in the future.

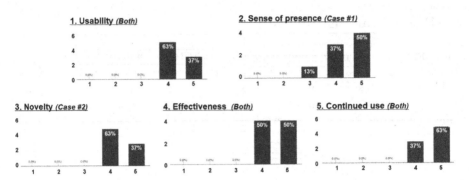

Fig. 14. Results of the participant questionnaire.

6.3 Discussion

From the results of the preliminary evaluation, we expect that our system will increase the motivation of walking exercise. However, we also found several issues and limitations in this initial stage of the system. The followings are the discussion issues:

1. **HoloLens 2 for walking exercise:** We believe wearing an HMD should be similar to wearing sports goggles, with minimal inconvenience. To investigate this, we compared the weights of various devices. The weight of HoloLens 2 has a significant disadvantage, with an average weight of 556 g, compared to sports goggles, with an average weight of 35 g. However, safety helmets used on construction sites weigh 300 g on average; hence, we can infer that the HoloLens 2 can be worn for long periods of time. Finally, since the target of this study is walking exercise, which differs from running, we believe that HoloLens 2 will not limit.

2. **Unexpected movement of avatar:** We utilized the spatial awareness of HoloLens 2 to place the avatar in the physical space in our system. However, a time delay between the display of the avatar and the space calculation occurs due to the computational limitations of HoloLens 2. Additionally, our system used the coordinate system of the HoloLens 2 camera to synchronize the movement of the avatar and the user. The proposed method uses only the "z" value of the 3D coordinate system; thus, when the user's "x" and "y" axes are changed, it is necessary to calibrate the "z" value required for the movement of the avatar. However, because the calibration value is not applied at this stage, so unexpected movement appears.

3. **Restricted interaction with avatar:** We found that the interaction between the user and the avatar is relatively one-sided. The interactions implemented in this prototype system only allow the user to interact with the avatar through the situation and interface specified in advance during the development process. Thus, depending on the situation, the user may feel that their virtual partner is acting out of context. To address this, complicated real-time calculations are required, which is challenging for the limited

computational power of the HoloLens 2. Therefore, it is necessary to consider a combination of devices and technologies to improve the system.

7 Conclusion

We designed an AR system to increase the motivation of walking exercise. Specifically, a 3D personalized avatar was implemented as a virtual partner in AR. We designed a novel interaction that enables a user to experience a realistic walking experience with a virtual partner for two different use cases. In Case #1, we designed interactions between a user and an avatar. In Case #2, we designed a novel method of movement synchronization between user and the avatar, using only the HMD without additional sensors, to enable a user to walk together with a remote user via their respective avatars.

We investigated the effect of our system with a qualitative preliminary evaluation. The results of the questionnaire outlined a positive response from most of the participants. These results support the idea that novel interactions in walking exercise scenes between a user and an avatar, while walking, can increase the motivation of walking exercise. In addition, some participants showed an interest in the system, demonstrating the potential of the proposed system to make a repetitive physical world walking exercise more entertaining. In the future, we plan to investigate a quantitative evaluation [27] by, for example, comparing the duration and distance of a user's walking exercise with or without our system. We believe that the above two factors are important to confirm and quantify the increase in a user's motivation.

References

1. Milgram, P., Kishino, F.: A taxonomy of mixed reality visual displays. IEICE Trans. Inf. Syst. **77**(12), 1321–1329 (1994)
2. Azuma, R.: A survey of augmented reality. Presence: Teleoperators Virtual Environ. **6**(4), 355–385 (1997)
3. Baldi, T., Paolocci, G., Barcelli, D., Prattichizzo, D.: Wearable haptics for remote social walking. IEEE Trans. Haptics **13**(4), 761–776 (2020)
4. Plante, T., Frazier, S., Tittle, A., Babula, M., Ferlic, E., Riggs, E.: Does virtual reality enhance the psychological benefits of exercise. J. Hum. Mov. Stud. **45**(6), 485–507 (2003)
5. Karunarathne, D., Morales, Y., Nomura, T., Kanda, T., Ishiguro, H.: Will older adults accept a humanoid robot as a walking partner. Int. J. Soc. Robot. **11**(2), 343–358 (2019)
6. Hanson, S., Jones, A.: Is there evidence that walking groups have health benefits? A systematic review and meta-analysis. Br. J. Sports Med. **49**(11), 710–715 (2015)
7. Yang, P., Dai, S., Xu, H., Ju, P.: Perceived environmental, individual and social factors of long-distance collective walking in cities. Int. J. Environ. Res. Public Health **15**(11), 2458 (2018)
8. Kilduff, G., Elfenbein, H., Staw, B.: The psychology of rivalry: a relationally dependent analysis of competition. Acad. Manag. J. **53**(5), 943–969 (2010)

9. Futami, K., Terada, T., Tsukamoto, M.: A method for behavior change support by controlling psychological effects on walking motivation caused by step count log competition system. Sensors **21**(23), 8016 (2021)

10. Mueller, F., O'Brien, S., Thorogood, A.: Jogging over a distance: supporting a "jogging together" experience although being apart. In: CHI'07 Extended Abstracts on Human Factors in Computing Systems, pp. 2579–2584 (2007)

11. Murata, H., Bouzarte, Y., Kanebako, J., Minamizawa, K.: Walk-in music: Walking experience with synchronized music and its effect of pseudo-gravity. Adjunct Publication of the 30th Annual ACM Symposium on User Interface Software and Technology, pp. 177–179 (2017)

12. Nomura, T., Kanda, T., Yamada, S., Suzuki, T.: The effects of assistive walking robots for health care support on older persons: a preliminary field experiment in an elder care facility. Intel. Serv. Robot. **14**(1), 25–32 (2021). https://doi.org/10.1007/s11370-020-00345-4

13. Fasola, J., Mataric, M.: Using socially assistive human-robot interaction to motivate physical exercise for older adults. Proc. IEEE **100**(8), 2512–2526 (2012)

14. Norouzi, N., Kim, K., Lee, M., Schubert, R., Erickson, A., Bailenson, J., Bruder, G. and Welch, G.: Walking your virtual dog: analysis of awareness and proxemics with simulated support animals in augmented reality. In: 2019 IEEE International Symposium on Mixed and Augmented Reality (ISMAR), pp. 157–168 (2019)

15. Kim, H., Lee, M., Kim, G., Hwang, J.: The impacts of visual effects on user perception with a virtual human in augmented reality conflict situations. IEEE Access **9**, 35300–35312 (2021)

16. Lee, M., Kim K., Daher, S., Raij, A., Schubert, R., Bailenson, J. and Welch, G.: The wobbly table: increased social presence via subtle incidental movement of a real-virtual table. In: 2016 IEEE Virtual Reality (VR), pp. 11–17 (2016)

17. Erickson, A., Bruder, G., Wisniewski, P., Welch, G.: Examining whether secondary effects of temperature-associated virtual stimuli influence subjective perception of duration. In: 2020 IEEE Conference on Virtual Reality and 3D User Interfaces (VR), pp. 493–499 (2020)

18. Chang, K., Zhang, J., Huang, Y., Liu, T., Sung, Y.: Applying augmented reality in physical education on motor skills learning. Interact. Learn. Environ. **28**(6), 685–697 (2020)

19. Koulouris, J., Zoe, J., James, B., Eamonn, O. and Christof, L.: Me vs. Super (wo)man: effects of customization and identification in a VR exergame. In: Proceedings of the 2020 CHI Conference on Human Factors in Computing Systems, pp. 1–17 (2020)

20. Praetorius, A., Krautmacher, L., Tullius, G., Curio, C.: User-avatar relationships in various contexts: does context influence a users' perception and choice of an avatar? Mensch Und Comput. **2021**, 275–280 (2021)

21. Wang, X., Wang, Y., Shi, Y., Zhang, W., Zheng, Q.: AvatarMeeting: an augmented reality remote interaction system with personalized avatars. In: Proceedings of the 28th ACM International Conference on Multimedia, pp. 4533–4535 (2020)

22. Fairchild, A., Campion, S., Garc, A., Wolff, R., Fernando, T., Roberts, D.: A mixed reality telepresence system for collaborative space operation. IEEE Trans. Circuits Syst. Video Technol. **27**(4), 814–827 (2016)

23. Ng, Y., Ma, F., Ho, F., Ip, P., Fu, K.: Effectiveness of virtual and augmented reality-enhanced exercise on physical activity, psychological outcomes, and physical performance: A systematic review and meta-analysis of randomized controlled trials. Comput. Hum. Behav. **99**, 278–291 (2019)

24. Orts-Escolano, S., Rhemann, C., Fanello, S., Chang, W., Kowdle, A., Degtyarev, Y., Kim, D., et al.: Holoportation: Virtual 3D teleportation in real-time. Proceedi
25. Pejsa, T., Kantor, J., Benko, H., Ofek, E., Wilson, A.: Room2room: enabling life-size telepresence in a projected augmented reality environment. In: Proceedings of the 19th ACM Conference on Computer-Supported Coperative Work & Social Computing, pp. 1716–1725 (2016)
26. Freeman, G., Zamanifard, S., Maloney, D. and Adkins, A.: My body, my avatar: how people perceive their avatars in social virtual reality. Extended Abstracts of the 2020 CHI Conference on Human Factors in Computing Systems, pp. 1–8 (2020)
27. Lee, C., Richard, K., David, P., Christian, S.: Walking the walk: a phenomenological study of long distance walking. J. Appl. Sport Psychol. **23**(3), 243–262 (2011)

Information in Virtual and Augmented Reality

Augmented-Reality-Based Real-Time Patient Information for Nursing

Agostino Di Dia, Tim Riebner, Alexander Arntz$^{(\boxtimes)}$ [ID], and Sabrina C. Eimler [ID]

Institute of Computer Science, Hochschule Ruhr West University of Applied Sciences,
Bottrop, Germany
{agostino.didia,tim.riebner}@stud.hs-ruhrwest.de,
{alexander.arntz,sabrina.eimler}@hs-ruhrwest.de

Abstract. While the usage of digital systems in the medical sector has increased, nursing activities are still mostly performed without any form of digital assistance. Considering the complex and demanding procedures the medical personnel is confronted with, a high task load is expected which is prone to human errors. Solutions, however, need to match staff requirements and ideally involve them in the development process to ensure acceptance and usage. Based on desired application scenarios, we introduce a concept of an augmented reality (AR)-based patient data application that provides context-relevant information for nursing staff and doctors. Developed for the Hololens 2, the application allows the retrieval and synchronization of the patient data from the host network of the respective hospital information system. For this purpose, a system infrastructure consisting of several software components was developed to simulate the exchange between the AR device and the independent hospital environment. The paper outlines the conceptual approach based on requirements collected from nurses, related work, the technical implementation and discusses limitations and future developments.

Keywords: Augmented reality · Medical application · Nursing support · Hospital information system

1 Introduction

In the process of digitization in various industries and specialized areas, the question arises of to what extent digitization could also improve processes in hospitals and clinics. However, it is clear that the clinical sector in Germany has catch-up potential in terms of digitization. The introduction of a standardized digital patient file has already been postponed for years [19]. The purpose of digitization is basically to digitalize workflows as well as business processes whilst avoiding analog procedures as far as possible or, in the best case, replacing them as optimally as possible [15]. The process of optimizing workflows often interferes with the everyday lives of many employees. With optimized work processes, employees may first have to get used to new procedures and this can lead to

S. Yamamoto and H. Mori (Eds.): HCII 2022, LNCS 13306, pp. 195–208, 2022.
https://doi.org/10.1007/978-3-031-06509-5_14

pressure on employees as they have to learn new structures and work plans [17]. The pressure that care workers might feel in adapting to new structures could then lead to insecurities or even mistakes. Especially in the area of patient care or patient medication, mistakes should be avoided in order not to endanger patients' well-being. The question is, therefore, which processes can be optimized in the context of medical care for patients and, if possible, in such a way that nurses and doctors do not have to expect any great difficulties in adapting to new technologies.

The PARCURA project pursues the idea of a participatory design process in the implementation of AR-technology in nursing. Together with hospital staff and researchers of different disciplines, the idea is to include multiple perspectives and requirements in the development process. In order to identify scenarios that medical staff envisions to be supported by AR-technology, collect requirements, and decide on a suitable technical device, we conducted two studies [8]. In study 1, nurses had the opportunity to explore the Moverio BT-200 and Hololens 2 and were subsequently asked to fill in a questionnaire, asking them, among other topics, for their impression on both devices and potentials for reducing workload and increasing quality of work. In study 2, an online questionnaire distributed among all hospital staff collected application scenarios besides looking into personal and motivational aspects of the usage of AR-devices in the hospital environment. Results showed a preference for the Hololens2 device among the sample. People positively rated the graphics and intuitive handling, although they considered the device to be too large and heavy. In the data collections, patient data retrieval (medication, vitality parameters) and documentation were among the most frequently mentioned potential aspects for the device reducing workload and supporting quality of work. Participants saw the potential of time and walking distance savings resulting from using AR technology.

Thus, a major focus is to be placed on the flood of information that is associated with the medication of patients. The presentation of current patient data offers a possible optimization and therefore a digitization opportunity. This could enable doctors and nurses to visualize information digitally during ward rounds or when directly dispensing medication, thus eliminating the management and workload of carrying the corresponding patient files to the respective patients. The focus of the visualization should be on a context-free presentation. When using such a technology, users should always have free hands in order not to be hindered in the possible treatment of patients. Furthermore, users should not be completely distracted when using such a visualization. In order to achieve this, an application for the Hololens 2 [13] is to be designed with the help of augmented reality (AR) technology, which allows users to visualize patient data context-free. The aim of this paper is to demonstrate the potential of an AR application in the clinical field hence encouraging further research projects in this area. For this purpose, an overall system is designed and developed that functions completely independently and does not contain any further dependencies. The overall system consists of several components, including a back-end system, the associated database, a web application for managing patient information, and the Hololens application for visualizing the managed data.

2   State of the Art

In order to obtain an up-to-date overview of the digital status of the medical sector, a literature search was first conducted using the terms "digitalization medication". The focus was on results from German-speaking countries in order to check the regional status. It was found that there is a lack of willingness to promote digitalization in the medical sector [20]. The lack of willingness is reasoned with the fact that potential users lack proof that digitization will bring a positive outcome for them. Additionally, it is criticized that it seems almost impossible that several different systems can communicate seamlessly with each other [20]. Therefore, a current acute problem is the lack of willingness for digitalization, as well as the readiness and acceptance to implement it accordingly. The question that arises subsequently is whether there are already successful digital applications that can serve as positive examples to promote further research work in this area, as well as to show medical workers as a positive example to encourage digitization of the sector. With the help of applications that focus on not overwhelming the user and allow context-free user interactions, it might be possible to convince skeptics.

Accordingly, a further literature search was conducted using the keywords "augmented reality medicine" to explore the current status of the implementation of AR technology in the medical sector. The published research shows that there are already some successful research projects dealing with the medical sector and a possible optimization using AR. Among other things, there is already an application that visually supports surgeons in the operation of tumors [11]. AR technology is also used to develop simulations. With the help of these simulations, medical students can learn certain medical procedures [12] before they have to apply them in practice. Support for medical staff with the help of AR glasses was also discussed. For example, concepts have already been presented for the development of an intelligent AR-system as a medication management system [10]. A system was also developed to support patients in taking their medication themselves, in order to provide support for the pillboxes [3]. The published literature shows that often very specific use cases are being supported with the help of AR applications. Especially very graphically complex applications that are also intended to help with complex procedures, such as surgery. In the case of on-demand medication, it is primarily the patients who are assisted in taking the medication themselves, while supported in setting up a theoretical framework for an administration system. The innovative point of the present work is that a completely independent system is being designed and developed, which brings together several factors. On the one hand, the administration of patient data, and on the other hand, the visualization of this data for the medical staff, with regard to the fact that the visualization takes place in such a way that the user is not restricted in his actions.

3 Architecture

The designed application consists of four main components: the front end, the Hololens application, the back end, and the database.

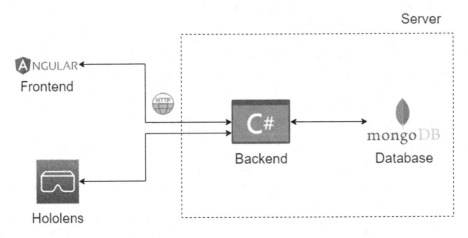

Fig. 1. Shows the overall architecture of the entire system and how the individual components are connected to each other [1, 16].

The database is used to store the required entities of the application. The back-end system communicates with the database and serves the entities via interfaces that have been developed accordingly. The Hololens was used to enable a hands-free AR experience [9]. This allows hospital staff to continue to apply medications or perform wound care during patient visits in addition to using the AR application. It is shown in previous research that users consider an augmented reality experience to be good if they do not have to use additional devices by hand [2].

The front-end application is designed to interact and edit the entities. The hospital staff can insert new patients into the web application as well as edit their medications. With the help of the front-end application, interaction with the data is made possible without requiring any specific technical expertise. The front end communicates with the back end system through the defined interfaces to access the required entities. When an entity is read, written, or deleted, the front end sends this request to the back end, which then performs the operation on the database.

The Hololens application is mainly used to read specific entities. The application communicates as the front end acts with the back end, but independently of the front end. The Hololens application receives all patients from the back end and visually prepares this information. The user can choose a patient on the user interface (UI), at which point the Hololens application sends another request to the back end. The selected patient's hospitalization information is then loaded and the patient's medical record is made visible.

At the beginning of the research work, there was no previous work on which to build technologically. Consequently, a technological basis had to be developed in order to be able to achieve the goals of the paper. The following chapter describes how the implementation of the presented architecture, see Fig. 1, was realized.

4   Implementation

4.1   Back End

In order to develop the Hololens client and the back end in the same programming language, the .NET 5 framework has been used for the back end. This allows developers who are already familiar with .NET to contribute to both the back end and the Hololens application. The back end is developed using the domain-driven design approach. With the help of domain-driven design, it is possible to implement new features into the application relatively simple and fast [14]. In addition, the domain-driven design approach supports developers' understanding of the context of the application [14]. Each domain is represented by an entity.

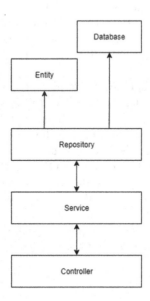

Fig. 2. Shows the back end pattern used to load individual entities from a database

They are implemented by the three-level pattern, see Fig. 2. The controllers define the interfaces of the back end. If a client sends a request, a function is called within the addressed controller. Each client calls the same controller, which saves development time because explicit interfaces do not have to be developed for each individual client.

Each controller also holds an instance of a defined service. A service is used to execute the application's actual logic. In doing so, a service executes the required algorithms, which are needed accordingly, in order to be able to communicate with the database. Each service also holds an instance of a repository, which in return is connected to the database. Via the repository instance, the service can then only access the respective released areas of the database and read, write and also delete entities. This also ensures that no controller, which is publicly available, has direct access to the database and only has to manage the requests.

The application programming interface (API) was developed according to the OpenAPI 3 specification so that the clients can also communicate correctly with these according to the defined interfaces [18]. Developers can use the Swagger editor to visualize the API. The defined standard allows all clients to implement them explicitly. The method reduces errors, among other benefits, because the Swagger documentation is generated directly from the existing code and developers do not have to read potentially outdated documentation that has been written separately and that has to be updated manually [7].

The communication of the requests between client and server is done via the HTTP network protocol, as this is an established standard used in almost every web application nowadays. As the context of the application deals with the use in a hospital, connection problems between the clients and the servers had to be considered very likely, as there are still hospitals that do not have a functioning area-wide WLAN infrastructure [19]. Therefore, if a client with the Hololens is in a section of a hospital that may have a poor network connection, it must be assumed that requests to the back end will take a longer time to arrive. In order to take into account higher latency times, high timeouts had to be set for requests as well as for responses, so that the clients do not automatically receive a timeout error message from the back end in case of a bad connection.

By using the OpenAPI specification, JSON was used as the data structure. Therefore, MongoDB was used as a database to be able to persist the data directly in a flexible way. For each domain, a collection was created in the database. To keep track of the activities on the server, a corresponding log entry is persisted in the database for each request, which is executed in a new thread. For all entries, a reference to the patient is stored, to provide an overview of all activities per patient.

4.2 Data Structure

In order to be able to simulate a reality-like infrastructure for the application, a data structure had to be designed that represents the most important information in a hospital context.

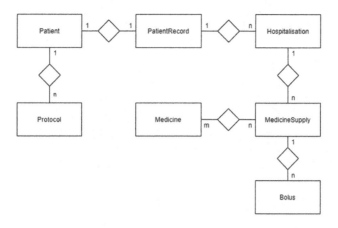

Fig. 3. The relations shown demonstrate how the entities interact with each other.

The entities shown in Fig. 3 indicate the context of the hospital management application. A patient has a list of protocols, which is the accessible data of the individual patient. For example, when a patient receives a bolus, e.g. the rapid administration of medication, this process is created as a protocol. The protocol stores, amongst other things, the time stamp when the bolus entry was made in the system. This process is completely automated. Each patient has a patient record. A patient's stay in the hospital is stored in the patient file. This is represented by "Hospitalisation". It stores when the patient was hospitalized and when the patient was released. The medication provided for the current treatment is stored in the "MedicationSupply" entity. The administration of the medication can take place over a defined period of time. Relation to the administered medication is created. All medications are stored once in the system and can be selected in the medication administration and used accordingly. If a medication is administered for a longer period of time and a higher dose is administered once regularly or irregularly, this is stored as a bolus. For example, if morphine is given by a pump over a longer period of time for pain and the patient temporarily experiences higher pain, then a bolus can be given to quickly relieve the patient's pain.

4.3   Request Procedure

The following section deals with the general sequence of a request to the back end and the underlying components.

A sequence on the back end always runs as shown in Fig. 4. A client first sends an HTTP request via the predefined interfaces to an explicit controller that is accessed via a defined URL. As already described, each controller holds an instance of a service that is created using dependency injection [21]. The injected service then executes the desired function, which is called by the controller. The function invocation triggers an event. The event is then used to generate the log entries, which ensure that every action performed with the API is verifiable.

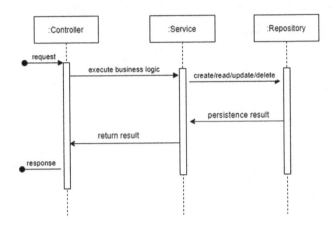

Fig. 4. Demonstrates the flow of an HTTP request to a controller.

The manipulation of the data is then performed using the instance of a repository that each service contains. The database operations are used to allow hospital staff to manage and manipulate the application's datasets. If an internal application error occurs, the controller sends a corresponding error message to the requesting client, otherwise, the controller passes the result of the request.

The next section shows the implementation of the front-end application. The structure of the application will be discussed.

4.4 Front End

The front end was completely implemented in the Angular framework. This allows the application to be used in the browser and can be implemented as a progressive web app. For every entity, a table was created in which create, read, update and delete operations can be executed (Fig. 5).

Each table was developed as a visual component consisting of several HTML components. Those components use services that have the purpose of sending server requests such as GET and POST for an entity. In addition, services can be used, for example, to execute business logic and therefore make the code more modular. Care was taken to comply with the single-responsibility principle, which is provided for Angular services according to the conventions. In the administration application, the patient file can be opened for each patient, in which all hospital stays are documented. Furthermore, the complete logbook of a patient can be opened. For every patient, it is documented which medications were administered over a certain period of time and when a bolus was set. These entries can be newly created or changed. For this purpose, a medication list is managed in the system.

However, the front-end application is not the only client. The Hololens application is still a client application in the overall construct, which will be presented in the next section.

Fig. 5. The list page containing the patient information. The files presented in this image are mock-up patient data. Translation: (A) patient, (B) bolus, (C) medicine, (D) medicine supply, (E) user, (F) name, (G) surname, (H) age, (I) weight, (J) hospitalizations, (K) hospitalization beginning, (L) hospitalization end, (M) protocol.

4.5   Hololens

The Hololens application uses the Mixed Reality Toolkit published by Microsoft. The toolkit contains basic UI components that can be used to make a Hololens application interactive. The advantage of using the existing components is that they have already been proven in other AR applications. The UI components were used to load and display entities.

First, a prefab was created during the development of the patient overview. A prefab can consist of several components within the Unity environment. Basically, one can think of a prefab as a blueprint for a complex, coherent 3D object. In the case of the patient overview, the prefab consists of a grid object from the Mixed Reality Toolkit. This prefab then serves as a wrapper for all available patients that can be loaded. An additional prefab was created, which itself is an interactive button. This button holds a person's patient information and is displayed in the grid object. These prefabs are then marked as references in the PatientController class. As soon as the application is started, the Patient-Controller class loads all currently available patients from the server by sending a matching Representational State Transfer (REST) request. In order for the application to start, the PatientController has to load the required entities first. The complexity of the loading function results from this as $O(n^2)$. This results from the fact that for each patient button, the hospital visits are loaded directly for the required medical record, which is loaded when a patient is selected.

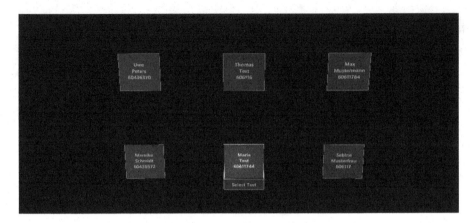

Fig. 6. The overview of patients available via the back end system seen through the AR device. The black background represents the environment where the AR content is embedded.

For each patient that has been loaded, a corresponding button is created, see Fig. 6, which takes over the properties from the referenced prefab. The list of objects is then dynamically loaded into the prefab grid object and then aligned accordingly so that the user of the application can also visually identify each patient. The name of the respective patient is then displayed within a button. When the buttons were created, additional functions were defined on the click events that are executed as soon as the user clicks on a button. The user can therefore select a patient by "touching" it and this calls up the defined function. When a user hovers over a patient button, the user is also shown a display that prompts him to click on the user. In this case, the user is shown the last name of the patient over whom he is currently hovering see Fig. 6.

This function then creates the medical record of the respective patient, which has also been created as a prefab beforehand. The medical record contains a list of all hospitalizations, see Fig. 7, as well as basic information about the patient. The patient record is designed in such a way that any objects or data could be displayed at any time. All that is needed is to load the information from the PatientController. The patient record of the Hololens client only serves as a wrapper to display information, which is then displayed within the individual tiles as needed. As a result, in the current version of the application, the entries of the hospital stays remain unsorted and are displayed according to how the backend system has stored the data. In order to not obstruct the view of the user, e.g. the hospital staff in an augmented reality environment, the user can move the patient's medical record component. It is also possible to fix the medical record to a position that is relative to the user. If the user of the Hololens moves his head, the fixed medical record moves in the direction of the head movement to resume the relative position to the user. During the development of the interface implementation in the Hololens application, appropriate certificates had to be

Fig. 7. Shows the patient record of the selected patient. Apart from the name of the patient and a unique ID, medical personnel can access age, weight as well as the beginning and end of the individual staying periods. Again the black background represents the individual environment, which is augmented with the UI elements.

installed in the client. As long as the certificates were not installed, no requests could be sent to the back end system and the corresponding controllers, as they were blocked. The required certificate must be stored in the operating system in order to guarantee access from the Hololens client to the back-end system.

The implementation of all individual components should be done in such a way that further research could build on the technological foundation that has been developed. The following section describes how the possible scalability in the overall system has been designed.

4.6   System Scalability

Since the entire software architecture consists of several components, one of the tasks of the research work was to keep the complexity as simple as possible so that possible maintenance and the scalability of the overall application would not be more difficult than necessary. Since the Unity engine had to be used to develop the Hololens 2 application, we also decided to develop the back end in such a way that the technological competencies could be divided between the two components. Consequently, the decision was made to use the .NET framework for the back end as well. This also proved to be a good decision during development, as it simplified the processes for serializing and deserializing the entities sent to the Hololens application via the REST interface. This design allows developers who are familiar with C# to contribute directly to the back end as well as the Hololens application without having to learn a new language. In order to keep the complexity as low as possible, we also decided to use Angular as the front-end framework. This decision was made because the Angular framework, unlike the other established frameworks such as React or VueJS, relies on Typescript as the programming language. Typescript, unlike Javascript, relies on object-oriented concepts and can therefore be adapted very quickly by developers who are familiar with it.

By using the Angular front end, new modules can always be developed and therefore managed in a clear manner, even for larger-scale projects. Modularisation thus also enables expansion and maintenance based on specific use cases. In addition, new components can be developed independently of other components at any time.

The back end was developed RESTless so that it can be scaled independently of all clients. In case of high network traffic, the back end can be started in multiple instances and listen to different ports. If a load-balancer distributes the network load to different instances, the back end can theoretically scale infinitely with any number of system resources [4]. Since the front end uses client-side rendering and was developed in Angular, the front end is compiled into several static HTML and Javascript files [6]. This allows the front end to be made available via a web server independent of the back end. MongoDB can be deployed in a cluster and scaled horizontally across replica sets [5].

The system has been developed to be as scalable as possible, but with the current implementation of the overall system also comes some limitations that are described in the next section.

4.7   Limitations

One limitation of the project involves the design of the AR solution, as the implementation is limited exclusively to the Microsoft Hololens 2. Smartphones or other devices that support AR as a feature cannot run the application because the Mixed Reality Toolkit, which is an explicit framework for Hololens, is used. Due to the acute pandemic, it was also difficult to conduct user tests with appropriate participants with medical backgrounds. However, considering the sensitive subject of the usage of the AR application by nursing personnel involving direct patient interaction, user tests to validate the application are planned for the next iteration of the development process. Another major challenge for the implementation of such a system is the fact that current hospital information systems (HIS) are closed systems and therefore do not offer interfaces to enable data synchronization. However, the presented research work could help to identify the potential of an AR application and to design corresponding systems more openly so that, in the best case, hospitals can also benefit from digitalization with corresponding mobile devices and that workflows can be optimized. To conclude the present work, a conclusion will assess the research result, taking into account the current implementation.

5   Conclusion and Outlook

With the advance of digitalization, the medical sector continues to ask itself which areas and especially, which processes can be further optimized. One possible implementation of optimization of a current scenario is the flood of information that may occur per patient for the medical staff. Using a possible visualization of patient data with the help of context-free user handling, medical staff could be supported in the overview of patient data.

This paper demonstrates that AR technology can be used to enable the context-free visualization of patient information. This can reduce the administrative burden of paper document-based patient records. However, it also shows that other factors need to be taken into account before such an application can be implemented properly and ready for production. On the one hand, data protection issues must be clarified, namely to what extent the storing of patient information must be explicitly applied in such a procedure. Also, the extent to which the caregivers and doctors may have access to the corresponding visualizations of the patient data must be investigated. The current implementation, however, allows the implementation of different roles that can have corresponding user rights to read and write data. Another additional question is whether current HIS's are still up to date and whether they should not have interfaces to simplify possible digitalization procedures and therefore save development time.

Acknowledgments. The presented work is partly supported by the PARCURA project funded by the Federal Ministry of Education and Research Germany. The authors thank Stefan Geisler, Nils Malzahn, Veronica Schwarze, Pasquale Hinrichs, and Dustin Keßler for comments in the development process and reviews of earlier versions of the manuscript. Presentation of this work is funded by the initiative for quality improvement in teaching of the Institute of Computer Science.

References

1. Angular: Angular web platform (2022). https://angular.io
2. Arntz, A., et al.: Navigating a heavy industry environment using augmented reality - a comparison of two indoor navigation designs. In: Chen, J.Y.C., Fragomeni, G. (eds.) HCII 2020. LNCS, vol. 12191, pp. 3–18. Springer, Cham (2020). https://doi.org/10.1007/978-3-030-49698-2_1
3. Blusi, M., Nieves, J.C.: Feasibility and acceptability of smart augmented reality assisting patients with medication pillbox self-management. Stud. Health Technol. Inform. **264**, 521–525 (2019)
4. Chieu, T.C., Mohindra, A., Karve, A.A., Segal, A.: Dynamic scaling of web applications in a virtualized cloud computing environment. In: 2009 IEEE International Conference on e-Business Engineering, pp. 281–286. IEEE (2009)
5. Chodorow, K.: MongoDB: The Definitive Guide: Powerful and Scalable Data Storage. O'Reilly Media, Inc. (2013)
6. Clow, M.: Introducing Webpack. In: Angular 5 Projects, pp. 133–137. Apress, Berkeley, CA (2018). https://doi.org/10.1007/978-1-4842-3279-8_10
7. Ed-douibi, H., Cánovas Izquierdo, J.L., Cabot, J.: Example-driven web API specification discovery. In: Anjorin, A., Espinoza, H. (eds.) ECMFA 2017. LNCS, vol. 10376, pp. 267–284. Springer, Cham (2017). https://doi.org/10.1007/978-3-319-61482-3_16

8. Eimler, S., Volk, J., Schwarze, V., Geisler, S., Arntz, A.: In the eye of the beholder: introducing data glasses in nursing considering ideas from uses and gratifications and self determination theory. 12. In: Conference of the Media Psychology Division of the German Psychological Society, 8th-10th September 2021, Aachen (2021)

9. Evans, G., Miller, J., Pena, M.I., MacAllister, A., Winer, E.: Evaluating the Microsoft Hololens through an augmented reality assembly application. In: Degraded Environments: Sensing, Processing, and Display 2017, vol. 10197, p. 101970V. International Society for Optics and Photonics (2017)

10. Guerrero, E., Lu, M.H., Yueh, H.P., Lindgren, H.: Designing and evaluating an intelligent augmented reality system for assisting older adults' medication management. Cogn. Syst. Res. **58**, 278–291 (2019)

11. Ha, H.G., Hong, J.: Augmented reality in medicine. Hanyang Med. Rev. **36**(4), 242–247 (2016)

12. Lee, S., et al.: Augmented reality intravenous injection simulator based 3d medical imaging for veterinary medicine. Vet. J. **196**(2), 197–202 (2013)

13. Microsoft: Hololens documentation (2020). https://www.microsoft.com/de-de/hololens

14. Millett, S., Tune, N.: Patterns, Principles, and Practices of Domain-Driven Design. Wiley, Indianapolis (2015)

15. Mitchell, M., Kan, L.: Digital technology and the future of health systems. Health Syst. Reform **5**(2), 113–120 (2019). https://doi.org/10.1080/23288604.2019.1583040

16. MongoDB: Mongodb database (2022). https://www.mongodb.com/de-de

17. Öberg, U., Orre, C.J., Isaksson, U., Schimmer, R., Larsson, H., Hörnsten, Å.: Swedish primary healthcare nurses' perceptions of using digital eHealth services in support of patient self-management. Scand. J. Caring Sci. **32**(2), 961–970 (2018). https://doi.org/10.1111/scs.12534

18. Patro, A., Banerjee, S.: Coap: A software-defined approach for home WLAN management through an open API. In: Proceedings of the 9th ACM Workshop on Mobility in the Evolving Internet Architecture, pp. 31–36 (2014)

19. Pohlmann, S., et al.: Digitalizing health services by implementing a personal electronic health record in Germany: qualitative analysis of fundamental prerequisites from the perspective of selected experts. J. Med. Internet Res. **22**(1) (2020). https://doi.org/10.2196/15102

20. Poncette, A.-S., Meske, C., Mosch, L., Balzer, F.: How to overcome barriers for the implementation of new information technologies in intensive care medicine. In: Yamamoto, S., Mori, H. (eds.) HCII 2019. LNCS, vol. 11570, pp. 534–546. Springer, Cham (2019). https://doi.org/10.1007/978-3-030-22649-7_43

21. Prasanna, D.R.: Dependency injection. Safari Books Online, Manning, Greenwich, Conn (2009). http://proquest.tech.safaribooksonline.de/9781933988559

UTAUT Within Service Operation – the Relevance of Information Technology Acceptance on Service Quality

Katja Gutsche[✉] and Santina Schlögel

Furtwangen University, Robert-Gerwig Platz 1, 78120 Furtwangen, Germany
{Katja.gutsche,Santina.schloegel}@hs-furtwangen.de

Abstract. Service operation, especially in the field of industrial services like maintenance, increasingly depends on an easy and available access to information on technological, legal and safety requirements to be respected during service operation. As digitalization advances more technical options for such information providence become available. More advanced systems like mobile applications and Augmented-Reality-solutions allow a more individual, adaptive information providence as they are categorized as smart tools which come with an increased human-computer-interaction level. More advanced technologies promise a better work outcome. This paper addresses the relevance of technology acceptance in the field of industrial service operation on the service outcome, measured by specific service quality parameters. As the UTAUT is used for measuring the technology acceptance level, the paper also questions the suitability of the defined influencing parameters within UTAUT to predict technology acceptance within the field of service operation.

Keywords: Technology acceptance · UTAUT · Service quality · Augmented reality · Service operation · Information technology

1 Motivation

Service operation, especially in the field of industrial services like maintenance, increasingly depends on an easy and available access to information on technological, legal and safety requirements to be respected during service operation. Access can be provided through paper, pdf, video, mobile applications or immersive technologies. Especially smarter information technologies like augmented reality promise positive effects on service delivery and quality. As the options of assisting information technology widen and become more available, it must be analyzed on which information tool supports best in achieving a high service quality level and therefore meeting the customer requirements. As service business is people's business, such a decision must respect the service operators attitude towards using the information technology. For technologies to improve the output, they must be accepted by employees. Acceptance is the willingness of an operator to adopt to innovations. There are different acceptance models, which are to help in understanding the causes of an individual to adopt or not to adopt to innovations.

S. Yamamoto and H. Mori (Eds.): HCII 2022, LNCS 13306, pp. 209–221, 2022.
https://doi.org/10.1007/978-3-031-06509-5_15

The Unified Theory of Acceptance and Use of Technology (UTAUT) is well accepted and helpful in decisions on information technology rollouts within the service domain. This paper is based on a broad empirical study, where actual service technicians were subjects. Within the study 30 service technicians from different industries in Germany were asked to use three different kinds of information technologies – video, mobile application and Augmented Reality (AR) solution. The three tools differ in their levels of innovation and diffusion rates.

2 Scientific Approach

The study took place to analyze the effect of information technology (IT) acceptance on service quality. To do so, firstly the appropriateness of the UTAUT for explaining technology acceptance in the field of service operation was looked at. With the help of UTAUT, enhancing and limiting factors determining information technology acceptance within service operation are identified. Then differences in acceptance of video, mobile application and AR solution are identified. Differences in service quality depending on the used information technology and its level of acceptance were analyzed (Fig. 1).

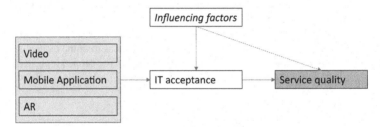

Fig. 1. Analyzing frame

The following research questions come along with the scientific approach:

1) Research Question 1: Is the UTAUT an appropriate tool to predict technology acceptance in the field of industrial service operation?
2) Research Question 2: How much can service quality be improved by smart information technology and which relevance plays technology acceptance?

To address RQ 1 the explanatory factors of the UAUT model [1] were examined. To answer RQ 2 the following hypotheses were investigated:

- H1: The smarter the technology, the higher the acceptance.
- H2: The higher the acceptance, the higher the service quality.

  - H2.1: The higher the acceptance, the lower the number of errors.
  - H2.2: The higher the acceptance, the higher the compliance with safety instructions.
  - H2.3: The higher acceptance, the lower the time required.

3 Technology Acceptance, Industrial Service Operation and Service Quality

3.1 Technology Acceptance – UTAUT

Acceptance in general is the positive attitude of individuals or groups towards innovation and progression within workplaces, companies or societies. The acceptance of innovation often comes along with changes in technology use, therefor technology acceptance must be addressed. There are numerous models, which were developed based on empirical studies, to measure technology acceptance [1, 2, 3, 4, 5, 6, 7]. Within these models technology acceptance is defined by the behavioral intention to repeated use of the technology.

The Unified Theory of Acceptance and Use of Technology (UTAUT) is a well-accepted model. As shown in Fig. 2, within UTAUT the behavioral intention depends on performance expectancy, effort expectancy, social influence and facilitating conditions, whereas gender, age, experience and voluntariness of use are moderating factors upon these influencing factors. Behavioral intention is seen as the direct indicator for use behavior (see Fig. 2.).

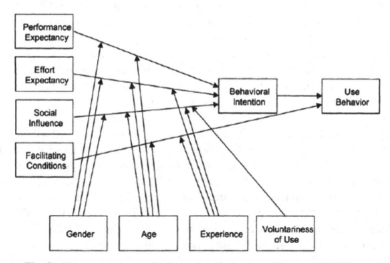

Fig. 2. User Acceptance of Information Technology Theory (UTAUT) [1]

To have a clear understanding of UTAUT, the list of influencing factors as identified by Venkantesh et al. [1] is given.

1. *Performance expectancy*: The performance expectancy questions a person's belief that the system used can help improve work performance.
2. *Effort expectancy*: Effort expectancy includes a person's assessment of how easy it is to use and interact with the system in use.
3. *Attitude toward using technology*: this factor captures a person's attitude toward the system being used, and thus their affective attitude toward it.

4. *Facilitating conditions*: The Facilitating conditions include questions about whether all the resources and necessary infrastructure are in place to use the system.
5. *Self-efficacy*: This factor asks whether the user is able to complete a task with the help of the system under certain conditions.
6. *Social influence*: Social influence asks whether the user believes that other people think he should use the system.
7. *Anxiety*: This factor includes questions about anxiety about using the system.

The UTAUT comes with a questionnaire of 30 items clustered into the seven influencing factors plus the behavioral intention itself.

3.2 Information Technology Within Industrial Service Operation

Industrial services must assure a safe, economic and compliant operation of industrial assets as i.e. paper mills, power plants or trains. Typical industrial services are professional training, maintenance, overhaul or disposal services addressing the needs of the industrial asset along its life cycle. They are characterized by a low level of repetitive tasks and heterogeneous, highly customized environment which requires human work. Industrial services belong to the group of services with a high degree of labor intensity and a high degree of interaction and customization [8]. Consequently, they belong to the most demanding services. Challenges within service operation arise amongst others from the variety of physical assets (i.e. manufacturing machines) and asset properties (i.e. software, functionality), hazardous work environments and high compliance requirements. Especially the trend towards automation and digitalization within the industry sector comes with change for industrial service operation.

Smart technologies as promising tools to ease the work and achieving better service outcome [9], come along with an increase in human-computer-interaction within service operation. Whereas service instructions were primarily provided paper-based in the past, a shift towards more advanced, smarter information technologies can be seen. Service instructions as an information product enables the user to carry out necessary actions on a physical product safely and without risk [10]. Within service operation they are highly relevant for successful service operation. Currently, Mixed Reality (MR) applications are the most advanced tools. It is seen as the smartest technology within technical documentation. MR-based information products give an automated step-by-step guidance depending on the service object and previous working steps. Through the use of object recognition the technician gets detailed, accurately fitting information helping to fulfil the work routine. Video guidance belongs to the smart technologies as it allows, at least on a low level, a data collection, analysis and treatment. In-between Mixed Reality and video, mobile applications are ranked. Service information are more structured, allow individual interaction, demand for approval of safety instructions but do not use periphery data as mixed reality does (Fig. 3).

Service operation is evaluated by looking at service productivity and service quality [11]. This paper focuses on the effect of smart information technology on service quality, as this is also one indicator for service productivity measurements [12].

level of data collection, interconnectivity and analysis (qualitative ranking)

Fig. 3. Information tools ranked by level of data collection, interconnectivity and analysis

3.3 Service Quality

From the customer perspective the service result can best be described by the understanding of service quality. Quality in general describes how well requirements towards a product or process are met [13]. Service quality is understood as the ability of a service provider to meet customer expectations and fulfil the customer requirements towards a primarily intangible service product under the involvement of the service customer [14]. The SERVQUAL instrument sums up different ways of how to characterize service quality and defines (1) tangibles, (2) reliability, (3) responsiveness, (4) assurance, (5) empathy as quality elements [15, 16, 17]. Not all of the service quality elements are directly influenced by the use of different information tools. A change in service reliability, responsiveness and assurance are expected when changing the technology on which the information product is based on (Table 1).

Table 1. Effects of information tools on service quality [18]

	effected by information tool?
Tangibles	
Reliability	x
Responsiveness	x
Assurance	x
Empathy	

There are several models on how to quantify service quality [14]. As the customer-oriented SERVQUAL questionnaire [16] would be too powerful, this study measures service quality by looking at the quantitative parameters (1) "duration", (2) "risk" and (3) "number of errors". These three indicators build a customer-oriented, objective service quality measure. The three parameters reflect in extracts the effects on reliability, responsiveness and assurance (cf. Table 1) by the use of the three different information tools (cf. Fig. 3). Service quality as measured within this study was calculated as described in Eq. 1:

$$Service\ quality = \frac{duration}{1 + risk + error} = \frac{\frac{target\ time}{actual\ time}}{1 + \left(1 - \frac{f.i}{g.i}\right) + error} \tag{1}$$

Duration

For measuring the quality parameter "duration", a target time was defined ex-ante and set in relation to the actual time the subject needed (Eq. 2).

$$duration = \frac{target\ time}{actual\ time} \tag{2}$$

Risk

"Risk" was measured by comparing the number of safety instructions followed (f.i.) by the subject to the number of the ones given (g.i.) (cf. Eq. 3).

Within this study, two safety instructions were given. Consequently, if "all" safety instructions were followed a two, if "only partially" a one, and if "none" a zero was put into Eq. 3. In case of the subject following all given safety instructions, the risk is zero.

$$risk = 1 - \frac{f.i}{g.i} \tag{3}$$

Error

Errors were simply counted. The more errors the subject made during service operation, the worse the service quality, so this was added to the denominator (cf. Eq. 1).

4 Study

4.1 Experimental Setting

A total of 30 real service technicians participated in the study (n = 30). All subjects were asked to repair a chain saw. They were asked to fulfill the task as quickly as possible. None of the subjects had ever done this repair before. The 30 participants were divided into three groups. There were 10 participants in each group. Each group worked on the same repair scenario, one group doing so with the help of video instruction, the second group with APP instruction, and the last with the help of augmented reality.

- The video instruction using picture and voice had a total length of 10 min, all information were given as one sequence, subjects could pause or rewind the video wherever needed.
- Within the mobile application 23 information sequences were given using video, picture and sound. The subjects are free to re-run and stop sequences as well as pushing the help button for receiving further information using touch functionality implemented on the given tablet device.
- The Augmented Reality application was installed on the first generation Microsoft Hololens®. Through the use of object recognition the technician gets detailed, accurately fitting information within 20 sequences helping to fulfil the work routine which the technician confirms and executes. Besides AR information this solution had sound, picture and video information as well as help buttons integrated. The objects could pause, re-play or stop the assistive tool by gesture or voice control. The subjects using the AR solution got a brief introduction in how to operate the Microsoft Hololens®.

4.2 Sample Description

The number of participants included one woman and 29 men. This also represents the real circumstances, as women are still very rare as service technicians. The average age of the participants was 40 years. The distribution of age groups and genders by technology used are shown in a chart below (Fig. 4).

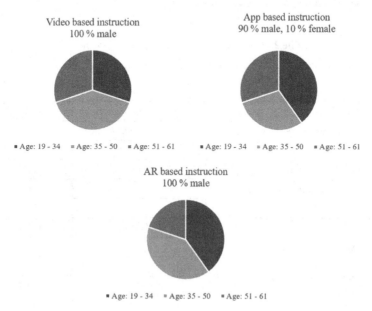

Fig. 4. Age and gender distribution by group

The participants in the study came from three different industry sectors: Mechanical Engineering, Electronics and Automotive. The distribution in the three technology groups is similar, with mechanical engineering representing the largest share in all areas.

4.3 Findings

RQ 1: Is the UTAUT an appropriate tool to predict technology acceptance in the field of industrial service operation?

To answer this research question, the correlation between the influencing factors and behavioral intention (acceptance) (cf. Fig. 2) were determined. As seen in Table 2, there is a statistically significant correlation between the performance expectancy and acceptance. The expected benefit of the technology and acceptance have a statistically significant strong positive correlation with each other, $r = 0.475$, $p < .05$. With the correlation coefficient of 0.475, a significant dependence of both variables could be determined. A statistically significant relationship was also found between effort expectancy and acceptance. Effort expectancy and acceptance had a statistically significant strong positive correlation with each other, $r = 0.522$, $p < .05$. Attitude toward using the technology and acceptance correlate weakly positively with each other, but not statistically significantly. Facilitating conditions and acceptance correlate statistically significantly strongly positively with each other, r = 0.586, p < .05. Self-efficacy and acceptance do not have a statistically significant correlation; they only correlate weakly positively with each other. Social influence and acceptance have weak positive correlation with each other, but also not statistically significant. Anxiety about technology and acceptance do not have a statistically significant correlation either. They correlate weakly negatively with each other, but not statistically significantly.

Table 2. Correlation of the factors and acceptance

Correlation		
Performance expectancy	Correlation coefficient	,475**
	Sig. (2-sided)	0,008
	N	30
Effort expectancy	Correlation coefficient	,522**
	Sig. (2-sided)	0,003
	N	30
Attitude toward using technology	Correlation coefficient	0,290
	Sig. (2-sided)	0,120
	N	30
Facilitating conditions	Correlation coefficient	,586**
	Sig. (2-sided)	0,001
	N	30
Self-efficacy	Correlation coefficient	0,059
	Sig. (2-sided)	0,757
	N	30
Social influence	Correlation coefficient	0,139
	Sig. (2-sided)	0,527
	N	23
Anxiety	Correlation coefficient	- 0,132
	Sig. (2-sided)	0,486
	N	30

To sum up, technology acceptance by service technicians is primarily dependent on:

- performance expectancy
- effort expectancy
- facilitating conditions

The emergent model can be seen in Fig. 5.

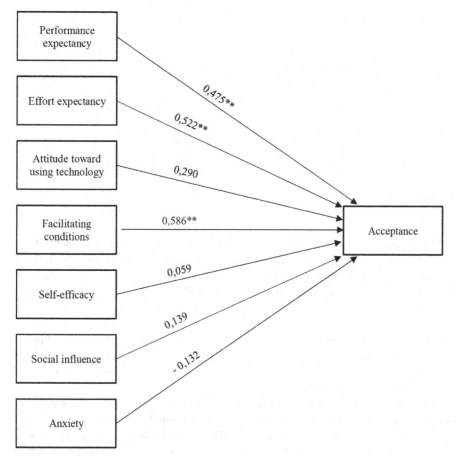

Fig. 5. Influencing factors on technology acceptance for service technicians (**0.001 < p < 0.01, otherwise p > 0.05)

RQ 2: How much can service quality be improved by high tool acceptance?
H1: The smarter the technology, the higher the acceptance.

The technology acceptance is statistically significantly different for the three different information technologies examined, $F(2, 27) = 8.314$, $p < 0.002$.

A post-hoc test was performed to examine differences between groups (Table 3).

Table 3. Post-hoc-test – technology used and acceptance

Turkey post-hoc test						
(I) Information technology		Mean value difference (I-J)	Standard error	Sig.	95% confidence interval	
					Lower limit	Upper limit
Video	APP	0,20000	0,41821	0,882	-0,8369	1,2369
	AR	1,56667*	0,41821	0,002	0,5298	2,6036
APP	Video	-0,20000	0,41821	0,882	-1,2369	0,8369
	AR	1,36667*	0,41821	0,008	0,3298	2,4036
AR	Video	-1,56667*	0,41821	0,002	-2,6036	-0,5298
	APP	-1,36667*	0,41821	0,008	-2,4036	-0,3298

The post-hoc test showed that there was a statistically significant difference between the Video and AR groups as well as between the App and AR groups. The Turkey post-hoc test showed a significant difference ($p < .05$) in acceptance between the video technology group and the AR instruction group (1.57, 95% CI [0.53, 2.60]). The group with the video instruction rated 1.57 points better on average on the Likert scale for acceptance than the group with the AR instruction. In addition, the Turkey post-hoc test showed a significant difference ($p < .05$) in acceptance between the technology group app and the group with the AR instruction (1.37, 95% CI [0.33, 2.40]). The app-instruction group rated 1.37 points higher on average on the Likert scale for acceptance than the AR-instruction group.

There were no statistically significant correlations between the video and app instruction group. Augmented reality remains far behind expectations here, as both APP instruction and video instruction were rated better. Therefore, the hypothesis H1 set up at the beginning must be rejected, as AR as the smartest technology (cf. Fig. 3) was rated worse.

H2: The higher the acceptance, the higher the service quality.

To find out whether service quality can be predicted by the acceptance of the technology used, a linear regression was performed (Table 4).

Table 4. Linear Regression – acceptance and service quality

Model Summary				
Model	R	R^2	Corrected R^2	Standard error of the estimator
1	,040[a]	0,002	-0,034	0,23876

The R^2 indicates that only 0.2% of service quality is explained by acceptance. Therefore H2 must be rejected.

To study if one or two of the three service quality criteria as defined in Eq. 1 are dependent on the technology acceptance, the following sub-hypothesis were set.

H2.1: The higher the acceptance, the lower the number of errors.

H2.2: The higher the acceptance, the higher the compliance with safety instructions.

H2.3: The higher acceptance, the lower the time required.

The correlations between acceptance and the individual factors of service quality (duration, safety, number of errors) were not statistically significant (cf. Table 5).

- Time required and acceptance correlate moderately negatively, but not statistically significant.
- Safety instructions followed and acceptance correlate weakly positively, but not statistically significant.
- Number of errors and acceptance moderately positive, but not statistically significant.

Table 5. Correlation – acceptance and duration, safety, number of errors

Correlation				
				acceptance
Pearson - Correlation	duration	Correlation coefficient		-0,244
		Sig. (2-sided)		0,194
		N		30
Spearman - Rho	safety	Correlation coefficient		0,114
		Sig. (2-sided)		0,549
		N		30
Spearman - Rho	number of errors	Correlation coefficient		0,211
		Sig. (2-sided)		0,264
		N		30

5   Conclusion, Outlook, Limitations

As improvements in information technology use shall ease the work situations and improve the service quality level, the given results are not only a help for rollout-projects, but also give advices for further developments of information technology for service operation use. The findings of this study are as summarized and pictured in Fig. 6 (in correspondence to Fig. 1).

The study showed that UTAUT is only partially an appropriate tool to predict technology acceptance in the field of industrial service operation. Three out of seven influencing factors show statistically significant and strong positive correlation. Technology acceptance by service technicians is higher the higher performance expectancy, effort expectancy and facilitating conditions are.

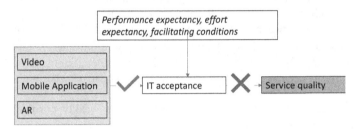

Fig. 6. Resulting frame

The study also showed that the difference of information technology (IT) acceptance is statistically significant. However, it cannot be said that the smarter the technology the higher the acceptance. Augmented reality, as the smartest technology within this study, underachieved. The expected performance and effort gains could not be achieved by AR at that point in time. Further advances in the technology implementation might lead to a shift.

The assumption that higher IT tool acceptance leads to better service quality could not be supported by the empirical data; neither for the entire indicator nor for the single quality parameters (time, safety, errors). A more detailed measure of service quality might show different results.

6 Limitations

This study is based on a small number of subjects of only 30 persons. To obtain more meaningful results, it would make sense to examine a larger sample size. This would also allow more variables to be included in the study. It could e.g. be investigated whether younger subjects show a higher acceptance towards smarter technologies than older ones.

In the augmented reality scenario, an older AR technology was used. With a more advanced, newer AR technology vehicle AR might perform better. This effect will be investigated in further studies.

The effect of technology acceptance was only measured be looking at three quality dimensions – time, error rate and safety level. However, service quality is determined by many more factors. Also are there indirect effects, like stress reduction for the service worker [19, 20], which can increase the level of customer perceived quality.

References

1. Venkatesh, V., Morris, M.G., Davis, G.B., Davis, F.D.: User acceptance of information technology – toward a unified view. MIS Quart. **27**(3), 425–478 (2003)

2. Venkatesh, V., Davis, F.D.: A theoretical extension of the technology acceptance model – four longitudinal field studies. Manag. Sci. **46**(2), 186–204 (2000)
3. Goodhue, D.: I/S attitudes: toward theoretical and definitional clarity. ACM SIGMIS Database **19**(3–4), 6–15 (1988)
4. Goodhue, D.L., Thompson, R.L.: Task-technology fit and individual performance. MIS Quart. **19**(2), 213–236 (1995)
5. Fischbein, I., Ajzen, I.: Belief, attitude, intention and behaviour: an introduction to theory and research. Philos. Rhetor. **10**(2) (1977)
6. Davis, F.D.: Perceived usefulness, perceived ease of use, and user acceptance of information technology. MIS Quart. **13**(3), 319–339 (1989)
7. Ajzen, I.: The theory of planned behavior. Organ. Behav. Hum. Decis. Proc. **50**(2), 179–211 (1991)
8. Schmenner, R.W.: How can service business survive and prosper? Sloan Manag. Rev. **27**(3), 21–32 (1986)
9. Gutsche, K., Eigenstetter, M.: Service productivity in a smart production – humans and automation in industrial maintenance. wt Werkstattstechnik online **109**(7–8), 514–521 (2019)
10. Oehmig, P.: Wie Sie eine benutzergerechte Technische Dokumentation (ein Informationsprodukt) planen, konzipieren und gestalten. Euroforum Verlag (2011)
11. Heskett, J.L., Jones, T.O., Loveman, G.W., Sasser, E., Schlesinger, L.A.: Putting the service-profit chain to work. Harv. Bus. Rev. **72**(2), 164–174 (1994)
12. Grönroos, C., Ojasalo, K.: Service productivity: toward a conceptualization of the transformation of inputs into economic results in services. J. Bus. Res. **57**(4), 414–423 (2004)
13. ISO 9000.: Quality Management Systems — Fundamentals and Vocabulary. Beuth, Berlin (2015)
14. Bruhn, M.: Qualitätsmanagement für Dienstleistungen. Springer, Heidelberg (2020)
15. Zeithaml, V.A., Parasuraman, A., Berry, L.L.: Qualitätsservice. Was Ihre Kunden erwarten – was Sie leisten müssen. Frankfurt a. M. (1992)
16. Parasuraman, A., Zeithaml, V.A., Berry, L.L.: SEVQUAL: a multiple-item scale for measuring consumer perceptions of service quality. J. Retail. **64**(1), 12–40 (1988)
17. Grönroos, C.: A Service Quality Model and its Marketing Implications. Eur. J. Mark. **18**(4), 36–44 (1984)
18. Gutsche, K., Weltin, M.: Smart tool use in knowledge intensive work situations – an information technology review. In: Leitner, C., Ganz, W., Satterfield, D., Bassano, C. (eds.) Advances in the Human Side of Service Engineering. AHFE 2021. Lecture Notes in Networks and Systems, vol. 266. Springer, Cham (2021)
19. Lazarus, R.S., Folkman, S.: Stress, Appraisal and Coping. New York (1984)
20. Dean, A.M., Rainnie, A.: Frontline employees' views on organizational factors that affect the delivery of service quality in call centers. J. Serv. Mark. **23**(5), S. 326–337 (2009)

The Elf-AR-QA System Based on IoT Cross-Media and Discussion of Emotional and Pleasure Design

Yu-Hsiung Huang[1], Chih-Wei Liao[2], and Su-Chu Hsu[3(✉)]

[1] Department of New Media Art, Taipei National University of the Arts, Taipei 11201, Taiwan
eric@techart.tnua.edu.tw
[2] International Intercollegiate Master Program – Division of Techart, National Tsing Hua University, Hsinchu 30013, Taiwan
[3] Research Center for Technology and Art, National Tsing Hua University, Hsinchu 30013, Taiwan
suchu@mx.nthu.edu.tw

Abstract. Taiwan's Hsinchu Assembly Hall is a historic building leftover from the Japanese occupation. Recently, "Memory Texture Interactive Experience Museum in Hsinchu Assembly Hall" was held after reconstruction. It integrates different technologies to allow people to learn the history and architecture of Hsinchu Assembly Hall. In this case, we developed the Interactive Elf-AR-QA system on the interactive experience museum, which is based on IoT Cross-Media System we created before. In the system, we used the knowledge of Hsinchu Assembly Hall as its data and used the smartphone as a tangible user interface. Using their own smartphones, the audience can participate with the exhibits by the "fish" and "pour" actions. The "fish" action can collect and answer question data of the exhibit art-works. The "pour" action can deliver the result into the iPad, where the audience can get the Elf number corresponding to the correct answers and then start to play the AR game based on our interactive Elf-AR-QA system in the Stone Lantern. This research used marker-based AR technology to augment cute Elf creatures on the Stone Lantern surface. In our system, we designed the "crack" pattern as the AR marker, which subtly conforms to the feature of the Stone Lantern and the demand for AR recognition. The iPad's tangible feature also allows the audience to explore the Elf creatures among the Stone Lantern.

This research integrates the cultural knowledge of Hsinchu Assembly Hall into the QA System, and according to the result audience can play with the Interactive Elf-AR system on the Stone Lantern; such application is rare in museums in Taiwan. This research also discussed emotional design and pleasure theory and produced questionnaires for verification. The result shows the Elf design's success and proves that the system did increase the motivation of the audience, which made them want to know more about the culture of Hsinchu Assembly Hall. After the experience, the audience did gain pleasure. We hope that through this kind of interactive design, we can increase the motivation to understand Taiwan's culture and history and get exciting and enjoyable experiences in the process. In the future, we also hope that this system and research can be applied to more cultural and creative industries.

© The Author(s), under exclusive license to Springer Nature Switzerland AG 2022
S. Yamamoto and H. Mori (Eds.): HCII 2022, LNCS 13306, pp. 222–237, 2022.
https://doi.org/10.1007/978-3-031-06509-5_16

Keywords: IoT cross-media · Tangible user interface · Augmented reality · Emotional design · Pleasure theory

1 Introduction

In recent years, with the improvement of the hardware conditions of mobile devices such as mobile phones, Augmented Reality (AR) technology has also been widely used in various fields. The technical characteristics of AR make it easy to combine with applications in multiple areas, such as medical, military, education, entertainment, etc. In the cultural industry, it has become a trend to apply augmented reality technology to enhance the participation experience in heritage museums.

Taiwan's Hsinchu Assembly Hall commissioned us to build a permanent "Memory Texture – Interactive Experience Hall" exhibition. The development structure of the interactive experience hall is based on the "IoT Cross-Media System" we have developed in the past and combined with AR technology to create the "Elf-AR-QA System". IoT Cross-Media System was developed by FBI Lab [1, 2]. The system is designed by combining the IoT and interactive sensing technology, which can connect the digital content of all exhibits in the exhibition hall, allowing the public to use their mobile phones to interact with the exhibits by the gestures of "fishing" and "pouring". On this basis, we designed the content of the exhibition hall into questions and let the participants fish them out with their mobile phones; then, they poured in the Stone Lantern cultural relics and got the elves who answered the correct number of questions. Finally, the participant finds the elves in the stone lantern artifact with a tablet through the AR interactive system. The system integrates several multimedia technologies and applications to stimulate the public's learning of historical monuments and architectural knowledge.

In addition, we also discussed Donald Norman's emotional design and Lionel Tiger's theory of pleasure. We conducted a questionnaire survey to analyze whether our design affects people's motivation to use during the experience and the pleasure after use. We look forward to combining the historic buildings of the Hsinchu Assembly Hall with emerging technologies to create a culturally contemporary feel to the historic buildings and give the assembly hall new life and vitality.

2 Related Work

This paper mainly explores the application of augmented reality in museums and understands whether participants can obtain pleasant feelings from it. Therefore, this chapter will consist of three parts: augmented reality, tangible user interface and design theory.

2.1 Discussion of References Related to Augmented Reality

With the development of augmented reality technology, more and more cases have been applied to cultural industries such as museums and art galleries in recent years. For example, in 2017, the Franklin Institute in Philadelphia held the Terracotta Warriors theme exhibition [3]. At that time, they combined augmented reality technology with ancient cultural relics – Terracotta Warriors; the public can directly identify the sculptures of Terracotta Warriors and Horses through the AR system in the mobile app provided by the museum and generate 3D models of the cultural relics and other Artifact details. The use of markers in augmented reality includes marker-based, marker-less, and location-based. Vuforia is an augmented reality software development kit. It used the "product photo" in the magazine as an identification reference. When a customer points the lens of the tablet computer at the magazine, the 3D image of the product will appear on the screen: model and product details [4]. IKEA, a well-known homeware retailer, has developed an app IKEA Place [5], that uses marker-less augmented reality to facilitate customers to purchase furniture. The most well-known case of location-based augmented reality is the mobile game "Pokemon Go" released by Niantic on Android and iOS platforms in 2016 [6]. Google Map also uses location-based augmented reality technology to guide users. After users turn on the navigation function in Google Map, the application will detect the user's location and use landmark-shaped icons on the screen. Signs give directions to the user [7].

This research mainly uses marker-based augmented reality. Like most of the current marker-based augmented reality applications in museums and other cultural industries, obvious markers are also used as reference objects so that users can clearly understand Know which feature points to identify as locations that can be interacted with. In this study, we specially designed several "crack marks" on the antique stone lantern sculpture as identifiable reference objects and deliberately let the marks blend into the antique stone lantern sculpture inconspicuously, in line with the stone lantern as a The mottled material characteristics of historical relics themselves. With the features of the shape of the "crack" itself, several different patterns can be designed as reference objects for AR identification. This creates a sense of anticipation in the process of exploring unknown treasures and looking for elves and a sense of surprise after finding them.

2.2   Discussion of References Related to Tangible User Interface

The research on interactive experience in this paper belongs to the application of the Tangible User Interface. Hiroshi Ishii of MIT Media Lab first introduced the concept of Tangible User Interface (TUI) in 1997. Proposed in 2009, Ishii believes that humans have mastered the complex capabilities of perceiving and manipulating objects in the physical environment, but these capabilities cannot be applied to traditional graphical user interfaces (GUIs). Therefore, Ishii proposed the Tangible User Interface (TUI), which endows digital information with tangible entities, allowing people to directly interact with virtual information in the physical environment [8]. Sifteo Cubes, designed by David Merrill and Jeevan Kalanithi, is an application of a Tangible User Interface [9]. Sifteo Cubes are a group of tiny computers with sensors, a display interface, and wireless communication functions. These small blocks, like building blocks, communicate wirelessly through sensors and can sense other small blocks adjacent to them so that they can have some interesting interactive applications with other blocks through the display interface. The ReacTable, designed by Sergi Jordà et al., is also an application of a Tangible User Interface. ReacTable is a desktop electronic musical instrument. It can generate rhythm or melody by placing tactile objects on the electronic table. In addition, objects can also interact with each other and produce different music [10].

In this research, we regard smartphones and tablets as Tangible user interfaces, allowing participants to input data through their mobile phones and hold the mobile phone to perform a "fishing" action at a designated location to obtain the question and answer questions. After answering the question, the participants held the mobile phone to do the "pour in" action to get the corresponding number of elves; the tablet computer was used to find the elves.

2.3 Discussion of References Related to Design Theory

Donald Norman takes the user's desire to use the product as a product design principle, elaborates on it, and proposes three levels of emotional design [11]: Visceral Design, Behavioral Design, and Reflective Design. In this study, we hope that the "Elf-AR-QA System" can arouse participants' desire to explore and experience actively. This study designed a questionnaire based on Donald Norman's three emotional-level design principles to examine the "Elf-AR-QA System" to analyze and understand whether our design can attract participants to use and which design elements are the key factors of influence. Lionel Tiger put forward the theory of pleasure in human emotions. He analyzed the factors and types of pleasure in human beings [12], namely physio-pleasure, socio-pleasure, psycho-pleasure, and ideo-pleasure. Based on the framework of the four pleasure theories proposed by Tiger, Patrick W. Jordan also used the four pleasure theories to reinterpret product design in 2000 [13]. This research reinterprets the concept of product design based on Patrick W. Jordan's four pleasure theories. We analyze the "Elf-AR-QA System" product design and design a questionnaire for learning about the people who visit the exhibition in the public hall., whether you can really enjoy the fun of exploration and interaction.

3 Creative Interactive Design Based on the Augmented Reality of IoT Cross-Media

3.1 Introduction to Memory Texture Interactive Experience Museum in Hsinchu Assembly Hall

In the permanent exhibition of "Memory Texture Interactive Experience Museum in Hsinchu Assembly Hall," we mainly develop "Elf-AR-QA System on IoT Cross-Media" [8]. The operation process of this system is divided into three parts, namely the mobile phone QA system, the IoT server, and the tablet AR system. After the mobile phone QA system is completed, the audience can put the mobile phone close to the induction area of the scene and make a "pour in" gesture, the data will be transferred from the mobile phone to the server-side of the IoT, and the server-side will send it to the tablet after receiving the data. Start playing. When the tablet computer receives the data from the server, according to the number of questions answered correctly by the audience, the AR game is started from a randomly obtained number of sprites. The following will explain the actual operation process of the "Elf-AR-QA System" on IoT Cross-Media:

1. After entering the exhibition hall, visit and read the content of the exhibition board, and then scan the QR Code on the exhibition board to enter the webpage to answer the questions, as shown in Fig. 1.
2. Hold the mobile phone and make the "fishing" gesture at the designated position in Fig. 2, fish out the question like a fish, and then enter the answering page on the mobile phone to start answering the question.
3. Figure 3 shows the answering page on the mobile phone. The questions include three question groups: "Documentary of the Age," "Glossary of Architecture," and "Show-case of Cultural Relics." Each question group will randomly select four questions for answering.

Fig. 1. (Left): Visiting the exhibition board at "Hsinchu Public Hall – Chronicle"

Fig. 2. (Middle): Participants fishing questions with their mobile phones

Fig. 3. (Right): Participants answering questions with their mobile phones

4. According to the number of questions answered correctly, you will get the corresponding number of "Spirit Seeds" after answering all questions, as shown in Fig. 4. Move the "elf seed" in the mobile phone to the sensing area next to the stone lantern and make a "pour in" gesture, as shown in Fig. 5, and the "elf seed" will be transferred to the iPad.
5. Pick up the iPad and start playing "Stone Lantern AR Elf," explore around the surface of the stone lantern cultural relic, and point the lens of the tablet at the "crack," and the Elf will appear, as shown in Fig. 6.
6. After finishing the game, the iPad back where it was picked up for the next participant to use.

Fig. 4. (Left): The participant gets the seeds

Fig. 5. (Middle): The participant pours the seeds with the mobile phone

Fig. 6. (Right): The participant uses the camera of the iPad to aim at the crack, Elf appears in the AR system

3.2 Design of "Interactive Elf-AR System on the Stone Lantern"

The entire exhibition hall is divided into five exhibition areas, and each exhibit in each exhibition area has a QR-Code for the public to scan directly for further introduction of the exhibits; HTTPS communication mode is adopted between the mobile phone and the webserver. Each exhibition area has a "fishing" sensor node, which allowing people to answer questions. The MQTT communication mode is used between the "fishing" sensor node and the IoT server. After answering the questions in the five exhibition areas,

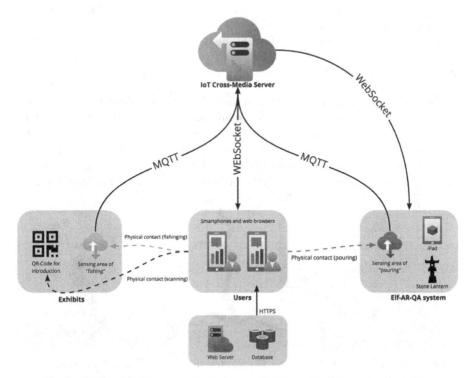

Fig. 7. Architecture diagram of IoT cross-media QA + AR system communication

the public walked to the "injection" sensor node in front of the "Stone Lantern" work to do the pouring action to obtain cute sprites; at this time, MQTT communication was also used between the "injection" sensor node and the IoT server. Model. The public picked up the tablet and pointed it at the "crack" mark on the "stone lantern" to find the elf. At this time, the AR tablet and the IoT server adopted the WebSocket communication mode. Figure 7 is the architecture diagram of the system communication we designed in the interactive experience hall.

This system uses the Unity3D game engine to create the interactive process of the game and uses the plug-in Vuforia for AR identification. Finally, it is combined with the socketIO system to link with other exhibits in the venue.

3.3 Design of "Crack" AR Marker and "Stone Lantern Elf"

This section consists of two parts. The first part is to introduce the role of the "crack" AR marker in this system. It will detail its identification principle, design concept, and production process. The second part will introduce the elf animation in the Stone Lantern interactive AR game, including appearance, action script, design concept, and background setting.

"Crack" AR Marker. This system uses marker augmented reality as the main application. Considering that the pattern recognized by AR needs to be complex enough to generate enough feature points and because the pattern on the surface of the stone lantern needs to be integrated into the shape of the stone lantern cultural relic as much as possible without being obtrusive, the system finally adopts the "crack" pattern. They are used as an AR identification mark. Figure 8 below shows the detailed pictures, identification picture, and characteristic points of one of the "crack" marks on the stone lantern.

The "crack" feature points all appear at the sharp corners of the pattern. Therefore, in the process of designing the pattern, this study tries to increase the number of pattern corners to ensure that there are enough feature points, and the relative positions of the corners between different patterns are different to a certain extent, to avoid the problem that the patterns are too similar to cause identification errors. Figure 9 below shows the location map of a total of 12 "crack" marks on the stone lantern and their numbers.

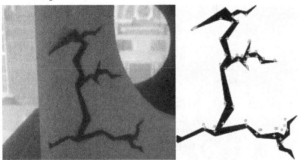 

Fig. 8. Detail of the "crack" mark (left), identification diagram and its feature points (middle)

Fig. 9. The position of the "crack" mark (right)

Design of "Stone Lantern elf". Regarding the design concept of the elf, it comes from the material and shape of the stone lantern and its characteristics as a cultural relic. The main design is to hope that the elf's appearance tends to be planted or jump out of the stone lantern, with funny animation and sound effects. We designed 12 elves to attract users to find them, hoping to inspire the public to participate in quiz learning to get more elves as rewards, as shown in Fig. 10.

Related video links: https://youtu.be/PnIw7mY7-pM.

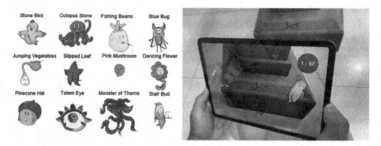

Fig. 10. Appearance and test screenshot of stone lantern elves

3.4 Discussion on Emotion and Pleasure Design

Donald Norman believes that how a product is designed and used also has a significant impact on the emotional level of the user's "desire to use." To analyze the influence of emotion on design, Donald Norman divides the emotional design into three levels to discuss, including "visceral design," "behavioral design," and "reflective design" [11]. Most discussions on emotional design focus on product analysis. However, this study believes that the concept of emotional design can also be applied to the design and analysis of "interactive experience systems."

A. **Visceral Design**

   It discusses the most intuitive feeling of design. Donald Norman believes that a good design at the instinctual level should attract the user's attention by making the user curious and then using the product. In this study, the funny appearance animation and sound of "Stone Lantern elf" can attract visitors to go and learn more about the exhibit and how to interact with it. The "stone lantern elf" design can immediately attract the user's attention, so it meets the design requirements at the instinct level.

B. **Behavioral Design**

   It mainly discusses the use of the product. Donald Norman believes that good behavioral design is about making the user use the product easily and smoothly, thereby producing a pleasant experience. In this study, the smooth operation process and the easy-to-understand interface design can allow users to play smoothly, thus meeting the design requirements at the behavioral level.

C. **Reflective Design**

It discusses the message, cultural meaning, etc., that the product designer wants to convey through the product. In this research, the use of an enjoyable interactive experience allows visitors to gain a little knowledge of Hsinchu Guildhall after the interactive play experience, conveying the original intention of the historical connotation of the Guildhall, thus satisfying the reflection level in emotional design.

Anthropologist Lionel Tiger divided human pleasure into four aspects: physio-pleasure, socio-pleasure, psycho-pleasure, and ideo-pleasure [12]. Patrick W. Jordan quoted the concept of Tiger's four pleasures framework, reinterpreted the meaning of these four pleasures in design, and described how to make users feel pleasure after using the product through product design [13]. It will be explained in detail below.

A. **Physio-Pleasure**

"Physio-Pleasure" starts from the human body senses, such as hearing, touch, smell, taste, etc. In product design, physical pleasure can also arise from using a product. In this study, we designed "stone lanterns elf" and gave them lifelike animation and sound to attract the audience and bring them physical pleasure.

B. **Socio-Pleasure**

Socio-Pleasure, as the name suggests, refers to the pleasure that can be produced when socializing, including belonging, social-enabler, and community self-identification. From the perspective of product design, the connection between the product and the user shapes the user's social identity. In this study, we created a topic through the experience of finding spirits, allowing visitors to communicate with others and gain social pleasure from it.

C. **Psycho-Pleasure**

"Psycho-Pleasure" comes from the pleasures of cognition, discovery, anticipatory psychology, etc., that can satisfy such needs. From the product design perspective, the ease of use, usability, and other product factors can help psychological pleasure. In this research, we use the intuitive operation of the system interface and the smooth operation of the system functions to satisfy the audience's psychological pleasure for the "Stone Lantern Elf Interactive AR System."

D. **Ideo-Pleasure**

"Ideo-Pleasure" comes from feelings that cannot be brought by the other three pleasures, such as aesthetics, culture, and value. From the product design perspective, the product's cultural connotation, the concepts conveyed behind it, and the added value can all satisfy the sense of pleasure. In this study, visitors learn new knowledge through play and gain an understanding of fulfillment in the process, resulting in a pleasant feeling.

3.5   Analysis and Discussion of Questionnaire Results

Limitations of Questionnaire Research. "Memory Texture Interactive Experience Museum in Hsinchu Assembly Hall" was completed in May 2020. However, due to the COVID-19 epidemic, the museum could not be officially opened, which also made the evaluation of this study difficult. In consideration of compromise, this time, we used a small sample size of 24 people, 16 women and 8 men. And in the subsequent statistical analysis, the single-sample T-test suitable for a small sample size was used as the statistical method for analysis.

Analysis of Descriptive Statistics of Questionnaire Results. To carry out quantitative analysis, the answer is digitized in the form of scores in this study, among which "very much" is 3 points, "yes" is 2 points, "not quite" is 1 point, and "nothing at all" is 0

Table 1. Descriptive statistics for men and women of the questionnaire results

Questionnaire content	Applicable theory	Minimum		Maximum value	Average	Standard deviation
1. Does the appearance of the stone lantern attract your attention and want to interact with it?	Emotion Design: Visceral Design	Male	1	3	2.08	0.654
		Female				
2. Does the "elf animation" in the shape of a stone lantern attract you and make you want to interact with it?	Emotion Design: Visceral Design	1		3	2.25	0.676
3. Is the user interface design of the "Stone Lantern elf Interactive AR System" easy to operate?	Emotion Design: Behavioral Design	1		3	2.13	0.537
4. Does the elf animation appearing in the "crack" of the stone lantern attract you?	Emotion Design: Reflective Design	0		3	2.42	0.830
5. Does the way of "getting the number of elves" as a reward motivate you to learn about the historical background of Hsinchu Assembly Hall?	Emotion Design: Reflective Design	1		3	2.42	0.584

(*continued*)

Table 1. (*continued*)

Questionnaire content	Applicable theory	Minimum		Maximum value	Average	Standard deviation
6. Did the experience of finding elves with a group of participants bring you a pleasant feeling of "community communication"?	Pleasure Theory: Socio-Pleasure	1	3		2.17	0.702
7. Does elf's "appearance animation" and "sound" design bring you a pleasant feeling?	Pleasure Theory: Physio-Pleasure	1	3		2.46	0.658
8. During the experience, different elves will appear in "different cracks." Does this give you a sense of expectation and surprise?	Pleasure Theory: Psycho-Pleasure	0	3		2.46	0.833
9. In this system, the background knowledge of Hsinchu Assembly Hall was designed as a question, and the number of correct answers to the question was converted into the number of elves, and then participates in catching the elves in an interesting AR interactive way. Does this design bring you a pleasant feeling?	Pleasure Theory: Ideo-Pleasure	1	3		2.21	0.658

(*continued*)

Table 1. (*continued*)

Questionnaire content	Applicable theory	Minimum		Maximum value	Average	Standard deviation
10. Is the interactive way of elf appearing when you point the "iPad camera at the crack" that impresses you?	Pleasure Theory: Ideo-Pleasure	1	3		2.33	0.637

points. Table 1 is the descriptive statistics of the questionnaire, including the minimum, maximum, mean, and standard deviation of each item in the 24 valid samples.

In Table 1, we can find and get some analysis results:

(1) Question 1: "Does the appearance of the stone lantern attract your attention and want to interact with it?" The average score obtained is 2.08, which is the lowest score in this statistics, indicating that in the design of the instinct level, the stone lantern. The shape itself did not attract much attention from the participants. This result was somewhat unexpected. After analysis and discussion, we feel that this result is also good. When the participants picked up the iPad, they found that the stone lanterns that did not attract attention at first could run out of cute elves, and the surprise generated by such unexpected contrasts would be tenser. And this also echoes question 8: "During the experience, different elves will appear in "different cracks." Does this give you a sense of expectation and surprise?" and question 10 "Is the interactive way of elf appearing when you point the "iPad camera at the crack" that impresses you?", the two questions received an average score of 2.46 and 2.33 respectively, both of which are relatively high scores, indicating that the participant's experience of the generation of elves in the crack of the stone lantern is rather satisfied and pleasant on a psychological and conscious level.

(2) In the table, the questions that mention the elf have relatively high scores, including question 2: "Does the "elf animation" in the shape of a stone lantern attract you and make you want to interact with it?", Question 4: "Does the elf animation appearing in the "crack" of the stone lantern attract you?", Question 7: "Does elf's "appearance animation" and "sound" design bring you a pleasant feeling?" and Question 8: "During the experience, different elves will appear in "different cracks." "Does this give you a sense of expectation and surprise?", the three questions scored 2.25, 2.42, 2.46 and 2.46, respectively. This shows that the design of the elf character is very successful. The designs in "Visceral Design" and "Reflective Design" are attractive to participants and motivate them to operate and use the system. It does bring participants a high psychological and physical pleasure after the operation.

(3) Question 3: "Is the user interface design of the Stone Lantern elf Interactive AR System easy to operate?" got a low score of 2.13, and its standard deviation of

0.537 was the lowest in the table. It means that participants generally believed that although the interface design was indeed easy to operate and use, it was not very attractive, and there was still room for improvement.

(4) Question 6: "Did the experience of finding elves with a group of participants bring you a pleasant feeling of community communication?" The score was 2.17. It means that the participants did not derive much social pleasure from the system. However, the standard deviation of 0.702 for this question indicates that the participants' views are biased towards polarization, which falls short of the expectations of this study. Our review will cause such a phenomenon, mainly because the venue cannot be opened for participants to experience in a group way due to the epidemic situation. As a result, the participants cannot officially open a group of people to participate in the exhibition hall. The interviewed participants are very. It is difficult to understand the pleasant feeling of "community communication" brought by this system in community communication and interaction.

(5) In this questionnaire, there are questions about the design of elves to encourage participants to understand the culture of the Hsinchu Assembly Hall. Question 5: "Does the way of getting the number of elves as a reward motivate you to learn about the historical background of Hsinchu Assembly Hall?", and Question 9: "In this system, the background knowledge of Hsinchu Assembly Hall was designed as a question, and the number of correct answers to the question was converted into the number of elves, and then participates in catching the elves in an interesting AR interactive way. Does this design bring you a pleasant feeling?" get The scores were 2.42 and 2.21. The standard deviations were 0.584 and 0.658, respectively, which indicated that the participants had the same opinion. Most of them agreed that on the "Reflective Design" design, the elf could indeed provide incentives to attract them to understand the culture of Hsinchu Assembly Hall and in the "Reflective Design" design. Ideo-Pleasure can also be obtained during this process.

(6) There is a rather interesting phenomenon in the table. Question 4: "Does the elf animation appearing in the "crack" of the stone lantern attract you?" and Question 8 "During the experience, different elves will appear in "different cracks." Does this give you a sense of expectation and surprise?" there are answers with 0 points. That is, they do not agree at all, and this also causes the standard deviation to increase. The difference between these two questions and other questions is that they both mentioned "cracks." The results showed that the design of the crack itself did not bring the participants attractiveness or pleasure after the operation, but different sprites appeared in various cracks. The above is to get a sense of surprise to the participants, indicating that the combined use of cracks and sprites is still popular with participants.

This questionnaire also uses the "Single-Sample T-Test" for statistical analysis, mainly because the sample size of the questionnaire is small (less than 30). Moreover, this study hopes to statistically understand the specific extent of the overall interactive experience of the "Elf-AR-QA System" that produces attractive and pleasant feelings for ordinary participants. According to the questionnaire's content, if the average value of the questionnaire results is greater than or equal to 2, it means that the system has a pleasant feeling or desire to use the system; Use desire. This study sets the null hypothesis H0: mean = 1.9. In statistics, the goal of statistical analysis is to reject the null hypothesis and express the degree of rejection through a significant value, where the smaller the significant value, the higher the degree of rejection. In general, if the significant value is lower than 0.05, it means that the significance is high, that is, rejecting the null hypothesis.

Based on the above, under the premise that the average scores obtained by this questionnaire question are all greater than 2, the lower the significant value, the higher the degree of recognition of the general participants. The statistical results are shown in Table 2. The table shows the significant value of each question and the difference between the average and 1.9 when the test value is 1.9.

Table 2. One-sample T-test for the questionnaire results of "Elf-AR-QA system"

Questionnaire content	Test value = 1.9	
	Salience	Mean difference
1. Does the appearance of the stone lantern attract your attention and want to interact with it?	0.183	0.183
2. Does the "elf animation" in the shape of a stone lantern attract you and make you want to interact with it?	0.018	0.350
3. Is the user interface design of the "Stone Lantern elf Interactive AR System" easy to operate?	0.052	0.225
4. Does the elf animation appearing in the "crack" of the stone lantern attract you?	0.006	0.517
5. Does the way of "getting the number of elves" as a reward motivate you to learn about the historical background of Hsinchu Assembly Hall?	0.000	0.517
6. Did the experience of finding elves with a group of participants bring you a pleasant feeling of "community communication"?	0.076	0.267
7. Does elf's "appearance animation" and "sound" design bring you a pleasant feeling?	0.000	0.558
8. During the experience, different elves will appear in "different cracks." Does this give you a sense of expectation and surprise?	0.003	0.558
9. In this system, the background knowledge of Hsinchu Assembly Hall was designed as a question, and the number of correct answers to the question was converted into the number of elf, and then participates in catching the elves in an interesting AR interactive way. Does this design bring you a pleasant feeling?	0.031	0.308
10. Is the interactive way of elf appearing when you point the "iPad camera at the crack" that impresses you?	0.003	0.433

Combining the data in the table above, we get the following analysis results:

(1) According to the statistical results in Table 2, question 4: "Does the elf animation appearing in the "crack" of the stone lantern attract you?" and question 5: "Does the way of "getting" both belong to "Reflective Design" the number of elves" as a reward motivate you to learn about the historical background of Hsinchu Assembly Hall?". The mean difference for both questions was 0.517; in terms of significance, question 5 was 0.000 less than question 4's 0.006. Comprehensively displayed in "Reflective Design," the system uses elves as an incentive to motivate people to understand the culture of Hsinchu Assembly Hall, which is more attractive to the general public.

(2) In Question 7: "Does elf's "appearance animation" and "sound" design bring you a pleasant feeling?" and Question 8: "During the experience, different elves will appear in "different cracks." Does this give you a sense of expectation and surprise?", the average difference between the two questions is also 0.558. However, in terms of significance, the 0.000 of question 7 is less than 0.003 of question 8, which means that the psychological pleasure brought to the public by the two, the appearance and sound design of the elf itself is more effective than the sense of expectation and surprise created by multiple elves. Make the people happy.

(3) Question 5: "Does the way of "getting the number of elves" as a reward motivate you to learn about the historical background of Hsinchu Assembly Hall?" and Question 7: "Does elf's "appearance animation" and "sound" design bring you a pleasant feeling?", the scores for both questions are 0.000, which are the two items with the best significance in the table. The results of this questionnaire once again verified the success of the elf design and also verified that the elf can effectively drive the desire of the public to know more about the culture of Hsinchu Assembly Hall.

The research results show that in terms of the desire to use "emotional design," the general public's game reward mechanism for the "Elf-AR-QA System" using "the number of elves obtained" as an incentive has indeed stimulated the public's motivation to learn the Hsinchu Public Hall. And the use of the low attractive "stone lantern appearance" to lay out the two interactive elements of "elf animation" and "elf appearing in cracks" has also responded quite well to the public. It has a high appeal and shows the success of the pixie exterior styling design. However, the results of the public's "AR system user interface design" were not as expected, indicating that there is still room for improvement in the future.

4   Conclusion

The "Elf-AR-QA System" of this research is based on the IoT Cross-Media System. It is connected with a question answering system with historical and cultural knowledge as the main content, providing the public with a pleasant interactive experience and incentives for active learning. Our system generates object links for multiple exhibitions works in the museum, allowing the public to use their mobile phones to use the gestures of "fishing" and "pouring" to obtain the questions of the exhibit. We also used "Stone Lantern AR Elf" as a reward for completing their answers. Based on Lionel Tiger's four pleasure theories and Donald Norman's three-level effective design, we design related questions of the "Elf-AR-QA System" to conduct a questionnaire survey for the public. We verified that the system can really bring them the incentives to participate and the pleasure after participation through the questionnaire.

This study used marker-based augmented reality, and we hope to change it to a marker-free augmented reality in the future. We hope to increase the public experience of watching the elf animation, such as allowing the elf to travel through the stone lantern or interact with the public. In the future, we will continue to develop the multiplayer system so that the sprites found by users can be interchanged. It will increase the fun of interaction.

Recently many IoT and augmented reality applications appear in museums or cultural monuments. We hope that our executive experience can be applied to more fields in the future. We look forward to combining different media in the future to create more interesting interactive methods, which can be applied to exhibitions or performances or even other cultural and creative industries.

References

1. Liu, S.-T., Hsu, S.-C., Huang, Y.-H.: Data Paradigm Shift in Cross-Media IoT System. In: Yamamoto, S., Mori, H. (eds.) HCII 2020. LNCS, vol. 12185, pp. 479–490. Springer, Cham (2020). https://doi.org/10.1007/978-3-030-50017-7_36
2. FBI Lab. In 2019 Tsing Hua Effects - IoT Cross-Media Technology and Art Festival. https://techart.nthu.edu.tw/THE2019/. Last accessed 28 Sep 2021
3. Franklin Institute. Terracotta Warrior Exhibition. https://www.fi.edu/augmented-reality. Last accessed 28 Sep 2021
4. Vuforia Engine. Develop AR Experiences With Vuforia Engine. https://www.ptc.com/en/products/vuforia/vuforia-engine. Last accessed 24 Sep 2021
5. Inter IKEA Systems. IKEA Place. https://apps.apple.com/us/app/ikea-place/id1279244498#?platform=iphone. Last accessed 24 Sep 2021
6. Niantic, Inc. Pokemon Go. https://apps.apple.com/tw/app/pok%C3%A9mon-go/id1094591345. Last accessed 29 Sep 2021
7. Google. Augmented Reality. https://arvr.google.com/ar/. Last accessed 29 Sep 2021
8. Ishii, H., Ullmer, B.: Tangible bits: towards seamless interfaces between people, bits and atoms. In: Proceedings of the ACM SIGCHI Conference on Human factors in computing systems, Atlanta, GA, USA, 22–27 Mar (1997)
9. Merrill, D., Kalanithi, J.: Siftables: toward sensor network user interfaces. In: Proceedings of the 1st International Conference on Tangible and Embedded Interaction (TEI 2007), Baton Rouge, Louisiana, USA, 15–17 Feb (2007)
10. Jorda, S., Geiger, G., Alonso, M.: The reacTable: exploring the synergy between live music performance and tabletop tangible interfaces. In: Proceedings of the 1st International Conference on Tangible and Embedded Interaction (TEI 2007), Baton Rouge, Louisiana, USA, 15–17 Feb (2007)
11. Norman, D.: Emotional Design: Why We Love or Hate Everyday Things. Basic Books, New York (2005)
12. Tiger, L.: The Pursuit of Pleasure. Taylor & Francis, London (1992)
13. Jordan, P.: W: Designing Pleasurable Products: An Introduction to the New Human Factors. Taylor & Francis, London, London (2000)

Natural Involvement to Video Conference Through ARM-COMS

Teruaki Ito[✉] and Tomio Watanabe

Faculty of Computer Science and System Engineering, Okayama Prefectural University, 111 Kuboki, Soja 719-1197, Okayama, Japan
tito@ss.oka-pu.ac.jp

Abstract. The authors have proposed an idea of augmented tele-presence system called ARM-COMS (ARm-supported eMbodied COmmunication Monitor System), which detects the orientation of a subject face by face-tracking based on image processing technique, and mimics the head motion of a remote person to behave as if its avatar makes interaction during video communication. In addition to that, ARM-COMS makes appropriate reactions by audio signals during talk when a remote person speaks even without any significant motion in video communication.

Based on the basic idea of ARM-COMS, this study implemented an advanced prototype system using ROS platform for natural video conference involvement. This paper describes the prototype system developed in this study, shows how the basic procedure was implemented, and discusses the natural involvement targeted by this approach.

Keywords: Embodied communication · Augmented tele-presence robotic arm · Robot operating system · Natural involvement

1 Introduction

The impact of pandemic occurred in 2019 and spread worldwide has dramatically changed people's lifestyle. Under these circumstances, personal video communication tools [1] are now commonly used by many people not only for personal communication but also business meeting, conference, telework, healthcare [14], etc. Considering the expansion of Society 5.0 [21] technologies [12], further enhancement of function in communication [10] is being expected by enhanced ICT (Information and Communication Technology) technologies, such as AR/VR or Metaverse [2] tools. However, video communication tools still leave several critical issues, such as the lack of tele-presence feeling for participants, the lack of relationship feeling during video communication as opposed to a typical face-to-face communication.

This study focuses on the idea of motion-enhancement display where physical motion corresponding to the virtual content shown on a monitor screen provides a sense of reality. For example, physical rotation of the monitor device showing a rotating football gives much more sense of reality than just showing a rolling football on the monitor screen.

S. Yamamoto and H. Mori (Eds.): HCII 2022, LNCS 13306, pp. 238–246, 2022.
https://doi.org/10.1007/978-3-031-06509-5_17

This study proposes an idea of motion-enhanced display applied to video communication system, and developing a system called ARM-COMS (ARm-supported eMbodied COmmunication Monitor System) [6, 8, 21] for human-computer interaction through remote individuals' connection with augmented tele-presence systems. The challenge of this idea is to use the human body movement of a remote person as a non-verbal message [4] for sharing the connected communication, and to design a cyber-physical media using ARM-COMS for connected remote communication [6].

After briefly explaining the research background, this paper describes the system framework which is the goal of this research. Then, this paper introduces the prototype system which is currently under development, report the results of operation experiments conducted using this prototype system, and discusses the natural interaction in video conference system through ARM-COMS.

2   Research Background

Personal video communication tools are commonly used by many people not only for personal communication but also business meeting, conference, telework, etc. However, these communication tools address three types of critical issues, which are the lack of tele-presence feeling for participants, the lack of space sharing in communication, and the lack of connected feeling during video communication as opposed to a typical face-to-face communication.

As for the lack of tele-presence feeling for participants, various ideas of robot-based remote communication systems have been proposed, such as tele-presence robots. Primitive functions, such as face image display of an operator, tele-operation to move around, or tele-manipulation are available by explicitly remote-control.

The lack of space sharing in communication is another open issue. Virtual avatar is a promising approach to share the virtual space instead of physical space. Anthropomorphization [18] is a new idea to show the telepresence of a remote person in communication system. Even though the physical space sharing is not possible, virtual space sharing is available.

The lack of connected feeling with talking partners, is another big challenge in remote video communication [24]. The author focuses on an idea of enhanced motion display where physical motion corresponding to the virtual content shown on a monitor screen provides a sense of reality. For example, physical rotation of the monitor device showing a rotating football gives a sense of reality than just showing a rolling football on the monitor screen. The active display has the effect of strengthening the presence by emphasizing the movement of physical objects. Recently, an idea of robotic arm-type systems draws researchers' attention [25]. For example, Kubi [9], which is a non-mobile arm type robot, allows the remote user to "look around" during video communication by way of commanding Kubi where to aim the tablet with an intuitive remote control over the net. However, this motion is operated by explicitly remote-control.

This study applies the idea of active display to video communication system where the motion of the talker on the other side is the trigger to physically control the display motion. Figure 1 shows the basic idea of ARM-COMS, where the active display on the right side is automatically controlled by the head-motion of the talker on the left side. The subject and ARM-COMS are located in physically separated locations.

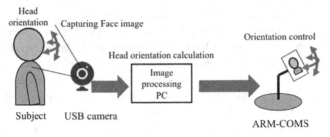

Fig. 1. Basic idea of ARM-COMS

As opposed to the original idea of motion-enhanced active display, the object on the screen is the remote person shown as Subject B in Fig. 2 with whom Subject A communicates. In this idea, this motion-enhanced display utilizes the display itself as the communication media which mimics the motion of human head to enhance presence in remote communication.

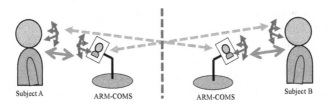

Fig. 2. Basic interaction in video conference through ARM-COMS

The idea has been implemented as an augmented tele-presence system called ARM-COMS as shown in Fig. 2 [23]. In order to mimic the head motion using the display [4], ARM-COMS detects the orientation of a face by face-detection tool [19] based on an image processing technique [6]. However, ARM-COMS does not make appropriate reactions if a remote talker speaks without head motion in explicit motion. In order to solve this problem, a voice signal usage [11] in local interaction is used so that ARM-COMS makes an appropriate action [7] even when the remote partner does not make any head motion.

3   System Reconfiguration

3.1   Basic Concept

ARM-COMS is composed of a tablet PC and a desktop robotic arm. The table PC in ARM-COMS is a typical ICT device and the desktop robotic arm works as a manipulator of the tablet, of which position and movements are autonomously manipulated based on the behavior of a human user who communicates with remote person through ARM-COMS. This autonomous manipulation of ARM-COMS is controlled by the head movement, which can be recognized by a general USB camera by the idea of FaceNET

[20]. Then it is processed by the image processing library OpenCV [16], the face detection tool OpenFace [17], which uses Constrained Local Network Field (CLNF) composed of point distribution mode, patch expert, and fitting. Then, an image analysis for face detection is conducted by Haar Cascade face detector, which uses difference in brightness using a variety size of rectangles. Then 68 landmarks are defined using dlib library [3], and orientation of subject head is estimated by OpenFace tool. Using this orientation data, ARM-COMS can be controlled.

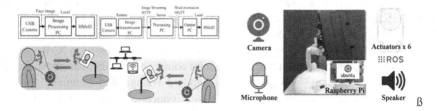

Fig. 3. Basic framework of ARM-COMS system

In this study, an extended design of robotic arm system was studied and implemented as shown in Fig. 3. The manipulator of the robotic arm is composed of six sets of servo motors with a motor controller, single board computer installed Ubuntu [13, 22], equipped with a speaker and a microphone, and a camera.

3.2 System Configuration for a Prototype System

The original prototype of ARM-COMS was implemented based on MQTT communication process environment. In this study, the extended prototype was implemented using ROS (Robot Operating System) [5] middleware. ROS provides a variety of robot operation tools [15], including hardware abstraction, device drivers, libraries, visualization tools, message communication packages, etc., which help developers to build robot applications in an effective manner. For this study, a new configuration using ROS was

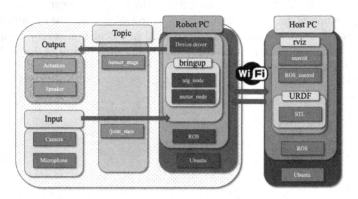

Fig. 4. ROS-based configuration of ARM-COMS system

designed based on the assignment of the roles between the host PC and the robot PC as shown in Fig. 4.

In order to use rviz simulator [19], 3D model for ARM-COMS was designed and built using 3D CAD software as shown in the left figure of Fig. 5. Then, the assembly model completed by adjusting the size, position, and axial direction with Blender software is shown in the middle figure of Fig. 5. This model is identical to the physical model shown in the right figure of Fig. 5.

The completed model data cannot be used as it is in rviz simulator. It is required to create a model definition program called URDF (Unified Robotics Description Format) [23] in the ROS workspace so that the model data for each part could be called in rviz. URDF is a program written in XML format, which is a markup language for describing the appearance and structure of sentences. 3D models can be expressed in XML, which defines the link representing each part and the joint composed of links. The above model data was moved to the same package as STL (Standard Triangulated Language) format, and the data was referenced directly from URDF. Connection type of each part at the joint was defined as fixed or variable. In variable type connection, a movable object was specified from the parent-child connection relation, and its movable direction was defined. In this way, 3D model of ARM-COMS was manipulated in rviz simulater.

Fig. 5. CAD model, Blender model, and physical model of ARM-COMS system

In the control of the robot arm, the control of moving the tip of the arm to a certain point is normally performed. By controlling the arm by inverse kinematics, the movement between two points at the tip can be made smooth and short. Since the motion trajectory of the 6-axis robot arm has various conditions and its calculation is very complicated, this study uses the motion trajectory creation plug-in called moveit of the ROS tool to automatically calculate on rviz.

Fig. 6. rviz simulation for ARM-COMS positioning

Operation of the 6-axis actuators was verified using the rviz simulator as shown in Fig. 6. Target posture and motion planning were designed by GUI operation as shown in Fig. 6. Moving the light blue sphere using dragging operation with a mouse device, the parameters of the arm are automatically calculated so that the tip (display) of the model positioned to the center of the sphere.

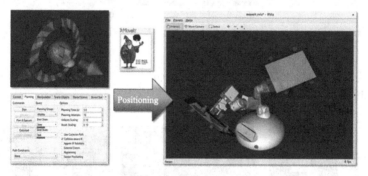

Fig. 7. Positioning definition for ARM-COMS

It was confirmed that the robot arm operates normally on the simulation by executing the procedure defined as mentioned in Fig. 7, and that the robot moves from the start posture to the target posture over several tens of frames. Figure 8 shows how the positioning was defined.

Fig. 8. Confirmation of ARM-COMS positioning

4   Experiment and Future Work

Basic motion definition was set to ARM-COMS with moveit definition, which includes one actuator motion such as "Nodding", "Sideway-shake" or "Head-tilting", and two actuators motion such as "Lean-forward", "Vertical motion", or "Diagonal upward" as shown in Fig. 9.

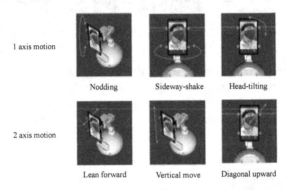

1 axis motion	Nodding	Sideway-shake	Head-tilting
2 axis motion	Lean forward	Vertical move	Diagonal upward

Fig. 9. Predefined motion examples of ARM-COMS

The predefined motion of "Nodding", for example, corresponds to the nodding of a human subject as shown in Fig. 10.

Fig. 10. Implemented action of ARM-COMS motion as "Nodding"

In the previous study, ARM-COMS motion was dynamically generated by the head motion of a subject using the face tracking program based on the image processing technique. This means that ARM-COMS mimics the head-motion of its master subject as if it were an avatar. Since the human subject does not always make head-motion explicitly, tiny motion needs to be amplified, which makes the noise inclusion in ARM-COMS motion. Voice signal is also used to generate a motion when explicit head-motion is not recognized.

Figure 11 shows an example of video conference interaction based on the dynamically generated ARM-COMS motion in such a way as mentioned above. In this example, head-motion as well as local and remote voice signals [11] were used to generate the motion of ARM-COMS. It was confirmed that the interaction with ARM-COMS is very straight and corresponding to the human subject quite well. However, it was very difficult to control the motion. Low noise filtering allows too much sensitive motion, whereas high noise filtering makes the reaction dull. One solution would be a combination of dynamically generated motion and predefined motion. However, there are many open issues for this combination of motion.

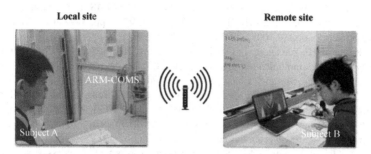

Local site   **Remote site**

Fig. 11. Video conference interaction through ARM-COMS

The next step in this study is to make an objective evaluation on the impression of the predefined motion using a Kansei engineering approach to generate a natural motion which would allow a natural video conference interaction through ARM-COMS. Then, further study will continue to design a method to make an appropriate combination of dynamic generated motion with predefined ones.

5   Concluding Remarks

This study focuses on the idea of motion-enhancement display where physical motion corresponding to the virtual content shown on a monitor screen provides a sense of reality. Previous study worked the first prototype of ARM-COMS and implemented this idea. This study implemented an extended prototype system using ROS platform and evaluated the predefined motion with a simulation experiment. This prototype system will be the experimental platform for the next step of this study.

Acknowledgement. This work was partly supported by JSPS KAKENHI Grant Numbers JP19K12082 and Original Research Grant 2021 of Okayama Prefectural University. The author would like to acknowledge Dr.Takashi Oyama, Mr.Shuto Misawa, Mr.Kengo Sadakane for implementing the basic modules, and all members of Kansei Information Engineering Labs at Okayama Prefectural University for their cooperation to conduct the experiments.

References

1. Bertrand, C., Bourdeau, L.: Research interviews by Skype: a new data collection method. In: Esteves, J. (Ed.) Proceedings from the 9th European Conference on Research Methods, pp. 70–79. IE Business School, Spain (2010)
2. Dionisio, J.D.N., Burns III, W.G., Gilbert, R.: 3D virtual worlds and the metaverse: Current status and future possibilities. ACM Comput. Surv. **45**(3), 1–38. Article no. 34. https://doi.org/10.1145/2480741.2480751

3. Dlib c++ library.: http://dlib.net/

4. Ekman, P., Friesen, W.V.: The repertoire or nonverbal behavior: categories, origins, usage, and coding. Semiotica **1**, 49–98 (1969)

5. Gerkey B., Smart, W., Quigley, M.: Programming Robots with ROS. O'Reilly Media (2015)

6. Ito, T., Watanabe, T.: Motion Control Algorithm of ARM-COMS for Entrainment Enhancement. In: Yamamoto, S. (ed.) HIMI 2016. LNCS, vol. 9734, pp. 339–346. Springer, Cham (2016). https://doi.org/10.1007/978-3-319-40349-6_32

7. Ito, T., Kimachi, H., Watanabe, T.: Combination of Local Interaction with Remote Interaction in ARM-COMS Communication. In: Yamamoto, S., Mori, H. (eds.) HCII 2019. LNCS, vol. 11570, pp. 347–356. Springer, Cham (2019). https://doi.org/10.1007/978-3-030-22649-7_28

8. Ito, T., Oyama, T., Watanabe, T.: Smart Speaker Interaction Through ARM-COMS for Health Monitoring Platform. In: Yamamoto, S., Mori, H. (eds.) HCII 2021. LNCS, vol. 12766, pp. 396–405. Springer, Cham (2021). https://doi.org/10.1007/978-3-030-78361-7_30

9. Kubi.: https://www.revolverobotics.com

10. Kumar, A., Haider, Y., Kumar, M., et al.: Using WhatsApp as a quick-access personal logbook for maintaining clinical records and follow-up of orthopedic patients. Cureus **13**(1), e12900 (2021). https://doi.org/10.7759/cureus.12900

11. Lee, A., Kawahara, T.: Recent development of open-source speech recognition engine Julius. In: Asia-Pacific Signal and Information Processing Association Annual Summit and Conference (APSIPA ASC) (2009)

12. Lokshina, I., Lanting, C.: A Qualitative Evaluation of IoT-Driven eHealth: Knowledge Management, Business Models and Opportunities, Deployment and Evolution. In: Kryvinska, N., Greguš, M. (eds.) Data-Centric Business and Applications. LNDECT, vol. 20, pp. 23–52. Springer, Cham (2019). https://doi.org/10.1007/978-3-319-94117-2_2

13. Helmke, M., Elizabech, J., Rey, J.A.: Official Ubuntu Book, 9th edn. Pearson (2016)

14. Medical Alert Advice.: www.medicalalertadvice.com. Accessed on 23 Feb 2021

15. Quigley, M., Gerkey, B., Smart, W.D.: Programming Robots with ROS: A Practical Introduction to the Robot Operating System. O'Reilly Media (2015)

16. OpenCV.: http://opencv.org/

17. OpenFace API Documentation.: http://cmusatyalab.github.io/openface/

18. Osawa, T., Matsuda, Y., Ohmura, R., Imai, M.; Embodiment of an agent by anthropomorphization of a common object. Int. J. Web Intell. Agent Syst. **10**, 345–358 (2012)

19. Rviz.: https://carla.readthedocs.io/projects/ros-bridge/en/latest/rviz_plugin/

20. Schoff, F., Kalenichenko, D., Philbin, J.: FaceNet: a unified embedding for face recognition and clustering.In: IEEE Conf. on CVPR 2015, pp. 815–823 (2015)

21. Society 5.0.: https://www.japan.go.jp/abenomics/_userdata/abenomics/pdf/society_5.0.pdf. Accessed on 23 Feb 2021

22. Ubuntu.: https://www.ubuntu.com/

23. urdf/XML/Transmission.: http://wiki.ros.org/urdf/XML/Transmission. Accessed on 16 Feb 2020

24. Watanabe, T.: Human-entrained embodied interaction and communication technology. In: Fukuda, S. (eds) Emotional Engineering. Springer, London. https://doi.org/10.1007/978-1-84996-423-4_9 (2011)

25. Wongphati, M., Matsuda, Y., Osawa, H., Imai, M.: Where do you want to use a robotic arm? And what do you want from the robot ? In: International Symposium on Robot and Human Interactive Communication, pp. 322–327 (2012)

Analysis of Nonverbal Interaction Among Competitive Ballroom Dance Couple

Kinesiology and Time-Frequency Analysis

Yosuke Kinoe[(⊠)] and Mari Sato

Hosei University, 2-17-1 Fujimi, Chiyoda City, Tokyo 102-8160, Japan
kinoe@hosei.ac.jp

Abstract. This paper describes an empirical study that investigated non-verbal interactions among a competitive ballroom dance couple. We proposed a new methodology for empirical dance research, which combines the precise 3D motion analysis of dancing with time-frequency analysis. Two skilled competitive ballroom dancers' couple participated. Dancers' 3D movements while dancing the first half of the Natural Turn of the Waltz following its preparation steps were captured using Mocap. The analysis revealed insightful findings.

The meaningful non-verbal interactions among a dancing couple were identified at least at the timings just before they initiated or just before they changed their dancing movements significantly and synchronously. The prime modality of the interactions was somatosensation (tactile/pressure sensation).

The results include that: (a) the couple could feel each other's movements whose frequencies over 0.4 Hz became almost completely quiet, at least at the leader's right shoulder via body contact and at the partner's right temple at the timing (e.g. 0.8 s) just before they initiated dancing sequence simultaneously; (b) the leader made a lead communication with very slight movements less than a few millimeters forward at least at both wrists of either side simultaneously, so that the partner could feel those slight changes of the pressure via the body contacts, at the timing (e.g. 0.6 s) just before the couple initiated their large steps for making a turn. This study indicated that the stable closed hold with light constant body contacts enabled very sensitive non-verbal interactions of a faster style among a dancing couple.

Our methodology was effective to identify precisely particularly slight non-verbal interactions among a couple and the timing of its occurrence.

Keywords: Kinesiology · Non-verbal communication · Ballroom dance · Time-frequency analysis

1 Introduction

Phenomena of dancing comprise two basic components: spatial movements and temporal transformations. It develops in space and time [14]. In this paper, we proposed a new methodology for empirical dance research, which combines those two components: the precise 3D movement analysis of dancing and time-frequency analysis. That was quite effective to investigate particularly the timing and harmonization of dancing movements of competitive ballroom dance.

Dance is a fundamental form of human movement for the expression of tradition, culture, and social relationships. It involves nonverbal bodily communication with aesthetic value [15]. Ballroom dance is a class of coordinated partner dances, which typically refers to the ten dances of Standard (*e.g.* Waltz, Quick-step) and Latin (*e.g.* Cha-cha, Samba) [17]. One of the salient features of the international style of Standard category (*e.g.* Waltz, Foxtrot, Quickstep) is the hold position [10, 15] (see Fig. 8) with close positional relation of a dancing couple.

1.1 Empirical Study of Competitive Ballroom Dancing

Competitive ballroom dance is a competitive form of ballroom dance that rigorously standardizes its steps, postures, poise and techniques [4]. Competitive ballroom dancing, also known as Dancesport, requires to combine athletes' physical energy, precision, harmony and synchronization in couples' movements with a particular emphasis on the aesthetic components [19]. It comprises forceful and rapid movements and strongly demands physical and mental condition and preparations especially in the competition [8, 15].

Several insightful previous studies investigated; for example, on a comparison of motion speed of top-ranked ballroom dancers [12], the trajectory of dancing pairs' movements [19], and partnering effects on step length [18]. Despite the popularity of ballroom dance, limited amounts of previous literatures investigated ballroom dancers' movements (*e.g.* [15, 18]), especially in relation to biomechanics and kinesiology.

Competitive dance couples are required to precisely harmonize their body movements. However, verbal and nonverbal communication among a dance couple is limited. The question is *how a competitive ballroom dance couple achieves their well-coordinated motions without exchanging explicit signals.*

1.2 Co-creation Model of Dance Communication

Two different models of dance communication are shown in Fig. 1. The SMCR (source, message, channel, receiver) based model is a conventional sequential model of dance communication (Fig. 1-a). In this paper, to clarify essential components of co-creation of dancing, we propose the "Co-creation Model of Dance Communication" (CMDC). The CMDC model emphasizes five components of co-creation: (i) co-creation by a choreographer and dancers, (ii) co-creation by dancers, (iii) co-creation by dancers and audiences, (iv) co-creation among audiences including critiques, and (v) co-creation by audiences and a choreographer (Fig. 1-b). The audiences involve judges, critics, other choreographers and other dancers. The CMDC model doesn't assume a completed dance performance in advance, like a live performance by Jazz players. Dance develops and evolves via *autopoietic* processes [9] of co-creation I, II, III, IV and V.

(a) SMCR-based model of dance communication (revised from [5])

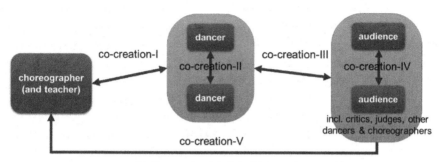

(b) Co-creation Model of Dance Communication

Fig. 1. Model of Dance Communication. (a) SMCR (source, message, channel, receiver) based model. (b) Co-creation Model of Dance Communication (CMDC). Dance evolves via *autopoietic* processes of co-creation I/II/III/IV/V.

1.3 Our Approach

Focus on Non-verbal Interactions of Dance Couples during Dancing. Most previous studies on ballroom dance concentrated to dancing performance expressed explicitly for audiences including judges, namely, external interactions in the co-creation III. On the other hand, little emphasis had been placed on internal interactions of a dance couple in the co-creation II. In fact, top-level competitive dance couples seldom exchange unnecessary explicit cues perceivable to audiences and judges. However, we assume that some kind of couple's interactions of co-creation II play an important role to achieve quality dance performance of co-creation III.

This paper investigates non-verbal interactions among a competitive ballroom dance couple. By using a metaphor of synchronized swimming, our interests can be compared with swimmers' serious efforts underwater not only their elegant appearance presented to the judges and audiences. Although a ballroom dance couple on the stage synchronizes their movements as one, all should be done by nonverbal communication. On the other hand, higher-level cognitive processing of visual and/or audible interactions is probably too slow for the requirements of modern competitive ballroom dancing. Non-verbal communication of a faster style is essential.

Kinesiological Study using MoCap. Kinesiological analysis falls into three categories: structural, biomechanical and neuromuscular analyses [3]. This study addresses first two aspects. In order to identify various levels of body movements including even the movements of a millimeter of size [7], optical motion capture system was adopted. 3D movements of a dancing couple are captured with synchronized high-speed cameras from multiple directions. Figure 2 shows a set of twenty-five anatomical landmarks of skeletal system [11] chosen for motion analysis of ballroom dancers.

The Combined Analysis Method. In this study, in order to investigate couple's non-verbal interactions involving very slight bodily movements, we proposed a new methodology which combines the precise 3D motion analysis of dancing movements and time-frequency analysis. The details will be described in Sect. 3.

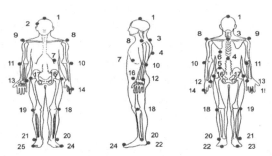

Fig. 2. The set of anatomical body-landmarks used for capturing dancer's 3D movement (common to leader/partner). 1: Vertex, 2: Temple (R), 3: C7 (Cervical Vertebra VII), 4: Th8 (Thoracic Vertebra VIII), 5: Spina Illiaca posterior superior (L), 6: Scapula, 7: Rib11, 8/9: Acromion (L/R), 10/11: Epicondylus lateral (L/R), 12/13: Wrist medial (L/R), 14/15: Middle finger base joint (L/R), 16/17: Trochanter major (L/R), 18/19: Condylus lateral (L/R), 20/21: Outer ankle-bone (L/R), 22/23: Heel (L/R), 24/25: Little toe tip (L/R).

2 Experiment

The purpose of the experiment was to investigate non-verbal bodily interactions made among a competitive ballroom dance couple during dancing.

2.1 Materials and Methods

Participants. Two skilled amateur competition dancers, a dance couple of modern ballroom dancing (a leader and a partner) (age range: 22–23; 173 cm and 169 cm tall respectively), participated. The dance couple was certified as grade B (standard) by East Japan Ballroom Dance Federation, who were finalists in the quickstep division of Japan University Ballroom Dance Competition. Dance experiences of the leader and the partner were four years and their couple experience was two years. The couple trained 9 h/week on the average. After explaining about the experiment, a written informed consent was signed to agree to participate in this study, prior to the experiment. The participants declared that they were free of orthopedic injuries and illness.

Task. The Natural Turn of the Waltz [10] was adopted as the task. This is one of the most basic and popular figure in modern ballroom dancing and has been frequently used in competition dancing and professional examinations. The participants were asked to perform the first half of the Natural Turn of Waltz (count 1 to 3) following its preparational steps (count 1 to 3). Figure 3 describes the footwork positions of the task of a dance routine. The task can be divided into nine phases. The phase N1 (Natural Turn count 1) contains the Contrary Body Movement (CBM), the action of turning the opposite hip and shoulder towards the direction of the moving leg, which is used to commence all turning movements [10]. The phases and the detailed descriptions of the movements of the legs and feet is explained in Table 1.

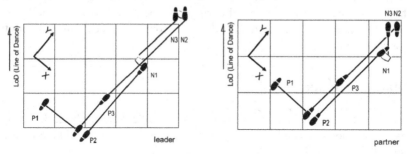

Fig. 3. Footwork positions of the task, a dance routine for a dance couple. This routine consisted of 9 phases: approaching and establishing body contact (B1–3: not appeared in the chart), preparation steps count 1-2-3 (P1–3), and the Natural Turn of the Waltz count 1-2-3 (N1–3).

Table 1. Phases and description of a dance routine used in the experiment.

#	Phases	Description (movement of the legs and feet)	
		Leader	Partner
B1–3	Body contact	Approaching and establishing body contact	
P1	Preparation - count 1	L.F. to the left side	R.F. to the right side
P2	Preparation - count 2	R.F. to the right side	L.F. to the left side
P3	Preparation - count 3	L.F. forward	R.F. backward
N1	Natural Turn - count 1	R.F. forward	L.F. backward
N2	Natural Turn - count 2	L.F. to the left side	R.F. to the right side
N3	Natural Turn - count 3	Close R.F. to L.F	Close L.F. to R.F

Note: L.F (left foot); R.F (right foot)

Procedure. The participants (a competition dance couple) stood quietly on floor apart at approximately 2.5 M distance. The participants were asked to perform the task of a dance routine at their preferred pace without musical accompaniment in the same style they usually practice for the competition. They wore their own dance shoes. The participants were allowed to repeat performing the task until they were satisfied.

2.2 Data Collection

3D motion data of a dance couple's anatomical landmarks (Fig. 2) were captured from different directions with eight synchronized cameras with time-stamp at a one-100th seconds accuracy, by using an optical motion capture system, Simi Motion 3D (100 fps), Germany. The recording contained additionally 2–4 s before and after each trial. According to the calibration, standard deviation of motion tracking error was 0.70 mm.

The data collection was performed during daytime between December 2019 and January 2020, in Tokyo. The session in which the couple was best satisfied with their dance was performed on the last day.

3   Analysis Method

3D motion data of a competitive ballroom dance couple were analyzed by applying our analysis method that combined the precise 3D motion analysis and time-frequency analysis [2].

3.1   Analysis 1. Motion Analysis of Anatomic Landmarks, Segments, Angles

3D Movements of Anatomic Landmarks. In the analysis-1, we analyzed 3D movements of the predefined set of anatomical landmarks (see Fig. 2) according to the motion data tracked with GCS (global coordinate system). Figure 4-(a) shows an example of 3D motion analysis of anatomical landmarks (leader's left ankle).

3D Movements of Body-Segments. Based on human musculoskeletal model, we analyzed the movements of a dancer's body segments such as head, neck, trunk, shoulders, upper arms, forearms, hands, legs, and feet [6]. LCS (local coordinate system) was employed. Figure 4-(b) shows an example of 3D motion analysis of body segments (leader's head).

Joint Angles. Figure 4-(c) shows an example of analysis of joint angles (angle of the flexure of partner's neck). That joint angle was calculated with three 3D positions of anatomical landmarks (i.e. Vertex, C7, Th8).

3.2   Analysis 2. Comparison of Corresponding Movements of a Dance Couple

One of the most attractive and visible element of competition dance performance is the movements of dancing couples in unison. We compared the movements of a pairs of corresponding anatomic landmarks of the dance couple.

Figure 5 shows an example that compares the movements of the leader's left Acromion and the partner's right Acromion. The chart indicates that the movements (Y-direction) of two corresponding Acromion of the couple moved synchronously throughout their performance after they completed the phase B3 (i.e. body contact).

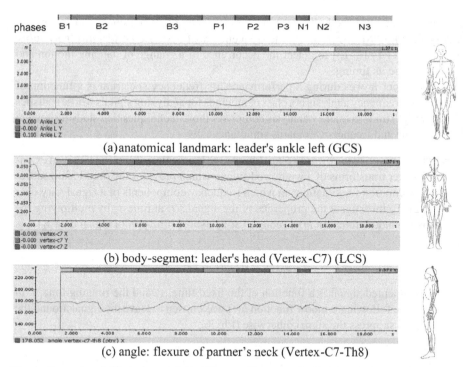

Fig. 4. Examples of 3D motion analysis: (a) a specific anatomical landmark (leader's Ankle left) and (b) a specific body segment (leader's head i.e. Vertex-C7), and (c) a specific joint-angle (angle of the flexure of partner's neck i.e. Vertex-C7-Th8).

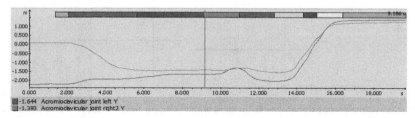

Fig. 5. Comparison of the corresponding movements of the dancing couple: the leader's left Acromion vs. the partner's right Acromion (Y).

3.3   Analysis 3. Time-Frequency Analysis of Dancer's Movements

During a dancing performance, a dancer varies her/his movement such as its speed and rhythm. 3D motion data of a dancer can be regarded as a time-varying signal. The analysis-3 provides with further detailed analysis method for clarifying the occurrence and timing of a change of a dancer's movement. An example is explained below.

Detection of a Change of a Dancer's Movement. Figure 7-(a) shows an example of a time domain representation of the partner's movement at Th8. According to the chart, the partner's Th8 began moving significantly at approximately 13.8 s, but until then its movement seemed smooth. There was no quick and significant change of movement during 12–14 s. We focused on time-frequency analysis based on short-time Fourier transform (STFT) [2, 13] to detect the occurrence of a change of dancing motion and also determine its timing.

As a dancer moves during a performance, its frequency spectrum is a function of time. Time–frequency analysis is a class of methods for analyzing signals whose statistics vary in time. Time–frequency analysis comprises those techniques that study a signal in both the time and frequency domains simultaneously.

Short Time Fourier Transform (STFT). Short-time Fourier transform (STFT) is an extension of Fourier transforms of a windowed signal, which provides the time-localized frequency information for situations in which frequency components of a signal vary over time [1, 2]. To investigate the properties of the signal $s(t)$ at time τ, by multiplying the signal by a window function $h(t)$, centered at τ, a short-time part of signal data $s_\tau(t)$ is produced,

$$s_\tau(t) = s(t)h(t - \tau) \tag{1}$$

The segmented signal is a function of the fixed time, τ, and the running time, t. In this study, the following window function $h(t)$ was chosen to leave the signal around the time τ but to suppress the signal otherwise (Fig. 6).

$$h(t) = \begin{cases} 1, & \text{for } t \text{ near } \tau \\ 0, & \text{otherwise} \end{cases} \tag{2}$$

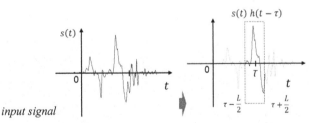

Fig. 6. Short-time part of signal data segmented with a window function $h(t)$ centered about time τ, for the input signal $s(t)$.

For the input signal $s(t)$, short-time Fourier transform is given by

$$\text{STFT}\{\, s(t)\} = S_\tau(\omega) = \frac{1}{2\pi} \int_{-\infty}^{\infty} s(t)h(t - \tau)\, e^{-jwt} dt \tag{3}$$

where ω denotes angular frequency. For each different time we obtain a different spectrum and the totality of these spectra is the time-frequency distribution, Psp. The magnitude squared of the STFT yields the *spectrogram* representation of the power spectral density of the function. The power spectral density at time τ is calculated by

$$Psp(\tau,\omega) = |S_\tau(\omega)|^2 = \left| \frac{1}{2\pi} \int_{-\infty}^{\infty} s(t)h(t - \tau)e^{-jwt} dt \right|^2 \tag{4}$$

Figure 7-(b) shows an example of time-frequency analysis based on STFT. It contains two types of representations of the analysis results: spectrograph (left) and 2D time-frequency diagram (right). The same motion data with Fig. 7-(a) was used. The charts of time-frequency analysis revealed the occurrence of a change of the partner's Th8 movement (x-axis) at 13.2 s (Fig. 7-(b)).

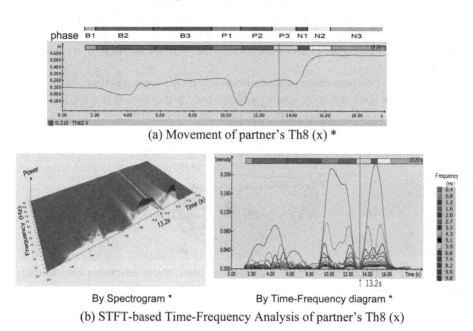

(a) Movement of partner's Th8 (x) *

By Spectrogram *   By Time-Frequency diagram *

(b) STFT-based Time-Frequency Analysis of partner's Th8 (x)

Fig. 7. Time-Frequency Analysis of movements. (a) Movement of partner's Th8 (x-axis). No significant change of movement was observed during 12–14 s. (b) Two types of representations of STFT-based time-frequency analysis: Spectrograph (left) and 2D time-frequency diagram (right). Either diagram shows a significant change of Th8 movement (x-axis) at 13.2 s. Note (*): the same data was used.

4   Analysis of Non-verbal Interactions Among Dancing Couples

The analysis diverges into various aspects of ballroom dancing. To focus on the harmonization of couple's movements, this paper narrowed down analysis viewpoints to specific topics: (a) stability of the hold and body contact; (b) the occurrence and its timing of non-verbal interactions and lead communication, (c) comparison of corresponding movements of a couple; (d) couple's continuous adjustments of individual movement; and (e) a role of body contact in achieving the unity of couple's movements.

4.1 The Hold and Body Contact

A leader and a partner approach each other in the phase B1 & 2, and then begin establishing their standing position in the phase B3. Before starting their motions, a dance couple completes building the hold. In a typical style of the closed position, body contact is lightly made at four or five body-parts/areas (Fig. 8): (1) a leader's right hand–a partner's left scapula, (2) a leader's right forearm-a partner's left forearm, (3) a grip between a leader's left hand and a partner's right hand, (4) a leader's right upper arm-a partner's left hand, and (5) the region of abdomen (around the pit of the stomach) of a leader and a partner.

Competition ballroom dance couples should pay their attention to the hold. Because an inappropriate hold and body contact will not only give a dancer and the judges an appearance of bad style, but also seriously affect the balance [10].

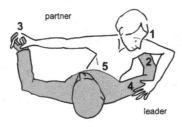

Fig. 8. The hold (the closed position). A competition dance couple establishes body contacts typically at five areas (1–5).

The Hold for the Leader. The sustainability of the joint-angle of the leader's left elbow is one of a useful parameter that represents the leader's hold of good style. Figure 9-(a) shows the joint angle made by leader's Acromion-Epicondylus-Wrist (left) (AcEpWr-L-ldr). We focused on the phases after P3 when the couple initiated their sequential movements of Natural Turn. The chart indicates that the joint-angle AcEpWr-L-ldr had been maintained constant around 90–100 degree, which engendered the appearance of good style, except a short time in initial phase of a turn.

The Hold for the Partner. The joint-angle of the partner's neck is another useful parameter. Figure 9-(b) shows the joint angle made by the partner's Vertex-C7-Epicondylus (right) (VtC7Ep-R-ptn). After the partner began the Natural Turn count 1 (N1), the chart indicates that the joint-angle VtC7Ep-R-ptn had been maintained around 100 degree that engendered the appearance of good style and poise even while the partner made turning.

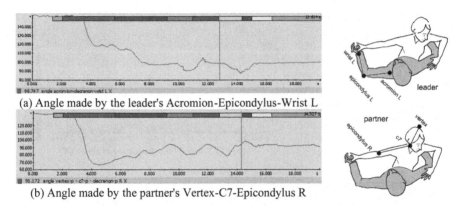

(a) Angle made by the leader's Acromion-Epicondylus-Wrist L

(b) Angle made by the partner's Vertex-C7-Epicondylus R

Fig. 9. Examples of the joint angles for the hold (leader and partner).

The hold and an appropriate body contact provide a dance couple with the foundation of non-verbal interactions among them.

4.2   Interaction When the Couple Initiates and Changes Their Movements

Just before Starting Movements. Dance couples begin dancing soon after they finalize their dancing positions. When couples synchronously start their movements, they don't use externally perceivable cues such as music, counting, and a wink. The question is, *how can a dance couple decide the appropriate timing for starting a dance?*

Video data showed that the dance couple gradually quieted individual motion generally while they established the hold in the phase B3. The dance couple seemed to suppress some specific movements of their bodies. Several parts related to the hold were chosen for further investigation using the time-frequency analyses.

Exchanging the Moment of "Silence" Each Other. Figure 10 shows (a) the movements (X,Y) and (b) the STFT-based time-frequency analysis chart of the leader's right Acromion (X). This part was chosen because the change of its movement should be easily perceived via the body contact #4 by the partner. The time-frequency analysis revealed that the movement at most of frequencies suppressed quickly at 8.5 s.

Likewise Fig. 10 (c, d) show the movements (X,Y) and the STFT-based time-frequency analysis chart of the partner's right Temple (X). This part was chosen because its movement should be closely perceived by the leader after they finalized the body contacts. The time-frequency analysis revealed that the movement at most of frequencies suppressed quickly at 8.9 s.

Detecting The Quiescent State Using Time-Frequency Analysis. The charts indicated that at first the movement of the leader's right shoulder became quiet, followed by the movement of partner's head. Then, the couple immediately started dancing at 9.7 s (see Fig. 15-b). The result indicated that the dance couple perceived and exchanged the moment of "silence" just before they start their movements. The STFT-based time-frequency analysis revealed the occurrence of the quiescent state in the movements.

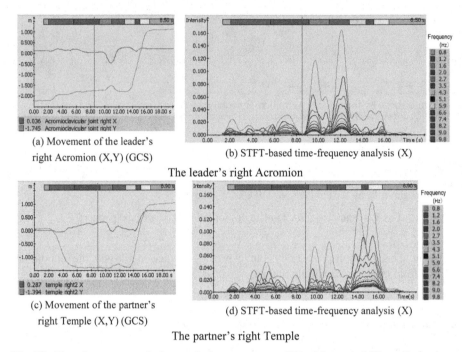

(a) Movement of the leader's right Acromion (X,Y) (GCS)

(b) STFT-based time-frequency analysis (X)

The leader's right Acromion

(c) Movement of the partner's right Temple (X,Y) (GCS)

(d) STFT-based time-frequency analysis (X)

The partner's right Temple

Fig. 10. Time-frequency analysis reveals the occurrence of "the Moment of Silence" of a dance couple. Particular the movements of most frequencies became quiet at (b) the leader's right Acromion (X) at 8.5 s, and (d) the partner's right Temple (X) at 8.9 s.

Lead Communication (Just Before Changing the Movements). 3D motion data indicated that the couple quickly moved their legs (forward for the leader; backward for the partner) simultaneously around 13.4 s in the middle of the phase P3. However, 3D motion analysis using GCS doesn't indicate significant movements of the leader's landmarks until then. Examples are shown in Fig. 11-(a, c).

Non-verbal Interaction Before the Couple Change the Movements. Further investigation of the couple's non-verbal interaction was conducted by applying time-frequency analysis. We especially focused on "lead communication" just before the couple made that change of their movements. The leader's left and right Wrists were chosen as candidates. They were located at the body contacts #3 and #1 areas respectively.

Figure 11-(b, d) show the results of STFT-based time-frequency analysis for those two landmarks. The charts revealed that the changes of the movements of most frequencies occurred (b) at the leader's wrist left (Y) at 12.8 s and (d) at the leader's wrist right (Y) at 12.6 s. The analysis revealed that the leader's different wrists, located at L and R sides, slightly moved to the almost same direction almost simultaneously.

Invisible Interactions Perceivable Only by the Couple. The leader's movements at Wrist L/R were very slight. Those motions are invisible by the judges and audiences. On the other hand, even slight movements of the leader's Wrists should be able to change a pressure or touch-feeling through their body contacts #1 and 3 with the partner. The

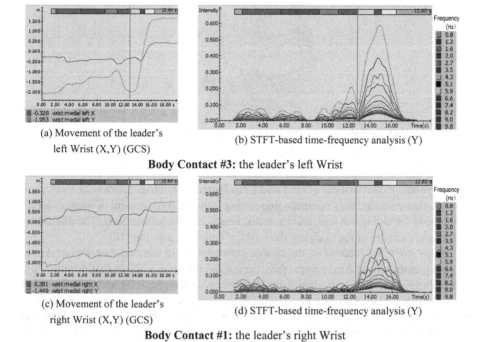

(a) Movement of the leader's
left Wrist (X,Y) (GCS)

(b) STFT-based time-frequency analysis (Y)

Body Contact #3: the leader's left Wrist

(c) Movement of the leader's
right Wrist (X,Y) (GCS)

(d) STFT-based time-frequency analysis (Y)

Body Contact #1: the leader's right Wrist

Fig. 11. Movements of leader's left Wrist (body contact #3) and right Wrist (body contact #1). During 12.3–13.4 s, those movements seemed smooth until the couple began moving significantly at 13.4 s. However, time-frequency analysis chart revealed that quick but small movements of most frequencies significantly *changed* at (b) the leader's left Wrist (Y) at 12.8 s, and (d) the leader's right Wrist (Y) at 12.6 s. Those two different body parts of the leader moved to the almost same direction almost simultaneously.

results suggested that this dance couple made lead communication including the change and the direction of dancing movements at least at the phase P3, by slightly changing pressure and perceiving the change of touch-feelings through their body contacts (Fig. 12). That interaction among the dance couple was quite different from other styles of non-verbal communication such as the leader's tapping on the partner's body parts or exchange of their facial expressions. Immediately after the leader made a lead communication (12.6–12.8 s) by conveying very slight movements less than a few millimeters at the body contacts, the couple initiated significant movements to the same direction simultaneously (13.4 s).

4.3 Awareness of a Sense of Unity in Couple's Corresponding Movements

For audiences including the judges, one of the most attractive and visible element of competition dance performance is a couple's harmonized movements. In this section, we compared the movements of a pairs of corresponding anatomic landmarks and segments of the couple.

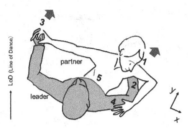

Fig. 12. The leader's slight movements at the body contacts #1 and #3 just before the dance couple moved quickly along almost the Y-axis (+).

Corresponding Movements of Feet and Legs During Dancing. Once ballroom dance couples start dancing, they continue fine-tuning individual movement of various levels of the body including the legs, trunks, arms, heads, and the whole body. The alignment of feet and carriage of the body are the basis of ballroom dancing [10].

In this study, we focused on the couple's corresponding feet, the leader's left Ankle and the partner's right Ankle, especially during the phases P2-N2. In that duration, the couple began a sequence of significant movements in the phase P3 and then they also mostly completed their turning movements in the phase N2. Figure 13 shows an example photo of the couple's dancing movement of the preparation step count 3 (P3). The photo shows that the leader made his large step with his left foot forward and the partner made her large step with her right foot backward simultaneously at that timing. The couple made their Natural Turn after that.

Fig. 13. An example photo of the couple's dancing movement of the preparation step count3 (P3). At that timing, the leader made his large step with his left foot forward and the partner simultaneously made her large step with her right foot backward.

Figure 14 summarizes a trace of the corresponding movements of the leader's left Ankle and the partner's right Ankle, between the phases P2 and N2 (12.3–16.6 s). It contained a turn movement. A comparison of those movements (Y) (the leader's left Ankle vs. the partner's right Ankle) is shown in Fig. 15-(a). Those charts illustrate that the couple made harmonized movements of their corresponding feet, even when they both made a turn as well as large steps forward (i.e. step backward by the partner). Please note that Fig. 15-(a) also shows that the couple made changes of their dancing motions several times, for example by speeding up and down synchronously at approx. 13.4 s, 14.7 s, and 15.5 s.

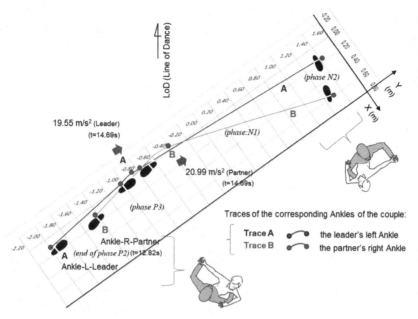

Fig. 14. Traces of the movements of the couple's corresponding feet: the leader's left Ankle and the partner's right Ankle, during the phases P2-N2 containing a turn movement.

Couple's Continuous Adjustments of the Corresponding Movements. The traveled distance of the leader's left ankle was approx. 3.5 M that was 0.8 M longer than the partner's right Ankle (2.7 M) during the phases P2-N2 (see Fig. 14). Nevertheless the couple is required to start simultaneously and to complete their turn at the same time. A simple synchronization is insufficient to achieve it. Therefore, the couple should make some sort of adjustments in the interim.

Figure 15-(b, c) show the acceleration of the movements of the couple's corresponding Ankles: (b) the leader's left Ankle and (c) the partner's right Ankle. The couple quickly accelerated the movements of those corresponding ankles simultaneously (14.7 s) by almost the same acceleration (20.3 ± 0.7 m/s^2) and also immediately decelerated those movements. Further investigation was conducted by combining Fig. 14 and 15-(a, b, c).

According to the result, a process of the couple's adjustments in that duration can be described as following: (1) the leader lead the dancing motion and the partner followed it almost simultaneously (13.3–13.4 s). Until 14.0 s, the acceleration and deacceleration of the leader's Ankle was higher than the partner's; (2) the couple's corresponding movements of their Ankles changed their speed simultaneously at 14.7 s by almost the same acceleration (20.3 ± 0.7 m/s^2); (3) the partner deaccelerated her right Ankle slightly earlier and the leader deaccelerated his left Ankle slightly later; (4) the leader's Ankle caught up with the partner's Ankle and overtook it slightly; and (5) as a result, the couple could reach the pre-designated positions and complete their corresponding

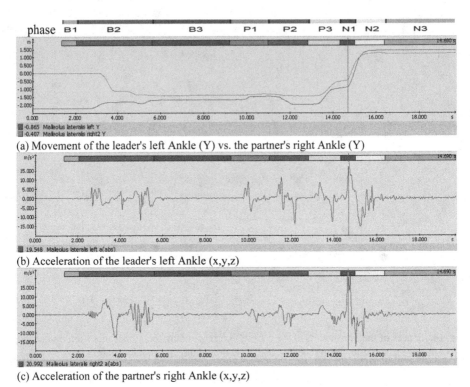

(a) Movement of the leader's left Ankle (Y) vs. the partner's right Ankle (Y)

(b) Acceleration of the leader's left Ankle (x,y,z)

(c) Acceleration of the partner's right Ankle (x,y,z)

Fig. 15. Comparison of the movements and those accelerations of the couple's corresponding anatomical landmarks. (a) The movements of the leader's left Ankle vs. the partner's right Ankle. (b, c) The accelerations (Y) of the leader's left Ankle and the partner's right Ankle. The couple simultaneously and quickly accelerated the movements of those corresponding ankles (14.7 s) by almost the same acceleration (20.3 ± 0.7 m/s^2), and immediately decelerated them.

movements of Ankles at the same time (N2). Thus a sense of unity is realized by the couple's continuous adjustment of their corresponding movements.

The Unity of Dancing Movements as a Result. The unity of the couple's dancing movements is one of the visual achievements. Especially the alignment of the couple's knees can be easily perceived by the audience. Figure 16 shows an example of a comparison of the corresponding movements (Y) of the leader's left Condylus and the partner's right Condylus.

The result revealed that the leader's left Condylus and the partner's right Condylus were almost exactly in alignment since they started dancing. The couple's corresponding knees actually changed motion speed at least four times, however, the couple changed their movements simultaneously and moved like a single body segment. Similar results were also obtained for the couple's corresponding Trochanters.

The unity of dancing movements is not the goal of the couple's dancing movements but a result. This study suggested that the continuous appropriate adjustment of the couple's corresponding feet provided a solid basis of synchronizing the corresponding movements of not only the couple's legs but also the couple's movements of lower half

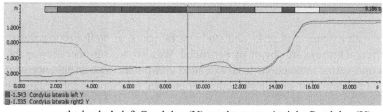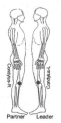

the leader's left Condylus (Y) vs. the partner's right Condylus (Y)

Fig. 16. Comparison of the corresponding movements of the dancing couple. The leader's left Condylus (Y) vs. the partner's right Condylus (Y).

of their bodies. That is also expected to provide with a foundation of external expressions produced by the couple's upper half of their bodies.

4.4 The Closed Hold with Body Contact as a Foundation of Interactions

Finally, we investigated a precise positional relation of the couple's bodies especially their center of bodies.

Keeping Constant Close Distance between a Dancing Couple. Figure 17 shows the distance between the leader's Th8 and the partner's Th8. The chart indicated that the couple's Th8 had been maintained constantly close (approx.47 cm) during dancing even while making a turn. Notably, the result implies that the couple maintained light pressure at almost same level at the center area of their bodies without pushing and pulling each other's body. That enabled slight nonverbal interactions during dancing.

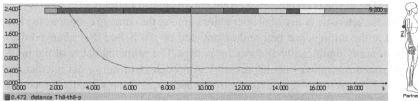

Fig. 17. The distance between the leader's Th8 and the partner's Th8. The distance kept close constantly during dancing even while making a turn.

To maintain light stable body contact is a key for creating a unity of couple's dancing. Adequate control of their body contacts particularly at the center of body such as abdominal region plays more important role in modern style of competition ballroom dancing and dance sports. A sense of unity was realized by the couple's continuous adjustment of maintaining light contact pressure of the same level by slightly modifying directions, velocity and accelerations of their corresponding movements.

5 Discussion

Further studies with extension of tasks and study participants, as well as comparative studies with different settings are obviously beneficial. We also stress further deep analyses of couple's non-verbal interactions from extended viewpoints, with an enhancement of the accuracy of analysis of spatial and temporal characteristics of couple's dancing movements.

A part of our empirical findings especially on lead communication partially complied with introductory descriptions [10, 16] written by the British legends of competitive ballroom dancers who established foundations of competitive ballroom dancing. This result might be a reflection that most ballroom dancers and teachers had been trained according to those basic principles.

Support Tool for Dance Education/Training. On the other hand, more importantly, our study also suggested the possibility of a new methodology and tool, beyond video-recording. It is expected to enable dancers to evaluate their dance performances by themselves quantitatively in detail from various viewpoints. It will also be useful for stimulating the co-creation I and II by dancers and teachers, i.e. dance education and training.

6 Concluding Remarks

This paper investigated non-verbal interactions among a competitive ballroom dance couple during dancing. We proposed a new methodology for empirical dance research, which combines the precise 3D motion analysis of dancing and STFT based time-frequency analysis. 3D movements of a skilled competition dance couple while dancing the first half of the Natural Turn of the Waltz following its preparation steps were captured using Mocap. The analysis results revealed several insightful findings.

First, the characteristic non-verbal interactions among the dancing couple were identified at least at the timings just before they initiated or just before they changed their dancing movements significantly and synchronously. The prime modality of the interactions was somatosensation (tactile/pressure). Although most nonverbal interactions were very slight movements and invisible to the audiences, however only the couple could perceive them via tactile/pressure sensation, for example.

Second, the combined precise analyses revealed that: (a) The couple could *feel* each other's movements whose frequencies over 0.4 Hz became almost completely quiet, at least at the leader's right shoulder (via body contact #4) and at the partner's right temple (by viewing closely) at the timing (*e.g.* 0.8 s) just before they initiated dancing sequence simultaneously (phase B3); (b) The leader made a *lead communication* with very slight movements less than a few millimeters at least at both wrists of either side simultaneously, so that the partner could feel those slight changes of the pressure via the body contact #3 and #1, at the timing (*e.g.* 0.6 s) just before the leader made his large step forward for making a turn (phase P3); (c) *A sense of unity* was realized by the couple's continuous adjustment of maintaining light contact pressure of the same level by slightly modifying directions, velocity and accelerations of their corresponding movements; (d) A continuous maintenance of the closed hold with a light and close body contacts involving especially #5 were confirmed throughout dancing even while making a turn.

Third, the above empirical results indicated that the stable closed hold with light constant body contacts was a foundation that enabled very *sensitive non-verbal interactions of a faster style* among a dancing couple.

Our methodology was effective to precise investigation especially on temporal characteristics and the harmonization of couples' movements of competitive ballroom dances. Future enhancements include extensions of task and study participants, standardization of the analysis, more precise time-frequency analysis, and development of a tool useful for dancers' co-creation I and II, i.e. dance education and training.

Acknowledgement. The authors thank study participants and K.Yoshikawa especially for the contributions to our experiment. We thank NS, SS and YT for their insightful implications to our model of dance communication as well as the dance concepts.

References

1. Cohen, L.: Time-Frequency Analysis. Prentice Hall (1995)
2. Gröchenig, K.: Foundations of Time-Frequency Analysis. Birkhaeuser (2013)
3. Haas, J.G.: Dance Anatomy, 2nd edn. Human Kinetics, Champaign (2018)
4. Imperial Society of Teachers of Dancing: The Ballroom Technique, 10th edn. ISTD, London (1994)
5. Kataoka, Y.: Dance and Dance Education (*in Japanese*). Taishukan, Tokyo (2007)
6. Kinoe, Y., Akimori, Y., Sakiyama, A.: Postural movement when persons feel uncomfortable interpersonal distance. In: Yamamoto, S., Mori, H. (eds.) Human Interface and the Management of Information. Information in Intelligent Systems. Lecture Notes in Computer Science LNCS, vol. 11570, pp. 357–371. Springer, Cham (2019). https://doi.org/10.1007/978-3-030-22649-7_29
7. Kinoe, Y., Akimori, Y.: Appeal of inconspicuous body movements during spatial invasion. In: Yamamoto, S., Mori, H. (eds.) Human Interface and the Management of Information. Interacting with Information HCII 2020. Lecture Notes in Computer Science LNCS, vol. 12185, pp. 175–193. Springer, Cham (2020). https://doi.org/10.1007/978-3-030-50017-7_12
8. Liiv, H., Jürimäe, T., Klonova, A., Cicchella, A.: Performance and recovery: stress profiles in professional ballroom dancers. Med. Probl. Perform. Artists **28**(2), 65–69 (2013)
9. Maturana, H.R., Varela, F.J.: The Tree of Knowledge: The Biological Roots of Human, revised Shambhala, Boston (1992)
10. Moore, A.: Ballroom Dancing, 10th edn. Methuen Drama, London (2002)
11. Neumann, D.A.: Kinesiology of the Musculoskeletal System, 3rd edn. Elsevier (2016)
12. Prosen, J., James, N., Dimitriou, L., Perš, J., Vučković, G.: A time-motion analysis of turns performed by highly ranked Viennese waltz dancers. J. Hum. Kinet. **37**(1), 55–62 (2013)
13. Sejdić, E., Djurović, I., Jiang, J.: Time-frequency feature representation using energy concentration: an overview of recent advances. Digit. Signal Process. **19**(1), 153–183 (2009)
14. Silva, A.H., Bonorino, K.C.: BMI and flexibility in ballerinas of contemporary dance and classical ballet. Fit. Performance J. **7**(1), 48–51 (2008)
15. Vaczi, M., et al.: Ballroom dancing is more intensive for the female partners due to their unique hold technique. Physiol. Int. **103**(3), 392–401 (2016)

16. Wessel-Therhorn, O.: The Irvine Legacy. DSI London (2009)
17. World Dance Council: WDC Competition Rules (2020). https://www.wdcdance.com/competitive-dance/
18. Yoshida, Y., Bizokas, A., Demidova, K., Nakai, S., Nakai, R., Nishimura, T.: Partnering effects on joint motion range and step length in the competitive waltz dancers. J. Dance Med. Sci. **24**(4), 168–174 (2020)
19. Zaletel, P., Kajtna, T.: Motivational structure of female and male dancers of different dance disciplines. Acta Gymnica **50**(2), 68–76 (2020)

Application and Improvement of VR Content Creation Support System in Classes

Riku Koyama[1]([✉]), Teruhiko Unoki[2], Toru Kano[3], and Takako Akakura[3]

[1] Department of Information and Computer Technology, Graduate School of Engineering, Tokyo University of Science, 6-3-1 Niijuku, Katsushika-ku, Tokyo 125-8585, Japan
`4621511@ed.tus.ac.jp`

[2] Research and Development Center, PHOTRON LIMITED, 1-105 Jinbocho Kanda, Chiyoda-ku, Tokyo 101-0051, Japan
`unoki@photron.co.jp`

[3] Department of Information and Computer Technology, Faculty of Engineering, Tokyo University of Science, 6-3-1 Niijuku, Katsushika-ku, Tokyo 125-8585, Japan
`{kano,akakura}@rs.tus.ac.jp`

Abstract. One of the reasons for virtual reality (VR) not being widely used in the field of education is that its handling requires specialized knowledge and the installation of VR equipment, which can be a burden for teachers. Therefore, we developed a system that allows teachers to easily create VR learning contents, which have been attracting attention in recent years. However, a problem with this system is encountered when the contents consist only of events reproducible in real and do not make use of the characteristics of VR. In this study, we develop a support system for creating VR learning contents that enables object manipulation in the VR space with only simple editing operations on a personal computer. Then, based on the evaluation by subject with teaching experience, we examine ways to improve the system to make it easier to use. Additionally, based on the results of the interviews with the subject, we consider ways to improve the system further.

Keywords: Virtual reality · Teaching material development · Teaching aid · Object manipulation · e-learning

1 Introduction

1.1 Research Background

In recent years, the development of information technology has led to a rapid increase in the use of information in all areas of society. In this context, Information and Communication Technology (ICT) has been utilized in the field of education, and e-learning has been introduced in many companies and educational institutions [1]. One of the advantages of e-learning is the ease of collecting learning logs as well as the reduction of time and space constraints. Moreover, according to Tominaga et al. [2], e-learning has been confirmed to have the same or better effect than conventional learning methods, and it is expected to become more widespread in the future. However, as e-learning becomes

© The Author(s), under exclusive license to Springer Nature Switzerland AG 2022
S. Yamamoto and H. Mori (Eds.): HCII 2022, LNCS 13306, pp. 267–279, 2022.
https://doi.org/10.1007/978-3-031-06509-5_19

more widespread, problems are beginning to emerge. These problems include the loss of tension due to the absence of a teacher and increase in dropouts due to the difficulty of maintaining motivation [3]. One of the possible solutions to the problem of maintaining motivation in e-learning is the virtual reality (VR) class using Head Mounted Display (HMD), where 3D avatars that reproduce the movements of the teacher and students are displayed on the HMD, and the class is held in a classroom reproduced in VR space.

1.2   Related Research

Baba et al. [4] studied the presence of teachers and other students in an e-learning environment where class images are viewed. They developed a VR lecture system in which a teacher avatar and other students are placed in a VR space. As shown in Fig. 1, by wearing an HMD, the learner can study in the learning space reproduced by the avatar and the classroom. Interactions are implemented in such a manner that when the learner looks at the avatar, the avatar smiles back at the learner, creating a more natural classroom environment. Additionally, the learner can control the progress of the class by using a controller and take notes by projecting images of the real space onto the VR space.

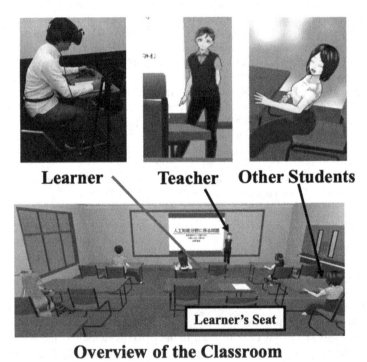

Fig. 1. System overview of VR lecture system [4]

The results of the evaluation experiment suggested that the system improved the motivation to learn and prevented the loss of concentration. However, when creating a

VR class, the teacher needs to wear a device for motion tracking when recording the class, which is a burden for the teacher. Yano et al. [5] developed a class delivery system using VR to increase the realism of the delivered class. From the results of the class practice, students' responses were generally favorable, suggesting the usefulness of the system. However, teachers need to have knowledge of VR, and this can be a challenge for teachers who are not familiar with VR.

1.3 Purpose of This Research

In this study, we will develop a system that allows anyone to easily create VR contents that take advantage of the characteristics of VR, without the teacher having to wear VR equipment when recording a lecture. In addition, we will conduct an evaluation experiment with subject who has teaching experience, and based on the results of the interviews, we will discuss how to improve the system to make it easier to use.

2 Development of Systems

2.1 System Overview

Flow of the System. Figure 2 shows a flow of the system, which briefly describes the process of creating VR contents. In step 1, the teacher launches the system. In step 2, the teacher records a lecture. The system creates an animation of the teacher avatar based on the lecture video obtained from the recording (see Sect. 2.3). Then, we automatically generate the VR contents by assigning the obtained animation and voice to the teacher avatar in the VR space. In step 3, the teacher edits the VR contents by moving objects in and out of the generated VR contents at arbitrary timing. If necessary, teacher puts on the HMD and freely watches the VR contents.

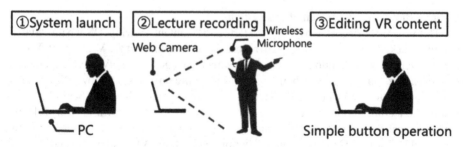

Fig. 2. Flow of the system

This system application is configured so that all the processes necessary to create VR contents can be completed within the application. With the system described above, VR contents can be created with a simple button operation and does not require the need to wear VR equipment.

Duration of VR Contents. In this system, the VR contents created by the teacher are supposed to be used as a part of the class. For this reason, the minimum length of the VR content is 20 s and maximum is 5 min.

Theme of VR Contents. The theme of the VR contents can be freely set by the teacher. Figure 3 shows an example of objects that can be selected by the teacher. From left to right, 3D objects of earth, skeleton, and lion can be seen. In this case, the theme is "celestial bodies," which is taught in junior high school classes, and an object of the earth has been set. The teacher creates the VR contents using the Earth object.

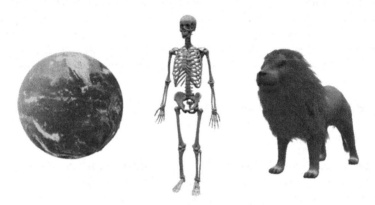

Fig. 3. Examples of selectable objects

2.2 Title Screen

Figure 4 shows the title screen of this system.

This screen consists of two buttons: "Start" and "Content Viewing." When the "Start" button is clicked, the screen switches to record the lecture and edit the VR content. When the "Content viewing" button is clicked, the screen changes and the VR content created by the teacher can be viewed. Therefore, the flow of the screen is as follows: First, press the "Start" button to switch to the lecture recording screen (shown in Sect. 2.3) and record the lecture. Then, switch to the content editing screen (shown in Sect. 2.4), in which the teacher can edit the VR content. After that, return to the title screen shown in Fig. 4, and click the "Content Viewing" button to check the VR content created.

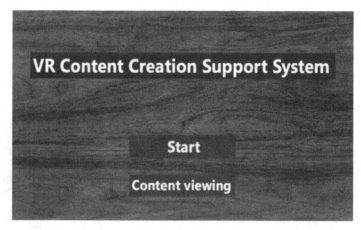

Fig. 4. System title screen

2.3 Lecture Recording Screen

Figure 5 shows the system screen during lecture recording.

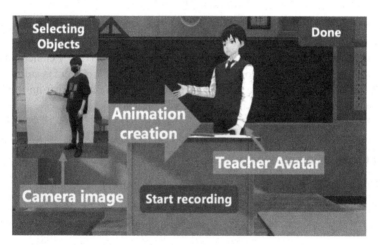

Fig. 5. System screen during lecture recording

To record the lecture video, first, the teacher wears a wireless microphone and prepares a camera to capture the lecture. Next, the teacher selects an object to be displayed in the VR content, as shown in Fig. 5. Then, the teacher presses the "Start Recording" button to start recording the lecture. The teacher gives the lecture in real space, keeping in mind the movement of the objects in and out of the VR space. The system creates the motion of the teacher avatar in real time based on the lecture video captured by the camera and reflects it on to the teacher avatar on the screen. This allows the teacher to see how their lectures are reflected in the VR space while giving the lecture.

Animation Creation Procedure. Figure 6 shows the procedure for creating an avatar animation.

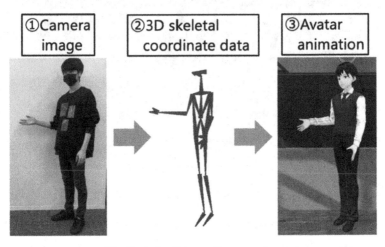

Fig. 6. Animation creation procedure

To create the animation of the avatar, we use "ThreeDPoseTracker" [7], which is an application distributed to the public. In this application, the 3D skeletal coordinate data of the body is obtained by estimating the skeletal structure based on the camera image of the teacher. Finally, when the "Done" button is pressed, the VR content is automatically generated by assigning the voice and avatar animation data obtained from the lecture recording to the teacher avatar in the VR space.

2.4   VR Content Editing Screen

Figure 7 shows the system screen when editing VR content.

Fig. 7. System screen when editing VR content

The system screen during editing is like the user interface of video editing tools, allowing teachers to operate it intuitively. At the bottom of the screen, there are "play/pause" and "forward/backward 10 s" buttons, as well as a seek bar and playback time, allowing the user to move to the desired timing of the VR content. In addition, by pressing the "Object Appearance/Disappearance" button, the teacher can move objects in and out of the automatically generated VR content at any timing. The timing of object insertion/removal is saved as data, and the data are used to reflect the object appearance/disappearance in the VR content. Additionally, it is possible to move the viewpoint by dragging the mouse, and to move in the VR space by pressing the WASD key, so that the teacher can edit the VR contents from any viewpoint. Finally, when the teacher finishes editing the VR content and presses the "Finish" button, the edited VR contents are saved in the system and the title screen (Fig. 4) appears.

2.5 VR Content Viewing Screen

Figure 8 shows the VR content viewing screen.

Fig. 8. VR content viewing screen

By clicking the "Content Viewing" button on the title screen (Fig. 4), the teacher can view the VR content created by this system. By entering the pre-assigned keys, the teacher can repeatedly view the VR content. The teacher can either view the content on the 2D screen of the system, or wear the HMD and view it in the VR space.

The VR space is configured to resemble a school classroom as shown in Fig. 9. We set up a general-purpose learning space so that both teachers and learners would feel comfortable when viewing the VR content. Unity, a game development platform, is used to construct the VR space.

Fig. 9. Space built within the VR content

3   Evaluation Experiment

3.1   Experimental Outline

In this paper, we discuss the potential improvements to this system from the viewpoint of a subject who has experience as a teacher. For this reason, we conduct an evaluation experiment with a university teacher as a subject. The content of the experiment is a questionnaire and an interview after the subject has used the system. The questionnaire employs a five-point scale with 1 as a highly negative evaluation and 5 as a highly positive one. In addition, the questionnaire primarily consists of items asking about the experience of using the system when "recording lecture," "editing VR contents," and "viewing VR contents," and items asking about the evaluation of the system. The interview consists of "good points," "points for improvement," and "opinions and impressions" about the system. In this study, the theme of the lecture was "celestial bodies." The lecture was conducted to create a situation in which the rotation of the earth is to be explained. The following are the items to be explained in the lecture.

- The earth rotates on its axis.
- The earth rotates once a day.
- The earth rotates from west to east.
- The rotation of the earth causes "diurnal motion."

Figure 10 shows how a teacher uses this system to record a lecture. The device used to view the VR content created by the teacher is an HMD-type HTC Vive Pro Eye. This device can manipulate the objects in the virtual space in the same way as in the real space, in conjunction with the movement of the main body and the controller operation.

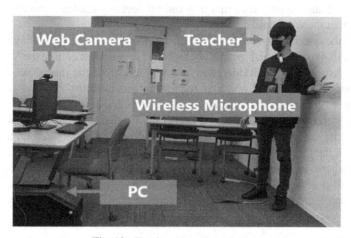

Fig. 10. Teacher recording a lecture

3.2 Experimental Results

The length of the content created by the teacher was 53.94 s. It took about 1 min to record the lecture and about 2 min to edit it. Therefore, if we include the time for viewing the VR contents, it took about 4 min to complete the creation of one VR content.

We describe the results of the questionnaire and interviews. Table 1 shows some excerpts from the questionnaire.

Table 1. Questionnaire Results

No.	Question	Evaluation
7	I did not feel tired during the recording of the lecture in this experiment	5
8	It was not difficult to operate the equipment used for recording the lecture	5
12	I did not feel tired when editing the VR contents	5
13	The editing of the VR contents in this system is easy	4
14	It was not difficult to control the appearance and disappearance of objects	5
17	The avatar reproduced in the VR had the movement that you intended	4
18	The objects reproduced in the VR had the movements that you intended	5
19	The VR contents were created exactly as you had imagined	4
21	I would like to create VR contents using this system and give lessons to students using the VR contents	4

First, in the questionnaire items (No. 7, 8) concerning the recording of the lecture of our system, the subject answered that they did not feel any burden when recording the lecture and that there were no difficult operations.

Next, in the questionnaire items (No. 12, 13, 14) concerning the editing of the VR contents of this system, the subject did not feel any burden when editing the VR contents and did not have any difficult operations. In addition, from the interviews during the editing process, we obtained opinions requesting a cut editing function for the VR contents and a function on the seek bar to check the status of the objects and avatars.

Finally, in the questionnaire items (No. 17, 18, 19) that asked whether the VR contents created by this system performed the actions intended by the teacher, the subject answered that they were able to create VR contents that generally performed the actions intended by them. In addition, the ability to check the created VR contents on the spot was evaluated positively. However, there was a request for improving the positions of the objects and avatars in the created VR contents as these were slightly misaligned.

3.3 Discussion

As for the overall usability of this system, the subject answered that they felt little burden and did not need to perform difficult operations; hence, we believe that the objective of enabling teachers to easily create VR contents was largely achieved. In addition, the questionnaire item No. 21, "I would like to create VR contents using this system and give lessons to students using the VR contents," was answered in the affirmative. Therefore, we believe that the created VR contents have sufficient usefulness as learning contents for the subject, and the objective of being able to create VR contents that take advantage of the characteristics of VR has been largely achieved.

Based on the above results, we suggest the prospects of the system. The first is to adjust the UI of the system. This system also serves as an editing tool for VR contents. Therefore, to make it easier for teachers to create VR contents, we need to adjust the UI of the application to make it easier to use. For example, we need to implement AI that can automatically provide operation instructions and comments when the system user has trouble operating the system and introduce an application design for people who are not familiar with machine operation. The second is to develop a system that can create VR contents on the Web. This system is configured as a single application, but by implementing it so that it can be used on the Web, it will be possible to use this system more easily. The third is the addition of functions that take advantage of the characteristics of VR. In addition to the current function that allows the user to move objects in and out of the room, we can add a function that automatically performs operations in the VR space according to the teacher's avatar. For example, when the teacher points to an object, the object being explained will be highlighted. Thus, by implementing a function to automatically edit the VR contents, we can expect to increase the value of the VR learning contents without increasing the burden on the teacher.

3.4 Improvement of the Lecture Recording Screen

From the results of the evaluation experiment of this system, the mental burden on the teacher due to the absence of the students during the recording of the lecture was raised as an issue. As a solution to this problem, we propose a system in which a virtual student avatar is placed in the VR space, and the teacher can record the lecture while looking at the avatar. The virtual student avatar plays back a predetermined animation. Specifically, we prepared several animations of gazing at the teacher or objects, or taking notes, and played them back randomly. Simultaneously, the animation of the students nodding their heads is dynamically played back based on the audio data obtained from the teacher during the lecture recording. In this way, we can reproduce more natural movements of the students during the lecture.

Figure 11 shows the system with the virtual student avatars. We prepared several virtual student avatars that are young and wear school uniforms, considering the situation of a school class. However, the roles and effects of the avatars themselves have not been considered in this system and need to be investigated in the future.

Fig. 11. Lecture recording screen with virtual student avatars.

4 Conclusion

4.1 Summary

In this study, we developed a support system for creating VR learning contents that enables object manipulation in the VR space with only simple editing operations on a personal computer. As a result of an evaluation experiment on subject with teaching experience, it was found that the teacher could easily create VR contents in a short period of time because there was little burden in recording the lecture and editing the VR contents, and no specialized knowledge was required. In addition, the practicality of the VR contents that can be created by this system was suggested. Based on the results, we studied how to improve the system so that teachers can use it more easily. Specifically, we proposed a system in which a virtual student avatar is placed in the VR space so that the teacher can watch the student while recording the lecture. We believe that this system can solve the mental burden on the teacher due to the absence of students when recording a lecture.

4.2 Future Tasks

In the future, we will develop a system that enables teachers to create VR contents more easily than is possible in the current system. Specifically, we will introduce application designs and UI principles that will make it easier for teachers to use this system. In addition, we are developing a system that uses action recognition and voice recognition to dynamically manipulate the virtual student avatars in response to the teacher's words and actions during lecture recording. This will improve the interaction between the virtual student avatar and the teacher, and make the teacher feel as if he or she is teaching the students, which will improve the ease of teaching.

Acknowledgements. We would like to thank Editage (www.editage.com) for English language editing.

References

1. Yano Research Institute Co., Ltd.: Conducted e-learning market research. https://www.yano.co.jp/pressrelease/show/press_id/2404. Accessed 11 Nov 2021
2. Tominaga, A.: Effects of Blending Lessons Combining E-Learning and Peer Response on Writing Skills. Waseda University Press, Tokyo (2014).(in Japanese)
3. Japan e-Learning Consortium: 2019 Investigation Committee Report. https://www.elc.or.jp/files/user/doc/eLearningReport_2019.pdf. Accessed 11 Nov 2021
4. Baba, T., Tokunaga, T., Kano, T., Akakura, T.: Development of VR learning spaces considering lecture format in asynchronous e-learning. In: Yamamoto, S., Mori, H. (eds.) HCII 2020. LNCS, vol. 12184, pp. 350–362. Springer, Cham (2020). https://doi.org/10.1007/978-3-030-50020-7_25
5. Yano, K.: Extending the video conferencing system to VR space to deliver online classes with a more live feel. In: 2020 PC Conference, CIEC, pp. 247–250, Japan (2020). (in Japanese)
6. Koyama, R., Unoki. T., Kano, T., Akakura, T.: Proposal of VR class creation system using skeleton pose estimation technology. In: IEICE General Conference, Information and System Society Special Project, Student Poster Session Preprints, p. 141 (2021). (in Japanese)
7. Yukihiko, A.: USB Camera Motion Capture ThreeDPoseTracker Description. https://qiita.com/yukihiko_a/items/43d09db5628334789fab. Accessed 10 Feb 2022

VisionPainter: Authoring Experience of Visual Impairment in Virtual Reality

Kiyosu Maeda[1,3]([✉]), Kazuma Aoyama[2,3], Manabu Watanabe[4],
Michitaka Hirose[5], Kenichiro Ito[3], and Tomohiro Amemiya[2,3]

[1] The Graduate School of Interdisciplinary Information Studies,
The University of Tokyo, Tokyo, Japan
`kiyosu775@g.ecc.u-tokyo.ac.jp`
[2] The Graduate School of Information Science and Technology,
The University of Tokyo, Tokyo, Japan
[3] Virtual Reality Educational Research Center,
The University of Tokyo, Tokyo, Japan
[4] The Graduate School of Frontier Sciences, The University of Tokyo, Tokyo, Japan
[5] Research Center for Advanced Science and Technology, The University of Tokyo,
Tokyo, Japan

Abstract. We present an authoring system and VR viewer that simulate various types of visual impairments. As we all have different visual acuities, it is important for sighted people to understand how people with low vision see. One of the ways to understand their residual vision is to experience it through displays, goggles, and head mounted displays. Although existing research has shown that vision simulation systems are helpful for instilling empathy in non-visually impaired people, they can only handle one or a few specific visual impairments, or it has been difficult for users to change the types of impairment or adjust the severity in real time. In contrast, we propose VisionPainter, 2D authoring application to create a wide variety of vision impairments through painting a viewer with several brush tools that can simulate visual functions. The paintings are transformed into corresponding filters, and reflected in virtual reality viewers immediately. We discuss application scenarios of the system in which it creates novel interactions over existing approaches.

Keywords: Visual impairment · Virtual reality · Authoring

1 Introduction

Having empathy, understanding others' experiences and emotions is essential for social interactions [16]. Despite its importance, it is particularly difficult for those who do not have any impairment to imagine those who have one. For example, people tend to misperceive impaired people who use assistive technologies as having comparable abilities even though they actually do not [30]. One of the ways to foster empathy is to use systems that simulate others' experiences. These systems enable users to improve their attitudes toward impaired people [10] and enhance their altruistic behaviors [5]. These systems and applications to understand disorders [7,14,25,33], such as aphasia, schizophrenia, and dementia, are deployed in various modalities (e.g., wearable devices [22], desktops [27], videos [3], mixed reality [18], and games [13]).

Visual impairments are particularly common among those impairments. There are 2.2 billion visually impaired people around the world as of 2019, according to the WHO report [38]. They have various sight impairments depending on their diseases, including myopia [24], color blindness [11], age-related macular degeneration (AMD) [20], cataracts [19], and glaucoma [36]. They have difficulty in being understood regarding their level of stress and discomfort in their daily lives by others including their own friends and family members, which leads to insufficient empathy [8]. In addition to those who have a close relationship with visually impaired people, such insufficient empathy is also crucial for designers who want to create an inclusive product [9], caregivers who take care of elderly people with visual impairments, and teachers who need to provide inclusive schooling environments [23].

Existing research has tackled this problem by developing visual impairment simulators running on various platforms such as browsers [17], smartphone applications [22], and head mounted displays [20]. They can simulate almost all types of visual impairments: myopia [21], color blindness [11], and AMD [20], and through user studies, they have been proven to be effective to obtain visual impairment experiences, which could be helpful for designers when considering the accessibility of their products [17]. Utilizing virtual reality (VR) environments especially has better effects on the perception of non-visually impaired users [15], and some simulators are already deployed on social VR platforms [1]. Despite their effectiveness, these simulators have a few disadvantages. First, each simulator supports only one or a few visual impairments. Second, it is difficult to adjust the severity of visual impairments immediately. To experience various visual impairments with different degrees of severity, users had to switch applications and physical goggles, or change the internal parameters of the systems. Moreover, it is also difficult to share the simulation results among multiple users, which prevents rapid iterations.

In this study, we developed VisionPainter, an authoring tool and VR viewer that simulate various types of visual impairments with different degrees of severity immediately. The authoring tool enables users to use brushes as a view-painting tool. There are several brushes such as a color brush, a blur brush, and a distortion brush to visualize various types of visual impairments. For example, a color brush is used when users want to visualize AMD and tunnel vision. Users can easily change sizes, opacities, and intensities of the brushes, which means that they can adjust the severity of visual impairments. When users paint a viewer, the system translates the painted areas into a gray-scale filter that describes where they painted. The authoring application sends filter information including the latest filter to a server whenever users update them. Viewer applications connected to the server receive those filters, and render the left and right views in real time. Because filters can be overlaid with each other, users can create an expressive vision not limited to existing solutions. Furthermore, the system can render those filters based on the gaze directions, although this feature is supported only when using a specific device. The viewer can be deployed to many types of VR devices, such as an HMD or smartphones.

In addition to its advantages over previous approaches, this system creates new interactions. Multiple users can connect to the same authoring tool, which will be helpful for teachers who want to teach their students about visual impairments using simulators, and for families with a person who has low vision to deeply understand his/her vision in their daily lives. Furthermore, since the system has two components: the authoring tool and the viewer, it facilitates uses with two people. For example, designers using the authoring tool can paint a more realistic vision based on feedback from experts or visually impaired people. This is consistent with an encouragement in which users need partnerships when creating an inclusive design [6]. We describe these features that produce novel interactions over previous studies.

2   Related Work

In this section, we introduce existing research and systems related to this study. First, we describe the importance of empathy building in people, and how they foster empathy through empathy tools. Second, we introduce visual impairments and the problems visually impaired people face. Finally, we review studies on visual impairment simulators with various platforms.

2.1   Empathy Building

Empathy is the ability to understand other's experiences and emotions [16]. Not having empathy will lead to wrong attitudes toward people with disabilities. Shinohara and Wobbrock [30] found that people tended to believe that assistive technologies made impaired people "normal" while it is not the truth, which led to an insufficient amount of empathy.

One of the ways to build empathy is to use empathy tools that simulate others' experiences, and researchers have proposed and evaluated various empathy tools [7,13,18,42]. Kors et al. [18] simulates a refugee's journey through a mixed-reality game. The Dyslexperience [42] provides a multimodal experience of dyslexia by which people have difficulty in reading and writing texts. Although some studies have not confirmed the effectiveness of the proposed systems through experiments, much research has found that these empathy tools are helpful for people, caregivers, teachers, and designers to understand the experiences of people with disabilities.

Some studies have investigated the literature on empathy or empathy tools in the context of Human-Computer Interaction [28,41]. Paratte et al. [28] analyzed publications about empathy tools and found three dimensions to describe these empathy tools: the amount of agency (how freely users can choose various options during their experiences), the user's perspective (first-, second-, and third-person perspectives), and the type of sensations (creating or limiting sensor inputs).

Despite the benefit of empathy building as mentioned above, some studies have pointed out that empathy tools themselves are not enough for designers [6,32,34]. Bennett and Rosner [6] indicated that empathy building did not necessarily work due to a concealment of various important elements such as an affective understanding and personal capacity. Based on their analysis, they proposed commitments to enhance "being with" experiences rather than "being like" experiences during a design process.

2.2   Visual Impairment

Visual impairments are particularly common among those impairments in the world as we mentioned in the introduction. There are various types of visual impairments. For example, people with myopia have a lower ability to see far-away objects [24]. Color blindness is another type of visual impairment that makes it difficult for people to distinguish between certain colors. In addition to various types of impairments, their severity differs from person to person. We also introduce other visual impairments briefly in a later section.

It is difficult for those who do not have any impairment to understand the inconveniences and challenges visually impaired people face as with other types of impairments. For example, sighted people who want to help visually impaired people navigate often give wrong feedback although they think it is right due to a lack of understanding [39]. This is true not only to strangers but also to closely related people. Existing research has indicated that even sighted people have difficulty in knowing the needs of their partners with vision impairments [8].

2.3   Visual Impairment Simulator

Existing research has proposed visual impairment simulators to experience visual impairments [11,12,17] as we introduced in the last section. Flatla et al. [11] proposed a color blindness simulation tool to understand the experience of having color blindness. They simulated personalized symptoms of color blindness based on an empirical model, which were shown to be more accurate than the standard model. Kamikubo et al. [17] developed a gaze-contingent tunnel vision simulator to accelerate the prototyping of accessible products.

These systems run on various platforms: physical goggles [12,40,43], displays [17], smartphones [22], and VR (head mounted displays) [2,4,20,21,36,37]. Wood et al. [40] indicated that cataract and blurring conditions simulated with goggles degrade the driving performance under nighttime conditions. MacAlpine and Flatla [22] proposed a personalized simulator of color blindness running on mobile devices in real time.

Among these platforms, VR has been shown to be particularly effective to induce long-term empathy due to its embodiment and immersion [15]. Ahn et al. [2] showed that an experience of red-green color blindness in VR encouraged participants to have favorable attitudes toward people with disability. XREye [20] is a system that simulates seven common visual impairments with eye-tracking.

As well as simulators, visual impairment experiences have been integrated into VR games. For example, Myopic Bike and Say Hi [21] are two virtual reality games that allow users to experience myopia for enhancing empathetic feelings.

While these systems have been effective, there are a few disadvantages. First, each system only supports one or a few visual impairment types. Using goggles to experience the tunnel vision, for example, we have to change lenses or goggles to experience cataracts. Second, it is difficult to change the severity of the impairments. It is desirable for a system to provide more flexible experiences in which users can freely change the types or adjust the severity in real time. In the next section, we introduce our system and how it overcomes these disadvantages.

3   System

We developed VisionPainter, an authoring tool and a VR viewer in which users can create various types of vision changing their severity with a 2D painting interface, and see those vision in VR in real time. In this section, we introduce how to use these tools to create and simulate an experience of visual impairment. This system is implemented in Unity 2019.4.18f, and deployed in Windows 10 for the authoring tool and HTC Vive Pro Eye[1] and Android devices for the VR viewer.

3.1   Authoring Tool

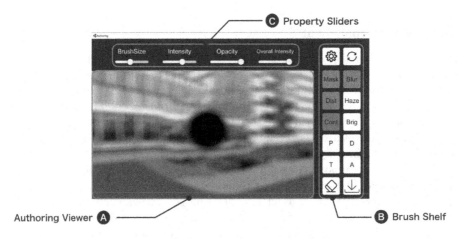

Fig. 1. Authoring tool of the system. (A) Authoring Viewer, where users paint with brushes, (B) Brush Shelf, where users select or change the brush types, (C) Property Sliders, where users adjust the brush size, intensity, and opacity.

---

[1] https://htcvive.jp/item/99HARJ006-00.html.

Figure 1 describes a user interface of the authoring tool. There are three components: Authoring Viewer (Fig. 1A), Brush Shelf (Fig. 1B), and Property Sliders (Fig. 1C).

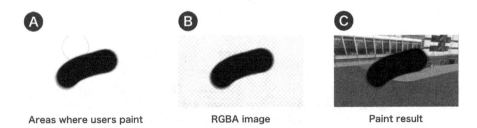

Areas where users paint   RGBA image   Paint result

Fig. 2. Authoring brush of the system. (A) Users drag the selected brush in the viewer. (B) The area where they have painted is translated into an RGBA image. (C) The system applies brush effects to each pixel through shaders. In this case, the mask effect is applied to the viewer.

This is an authoring viewer where users paint their vision with a brush. As described in the figure, there is a brush marker that represents the size of the brush. When users drag this marker in the viewer, they can paint the viewer (Fig. 2A). The system translates the area where they have painted into a 640 × 360 pixel RGBA image in real time (Fig. 2B). In this image, RGBA values in the painted pixels are (0.0, 0.0, 0.0, 1.0), while RGBA values in non-painted pixels are (0.0, 0.0, 0.0, 0.0). When we define an alpha value of a filter image in a pixel p as α_p, α_p takes a value of between 0.0 and 1.0, which can be changed with an opacity slider and an intensity slider, as we describe in the later section. The system applies brush effects to each pixel p through several shaders in Unity, scripts to calculate the color of each pixel. The calculation method in these shaders is described as follows:

$$V'_p = C_p * (1 - \alpha) + C'_p * \alpha \tag{1}$$

where V'_p is a final result of an RGBA value at pixel p, C_p is an RGB value of the original viewer at pixel p, and C'_p is an RGB value after being applied a brush effect at pixel p. Equation (1) is calculated for the number of brush types. Figure 2C describes the result when users paint the authoring viewer with a mask brush. As we can see, the painted area becomes invisible with black colors. In the next section, we introduce the brush shelf, 10 brush types the system supports, and how C'_p is calculated for each brush effect.

Brush Shelf. Figure 1B shows a brush shelf. There are several types of brushes: mask, blur, distortion, haze, brightness, contrast, color blindness, and eraser. Each brush has three modes: paint mode (marked as orange), visible mode (marked as blue), and non-select mode (marked as white). Users can paint the viewer with a brush which is in the paint mode. While the system applies brush effects to the viewer in the paint and visible modes, it does not apply them in the non-select mode. The visible and non-select modes are switched by pressing the brush buttons. Holding the brush button down for a second changes the mode into the paint mode. To lift the paint mode, users need to press the button (Fig. 3).

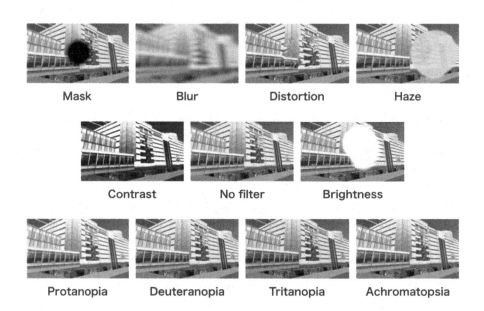

Fig. 3. Brush types. There are 10 brushes: Mask, Blur, Distortion, Haze, Brightness, Contrast, and Color Blindness (there are four types: Protanopia, Deuteranopia, Tritanopia, and Achromatopsia).

Mask Brush. Users can paint the authoring viewer in black with this brush. This brush can be used to simulate a few types of visual impairments, such as AMD and a tunnel vision, which have a blind spot symptom. Here, C'_p for this brush is simply described as (0.0, 0.0, 0.0, 1.0) independent of the original color C_p. Since the size and position of blind spot areas differ depending on the individual and severity of the impairments, existing systems have difficulties in adjusting this type of vision. On the other hand, this system allows users create blind spot areas changing their size and severity.

Blur Brush. This brush can be used for nearsightedness and farsightedness with which it is difficult to see nearby or far-away objects. Gaussian blur is applied to where users paint with this brush. The strength of the blur can be modified through an opacity slider whose value corresponds to the kernel size (k) of Gaussian blur with five grades $(k = 3, 5, 7, 9, 11)$. At this time, we do not consider the distance of objects in a virtual reality environment for applying blur filters. This is because it is difficult to measure the distance when using 360-degree photos or see-through view in real time as the background of the viewer.

Distortion Brush. This brush allows users to create a distorted vision. This brush is used for simulating AMD or diabetic maculopathy, which causes damage to the macula due to the leaking of blood vessels near or the presence of protein near or on the macula, respectively. According to a random gray-scale noise map generated by the system, each original pixel position of the filter image is shifted. For example, when one pixel p_i at position (x, y) corresponds to a gray-scale value $g_i (0 \leq g_i \leq 255)$ in the noise map, C'_{pi} will take the value of the original pixel color at position $(x + cos(g_i/255 * 2\pi), y + sin(g_i/255 * 2\pi))$.

Haze Brush. This brush simulates opaque vision and is used to simulate cataracts where the eye lens becomes cloudy, which causes blurry or hazy vision. The system simply multiplies gray colors with areas where users paint with this brush. By default, C'_p is set to (0.7, 0.7, 0.7, 1.0) independent of the original color as with the mask brush.

Contrast Brush This brush enables users to change the contrast of the viewer. The contrast of one's vision is reduced when people suffer from cataracts and AMD, as indicated in [19, 20]. The system uses a sigmoid function to achieve a reduced contrast as follows:

$$C'_p = \frac{1}{1 + e^{-aC_p}} \tag{2}$$

where a is set to 10.0 by default.

Color Blindness Brushes. These brush types are used to visualize four types of color blindness: Protanopia, Deuteranopia, Tritanopia, and Achromatopsia. People usually have three types of sensitive cones (short-wavelength, middle-wavelength, and long-wavelength) to perceive colors [29]. On the other hand, people with color blindness lack one or more cones and cannot distinguish certain colors. For example, people with protanopia do not have long-wavelength cones, which makes it difficult to perceive red [11]. The system simulates four types of color blindness by applying rotation matrices to each pixel that has RGB values.

Eraser brush In addition to the various types of brushes, the system also provides an eraser brush to literally erase brush effects. Users switch from paint mode to eraser mode by clicking the eraser button. The eraser button is marked as blue at this time. This eraser effect is applied only to a brush in the paint mode (a brush marked as orange). The pixel colors in an applicable filter image become (0.0, 0.0, 0.0, 0.0) after users paint with the eraser brush.

Reset Button. When users want to erase the brush effects all at once, they can use this reset button. As with the eraser button, it is applied by simply clicking the button, and all filters are initialized. This means that the α value at each pixel in the filter images becomes 0.0.

Save Button. Users can also save the results with this button. When pressing this button, the system saves the gray-scale filter images of each brush in local storage. These images are linked with a timestamp that represents when they are saved.

Setting Button. When users press this button, the system displays the setting panel. Here, users can set an author id, a server address, and a background of the viewer from several options (e.g., 360-degree photos or 3D cities). The author id and the server address are needed to connect the server which sends filter information to viewers acquired from the authoring tool. Users can set the author id with a string value. The setting panel also provides the past filters they saved with the save button from a list of timestamps that are linked with filter images in the local storage. When a timestamp is clicked, the corresponding filters are applied to the authoring viewer.

Property Sliders. Here, users can change the brush size, brush intensity, brush opacity, and overall opacity. The brush size represents the radius of the brush, ranging from 1 to 100 pixels. The brush opacity value corresponds to α of the brush, which can be taken between 0 and 1, as we described in the authoring viewer. This value is applied to all paintings after the value changes. That means that α is not applied to the painting results before the value changes. Each brush type has its own opacity value. The brush intensity slider is used to change the hardness of the brush edge, ranging from 0.0 to 1.0. When this slider value is small, the brush edge becomes soft, which means α at the edge of the brush is closer to 0.0. While the opacity value slider is applied to the subsequent paintings, an overall opacity slider is applied to the current filters. When we define this slider value as o, ranging between 0.0 and 1.0, α_p will be $\alpha_p * o$.

Using these components in the authoring tool, we now describe how users create a vision, as depicted in Fig. 1. There are a few symptoms such as blur, black and distorted areas at the center, which are commonly seen in AMD. First, a user selects the mask brush as the paint mode and changes the brush size to 50 pixels. The user also sets the brush intensity slider value to 0.6 so that the edge of the brush will be softer and then paints the center of the viewer with this mask brush. Next, he selects the blur brush in paint mode and changes the opacity slider value to simulate a medium-level of blurry vision. The user paints all areas of the viewer with this brush. Those filters can be overlaid with each other. The processing order in Unity shaders is as follows: color blindness, distortion, blur, brightness, haze, contrast, and mask. Finally, the user paints the viewer around the center with the distortion brush. After finishing the painting, the user can save these filters with the save button so as to look back at them later.

3.2 Viewer

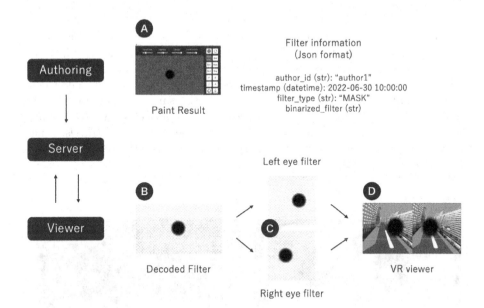

Fig. 4. Architecture of the system. After users paint the authoring viewer (A), the authoring tool sends the filter information to the server. The viewer obtains the filter information from the authoring tool through the server (B). Then, the viewer creates left and right filters (C), applying those filters to the VR view (D).

Users can see the painted vision through the viewer. The viewer applies the filters that are created in the authoring tool. Figure 4 introduces how the viewer obtains and applies these filters. First, after the authoring viewer is painted (Fig. 4A), the authoring tool sends the filter information in json format to the server, which is currently deployed on Heroku. The filter information consists of four variables: the author id, a filter type, timestamp, and a binarized filter encoded from the filter image. The authoring tool only sends a filter selected as the paint mode in each send. In the case of Fig. 4A, the filter type in the filter information is set to "MASK" because the authoring viewer is painted with the mask brush.

The server holds the filter images associated with filter types and the author id. In other words, there are 10 filter images for each author id in the server. Since these images are updated whenever they are sent from the authoring tool, all filters are kept to be synchronized with those in the authoring tool.

The viewer regularly checks the server and when it detects the latest filter information based on the timestamp, the viewer receives the information from the server. At this time, the users need to specify the author id. After the viewer receives the filter information, it decodes the binarized filter into a 640×360

pixel RGBA filter (Fig. 4B) and creates left and right filters from a decoded filter image, as shown in Fig. 4C. Since left and right views in VR are different due to a binocular parallax, the viewer crops the decoded filter image into a 360 × 360 pixel square with some x-axis pixel offsets that are adjustable in the viewer. The system supports both dual and single eye modes. In dual eye mode, the viewer applies the same filters to the left and right views. On the other hand, it can apply different filters to each eye in single eye mode.

Figure 4D shows how the viewer renders the filters with HMDs. The calculation method to apply filters to the vision is the same as that used by the authoring tool (see Sect. 3.1). The viewer can be deployed on Android smartphones (Fig. 5A, using Google Cardboard[2] to see the viewer) and HMDs. When the system renders the viewer on a smartphone, it adjusts the rendered images with distortion correction.

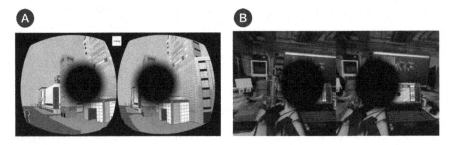

Fig. 5. The smartphone view (A) and the see-through view (B) with the mask and color blindness brushes applied.

When the users have HTC Vive Pro Eye, they can access two features. First, the viewer can support eye tracking. The system can adjust the position of the filters according to the gaze positions. Since there has been little research that supports eye tracking [20], it will provide users with a more immersive experience than existing systems. Second, it can simulate visual impairments with a see-through view for the background (Fig. 5B). This see-through view promotes an active experience with higher agency [28]: Users can interact with real-world objects and people, as described in [26], by which users experience an embodied and active egocentric child vision. Figure 4C shows a see-through view with the mask and color blindness brushes applied.

4   Discussion

In this section, we first discuss the application scenarios of the system. These scenarios will enable users to experience new interactions over existing visual impairment simulators. We also describe the limitations, and future work of the study.

---

[2] https://arvr.google.com/cardboard/.

4.1   Application Scenario

Since the viewer can get filter information from the server by specifying an author id as described in Sect. 3.2, multiple users can connect viewers to the same authoring tool via the server simultaneously as long as they have devices for the number of people. This means that the system will be appropriate to be deployed in places where there are many users such as a classroom. While existing systems require users to manipulate by themselves or wait for instructions when they want to change the filters or severity, this system only requires the manipulation of the authoring tool to change such parameters. Painting the authoring viewer updates all viewers connected to the server with the same author id. This scalability will be helpful for teachers who conduct lessons to their students about visual impairments using simulators.

Users can save and load the filter images they painted as described in Sect. 3.1, which makes it easier for them to see progress of visual impairments or compare symptoms with others. This feature will be helpful for users to deeply understand that the severity of visual impairments differs depending on people and time. Although in the current situation, users can only save filters in their local storage, we will provide them with a feature to save filters to the server. This feature will allow the server of the system to function as a gallery in which users can post, see, or even download various visual impairment filters created by others.

The system induces a pairing experience in which one person uses the authoring tool and another uses the viewer. For example, a designer pairs up with an expert or a visually impaired person, and iterates a design process to create a more realistic vision with the system through feedback from them. This is consistent with existing research that claims the importance of design process with people with disabilities [6]. Furthermore, users can experience different perspectives at the same time during collaboration. As well as using the authoring tool to see visions with a first-person perspective, users can also experience the third-person perspective by looking at a pair of users with VR viewers. While it has been indicated that the perspective is an important aspect of an empathy tool, it has not been deeply explored how the different perspective affects empathetic behaviors [28]. The system enhance such investigations to understand the effect of first-person and third-person perspectives on users' empathy.

4.2   Limitations and Future Work

The system still can not simulate some visual impairments accurately. When painted with the blur brush, the system applies Gaussian blur to the viewer equally regardless of the distance to simulate myopia with several discrete level of strength by changing the kernel size. However, we need to consider that those who have myopia can see near objects and can not see far-away objects well while people with hyperopia have difficulty in seeing near objects. Furthermore, the color blindness filters in the system are simulated with approximate values using rotation matrices, and not personalized as in [11]. We will improve the simulation accuracy of these types of visual impairments based on existing research and theories. For example, we will apply blur to the viewer with different strengths based on the distances between the camera and objects. In future work, we will evaluate the realism of the improved simulated vision created by this system with user studies.

While the system enables users to simulate various visual impairments, it is expected that it might take time for them to get used to the authoring tool due to its multi-functionality. In other words, beginners might confuse how they select or combine appropriate brushes and their properties to simulate various visual impairments on the authoring user interface. This problem will be solved by using the server as a gallery in which there are filters created by others as we discussed in Sect. 4.1. Users can simply download sample filters from the server and apply them to the viewer without any training or experience.

We will enhance the system so that the viewer will be easily integrated into other applications such as VR games. While some studies have developed systems that allow users to play games with some visual impairments [21], the strength of our system is to provide them with more flexible experiences in which they can change the type or severity of a visual impairment even during playing games. Here is the future scenario of how game developers incorporate this feature of the system into their games. To integrate the system into VR games created by Unity, game developers first import the viewer of this system as a unitypackage, a package format used in Unity. Then, they attach a script that connects the games with the server (they need to specify the server address and an author id) and processes filter images from the server to a camera object. Similarly, this feature will allow the system to be combined with other modalities to experience visual impairments such as a white cane and a guide dog [31, 35]. We believe that our system will accelerate the development and evaluation of VR games and multimodal experiences as empathy tools for those with visual impairments.

5   Conclusion

We proposed VisionPainter, an authoring and viewer system to create and simulate various visual impairment experiences. Users can paint and process vision with several types of brushes, and observe the painted vision through VR viewers simultaneously. This system can support various visual impairments, changing their severity immediately. Furthermore, we introduce some new application scenarios of the system such as scalable usage in a classroom, saving and loading past filters, integration into games, and pairing experiences. We believe that the system will build a bridge of mutual understanding among people with a wide variety of vision types.

References

1. NearSighted   Classroom   -   VRChat.   https://vrchat.com/home/world/wrld_ce96014b-bb0a-4060-9d09-1672824570ea

2. Ahn, S.J., Le, A.M.T., Bailenson, J.: The effect of embodied experiences on self-other merging, attitude, and helping behavior. Media Psychol. **16**(1), 7–38 (2013). https://doi.org/10.1080/15213269.2012.755877

3. Aitamurto, T., Zhou, S., Sakshuwong, S., Saldivar, J., Sadeghi, Y., Tran, A.: Sense of presence, attitude change, perspective-taking and usability in first-person split-sphere 360 video. In: Proceedings of the 2018 CHI Conference on Human Factors in Computing Systems, pp. 1–12 (2018). DOIurl10.1145/3173574.3174119

4. Ates, H.C., Fiannaca, A., Folmer, E.: Immersive simulation of visual impairments using a wearable see-through display. In: Proceedings of the Ninth International Conference on Tangible, Embedded, and Embodied Interaction, pp. 225–228 (2015). https://doi.org/10.1145/2677199.2680551

5. Batson, C.D., Batson, J.G., Slingsby, J.K., Harrell, K.L., Peekna, H.M., Todd, R.M.: Empathic joy and the empathy-altruism hypothesis. J. Personal. Soc. Psychol. **61**(3), 413–426 (1991). https://doi.org/10.1037/0022-3514.61.3.413

6. Bennett, C.L., Rosner, D.K.: The promise of empathy: design, disability, and knowing the "other". In: Proceedings of the 2019 CHI Conference on Human Factors in Computing Systems, pp. 1–13 (2019). https://doi.org/10.1145/3290605.3300528

7. Berezina-Blackburn, V., Oliszewski, A., Cleaver, D., Udakandage, L.: Virtual reality performance platform for learning about dementia. In: Companion of the 2018 ACM Conference on Computer Supported Cooperative Work and Social Computing, pp. 153–156 (2018). https://doi.org/10.1145/3272973.3274043

8. Branham, S.M., Kane, S.K.: Collaborative accessibility: how blind and sighted companions co-create accessible home spaces. In: Proceedings of the 33rd Annual ACM Conference on Human Factors in Computing Systems, pp. 2373–2382 (2015). https://doi.org/10.1145/2702123.2702511

9. Dandavate, U., Sanders, E.B.N., Stuart, S.: Emotions matter: user empathy in the product development process. In: Proceedings of the Human Factors and Ergonomics Society Annual Meeting, vol. 40, No. 7, pp. 415–418 (1996). https://doi.org/10.1177/154193129604000709

10. Fazio, R.H.: Multiple processes by which attitudes guide behavior: the mode model as an integrative framework. In: Advances in Experimental Social Psychology, vol. 23, pp. 75–109 (1990). https://doi.org/10.1016/S0065-2601(08)60318-4

11. Flatla, D.R., Gutwin, C.: "So that's what you see": building understanding with personalized simulations of colour vision deficiency. In: Proceedings of the 14th international ACM SIGACCESS Conference on Computers and Accessibility, pp. 167–174 (2012)

12. Goodman-Deane, J., Waller, S., Collins, A.C., Clarkson, J.: Simulating vision loss: what levels of impairment are actually represented? In: Contemporary Ergonomics and Human Factors 2013: Proceedings of the International Conference on Ergonomics & Human Factors, p. 347 (2013)

13. Gerling, K.M., Mandryk, R.L., Birk, M.V., Miller, M., Orji, R.: The effects of embodied persuasive games on player attitudes toward people using wheelchairs. In: Proceedings of the SIGCHI Conference on Human Factors in Computing Systems, pp. 3413–3422 (2014). https://doi.org/10.1145/2556288.2556962

14. Hailpern, J., Danilevsky, M., Harris, A., Karahalios, K., Dell, G., Hengst, J.: ACES: promoting empathy towards aphasia through language distortion emulation software. In: Proceedings of the SIGCHI Conference on Human Factors in Computing Systems, pp. 609–618 (2011). https://doi.org/10.1145/1978942.1979029

15. Herrera, F., Bailenson, J., Weisz, E., Ogle, E., Zaki, J.: Building long-term empathy: a large-scale comparison of traditional and virtual reality perspective-taking. In: PloS One, p. e0204494 (2018)

16. Hoffman, M.L.: Empathy and Moral Development: Implications for Caring and Justice. Cambridge University Press, Cambridge (2001)
17. Kamikubo, R., Higuchi, K., Yonetani, R., Koike, H., Sato, Y.: Rapid prototyping of accessible interfaces with gaze-contingent tunnel vision simulation. In: Proceedings of the 19th International ACM SIGACCESS Conference on Computers and Accessibility, pp. 387–388 (2017)
18. Kors, M.J., Ferri, G., Van Der Spek, E.D., Ketel, C., Schouten, B.A.: A breathtaking journey. On the design of an empathy-arousing mixed-reality game. In: Proceedings of the 2016 Annual Symposium on Computer-Human Interaction in Play, pp. 91–104 (2016). https://doi.org/10.1145/2967934.2968110
19. Krösl, K., et al.: CatARact: simulating cataracts in augmented reality. In: 2020 IEEE International Symposium on Mixed and Augmented Reality (ISMAR), pp. 682–693 (2020). https://doi.org/10.1109/ISMAR50242.2020.00098
20. Krösl, K., Elvezio, C., Hürbe, M., Karst, S., Feiner, S., Wimmer, M.: XREye: simulating visual impairments in eye-tracked XR. In: IEEE Conference on Virtual Reality and 3D User Interfaces Abstracts and Workshops (VRW), pp. 830–831 (2020)
21. Li, X., Tang, X., Tong, X., Patibanda, R., Mueller, F., Liang, H.N.: Myopic bike and say hi: games for empathizing with the myopic. In: Extended Abstracts of the 2021 Annual Symposium on Computer-Human Interaction in Play, pp. 333–338 (2021). https://doi.org/10.1145/3450337.3483505
22. MacAlpine, R., Flatla, D.R.: Real-time mobile personalized simulations of impaired colour vision. In: Proceedings of the 18th International ACM SIGACCESS Conference on Computers and Accessibility, pp. 181–189 (2016). https://doi.org/10.1145/2982142.2982170
23. Metatla, O., Cullen, C.: "Bursting the assistance bubble" designing inclusive technology with children with mixed visual abilities. In: Proceedings of the 2018 CHI Conference on Human Factors in Computing Systems, pp. 1–14 (2018). https://doi.org/10.1145/3173574.3173920
24. Morgan, I.G., Ohno-Matsui, K., Saw, S.M.: Myopia. Lancet **379**(9827), 1739–1748 (2012). https://doi.org/10.1016/S0140-6736(12)60272-4
25. Nishida, J., Suzuki, K.: BioSync: a paired wearable device for blending kinesthetic experience. In: Proceedings of the 2017 CHI Conference on Human Factors in Computing Systems, pp. 3316–3327 (2017). https://doi.org/10.1145/3025453.3025829
26. Nishida, J., Matsuda, S., Oki, M., Takatori, H., Sato, K., Suzuki, K.: Egocentric smaller-person experience through a change in visual perspective. In: Proceedings of the 2019 CHI Conference on Human Factors in Computing Systems, pp. 1–12 (2019). https://doi.org/10.1145/3290605.3300926
27. Papini, G.P.R., Fontana, M., Bergamasco, M.: Desktop haptic interface for simulation of hand-tremor. In: IEEE Transactions on Haptics, pp. 33–42 (2015). https://doi.org/10.1109/TOH.2015.2504971
28. Pratte, S., Tang, A., Oehlberg, L.: Evoking empathy: a framework for describing empathy tools. In: Proceedings of the Fifteenth International Conference on Tangible, Embedded, and Embodied Interaction, pp. 1–15 (2021). https://doi.org/10.1145/3430524.3440644
29. Sharpe, L.T., Stockman, A., Jägle, H., Nathans, J.: Opsin genes, cone photopigments, color vision, and color blindness. Color vision: From genes to perception, pp. 3–51 (1999)
30. Shinohara, K., Wobbrock, J.O.: In the shadow of misperception: assistive technology use and social interactions. In: Proceedings of the SIGCHI Conference on Human Factors in Computing Systems, pp. 705–714 (2011)

31. Siu, A.F., Sinclair, M., Kovacs, R., Ofek, E., Holz, C., Cutrell, E.: Virtual reality without vision: a haptic and auditory white cane to navigate complex virtual worlds. In: Proceedings of the 2020 CHI Conference on Human Factors in Computing Systems, pp. 1–13 (2020). https://doi.org/10.1145/3313831.3376353
32. Spiel, K., Frauenberger, C., Hornecker, E., Fitzpatrick, G.: When empathy is not enough: assessing the experiences of autistic children with technologies. In: Proceedings of the 2017 CHI Conference on Human Factors in Computing Systems, pp. 2853–2864 (2017). https://doi.org/10.1145/3025453.3025785
33. Tichon, J., Banks, J., Yellowlees, P.: The development of a virtual reality environment to model the experience of schizophrenia. In: International Conference on Computational Science, pp. 11–19 (2003). https://doi.org/10.1007/3-540-44863-2_2
34. Tigwell, G.W.: Nuanced perspectives toward disability simulations from digital designers, blind, low vision, and color blind people. In: Proceedings of the 2021 CHI Conference on Human Factors in Computing Systems, pp. 1–15 (2021). https://doi.org/10.1145/3411764.3445620
35. Tzovaras, D., Moustakas, K., Nikolakis, G., Strintzis, M.G.: Interactive mixed reality white cane simulation for the training of the blind and the visually impaired. In: Personal and Ubiquitous Computing, pp. 51–58 (2009). https://doi.org/10.1007/s00779-007-0171-2
36. Väyrynen, J., Colley, A., Häkkilä, J.: Head mounted display design tool for simulating visual disabilities. In: Proceedings of the 15th International Conference on Mobile and Ubiquitous Multimedia, pp. 69–73 (2016). https://doi.org/10.1145/3012709.3012714
37. Werfel, F., Wiche, R., Feitsch, J., Geiger, C.: Empathizing audiovisual sense impairments: interactive real-time illustration of diminished sense perception. In: Proceedings of the 7th Augmented Human International Conference, pp. 1–8 (2016). https://doi.org/10.1145/2875194.2875226
38. World Health Organization: World report on vision (2019)
39. Williams, M.A., Galbraith, C., Kane, S.K., Hurst, A.: "Just let the cane hit it": how the blind and sighted see navigation differently. In: Proceedings of the 16th International ACM SIGACCESS Conference on Computers & Accessibility, pp. 217–224 (2014). https://doi.org/10.1145/2661334.2661380
40. Wood, J., Chaparro, A., Carberry, T., Chu, B.S.: Effect of simulated visual impairment on nighttime driving performance. In: Optometry and Vision Science, pp. 379–386 (2010)
41. Wright, P., McCarthy, J.: Empathy and experience in HCI. In: Proceedings of the SIGCHI Conference on Human Factors in Computing Systems, pp. 637–646 (2008)
42. Yong, Z.F., Ng, A.L., Nakayama, Y.: The Dyslexperience: SSE of projection mapping to simulate dyslexia. In: 2019 International Conference on Multimodal Interaction, pp. 493–495. https://doi.org/10.1145/3340555.3358657
43. Zagar, M., Baggarly, S.: Low vision simulator goggles in pharmacy education. In: American Journal of Pharmaceutical Education (2010)

Enhancing Mall Security Based on Augmented Reality in the Post-pandemic World

Like Wu and Jiro Tanaka$^{(\boxtimes)}$

Waseda University, Kitakyushu, Japan
WuLike@fuji.waseda.jp, jiro@aoni.waseda.jp

Abstract. COVID-19 has shocked the retail industry, customers' concerns for their health and safety are taking business away from shopping malls. Mall owners are thinking of finding new ways to bring their business back in this post-pandemic world. How to protect customers from COVID-19 in shopping malls has been a problem. This study presents an enhanced mall security system to help enforce wearing masks and proper social distancing in shopping malls using augmented reality (AR). We created a novel visualization way: Radar vision to display detected people in the perspective of mall guards, to help guards react quickly to violations, and better enforce the mandatory rules. When the mall guards wearing hololens activate the radar vision function, they can see all people violating wearing masks or social distance mandates through the wall. Mall guards can use gaze to select the target person and then use the voice command to activate the navigation arrow to help them quickly go to the scene. In addition to helping mall guards to enforce mandates, the system also provides assisted functions to protect customers. When the violation situation appears around a customer, the system will alert them to avoid and show an avoidance arrow until the user goes in the correct direction. We demonstrated a preliminary system with four surveillance cameras in our school building area. The pilot study shows that our system can effectively detect and display radar images, increasing the efficiency of mall guards and reducing customer safety concerns.

Keywords: Augmented reality · See through the wall · COVID-19 · Shopping mall

1 Introduction

Coronavirus disease (COVID-19) is an infectious disease caused by the SARS-CoV-2 virus. The virus was first detected in the city of Wuhan in December 2019. On 30 January 2020, the world health organization (WHO) declared the outbreak a public health emergency to draw international attention. The statistics by WHO on 13 January 2022 confirm 312 million infected people and a massive number of deaths worldwide.

The retail industry was then shocked by the COVID-19 crisis. Shopping malls suddenly lost customers because the world had to lock down for the prevention of the virus's spreading [1]. As restrictions began to lift, mall owners have been thinking of finding new ways to bring their business back. As a result of the isolation measures, customers accelerated the shift in spending patterns to online shopping. With the emergence of new virus variants repeatedly appearing [2], customers' concerns for their health and safety are taking business away from shopping malls. Their expectations for offline shopping have changed to demand more safety than they do convenience and the price of the goods [3]. Safety is the overriding priority for customers returning to the shopping malls. The key to getting customers back to the malls is to create a safe shopping environment for mall owners and retail store owners, to invest in safe ways to protect their customers. Many retailers are looking for some precaution ways to impose into shopping malls to limit the virus spread.

Based on the advice by the WHO, there are several rules that people should follow outdoors to protect themself and others: 1. keeping social distance of more than 1 m, and avoiding crowded places. 2. wearing fitted masks correctly. Many research works have proved that wearing masks and social distancing are effective approaches for controlling the spread of infectious diseases such as influenza, MERS, and COVID-19. However, controlling the spread of the virus in public places such as shopping malls is a problem. Although shopping malls worldwide imposed mandatory wearing of masks and social distancing to limit the transmission of COVID-19, there are still several individuals who are not abiding by the rules. Shopping malls usually have higher foot traffic than other public places. It is not sufficient to rely on mall guards alone to enforce the mandates. To address customers' concerns for their health and safety in offline shopping, this study focuses on helping malls enforce mandates for COVID-19 prevention. We made an enhanced mall security system based on augmented reality. With the radar vision of the system, the mall guards on patrol can see people who violate the mandates, no matter how many walls separate them. They can also go to the scene quickly with aid of the system to maintain the mandates. However, this system provides user protection functions to help general users avoid high-risk situations.

2 Related Work

2.1 Medical Research

After the WHO published the health recommendation for the public, many researchers have proven that wearing a mask and maintaining social distance are two significant effective ways for reducing the transmission of the COVID-19 virus. Eikenberry et al. [4] developed a compartmental model to assess the impact of community-wide mask use on the spread of COVID-19. They used COVID-19 transmission data from Washington state and New York City. The simulation result of the data demonstrated that even if the mask's performance was not good, it can still reduce the spread of the virus and decrease mortality. Berry C, Berry H, and Berry R [5] explored the relationship between mask mandates and COVID-19 infection rates using a large dataset collected by government agencies. The result suggested that mask mandates significantly impacted on reducing the spread of COVID-19 during the early summer of 2020 in the United States. Thu et al. [6] assessed the effectiveness of the social distancing measures in 10 countries through the confirmed cases and deaths. They demonstrated that after the government announced the highest level of social distance measure, the effect of this measure resulted in the number of people infected after 1 to 4 weeks.

2.2 Indoor Localization

Our research requires devices to have the ability to locate specific people in the building. There are several positioning methods. Kulyukin et al. [7] proposed a robot-assisted indoor navigation system based on radio frequency identification (RFID) technology. These types of passive RFID tags can give the robots stimulation at the right place and assist them in taking the right path. Chumkamon, Tuvaphanthaphiphat, and Keeratiwintakorn [8] proposed an RFID-based system to support the visually impaired to reach the target location correctly. The RFID chips are filled with location information that they import.

Some studies use wireless signals for localization. Barsocchi et al. [9] proposed a wireless network-based positioning algorithm. They measured the received signal strength indicator (RSSI) and then translate it into distance data. By using a calibration method, their system can locate the mobile device's location. Because of wireless networks' wide distribution and applicability, these signal strength-based measurement and localization methods have further research. Another positioning technology has emerged in indoor positioning, named ultra-wideband (UWB). UWB is a radio technology that can use a low energy level for short-range, high-bandwidth communications over a large portion of a radio spectrum [10]. It has good accuracy and good anti-jamming performance. Its disadvantage is that it is high costly to apply to the actual environment.

In addition to signaling positioning techniques, computer vision for localization has also been studied. Cooper and Hegde [11] used low-cost webcams paired with a series of algorithms to detect people in a video stream and determine their location. The research showed that the method achieved 95% accuracy of people detection and half-meter positioning accuracy. This system can be applied to a large area such as a shopping mall.

2.3 Object Detection

Research on artificial intelligence (AI) has been a hot topic in recent years. Among the many subfields of artificial intelligence, the object detection method has been widely used. The mainstream algorithms are divided into two types: one-stage methods and two-stage methods.

As for one-stage methods, Liu et al. [12] presented single short multibox detector (SSD) for detecting objects in images only using a single deep neural network. The core of this algorithm is the multiscale feature map. Convolutional layers convert the original image, and this data is called a feature map, which contains the information of the original image. The SSD network contains multiple convolutional layers, and the feature map is used to locate and detect the objects in the original image. Redmon et al. [13] presented you only look once (YOLO) for detecting the object. YOLO redefines object detection as a regression problem. It applies a single convolutional neural network (CNN) to the entire image, divides it into grids, and predicts class probabilities and bounding boxes for each grid. This algorithm can also predict the probability of the presence of objects in the bounding box and it is significantly fast.

As for two-stage methods, Ren et al. [14] proposed a fast region-based convolutional network (Fast R-CNN) method for object detection. In Fast R-CNN, the ssp layer of the last convolutional layer is changed to the ROI Pooling layer. Moreover, the multi-task loss function (MTLF) was proposed. These improvements make CNN faster.

After the COVID-19 outbreak, these AI echniques have also been of great help in reducing the virus transmission. Boyko, Abdelpakey, and Shehata [15] propose a multi-object tracking social distancing violation detector that improves accuracy by adding more group detection. Bhambani, Jain, and Sultanpure [16] proposed a YOLO-based deep learning solution to help enforce the social distance and wearing masks in public.

2.4 Augmented Reality on Occlusion Management

Augmented reality technology has received unprecedented growth in recent years. The AR market is growing rapidly, and more research on AR close to people's life has emerged. The ability to see invisible things is one of the features of AR. Wu and Popescu [17] used an RGB-D sensor to dynamically capture the hidden content to provide X-ray vision to improve exploration efficiency in VR and AR scenes. Kameda, Takemasa, and Ohta [18] integrated the images from remote surveillance cameras into the user's hand-held device screen to achieve the augmented reality effect of displaying invisible life information inside the building. Avery, Sandor, and Thomas [19] proposed an augmented reality system with multi-view modes. This system has two types of visualization methods. The edge overlay visualization makes AR objects appear behind walls rather than in front of the user. The tunnel cut-out visualizations make the object to be displayed more realistic by providing occluding layers between the user and the remote location. Zollmann et al. [20] evaluated various methods for implementing x-ray view in augmented reality. Their research results showed that image-based ghosting can help users understand the depth order between physical and AR objects.

3 Goal and Approach

Mall owners should ensure a safe environment to keep their business relevant in this post-pandemic world. This study therefore aims to create an AR system to assist malls in maintaining a safe shopping environment to address customers' health and safety concerns in this post-pandemic world. To achieve this goal, we present an AR-based mall security system to help enforce wearing masks and social distancing in the shopping mall.

This system has three enhancement functions based on AR technology.

The first function is Radar vision. It is a novel visualization method to see the unmasked people or crowd gathering through the wall (see Fig. 1).

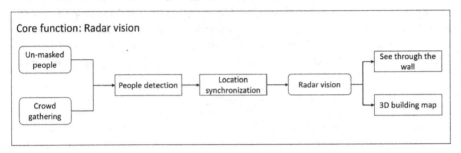

Fig. 1. Radar vision flow chart

The second function is AR tracking. After mall guards grasp position information of violative people, they can use eye-tracking to select the target person they want to track, and turn on the auxiliary navigation arrow heading to the target position.

The third function is user protection. When the violation situation appears around the customer, the system will alert them to avoid and show an avoidance arrow until the user goes in the correct direction.

4   System Design

4.1   System Overview

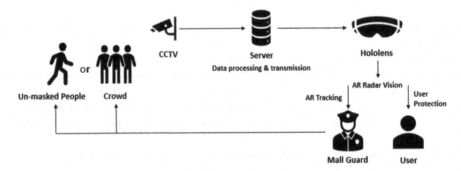

Fig. 2. Overview of the system

This system uses three types of hardware: CCTV cameras, servers, and Hololens. The system detects two violations in a mall: un-masked people and crowd gathering. First, the CCTV cameras collect the input video sequences and pass them to the server with a deep neural network model. The model's output would be the detected violative people in the scene. Then the server will transfer the people's position data to the Hololens to open the AR Radar vision. The radar vision can support the AR tacking function to help mall guards and avoidance suggestions to customers (Fig. 2).

4.2   System Hardware

Hololens2   Camera   Laptop PC

Fig. 3. System hardware

To allow users to free their hands and not hinder their regular security work or shopping activities, the system uses mixed reality smartglasses to display the hologram content. We used Microsoft hololens 2 as the mixed reality smartglasses. Hololens 2 is a wireless, ergonomic self-contained holographic device. In addition to displaying augmented reality content, it can also provide real-world environmental awareness in mixed reality applications. We also used the monocular camera as CCTV cameras to capture video information from the scene. This video information is transmitted directly to the server. In addition to the above two hardware devices, the system also requires a server to process and transfer data. Here we use a laptop PC as a server. We connected the webcam to the laptop PC and kept the laptop and hololens on the same local network for data transmission. These three devices are shown in Fig. 3.

4.3   Radar Vision

Concept diagram   **Implementation diagram**

Fig. 4. Radar vision

In this system, we present a Radar vision: a novel visualization way to help mall guards keep track of the movement of detected people in a mall. Compared to ordinary radar machines, this Radar vision gives mall guards an enhanced vision to observe the violative people through the wall (see Fig. 4). It is like Superman's X-ray vision in the comics.

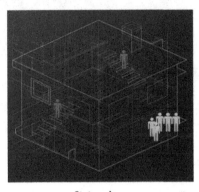

Status view

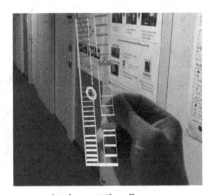
Implementation diagram

Fig. 5. Status view

In addition to the X-ray view, the system provides a status view of the shopping mall. It helps mall guards get a quick, clear idea of what is going on in the mall. This status view is not like a bird's-eye view that the exterior of the building will block. It can directly view the internal structure of the building and get clear position information of the marked people. The red human-shaped small image indicates people not wearing a mask. The yellow multi-person image indicates a crowd gathering in that place (see Fig. 5).

This Radar vision consists of three main components: people detection, location synchronization, and radar image visualization. First, The system keeps monitoring unmasked people and crowd gathering based on a complete surveillance system in the mall. Second, by setting landmarks for location mapping and distance estimation of the detected people's location, the system can synchronize the people's location to the virtual world in Hololens. Third, we use the hologram avatar to represent the detected people to visualize the person's radar image. Next, we explain these three components in detail.

People Detection

For fundamental security reasons, shopping malls usually are equipped with a complete surveillance system. The people detection functions take advantage of this surveillance system. The CCTV cameras in the shopping mall collect the input video and pass them

Fig. 6. People detection

to the server with a deep neural network model. Therefore, we can enhance the cameras in the mall. These enhanced CCTV cameras can monitor people and determine whether people comply with epidemic prevention measures or not (see Fig. 6). Finally, mark these people for other functions.

Location Synchronization

After the monitoring system detects the violative persons, it then helps the user's device locate where the person is. Because the world in Hololens is virtual, and the violative person's location is in the real world. Therefore, to synchronize the location of the violative person into the virtual world, we established a mapping from the real world to the virtual world through virtual landmarks.

Landmarks: Similar to outdoor navigation, where landmarks such as famous buildings, rivers, and bridges are used for localization, landmarks are also a great help for indoor localization. In this system, we chose the Azure spatial anchor service to create landmarks in the building. Spatial anchor is a cross-platform developer service that allows users to create objects that persist in their location on the cloud. We placed spatial anchors scattered in the building, and through the connection of these points, a virtual map network was formed.

When the camera detects the violative person's location, the system compares it with the location of the preset spatial anchor points. The system chooses the closest anchor to the violative person to be his position.

Radar Image Avatar

After some people are detected, the ordinary radar machine can only display light dots on a 2D screen. This system enables users to locate detected people through the wall. Therefore, we designed a human-shaped radar avatar to represent the detected people (see Fig. 7). This avatar comes with holographic effects, and it will be displayed at the location of the detected people based on the mapped landmarks.

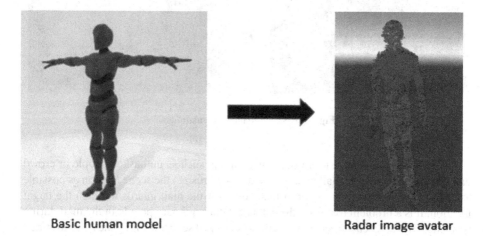

Basic human model   Radar image avatar

Fig. 7. Radar image avatar

4.4 AR Tracking

Mall guards ensure the safety of everyone at a mall. They work for the shopping mall, patrolling the premises checking surveillance equipment. In the post-pandemic world, the mall guards were given new duties to maintain virus prevention and control regulation in the mall while patrolling. The specific measures are as follows: First, evacuating the gathered crowds in a timely way. Second, identifying people who have taken off their masks in a mall and observing whether it is necessary to ask them to leave the mall.

When the system detects violations in a mall, it sends a warning message to mall guards. They can then open Radar vision to see radar images of violative people, getting a general idea of these people's position. Then mall guards can use eye-tracking to select the target people to track and activate the spatial arrow heading to the target (see Fig. 8).

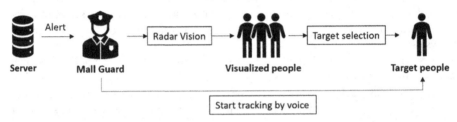

Fig. 8. AR tracking

4.5 User Protection

Fig. 9. Risk avoidance for customers

When there is a high risk of infection situation, such as unmasked people or crowd gathering in the mall, the mall guards on patrol will rush to the scene as soon as possible to address the situation. However, it takes time for the mall guards to reach the target location. It is a problem to ensure the safety of other ordinary people in the mall during this time. To protect customers in time, the system will send a warning message to attract the customers' attention. The system will also temporarily activate the Radar vision to help them clearly perceive high-risk situations nearby (see Fig. 9).

5   Implementation

We developed the main application of this system on Unity 2020 and used C sharp as the development language for the main application. We used python to build the people detection program to run on the server-side.

5.1   Radar Vision Visualization

We presented Radar vision as a type of new X-ray visualization method. It uses surveillance cameras to capture people out of view and displays a radar image avatar at the detected people's location to achieve an X-ray vision with spatial information. This method is different from the previous X-ray visualization method, which directly fuses the camera video information. Our visualization method is based on spatial anchors. It has factual geospatial information, making it more stable and more realistic than previous studies [17, 18]. The implementation steps are explained below.

Radar Image Avatar Generation
Generation of the radar image avatar is an essential part of radar vision visualization. This avatar represents the detected people and displays them as radar images. To allow users to see realistic radar effects. First, we determined a realistic 3D human character model from Mixamo.com. This model is high-quality and full-rigged, then we applied idle action to this model to make it appear more natural. Next, we used a Holo special effects package from the unity store to achieve a realistic effect. This Holo fx pack has many holographic and radio interference effects. It helps us to make this avatar a realistic radar effect (see Fig. 10). Finally, because this system's core is a through-wall perspective, to ensure the interaction experience, this avatar should not be blocked by

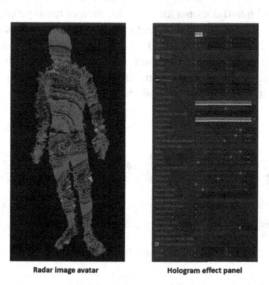

Radar image avatar   Hologram effect panel

Fig. 10. Radar image avatar

the system's UI components. We made a unity shader component to let the avatar always be at the forefront.

3D Building Map

This system is to be deployed in shopping malls. In theory, we can apply it to any building of interest. This study selected the IPS school building as the shopping mall to prototype and demonstrated this system. To realize the status view, we required a 3D map model of the IPS building. Therefore, we modeled the IPS building manually based on the IPS building plan structure (see Fig. 11).

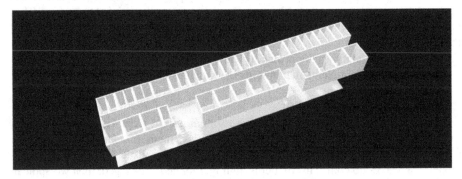

Fig. 11. School building 3D model

Location Mapping

When the server with a surveillance system captures un-masked people or crowd gathering status, the mall guard does not know the location of these people. In this system, we provided a location synchronization method to synchronize the place of the tagged people in reality to the virtual world. This method allows the device to know the location of these people. We divided the school building area based on the distribution area of the CCTV cameras. We arranged webcams in three main areas to act as surveillance cameras to demonstrate this system, our laboratory and two lobbies were near the stairs (see Fig. 12).

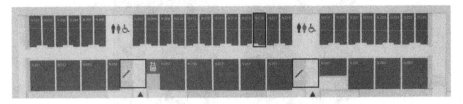

Fig. 12. School building area

Then we went to these three selected monitoring areas to create local spatial anchors and upload the local spatial anchors to the cloud service (see Fig. 13). Thus, multiple Hololens observe the same persisted avatar over time. Finally, we classified these anchors to the corresponding camera monitoring area. Therefore, the system could form a virtual location network of these three areas based on presetting this positional relationship.

PartitionKey	RowKey	Timestamp	SpatialAnchorId	Name
main	Lobby 1.1	2021-10-02T10:39:49.30...	de5baa3a-8512-4aa1-9...	Lobby 1.1
main	Lobby 1.2	2021-10-02T11:29:46.71...	d5d55d42-a3c9-4d4c-8...	Lobby 1.2
main	N216	2021-09-15T06:02:37.21...	2ecf649a-de14-4487-8a...	N216

Fig. 13. Cloud spatial anchors

In the 3D building map in the status perspective, we also placed a series of anchor points. The yellow sphere (see Fig. 14) implies that these anchor points represent the azure spatial anchors we set in the study area. By these anchor points in a 3D map, we can also synchronize the location in the actual building area to the 3D representative map of the building.

Fig. 14. Anchors in 3D building map

Interval Distance Estimation

To determine the position of the detected people, we should know the interval distance between the people and the CCTV camera. There are two prevalent technologies for ranging distance: binocular cameras ranging and Lidar camera ranging. They are common in smart cars with safety assistance. However, our system will be deployed in the shopping mall or other public places. Owing to the cost factor, these public places are equipped with binocular cameras or Lidar cameras. We used the monocular solution to enable our apply to all public places using only a general CCTV camera. To realize the monocular distance estimation, first, we did camera calibration work to determine the focal length of the camera and position of the optical center in the imaging plane. We knew these two parameters from calibration, the pixel value of the bottom (P_Bottom) of the detected people in the imaging plane and the mounting height of the camera. Thus we can calculate the distance between the detected people and camera. The principle diagram is shown in Fig. 15.

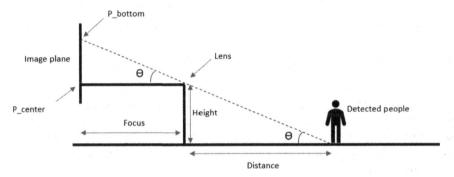

Fig. 15. Monocular ranging solution

The distance measurement formula is as follows:

$$tan\theta = \frac{H}{Dis} = \frac{|P\_bottom - P\_center|}{f} \tag{1}$$

Display Radar Image Avatar

The final step in realizing the radar vision is to display the radar image avatar to the corresponding location. The distance (C_A_distance) from the anchor to the camera and the distance (C_P_distance) from the detected people to the camera is known, Therefore, we can determine the closest anchor to the detected people by comparing these two distances. Then we let the radar image avatar be displayed on the location of this anchor (see Fig. 16). Thus, people with radar vision activated can see the radar image displayed through the wall.

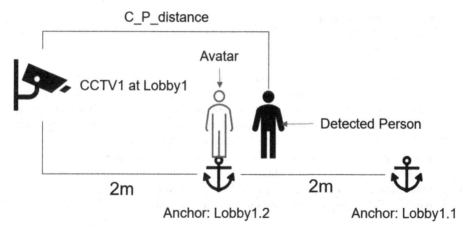

Fig. 16. Display radar image avatar

5.2 AI-Based Detection

To work with the surveillance system in the shopping mall to detect un-masked people and crowd gathering in real-time, we used OpenCV to develop the real-time people detection part in our system. Because there has been a deep neural networks module in the library of OpenCV, implementing forward pass (inferencing) with deep networks, pre-trained using some popular deep learning frameworks. Our system uses the YOLOv3 deep neural network model to do object-detection work based on the PyTorch framework.

Mask-Detection
Among object detection algorithms, one-stage methods such as SSD and YOLO are generally faster than two-stage methods, such as CNN and RCNN [12–14]. The YOLO detector achieves a fast speed and good accuracy in human face mask detection [16]. Referring to this study, we made a deep learning model trained by YOLO for mask detection. We selected an open dataset of medical masks to train our deep learning model. This dataset contained 1,148 pictures. In these pictures: some people were wearing masks, some were not, or some were not wearing masks properly. These pictures have been annotated corresponding to the label mask, none, poor. After we trained the model, we loaded this pre-trained model to perform a forward pass for the whole network to compute the output result.

Social Distance Detection
We used the YOLO with COCO model to detect people in the CCTV video stream for social distance detection. The MS COCO dataset is a large-scale object detection, segmentation, and captioning dataset published by Microsoft. The model trained with it also performs well in our system. When more than two people appear in the video stream, the system obtains the center point by object-detection model and uses the center point to calculate the Euclidean distance between two people. Suppose the Euclidean distance is greater than the presetting safe social distance, therefore, the system will determine these two people as a social distance violative.

6 System Interaction

6.1 Gesture Interaction

Gestures are a means of interaction in line with everyday human habits. People usually use gestures to convey some information or express a specific intention. The gestures can be divided into static gestures and dynamic gestures. Static gestures recognition considers the appearance features of a gesture at a certain point in time; for dynamic gestures recognition, it considers a series of people's actions over a while. Compared to static gesture recognition, it adds time information and action features.

In the context of augmented reality, the birth of gesture interaction provides a new way of interaction for augmented reality applications. Our system mainly uses dynamic gesture recognition to implement hand menu and manipulation of 3D building map.

Hand Menu
When the mall guards receive a warning message from the system, they can activate the hand menu by raising their left hand and looking into the palm of their hand. There are three buttons in the hand menu: the first button opens the radar vision, the second button activates the tracking function, and the third button opens the 3D building map (see Fig. 17).

Hand menu

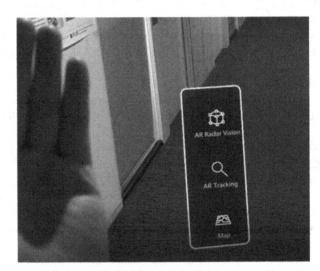

Gesture to call menu

Fig. 17. Hand menu

Gaze Interaction
In our system, to allow mall guards focus more on their work and improve tracking efficiency, we used eye-tracking technology to help them select people displayed by

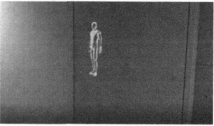

Normal radar image   Radar Image after Gaze selection

Fig. 18. Target selection by eye-tracking

radar vision. When the mall guards gaze on the radar image, the radar image turns its color from red to yellow to indicate that it has been selected (see Fig. 18).

Voice Interaction
When users use eye-tracking to select the target, it is not easy to move their gaze to their palm to activate the hand menu. We implemented the voice command in our system: "follow this person" as a trigger to activate the assisted navigation arrows (see Fig. 19).

MRTKSpeechCommandsProfile   SpeechinputHandler

Fig. 19. Voice command setting

7 Pilot Study

To explore the usability and effectiveness of our system, we conducted a pilot study in terms of functionality, learnability, efficiency, and impact. We gathered 12 volunteers to experiment with our preliminary system in the school building.

In the preparation of the experiment, we taught each volunteer the essential operation of the Hololens. Then we showed them a demo video of the system to familiarize them with the various interactions. In the experimental session, volunteers were asked to play three roles to experience the system. These three roles are mall guards, customer user without system, and customer user with the system. The mall guard task was to enforce mandates in the mall. Customer users without our system shopped freely in the mall. The customer users with the system were tasked with shopping in the mall, walking around, and avoiding violative people. These two customer users' experiences were in contrast.

After the experiment, we invited the 12 participants to complete the questionnaire. The experiment results are shown below:

The pilot study result (see Fig. 20) shows that our system can effectively detect and display radar images, increasing the efficiency of mall guards and reducing customer safety concerns.

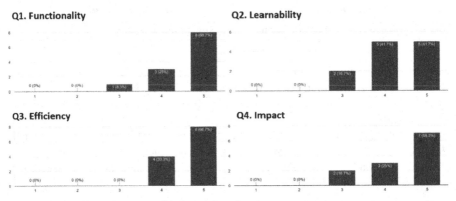

Fig. 20. Pilot study result

8   Conclusion and Future Work

Reaching a post-COVID-19 future for retail is an evolutionary process. Suppose mall owners hesitate too long in deciding the direction of their strategic development. In that case, they will lose the opportunity to grasp new markets retain loyal customers. They should evolve their business quickly to meet the demands of the "new-normal shopper."

In this study, to meet the consumer's demands for safe offline shopping, we enhanced the mall security system to help enforce wearing masks and proper social distancing in shopping malls using augmented reality. This study presents a new concept of visualization manner to monitor and maintain order in the shopping mall. It explores the image of the "Mall of the future" by reinvigorating the shopping environment in terms of safety.

In the future, The "mall" as we know it will change forever. Mall owners will rethink the entire customer journey and provide a seamless shopping experience. This direction will connect the online world to the individual stores within a mall, enhancing overall shopping experience for the user. The shopping mall is also a popular meeting hub. The social experience of the mall, such as dining out, is a point that cannot be replaced by online shopping. In the future, augmented reality can provide a safe shopping experience and balance consumers' desire for social interaction and a convenient shopping experience. Our work will continue to enhance the security aspect and use augmented reality as a bridge between the online world and the physical stores to get a glimpse of a future mall scene.

References

1. Pantano, E., Pizzi, G., Scarpi, D., Dennis, C.: Competing during a pandemic? Retailers' ups and downs during the COVID-19 outbreak. J. Bus. Res. **116**, 209–213 (2020)
2. Grant, R., et al.: Impact of SARS-CoV-2 Delta variant on incubation, transmission settings and vaccine effectiveness: results from a nationwide case-control study in France. Lancet Reg. Health – Europe **13**, 100278 (2021)
3. Sheth, J.: Impact of Covid-19 on consumer behavior: will the old habits return or die? J. Bus. Res. **117**, 209–213 (2020)
4. Eikenberry, S., et al.: To mask or not to mask: modeling the potential for face mask use by the general public to curtail the COVID-19 pandemic. Infect. Dis. Model. **5**, 293–308 (2020)
5. Berry, C., Berry, H., Berry, R.: Mask mandates and COVID-19 infection growth rates. In: 2020 IEEE International Conference on Big Data (Big Data), pp. 5639–5642 (2020)
6. Thu, T., Ngoc, P., Hai, N., Tuan, L.: Effect of the social distancing measures on the spread of COVID-19 in 10 highly infected countries. Sci. Total Environ. **742**, 140430 (2020)
7. Kulyukin, V., Gharpure, C., Nicholson, J., Pavithran, S.: RFID in robot-assisted indoor navigation for the visually impaired. In: 2004 IEEE/RSJ International Conference on Intelligent Robots and Systems (IROS), vol. 2, pp. 1979–1984 (2004)
8. Chumkamon, S., Tuvaphanthaphiphat, P., Keeratiwintakorn, P.: A blind navigation system using RFID for indoor environments. In: 2008 5th International Conference on Electrical Engineering/Electronics, Computer, Telecommunications and Information Technology, pp. 765–768 (2008)
9. Barsocchi, P., Lenzi, S., Chessa, S., Giunta, G.: A novel approach to indoor RSSI localization by automatic calibration of the wireless propagation model. In: VTC Spring 2009 - IEEE 69th Vehicular Technology Conference, pp. 1–5 (2009)
10. Alarifi, A., et al.: Ultra wideband indoor positioning technologies: analysis and recent advances. Sensors **16**(5), 707 (2016)
11. Cooper, A., Hegde, P.: An indoor positioning system facilitated by computer vision. In: 2016 IEEE MIT Undergraduate Research Technology Conference (URTC), pp. 1–5 (2016)
12. Liu, W., et al.: SSD: single shot multibox detector. In: Leibe, B., Matas, J., Sebe, N., Welling, M. (eds.) Computer Vision – ECCV 2016. ECCV 2016. Lecture Notes in Computer Science(), vol. 9905. Springer, Cham (2016). https://doi.org/10.1007/978-3-319-46448-0_2
13. Redmon, J., Divvala, S., Girshick, R., Farhadi, A: You only look once: unified, realtime object detection. In: 2016 IEEE Conference on Computer Vision and Pattern Recognition (CVPR), pp. 779–788 (2016)
14. Ren, S., He, K., Girshick, R., Sun, J.: Faster R-CNN: towards real-time object detection with region proposal networks. IEEE Trans. Pattern Anal. Mach. Intell. **39**(6), 1137–1149 (2017)
15. Boyko, A., Abdelpakey, M., Shehata, M.: GroupNet: detecting the social distancing violation using object tracking in crowdscene. In: 2021 IEEE Canadian Conference on Electrical and Computer Engineering (CCECE), pp. 1–5 (2021)
16. Bhambani, K., Jain, T., Sultanpure, K.: Real-time face mask and social distancing violation detection system using YOLO. In: 2020 IEEE Bangalore Humanitarian Technology Conference (B-HTC), pp. 1–6 (2020)
17. Wu, M., Popescu, V.: Efficient VR and AR navigation through multiperspective occlusion management. IEEE Trans. Visual Comput. Graph. **24**(12), 3069–3080 (2018)
18. Kameda, Y., Takemasa, T., Ohta, Y.: Outdoor see-through vision utilizing surveillance cameras. In: Third IEEE and ACM International Symposium on Mixed and Augmented Reality, pp. 151–160 (2004)
19. Avery, B., Sandor, C., Thomas, B.: Improving spatial perception for augmented reality x-ray vision. In: 2009 IEEE Virtual Reality Conference, pp. 79–82 (2009)

20. Zollmann, S., Grasset, R., Reitmayr, G., Langlotz, T.: Image-based X-ray visualization techniques for spatial understanding in outdoor augmented reality. In: Proceedings of the 26th Australian Computer-Human Interaction Conference on Designing Futures: The Future of Design, pp. 194–203 (2014)

Information in Complex Technological Environments

Development of the Biological Sensing Head Mounted Display

Yuki Ban$^{(\boxtimes)}$ and Masahiro Inazawa

Graduate School of Frontier Sciences,
The University of Tokyo, Kashiwa, Chiba, Japan
ban@edu.k.u-tokyo.ac.jp

Abstract. Measuring biometric information helps us estimate the users' excitement degree and their negative and positive emotions. By measuring a person's biometric information while experiencing the virtual reality (VR), it is possible to interactively change the content according to the estimated emotional state of the person. However, the hassle and discomfort of wearing the sensor interferes with the VR experience, and the body motion caused by the VR experience prevents accurate measurement. Therefore, some studies have developed devices that incorporate biometric measurement sensors into the head mounted displays (HMDs). Since we use HMDs by pressing them against our faces, biometric sensing by HMDs is resistant to body movements and can reduce the discomfort of sensor attachment. This paper introduces our research on HMDs with embedded sensors and our previous study as part of this project. This paper introduces the various biological sensing HMDs including our research and discusses VR applications using those HMDs.

Keywords: Head mounted display · Biological information · Sensing

1 Introduction

With the development of sensing technology, it has become possible to calculate various biological indices such as heart rate, respiration rate, and perspiration rate by measuring biological information. Various studies have suggested the possibility of estimating arousal, which indicates the degree of excitement and stress, and emotional valence, which means negative and positive states, using these biological indices [6,13,25,28,37].

In the field of Virtual Reality (VR), many systems incorporate biological measurement. They mainly use VR systems as devices that reproduce situations and present specific sensory stimuli and verify the stimulus's effects on the user's body by measuring and analyzing the biological responses [17,27]. In addition, by measuring the user's biological information during the VR content experience, we can estimate the user's level of arousal and interactively change the difficulty level and other aspects of the VR content accordingly [1].

S. Yamamoto and H. Mori (Eds.): HCII 2022, LNCS 13306, pp. 317–329, 2022.
https://doi.org/10.1007/978-3-031-06509-5_22

When measuring biometric information, attaching a sensor directly to the user's body is common. During the VR experience, it is necessary to attach a sensor in addition to the Head Mounted Display (HMD) to acquire electrocardiograph (ECG), photoplethysmogram (PPG), and respiratory wave forms, which are effective in estimating emotional state. In addition, many VR content experiences involve body movement, and the biometric sensor may shift due to the user's motion. For stable measurement, fixing the sensor to the body while experiencing VR contents is necessary. As described above, it isn't easy to measure biometric data using existing wearable sensors while experiencing VR.

Several studies have attempted to place sensors directly on the HMD to solve the problems of measurement load and body motion. Integrating the measurement sensors into the HMD makes it unnecessary to wear other wearable sensors, thus reducing the burden on the user. Moreover, when the user wears the HMD for VR experience, the HMD should be placed close to the face, not shifting even when the user moves their body. For this reason, we can reduce the wearing load of the sensor, which is used in close contact with the skin and avoids misalignment of the sensor due to body movement. In addition, because we always fix the HMD in the same position to focus on the presented image, there is no need to fine-tune the sensor position every time the VR content experience starts. Existing wristband-type wearable biometric measurement devices also satisfy the requirements for biometric sensing during VR content experience regarding low sensor wear load. However, biometric measurement with HMDs has the advantage of obtaining information such as respiratory waveforms and facial expressions, which cannot be obtained with wrist measurements. Due to the above advantages, various biological sensing HMDs have been developed.

This paper introduces the various biological sensing HMDs including our research and discusses VR applications using those HMDs.

2   Biological Sensing HMD

Table 1. Biological sensing HMDs.

Biological information	Measurement method	Measurement target	Reference
Gaze and pupil diameter	Pupil center corneal reflection	Eye	[2–4, 11, 24, 26]
Pulse wave	Photoplethysmogram	Nose skin	[15]
Pulse wave	Photoplethysmogram	Forehead skin	[2, 22]
Heart rate from head movement	Estimating Head	[12]	
Respiration	Estimating respiratory wave using temperature difference	Nose	[15, 20]
Respiration rate	Estimating from head movement	Head	[12]
Brain activity	Electroencephalogram	Head	[5, 18, 32, 35]
Brain activity	Near-infrared spectroscopy	Head	[4]

We can measure various types of biological information from the face and head where the HMD is worn, such as pulse wave, respiration, electroencephalogram (EEG), and cerebral blood flow. For each biometric, the researchers have been developing methods to measure it with the HMD. In this section, we summarize the advantages of measuring each biometric in VR, and the research of biological sensing HMDs (Table 1).

2.1   Gaze and Pupil Diameter

The most common biometric measurement function of HMDs available in the market is eye tracking [19]. By measuring the eyesight and gaze of the VR user wearing the HMD in real-time, it is possible to construct a more expressive and natural avatar and realize intuitive object selection and information input by gaze [11,24,26]. In addition, since the system can track where the user is focused, it can evaluate whether or not the user is interested in some virtual objects. In this way, we can generate a saliency map of the user in space so that it is also used to analyze purchasing behavior [10].

The Pupil Center Corneal Reflection (PCCR) method is mainly used for gaze measurement with built-in HMD [14]. This method generates a reflection point on the cornea and captures the reflection pattern. Usually, the near-infrared LEDs emit light to the cornea. The system identifies the lighting reflection points on the cornea and the pupil from the captured eye image. Then, it calculates the eye direction based on the light reflection points and other geometric features. HMDs such as the HTC Vive Pro Eye have near-infrared LEDs around the lens [3].

Since PCCR uses pupil detection, pupil diameter can be measured simultaneously with the gaze. The pupil diameter is an autonomic indicator, and we can estimate the level of excitement and stress by measuring it [9].

2.2   Heart Rate and Pulse Wave

Indices obtained from heartbeats and pulse waves are used to evaluate the autonomic nervous system. It has been confirmed that the R-R interval (RRI) and the R-R interval variability (RRV), calculated from the R-wave interval of the ECG and its variance, change significantly with mental stress load [6,13,25]. Using the pulse wave, we can also estimate the mental stress load with the peak interval of the PPG. Frequency analysis of the pulse wave yields the frequency spectrum of the RRI, and the area ratio between the 0.04–0.15 Hz (LF = Low Frequency) and 0.15–0.4 Hz (HF = High Frequency) regions is related to the autonomic nervous balance [8]. When the sympathetic nervous system is dominant, the HF component is suppressed, and the area ratio LF/HF becomes large. Conversely, when the parasympathetic nervous system is dominant, LF/HF becomes small. Thus, many research reports that the more relaxed a person is, the smaller the LF/HF value becomes. By measuring the pulse wave and calculating these physiological indices, we can estimate the emotional state of the VR user in real-time.

Researchers generally used a photoelectric sensor to measure a pulse wave. The volumetric pulse wave acquired by this sensor is called a photoplethysmo-gram (PPG). The PPG sensor comprises a LED and photodetector (PD) and measures pulse waves using the absorption characteristics of hemoglobin contained in the blood. This sensor irradiates a certain amount of light to the fingertip or ear and measures the difference in transmitted or reflected light as a volumetric pulse wave. There are two types of PPG sensors: a transmissive type that observes the light transmitted from the LED through the biological tissue and a reflective type that monitors the reflected light [29]. Both types of PPG sensors are often used because of their high absorbance of hemoglobin and low absorbance of biological tissue. The former can penetrate the combined blood volume changes of capillaries, small arteries, and arteries inside the skin layer. On the other hand, the latter has a high absorbance of hemoglobin and is less affected by ambient light, and has been confirmed to be resistant to the effects of body motion.

Considering the ease of integration into HMDs and the reduction of the effects of body movements, HMDs are often equipped with reflective PPG sensors that employ green light [2,15]. Some research has confirmed that the peak interval and variance of the PPG vary significantly with mental stress load and use these features to estimate the arousal level [23]. In many cases, the measurement position is the forehead, where the HMD is in contact with the skin, and stable measurement is possible due to the large flat contact area [22].

2.3   Respiration

Indices obtained from respiratory waveforms also evaluate the autonomic nervous system. The difference between the peak frequency of the power spectrum of the respiratory waveform and the center-of-gravity frequency indicates the instability of respiration. It can be used as an indicator of the degree of tension.

There are two methods for measuring respiratory waveforms: one is to indirectly calculate respiratory waveforms by measuring body movements caused by breathing, and the other is to measure exhalation information directly. The doppler radar and piezoelectric sensors were used to measure the displacement of the chest and changes in chest circumference for the measurement of body movements caused by breathing. These methods are not suitable for use in HMDs. On the other hand, there are some methods to measure exhalation information: breathing sound, CO_2 concentration, the temperature of exhaled air, and so on. These methods are uncomfortable for measurement in daily life because the sensors are placed near the face, but they are suitable for use in HMDs.

Hernandez et al. estimated heart rate and respiration rate using the accelerometer, gyroscope, and camera of google glass [12]. However, in addition to heart rate, variations in peak intervals of ECG or PPG, respiratory depth, and the ratio of exhalation to inhalation are necessary to estimate emotional states such as arousal. On the other hand, Kodama et al. focused on the fact that the temperature of the air inside the nose changed due to breathing and used a device that can insert a thermistor into the nostrils to measure the respiratory waveform of a person wearing glasses [20]. Although this method targets people wearing glasses, it can be applied to people wearing HMDs as most HMDs are worn with the nose exposed to the outside world.

2.4 Brain Activity

In addition to heartbeat and respiration, researchers have been conducting research on using Electroencephalogram (EEG) and near-infrared spectroscopy (NIRS) as biological information for estimating internal states such as emotions during VR content experiences. Applying a conductive paste when attaching electrodes is necessary for conventional EEG measurement, making it difficult to measure easily. However, with the development of active electrodes with built-in amplifiers and dry electrode chips, which do not require such advanced preparation, it has become possible to measure EEGs easily. Due to this development, EEG has begun to be applied to various educational, entertainment, and medical purposes [21]. Similarly, various HMDs equipped with EEG measurement sensors have been developed and used to estimate VR users' tension, attention, and mental state [32,35]. In addition, using this EEG measurement HMD, some studies have been researching the brain-computer interaction technology that has been incorporated into VR and technology that can control the movement in VR space only by thinking [5,18].

Some studies attempted to incorporate NIRS, which measures cerebral blood flow, into HMDs. NIRS is a method to measure changes in hemoglobin concentration in the blood of the brain and muscles using near-infrared light and evaluate the state of oxygenation in the blood and changes in cerebral blood flow [34]. Near-infrared light irradiated from a light source on the scalp's surface passes through the cerebral cortex close to the scalp while being absorbed and scattered and reaches a detector on the scalp at a distance from the light source. This method is easy to use in daily life because it is not affected by body movements as long as the light source and detector are close to the scalp. Therefore, there have been many efforts to combine VR and NIRS, mainly in cognitive neuroscience research. It has been used in human spatial cognition, navigation ability, and spatial memory research. In addition, it has been shown that the cerebral blood flow in the frontal lobe can be used to measure the degree of stress based on the difference in the concentration of oxygenated hemoglobin between the right and left sides of the brain [30]. It has also been used in research on quantifying mental load in flight simulators and driving simulators. In this context, an attempt to mount a NIRS measurement sensor on an HMD is underway. Some studies attached the NIRS sensor to the upper part of the cushion of the HMD and, measured prefrontal brain activity has been proposed [4].

3   Biological Information Measurement Device that Can Be Attached to Various HMDs

As described above, we have developed a method of estimating biometric data by integrating a sensor for biometric measurement into the HMD or by using

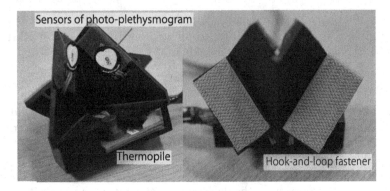

Fig. 1. Developed easy attachable biological information measurement device for Various HMDs

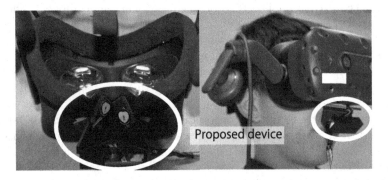

Fig. 2. Proposed device can be easily attached to various HMDs using hook-and-loop fastener

the default acceleration data of the HMD. As described above, there are several methods to measure biometric information while wearing an HMD, such as incorporating a sensor for biometric measurement in the HMD or estimating biometric information from information such as acceleration measured by default in the HMD. However, since many HMDs are already available in the market, rather than developing a new HMD with a built-in biometric sensor, it is better to build an external biometric sensing device that can be installed easily. It will reduce the cost of introducing sensing and help biometric sensing HMDs to be used in many scenes. Therefore, we have developed a photoelectric volumetric pulse wave and respiratory waveform measurement device that can easily attach to many HMDs [16].

Figure 1 shows the biometric sensing device we have developed. This device can measure photoelectric volumetric pulse wave and respiratory waveform, easily attached to an HMD using hook-and-loop fasteners (Fig. 2).

The photoelectric volumetric pulse wave is measured by applying an optical pulse wave sensor (SFE-SEN-11574, SwitchScience) to the nasal area. The wave-

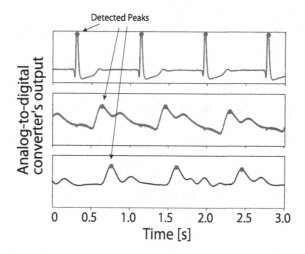

Fig. 3. Upper: electrocardiogram measured by commercially available sensors. Middle: pulse wave measured by commercially available sensors. Lower: pulse wave measured by proposed device.

length used was green light of 565 nm. A sponge was placed on the backside of the photoelectric volumetric pulse wave sensor so that the inclination angle of the device's nose and the user's nose may deviate slightly. In addition, since the size of the nose varies from person to person, the two photoelectric volumetric pulse wave sensors were placed in different positions. As a result, this device can measure the photoelectric volumetric pulse wave robustly to the nose shape.

We focused on the temperature change near the nostrils due to breathing and measured the respiratory waveform by placing a thermopile (10TP583T, SEMTEC Inc.) at the position where the exhaled air hits the nasal area. The reason for selecting the thermopile is that the changes in the respiratory waveform are usually less 1 Hz, so it was necessary to use a temperature sensor with a time constant of less than 0.5 s. The thermopile used in the proposed method satisfies this condition with a time constant of 15 ms. If a temperature sensor with a short time constant is used, there is a possibility that even a thermistor can measure respiration. Other methods of obtaining respiration include measurement of respiratory sound and measurement of CO_2 concentration [7]. The method using respiratory sound is not appropriate for measurement during VR experience because the sound of VR contents can be mixed as noise. In addition, CO_2 concentration has the disadvantage that it is difficult to change the concentration during shallow breathing. For these reasons, we selected the method of acquiring the change in temperature of exhaled and inhaled air.

We compared the biological waveforms measured using our proposed device with those using commercially available devices widely used for biometric measurement. The waveform peak should be measured with detectable accuracy for photoelectric volumetric pulse waves. An index based on the frequency analysis

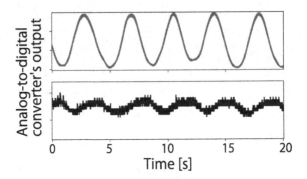

Fig. 4. Upper: respiration measured by commercially available sensors. Lower: respiration measured by proposed device.

of the waveform peak interval is widely used as an autonomic nerve index to evaluate a person's level of arousal and other emotional states. Figure 3 shows the proposed device can measure with the same accuracy as the ECG and the photoelectric volumetric pulse wave measured with commercial devices. Similarly, Fig. 4 shows that the period of the waveform measured by the commercial device and that measured by the proposed device are almost the same for the respiratory waveform. As a result of the user study comparing the features calculated from the waveforms obtained by wearing the proposed device with those obtained from commercial devices, the photoelectric volumetric pulse wave features could be calculated with an accuracy of less than 1% for the measurement data of 9 out of 14 users. As for respiration, it was possible to measure the respiratory peak frequency useful for evaluating arousal with an error of less than 0.6% when participants did not move. Details of the experiments and results can be found in our paper [15].

Since this device is used in close contact with the face, it can incorporate biometric sensors other than the photoelectric volumetric pulse wave and respiratory waveform obtained from the face. For example, some research suggested that nasal skin temperature indicates pleasant and unpleasant emotions [36]. The nasal skin temperature rises during pleasant emotions and falls during unpleasant emotions. By incorporating a thermistor in this device, we can measure the nasal skin temperature while wearing the HMD, and it may be possible to estimate the pleasant and unpleasant states during the VR experience (Fig. 5). Figure 6 shows the nasal skin temperature measured during a stress task while wearing the HMD. The nasal skin temperature drops while the user is engaged in the stress task, and this measurement result suggests that the device can measure the user's unpleasant emotions (Fig. 7).

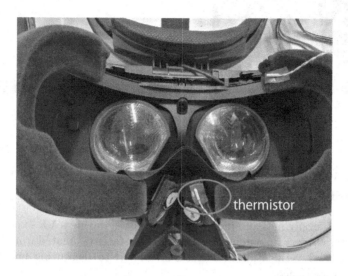

Fig. 5. Measuring the skin temperature of the nose while wearing an HMD.

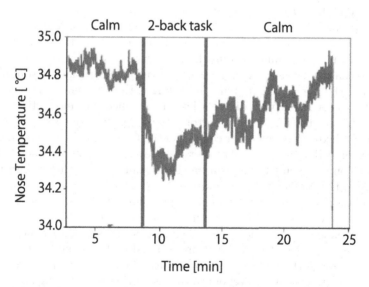

Fig. 6. The nasal skin temperature measured by the thermistor incorporated in the proposed device when performing a stress task called 2-back task while wearing the HMD. It can be confirmed that the skin temperature of the nose is lowered by the 2-back task and is raised at rest.

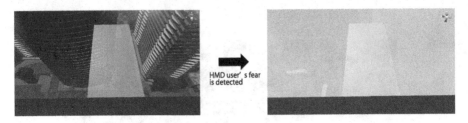

Fig. 7. When fear is detected, the fog becomes thicker and it becomes difficult to see below.

4   Application Potential of Biological Information Measurement During VR Experience

The ability to easily measure biometric information during a VR experience can develop interactive VR content based on human states estimated from biometric information and verification and research related to measuring human states during VR experiences.

For example, Ueoka et al. measured a user's heartbeat in horror VR content. They presented a faster-than-average pseudo-heartbeat by vibration to manipulate the impression of fear of the content and increase the actual heartbeat [33]. We have created VR content that interactively changes the degree of fear of horror VR, and high altitude VR based on heart rate and respiration rate measured using the proposed device [16] (Figure 1) A game that uses a wristwatch device to measure the heart rate and change the degree of fear in the content according to the fear level estimated from the heart rate has been released [1]. These systems estimate the user's fear level based on biometric data and adjust the fear level of the horror VR contents accordingly, thereby generating acceptable content for various users with different horror tolerance. The interactively changing contents are currently mostly horror-related, but we are looking forward to developing relaxing VR and other content in the future. There have been various researches on VR content to relax users. However, as far as we know, there is no research on enhancing the relaxation effect by presenting sensory information according to the user's emotional state.

In addition to these entertainment applications, there is a possibility that biometric data can be used for training applications using VR. Many training applications place a mental load on the trainee, such as customer service training, which may prevent the trainee from proceeding to the end of the training process or damage the trainee's mental health. Therefore, we propose an approach to estimate the stress level of the trainee during VR training based on the information obtained from the biometric sensing HMD and adjust the training level accordingly [31]. We developed a VR simulator for interpersonal customer service training and constructed a system that adjusts the training level by changing the attitude of the customer avatar according to the mental load of the trainee.

As described above, the number of applications where biometric information is actively used in VR systems increases. Therefore, it is expected that installing biometric sensors in HMDs will become even more popular in the future.

5   Conclusion

This paper summarizes the various approaches in the research field of biological sensing HMD. Moreover, we introduce our research on biometric sensing HMDs. This biometric sensing device can be attached to various HMDs and measures respiratory waveforms and pulse waves from around the user's nose. We also discussed the VR application of the biometric sensing HMD.

The estimation of emotions from biometric information varies significantly among individuals, making it difficult to estimate from a single index. Therefore, it is necessary to construct an HMD that can measure brain activity and autonomic indices to estimate the emotional state in an integrated manner from multiple biometric data. The future development of biometric sensing HMDs is expected to expand the possibility of dynamically generating content according to the user's emotional state and to help generate VR content with a higher sense of immersion.

Acknowledgments. This work was supported by Council for Science, Technology and Innovation, Cross-ministerial Strategic Innovation Promotion Program (SIP), Big-data and AI-enabled Cyberspace Technologies. (funding agency: NEDO)

References

1. Bring to Light. https://store.steampowered.com/app/636720/Bring_to_Light/. Accessed 30 May 2019
2. HP Omnicept & HP Reverb G2 Omnicept Edition. https://www.hp.com/us-en/vr/reverb-g2-vr-headset-omnicept-edition.html. Accessed 6 Feb 2022
3. HTC Vive Pro Eye. https://www.vive.com/us/product/vive-pro-eye/overview/. Accessed 11 Feb 2022
4. NeU-VR. https://neu-brains.co.jp/solution/neuro-marketing/neu-vr/. Accessed 6 Feb 2022
5. NextMind. https://www.next-mind.com/. Accessed 11 Feb 2022
6. Agrafioti, F., Hatzinakos, D., Anderson, A.K.: ECG pattern analysis for emotion detection. IEEE Trans. Affect. Comput. **3**(1), 102–115 (2012). https://doi.org/10.1109/T-AFFC.2011.28
7. Al-Khalidi, F.Q., et al.: Respiration rate monitoring methods: a review. Pediatric Pulmonol. **46**(6), 523–529 (2011)
8. Billman, G.E.: Heart rate variability-a historical perspective. Front. Physiol. **2**, 86 (2011)
9. Bradley, M.M., Miccoli, L., Escrig, M.A., Lang, P.J.: The pupil as a measure of emotional arousal and autonomic activation. Psychophysiology **45**(4), 602–607 (2008)
10. Chandon, P., Hutchinson, J., Bradlow, E., Young, S.H.: Measuring the value of point-of-purchase marketing with commercial eye-tracking data. INSEAD Business School Research Paper (2007/22) (2006)

11. Gupta, K., Lee, G.A., Billinghurst, M.: Do you see what I see? The effect of gaze tracking on task space remote collaboration. IEEE Trans. Visual Comput. Graph. **22**(11), 2413–2422 (2016)
12. Hernandez, J., et al.: BioGlass: physiological parameter estimation using a head-mounted wearable device. In: 2014 4th International Conference on Wireless Mobile Communication and Healthcare-Transforming Healthcare Through Innovations in Mobile and Wireless Technologies (MOBIHEALTH), pp. 55–58. IEEE (2014)
13. Hsu, Y.L., Wang, J.S., Chiang, W.C., Hung, C.H.: Automatic ECG-based emotion recognition in music listening. IEEE Trans. Affect. Comput. **11**(1), 85–99 (2017)
14. Hua, H.: Integration of eye tracking capability into optical see-through head-mounted displays. In: Stereoscopic Displays and Virtual Reality Systems VIII, vol. 4297, pp. 496–503. SPIE (2001)
15. Inazawa, M., Ban, Y.: Development of easy attachable biological information measurement device for various head mounted displays. In: 2019 International Conference on Cyberworlds (CW), pp. 1–8. IEEE (2019)
16. Inazawa, M., Hu, X., Ban, Y.: Biofeedback interactive VR system using biological information measurement HMD. In: SIGGRAPH Asia 2019 Emerging Technologies, SA 2019, pp. 5–6. Association for Computing Machinery, New York (2019). https://doi.org/10.1145/3355049.3360523
17. Ito, K., et al.: Evaluation of "dokidoki feelings" for a VR system using ECGs with comparison between genders. In: 2017 International Conference on Biometrics and Kansei Engineering (ICBAKE), pp. 110–114. IEEE (2017)
18. Juliano, J.M., et al.: Embodiment is related to better performance on a brain-computer interface in immersive virtual reality: a pilot study. Sensors **20**(4), 1204 (2020)
19. Kassner, M., Patera, W., Bulling, A.: Pupil: an open source platform for pervasive eye tracking and mobile gaze-based interaction. In: Proceedings of the 2014 ACM International Joint Conference on Pervasive and Ubiquitous Computing: Adjunct Publication, pp. 1151–1160 (2014)
20. Kodama, R., et al.: A context recognition method using temperature sensors in the nostrils. In: Proceedings of the 2018 ACM International Symposium on Wearable Computers, ISWC 2018, pp. 220–221 (2018). https://doi.org/10.1145/3267242.3267261
21. Li, B., Cheng, T., Guo, Z.: A review of EEG acquisition, processing and application. J. Phys. Conf. Ser. **1907**, 012045 (2021)
22. Luong, T., Martin, N., Raison, A., Argelaguet, F., Diverrez, J.M., Lécuyer, A.: Towards real-time recognition of users mental workload using integrated physiological sensors into a VR HMD. In: 2020 IEEE International Symposium on Mixed and Augmented Reality (ISMAR), pp. 425–437. IEEE (2020)
23. Mohan, P.M., Nagarajan, V., Das, S.R.: Stress measurement from wearable photoplethysmographic sensor using heart rate variability data. In: 2016 International Conference on Communication and Signal Processing (ICCSP), pp. 1141–1144. IEEE (2016)
24. Pai, Y.S., Dingler, T., Kunze, K.: Assessing hands-free interactions for VR using eye gaze and electromyography. Virtual Reality **23**(2), 119–131 (2019)
25. Rattanyu, K., Mizukawa, M.: Emotion recognition based on ECG signals for service robots in the intelligent space during daily life. J. Adv. Comput. Intell. Intell. Inform. **15**(5), 582–591 (2011). https://doi.org/10.20965/jaciii.2011.p0582
26. Song, G., Cai, J., Cham, T.J., Zheng, J., Zhang, J., Fuchs, H.: Real-time 3D face-eye performance capture of a person wearing VR headset. In: Proceedings of the 26th ACM International Conference on Multimedia, pp. 923–931 (2018)

27. Sullivan, C., et al.: The effect of virtual reality during dental treatment on child anxiety and behavior. ASDC J. Dent. Child. **67**(3), 193–6 (2000)
28. Taelman, J., et al.: Influence of mental stress on heart rate and heart rate variability. In: Vander Sloten, J., Verdonck, P., Nyssen, M., Haueisen, J. (eds.) 4th European Conference of the International Federation for Medical and Biological Engineering. IFMBE, vol. 22, pp. 1366–1369. Springer, Heidelberg (2009). https://doi.org/10.1007/978-3-540-89208-3_324
29. Tamura, T., Maeda, Y., Sekine, M., Yoshida, M.: Wearable photoplethysmographic sensors-past and present. Electronics **3**(2), 282–302 (2014)
30. Tanida, M., Katsuyama, M., Sakatani, K.: Effects of fragrance administration on stress-induced prefrontal cortex activity and sebum secretion in the facial skin. Neurosci. Lett. **432**(2), 157–161 (2008)
31. Tanikawa, T., Shiozaki, K., Ban, Y., Aoyama, K., Hirose, M.: Semi-automatic reply avatar for VR training system with adapted scenario to trainee's status. In: Stephanidis, C., et al. (eds.) HCII 2021. LNCS, vol. 13095, pp. 350–355. Springer, Cham (2021). https://doi.org/10.1007/978-3-030-90963-5_26
32. Tauscher, J.P., Schottky, F.W., Grogorick, S., Bittner, P.M., Mustafa, M., Magnor, M.: Immersive EEG: evaluating electroencephalography in virtual reality. In: 2019 IEEE Conference on Virtual Reality and 3D User Interfaces (VR), pp. 1794–1800. IEEE (2019)
33. Ueoka, R., AlMutawa, A.: Emotion hacking VR: amplifying scary VR experience by accelerating actual heart rate. In: Yamamoto, S., Mori, H. (eds.) HIMI 2018. LNCS, vol. 10904, pp. 436–445. Springer, Cham (2018). https://doi.org/10.1007/978-3-319-92043-6_37
34. Villringer, A., Planck, J., Hock, C., Schleinkofer, L., Dirnagl, U.: Near infrared spectroscopy (NIRS): a new tool to study hemodynamic changes during activation of brain function in human adults. Neurosci. Lett. **154**(1–2), 101–104 (1993)
35. Vourvopoulos, A., Niforatos, E., Giannakos, M.: EEGlass: an EEG-Eyeware prototype for ubiquitous brain-computer interaction. In: Adjunct Proceedings of the 2019 ACM International Joint Conference on Pervasive and Ubiquitous Computing and Proceedings of the 2019 ACM International Symposium on Wearable Computers, pp. 647–652 (2019)
36. Zenju, H.: The estimation of unpleasant and pleasant states by nasal thermogram. In: Forum on Information Technology, vol. 3, pp. 459–460 (2002)
37. Zhang, Q., et al.: Respiration-based emotion recognition with deep learning. Comput. Ind. **92**, 84–90 (2017)

Optimal Touchscreen Button Size and Button Spacing for Next Generation Fighter Aircrafts

Atakan Coskun[1,2]([✉]) [ID], Yeter Tuğba Çetin[1,3] [ID], Mehmetcan Fal[1,4] [ID], and Ertan Zaferoğlu[1,4] [ID]

[1] Turkish Aerospace, Ankara, Turkey
atakancoskun45@gmail.com
[2] Department of Instructional Technology, Middle East Technical University, Ankara, Turkey
[3] Department of Computer Engineering, Hacettepe University, Ankara, Turkey
[4] Department of Cognitive Science, Middle East Technical University, Ankara, Turkey

Abstract. The popularity of integrating touchscreen technology into next-generation fighter aircraft's flight decks has increased recently. Therefore, the touch button size and button spacing have gained importance in human factors. In this way, the current study aimed to investigate the optimal button size and button spacing for next-generation fighter aircraft's touchscreen. In accordance with that purpose, fourteen participants consisting of flight test engineers and pilots performed experimental tasks in a flight simulator on the six different keyboard designs consisting of three different sized buttons (12.7 mm, 15.87 mm & 19.05 mm) and two different sized spacing (1.65 mm & 2.54 mm). Dependent variables consisted of task completion time, total errors, subjective workload scale scores, and user preference. A button size of 12.7 mm and a button spacing of 2.54 mm are optimal when considered task completion time and workload. No significant difference was found in terms of total error. Participants mostly favored a button size of 15.87 mm. Optimal button size and button spacing can be affected by the factors such as maneuvering and pilot equipment (e.g., gloves). Hence, it is recommended that human factors researchers replicate this study by manipulating these factors, especially in simulator settings with jet fighter pilots.

Keywords: Button size · Button spacing · Touchscreen

1 Introduction

The touchscreen seems a part of life because it is employed in many different applications used in daily life, such as mobile phones, tablets, kiosk displays, ATMs, and home systems [1]. In recent years, the integration of touchscreen into flight decks has also started. For instance, Garmin G3000, an avionic system, implemented touchscreen technology into the flight deck [2]. Thales's integrated touchscreen has become the first touchscreen certified by European Union Air Safety Agency (EASA) in 2019 for Airbus A350 [3]. Besides, the USA Jet Fighter F-35 and French Jet Fighter Dassault Rafale have employed touchscreen screen displays rather than the traditional displays on the flight

© The Author(s), under exclusive license to Springer Nature Switzerland AG 2022
S. Yamamoto and H. Mori (Eds.): HCII 2022, LNCS 13306, pp. 330–342, 2022.
https://doi.org/10.1007/978-3-031-06509-5_23

deck [2, 21]. Briefly, the industry has considerable interest in moving cockpit controls to touchscreen [4]. Touchscreen technology is considered a piece of vital equipment in the flight decks of the next-generation aircraft. The first reason for the increasing popularity of touchscreen in the flight deck is that touchscreen display simplifies the complex avionic cockpit systems and pilots show a better performance on touchscreen [2, 6]. Secondly, touchscreen technology enables users to operate functions efficiently by inexperienced and disabled users, leading to less training than other input tools, such as the keyboard, trackball, and mouse. Thirdly, the touchscreen can decrease the size of a device, as traditional physical buttons in the flight deck can replace digital buttons [7]. Finally, unlike physical buttons, designers can easily adjust the touchscreen interface in the flight deck by changing button size, button spacing, and button shape via software [8]. However, button size and button spacing have become the two most critical factors affecting the efficiency of touchscreen [5, 7, 9]. If button size and button spacing are poorly designed, touchscreen use can turn into a disadvantage. Although some research studies [4, 7, 10, 11] have investigated touchscreen target size and spacing, there is a lack of consensus on optimal touchscreen button size and button spacing [10, 13]. For instance, American National Standards Institute [ANSI] and Human Factors and Ergonomics Society [HFES] suggest 9,5 mm at least for a button size, while ISO 9241–9 (ISO, 2000) recommends approximately 22 mm at least for that [10]. MIL-STD-1472H, defense design criteria standard, recommends 15 mm at least and 38 mm at most for a button size [12]. Moreover, some research [8, 14] recommended a 15–20 mm range for a usable touchscreen button size. Research [5] recommended approximately 12.7 mm for a touchscreen button size. Nevertheless, the current literature concludes that it may be useful to study the range of 13–20 mm for an optimal button size on a fighter aircraft's touchscreen. On the other hand, there are confounding results about touchscreen button spacing. Some studies [8, 10, 21] found no measurable effects of button spacing on user performance, whereas some [5, 15] indicated that button spacing has a measurable effect on user performance. In addition, there are a few research [5, 10] studying the range of 1–3 mm for button spacing. The gap between keys could be removed, but users generally want to see the presence of the gap between keys [13]. Fighter aircraft include complex avionic systems, so many functions have to be placed on touchscreen interfaces with a limited field. Therefore, the button size and button spacing need to be as small as possible. However, there is no common view on how small button size and button spacing should be. On top of it, the existing studies reported that further examination is needed in various touchscreen usage scenarios to determine the effects of touchscreen button size and button spacing on pilot performance [2, 13]. The number of studies investigating the touchscreen button size and button spacing in the flight deck is also spare [2]. As a result, it could not be possible for designers to find enough sources they can refer to for the button size and button size on fighter aircraft's touchscreens. Considering these literature gaps, the current study investigated the effect of three different button sizes (12.7 mm, 15.87 mm, and 19.05 mm) and two different button spacing (1.65 mm and 2.54 mm) on user performance in a fighter aircraft simulator setting. The current study suggested optimal button size and button spacing for the next-generation fighter aircraft.

2 Background

2.1 Button Sizes

Fitts's [16] study is the well-predicted one to show the effect of button size on user performance. Fitts's [16] model indicated that larger and closer targets need shorter movement time than smaller and further ones. However, larger button sizes can make it difficult for designers to fit flight controls and functions into fighter aircrafts' touchscreen with limited space. Therefore, button size should be as small as possible, especially for fighter aircraft's touchscreen. That is, optimal button size values for fighter aircraft's touchscreen are needed. The critical question is how small the target size should be considering the factors, such as pilot error and pilot performance. Some related works contributed to the identification of optimal target size. Avsar et al. [9] investigated the effect of touchscreen target size (5, 10, 15, 20 mm) on a helicopter flight deck as well as considering the vibration effect. The study found no significant differences for touchscreen target size between 15 mm and 20 mm. They suggested that *15* mm is the optimal size for touchscreen buttons for non-safety critical Electronic Flight Bag applications (EFB) and that *20* mm is optimal for safety-critical tasks on static displays. Tao et al. [7] studied button size, including 7.5 mm, 12.5 mm, 17.5 mm, 22.5 mm, and 27.5 mm. They pointed to *17.5* mm as the optimal size for touchscreen use. Jin et al. [1] reported that 16.51 mm square is acceptable for a touchscreen interface. Chen et al. [14] studied button size ranging from 10 to 30 mm with 5-mm increments; the results demonstrated that 15 mm is acceptable for healthy individuals. Similarly, Colle and Hiszem [8] studied touchscreen input's key sizes (10, 15, 20, 25 mm). They presented that a button size of 20 mm was sufficiently large for touchscreen input. Wang et al. [2] recommended a button size of 19 mm for a usable touchscreen. Dodd et al. [5] compared the effect of button sizes 6.35 mm and 12.7 mm on human performance in a flight deck simulator. They found that pilots made fewer errors on the 12.7 mm touch target size, and the workload level of pilots is acceptable for the 12.7 mm touch target size. The study also concluded that the muscle activity measured by EMG is lower for 12.7 mm when compared to a target size of 6.35 mm. Conradi et al. [17] recommended a button size of 14 mm for applications used while walking. Consequently, there is no common view in the current literature about touchscreen button size for optimal touchscreen. In addition, the participant groups mentioned above do not consist of pilots, except for Dodd et al.'s [5] study. Jin et al. [1] suggested designers who implement button size and button spacing guidelines to be conscious of the design's target population. Considering these, it is difficult for human factors practitioners to identify optimal touchscreen target size for touchscreen, especially in the flight deck of fighter aircraft. Further study about touchscreen uses in a flight deck seems worthwhile [18]. Therefore, the current study aimed to study the key sizes of 12.7 mm, 15.87 mm, and 19.05 mm in a simulated flight scenario with pilots and flight test engineers. As a result, the current study recommended an optimal button size for the touchscreen use in the flight deck of fighter aircraft.

2.2 Button Spacing

Some studies investigated the effect of the presence of gap size on user performance. Chen et al. [14], for instance, studied the effect of two button spacing: 1 mm and 3 mm.

They found that the gap size did not have a measurable effect on user performance. Similarly, Colle and Hiszem [8] investigated the effect of button spacing (1 mm and 3 mm) on user performance, and they found no significant difference between button spacing on user performance. Also, they found no significant difference in user preference for button spacing (1 mm vs. 3 mm). Likewise, Sesto et al. [10] found the same result about the effect of button spacing (1 mm vs. 3 mm) on user performance. Unlike the above-stated studies, Tao et al. [13] examined both presence (i.e., 2 mm) and absence of gap, but no effect was detected. These findings have a considerable implication in that button spacing could be removed to use the touchscreen area efficiently [13]. However, some studies [1, 13] recommended that designers avoid using no space between buttons. These studies indicated that users generally preferred using touchscreen buttons with the presence of space. In addition, button spacing on the touchscreen may significantly affect user performance in the flight deck. Dodd et al. [5] examined the effect of three different button spacing sizes (0.76 mm, 1.65 mm, and 2.54 mm) on user performance. They reported that touchscreen button size and button spacing significantly affect total errors and workload. Conti et al. [15] concluded that the larger target-element space (10 mm) was moved significantly faster than the medium (5 mm) and smallest target-element space (3 mm). To sum up, in the current literature, there are confounding results about the presence of button spacing and the gap size between buttons on the touchscreen. If the gap between buttons is needed, it is indefinite how small they should be. Studies, as mentioned earlier, generally examined the effect of button spacing sizes between 1–3 mm on user performance. The studies could not indicate a consensus view about button spacing size on the touchscreen. Further research is needed to investigate button spacing sizes (1–3 mm). Hence, the current study investigated the effect of button spacing sizes (1.65 mm vs. 2.54 mm) as well as button sizes (12.7 mm, 15.87 mm, and 19.05 mm) on user performance for the next-generation fighter aircraft. The current study aimed to answer the research question below:

What are the optimal button size and button spacing on the touchscreen in the next generation of fighter aircraft?

3 Methodology

3.1 Participants

Fourteen volunteer users aged 27–51 ($M = 35.86$, $SD = 8.08$) and consisting of pilots ($N = 7$) and flight test engineers ($N = 7$) participated in the study. The inclusion criteria for being a participant in the current study is that all participants must have at least one-year experience with F-16 aircraft in the simulator settings, and they must have no vision problem. All participants were right-handed.

3.2 Experimental Design

The effect of three different button sizes (12.7 mm, 15.87 mm, and 19.05 mm) and two different button spacing sizes (2.54 mm and 1.65 mm) were studied on user performance. The current study had a 3×2 research design. There were two independent variables and four dependent variables within-subject design.

Independent variables:

- Button sizes (12.7 mm, 15.87 mm, and 19.05 mm)
- Button spacing sizes (2.54 mm and 1.65 mm)

Dependent variables:

- Task completion time (passing time between first entry and last entry for each keyboard design)
- Total errors (the number of incorrect entries or missing entries)
- Subjective workload rating (one question Likert scale)
- Participants' preferences related to button sizes and button spacing sizes.

3.3 Study Setting and Instrumentation

The current study was conducted in a flight simulator environment (see Fig. 1). As the primary task, the participants were asked to fly from Atatürk Airport in İstanbul to Esenboğa Airport in Ankara in a flight simulation presented by Prepare 3D software. The participants are experienced in F-16 aircraft in simulation settings, so F-16 was selected for the study. The simulation was demonstrated on a 55-in. TV screen. The QWERTY touchscreen keypad was displayed to the participants in a 21.5-in. capacitive monitor as the secondary task. Users performed experimental tasks on the QWERTY

Fig. 1. Simulator setting

touchscreen keyboard, and their performance was logged by considering the metrics, such as task completion time and total errors. Instantaneous self-assessment (ISA) of workload technique was employed to measure workload. Users were asked a question to understand the users' preferences on six different keyboards. The question is, "which keyboard design would be your preference for a next-generation fighter aircraft among six keyboard designs?".

3.4 Experimental Tasks and Manipulated Stimuli

Experimental tasks included 9-line words entry, and their language was Turkish. The pilots were expected to type a 9-line word entry into the text area, as can be seen in Fig. 2. 9-line words were selected because a fighter pilot is expected to type a 9-line entry at most into the text area in a real-world condition. There were six different groups of 9-line words for each keyboard design. Six different keyboard designs (see Fig. 3 for an instance of keyboard designs) consisted of:

- Large – Large (LL, button size: 19.05 mm, button spacing size: 2.54 mm)
- Large – Small (LS, button size: 19.05 mm, button spacing size: 1.65 mm)
- Medium – Large (ML, button size: 15.87 mm, button spacing size: 2.54 mm)
- Medium – Small (MS, button size: 15.87 mm, button spacing size: 1.65 mm)
- Small – Large (SL, button size: 12.7 mm, button spacing size: 2.54 mm)
- Small – Small (SS, button size: 12.7 mm, button spacing size: 1.65 mm)

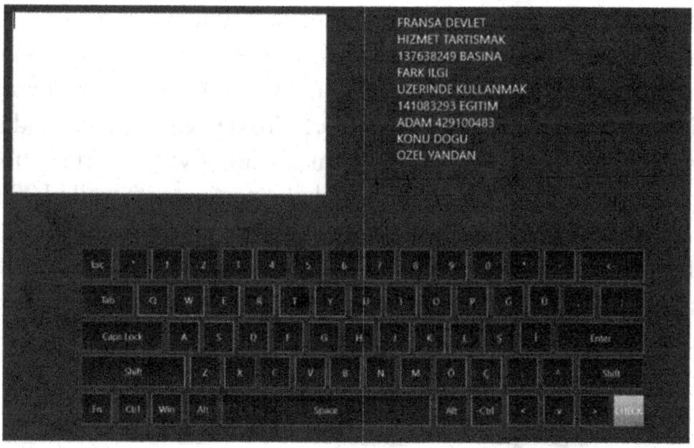

Fig. 2. An example of an experimental task for X user

The order of 9-line word entries in each keyboard design was randomly presented for each participant. The character number of a 9-line word group was the same for each keyboard. 9-line words entry were shown on the right, and participants used the "enter" button to write line by line. 9-line words entry consisted of numeric and non-numeric characters. The participants performed experimental tasks on six different keyboard

Fig. 3. An example for LS keyboard design

designs demonstrated randomly. Participants could use numeric and non-numeric characters on the keyboard, so keys (e.g., Esc, Tab, Caps Lock, Shift) were not allowed. However, that participants clicked these keys were counted as an error.

3.5 Data Collection Procedure

Before starting the study, participants were expected to read the consent form and sign it. Next, participants were informed about the purpose of the study and what they would perform within the study. After that, for the primary task, the participants sat down on the simulator and activated the engines of the F16 aircraft in the simulator to fly from Ataturk Airport in İstanbul to Esenboğa Airport in Ankara. Before pilots started flying, they performed a short demo session in which they typed one-line alphanumeric string three times. After taking off, the participants positioned the cruise at an 8,000–12,000 ft altitude. Later, they were requested to do secondary tasks given on touchscreen by attempting to stay at an altitude between 8,000–12,000 ft. In the cruise phase, the pilots performed the experimental tasks (entry of 9-line words) using six different keyboards, randomly presented to minimize the order effects. To decrease fatigue and boredom, the participants had the opportunity to rest two times while flying at cruise position. In the resting time, an interface was designed in which the participants waited 30 s for the next page. This interfaced appeared only two times for each pilot (see Fig. 4). Participants were asked to rate the ISA of workload scale after completing the tasks on each keyboard design. At the end of the study, they answered the question related to their preference for keyboard designs.

Fig. 4. Secondary task interface appearing during the experiment

3.6 Data Analysis

The keyboard interface was designed and programmed in Visual Studio 2017. Data logs captured by computers were produced in an excel file. The outputs consist of the pressed time of each word entry, received alphanumeric character, and target word. This enabled us to calculate error count and response time for the experimental task in each keyboard design. A 3 × 2 Repeated Measures ANOVA was applied to understand whether or not there is a significant difference between keyboard designs (LL, LS, ML, ML, MS, SL, and SS) in terms of response time and total error counts. A Friedman's test was applied to understand whether or not there is a significant difference between keyboard designs (LL, LS, ML, ML, MS, SL, and SS) in terms of subjective workload scores. Finally, a chi-square statistical analysis with Monte Carlo simulation was employed to understand whether or not there is a significant difference between users' preference distribution on the keyboard designs.

4   Results

4.1   Task Completion Time

Two-way repeated-measures ANOVA was implemented to understand the main and interaction effects of button size and button spacing on task completion time. ANOVA

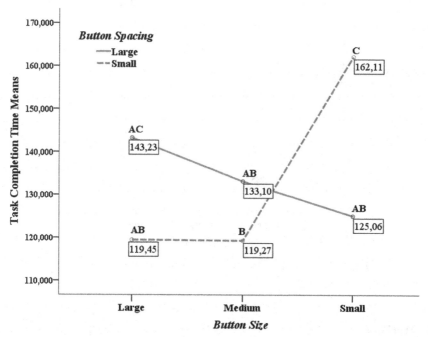

Fig. 5. Interaction for mean task completion time between button size and button spacing. Means with the different letters are significantly different, $p < .05$.

analysis revealed a significant interaction between button size and button spacing on task completion time, $F (2, 26) = 15.66, p < .05$, partial $\eta^2 = .546$, see Fig. 5. Post-hoc analysis using the Bonferroni test showed that mean task completion time on the SL keyboard design is statistically less than that on the SS keyboard design, $p < .05$. No significant difference was found between the SL keyboard design and other keyboard designs, including the LL, LS, ML, MS keyboard designs in terms of task completion time. These results suggested that the optimal button size is 12,7 mm and optimal button spacing is 2.54 mm on the touchscreen.

4.2 Total Errors

Two-way repeated-measures ANOVA was implemented to understand the main and interaction effects of button size and button spacing on total errors. ANOVA analysis revealed no significant interaction effect between button size and button spacing on total errors, $F (2, 26) = 3.31, p > .05$, see Fig. 6. Similarly, no significant main effect was found for button size, $F (2, 26) = .54, p > .05$ and for button spacing $F (2, 26) = .01, p > .05$.

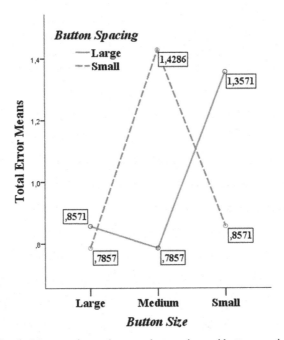

Fig. 6. Mean total error between button size and button spacing.

4.3 Workload

Instantaneous self-assessment of workload (ISA) technique reflects acceptable workload for ratings between 1–3 and high workload for ratings greater than 3. A Friedman's

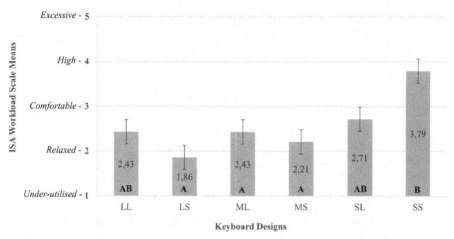

Fig. 7. Workload rating means for touch button size and touch button spacing. Different letters are significantly different, $p < .05$.

test indicated a significant difference in workload ratings between touch button size and touch button spacing, $p < .001$, see Fig. 7. Wilcoxon Signed-Rank tests with Bonferroni alpha correction demonstrated that workload on the SS keyboard design is statistically higher than the MS, ML, and LS keyboard designs, but no significant difference was found between the SS-LL keyboard designs, $p > .05$, and between the SS-SL keyboard designs in terms of workload ratings, $p > .05$. Similarly, no significant difference was found among the LL-LS-ML-MS-SL keyboard designs regarding workload ratings. Considering these results, the SL keyboard design has optimal touch button size and touch button spacing for the next-generation fighter aircraft.

4.4 User Preference

Most participants significantly preferred using a button size of 15.87 mm (72%, $\chi^2 = 9.57$, $p < .01$, see Fig. 8). The participants' preference indicated that the optimal button size might be 15.87 mm for fighter aircraft's touchscreen. There was no significant difference between the distribution of user preference on button spacing ($\chi^2 = 1.14$, $p > .05$). Similarly, no significant difference was found in the distribution of user preference by six different keyboard designs ($\chi^2 = 10.86$, $p > .05$).

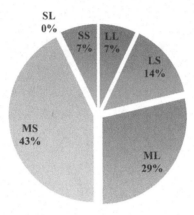

Fig. 8. Distribution of user preference by the keyboard designs.

5 Discussion

The current study aimed to investigate the optimal button size and button spacing on the touchscreen for next-generation fighter aircraft. For this purpose, the effect of three different button sizes (12.7 mm, 15.87 mm & 19.05 mm) and two different buttons spacing (2.54 mm & 1.65 mm) were investigated on user performance by considering task completion time, total errors, workload, and user preference. Generally, task completion time results showed a significant interaction effect between button size and button spacing. Similar results can be found in some studies [5, 7]. In contrast, this result is contradicted with the studies [8, 10, 13, 19], which suggested the removal of the gap between buttons. However, removing the gap between buttons may create a severe problem on the touchscreen of next-generation fighter aircraft. Pilots wear gloves, and they use the touchscreen with gloves. Glove-wearing may cause pilots to make more errors or extend completion time on tasks on the touchscreen with the adjacent buttons. Although wearing or not wearing a glove does not affect human performance on touchscreen [19], further research investigating the effect of button spacing on pilot performance, especially in-flight simulator scenarios with actual flight equipment (e.g., glove), is needed. Besides, task completion time results recommended 12.7 mm for optimal button size and 2.54 mm for optimal button spacing, which is in line with some studies [5, 19]. The recommended range is 15–20 mm for a minimally usable touchscreen in the current literature [2, 9, 13]. Yet, only a few investigated the effect of button size and button spacing in simulated flight deck settings on pilot performance, making it difficult to generalize the results for next-generation fighter aircraft. Subjective workload results supported the idea that 12.7 mm and 2.54 may become the optimal sizes for button size and button spacing, respectively, on the touchscreen of next-generation fighter aircraft. Instantaneous self-assessment of workload (ISA) technique demonstrated acceptable workload level for a button size of 12.7 mm and a button spacing of 2.54, which is parallel to Dodd et al. [5], who applied the Bedford workload rating scale. No significant difference was found among the keyboard designs in total error. This may be because the primary task (staying cruise position at an altitude between 8,000 – 12,000 ft) may not be challenging enough for pilots to make significant errors on the keyboard(s). That is, as the primary task may not contend for the same sources as the secondary task [20], a non-significant result was found among the keyboard designs in terms of total task errors. User preference results revealed that participants preferred using middle-sized buttons (15.87 mm) on the touchscreen in the flight deck, compared to large-sized buttons (19.05) and small-sized buttons (12.7 mm). Similarly, in Tao et al.'s [13] study, most participants preferred 15 mm button size, compared to 10 mm, 20 mm, and 25 mm button sizes. In Dodd et al.'s [5] study, participants preferred a button size of 12.7 mm, compared to a button size of 6.35 mm. In Jin et al.'s [1] study, the subjects primarily selected button sizes of 16.51 mm and 19.05 mm, compared to button sizes 11.43 mm, 13.97 mm, 21.59 mm, and 24.13 mm. This suggested that participants generally select the button sizes in the range of 13 mm–19 mm. However, more studies are needed about the pilots' preference on button sizes and spacing since the target population in many studies does not consist of pilots. After pilots experience touch button sizes and button spacing, especially in simulation scenarios, their preference should be asked and compared on different button sizes and button spacing.

6 Conclusion

This study aimed to explore the optimal touch button sizes and optimal touch button spacing for the next-generation fighter aircraft. Task completion time and subjective workload ratings concluded that a button size of 12.7 mm and a button spacing of 2.54 mm might be optimal sizes for the touchscreen of the next-generation fighter aircraft. Pilots' preference for button sizes showed that they generally prefer using a button size of 15.87 mm. Optimal button size and button spacing can be affected directly by the factors such as maneuvering and pilots' equipment (e.g., gloves). Therefore, in the future, this type of study should be replicated by manipulating these factors, especially in simulator settings with jet fighter pilots.

References

1. Jin, Z.X., Plocher, T., Kiff, L.: Touch screen user interfaces for older adults: button size and spacing. In: Stephanidis, C. (ed.) UAHCI 2007. LNCS, vol. 4554, pp. 933–941. Springer, Heidelberg (2007). https://doi.org/10.1007/978-3-540-73279-2_104
2. Wang, L., Cao, Q., Chang, J., Zhao, C.: The effect of touch-key size and shape on the usability of flight deck MCDU. In: the 8th International Conference on Advances in Computer-Human Interactions, pp. 234–238. IARIA, Lisbon, Portugal (2015)
3. Thales Homepage. https://www.thalesgroup.com/en/group/press-release/thales-integrated-touchscreen-becomes-worlds-first-product-its-kind-gain-easa. Accessed 07 Jan 2022
4. Cockburn, A., et al.: Turbulent touch: touchscreen input for cockpit flight displays. In: International Conference for Human-Computer Interaction, pp. 6742–6753. ACM, New York, NY, USA (2017)
5. Dodd, S., Lancaster, J., Miranda, A., Grothe, S., DeMers, B., Rogers, B.: Touch screens on the flight deck: The impact of touch target size, spacing, touch technology and turbulence on pilot performance. In: Proceedings of the Human Factors and Ergonomics Society Annual Meeting, vol. 58, no. 1, pp. 6–10. Sage CA: Los Angeles, CA: SAGE Publications (2014)

6. Stanton, N.A., Harvey, C., Plant, K.L., Bolton, L.: To twist, roll, stroke or poke? a study of input devices for menu navigation in the cockpit. Ergonomics **56**(4), 590–611 (2013)

7. Tao, D., Yuan, J., Liu, S., Qu, X.: Effects of button design characteristics on performance and perceptions of touchscreen use. Int. J. Ind. Ergon. **64**, 59–68 (2018)

8. Colle, H.A., Hiszem, K.J.: Standing at a kiosk: effects of key size and spacing on touch screen numeric keypad performance and user preference. Ergonomics **47**(13), 1406–1423 (2004)

9. Avsar, H., Fischer, J., Rodden, T.: Target size guidelines for interactive displays on the flight deck. In: 2015 IEEE/AIAA 34th Digital Avionics Systems Conference (DASC), pp. 3C4–1. IEEE (2015)

10. Sesto, M.E., Irwin, C.B., Chen, K.B., Chourasia, A.O., Wiegmann, D.A.: Effect of touch screen button size and spacing on touch characteristics of users with and without disabilities. Hum. Factors **54**(3), 425–436 (2012)

11. Tao, D., Diao, X., Wang, T., Guo, J., Qu, X.: Freehand interaction with large displays: effects of body posture, interaction distance and target size on task performance, perceived usability and workload. Appl. Ergon. **93**, 103370 (2021)

12. MIL-STD-1472H. http://everyspec.com/MIL-STD/MIL-STD-1400-1499/MIL-STD1472H-57041/. Accessed 09 Jan 2022

13. Tao, D., Chen, Q., Yuan, J., Liu, S., Zhang, X., Qu, X.: Effects of key size, gap and the location of key characters on the usability of touchscreen devices in input tasks. In: Harris, D. (ed.) EPCE 2017. LNCS (LNAI), vol. 10276, pp. 133–144. Springer, Cham (2017). https://doi.org/10.1007/978-3-319-58475-1_10

14. Chen, K.B., Savage, A.B., Chourasia, A.O., Wiegmann, D.A., Sesto, M.E.: Touch screen performance by individuals with and without motor control disabilities. Appl. Ergon. **44**(2), 297–302 (2013)

15. Conti, A.S., Kremser, F., Krause, M., An, D.J., Bengler, K.: The effect of varying target sizes and spaces between target and non-target elements on goal-directed hand movement times while driving. Procedia Manufact. **3**, 3168–3175 (2015)

16. Fitts, P.M.: The information capacity of the human motor system in controlling the amplitude of movement. J. Exp. Psychol. **47**(6), 381 (1954)

17. Conradi, J., Busch, O., Alexander, T.: Optimal touch button size for the use of mobile devices while walking. Procedia Manufact. **3**, 387–394 (2015)

18. Coutts, L.V., et al.: Future technology on the flight deck: assessing the use of touchscreens in vibration environments. Ergonomics **62**(2), 286–304 (2019)

19. Sun, X., Plocher, T., Qu, W.: An empirical study on the smallest comfortable button/icon size on touch screen. In: Aykin, N. (eds.) Usability and Internationalization. HCI and Culture. UI-HCII 2007. LNCS, vol. 4559, pp. 615–621. Springer, Berlin, Heidelberg (2007). https://doi.org/10.1007/978-3-540-73287-7_71

20. Stanton, N.A., Salmon, P.M., Rafferty, L.A., Walker, G.H., Baber, C., Jenkins, D.P.: Human Factors Methods: a Practical Guide for Engineering and Design, 2nd edn. Ashgate, England (2013)

21. Thomas, P.R.: Performance, characteristics, and error rates of cursor control devices for aircraft cockpit interaction. Int. J. Hum Comput Stud. **109**, 41–53 (2018)

Analysis of Customer Characteristics of Mobile Carrier Plans in Japan

Ayano Nagai[1]([⊠]) and Yumi Asahi[2]

[1] Graduate School of Management, Tokyo University of Science, Tokyo, Japan
8621508@ed.tus.ac.jp
[2] Department of Management, Tokyo University of Science, Tokyo, Japan
asahi@rs.tus.ac.jp

Abstract. Japanese mobile carriers offer very similar plans and prices, and it is not clear in which respects they are differentiating themselves and gaining a competitive advantage. The purpose of this study is to clarify who is interested in which carrier from two perspectives: personal attributes and values, and to find out the points of agreement and difference between the targets set by the communication service companies and the people who intend to use them. With regard to personal attributes, we were not able to find any differences among the carriers. However, from a value perspective, we were able to identify which people were most interested in each carrier. In order to further clarify the differences between the careers, it is necessary to conduct analysis that takes into account factors that may influence intention to use, such as the frequency and duration of Web use and the content of TV commercials.

Keywords: Customer feature analysis · TV commercial · Mobile carrier

1 Introduction

The rate of personal ownership of smartphones in Japan has been increasing year by year; in 2020, 69.3% of the population has a personal smartphone. Furthermore, the number of people who use the Internet on their smartphones is higher than those who use the Internet on their computers, at 68.3% in 2020. This indicates that the number of people who use the Internet on smartphones is expected to increase further in the future. Since the start of 4G service in 2015, the amount of data traffic has increased dramatically. Furthermore, with the launch of 5G service in 2020, faster communication speeds and higher capacity communication became possible. There is a need for improved communication technology, and communication technology is growing rapidly. As a result, further increase in data communication volume is expected in the future.

The increase in data communication volume could result in higher data communication charges or slower communication speed, which would be inconvenient. Therefore, some people (37.0%) are thinking of switching mobile carriers in order to keep their mobile contract plans low. The reasons given for switching to a lower rate plan or wanting to do so in the future are "because the rates are cheaper" and "because I can use more data capacity. However, there are many types of communication service companies and contract plans in Japan, and the contents of the plans are almost the same, making it difficult to understand the differences between communication service companies and plans. In marketing, it is said that differentiation can give a product or service a competitive edge, but the plans of telecommunication service companies often have similar contents and targets. In what ways do telecommunication service companies differentiate themselves and gain a competitive advantage?

The purpose of this study is to clarify who is interested in which carrier from two perspectives: personal attributes and values, and to explore the points of agreement and difference between the targets set by the communication service companies and the people who intend to use them.

2 Data Summary

In order to make comparisons, we will analyze the number of people who watched the TV commercials placed by each company and were affected by them in terms of their intention to use the service. More than 70% of the respondents learned about the new carrier plans of the three companies through the TV commercials, and it is said that TV

Table 1. Details of the target TVCM

	Ahamo	Povo	LINEMO
Actor	Nana Mori Fuju Kamio	(Many performers)	Tsubasa Honda Momonkey
Broadcast start date	February 24, 2021	February 4, 2021	March 6, 2021
Target	Twenties	Young people	Digital native generation that uses LINE frequently
Service concept	We have been working closely with young people in their 20s, known as Generation Z. generation, called Generation Z, and to grow together with them	A new concept plan that allows users to top up their voice calls and data capacity online depending on their mood of the day	"What a wonderful surprise."
TV commercial concept	Stylish, cool, admired	Let's use the video to convey that a new and free plan is about to begin	While lively dance, they expressed various numbers and messages through unique poses and dialogues to promote LINEMO's affordable rate service

commercials are effective in advertising the carriers at the stage of recognition. For this reason, TV commercials were used as a means of comparison. The details of the target TVCMs are described in Table 1.

The data used is single-source data from Nomura Research Institute, Ltd. Of the 2,500 questionnaires, 2,219 excluding missing values, TV commercial placement status data, and TV program viewing status data are used.

3   Analysis Method

First, we use TV commercial placement status data and TV program-specific viewing status data to extract those who have viewed the target CM. Next, the impact on intention to use is categorized into two types: "increased intention to use" when intention to use increases or remains unchanged from "definitely want to use" between the first and second survey dates, and "decreased or unchanged intention to use" when intention to use remains unchanged or declines.

Then, we analyze the characteristics of those whose intention to use increased from two points of view: personal attributes and value perspective. Decision tree analysis and binomial logistic regression analysis will be conducted. First, a decision tree analysis is conducted to visually represent the characteristics of those who have increased their intention to use. Next, we will conduct a binomial logistic regression analysis to deepen the interpretation of the decision tree analysis.

4   Result

4.1   Personal Attributes

Figure 1 and Table 2 show the results for ahamo as seen from the perspective of personal attributes.

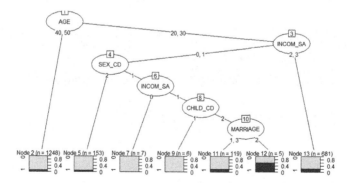

Fig. 1. Decision tree analysis (ahamo, personal attributes)

Table 2. Binomial logistic regression (ahamo, personal attributes)

	P-value	Odds ratio
Female	**0.0374**	*0.7803*
Thirties	0.9862	0.9971
Forties	**0.0250**	*0.6726*
Fifties	**0.0005**	*0.4998*
Married	0.8475	1.0348
Divorce/Bereavement	0.1177	0.5008
No children	0.7283	1.0622
Low income	0.4076	1.8633
Medium income	0.2727	2.2707
High income	0.2707	2.3100

Figure 1 and Table 2 show that women and those in their 40s and 50s are negatively affected, and furthermore, never married may have an effect.

Figure 2 and Table 3 show the results for povo as seen from the perspective of personal attributes.

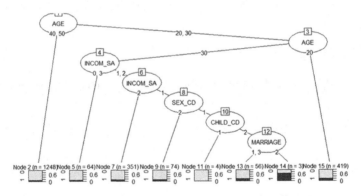

Fig. 2. Decision tree analysis (povo, personal attributes)

Table 3. Binomial logistic regression (povo, personal attributes)

	P-value	Odds ratio
Female	**0.0005**	*0.6430*
Thirties	**0.0382**	*0.6924*
Forties	**0.0000**	*0.4604*
Fifties	**0.0002**	*0.4721*
Married	0.7949	0.9499
Divorce/Bereavement	0.2050	0.5678
No children	0.1901	0.7799
Low income	0.1703	4.1173
Medium income	0.2159	3.5784
High income	0.1145	5.1459

Figure 2 and Table 3 show that women and those in their 30s, 40s, and 50s are negatively affected, and furthermore, never married may have an effect.

Decision tree analysis and binomial logistic regression analysis were conducted for LINEMO as well, but the decision tree analysis did not classify the results, and the binomial logistic regression analysis did not show significant results. Therefore, it can be said that classification is impossible and cannot be explained by the selected explanatory variables.

4.2 Value Perspective

Figure 3 and Table 4 show the results for ahamo as seen from the perspective of value perspective.

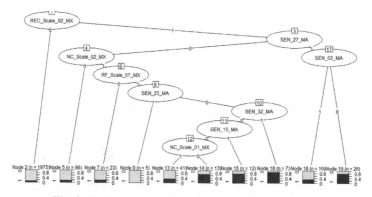

Fig. 3. Decision tree analysis (ahamo, value perspective)

Table 4. Binomial logistic regression (ahamo, value perspective)

	P-value	Odds ratio
Consider carefully whether the price is commensurate with the quality before buying	0.1066	0.8155
Choose products that are particular to your lifestyle	0.4197	1.1124
Buy products that are custom-made for oneself frequently	0.6737	0.8523
Tend to make expensive purchases with credit cards when they do not have enough cash or savings to spend immediately	**0.0008**	*1.7167*
Tend to ask the clerk right away if they can't find the product they are looking for	0.3084	0.8390
I prefer difficult tasks which require a lot of thinking to those which do not require much thinking	0.3900	1.1329
Tend to set goals that require a lot of thinking to achieve	**0.0068**	*1.5002*
Buy things that are in fashion	**0.0001**	*2.8540*
Get hurt sometimes by not being careful enough	0.8728	0.9803

F From Fig. 3 and Table 4, there is a positive effect on "those who buy things that are in fashion" and "those who tend to make expensive purchases with credit cards when they do not have enough cash or savings to spend immediately (may buy without carefully considering whether the price is commensurate with the quality)". However, if the item "those who tend to make expensive purchases with credit cards when they do not have enough cash or savings to spend immediately" does not apply to you, then it applies to "I tend to set goals that require a lot of thinking to achieve."

Figure 4 and Table 5 show the results for povo as seen from the perspective of value perspective.

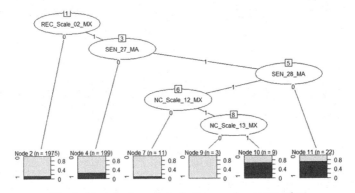

Fig. 4. Decision tree analysis (povo, value perspective)

From Fig. 4 and Table 5, there is a positive effect on "those who buy things that are in fashion" and "those who tend to make expensive purchases with credit cards when

Table 5. Binomial logistic regression (povo, value perspective)

	P-value	Odds ratio
Tend to make expensive purchases with credit cards when they do not have enough cash or savings to spend immediately	**0.0095**	*1.5622*
I save up money to buy things I like, even if it's expensive	0.5009	0.9039
I'm not satisfied unless I'm constantly thinking	0.7949	0.9613
Have many challenges that need to be solved in one's life	0.9213	0.9872
Buy things that are in fashion	**0.0000**	*2.9797*

they do not have enough cash or savings to spend immediately." However, if what they like is expensive, they are less likely to save money to buy it.

Figure 5 and Table 6 show the results for LINEMO as seen from the perspective of value perspective.

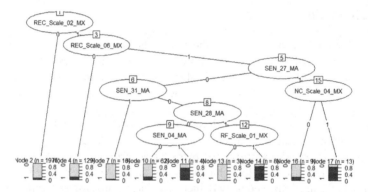

Fig. 5. Decision tree analysis (LINEMO, value perspective)

From Fig. 5 and Table 6, there is a positive effect on "those who buy what is in fashion" and "those who Tend to buy what the clerk recommends." However, it is possible that they tend to make expensive purchases with credit cards when they do not have enough cash or savings to spend immediately or savings, and it is also possible that they are less interested in learning new ways of thinking.

Table 6. Binomial logistic regression (LINEMO, value perspective)

	P-value	Odds ratio
Buy it even if the price is a little higher if a product is from a well-known brand or manufacturer	0.8040	0.9468
Tend to make expensive purchases with credit cards when they do not have enough cash or savings to spend immediately	0.0617	1.4047
I save up money to buy things I like, even if it's expensive	0.6256	0.9254
Tend to choose things that people around them say are good	0.6820	1.0896
I am not interested in learning new ways of thinking	0.9092	1.0187
Buy things that are in fashion	**0.0002**	*1.9834*
Tend to buy what the clerk recommends	**0.0069**	*1.6349*
When trying to achieve something important, I can't act according to my ideal	0.1176	1.2390

5 Consideration

In terms of personal attributes, overall, the results showed that the presence or absence of children and household income had no effect on intention to use the service, that being unmarried could have an effect, and that women and those in their 30s to 50s had a negative effect on intention to use the service. Therefore, there were no differences among the plans.

Regarding the value perspective, those who increased their intention to use ahamo tend to have high aspirations and think carefully before taking action. Therefore, we believe that we can provide more effective plans and advertisements by offering plans and campaigns that offer discounts for achieving goals, and by writing detailed descriptions of the plans and campaigns. People with increased intention to use povo are more likely to buy impulsively, and if what they want is expensive, some will give up and others will buy it without worrying about their savings. Therefore, it would be a good idea to run catchy advertisements that look good, keep the monthly fee low, and develop options that attract interest. People who have increased their intention to use LINEMO tend to be less pushy, more likely to buy on impulse, and more interested in what's trendy but less interested in what's new. Therefore, displaying recommended services in an easy-to-understand manner and actively communicating new services through SNS can be more effective.

6 Conclusion

The purpose of this study was to clarify what kind of people are interested in which carrier from two perspectives: personal attributes and values, and to explore the points of agreement and difference between the targets set by the communication service companies and the people with intention to use the service. However, it was not possible to clarify the impact of the changes in intention to use on the 20-somethings set by each company. Therefore, it is necessary to conduct an analysis that takes into account factors that may affect the intention to use, such as the frequency and duration of Web use and the content of TV commercials.

References

1. Ministry of Internal Affairs and Communications: Results of the 2020 Survey on Telecommunications Usage Trends (2021)
2. Ministry of Internal Affairs and Communications: Part 1: 5G Promotes Digital Transformation and the Construction of New Everyday Life, Ministry of Internal Affairs and Communications website. https://www.soumu.go.jp/johotsusintokei/whitepaper/ja/r02/html/nd1 31110.html. Accessed 11 Nov 2021
3. Ministry of Internal Affairs and Communications (MIC), Secretariat: Draft Direction of Study (Matters Related to Trends in the Telecommunications Market)(2021)
4. ahamo HP. https://ahamo.com/. Accessed 11 Nov 2021
5. povo HP. https://povo.jp/. Accessed 11 Nov 2021
6. LINEMO HP. https://www.linemo.jp/. Accessed 11 Nov 2021
7. LINE Research: [LINE Research Case Study] Mobile Phone Companies' New Plan Usage Intention Survey (1 Question Screening), LINE for Business, Published on 2 February 2021. https://www.linebiz.com/jp/column/service-information/litecase3/. Accessed 11 Nov 2021
8. Muramoto, S.: Why the New Rate Plans of the Three Major Mobile Carriers Look Almost Side by Side but Aren't, Nikkei XTECH, Published on 12 March 2021. https://xtech.nikkei.com/atcl/nxt/column/18/01112/031000014/. Accessed 11 Nov 2021
9. Senden Kaigi: ahamo launch: creating a 'freshness' not seen in docomo before, Senden Kaigi Digital Edition, Published on May 2021. https://mag.sendenkaigi.com/senden/202105/editors-pick/021269.php. Accessed 11 Nov 2021
10. Brain: TV commercial for KDDI's new povo rate plan, Brain Digital Edition, Published on May 2021. https://mag.sendenkaigi.com/brain/202105/up-to-works/021247.php. Accessed 11 Nov 2021
11. Softbank News Editor: Its name... LINEMO. Softbank announces the name of its online-only brand, Softbank News, Published on 18 February 2021. https://www.softbank.jp/sbn ews/entry/20210217_01. Accessed 11 Nov 2021
12. SOFTBANK CORP: SoftBank's New Brand LINEMO TV Commercial LINEMO Damon: Rates to Begin Airing Nationwide on Saturday, March 6, 2021, Starting with LINEMO Damon: Network, PR TIMES, Published on 3 March 2021. https://prtimes.jp/main/html/rd/p/000000035.000041498.html. Accessed 11 Nov 2021
13. CINRA.NET: Tsubasa Honda dances and performs with Momonkey in two new LINEMO commercials released sequentially, Pia, Published on 3 March 2021. https://lp.p.pia.jp/shared/cnt-s/cnt-s-11-02_2_4428ac46-c76d-4c3b-9ffe-8e267229a7c3.html. Accessed 11 Nov 2021

Adaptive Incremental Learning for Software Reliability Growth Models

Vidhyashree Nagaraju[1][(✉)], Shadow Pritchard[1], and Lance Fiondella[2]

[1] University of Tulsa, Tulsa, OK, USA
{vin5654,swp7196}@utulsa.edu
[2] University of Massachusetts Dartmouth, North Dartmouth, MA, USA
lfiondella@umassd.edu

Abstract. Software reliability growth models (SRGM) assist in software release decisions by quantifying metrics based on failure data collected during testing. Complexity of SRGM can increase significantly with increasing complexity of software, thus requiring faster and stable algorithms to identify model parameters. While previous studies have attempted to address this issue through application of machine learning (ML) algorithms, lack of sufficient data to train ML models. Moreover, it is important to assess software in an online manner as data becomes available, which is difficult since limited data is available towards the beginning of testing. Incremental learning [12] provides the possibility of applying machine learning algorithms in an online manner, however lack of large data towards the beginning of testing limits the efficiency. Therefore, this paper proposes an adaptive incremental learning that utilizes a model trained on historical data which can forecast failures for the present data. Historical data is selected based on the Granger causality test. Our results indicate that the adaptive incremental learning approach achieves significantly better accuracy on smaller sample sizes compared to simple application of neural networks.

Keywords: Software reliability · Software failure · Software reliability growth models · Neural network · Incremental learning

1 Introduction

Software reliability growth models (SRGM) [8] enable quantitative assessment of software by characterizing the failure data collected during testing. Specifically, non-homogeneous Poisson process (NHPP) [7] SRGM are the most commonly employed models. While software reliability growth models are important, efficient modeling of complex software systems increases the complexity of models. Increased model complexity presents a challenge in identifying robust and computationally efficient algorithms to identify model parameters.

Recent research attempts to address algorithmic challenges by improving upon numerical and statistical algorithms such as Newton-Raphson [3],

© The Author(s), under exclusive license to Springer Nature Switzerland AG 2022
S. Yamamoto and H. Mori (Eds.): HCII 2022, LNCS 13306, pp. 352–366, 2022.
https://doi.org/10.1007/978-3-031-06509-5_25

expectation maximization (EM) [27], and expectation conditional maximization (ECM) [26,40] algorithms. While these algorithms demonstrate improved stability and performance on models with relatively high complexity, lack of initial estimation selection strategy affects the performance with more complex models [25]. Additional research includes utilization of soft computing techniques [15,19] such as particle swarm optimization (PSO) [31] and the genetic algorithm [33]. To address these limitations, software reliability researchers have begun to explore the applicability of machine learning algorithms, specifically neural networks (NN) [17,18] to aid in failure prediction and reliability assessment given software failure data.

Applicability of neural networks to the problem of software reliability was initially demonstrated by Karunanithi et al. [17,18]. Study suggested neural networks exhibit predictive performance comparable to traditional software reliability models. Then, the scaling problem [16] of NN in software reliability prediction was discussed by adding a clipped linear unit in the output layer. Later studies proposed evolutionary neural network [14], which reported inefficient computation time, while other studies compare NN with parametric models [32] and simple linear regression [1] to validate the applicability of NN. The effectiveness of neural network applicability in characterizing software reliability data with changepoints [4] has also been studied, while [11] presented a mathematical description of software reliability estimation using the basic execution time model utilizing pattern mapping technique of artificial neural network (ANN). A genetic algorithm [36] was proposed as a precursor to NN models to identify the number of layers and neurons.

Several software reliability researchers have also attempted to derive the activation function based on NHPP SRGM to train NN and compare them with traditional models. In 2005, [35] proposed modified function from logistic growth curve model to train neural networks, while [2] proposed a neural network with logarithmic encoding and compared it with traditional NHPP models including the Goel-Okumoto (GO) [9], delayed s-shaped (DSS) [39], and inflection s-shaped (ISS) [29] models. Later, a dynamic weighted combination model [34] that is a sum of multiple NHPP models was utilized to formulate an activation function. A neural network based ensemble approach [41] was also proposed and compared to traditional models such as GO, Duane [23], and s-shaped models. ANN [6] was utilized to estimate parameters of the log power model with exponential testing effort function. A combination of the GO and generalized GO model [22] were used as the activation function for two nodes of the NN. Wang et al. [37] utilized a deep learning model based on recurrent neural network encoder-decoder, while Roy et al. [30] proposed an ANN based software reliability model trained by a novel PSO. Most recently, Wu et al. [38] proposed a systematic way of deriving activation function based on NHPP SRGM such as GO and DSS. Examples suggested that proposed models achieve better goodness-of-fit measures compared to traditional NHPP models.

Existing studies fail to address the issue of overfitting and the usability of models as well as accuracy of prediction when the sample size is smaller. Neural network models are only as good as the data and length of training data available, so application of NN to predict failures at early stages of testing with limited failure data is restricted. To address these challenges, this article proposes an adaptive incremental learning algorithm. The proposed approach enables utilization of a pre-trained model on data with a distribution similar or closer to the available data to enable better characterization of smaller datasets, especially during the beginning of testing. The model is incrementally trained as data becomes available by adding extra layers to the network while holding the previous layer parameters constant. The proposed algorithm is applied on real data taken from the Handbook of Software Reliability Engineering. Several activation functions including sigmoid, elu, relu, tanh, and exponential NHPP based functions are compared. Results suggest that the incremental learning performs better than application of neural networks alone and traditional NHPP models such as the Goel-Okumoto model. The adaptive incremental learning approach achieves significantly better accuracy with smaller sample size compared to simple application of neural networks with various activation functions.

The remainder of this paper is organized as follows: Sect. 2 describes models and methods utilized in this paper, while Sect. 3 presents application of incremental learning to software failure data. Section 4 reviews measures used to compare the models and Sect. 5 demonstrates the proposed concept through several examples. Section 6 provides conclusion and offers direction for future research.

2   Review of Models and Algorithms

This section reviews models and methods utilized in this paper including non-homogeneous Poisson process software reliability growth models as well as deep learning models.

2.1   NHPP SRGM

The non-homogeneous Poisson process is a stochastic process that counts the number of events observed as a function of time. In the context of software reliability, the NHPP counts the number of unique defects detected by time t. This counting process is characterized by a mean value function (MVF) $m(t)$, which characterizes the number of faults detected by time t and can assume a variety of forms. A general form of $m(t)$ can be written as,

$$m(t) = a \times F(t), \tag{1}$$

where a denotes the expected number of faults that would be discovered with indefinite testing and $F(t)$ is the cumulative distribution function (CDF) of a continuous probability distribution characterizing the software defect detection process.

The instantaneous failure rate of a NHPP SRGM is

$$\lambda(t) = \frac{dm(t)}{dt}. \tag{2}$$

Maximum Likelihood Estimation. Maximum likelihood estimation maximizes the likelihood function, also known as the joint distribution of the failure data. Let $\mathbf{T} = \langle t_1, t_2, \ldots, t_n \rangle$ denote a vector of individual failure times possessing density function $f(t_i; \Theta)$. The log-likelihood function is

$$LL(t_i; \Theta) = -m(t_n) + \sum_{i=1}^{n} \log \left[\lambda(t_i) \right], \tag{3}$$

where Θ is the vector of model parameters and $\lambda(t_i)$ is the instantaneous failure rate at time t_i. The MLE is found by numerically solving the following system of simultaneous equations:

$$\frac{\partial LL(\Theta)}{\partial \Theta} = \mathbf{0} \tag{4}$$

with an algorithm such as the Newton-Raphson method [3].

Goel-Okumoto SRGM (GO-NHPP). The MVF of the GO [9] model is

$$m(t) = a \left(1 - e^{-bt} \right) \tag{5}$$

where b is the fault detection rate.

Delayed S-shaped SRGM (DSS-NHPP). The MVF of the DSS SRGM is

$$m(t) = a \left(1 - (1 + bt)e^{-bt} \right) \tag{6}$$

where the term bte^{-bt} characterizes the delay in fault detection and reporting.

2.2 Neural Networks

A neural network is a machine learning approach made up of three components: (i) nodes, (ii) a learning algorithm, and (iii) size and shape of the network. Nodes, also referred to as neurons take in values and process before outputting a new value. The standard equation for how a node processes it's inputs is as follows:

$$f_i(X) = a_i \left(W_{i,j} \cdot X + b_i \right) \tag{7}$$

where $W_{i,j}$ is the weight for input from the jth node in the ith layer, $a_i(x)$ and b_i are activation function and bias of the ith layer respectively, and X is the vector of inputs. Figure 1 illustrates a single neuron with pre-activation and activation. Weights and bias for the neural networks in this paper are trained using back-propagation with the Adam [20] optimization algorithm. The goal of back-propagation is to minimize the total loss, in this case, the mean squared error.

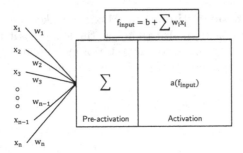

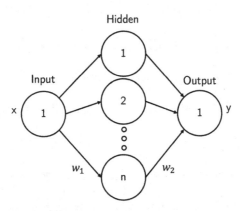

Fig. 1. Single neuron of an artificial neural network

In general, the structure of the network is comprised of the number of layers and number of nodes in each layer. Figure 2 shows an illustration of a neural network with a single hidden layer with one input and one output, and an undefined number of nodes for the hidden layer. In Fig. 2, each node is fully connected to all the nodes in the previous layer and outputs to all the nodes in the succeeding layer.

Fig. 2. Example of a neural network

Activation functions used in the hidden layer in Fig. 2 or $a(\bullet)$ shown in Fig. 1 can take several forms. Activation functions [5,28] utilized in this paper include:

Exponential Linear Unit (ELU). ELU is defined as

$$a(x) = \begin{cases} x & x > 0 \\ \alpha \left(e^x - 1\right) & x \leq 0 \end{cases} \tag{8}$$

where α is a positive constant value.

Rectified Linear Units (ReLU). ReLU is defined as

$$a(x) = \begin{cases} x & x > 0 \\ 0 & x \leq 0 \end{cases} \tag{9}$$

Alternatively, ReLU can be defined as $\max(0, x)$. ReLU is very similar to ELU except negative inputs and unlike ELU, ReLU becomes smooth sharply.

Sigmoid. Sigmoid exhibits important properties to be an activation function such as monotonicity, non-linearity, and produces output in a fixed range $(0, 1)$. The sigmoid activation function is defined as

$$a(x) = \frac{1}{1 + e^{-x}} \tag{10}$$

where x is a real value.

Tanh. Tanh produces a zero-centered output between $(-1, 1)$ and is defined as

$$a(x) = \frac{e^x - e^{-x}}{e^x + e^{-x}} \tag{11}$$

where x is a real-valued number.

GO-NN. A Goel-Okumoto activation function:

$$a(x) = 1 - e^{-bx} \tag{12}$$

where b is an additional parameter optimized during training by the network. GO activation is very similar to the elu activation defined above.

3   Adaptive Incremental Learning (AIL)

Application of software reliability growth models are limited due to the size of failure data collected during testing. Although statistical models are theoretically a better approach for data set with a smaller sample size, as more data becomes available, a reliability model which previously fit the data well may no longer be suitable when new data is added. While machine learning appears to be a viable solution, ML models are only as good as the training data, which may not work with small subsets of data specifically towards the beginning of testing. To address this challenge, an adaptive incremental learning approach is proposed.

Incremental learning is commonly applied to time series problems, where it is desirable to make predictions as new data is added without retraining the model on the entire time series. Algorithm 1 shows the standard implementation of the incremental learning (IL) [12] algorithm, which is an approach to training supervised learning models that inputs subsets of the data over time.

Algorithm 1. Incremental Learning (IL)

$ds1$
for $i = 1; i < \delta$ **do**
    $model.reset\_weights()$
    $model.fit(ds1[: training\_fraction])$
    $testing\_fraction < -(i+1) * length(ds1)/\delta$
    $model.predict(ds1[training\_fraction : testing\_fraction]$
end for

In Algorithm 1, $ds1$ indicates data set and δ indicates the percent of subset of the available data. This study assumes 10% of the overall data becomes available at a time and the next 10% is predicted.

Adaptive incremental learning (AIL) proposed in this paper follows two main steps:

– **(S.1)** Incremental learning is applied to neural networks by training on a set of data that is either a different data set with a similar shape or a subset of the data set. This is done by identifying historical or past data sets from similar projects and computing the F-score based on the Granger-causality test [10,13]. A smaller p-value indicates the ability of a model trained on a historical data set to forecast failures based on the new failure data. Let X_t and Y_t denote two time series data sets Let $F(X_t|I_{t-1})$ denote conditional probability distribution of X_t, where I_{t-1} consists of lag vectors of length L_x and L_y for X_t and Y_t respectively. Then, Y_t does not strictly Granger cause X_t if:

$$F(X_t|I_{t-1}) = F\left(X_t|\left(I_{t-1} - Y_{t-L_y}^{L_y}\right)\right) \tag{13}$$

Equation (13) suggests that past values of Y_t helps predict current and future values of X_t, if the equality does not hold.

– **(S.2)** Algorithm 2 summarizes the proposed adaptive incremental learning approach.

Algorithm 2. Adaptive Incremental Learning (AIL)

$ds1, ds2$
for $i = 1; i < \delta$ **do**
    $model.reset\_weights()$
    $model.fit(ds1)$
    $training\_fraction < -i * length(ds2)/\delta$
    $model.fit(ds2[: training\_fraction])$
    $testing\_fraction < -(i+1) * length(ds2)/\delta$
    $model.predict(ds2[training\_fraction : testing\_fraction]$
end for

In Algorithm 2, a neural network is trained on all of a similarly shaped failure data set and then using that trained model, a small portion of the data set to be tested is used to optimize the network. In the second case a small amount of data is used for training and then the model predicts the next few time steps. After the true values for the predicted data are gathered, the network is trained again by adding the new data to the model.

4   Goodness-of-Fit Measures

This section summarizes goodness of fit measures [21] to assist in model comparison based on information theoretic and predictive capability.

4.1   Mean Squared Error (MSE)

Mean squared error is defined as

$$MSE = \frac{1}{n} \sum_{i=1}^{n} (f(x_i) - y_i)^2 \tag{14}$$

where $f(x_i)$ is the predicted value and y_i is the actual value.

4.2   Mean Absolute Percentage Error (MAPE)

Mean absolute percentage error calculates the error as a percentage of how far off the predicted value is from the actual value

$$MAPE = \frac{1}{n} \times \sum_{i=1}^{n} \left| \frac{f(x_i) - y_i}{y_i} \right| \times 100 \tag{15}$$

where $f(x_i)$ is the predicted value and y_i is the actual value.

4.3   Predictive Mean Squared Error (PMSE)

Predictive mean squared error uses the same equation as MSE but only records results over the testing set of data of length n.

$$PMSE = \frac{1}{n-k} \sum_{i=k+1}^{n} (f(x_i) - y_i)^2 \tag{16}$$

where $f(x_i)$ is the predicted value and y_i is the actual value.

4.4   Predictive Ratio Risk (PRR)

The predictive ratio risk of a model is

$$PRR = \sum_{i=k+1}^{n} \left(\frac{f(x_i) - y_i}{f(x_i)} \right)^2 \tag{17}$$

where the term in the denominator penalizes underestimation of the number of defects more heavily than an overestimate.

4.5   Predictive Power (PP)

The predictive power of a model is

$$PP = \sum_{i=k+1}^{n} \left(\frac{f(x_i) - y_i}{y_i} \right)^2 \tag{18}$$

where the term in the denominator penalizes overestimation of the number of defects.

5   Illustrations

This section presents several examples to illustrate the application of machine learning algorithms specifically the incremental and adaptive incremental learning algorithms. Real data sets from the Handbook of Software Reliability Engineering [24] are utilized. First two examples compares traditional NHPP models with neural network models and assesses the multi-step predictive capability of these models. Final example illustrates the proposed AIL algorithm with IL method.

5.1   Assessment of Model Fit and Model Selection

This section compares models introduced in Sect. 2 based on goodness-of-fit measures described in Sect. 4 when applied to the CSR3 data with 108 failures.

Table 1 lists the MSE, MAPE, PMSE, PRR, and PP measures when the neural network and NHPP models were trained on 80% of the CSR3 data and tested on the remaining 20%. Highlighted values indicate better results and a difference of 2.0 is considered significant between models.

Table 1. Comparison of goodness-of-fit measures on CSR3 data

Model name	MSE	MAPE	PMSE	PRR	PP
Elu	**4.180**	**4.558**	15.283	**0.034**	0.037
ReLU	5.936	6.343	22.380	0.047	0.053
GO-NN	11.481	7.585	44.733	0.085	0.099
Sigmoid	18.381	7.780	85.900	0.238	0.181
TanH	24.812	6.249	118.503	0.345	0.252
GO-NHPP	38.228	17.270	**14.296**	**0.034**	**0.033**
DSS-NHPP	111.207	32.626	119.956	0.349	0.256

Table 1 suggests that the neural network model with Elu activation function attains better MSE, MAPE, and PRR values, suggesting better model fit and predictive capability. The GO-NHPP exhibits better values for predictive measures but are not statistically significant compared to Elu.

Figure 3 shows fits of models to the CSR3 data. The vertical line indicates the 80% of data used for training. Note that the DSS-NHPP is excluded for better presentation.

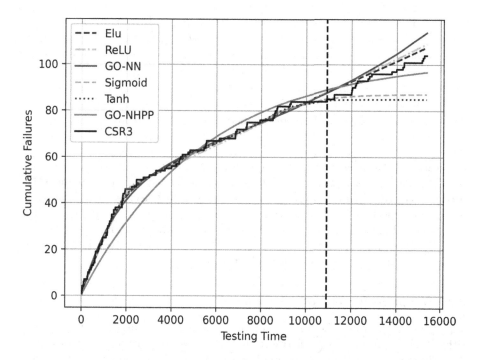

Fig. 3. CSR3 model fit on 80% of data

Observing models characterizing the CSR3 data before the vertical line Fig. 3 suggests relatively good fit by all models. However, estimations shown after the vertical line shows the predictive capability of these models. While all models seem to diverge quickly, Elu, ReLU, and GO-NHPP seem to estimate failures closely compared to other models, which agrees with results reported in Table 1. The Tanh and Sigmoid models fit the data well. However, they fail to predict more than two failures.

To assess the ability of a model to predict multiple failures with less error, Fig. 4 shows MSE and PMSE values of different models with varying size of training and test data. The training size is the difference between the length of the data and testing size.

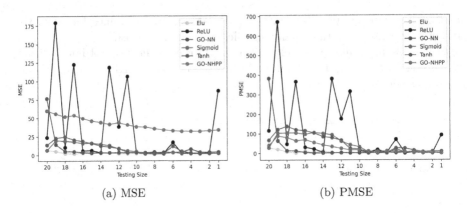

(a) MSE   (b) PMSE

Fig. 4. Multi-step prediction using CSR3 data

In first part of Fig. 4, Elu consistently maintains a smaller MSE value compared to all other models, which is closely matched by the GO-NN starting at the prediction of 18th failure. Tanh and sigmoid MSE values decrease slowly suggesting a better model fit and prediction for a smaller number of predictions, which agrees with Fig. 3. Similarly, the PMSE follows a similar trend, however, the GO-NHPP exhibits a better trend, suggesting better predictive ability despite reasonable approximation during model fitting.

5.2   Adaptive Incremental Learning

This section illustrates the application of adaptive incremental learning in Algorithm 2 and compares it with traditional incremental learning in Algorithm 1. The Elu model is chosen considering it's goodness-of-fit measures and multi-step prediction capability.

To select data sets for adaptive incremental learning algorithm demonstration, the Granger causality test value is computed for pairwise combinations of 10 failure times data sets from the Handbook of Software Reliability Engineering [24] as reported in Table 2. Combinations with significant p-values are reported. Data sets are sorted based on increasing p-values and the length of each data set is listed.

Table 2. Granger causality of software reliability datasets

ds1	ds2	p-value	ds1 length	ds2 length
CSR3	CSR1	2.89E−06	104	397
SYS2	CSR1	2.96E−06	86	397
S27	SS3	9.42E−05	41	278
SYS3	SS4	0.005563	207	197
CSR2	SYS1	0.008035	129	136
CSR3	SYS1	0.007538	104	136
CSR3	CSR2	0.002584	104	129
SYS3	CSR1	0.003249	207	397
S2	CSR1	0.005958	54	397
SYS2	CSR3	0.031280	86	104
CSR3	S2	0.034950	104	54
S2	CSR3	0.016660	54	104

In Table 2, CSR3 and CSR1 are chosen as this pair possesses the smallest p-value suggesting forecasting ability of a CSR3 trained model on CSR1 data.

Figure 5 shows the MSE and PMSE of CSR1 data when the model is trained on data with 10% increments and validated on the next 10%. The IL model starts with CSR1 data, while AIL utilizes a model that was previously trained on all of the CSR3 data.

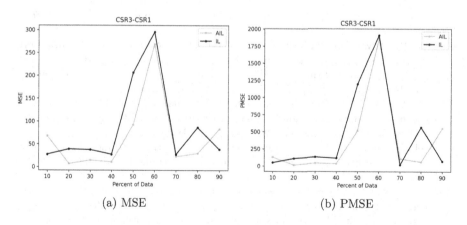

(a) MSE   (b) PMSE

Fig. 5. Adaptive incremental learning: CSR1 based on the CSR3 trained model

AIL in Fig. 5 shows relatively small MSE and PMSE values compared with the IL model. Specifically, the sudden increase in MSE and PMSE at 50% suggests a changepoint due to events such as transitioning from unit testing to integration testing is characterized by AIL 200 times better than IL.

6   Conclusion and Future Research

This paper proposed an adaptive incremental learning algorithm to characterize failure data collected during testing. The proposed approach is compared with a traditional incremental learning model and illustrations demonstrated that the AIL model can achieve 200 times better error value compared to the IL model. In addition, machine learning models are compared with NHPP SRGM as well as NHPP inspired activation function. Results suggested that machine learning models perform better based on information theoretic as well as predictive goodness-of-fit measures.

Acknowledgment. This work is supported by the University of Tulsa & Team8 Cyber Fellows program.

References

1. Aljahdali, S.H., Sheta, A., Rine, D.: Prediction of software reliability: a comparison between regression and neural network non-parametric models. In: Proceedings ACS/IEEE International Conference on Computer Systems and Applications, pp. 470–473. IEEE (2001)
2. Bisi, M., Goyal, N.K.: Software reliability prediction using neural network with encoded input. Int. J. Comput. Appl. **47**(22), 46–52 (2012)
3. Burden, R., Faires, J.: Numerical Analysis, 8th edn. Brooks/Cole, Belmont (2004)
4. Cai, K.Y., Cai, L., Wang, W.D., Yu, Z.Y., Zhang, D.: On the neural network approach in software reliability modeling. J. Syst. Softw. **58**(1), 47–62 (2001)
5. Clevert, D.A., Unterthiner, T., Hochreiter, S.: Fast and accurate deep network learning by exponential linear units (ELUs). arXiv preprint arXiv:1511.07289 (2015)
6. Dase, R., Pawar, D.: Application of artificial neural network for stock market predictions: a review of literature. Int. J. Mach. Intell. **2**(2), 14–17 (2010)
7. Farr, W.: chapter Software reliability modeling survey. In: Handbook Of Software Reliability Engineering, pp. 71–117. McGraw-Hill, New York (1996)
8. Farr, W., Smith, O.: Statistical modeling and estimation of reliability functions for software (SMERFS) users guide. Technical report NAVSWC TR-84-373, Rev. 2, Naval Surface Warfare Center, Dahlgren, VA (1984)
9. Goel, A., Okumoto, K.: Time-dependent error-detection rate model for software reliability and other performance measures. IEEE Trans. Reliab. **28**(3), 206–211 (1979)
10. Granger, C.: Investigating causal relations by econometric models and cross-spectral methods. Econometrica J. Econo. Soc. **37**, 424–438 (1969)
11. Gupta, N., Singh, M.P.: Estimation of software reliability with execution time model using the pattern mapping technique of artificial neural network. Comput. Oper. Res. **32**(1), 187–199 (2005)
12. He, J., Mao, R., Shao, Z., Zhu, F.: Incremental learning in online scenario. In: IEEE/CVF Conference on Computer Vision and Pattern Recognition, pp. 13926–13935 (2020)
13. Hiemstra, C., Jones, J.: Testing for linear and nonlinear Granger causality in the stock price-volume relation. J. Financ. **49**(5), 1639–1664 (1994)

14. Hochman, R., Khoshgoftaar, T.M., Allen, E.B., Hudepohl, J.P.: Evolutionary neural networks: a robust approach to software reliability problems. In: Proceedings The Eighth International Symposium on Software Reliability Engineering, pp. 13–26. IEEE (1997)

15. Hudaib, A., Moshref, M.: Survey in software reliability growth models: parameter estimation and models ranking. Int. J. Comput. Syst. 5(5), 11–25 (2018)

16. Karunanithi, N., Malaiya, Y.K., Whitley, D.: The scaling problem in neural networks for software reliability prediction. In: ISSRE, pp. 76–82 (1992)

17. Karunanithi, N., Malaiya, Y.K., Whitley, L.D.: Prediction of software reliability using neural networks. In: ISSRE, pp. 124–130 (1991)

18. Karunanithi, N., Whitley, D., Malaiya, Y.K.: Using neural networks in reliability prediction. IEEE Softw. 9(4), 53–59 (1992)

19. Kaswan, K., Choudhary, S., Sharma, K.: Software reliability modeling using soft computing techniques: critical review. J. Inf. Technol. Softw. Eng. 5, 144 (2015)

20. Kingma, D.P., Ba, J.: Adam: a method for stochastic optimization. arXiv preprint arXiv:1412.6980 (2014)

21. Kleinbaum, D., Kupper, L., Nizam, A., Muller, K.: Applied Regression Analysis and Other Multivariable Methods. Applied Series, 4th edn. Duxbury Press, Belmont (2008)

22. Lakshmanan, I., Ramasamy, S.: An artificial neural-network approach to software reliability growth modeling. Procedia Comput. Sci. 57, 695–702 (2015)

23. Littlewood, B.: Rationale for a modified Duane model. IEEE Trans. Reliab. 33(2), 157–159 (1984)

24. Lyu, M. (ed.): Handbook of Software Reliability Engineering. McGraw-Hill, New York (1996)

25. Nagaraju, V., Fiondella, L.: A hybrid model fitting approach incorporating particle swarm optimization and statistical algorithms. In: Reliability and Maintenance Engineering Summit (2021)

26. Nagaraju, V., Fiondella, L., Zeephongsekul, P., Jayasinghe, C., Wandji, T.: Performance optimized expectation conditional maximization algorithms for nonhomogeneous Poisson process software reliability models. IEEE Trans. Reliab. 66(3), 722–734 (2017)

27. Nagaraju, V., Fiondella, L., Zeephongsekul, P., Wandji, T.: An adaptive EM algorithm for the maximum likelihood estimation of non-homogeneous Poisson process software reliability growth models. Int. J. Reliab. Qual. Saf. Eng. 24(04), 1750020 (2017)

28. Nair, V., Hinton, G.E.: Rectified linear units improve restricted Boltzmann machines. In: ICML (2010)

29. Ohba, M.: Inflection S-shaped software reliability growth model. In: Osaki, S., Hatoyama, Y. (eds.) Stochastic Models in Reliability Theory. LNE, vol. 235, pp. 144–162. Springer, Heidelberg (1984). https://doi.org/10.1007/978-3-642-45587-2_10

30. Roy, P., Mahapatra, G.S., Dey, K.N.: Forecasting of software reliability using neighborhood fuzzy particle swarm optimization based novel neural network. IEEE/CAA J. Automatica Sinica 6(6), 1365–1383 (2019)

31. Sheta, A.: Reliability growth modeling for software fault detection using particle swarm optimization. In: Proceedings of the IEEE Congress on Evolutionary Computation, pp. 3071–3078 (2006)

32. Sitte, R.: Comparison of software-reliability-growth predictions: neural networks vs parametric-recalibration. IEEE Trans. Reliab. 48(3), 285–291 (1999)

33. Steakelum, J., Aubertine, J., Chen, K., Nagaraju, V., Fiondella, L.: Multi-phase algorithm design for accurate and efficient model fitting. Ann. Oper. Res. 1–23 (2021). https://doi.org/10.1007/s10479-021-04028-w

34. Su, Y.S., Huang, C.Y.: Neural-network-based approaches for software reliability estimation using dynamic weighted combinational models. J. Syst. Softw. **80**(4), 606–615 (2007)

35. Su, Y.S., Huang, C.Y., Chen, Y.S., Chen, J.x.: An artificial neural-network-based approach to software reliability assessment. In: TENCON 2005–2005 IEEE Region 10 Conference, pp. 1–6. IEEE (2005)

36. Tian, L., Noore, A.: Evolutionary neural network modeling for software cumulative failure time prediction. Reliab. Eng. Syst. Saf. **87**(1), 45–51 (2005)

37. Wang, J., Zhang, C.: Software reliability prediction using a deep learning model based on the RNN encoder-decoder. Reliab. Eng. Syst. Saf. **170**, 73–82 (2018)

38. Wu, C.Y., Huang, C.Y.: A study of incorporation of deep learning into software reliability modeling and assessment. IEEE Trans. Reliab. **70**, 1621–1640 (2021)

39. Yamada, S., Ohba, M., Osaki, S.: S-shaped reliability growth modeling for software error detection. IEEE Trans. Reliab. **32**(5), 475–484 (1983)

40. Zeephongsekul, P., Jayasinghe, C., Fiondella, L., Nagaraju, V.: Maximum-likelihood estimation of parameters of NHPP software reliability models using expectation conditional maximization algorithm. IEEE Trans. Reliab. **65**(3), 1571–1583 (2016)

41. Zheng, J.: Predicting software reliability with neural network ensembles. Expert Syst. Appl. **36**(2), 2116–2122 (2009)

Human Interfaces and Management of Information (HIMI) Challenges for "In-Time" Aviation Safety Management Systems (IASMS)

Lawrence J. Prinzel III[1]([✉]), Paul Krois[2], Kyle K. Ellis[1], Nikunj C. Oza[3], Robert W. Mah[3], Chad L. Stephens[1], Misty D. Davies[3], and Samantha I. Infeld[4]

[1] NASA Langley Research Center, Hampton, VA 23666, USA
{Lawrence.J.Prinzel,Kyle.K.Ellis,Chad.L.Stephens}@NASA.gov
[2] Crown Consulting, Inc, Aurora, CO 80016, USA
Paul.Krois@NASA.gov
[3] NASA Ames Research Center, Moffett Field, CA 94043, USA
{Nikunj.C.Oza,Robert.W.Mah,Misty.D.Davies}@NASA.gov
[4] Analytical Mechanics Associates, Hampton, VA 23666, USA
Samantha.I.Infeld@NASA.gov

Abstract. The envisioned transformation of the National Airspace System to integrate an In-time Aviation Safety Management System (IASMS) to assure safety in Advanced Air Mobility (AAM) brings unprecedented challenges to the design of human interfaces and management of safety information. Safety in design and operational safety assurance are critical factors for how humans will interact with increasingly autonomous systems. The IASMS Concept of Operations builds from traditional commercial operator safety management and scales in complexity to AAM. The transformative changes in future aviation systems pose potential new critical safety risks with novel types of aircraft and other vehicles having different performance capabilities, flying in increasingly complex airspace, and using adaptive contingencies to manage normal and non-normal operations. These changes compel development of new and emerging capabilities that enable innovative ways for humans to interact with data and manage information. Increasing complexity of AAM corresponds with use of predictive modeling, data analytics, machine learning, and artificial intelligence to effectively address known hazards and emergent risks. The roles of humans will dynamically evolve in increments with this technological and operational evolution. The interfaces for how humans will interact with increasingly complex and assured systems designed to operate autonomously and how information will need to be presented are important challenges to be resolved.

Keywords: In-time Safety · Data analytics · Human-autonomy teaming

1 Evolution of the National Airspace System (NAS)

As today's National Airspace System (NAS) rapidly expands with new and evolving aviation markets, a major challenge facing safety in design and operational assurance is how

This is a U.S. government work and not under copyright protection in the U.S.; foreign copyright protection may apply 2022
S. Yamamoto and H. Mori (Eds.): HCII 2022, LNCS 13306, pp. 367–387, 2022.
https://doi.org/10.1007/978-3-031-06509-5_26

humans will interact with increasingly autonomous systems. The increasing complexity of design and operations includes a wider mix and higher density of flying vehicles integrated with today's traditional aircraft and human operators managing ever-increasing flight information through dynamic interfaces for in-time identification, assessment, and mitigation of safety risks.

The evolution in the aviation markets involves introduction of different types of operations with an ever-widening array of aircraft from traditional passenger jets and General Aviation aircraft to new electric vertical takeoff and landing (eVTOL) vehicles. eVTOLs are designed and built by original equipment manufacturers (OEMs) and brought into service by traditional and entrepreneurial operators (e.g., airlines, cargo carriers, first responders, companies operating in the electronic commerce space, and air taxis). The Federal Aviation Administration (FAA) in its Vision 2035 described a concept aligning future airspace design that could accommodate different operational missions and vehicle performance characteristics for safe and efficient flight [1].

At the same time, the National Aeronautics and Space Administration (NASA) is envisioning and researching new concepts for how these types of operations could be integrated to work together as part of Advanced Air Mobility (AAM) [2]. The different domains comprising AAM are shown in Fig. 1. One emerging domain is urban air mobility (UAM) with its new and adaptive airspace, innovative vehicles, and other operational features [3]. UAM operates in low altitude airspace with vehicles carrying passengers and cargo between takeoff and landing sites that in some cases are called vertiports [4].

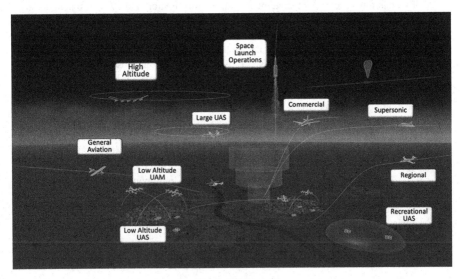

Fig. 1. AAM domains.

These concepts pose potential new critical safety challenges and risks with novel types of aircraft flying among traditional aircraft and helicopters, having frequent flights each day, within close proximity of one another carrying people and cargo, and in more congested and operationally complex airspace. This technological and operational evolution will be accompanied by changes in the roles of human operators. The interfaces designed for how humans will interact with increasingly complex and assured systems that operate semi-autonomously/autonomously and how information will need to be managed, accessed, presented, and acted on by humans are key considerations to assure that the in-time safety risks properly assessed and mitigated.

1.1 Addressing the New Safety Challenges

The need for a new and evolving paradigm to address the safety challenges in AAM was identified by the National Academies [5, 6]. They recommended an In-time Aviation Safety Management System (IASMS) to address risks in-time by focusing on integrating real-time risk monitoring, assessment, and mitigation with a more responsive time frame for detecting known risks and identifying emergent risks and latent patterns in safety trends. An IASMS will necessarily evolve over time as new automation systems are integrated in the NAS, which will require the roles of humans and automation to evolve accordingly in order to assure aviation safety.

IASMS will evolve to bridge today's safety management system (SMS) and the faster operations in AAM. The IASMS provides in-time risk monitoring, assessment, and mitigation in a manner that overcomes the brittleness of the current FAA system that will not scale according to how AAM will grow in complexity. The need for IASMS is compelled by the public having a low tolerance for aviation incidents and accidents, which has resulted from aviation's very high level of safety, as well as the importance of addressing regulatory shortcomings (e.g., the Boeing 737 MAX accidents [7]). FAA SMS regulations and advisory materials have significantly contributed to safety improvements. Prior to SMS, safety was emphasized such as with the expression of flying like you train and training like you fly, which flowed across key aspects of flying as Aviate, Navigate, and then Communicate.

To move toward the envisioned AAM future, NASA has been developing an IASMS concept of operation (ConOps) that builds from traditional commercial and other aviation operations and scales with the increasing complexity of new emerging and evolving operations across AAM domains [8, 9]. The IASMS ConOps is under the NASA Strategic Implementation Plan Thrust 5, called In-Time System-Wide Safety Assurance, that builds out adaptive in-time safety threat management. The IASMS features fully integrated hazard detection and risk assessment capabilities that can invoke trusted methods for dynamic, multi-agent planning, evaluation, execution, and monitoring of in-time risk mitigating response to safety hazards.

The safety risks addressed by IASMS are shown as an operational view in Fig. 2 [8]. IASMS is enabled by three higher-level functions of Monitor, Assess, and Mitigate that involve domain-specific safety monitoring and alerting tools, integrated predictive technologies with domain-level applications, and in-time safety risk management.

IASMS builds on conceptual and notional Services, Functions, and Capabilities (SFCs) that together enable the dynamic Monitor, Assess, and Mitigate functions with closely coupled interdependencies that are unique to the IASMS [9]. A safety risk that emerges during the life cycle phases of design or operations explains why a service is required to manage it. A service is useful for preventing or trapping a safety risk before harm can occur. A service could be provided by the vehicle, UAM system, and/or another agent in the architecture. A function represents what action is required by automation, automated systems, pilots, and other human operators. A function can integrate streams of information and data to ascertain what should be done and when to mitigate a risk as well as use predictive analytics to identify and project known and emerging trends from performance data. A capability involves how a particular risk type would be addressed by technology, including sensors and models that will detect, generate, validate, and distribute information and data across network architectures and be used by functions and services to monitor, assess, and mitigate those risks. The risks included in the operational view in Fig. 2 are shown in Table 1 with corresponding examples of SFCs and risk mitigations. SFCs could be distinguished as operational or safety, and an operational SFC may be used for safety, i.e., an operational SFC could be related to and inform risk monitoring, assessment, and mitigation to assure a safety margin or establish new ones. Example SFCs represent prototype models and techniques developed by NASA to demonstrate features and analyze model performance and test assumptions.

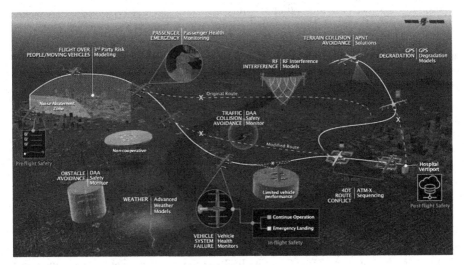

Fig. 2. IASMS operational view.

Table 1. IASMS safety risks, SFCs, and mitigations.

Safety Risks	Monitoring, Assessment, and Mitigation	Example SFCs
Flight Over People/Moving Vehicles	Vehicle maintains safe lateral and vertical distances around people and moving vehicles as established in its flight plan or as information is updated during flight, e.g., changes to route of flight or 3rd party risk assessment. If the risk cannot be reduced below threshold, then vehicle dwells in place until the risk subsides, flies a different route to the destination, returns home, or flies to another location	3rd Party Risk Modeling; cellular telephone data, public events monitoring
Obstacle Avoidance	Flight plan accounts for known obstacles as specified on aeronautical charts and maps, and other geographic information products to ensure safe lateral and vertical distances. DAA systems monitor planned operational trajectory to detect unanticipated obstacles to be avoided. In certain airspace, all vehicles use DAA	Detect and Avoid (DAA) Safety Monitor

(*continued*)

Table 1. (*continued*)

Safety Risks	Monitoring, Assessment, and Mitigation	Example SFCs
Weather	Flight plan checked before departure for current and forecast weather including temperature, wind direction, strength and gust, convective weather, precipitation, and icing. Microweather forecasting for urban flight planning. Pilot weather reports used to update flight plan. In-flight monitoring and assessment. If severe weather cannot be avoided in-flight, then vehicle dwells in place until the risk subsides, flies a different route to the destination, returns home, or flies to another location	Advanced Weather Models
Radio Frequency (RF) Interference	Operational systems monitor and assess RF interference for disrupting communications. If mitigation fails, then vehicle dwells in place until the risk subsides, flies a different route to the destination, returns home, or flies to another location	RF Interference Models
Global Positioning System (GPS) Degradation	Operational systems monitor and assess the quality of the GPS signal. If mitigation fails, then vehicle dwells in place until the risk subsides, flies a different route to the destination, returns home, or flies to another location	GPS Degradation Models

(*continued*)

Table 1. (*continued*)

Safety Risks	Monitoring, Assessment, and Mitigation	Example SFCs
Vehicle System Failure	Vehicle health monitoring systems continuously assess status and performance of on-board operational systems (e.g., battery power and propulsion performance). In case of failure, assesses hazard volume and emergency landing locations	Vehicle Health Monitors
Traffic Collision Avoidance	An on-board real-time operational system provides detect-and-avoid warning, determines maneuvers away from other airborne vehicles, and executes these maneuvers while communicating with other vehicles and Unmanned Aircraft System (UAS) Service Supplier (USS)	DAA Safety Monitor
Terrain Collision Avoidance	An on-board real-time operational system provides detect-and-avoid warning and maneuvering away from terrain to avoid controlled-flight-into-terrain (CFIT)	Alternative Positioning, Navigation, and Timing (APNT) Solutions
Route Conflict	On-board and/or ground-based operational systems provide safe sequencing and spacing between flights going/leaving the same destination vertiport/airport, as well as separation between vehicles having crossing trajectories including during climb/descent. In-flight monitoring and assessment. Risk mitigated in-flight through trajectory modification	Air Traffic Management – eXploration (ATM-X) Sequencing and Spacing

The IASMS will evolve to deliver a progression of SFCs that can assure safety as operations grow increasingly complex. The transformative changes in envisioned future aviation systems will necessitate new and emerging capabilities that enable innovative ways for humans to interact with data and manage information as cognitive requirements evolve. Complexity entails a multiplicity of dimensions with expected and unanticipated interactions. One depiction of these different dimensions is shown in Fig. 3.

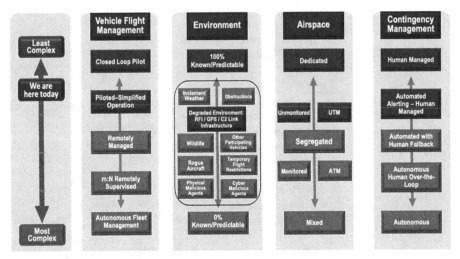

Fig. 3. Example factors of complexity.

SFCs involve data and information that contribute to what is referred to as safety intelligence. Safety intelligence can be considered knowledge of parameters of safety performance and issues gained through the analysis of available data and learning that enables improvements to safety management including risk management, safety assurance, and safety promotion activities [10].

The high level of safety in today's commercial operations has been achieved through the growth of safety intelligence by OEMs, commercial airlines, FAA, and others. The National Transportation Safety Board (NTSB) is recognized internationally for its vital work in identifying the causal and contributory factors of past aviation accidents and incidents, which is referred to as reactive safety or Safety I. Reactive safety provides intelligence of causal and contributory factors for what went wrong. The transition to proactive safety intelligence emphasizes the proactive detection of emergent risks that do not readily fit the patterns of causal factors of past accidents and incidents. Proactive analysis may identify unusual patterns or weak signals before accidents or incidents can occur [11]. Proactive analysis also identifies intervening action taken by the human to prevent or mitigate a hazard before it can cause an accident or incident and "save the operation," which is referred to as Safety II. Safety II emphasizes what the human does right in preventing or mitigating a risk during an operation. Progression of safety intelligence combines Safety I and II and integrates predictive analytics of future safety problems. Predictive models interpret data for future trends that could lead to unsafe conditions. These reactive, proactive, and predictive aspects of safety intelligence, as shown in Fig. 4, involve different types of information and data fusion as well as the dynamics of how humans interact and use that information.

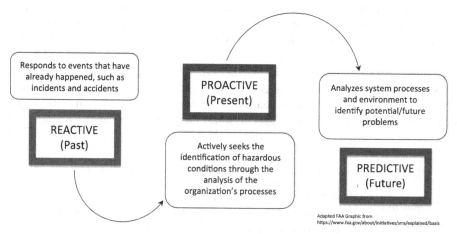

Fig. 4. Progression of safety intelligence.

2   HIMI Challenges

The IASMS provides risk management and safety assurance in a manner substantially more responsive in addressing known and emerging risks than with today's SMS. The FAA SMS regulation pertains to commercial airline carriers certificated under 14 CFR Part 121 and does not currently apply to any other category of aircraft operation. These other categories include helicopter operators (including medical transport), General Aviation, small Unmanned Aircraft Systems (sUAS) and commercial operators of smaller aircraft with limited passenger and cargo capability. IASMS would bring these and other AAM domains under its umbrella. To achieve a broader approach to risk management and safety assurance, the IASMS utilizes system-wide data that are aggregated and fused across the heterogenous data architectures belonging to the different commercial airline operators and other operators, although standards may require commonalities in architectures to provide appropriate, compatible, and consistent alerting and mitigation strategies.

A key thesis is that in the end state of AAM and during transformations to that end state, ensuring the safety of flight through separation provision will continue to be the responsibility of a separation provision service (such as a federated UAS Service Supplier relative to today's FAA air traffic control (ATC) service), a user (e.g., pilot), or an automated system. As shown in Fig. 5, in today's operations the pilot is responsible for ensuring safety of flight in flight conditions called Visual Flight Rules (VFR) and the FAA ATC service is responsible during flight conditions called Instrument Flight Rules (IFR). In the event of an accident or incident, either the pilot or the ATC service would be accountable for safety assurance with no division of responsibility between the two. In the future, assured automation may have responsibility for safety of flight for certain AAM operations [12]. Across these AAM transformations the roles of the human, separation service provider, and automation will change, e.g., changes to the pilot's role might be characterized as on-the-loop or over-the-loop (oversight role). In a fully assured autonomous operation the role of the human may be outside the mission operation and instead the human would be more of a system administrator monitoring the systems and handling outages and other technical administrative responsibilities. This poses critical challenges on the human exerting authority over and teaming with automation including bi-directional communication between the pilot and automation [13]. Transitioning to automation being fully responsible under VFR and IFR flight conditions requires development of new certification standards for safety assurance and other considerations.

Responsibility for Safety of Flight	Flight Rules		
	VFR	IFR	AAM
Human Pilot	Today	–	–
Service Provider	–	Today	–
Automation	Future Assured System?	Future Assured System?	Future Assured System

Fig. 5. Flight rules for safety of flight.

Being more responsive means the IASMS can scale for different operational positions with increasingly complex information being acted upon using more streamlined decision-making processes. A pilot flying on-board the aircraft represents a level of complexity that is well-understood in today's operations. A pilot remotely flying multiple vehicles using automated systems for certain critical risks such as Detect-and-Avoid (DAA) would necessitate different informational needs for the higher level of complexity. An operator working as a dispatcher controlling a fleet of highly autonomous vehicles flying different missions has unique informational needs and task complexity that can be specific to each operation. A safety manager and data analyst assessing post-flight vehicle performance data, safety reports, maintenance data, and other data sources may have other informational and data requirements. These are notionally shown in Fig. 6.

These processes entail fewer human decision-makers who each have the right knowledge at their level and who can trust the automated system. It provides information to humans monitoring operations in a manner to keep the humans attentive to the information and make off-nominal situations apparent.

A key attribute of an IASMS is that it supports the human to quickly manage known operational risks through highly automated information systems that integrate SFCs

Vehicle	Vehicle	Swarm of Vehicles	Multiple Independent Vehicles	Post-Flight Data Sources
↕	↕	↕	↕	↕
On-board Pilot	Remote Pilot	Remote Pilot	Dispatcher	Safety Manager & Data Analyst

Fig. 6. Notional operational positions.

across operators and federated architectures. SFCs would be distributed amongst on-board the vehicle, ground-based, and the cloud using digital twins for increased system reliability. These information systems would collect, aggregate, fuse, model, and distribute data that are used by IASMS functions.

3 Information Requirements

The information requirements for IASMS used by humans and automated systems can be organized according to 16 information classes as shown in Fig. 7 [14]. Each class of information is comprised of data parameters, for example, the information class of geospatial constraints involves data parameters of airspace boundaries, no-fly zones such as temporary flight restrictions, obstacles (type, location, extent), terrain, and operator-defined geofenced areas as stay-in regions.

Fig. 7. Classes of IASMS information.

Safety functions for highly autonomous operations monitor and assess these data for risks. Standards would establish minimum performance requirements for the quality of digital data. Data quality considerations include availability, latency, update rates, integrity, security, formats, implementation and service costs, bandwidth utilization, and standards [15].

The information class of safety reports includes data parameters from investigations of past accidents and incidents, and vetted reports from pilots and air traffic controllers about other safety concerns. Data sources of safety reports include the NASA Aviation Safety Reporting System (ASRS), Aviation Safety Action Program (ASAP), FAA Air Traffic Safety Action Program (ATSAP), Mandatory Occurrence Reporting System (MORS), Pilot Reports (PIREPS) about weather conditions, error and failure logs for equipment and functions, and maintenance logs including the age and history of critical components. These data sources are used today by different domains of the NAS and would be updated for UAM and urban UAS.

IASMS collects and fuses these data to monitor and detect known patterns of safety risk. An IASMS quickly identifies unknown risks that are different from recognized anomalies, precursors, and trends such as based on exceedances, latent safety risks not readily apparent, and emergent or unknown patterns [8, 9].

The potential for emergent risk necessitates innovative data analytical solutions involving machine learning and artificial intelligence (ML/AI) that can distinguish between proactive methods, that build on precedent, and predictive methods that currently are not resident or have limited application for commercial aviation SMS. These methods will involve human interaction to provide learning data during development and to provide a real-time interface with the AI at intermediate autonomy levels. A proactive SMS has the objective to identify precursors and anomalies and their likely causal factors that may lead to hazardous operations as posed through data markers and system behaviors. A proactive SMS attempts to preemptively mitigate the event before it manifests as an unsafe condition.

Predictive SMS derives from the International Civil Aviation Organization (ICAO) with its Annex 19 and Document 9589 that call for SMS to evolve to take advantage of advances in big data analytics with predictive analysis of safety indicators [16]. Outcomes of this approach are improved organizational processes and activities leading to faster collaborative decision-making, modelling and predicting of future operations and enhanced safety intelligence. Predictive SMS intends to take mitigating action based on the potential risk as determined from applying predictive analytics to normal operational data (i.e., not accident data) to reduce the risk of an accident that has not yet happened; to identify safety issues that have not yet occurred but probably will happen if left unaddressed; and to act based on actionable data including updating risk control strategies. Predictive safety management attempts to identify all possible risks in different scenarios based on both observed but also hypothesized situations to anticipate future risk controls, risk mitigation options, safety assurance, and organizational needs. Importantly, predictive SMS is complementary to and not a replacement for reactive and proactive SMSs. That is, all three SMSs represent important safety management approaches intended to work collectively and in an integrated manner to enhance aviation safety.

Lastly, an IASMS quickly informs system design as emergent risks are identified to establish effective risk controls to be enacted "in-time." In this context, an emergent risk was not identified during the design phase such as in hazard risk analysis or flight testing. When a risk is identified during operations, that information needs to loop back to design engineers to assess whether there might be a systemic flaw, perturbation, unforeseen condition, or other hidden risk that requires mitigation involving a change to equipment, systems, and/or procedures and training.

New and emerging capabilities are enabling new ways for humans to interact with data that have not been possible before. To achieve the objectives, the human's roles and responsibilities are envisioned to transform in pace with the equally transformative changes required to achieve the future aviation vision.

4   HIMI Design Considerations

Design of Human Interfaces and Management of Information (HIMI) will be critical to successful deployment of an IASMS. The interface with safety management data and information is the key portal through which human operators maintain situation awareness and team with increasingly autonomous systems for safety assurance and in-time risk management.

For example, traditional roles and responsibilities of pilots, dispatchers, and air traffic controllers as done today by these different professionals may blend into a single hybrid position simultaneously managing multiple flights, but with significantly more trustworthy decision aids and assured autonomous SFCs.

Challenges for the teaming of humans with automated systems correspond with the maturity needed for autonomy and complexity of the operation. Further, teams can exhibit emergent behavior and develop new structures and properties in more complex arrangements and across a larger range of missions, which provide opportunities to improve task delegation, decision making, and problem solving. Increasing complexity can result from and in turn drive the need for new group and machine learning capabilities as well as new collaborative modeling techniques. These challenges have a direct effect on how information would be managed and the human interface to it [17, 18]. Examples of these challenges include:

- Pilots successfully manage equipment malfunctions that occur in normal operations but insufficient system knowledge, flight crew procedure, or understanding of aircraft state may decrease their ability to respond to failure situations. This is a particular concern for failure situations which do not have procedures or checklists, or where the procedures or checklists are incomplete or have limited applicability.
- Pilots sometimes rely too much on automated systems and may be reluctant to intervene, and auto flight mode confusion errors can occur, for example, programming and usage errors with the aircraft Flight Management System.

Much of what is known today about humans teaming with automation is exemplified in the design and operation of aircraft flight management systems and automated and driver-assisted automobiles. One question is to what extent will standards, guidance, and lessons learned be extensible to the design of more complex teaming arrangements. For safety assurance, extensibility builds on trustworthy decision support, mitigation of bias in ML/AI systems, and operator proficiency [19, 20].

4.1 Trustworthy Decision Support with IASMS

Safety information analyzed and communicated over advanced AAM architectures pose a challenge of integrating IASMS SFCs with operational SFCs. For example, operational SFCs manage traffic flow within a corridor using 4-dimension trajectories for effective spacing between vehicles while safety SFCs perform Detect-and-Avoid ensuring strategic separation between vehicles that perform traffic flow management and collision avoidance to handle tactical separation with other vehicles and aircraft. Teaming of humans and automation includes consideration of developing shared experience to develop mutual trust. This experience enables calibrating understanding and expectations of how team members will perform across a range of operations and constraints [19].

4.2 Systemic Bias in IASMS

Systemic bias poses a challenge in the way algorithms analyze information and identify risk mitigations. AI bias occurs when the use cases and data used to train algorithms contain deviations not representative of normal operations. Considering that ML/AI systems can be opaque in which the parameters and models may not be easily understood by humans, these biases may not be detected.

4.3 Operator Proficiency with IASMS

Current guidance for flight deck systems and an understanding of design shortcomings provides an important framework in the design of automated systems. HIMI implications include ensuring flight mode awareness as part of an emphasis on flight path management, such as reducing the number and complexity of modes from the pilot's perspective and improving the feedback to pilots on mode transitions. Other factors for considerations include energy state awareness and skill degradation resulting from use of automated systems.

5 Data Analytics for In-time Safety

As IASMS data becomes increasingly more available, a challenge is how to support humans through trustworthy decision support in the context of substantially increased number of available data streams, volume of data, and more complex and nuanced factors that may impact operational safety. Today, safety managers and boards typically review these data sequentially in stovepipes. Only a small fraction of available safety data is analyzed and those that are mined often have time latencies in event occurrence, assessment, and any mitigation actions.

Transitions to in-time data analytics will fuse data to identify known precursors, anomalies, and trends, as well as emergent risks more quickly and effectively. This poses important challenges for the design of a system that can simultaneously leverage these data streams while teaming in ways that support the needs of the human decision maker. Data analytics can be applied to operational data that go beyond techniques used with current safety management and reactive and proactive SMS, to enable in-time predictive risk assessment, mitigation, and safety assurance. New SFCs for "in-time" tools and predictive data analytics could isolate existing and emergent patterns of underutilized, underexploited, and unidentified system-wide data types to inform the IASMS. An important consideration is that the data management system and how the information will be used by the human has to be considered from the initial IASMS design in ways that enable teaming paradigms that support the needs of the human decision maker. A human-centric approach would utilize innovative methods, procedures, and techniques to safely design, integrate, implement, and validate a human-system integrated IASMS capable of providing accessible system-wide predictive data analytics, effective "in-time" risk mitigation and safety assurance, and learning from all operations.

The complexity of the human interface with data analytics expands with the complexity of safety SFCs. Predictive SMS involves faster safety decision-making, accurate modelling and predicting future outcomes, and enhanced safety intelligence. Safety risks may appear as validated concerns known to designers and operators and known to be detected and mitigated by assured SFCs. Emergent risks may be unknown to designers and operators (e.g., an unexpected and surprising situation masked by unidentified but actionable data markers) with SFCs designed and developed to understand, adapt, and manage them through machine learning or artificial intelligence. Other risks could be recognized by designers or operators as potential latent safety risks even though these are outside the envelope for assured SFCs to detect and mitigate them. Lastly, there could be unforeseen risks that are not recognizable by designers or operators or by safety assurance SFCs and await discovery.

6 Integration of ML/AI in IASMS

As automated systems make use of machine learning and artificial intelligence to handle big data, the underlying algorithms will evolve in sophistication. This may exceed what humans are able to understand if HIMI is not considered early in the system design lifecycle of IASMS development. Research has shown the difficulties experts have in understanding the "black box" methods of neural networks and some other advanced data analytical capabilities. While pilots could be considered users and partners with automated systems, they will need a level of expertise with system design, which corresponds with the complexity of an operation, to understand performance requirements and limitations, interdependencies, and other considerations in operational and safety SFCs.

Human decision makers will be trained to trust a system and to the extent needed for their operation have knowledge and skill with how underlying algorithms work. Similarly, automated systems will need to be designed for an appropriate level of transparency through HIMI so the human can maintain situation awareness and possibly anticipate how risk is monitored, assessed, and mitigated. Designing for that level of transparency will be a significant challenge for IASMS due to its basis in ML/AI-enabled data analytics, for which some frequently used techniques are inherently opaque. Human-centered design of HIMIs, comprehensive human-system integration approach, and dedicated operator training on these systems are key to IASMS success.

HIMI is an important part of the path for assuring the safety performance of automated systems with the human monitoring and verifying/validating how data are analyzed, risks identified, and mitigations prioritized and executed. ML/AI would be used to intercede and disrupt the sequence of causal and contributing risk factors and better and more quickly inform system design as emergent hazards are identified as necessary to establish effective risk controls. Design parameters may be initially set for known operational considerations and constraints, but these parameters could also be configured to manage emergent unknowns that could occur. Part of the challenge in identifying patterns is the extensibility of models to interpret data to identify different emergent patterns that appear similar to but yet are different from known patterns.

Longer time frames using data from IASMS services may have implications to better inform needed or required changes to other parts of the aviation SMS. This could include, for example, changes in pilot training programs, flight procedures, equipment design, or the content of scheduled maintenance checks. As IASMS data analytics expands with the ever-increasing volume of disparate data, the path to predictive SMS is challenged by the need for data analytics that can evaluate and detect unknown vulnerabilities and discover precursors, anomalies, and other predictive indicators, as compared to more traditional safety metrics used such as exceedances in nominal flight data values and trends from the Flight Operations Quality Assurance (FOQA) program. These vulnerabilities are "needles in a haystack" that ML/AI methods can discover. Data analytics would use SFCs that fuse and integrate different types of information and present it using innovative displays and interfaces used by the human as part of human-autonomy teaming (HAT) for in-time assessment and decision-making.

Some ML/AI research has focused on the problems of anomaly detection and precursor identification in heterogeneous, multivariate, variable-length time series datasets within the aviation safety domain. This includes examining flight operational data sets, such as FOQA, where data objects are flights consisting of multivariate time series that include sensor readings and pilot inputs. One goal has been to detect anomalous flight segments that may represent potential unknown vulnerabilities. NASA has developed three algorithms for this task: the semi-Markov switching vector autoregressive model (SMS-VAR—jointly with the University of Minnesota), the Multiple Kernel Anomaly Detection (MKAD) algorithm, and a deep learning-based algorithm that can use pre-labeled anomaly data if available. NASA has found these algorithms to be complementary and expects that future IASMS will use and integrate multiple algorithms to leverage their relative strengths [21–23].

7   Use of Human-Autonomy Teaming in IASMS

HAT is expected to be a cornerstone for operator information requirements that supports development and use of design guidance. These information requirements will shape HIMI as well as procedures and training to avoid misuse, disuse, or abuse of interactions.

Today's baseline for HAT takes form that includes the aircraft Flight Management System (FMS) comprised of systems having varying levels of automation and it has been suggested that some 20% of normal flights necessitate the pilot taking action to handle malfunctions and other off-nominal conditions. It has also been suggested that only 10% of flights are completed based on the original flight plan entered into the FMS before departure.

Leading edge work with HAT considers the multiple approaches that provide viable solutions for teaming. New and different HIMI standards and guidelines may need to be developed and existing guidance updated to support the information requirements of an IASMS [24]. Some examples of these strategies include the following [25]:

- Playbook represents an organized pre-planned set of action plans that can be used as a checklist identifying what needs to be done and who has responsibilities for completing them, with options addressing specific circumstances of the situation.
- Terms of engagement that represent stepwise shifts toward increased use of automation. Automation could be purely advisory with the operator performing the action, to the automation identifying the action but allowing time for the operator to review and possibly override or change the action, to conditions under which automation automatically executes the action and may inform the human afterwards [26].
- Predictive timelines inform the operator about how the automation is monitoring and assessing the future environment and the mitigations that may be required to improve operator situation awareness and decision making.
- Flight trial planning used by the operator to assess "what if" changes to flight plans and viability of contingency management strategies.

Hurdles need to be overcome for autonomous systems to be effectively integrated. These include brittleness, perceptual limitations, hidden biases, and lack of a model of causation important for understanding and predicting future events [19]. At the same time, human use of complex automation can be constrained by poor understanding of what the automation is doing, high workload when trying to interact with AI systems, poor situational awareness, and performance deficits when intervention is needed, biases in decision making based on system inputs, and degradation of manual skills. To overcome these challenges the human must understand and predict the behaviors of the AI system, develop appropriate trust relationships with it, make accurate decisions based on input received from the system, and be able to exert control over the system in a timely and appropriate manner.

These challenges can be organized as a series of overarching higher-level HAT research questions for focusing on IASMS, as follows [27]:

- Teaming models: What models of multi-agent interaction best fit or align with multiple human roles in IASMS, and how should this fit be assessed?
- Shared situation models: Considering that IASMS has different users working on different timelines to assure different parts of safety, how can a common architecture be defined from network architectures (e.g., ground, air, cloud) with their respective SFCs to support a common knowledge base?

- Trust calibration: How can inter-agent trust be appropriately built, calibrated, and leveraged to establish roles, authority, and transitions of control? Steps toward defining an envelope of trust could include development of a detailed use case for a particular mission that would lead to system requirements for automated systems and operational requirements for development of procedures and training.
- Contingency management: How is the IASMS designed so that human-machine teams retain or improve upon current capabilities to identify, assess, and mitigate known risk and detect emergent risk such as from new or different patterns in performance data?
- Performance measurement: How can the IASMS measure performance of human-machine teams and identify improvements to system performance?
- Paths to operational approval: What are the contributions of IASMS to certification and operational approval of human-machine teaming concepts?

Teaming paradigms correspond with the tasks of the human shifted to automated systems. Humans are still expected to have critical safety analyst roles in the future aviation SMS up through the design and operation of an automatically assured fully autonomous monitoring, detection, and risk mitigation SMS.

8 Cognitive Engineering with ML-AI and HAT

As the aviation system transforms with AAM and the different safety assurance methods become more complex, integration of cognitive engineering with ML/AI and HAT raises a range of concerns about HIMI. These concerns are framed as questions including the following:

- Where are opportunities possible for new types of interactions and how might they reveal knowledge gaps in the design path for IASMS?
- How should best practices be leveraged?
- How should information be scaled for display and how should the human operator navigate through menus and other techniques for more details?
- How should safety dashboards be tailored for information requirements of different users?
- How should time critical information be pushed to the display even if it interrupts whatever was being displayed at that time?
- How much training and education should be required relative to the level of understanding needed of the underlying algorithms?

Transparency of AI behavior could be accomplished in real-time through effective visualizations of explanations of the detected risks and identified mitigations. These explanations would need to adapt to the skill level of the human that would consider their prior knowledge and experience as well as performance level such as fatigue [19]. Bias can be introduced in AI systems during development of algorithms, development of training sets, and decision biases. As bias effects the performance of the AI system, over time it can affect the human operator in managing risk information. Processes and methods will be used in the design, testing, verification, and validation of evolving AI systems to detect AI blind spots and edge cases.

9 Data Visualization

Data visualization is important for aligning what, how, when, and why humans use safety data and their interactions with the information from automated systems. Data visualization scales from low complexity with the human pilot flying on-board or remotely operating a single vehicle using a ground control station. At higher levels of data visualization complexity, the data architecture expands through data delivered to the human pilot remotely managing a swarm of synchronized vehicles or multiple vehicles having asynchronous missions. The data architecture would expand with an interface with a federated air traffic management system involving other operators participating in the exchange of data through common services. Other types of data in the architecture having intersections with risk management include current and forecast weather, reports of weather conditions from pilots, geographic information systems data such as obstructions, airspace configuration such as temporary flight restrictions, corridor data such as congestion and slot management, and safety margins.

Data visualization represents the portal through which the human pilot or fleet manager develops and maintains situation awareness. The paradigm of the human pilot seated on the flight deck looking at aircraft controls and displays and out the window for other traffic is overtaken by the human looking at displays presenting different types of data. For example, data visualization for the fleet manager would be different from today's pilot looking at the cockpit display of traffic information (CDTI). Similarly, data visualization would be different from today's air traffic controller looking at the "radar" situation display. Data visualization as part of the design of an IASMS and HAT would involve a portfolio of decision-maker-centric strategies and innovative collaborative human interface techniques integrating data streams across distributed architectures while enabling modular and flexible approaches that meet operational requirements and respect and preserve operator-specific knowledge and skills.

10 Summary and Conclusions

Rapid changes to the NAS pose significant challenges to the design of HIMI for safety assurance in operations and design. Safety in design and operational safety assurance are critical factors for how humans will interact with increasingly autonomous systems. Future concepts for AAM pose potential new critical safety risks with novel types of aircraft and other vehicles having different performance capabilities flying in increasingly complex airspace and using adaptive contingencies to manage normal and non-normal operations. The roles of humans will dynamically evolve with this technological and operational evolution. The interfaces for how humans will interact with increasingly complex and assured systems designed to operate autonomously and how information will need to be presented to assure in-time safety, are important challenges to be resolved.

Acknowledgement. The authors extend their appreciation to Ms. Laura Bass for her contributions in the development of this paper.

References

1. MITRE Corporation: The Future of Aerospace: Interconnected from Surface to Space. FAA Managers Association Managing the Skies **18**(1), 12–15 (2020)
2. Verma, S., ET AL.: Lessons learned: using UTM paradigm for urban air mobility. In: 39th Digital Avionics Systems Conference (DASC), Virtual Event (2020)
3. Federal Aviation Administration: Unmanned Aircraft Systems (UAS) Traffic Management (UTM) Concept of Operations v2.0. FAA, Washington, DC (2020)
4. Patterson, M., et al.: An initial concept for intermediate-state, passenger-carrying urban air mobility operations. In: AIAA Sci Tech (2021)
5. National Academies of Sciences, Engineering, and Medicine: In-time Aviation Safety Management: Challenges and Research for an Evolving Aviation System. The National Academies Press, Washington, DC (2018). https://doi.org/10.17226/24962
6. National Academies of Sciences, Engineering, and Medicine: Advancing Aerial Mobility: A National Blueprint. The National Academies Press, Washington, DC (2020). https://doi.org/10.17226/25646
7. U.S. Department of Transportation Office of Inspector General: Weaknesses in FAA's Certification and Delegation Processes Hindered Its Oversight of the 737 MAX 8. Report No. AV2021020. Washington, DC (2021)
8. Ellis, K., Krois, P., Koelling, J., Prinzel, L., Davies, M., Mah, R.: A concept of operations and design considerations for an in-time aviation safety management system (IASMS) for advanced air mobility (AAM). In: AIAA Sci Tech (2021)
9. Ellis, K., et al.: Defining services, functions, and capabilities for an advanced air mobility (AAM) in-time aviation safety management system (IASMS). In: AIAA Aviation (2021)
10. Daeschler, R.: The need for Safety Intelligence based on European safety data analysis. In: OPTICS Workshop (2015). http://www.optics-project.eu/optics1/wp-content/uploads/2015/04/04_R-Daeschler_The-need-for-Safety-Intelligence-based-on-European-safety-data-analysis_OPTICS-2nd-Workshop.pdf
11. Ellis, K., et al.: An approach for identifying IASMS services, functions, and capabilities. In: IEEE Digital Avionics Systems Conference (2021)
12. Bradford, S.: Foundation – global air traffic management concept of operations, ICAO document 9854, panel on operational sustainability in an increasingly congested and heterogeneous airspace. In: SCI TECH Forum, Virtual Event: AIAA (2022)
13. Lachter, J., Hobbs, A., Holbrook, J.: Thinking outside the box: the human role in increasingly automated aviation systems. In: International Symposium on Aviation Psychology (2021). https://ntrs.nasa.gov/citations/20210011929
14. Young, S., et al.: Architecture and Information Requirements to Assess and Predict Flight Safety Risks During Highly Autonomous Urban Flight Operations. National Aeronautics and Space Administration Langley Research Center, Hampton, VA (2020). NASA/TM-2020-220440. https://ntrs.nasa.gov/citations/20200001140
15. American National Standards Institute: Standardization Roadmap for Unmanned Aircraft Systems, Version 1.0 (2018)
16. International Civil Aviation Organization: Safety Management, Standards and Recommended Practices–Annex 19. In: Convention on International Civil Aviation, 2nd Edition. ICAO: Montreal (2016)
17. Flight Deck Automation Working Group: Operational Use of Flight Path Management Systems. Performance-based operations Aviation Rulemaking Committee/ Commercial Aviation Safety Team (2013). https://www.faa.gov/aircraft/air_cert/design_approvals/human_factors/media/oufpms_report.pdf

18. Federal Aviation Administration: Summary of the FAA's Review of the Boeing 737 MAX. FAA, Washington, DC (2020). https://www.faa.gov/foia/electronic_reading_room/boeing_reading_room/media/737_RTS_Summary.pdf
19. National Academies of Sciences, Engineering, and Medicine: Human-AI Teaming: State of the Art and Research Needs. The National Academies Press, Washington, DC (2021). https://nap.edu/26355
20. Wojton, H., Sparrow, D., Vickers, B., Carter, K., Wilkins, J., Fealing, C.: DAAWorks2021: characterizing human-machine teaming metrics for test and evaluation. institute for defense analyses (2021). https://www.ida.org/-/media/feature/publications/d/da/dataworks-2021-characterizing-human-machine-teaming-metrics-for-test-and-evaluation/d-21564.ashx
21. Das S., Matthews, B., Srivastava, A., Oza, N.: Multiple kernel learning for heterogeneous anomaly detection: algorithm and aviation safety case study. In: Proceedings of the SIGKDD International Conference on Knowledge Discovery and Data Mining (KDD-2010), pp. 47–56 (2010). https://doi.org/10.1145/1835804.183513
22. Melnyk, I., Banerjee, A., Matthews, B., Oza, N.: Semi-Markov switching vector autoregressive model-based anomaly detection in aviation systems. In: Proceedings of the ACM SIGKDD International Conference on Knowledge Discovery and Data Mining (KDD) (2016)
23. Memarzadeh, M., Matthews, B., Avrekh, I.: Unsupervised anomaly detection in flight data using convolutional variational auto-encoder. Aerospace 7, 115. https://doi.org/10.3390/aerospace7080115
24. Federal Aviation Administration: Avionics Human Factors Considerations for Design and Evaluation. AC No: 00–74. FAA, Washington, DC (2019). https://www.faa.gov/documentLibrary/media/Advisory_Circular/AC_00-74.pdf
25. Brandt, S., Lachter, J.B., Russel, R., Shively, R.J.: A human-autonomy teaming approach for a flight-following task. In: Baldwin, C. (ed.) Advances in Neuroergonomics and Cognitive Engineering. AHFE Advances in Intelligent Systems and Computing, vol. 586, pp. 12–22. Springer, Cham (2017). https://doi.org/10.1007/978-3-319-60642-2_2
26. Parasuraman, R., Sheridan, T.B., Wickens, C.D.: A model for types and levels of human interaction with automation. IEEE Trans. Syst. Man Cybernet. - Part A: Syst. Hum. 30(3), 286–297 (2000)
27. Holbrook, J.B., et al.: Enabling urban air mobility: human-autonomy teaming research challenges and recommendations. In: AIAA AVIATION Forum, Virtual Event: AIAA (2020)

Evaluation of Riding Instability of a Bicycle with Children as Passengers Using the Relationship Between Handlebar Angle and Roll Angle

Syun Takagi$^{(\boxtimes)}$, Makoto Oka, and Hirohiko Mori

Tokyo City University, 1-28-1 Tamazutsumi, Setagaya-ku, Tokyo, Japan
g2081432@tcu.ac.jp

Abstract. This paper proposes indices to evaluate the riding instability of bicycles of riding children together. We propose two indices that focus on the relationship between handlebar angle and roll angles and discuss the advantages and disadvantages of each index. The experimental data of bicycles in various conditions were used to investigate the characteristics of each index, and the relationship between the proposed index and subjective feelings of riding instability was also investigated. The results showed that the evaluation of riding instability using singular spectral transformation, which focuses on the change in the relationship between handlebar angle and roll angle, can evaluate the difficulty of driving caused by riding with children together on the paved road. The handlebar roll ratio, which evaluates the independent swing of the handlebar angle, was found to be appropriate as an index to evaluate the difficulty of handlebar operation. It was also found that the handlebar roll ratio is an index that also reflects the disturbance of bicycle behavior due to habituation of operation and the influence of the road surface.

Keywords: Bicycle · Instability evaluation · Objective evaluation

1 Introduction

Bicycles are often used for short and medium distance travel. In Japan, the bicycles specially designed to carry up to two children (CC bicycle: to carry children bicycle Fig. 1 and Fig. 2) are also widely used in traveling with children. However, it is more difficult to maintain the stability of children bicycles compared to ordinary bicycles because they are heavy. In particular, the accidents of CC bicycles have become a big problem. For example, children passengers sometimes injure when the bicycle is fallen off.

In order to prevent fallen accidents, it is required to establish a method to evaluate riding instability based on bicycle behavior. If the index for evaluating riding instability can be established, the index can be used to map running situations to running instability, and more detailed quality evaluation and road safety evaluation can be investigated.

© The Author(s), under exclusive license to Springer Nature Switzerland AG 2022
S. Yamamoto and H. Mori (Eds.): HCII 2022, LNCS 13306, pp. 388–403, 2022.
https://doi.org/10.1007/978-3-031-06509-5_27

Fig. 1. Front type CC bicycle Quoted from reference [1]

Fig. 2. Rear type bicycle Quoted from reference [1]

Such efforts will make it possible to design bicycles with less risk of falling off and to improve roads.

At this moment, there are no objective methods to evaluate the running instability of CC bicycles. Currently, when the designer or developers evaluate the riding instability of bicycles, they evaluate them only from the subjective feelings. Although there are safety standards for CC bicycles, there are no numerical objective evaluation items for riding stability in those standards. As for the research on riding stability, there are some researches on detecting wobbling and predicting falls based on the behavior of bicycles [2, 3], but the methods proposed in these researches can be used only in very limited situations.

In this study, we propose two indices to evaluate the driving instability of CC bicycles and discuss the characteristics of the proposed indices. One of the proposed indices uses a singular spectral transform (SST) that detects changes in the relationship between handlebar angle and roll angle. The other is the handle per roll (HPR), which evaluates the wobble of the independent roll of the handlebar by comparing the roll angle with the handlebar angle.

2 Related Works

In investigating the riding characteristics of bicycles, handlebar angle and roll angle during riding are often measured. For example, Saito et al. [4] measured the acceleration of handlebar angle and roll angle and analyzed the difference of the riding characteristics between the elderly and the young people using their spectrum.

The spectrum of handlebar angle and roll angle are also used for detecting bicycle staggering and evaluating riding instability. Suzuki et al. [3] have created a classifier that uses the spectrum of handlebar angle and roll angle as features to classify riding data under the conditions where bicycles tend to wobble and stable riding data to detect wobbling. In a survey on CC bicycles conducted by the Consumer Affairs Agency of Japan [1], the power spectrum of handlebar angle was used to evaluate riding instability in order to investigate the relationship between the bicycle design characteristics and the fallen risk. However, the classification accuracy of Suzuki et al.'s method is very low, and it is difficult to apply the method to the prevention of fallen accidents of CC bicycles because the target bicycle is one type of general bicycle. In addition, the power spectrum of handlebar angle used in the survey by the Consumer Affairs Agency does not reflect the subjective feeling of difficulty and fear in driving, and it is not clear whether the power spectrum represents their riding instability.

The relationship between handlebar angle and roll angle has been used in research on fallen prediction. For example, Matsui et al. [2] predicted bicycle falls based on the correlation between handlebar angle and roll angle. Normally, when a bicycle turns, it is necessary to turn the handlebars as well as to tilt the bicycle's body in the direction of the desired direction. The method proposed by Matsui et al. focuses on the relationship between the handlebar angle and the roll angle, and the bicycle will be fallen off in few seconds when the negative correlation between the handlebar angle and the roll angle is observed. However, Matsui et al.'s method predicts falls only for slalom riding and is not a method that can be applied for other riding behaviors.

As we have discussed above, there are many analyses of driving behavior using handlebar angle and roll angle, they showed these two values are extremely useful to evaluate riding instability. Since the handlebar angle and roll angle are very easy to measure, if we can evaluate the riding instability from these two values, this method can be applied to various issues. For example, Saito et al. [5] and Usami et al. [6] have proposed a method for estimating the riding conditions of a bicycle and road surface using acceleration and gyro sensors as the sensor networks. If the evaluation of driving instability by handlebar angle and roll angle is established, we can easily find the traffic risks of the public roads from a lot of the data mounted sensors on the commercial bicycles.

As described above, no index for evaluating driving instability applicable to CC bicycles has been established so far. In addition, handlebar angle and roll angle, which are related to fallen prediction and wobble detection, should be used to evaluate riding instability. If it becomes possible to evaluate driving instability from handlebar angle and roll angle, the method can be applied to road safety evaluation.

3 Proposal of Indicators

In general, there is a relationship between the handlebar angle and the roll angle of a bicycle. For example, when turning, it is necessary to turn the handlebars while tilting the vehicle in the turn to the desired direction. The two indices proposed in this study focus on such a linkage between handlebar angle and roll angle.

3.1 Evaluation of Driving Instability Using Singular Spectral Transformation (SST Evaluation)

SST evaluation detects sudden changes in the relationship between handlebar angle and roll angle. The method of evaluating driving instability by SST is shown in Fig. 3

In the SST evaluation, the relationship between the handlebar angular velocity and the roll angle is expressed by the regression equation. As shown in the Fig. 4 there is a positive correlation between handlebar angular velocity and roll angle. Therefore, the relationship between handlebar angular velocity and roll angle is expressed by a linear equation.

The regression equation to be created is as follows, where the estimated roll angle at time t is $\hat{\phi}_t$ and the angular velocity of the handlebar is hv_t

$$\hat{\phi}_t = a \times hv_t + b \tag{1}$$

Let the residual time series be error$_t$, and let the actual measured roll angle be ϕ_t.

Create a regression equation to estimate roll angle from handlebar angular velocity.

↓

Calculate the residual between the actual roll angle and the estimated roll angle using the regression equation

↓

Perform SST on the residual time series and calculate the degree of anomaly$(a(t, \; k))$.

Fig. 3. Calculation procedure of SST evaluation

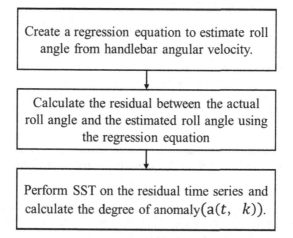

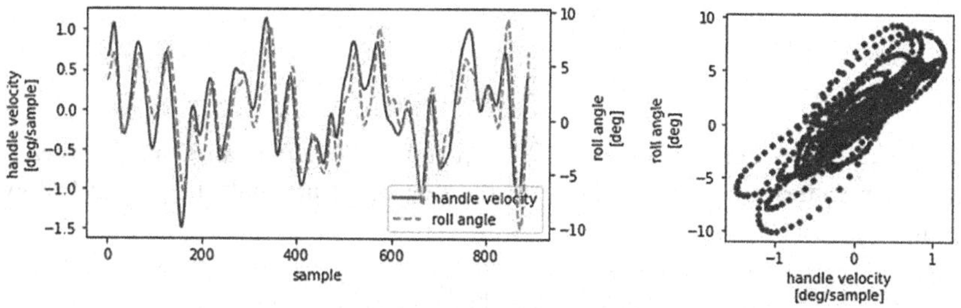

Fig. 4. Relationship between handlebar angular velocity and roll angle

$$\text{error}_t = \hat{\phi}_t - \phi_t \tag{2}$$

After creating the residual time series, the degree of anomaly is calculated for the residual time series using the singular spectrum transformation.

In singular spectral transformation, an arbitrary time series x_t is transformed into the matrix shown in the following equation, and singular value decomposition is performed on the matrix.

$$X = \begin{pmatrix} x_t & x_{t+1} & \cdots & x_{t+N-1} \\ x_{t+1} & x_{t+2} & & x_{t+N} \\ \vdots & & & \vdots \\ x_{t+M-1} & x_{t+M} & \cdots & x_{t+N+M-1} \end{pmatrix} \tag{3}$$

$$X = U\Sigma^{1/2}V^{\top} \tag{4}$$

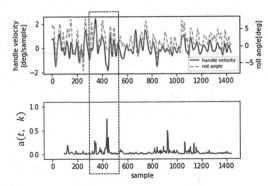

Fig. 5. Example of abnormality time series the upper figure shows the handlebar angular velocity and roll angle time series, and the lower figure shows the corresponding abnormality time series

In the SST evaluation, two time series are extracted from the time series data at different times, and the transformation of Eq. (4) is performed. When we consider calculating the instability at a certain time t for a time series x_t

$$X_t = U_t \Sigma_t^{\frac{1}{2}} V_t^\top \tag{5}$$

$$X_{t-k} = U_{t-k} \Sigma_{t-k}^{\frac{1}{2}} V_{t-k}^\top \tag{6}$$

After decomposition, the eigenvectors corresponding to up to an arbitrary eigenvalue (nth singular value) are used to calculate the degree of anomaly using the following equation:

$$a(t, k) = 1 - \|U_t^{(n)\top} U_{t-k}^{(n)}\|_2 \tag{7}$$

where $\|U_t^{(n)\top} U_{t-k}^{(n)}\|_2$ is the spectral norm and is obtained from the square root of the largest eigenvalue λ of $\left(U_t^{(n)\top} U_{t-k}^{(n)}\right)^\top \left(U_t^{(n)\top} U_{t-k}^{(n)}\right)$.

In this study, we perform these processes on the time series $error_t$ and create an anomaly time series from the residual time series. The anomaly time series in Eq. (7) is the SST evaluation in this study, and it is an index to detect the moment when the relationship between handlebar angular velocity and roll angle suddenly changes. In this study, M = 50 and N = 25 in Eq. (3) and k = 20 in Eq. (6) were used to calculate the anomaly level, and up to the second singular value was used to calculate the anomaly level.

An example of the abnormality time series is shown in Fig. 5. Figure 5 shows a graph of the handlebar angular velocity and roll angle during slalom driving, and the corresponding time series of the degree of abnormality. At time 400 in Fig. 5, the handlebar angular velocity and roll angle do not change in the same way. The degree of abnormality at that time becomes larger.

3.2 Handle Per Roll (HPR)

The HPR evaluates how large the roll wobble is relative to the handlebar wobble. There is an interlocking relationship between handlebar angle and roll angle. Therefore, the index focuses on wobbles where only the handlebar changes without changing the roll inclination.

When HPR at time t is set as HPR(t), it is obtained by the following equation

$$HPR(t) = \log_{10} \frac{\sum_{k_h} |H(t, k_h)|}{\sum_{k_r} |R(t, k_r)|} \tag{8}$$

where $H(t, k_h)$ and $R(t, k_r)$ are the short-time Fourier transforms of the handlebar angle time series and the roll angle time series, and t and k are the time and frequency respectively. In HPR, the ratio of the spectrum in a specific frequency band is obtained by setting k_h and k_r. In this study, the band of the handlebar angles is set about 0.93–1.51[Hz], and the one of the roll angles is done 0.54–1.22[Hz]. In performing the STFT, the time series was cut out in a Blackman window with a window width of 128, and zero-padded so that the data length was 1024.

4 Data Used for Validity Verification

In this study, we used two sets of data to validate the indicators. In Sect. 4.1, we will show about the data to check whether the two proposed indicators can be used to evaluate the driving instability. Section 4.2 describes the experiments we conducted, for further validity investigation.

4.1 The Data for Investigation on the Effectiveness of Indicators

We checked how the proposed index would behave under varying conditions of the number and the position of children riding with us and varying course conditions.

In this data [7], the riding behaviors of various CC bicycles in various running conditions are recorded. The data were obtained by slalom riding under the conditions of the riding children position and the number of the children as the passengers, moving speed, and course conditions using 4 types of CC bicycles with electric assist and 4 types of CC bicycles without electric assist. In the runway, the pylons are placed at intervals of 5.6 m and the participants were asked to run the slalom course three times in each trial. Children's ride the position in three conditions (children condition) of only front seat (F)/only rear seat (R)/and front and rear seats (FR), and the running speed is in two conditions of low speed/high speed. The conditions of the running road surface were on flat ground and the courses including steps and slopes. Here. we will introduce the results of the flat ground and the steps. The subjects involved in this experiment were one male in his twenties and two females in his thirties who had experience using CC bicycles in their daily life.

The behavior of the bicycle is measured by a rotary encoder for the handlebar angle, and the roll angle is estimated using a Kalman filter from the accelerometer and gyroscope sensors attached to the vehicle body. Raspberry Pi 3 Model B+ is used to control the sensor and acquire the values. Sampling frequency was 50 [Hz]. For the handlebar angular velocity, the first-order difference of the handlebar angle is used. A low-pass filter of 2.25 Hz is applied to the handlebar angle and roll angle.

The regression equation used for SST evaluation was estimated using data obtained during flatland slalom driving.

4.2 The Data for Investigating the Relationship Between Subjective Evaluation, Stable Driving Data and Unstable Driving

In order to confirm the relationship between the proposed index and subjective evaluation and the change of the index in stable riding, we conducted an experiment and collected the data. Most of the data in Sect. 4.1 are obtained from slalom runs. For the subjective evaluation, we also asked various questions such as "difficulty in driving" and "fear of driving".

Most of the driving data in Sect. 4.1 is corrected in the slalom riding, which is a very special type of riding data. In addition, all the data were run under some conditions that made the running unstable. In addition to it, considering the application of the index to quality evaluation, it is necessary to know in detail the relationship between the subjective perception of driving instability and the index. The following questions should be investigated a validity of an index to evaluate driving instability: (1) How do the indicators change in being compared under stable and unstable running conditions?, (2) How the indices changes when the subjects are made to perform general driving, rather than special driving paths such as slalom driving?, (3) What relationships with subjective evaluation are there?

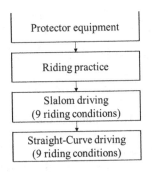

Fig. 6. Experimental procedure

The experimental procedure is shown in Fig. 6. There are nine riding conditions and two course conditions for the experiment. The running conditions are for the bicycles to be ridden and for the children to be carried. As for the bicycles, there are three types of bicycles: a standard bicycle (N), a front type CC bicycle (CF), and a rear type CC bicycle (CR). as for the CC bicycle, there is an additional condition regarding how to carry the children, which is not carried (N), front (F), rear (R), or front and rear (FR). The conditions for these bicycles and the conditions for carrying children are combined into the running conditions. Instead of children in the front, 15 kg of gravel was placed in a sandbag, and instead of children in the rear, 20 kg of sand was placed in a sandbag.

And the course conditions include slalom driving and straight curve driving. Slalom riding has been used in past many bicycle researches [1–3], and it requires meandering while constantly adjusting the handlebar angle. Under the slalom course in this experiment, the subjects were asked to slalom three times between marker cones placed at intervals of 5.6 [m] (Fig. 7), then make a U-turn and slalom three times again. Slalom riding is a special type of riding behavior that is not usually performed in riding a bicycle in the city. Therefore, though it must be an appropriate method for evaluating riding instability, it may not be suitable for the evaluation of usual situations in the city. In the straight/curved course, the bicycle travels in a straight line and turns left repeatedly (Fig. 8). In this study, a straight/curve condition was supposed the riding behavior in a city, especially the behavior of bicycles when they turn at an intersection after riding straight in the city. In the experiment, we asked the participants to ride straight for 10[m] on a 2.0[m] wide road, and then turn left, for seven times.

The procedure shown in Fig. 6 was used for the experiment. The subjects wore a protector to avoid the risk of falling off, and then they were asked to practice riding the bicycle with children until they felt they accustomed with it. After the practice, they drove the slalom course (2 times in each of the 9 conditions), followed by the straight curve course (2 times in each of the 9 conditions). The order of the running conditions was presented randomly by each subject. After each run, the subject was asked to make a subjective evaluation of driving instability. In this experiment, four subjects, all of whom had never used a CC bicycle before, were involved.

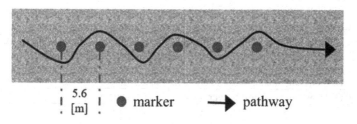

Fig. 7. Slalom condition

To measure the driving behavior, the handlebar angle/angular velocity was measured from the gyro sensor attached to the vehicle body and handlebar, and the roll angle was estimated from the Kalman filter using the values from the accelerometer and gyro sensor attached to the vehicle body. Raspberry Pi 3 Model B+ is used to control the sensor and acquire the values. Sampling frequency was 50 [Hz]. During the analysis, a band-pass filter of 0.02–2.25 [Hz] was applied to the handlebar angle, and a low-pass filter of 2.25 [Hz] was applied to the roll angle. (4th order Butterworth filter).

For the subjective evaluation, the participants were asked to answer nine questions about the degree of difficulty of riding and the degree of carefulness of riding as described in Table 1. Questionnaire items for subjective evaluation on a five-point scale, with 1

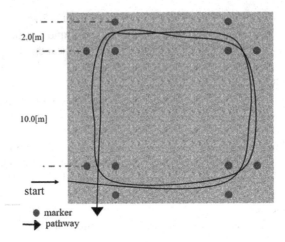

Fig. 8. Straight/curve condition

indicating no feeling at all and 5 indicating a strong feeling. The scores were standardized when used the analysis for each subject in the analysis.

Table 1. Questionnaire items for subjective evaluation

q1	Difficulty in driving
q2	Fear of driving
q3	Feeling wobbly at the handlebar
q4	Felt the body of the bicycle wobble
q5	Had difficulty controlling the handlebar
q6	Difficulty in controlling the leaning of the bicycle
q7	Felt unstable when turning
q8	Driving was unstable
q9	Did not have enough power to turn

5 Results

5.1 Research on the Effectiveness of Indicators

We applied the proposed index to the data described in Sect. 4.1 and compared the results among various conditions. In this paper, we describe the results that are relevant to the purpose of this study.

Figure 9 shows the average values of the SST evaluation by Eq. (7) for each of the flat road riding data described in Sect. 4.1, and compares them for each running condition. As the result of multiple comparisons (Steel-dwass method: $\alpha = 0.05$), the SST evaluation was the largest in FR condition in children position, and there were significant differences among all conditions.

Figure 10 shows the HPR calculated by Eq. (8) for the data described in Sect. 4.1, and the average values for each driving data are compared for each course condition.

As the result of multiple comparisons (Shaffer method: $\alpha = 0.05$), significant differences were observed among all conditions, with the slalom condition including a 5 cm steps having the highest HPR.

5.2 Investigating the Relationship Between Subjective Evaluation, Stable Driving Data and Unstable Driving

This section describes the results of the analysis of the data described in Sect. 4.2. First, the results of the analysis on the subjective evaluation are described first to confirm the relationship between each condition and instability, and then the results of applying the proposed index are described.

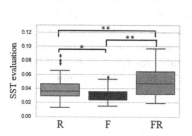

Fig. 9. SST evaluation (Comparison of children conditions)

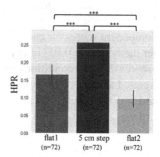

Fig. 10. HPR (Comparison of road condition)

5.2.1 Results of Subjective Evaluation

We checked the scores of the questionnaires about the subjective feelings of the riding instability in this experiment. First, we performed a principal component analysis on the obtained scores to examine the relationship be-tween each questionnaire item. A one-way ANOVA was then conducted on the ob-tained principal component scores, using the running conditions as a factor.

Table 2 summarizes the eigenvectors of the principal component analysis for the questionnaire items. Checking the eigenvectors of the first principal component in Table 2, we can see that most of the questionnaire items are aggregated in the first principal component. Since the questionnaire items in this study were designed to ask about the difficulty of driving and the degree of attention to the investigation, the first principal component score is interpreted as the ease of driving. Since the contribution of the first principal component was 0.659, we can see that the first principal component can explain most of the subjective evaluation. Therefore, we focused our analysis on the first principal component score.

Table 2. A summary of the elements of the eigenvector for each principal component score

	q1	q2	q3	q4	q5	q6	q7	q8	q9
PC1	-0.343	-0.390	-0.354	-0.226	-0.386	-0.281	-0.305	-0.349	-0.335
PC2	-0.033	-0.175	-0.411	0.646	-0.274	0.531	0.157	-0.003	-0.033
PC3	0.381	0.332	-0.477	-0.252	-0.207	-0.191	0.455	0.219	-0.345
PC4	0.338	0.160	-0.171	0.056	0.023	0.114	-0.802	0.375	-0.173
PC5	0.031	-0.074	-0.403	0.062	-0.115	-0.400	-0.063	0.168	0.788
PC6	0.459	-0.171	0.371	0.504	-0.270	-0.507	0.013	-0.119	-0.155
PC7	-0.500	0.402	-0.167	0.454	0.363	-0.401	-0.020	0.083	-0.234
PC8	0.367	0.187	-0.288	0.041	0.387	0.043	-0.100	-0.760	0.084
PC9	0.159	-0.671	-0.195	-0.001	0.605	-0.097	0.134	0.251	-0.173

In Fig. 11. Mean first principal component scores for each running condition (Horizontal axis: "bicycle condition" "children condition") shows the average of the first principal component scores for each running condition. The results of multiple comparisons (Shaffer method: $\alpha = 0.05$) indicate that all conditions without children is significantly larger scores than the conditions with children. Therefore, the first principal component is interpreted as the axis of ease of driving. This indicates that running without children on board was the condition that facilitated stable running, while running with children on board was a condition that facilitated unstable running.

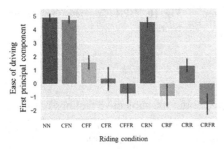

Fig. 11. Mean first principal component scores for each running condition (Horizontal axis: "bicycle condition" "children condition")

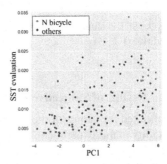

Fig. 12. Scatter plots of first principal component scores and SST evaluation

5.2.2 Results of SST Evaluation

Figure 12 Scatter plots of first principal component scores and SST evaluation. It indicates the SST evaluation values become larger as the subjective feelings become easier to ride, especially for ordinary bicycles.

The correlation coefficient between the first principal component score and the SST evaluation was calculated to be $r = 0.474$. This indicates that, overall, the SST evaluation tends to be large in situations where riding is easy. In the results of Sect. 5.1, SST ratings increased under conditions of driving instability, but the opposite trend was observed in the present results. In other words, the SST evaluation may be a valid indicator on flat driving roads, such as the data used in Sect. 5.1.

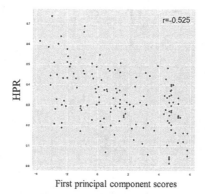

Fig. 13. Scatter plots of first principal component scores and HPR

5.2.3 Results of HPR

Figure 13 shows the relationships between the first principal component scores and HPR. The first principal component score is related to the ease of riding. Therefore, it can be said that the easier the driving becomes, the smaller the HPR becomes.

In order to examine the relationship between HRP and each questionnaire item, scatter plots of the various questionnaire items are shown in Fig. 14. Scatter plots and correlation coefficients of each questionnaire item and HPR and each correlation coefficient were calculated. They show that the correlation coefficients of "q3: Feeling wobbly at the handlebar" and "q5: Had difficulty controlling the handlebar " are more than 0.55. They indicates that the HPR takes a large value when the difficulty of handlebar operation increases.

A three-way analysis of variance was performed on the HPRs using running conditions, driving path (slalom, straight-curve), and number of trials (first, second) as factors, and an interaction was found between driving path and number of trials ($p < 0.10$). Figure 15 Comparison of the average value of HPR, course conditions and number of trials orders.

As the result of the simple main effect test, a main effect was observed for the number of trials in the slalom running condition ($p < 0.05$), and a main effect was observed for the running path in the first and second trials ($p < 0.05$). In the experiment, the first and second trials of slalom running were performed, followed by the first and second trials of straight curve driving. Therefore, this result means that the HPR is getting smaller as the number of trials increases. In summary, HPR can be an indicator of the difficulty of steering. In addition, it was found that it is an index that decreases with habituation because it decreases as the number of trials increases.

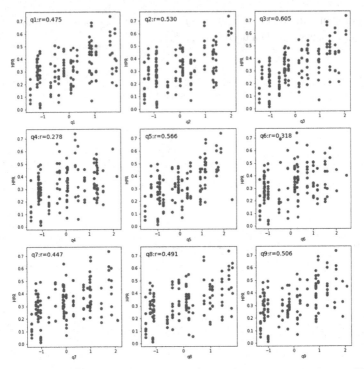

Fig. 14. Scatter plots and correlation coefficients of each questionnaire item and HPR

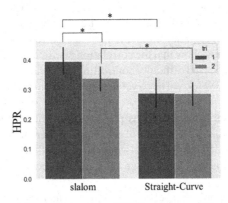

Fig. 15. Comparison of the average value of HPR, course conditions and number of trials

6   Discussion

6.1   Effectiveness and Application of SST Evaluation

Based on the results of the investigation, the SST assessment can be said to be a valid indicator to reflect the riding instability caused by the way of riding children passengers. As a result of comparing the SST evaluation for each children condition in Sect. 5.1, it was found that the FR condition showed the highest value. The data used for the analysis in Sect. 5.1 is a slalom ride on a flat road. Therefore, there are no irregular impacts or other characteristics of the road surface that would threaten the stability of the bicycle. As a result, the difficulty in controlling the bicycle caused by carrying an children in front and behind worked to change the relationship between handlebar angular velocity and roll angle, resulting in a larger SST evaluation in the FR condition.

From the experimental results in Sect. 5.2, the SST evaluation did not reflect the driving instability. This may cause because the experiment was conducted on an uneven sports field. The unevenness of the road surface must affect not only the stability of the bicycle, but also the subject's attitude of riding. As the data used for the analysis in Sect. 5.1 was obtained in riding on asphalt with little disturbance that affects the stability of the bicycle. On the other hand, the experiment in Sect. 5.2 was conducted on a dirt ground. Therefore, it is thought that the unevenness of the ground caused irregular forces to be applied to the handlebars that made the handlebars shake from side to side in riding. This vibration was also observed when the authors rode the bicycle in the preliminary experiment, so it is considered that the force applied to the handlebars to the left and right and the vertical vibration were larger in this experiment than when the bicycle was ridden on the asphalt. When the children on board, the subject consciously stabilized the bicycle so that the riding behavior itself would not change significantly in order to cope with the irregular wobbling of the handlebars. On the other hand, in the case of an ordinary bicycle that is ridden regularly or without children, it is easy to return the bicycle to a stable state even if there is a slight wobble. Compared to the situation with a child in the front and the rear seat, therefore, there was no need to be nervous about the handlebar operation, and even in the running condition where the relationship between the handlebar angular velocity and the roll angle changed, there was no mental effort to drive or difficulty in driving.

This problem must be improved by combining SST with biometric measurements. Section 5.2 shows that there are situations where the bicycle behavior itself appears to be stable due to the driver's effort, even though driving is difficult. In such situations, the driver's muscle activity while bicycling may be different from that in situations where driving stability is not a concern (e.g., when excessive force is used to control the steering wheel). By measuring SST and EMG simultaneously, we can distinguish whether the observed changes in SST ratings are due to driver effort or It will be possible to distinguish whether the observed changes in SST ratings are due to driver effort or not.

6.2 Effectiveness and Application of HPR

HPR can be said to be an index for evaluating the difficulty of handlebar operation. Section 5.1 showed that there was a correlation between the scores of the questions on handlebar operation and HPR, and HPR took a large value under conditions where handlebar operation was difficult. HPR took a large value when there was little roll wobble and the handlebar wobbled. HPR is an indicator that takes a large value when the roll wobble is small and the handlebar wobbles. These results must indicate that this sign appears in the bicycle behavior under the conditions where handling is difficult or the rider's attention is focused on the handlebars.

The HPR may also be an index that reflect the degree of skill of riding. From the results of the three-way ANOVA in Sect. 5.2, it was found that the value of HPR became smaller as the number of trials increased. The decrease in HPR with decreasing number of trials is most likely due to the effect of habituation. HPR is a measure of steering wheel wobble relative to roll wobble. Therefore, it may reflect that the extra wobble of the steering wheel was reduced by habituation. As for the subjective evaluation, although not described in this paper, there was no change in the subjective evaluation scores following the increase in the number of trials. Therefore, the HPR may be a driving instability evaluation with higher resolution than the subjective evaluation.

The HPR can also be applied to the course safety evaluation. In Sect. 5.1, we compared the HPR for different course conditions. The results showed that the HPR was larger in slalom runs containing 5 cm steps. In Japan, there is a step about 5 cm at the boundary between the roadway and the sidewalk, and this step is often a factor in bicycle accidents. The result suggests that HPR can be used as the index of evaluating traffic safety, because the HPR value becomes large in such a riding situation where fallen-off accidents are likely to occur can be interpreted. If bicycles whose behavior can be measured become commercially available in the future, it may be possible to interpret that there is some danger at high HPR by mapping the riding position to the HPR.

From the discussion so far, it can be said that HPR is an indicator of the riding behavior when the handlebar operation becomes difficult. This means that HPR may be able to be used as an indicator to detect not only bumps, but also traffic volume, road width, and other driving environments that tend to make the steering difficult.

7 Conclusion

Two indices focusing on the relationship between the handlebar angle and the roll angle were proposed as indices for evaluating the riding instability of bicycles with children. The SST evaluation, which responds to sudden changes in the relationship between the handlebar angular velocity and the roll angle, was found to be effective as an index reflecting the riding instability caused by riding with children. This index is expected to be able to evaluate driving instability in more detail by combining it with biometric measurements. HPR, which focuses on the wobble of handlebar angle and roll angle, was found to be effective as an index to evaluate the difficulty of handlebar operation. The HPR may also be applied to the evaluation of road safety.

References

1. Japan Consumer Affairs Agency: In accordance with the provisions of Article 23, Paragraph 1 of the Consumer Safety Act Report on investigation of cause of accident, etc. Accidents involving electrically power assisted bicycles while riding with children (2020)
2. Matui, K., Mori, H.: Detection of dangerous behavior of bicycles. In: The 73rd National Convention of IPSJ (2011)
3. Suzuki, K., Sato, T.: Bicycle Wobbling Detection Method Compared with Stable Drives, DEIM Forum (2018)
4. Saitou, K., Inoue, S., Hosoya, S., Kiyota, M.: The Characteristics of cycling by elderly from the point of view of steering and rolling motion. Japan. J. Ergon. **39**(5), 241–249 (2003)

5. Saito, H., Sugo, K., Aida, H., Thepvilojanapong, N., Tobe, Y.: Accidents involving electrically power assisted bicycles while riding with children. IPSJ **53**(2), 770–782 (2012)
6. Usami, Y., Isikawa, K., Takayama T., Yanagisawa, M., Togawa,N.: Improving bicycle behavior recognition using smartphone-based sensors. In: Multimedia, Distributed, Cooperative, and Mobile Symposium (2019)
7. Japan Consumer Affairs Agency: Survey data on accidents involving infants riding electrically power assisted bicycles. https://www.caa.go.jp/policies/council/csic/report/report_016/. Accessed 25 Feb 2022

First-Person View Drones and the FPV Pilot User Experience

Dante Tezza[1](✉) and Marvin Andujar[2]

[1] St. Mary's University, San Antonio, TX 78228, USA
dtezza@stmarytx.edu
[2] University of South Florida, Tampa, FL 33620, USA
andujar1@usf.edu

Abstract. First-person view (FPV) drones provide an immersive flying experience to pilots and are becoming popular for recreational purposes. In this paper, we study FPV pilots' flight preferences and how they interact with drones. First, we conducted an online survey with 515 pilots. We found that most pilots build their drones, have five drones or more, fly for three years or less, fly one to five hours per week, and prefer acrobatic flight mode. We present pilots' preferences in equipment, background, involvement with social media, competitions, and sponsorship. We also show the results of a second user study in which we interviewed five experienced pilots. We discuss their flight preferences, the correlation between FPV flying and social media presence, and how to improve the FPV user experience. Our results allow the understanding of FPV pilots' culture and how they interact with drones, enabling future work in the field.

Keywords: Drones · Human-drone interaction · Human-robot interaction · User experience

1 Introduction

Often we hear people express their desire to fly; the idea of seeing and exploring the world from the skies has fascinated humans for centuries. The Wright brothers achieved the first successful controlled flight in 1903 [24], and since then, aviation has been evolving and becoming ubiquitous in society. Unmanned aerial vehicles (UAV), also known as drones, are commonly seen in a broad range of applications (e.g., photography during extreme sports, natural disaster response, racing, and agriculture, among others), and their adaption is expected to continue to increase [20]. However, drones are remotely operated by a human on the ground. Generally, they cannot provide an immersive experience, which is an important aspect in the remote operation of robots [1]. Recently, a new type of flying has emerged, which allows users to control their drones as if they were flying onboard the aircraft [21,23]. This immersive type of drone flying is known as First-Person View, or simply FPV flying, and it is emerging as a popular recreational activity (e.g., drone racing).

© The Author(s), under exclusive license to Springer Nature Switzerland AG 2022
S. Yamamoto and H. Mori (Eds.): HCII 2022, LNCS 13306, pp. 404–417, 2022.
https://doi.org/10.1007/978-3-031-06509-5_28

FPV drones are equipped with a camera connected to a video transmitter which broadcasts the image to a pilot's goggles. This gives pilots a real-time view as if they were sitting on top of the drone, thus creating an immersive experience similar to virtual reality (VR), giving the sensation of free flight. FPV drones are growing in popularity and being used by hobbyists, video creators, and professional drone racers. Although drones broadcasting images in real-time have been studied in applications like search and rescue and disaster relief, there is a lack of research on the community of pilots who fly FPV recreationally [21].

This paper presents the results of two user studies with FPV pilots. First, we conducted an online survey with 515 FPV pilots to understand their user experience when flying FPV drones. Additionally, in this survey, we elicited research questions for further investigation in a follow-up study. We found that most pilots build their drones, have at least five drones, fly for three years or less, fly one to five hours per week, and prefer acrobatic flight mode. We also present pilots' preferences in equipment, background (e.g., gaming experience, previous RC hobbies), their involvement with social media, competitions, and sponsorship. In a follow-up study, we interviewed five experienced pilots to better understand the online survey results. More specifically, we further discussed their flight preferences, the correlation between FPV flying and social media presence, and how to improve the FPV user experience. Our results allow researchers on human-drone interaction (HDI) to understand how FPV pilots interact with drones. Such understanding guides further development in FPV technologies, and it also serves as a foundation for future research in the field.

2   Related Work

2.1   Human-Drone Interaction

Although some knowledge can be derived from the field of human-robot interaction, the drone's unique characteristic to freely fly in a 3D space and unprecedented shape makes human-drone interaction a research topic of its own [20]. Drones are becoming ubiquitous in our society, and there are unique differences in how users interact with drones compared to other types of robots (e.g., humanoids). Therefore, it is important to understand how humans can interact with them. Current human-drone interaction research has focused on developing natural interaction [4], and new control modalities(gesture [18], speech [12], brain-computer interfaces [14,22], and multi-modal interfaces [8]). Additionally, researchers are enhancing human-drone communication by adding new channels of information, such as using LEDs to communicate directionality [19], and drone's movement to acknowledge system attention [9]. Further examples of research in the field are evaluation of interaction distances [5], social drones [3], and the use of drones for somaesthetics [11]. Even though there is literature on human-drone interaction, such work targets drones in general and lacks focus in FPV drones. One work explored the learning experience of becoming a FPV pilot [23]. The authors found that most pilots (89%) recommend using flight simulators to learn FPV. Most (59%) learned how to fly in angle mode before switching to acrobatic, and those new pilots should seek help FPV community when starting.

(a)   (b)   (c)

Fig. 1. (a) FPV goggles, (b) FPV pilot, and (c) image displayed on goggles.

2.2   The FPV Drone Racing Sport

Drone racing began in the year 2014 in Australia [25]. As racers shared videos of the races via social media, people worldwide quickly became interested, which led to the Entertainment and Sports Programming Network (ESPN) beginning to televise these events in 2016. Since then, ESPN has continued to provide coverage of the now professional sport [16]. However, drone racing is still young, and research into the topic is lacking [2]. Previous work investigated 18 crashes from the 2016 racing season through analysis of 514 min of video footage to determine what caused them [2]. Furthermore, the Augmented FPV Drone Racing System described in [17] proposes several ways in which the drone racing spectator experience can be enhanced. In addition to allowing spectators to view the race using a FPV headset, as mentioned in [2], this system also puts forward an LED persistence of vision (POV) display attached to each drone, autonomous commentaries, and a motion capture and projection mapping scheme.

3   FPV Flying

First-Person View (FPV) flying differs from traditional line-of-sight (LOS) flying, in which the pilot controls the drone from a third-person view. FPV creates an immersive experience as if the pilot was on board the aircraft by sending commands through a remote controller and receiving visual feedback from the camera on the goggles, as seen in Fig. 1.

While non-FPV drones are commonly equipped with sensors to allow higher levels of navigation and automation (e.g., GPS, compass), FPV drones are equipped with bare-bone hardware consisting of a propulsion system, camera, and power supply [2]. These drones usually have a high thrust-to-weight ratio, making them very agile and capable of reaching over 100 mph. Nonetheless, they are also equipped with frames strong enough to endure crashes. Examples of FPV drones for indoor and outdoor uses can be seen in Fig. 2. Similarly, flight controller software used for FPV flying such as Betaflight and FlightOne focus on

Fig. 2. Two types of FPV drones: 5-in. outdoors drone (left), and 65 mm designed for indoor use (right).

cutting-edge flight performance [6] and usually do not have advanced navigation features such as autonomous flying.

3.1 FPV Remote Controllers and Flight Modes

The remote controller (RC) provides the control interaction between the pilot and the drone. Two factors influence how FPV pilots interact with the RC itself: the form of grip and RC mode. There are three primary forms of grips in which the pilot holds the controller, which are displayed in Fig. 3. Additionally, according to [21] there are four RC modes that dictate how the RC gimbal sticks are translated to drone commands, and two main flight modes commonly used by FPV pilots: angle and acrobatic.

3.2 FPV Racing and Freestyle

FPV flying can be divided into two categories: racing and freestyle. Drone racing is an emerging and competitive sport in which pilots fly FPV drones in complex 3D courses against each other, aiming to be the fastest pilot on the track [2]. Drone racing is significantly more complex than flying non-FPV drones as it requires long practice periods and a high level of skills [15]. Freestyle flying is a broader concept, as there are no specific rules or competitions for this category. There is no previous formal definition of freestyle flying; therefore, we derive its

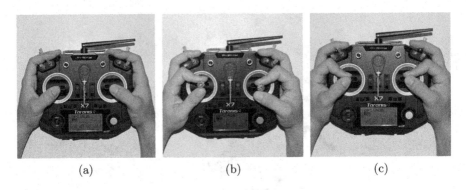

Fig. 3. Types of remote controller grip: (a) Thumb, (b) Pinch, and (c) Hybrid.

definition from another extreme activity, freestyle BMX; where its competitors spend their time performing tricks and stunts rather than racing [13]. Similarly, we define freestyle flying as the category where pilots fly FPV drones to explore spaces and perform tricks and stunts.

4   Study 1 - Surveying FPV Drone Pilots

4.1   Study Design and Procedure

Our first study consisted of a 51-question survey administered via Qualtrics for four months. Questions were related to pilots' backgrounds (e.g., gaming experience, previous hobbies) and how they impact their current flight preferences, previous hobbies and gaming experience, age, and how long they have been flying. Furthermore, we surveyed pilots' flight preferences (flight modes, remote controller grips, and flight simulators), flight controller software, and hardware (batteries, frames, propellers, goggles, remote controllers) preferences. A link to the survey was posted on FPV related groups on Facebook, Twitch, Discord, Twitter, and Reddit. Before completing the survey, participants had to sign an informed consent form digitally.

4.2   Participants

A total of 515 FPV pilots completed the survey. Of these, 505 (98.06%) participants were male, 5 (0.97%) were female, and 5 (0.97%) did not identify as neither male nor female. Additionally, 79 (15.34%) were 18 to 24 years old, 133 (25.83%) were 25 to 34, 176 (34.17%) were 35 to 44, 87 (16.89%) were 45 to 54, 34 (6.60%) were 55 to 64, and 6 (1.17%) were at least 65 years old.

4.3   FPV Pilot Flying Preferences

Flying Categories, Flight Modes, and Remote Controllers. Our analysis of the 515 FPV pilots shows that 43.08% of them fly freestyle only, 8.33% fly

Table 1. Pilots' flight preferences broken down by categories.

	All participants	Freestyle pilots	Racing pilots
Flight mode			
Angle	6.10%	8.02%	14.63%
Acrobatic	92.07%	90.09%	82.93%
Unknown	0.41%	0.47%	0.00%
Other	1.42%	1.41%	2.44%
Controller grip			
Thumb	53.46%	52.36%	51.22%
Pinch	20.9.%	21.70%	19.51%
Hybrid	24.80%	25.47%	29.27%
Unknown	0.81%	0.47%	0.00%
Controller mode			
Mode 1	6.10%	6.13%	12.20%
Mode 2	87.40%	88.21%	80.49%
Mode 3	0.81%	0.47%	0.00%
Mode 4	1.02%	0.47%	0.00%
Unknown	4.67%	4.72%	7.32%

only for racing purposes, and 48.57% fly both racing and freestyle. Table 1 breaks down the flight preferences among these groups. Over 90% of the pilots surveyed selected acro as their main flight mode, suggesting that this is the best-suited flight mode for these flight modalities. To understand the reason why this flight mode is the favorite among FPV pilots, we further evaluate this topic in the second study (see Sect. 5). Furthermore, we looked into whether gamers and pilots with previous RC hobbies preferred racing or freestyle flying; we found no significant differences in their inclinations.

The grip can influence the pilot's interaction with the drone in terms of control latency, accuracy, and comfort. Data in Table 1 shows the majority of pilots (53.46%) prefer to hold their controllers using the "thumb grip", followed by hybrid (24.80%) and pinch (20.9%). Additionally, our results show that controller mode 2 is the preferred RC mode for most pilots (87.40%). The form of grip is another topic that we investigated in the follow-up interviews, and results are presented and further discussed in Sect. 5.

Equipment Preferences. As seen in Table 2, it is common for pilots to own multiple drones, with the majority of pilots owning at least five drones. Results also demonstrate that most FPV pilots build their drones as 481 (93.4%) participants stated they had built at least one drone before. Additionally, Table 3 displays equipment preferences for each flying categories (freestyle vs racing). Results demonstrate that 4-cell batteries and 5 to 5.9-in. propellers are the most

Table 2. Number of drones owned by pilots, broken down by flying categories.

Number of drones	All participants	Freestyle pilots	Racing pilots
1	2.85%	2.83%	4.88%
2	8.94%	10.38%	7.32%
3	13.21%	16.51%	14.66%
4	12.20%	14.15%	7.32%
5 or more	62.80%	56.13%	65.85%

Table 3. Equipment preferences broken down by pilot categories.

	All participants	Freestyle pilots	Racing pilots
Flight controller			
BetaFlight	68.03%	67.74%	80.85%
CleanFlight	5.45%	4.66%	2.13%
Kiss	5.76%	6.09%	4.26%
FlightOne	5.78%	3.94%	6.39%
Other	14.56%	16.85%	6.39%
Unknown	0.45%	0.72%	0.00%
Battery size			
1 Cell	12.64%	12.54%	9.26%
2 Cell	8.18%	7.52%	3.70%
3 Cell	12.89%	12.85%	7.41%
4 Cell	51.55%	55.17%	55.56%
5 Cell	5.08%	6.27%	0.00%
6 Cell	9.67%	5.64%	24.07%
Propeller size			
< 2 in.	14.64%	14.10%	10.91%
2.0 to 2.9 in.	11.28%	10.11%	9.09%
3 to 3.9 in.	11.50%	11.44%	7.27%
4 to 4.9 in.	6.07%	5.32%	1.82%
5 to 5.9 in.	45.34%	44.95%	67.27%
6 to 6.9 in.	6.62%	8.78%	0.00%
>= 7 in.	4.56%	5.32%	3.64%
Frame type			
H	4.88%	5.66%	2.44%
X	54.07%	59.43%	46.34%
Stretch X	26.83%	16.98%	46.34%
Wide X	6.10%	9.43%	0.00%
Other	4.27%	2.83%	2.44%
Unknow	3.86%	5.66%	2.44%

used among pilots. This combination is common among racers because it falls under the requirements to compete in racing leagues. Additionally, a probable

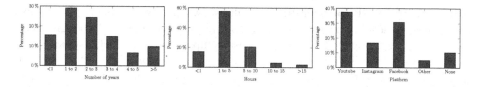

Fig. 4. Number of years each pilot has been flying, hours spent flying per week, and social media preferences.

cause why this is the main choice for freestyle pilots is because it leads to the smallest drone capable of carrying a high-definition action camera (e.g., GoPro) without heavily impacting flight performance. Lastly, we found that Betaflight is vastly the most used flight controller software, which we attribute to its cutting edge flight performance, and for being a free and open-source project with a team of developers actively collaborating with the FPV community.

4.4 Understanding the FPV Community Culture

Pilots' Gaming and RC Hobbies Background. Of the 515 participants, 414 of them reported playing video games regularly. A likely explanation for this high number is the similarity between video games and FPV flying. Players and pilots share comparable remote controllers and watch their activities through a screen. Similarly, 367 out of the 515 participants stated they had at least one other RC hobby before flying multi-rotor drones. Remote-controlled cars were the most common previous hobby (29.17%), followed by fixed-wing aircraft (18.92%), helicopters (14.85%), and boats (7.10%).

Social Media Preferences. FPV flying allows pilots to create and share a new form of audiovisual content on social media platforms. To better understand pilots' social engagement, we evaluated pilots' social media preferences. Our results demonstrate that 89.71% of participants post flight footage on at least one platform. As seen in Fig. 4, YouTube is the favorite platform; however, Facebook and Instagram are also popular among drone pilots. We further explored the correlation between FPV flying and social media presence in the follow-up study, presented in Sect. 5.

Amount of Time Spent Flying. As seen in Fig. 4, the majority of pilots have been flying for somewhere between one and three years. Additionally, less than 10% of pilots have been flying for more than five years. This is expected as FPV drone flying is a relatively new flight modality, only gaining popularity recently, as mentioned in Sect. 2. Moreover, Fig. 4 shows that the majority (56.50%) of pilots spend between 1 and 5 h per week flying.

Competition and Sponsorship. Results show that 80% of racing pilots compete at some level, compared to only 13% of freestyle pilots. Although there are official FPV racing leagues that host competitions, no such leagues exist for freestyle pilots. This is also a plausible explanation for why most sponsored pilots are racers, as these competitions are often televised and draw sponsorships. Results show that 15% of racing pilots receive some sort of sponsorship while only 3% of freestyle pilots do. As FPV sports continue to grow in popularity, we expect official freestyle competitions and sponsorship to emerge.

Relation to Acrophobia. Out of the 515 participants, 138 (26.8%) of them declared fear of heights before flying FPV drones. However, 29 of the 138 (21%) no longer suffer from such fear, suggesting that FPV flying may be an option for acrophobia treatment. This statement is supported by 20 pilots who stated that FPV flying helped them overcome their fear. When asked how FPV impacted their fear of heights, pilots answered with comments such as "being behind the goggles for several years helped me to cope with a mild fear of heights", "My fear has been greatly reduced from repeated exposure while flying FPV", and "I would get vertigo even on the ground prior to FPV. However, after a year or so of FPV, I noticed the vertigo was gone, and I was able to keep my balance better while I was on ladders or high edges." Combined, the above results suggest that FPV has the potential to treat acrophobia. As FPV flying has similarities to VR systems, this finding is supported by the fact that VR is currently used for such purposes [7,10].

5   Study 2 - Evaluating FPV Pilots User Experience Through Interviews

5.1   Study Design and Procedures

To further understand the online survey results, we conducted interviews with experienced FPV pilots. A researcher remotely interviewed each pilot for approximately 30 min. Prior to each interview, the pilot received the informed consent form and provided verbal consent to participate in this study. Each interview was audio recorded for post-analysis. The interview consisted of the following questions:

- Why do FPV pilots prefer acrobatic flight mode, and what are the advantages of this flight mode when compared to a self-level flight mode (angle)?
- What are the advantages and disadvantages of each remote controller grip (thumbs, pinch, hybrid)?
- What are main factors that explain the strong correlation between FPV flying and social media presence?
- How to improve the user experience for FPV pilots?

5.2 Participants

Five FPV pilots participated in this study. Recruitment was also performed solely online on FPV related groups on Facebook. All five participants were at least 18 years old. Additionally, all participants were experienced FPV pilots who have been flying for at least four years, and all of them stated additional involvement in the FPV community: owner of a FPV store, designer and manufacturer of electronic FPV components, professional racer, owner of a large FPV Youtube channel, and professional video content creator.

5.3 Results and Discussion

Flight Mode. Acrobatic (acro) flight mode is the most common flight mode in both racing and freestyle flying. As seen in Sect. 4, 90% of pilots fly acro as their main flight mode, suggesting that this flight mode is the best suited for FPV drones. All five participants stated that FPV pilots desire freedom of movement during flight, which cannot be achieved in other flight modes. Acro flying provides this freedom because the flight controller computer does not auto-level the drone, leaving complete control of the drone's attitude to the pilot. These characteristics allow pilots to explore spaces creatively, perform fast maneuvers, position the drone in any orientation for freestyle stunts, and create video content that wouldn't be possible with self-leveling flight modes. One of the pilots summarized this characteristic by forming an analogy to a Formula 1 car. He explained that the computer is still there with extremely advanced technologies "under the hood", but ultimately the control is in the pilot's hands. Other pilots' quotes expressing the advantages of acro mode are "provides freedom of movement", "it provides freedom during flights", and "it gives you full control and full benefits from drones".

Participants also discussed that acro flying has a steep learning curve. However, after the pilot understands the flight mode and builds muscle memory on the finger movements, acro flight mode becomes easier to control than others. Pilots also noted that the challenge of learning this flight mode makes the experience fun. Another advantage is that acro flight mode makes the drone behavior more predictable as the flight controller computer does not try to adjust the drone attitude without pilot command. The above acro flying characteristics allow pilots to feel more connected to the drone. Ultimately, this flight mode will enable racers to better maneuver around obstacles on the track and freestylers to perform stunts that would not be possible in other flight modes.

Remote Controller Grip. The majority of pilots (53.46%) prefer to hold their controllers using the "thumb grip" (see Table 1). The grip can directly impact the pilot's interaction with the drone. Therefore, we further investigated this matter in this second study. All participants stated that most beginners to FPV start their journey holding the thumb grip because "it feels like the right thing to do." More specifically, previous interaction with technologies like video-game controllers influenced how they held the FPV remote controller for the first time. However, 4 out of the 5 pilots switched to a pinch grip as they became more experienced. All 5 stated that a pinch grip provides more precise control, a higher perception of the gimbal sticks, and provides an overall better flight experience. An interesting response was that one pilot stated to suffer from "twitching hands" and that he could not precisely control drones with a thumb grip, however, switching to a pinch grip allowed him to overcome the physical constraint and feel more confident when piloting.

The single participant who still flies using a thumb grip also agreed that pinch provides more control. However, he did not shift to pinching because (1) he could not get used to the ergonomics of the grip, which could be due to his previous video-game experience, and (2) he prefers to have the index finger free to work on other remote controller switches. Another interesting fact raised by 3 of the 5 pilots is that the physical stick-ends of the gimbal play a significant role in the user experience as it directly changes the interface between the pilot, the remote controller, and ultimately the drone. Such responses demonstrate that new pilots are influenced by their experience with previous technologies, in this case how they previously held video game controllers. However, such influences might lead pilots to sub-optimal experiences with FPV drones as 4 out of 5 pilots with at least 4 years of experience switched their control grip to pinch. To enhance the FPV pilots' user experience, we suggest future studies quantitatively evaluate and compare each control grip.

Social Media. In this study, we also investigated the correlation between FPV flying and social media presence found in Sect. 4. First, 3 pilots expressed that flying FPV provides such a good experience that they want to share with family and friends. Pilots stated, "FPV makes me feel like I can fly", "it makes me feel like a fighter pilot", and "it feels like flying a jet". They post on social media to share their memories with others and to document their progress as pilots. They also stated that social media is "part of the new world", and posting on it is the new form of "picture albums". A pilot said, "we post for the same reason as we hang pictures on the wall of our houses, to remember our memories and share with others". This was supported by another pilot who defended that they post "for the same reasons why other communities post their hobbies and lifestyle to social media, it is the modern way of sharing good moments". As FPV flying is based on the visual feedback sent to the pilot's goggles, it is not surprising that pilots would like to share their videos demonstrating the sensation of flight with the community. FPV flying can also be considered a new form of artistic expression, as pilots tend to share their creativity through flight footage on social media.

Additionally, 3 pilots also stated that it is common to post on social media to meet other pilots. For instance, one of them stated "I started posting on social media to join the community of pilots, to be part of a group of individuals who share the same interest." This demonstrates that FPV drones are a technology that can bring people together. They also declared that social media is an excellent medium for seeking help within the community, receiving tips from more experienced pilots, asking for equipment recommendations, and even buying/sell and trade equipment. Finally, two of the pilots explained that social media allows them to trade drone parts with others, bringing a sense of nostalgia as it reminds them of trading cards as kids.

User Experience Improvement. Participants discussed how to improve the user experience in FPV. The main aspect raised by 3 out of the 5 pilots is the need to decrease the learning curve for beginners. Getting started with FPV can be challenging, which can steer new pilots away to other modalities. Tutorials, guides, and summer camps by different organizations can effectively introduce new users to the FPV community. Recently, FPV companies have been releasing bind-and-fly drones, which are FPV drones that are ready to fly out-of-the-box. Although the results from the online survey show that most pilots build their drones, a bind-and-fly drone might be a good option for a beginner that wants to learn how to fly before learning how to build FPV drones. Additionally, pilots often struggle to find legal and safe places to fly. Participants stated that regulations by the government agencies who regulate drones (e.g., FAA in the USA) are hard to read. Therefore, the user experience can also be enhanced by the demystification of current laws and the development of new ones that allow pilots to find flying fields that are both safe and legal.

Lastly, the user experience can be improved by advancements in software and hardware technologies. For instance, since the flying experience is based on the visual feedback in the pilot's goggles, increasing the FPV image quality can enhance the experience. One pilot explained that higher image quality combined with lower latency on the control link allows the pilot to feel more connected to the drone, increasing the overall user experience. In addition, software advancements such as better control algorithms can provide even higher levels of control. Another example of software advancement brought up during the interview that can help users is an auto-tuning feature for FPV drones. Although some pilots might enjoy tuning their quad-copters, some other pilots, especially beginners, consider tuning stressful.

6 Conclusion

First-Person View (FPV) drones provide a unique flying experience. FPV drones allow pilots to immerse themselves while flying, creating a sensation similar to what is experienced in virtual reality environments. In this paper, we surveyed 515 FPV pilots, aiming to understand the FPV community in-depth. Our results allowed us to evaluate different aspects of FPV flying and interactions between pilots and drones. We presented that the majority of pilots build their drones (93%), have 5 drones or more (62%), have been flying for 3 years or less (69%), and fly between 1 and 5 h per week (56%). We also presented that the majority of FPV pilots prefer acrobatic flight mode (92%), mode 2 remote controller mode (87%), thumbs controller grip (53%), and Betaflight flight controller software

(68%). We also discussed pilots' backgrounds and how they affect their experiences and their involvement with social media platforms, official competitions, and sponsorship.

To further understand the results from the first study, we conducted a follow-up study. We interviewed 5 experienced pilots to discuss some of the patterns found during the first study. More specifically, we confirmed that acrobatic flight mode provides the most advantages for FPV flying, discussed the benefits of different controller grips, the correlation between FPV and social media presence, and how to improve the FPV user experience. In conclusion, combining the results of these two studies, we provided an in-depth analysis of the FPV community and the pilot user experience.

References

1. Adalgeirsson, S.O., Breazeal, C.: Mebot: a robotic platform for socially embodied presence. In: Proceedings of the 5th ACM/IEEE International Conference on Human-Robot Interaction, pp. 15–22. IEEE Press (2010)
2. Barin, A., Dolgov, I., Toups, Z.O.: Understanding dangerous play: a grounded theory analysis of high-performance drone racing crashes. In: Proceedings of the Annual Symposium on Computer-Human Interaction in Play, pp. 485–496. ACM (2017)
3. Baytas, M.A., Çay, D., Zhang, Y., Obaid, M., Yantaç, A.E., Fjeld, M.: The design of social drones: a review of studies on autonomous flyers in inhabited environments. In: Proceedings of the 2019 CHI Conference on Human Factors in Computing Systems, pp. 1–13 (2019)
4. Cauchard, J.R., E, J.L., Zhai, K.Y., Landay, J.A.: Drone & me: an exploration into natural human-drone interaction. In: Proceedings of the 2015 ACM International Joint Conference on Pervasive and Ubiquitous Computing, New York, NY, USA, pp. 361–365. Association for Computing Machinery (2015). https://doi.org/10.1145/2750858.2805823
5. Duncan, B.A., Murphy, R.R.: Comfortable approach distance with small unmanned aerial vehicles. In: 2013 IEEE RO-MAN, pp. 786–792. IEEE (2013)
6. Ebeid, E., Skriver, M., Terkildsen, K.H., Jensen, K., Schultz, U.P.: A survey of open-source UAV flight controllers and flight simulators. Microprocess. Microsyst. **61**, 11–20 (2018)
7. Emmelkamp, P.M., Bruynzeel, M., Drost, L., van der Mast, C.A.G.: Virtual reality treatment in acrophobia: a comparison with exposure in vivo. CyberPsychol. Behav. 4(3), 335–339 (2001)
8. Fernandez, R.A.S., Sanchez-Lopez, J.L., Sampedro, C., Bavle, H., Molina, M., Campoy, P.: Natural user interfaces for human-drone multi-modal interaction. In: 2016 International Conference on Unmanned Aircraft Systems (ICUAS), pp. 1013–1022. IEEE (2016)
9. Jensen, W., Hansen, S., Knoche, H.: Knowing you, seeing me: investigating user preferences in drone-human acknowledgement. In: Proceedings of the 2018 CHI Conference on Human Factors in Computing Systems, p. 365. ACM (2018)
10. Krijn, M., Emmelkamp, P.M., Biemond, R., de Ligny, C.D.W., Schuemie, M.J., van der Mast, C.A.: Treatment of acrophobia in virtual reality: the role of immersion and presence. Behav. Res. Therapy **42**(2), 229–239 (2004)

11. La Delfa, J., Baytas, M.A., Patibanda, R., Ngari, H., Khot, R.A., Mueller, F.: Drone chi: somaesthetic human-drone interaction. In: Proceedings of the 2020 CHI Conference on Human Factors in Computing Systems, pp. 1–13 (2020)

12. Miyoshi, K., Konomura, R., Hori, K.: Entertainment multi-rotor robot that realises direct and multimodal interaction. In: Proceedings of the 28th International BCS Human Computer Interaction Conference on HCI 2014-Sand, Sea and Sky-Holiday HCI, pp. 218–221. BCS (2014)

13. Nelson, W.G.J.: Reading cycles: the culture of BMX freestyle. Ph.D. thesis, McGill University (2006)

14. Nourmohammadi, A., Jafari, M., Zander, T.O.: A survey on unmanned aerial vehicle remote control using brain-computer interface. IEEE Trans. Hum.-Mach. Syst. **48**(4), 337–348 (2018)

15. Ribeiro, R., Ramos, J., Safadinho, D., de Jesus Pereira, A.M.: UAV for everyone: an intuitive control alternative for drone racing competitions. In: 2018 2nd International Conference on Technology and Innovation in Sports, Health and Wellbeing (TISHW), pp. 1–8. IEEE (2018)

16. Rovell, D.: Drone racing league, ESPN reach broadcasting agreement, September 2016. https://www.espn.com/moresports/story/_/id/17544727

17. Sueda, K., Kitada, T., Suzuki, Y., Wada, T.: Research and development of augmented FPV drone racing system. In: SIGGRAPH Asia 2018 Posters, p. 9. ACM (2018)

18. Sun, T., Nie, S., Yeung, D.Y., Shen, S.: Gesture-based piloting of an aerial robot using monocular vision. In: 2017 IEEE International Conference on Robotics and Automation (ICRA), pp. 5913–5920. IEEE (2017)

19. Szafir, D., Mutlu, B., Fong, T.: Communicating directionality in flying robots. In: 2015 10th ACM/IEEE International Conference on Human-Robot Interaction (HRI), pp. 19–26. IEEE (2015)

20. Tezza, D., Andujar, M.: The state-of-the-art of human-drone interaction: a survey. IEEE Access **7**, 167438–167454 (2019)

21. Tezza, D., Caprio, D., Laesker, D., Andujar, M.: Let's fly! an analysis of flying FPV drones through an online survey. In: iHDI@ CHI (2020)

22. Tezza, D., Garcia, S., Hossain, T., Andujar, M.: Brain eRacing: an exploratory study on virtual brain-controlled drones. In: Chen, J.Y.C., Fragomeni, G. (eds.) HCII 2019. LNCS, vol. 11575, pp. 150–162. Springer, Cham (2019). https://doi.org/10.1007/978-3-030-21565-1_10

23. Tezza, D., Laesker, D., Andujar, M.: The learning experience of becoming a FPV drone pilot. In: Companion of the 2021 ACM/IEEE International Conference on Human-Robot Interaction, pp. 239–241 (2021)

24. Wright, O., et al.: How we made the first flight. Department of Transportation, Federal Aviation Administration, Office of . . . (1977)

25. Young, J.: Everything you need to know about drone racing, October 2018. http://www.droneguru.net/everything-you-need-to-know-about-drone-racing/

Coping with Variability in HMI Software in the Design of Machine Manufacturers' Control Software

Birgit Vogel-Heuser, Jan Wilch[✉], Adrian Dörfler, and Juliane Fischer

Technical University of Munich, Boltzmannstr. 15, 85748 Garching bei München, Germany
{vogel-heuser,jan.wilch,adrian.doerfler,juliane.fischer}@tum.de

Abstract. Due to customer-specific requirements that often change on short notice and vary tremendously, machine and plant manufacturers have to refactor their design processes and control software, especially for operator interfaces. Operator skills are crucial to operating complex systems, especially in case of a readjustment for new products or in case of a fault and the subsequent restart of the machine or plant.

The paper introduces the variability of human-machine-interface (HMI) software in relation to the variability of control software, generalizing from the application example of a lab-sized demonstrator. Primarily the manual mode is focused, used to cope with errors and prepare a machine restart after an error by manipulating selected mechanical elements.

The results of this paper are prerequisites and a first step to improve the design of both HMI and control software towards a holistic, modular approach instead of just trying to couple both on a very low level.

Keywords: Cyber-physical production systems · Control software design · HMI software · Variability

1 Introduction

Cyber-Physical Production Systems (CPPS) are mechatronic, long-living systems, consisting of mechanics, electrics/electronics, and software. They are usually controlled with Programmable Logic Controllers (PLCs) programmed in accordance with the IEC 61131-3 standard. Especially in the case of a readjustment for new products or fault diagnosis of the machine or plant, the skills and experience of operators are essential to control complex CPPS. For this purpose, operators can interact with the CPPS, e.g., to restart it after an error, via a human-machine interface (HMI). Moreover, due to customer-specific requirements, which often change on short notice, CPPS manufacturers have to cope with a high degree of variability. Thus, they frequently have to refactor their PLC control software, including the respective operator interfaces.

For analyzing and managing the variability of PLC-based control software, different approaches are available such as [1–3]. These approaches most often use modularity as the key to managing variability. The ISA 88 hierarchy is a common approach for

© The Author(s), under exclusive license to Springer Nature Switzerland AG 2022
S. Yamamoto and H. Mori (Eds.): HCII 2022, LNCS 13306, pp. 418–432, 2022.
https://doi.org/10.1007/978-3-031-06509-5_29

structuring PLC-based control software in a modular way (cp. Fig. 1, left). Call graphs provide an overview of functionality distribution and call dependencies of PLC software units (cp. Fig. 1, right). They support analyzing and optimizing the software units and their dependencies, including functionalities such as interfaces of the control software to the HMI as well as the distribution of diagnosis and fault handling implementations.

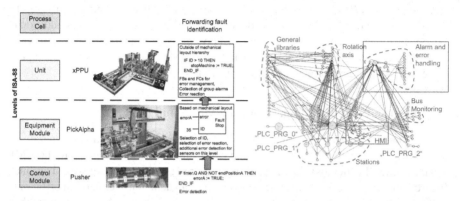

Fig. 1. Hierarchy of a lab size plant and its elements according to ISA 88 (left), forwarding of identified faults across the hierarchy levels (middle), graphical representation of control software calls, including alarm and error handling functionalities, and HMI (right)

Various approaches, including user studies, are available to develop HMIs, but there is a clear gap in the design of reusable HMIs to cope with the visualization's variability resulting from functional variability of CPPS control software. Additionally, HMI and control software are often designed by different teams using different tools and programming languages. This leads to separate reuse concepts and variability management instead of an integrated approach. A study of industrial CPPS shows that the interface between HMI and PLC is usually kept very lean and is not always designed to be flexible, which further complicates the handling of variability [4].

Modularity to enable reuse is different for control and HMI software, respectively, even if only one tool like CODESYS [5] is used for both. A CODESYS visualization is often chosen for local operator panels supporting troubleshooting after faults in manual mode. Reuse of existing visualization elements representing machine parts such as sensors, pushers, and slides is feasible but limited for elements that are composed of lower-level elements. Aggregating different sub-components may require a redesign of visualization elements, too.

The paper introduces the variability of HMI software in relation to the variability of control software using lab-sized application examples. Especially the manual mode is in focus to cope with faults and to prepare to restart the machine after a fault by manipulating selected mechanical elements and often hindering transparent code structures.

2 State of the Art in Extra-Functional PLC Software for CPPS

The control software of CPPS comprises two main parts: functional control software such as the control of actuators and extra-functional software implementing communication tasks, diagnosis, error handling, and operating modes. Thereby, extra-functional code parts make up around 50–75% of industrial control code [6] and cause complexity in the PLC software [7]. Additionally, due to the high variability of control software, its reuse is not a trivial task, and the close dependency on HMI software poses additional challenges. This section first illustrates the link between extra-functional control software and HMI. Subsequently, means for the visualization of variability and approaches for reusing extra-functional software parts are illustrated.

2.1 Linkage of Error Handling, Operating Modes and HMI

The extra-functional task *error handling,* which requires the intervention of operators, is used to illustrate the link of functional and extra-functional PLC software to the HMI software (cf. [8] for details). Error handling requires close connections to functional software parts, e.g., to trigger the emergency stop of an actuator in case of an error, and often references extra-functional tasks like operating mode change. Moreover, to enable operators to intervene and resolve an error if needed, the PLC communicates errors to the HMI via a usually leanly designed interface [4]. This interaction of a human operator with a CPPS is illustrated from an application perspective in Fig. 2.

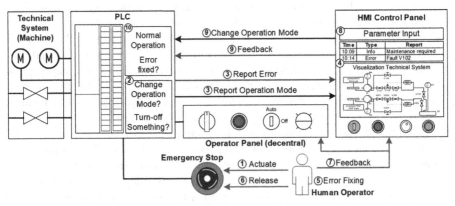

Fig. 2. Relationship between human operator and PLC, interacting via HMI in case of an error (emergency stop actuation by the operator until return to automatic mode) [8]

An error occurs and the operator pushes the physical emergency stop button at a machine of the CPPS (cf. Fig. 2, step 1). In the respective PLC program, the operating mode is changed accordingly and the machine is stopped either immediately or in controlled steps (2). Further, the PLC transmits the error to the HMI control panel (3). The operator monitors the machine status at the HMI control panel, which displays an error message (4). If required, the operator fixes the error, e.g., removing a jammed workpiece manually (5). Subsequently, the operator releases the actuated emergency stop switch (6) and then acknowledges the error situation via the HMI control panel (7, right fork, 8, 9) or a decentralized operator panel (7, left fork). After the acknowledgment, the PLC checks its status (10) and, if necessary, allows an organized restart in manual mode and a subsequent manual change to automatic mode once all interlocks are correctly parameterized. Alternatively, the operating mode can also be set back to automatic mode after the operator has acknowledged the error on the HMI panel (8), the PLC checks after transmission (9, 10).

This simple example regarding error handling and operating modes shows that PLC control software and HMI are strongly interlinked. However, they have fundamentally different implementation and code structures.

2.2 Visualization and Reuse of Variant-Rich Control Software

In the software engineering domain, family models are a well-established approach for planned reuse of variant-rich software systems, where software parts common to all variants are ideally implemented only once [9]. Family models represent a 150% model and form the basis for software configuration. Thereby, software parts classified as mandatory, alternative or optional are combined to build a specific software variant.

Recent research in the domain of CPPS targets the reengineering of variability in classical PLC control software. For example, Rosiak et al. use similarity metrics to identify variable and common parts documented in a family model [10]. Since a single visualization pattern like family models alone is not suitable to meet all user requirements of stakeholders handling CPPS software, different variability visualizations are proposed in [3]. Moreover, CPPS hardware causes additional software variants, which require approaches supporting the interdisciplinary character of CPPS, such as [2] and [11]. Yet, none of these consider the modularity and variability of HMI software.

2.3 Reuse in Extra-Functional Control Software

According to Güttel et al., a well-defined software artifact suitable for reuse, such as a software unit for controlling standard hardware, is characterized not only by standardized interfaces but also by the implementation of various operating modes and diagnostic options [12]. Only a small part of the control software fulfills functional requirements in the automatic operating mode. The logic for error handling, i.e., a part of the extra-functional software, is by far the larger part [6]. For the reuse of control code, the interface to the HMI, the software units for identifying and handling faults, and the software units for monitoring safety devices must thus be considered [12].

Regarding the HMI, Salihbegovic et al. [13] highlight its importance as a control software component and present an exemplary creation process. However, they do not consider variability. Urbas and Doherr [14] present a generation of the HMI from a model for the process industry that enables reuse through abstraction. For error handling, [15] and [16] work on a framework to investigate reliability in early development phases. Both integrate functional and extra-functional aspects at a high conceptual level in the process industry, but concrete control engineering aspects are not targeted.

Ladiges et al. [17] present the DIMA concept for modular process plants. This approach uses the PackML state machine to handle the operating modes and also includes HMI functionality. The approach is based on a standardization of all mechatronic trades, which can be combined at the interfaces for reuse. Prähofer et al. [18] present a framework based on which development environments can be created. It contains a graphical domain-specific language and is strongly visualization-oriented. Among other things, a variability model is included to identify reusable assets. However, the approach is focused on only one language and does not aim to distinguish between functional and extra-functional software.

3   Towards a Concept for Reuse of Variable PLC and HMI Software Modules

This section introduces a lab-sized application example, which is subsequently used to illustrate the challenges of a modularization principle targeting PLC and HMI software.

3.1   Lab-sized Application Example and Respective Visualization Elements

The extended Pick and Place Unit (xPPU) is a lab-sized demonstrator for CPPS, depicted in Fig. 3. It handles and manipulates workpieces (WP) of different colors, materials, and weights. The xPPU consists of various mechanical modules: a stack, which functions as WP storage, a crane for WP transportation, a stamp, a large sorting conveyor with three adjacent slides for WP sorting, and a conveyor system for re-feeding WPs from the large sorting conveyor back into the manufacturing process. To increase flexibility, the conveyor system contains a linear handling module (PickAlpha), which enables the manipulation of the WP sequence in the conveyor system. Also, the xPPU has various operating panels and safety equipment like a safety door and a light grid.

The production process starts with the crane, which picks up a WP from the stack and delivers it to the stamp, which stamps it with a symbol. Once the stamping process is finished, the crane picks up the WP again and places it onto the large sorting conveyor, which transports it to the appropriate slide. The conveyor system adds the possibility to manipulate the WP order and to add an additional processing step.

To illustrate the similarities and differences in PLC and HMI code modularization and variants, two mechanical modules are considered as key elements. The first is the large sorting conveyor controlled by an electric motor. Furthermore, it is equipped with various sensors such as light barriers and additional sensors to detect the WP position and type for its subsequent sorting onto an adjacent slide or the conveyor system. The sorting into slides is performed by pneumatic cylinders, which are allocated at the large sorting conveyor opposite of the slides. WPs can be moved from the large sorting conveyor to the conveyor system using a switch.

The second key element is the PickAlpha, reached after a WP enters the conveyor system from the large sorting conveyor via the switch. After being stopped, the gripper attached to the two linear axes can pick and place the WP to any position along the underlying conveyor. After that, the WP either exits the system through a slide or re-enters the large sorting conveyor.

As this system evolved and was extended over time, more and more components were added to the setup. Identical or similar objects like pneumatic cylinders, switches or sensors enable reuse in the PLC software and the visualization as their functionality often remains comparable.

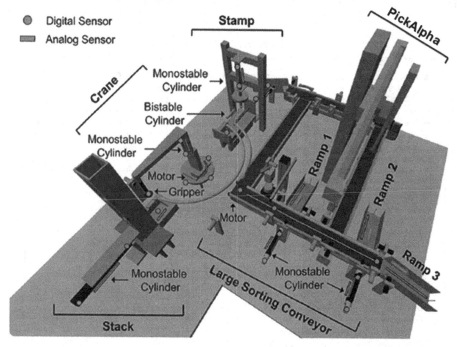

Fig. 3. 3D layout of xPPU with the key elements PickAlpha and conveyors [19].

As in traditional development processes, software engineers use their experience knowledge to specify control parameters of the xPPU in the PLC software. However, especially in complex CPPS, high performance and avoidance of errors cannot always be guaranteed. In the xPPU, the pneumatic pressure of the PickAlpha's gripper is an example for a control parameter. It needs to be set to a value, which enables picking up even the heaviest WPs. Similarly, the motion speed of the conveyors needs to be set to an appropriate value that allows a decently quick movement, which increases the xPPU's throughput but does not damage the WPs or the components during the sorting process. In case of an error, the operator sometimes needs to set these control parameters manually to fix the error and enable a return to automatic mode. As illustrated above, this error handling requires a close connection between PLC and HMI.

To enable manual CPPS control to handle an error or supervise the production process, the HMI needs to visualize the CPPS's hardware modules, including their variations. Moreover, due to safety reasons, an operator is only allowed to manually control the CPPS part visible from the position of the operating panel. Thus, HMI views from different angles of the same mechanical component are required and need to be selected depending on the position of the individual operating panels or, in case of decentral operator panels, depending on the operator's position moving through the CPPS.

By analyzing the mechanical hardware, including the operating panels for the xPPU's control and the PLC software of the xPPU, the required visualization elements of the HMI software were derived and documented. The schematic of the visualization elements, including their hierarchical dependencies, are depicted in Fig. 4.

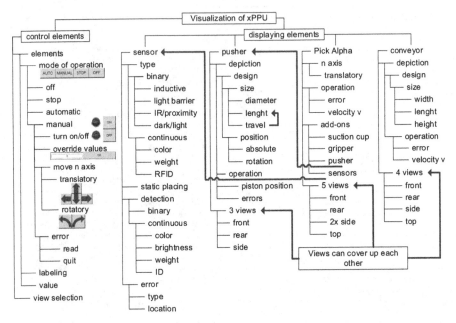

Fig. 4. Hierarchies of visualization elements of simple sorting plants and their dependencies

The components and hierarchical structure of the xPPU's hardware can be found in the corresponding PLC and HMI software. In addition to a purely *mechanical view*, extra-functional aspects such as the operating modes or error handling are crosscutting in the PLC software. Respectively, the HMI operating panel needs to enable the control of the CPPS via control elements linked to the PLC's I/Os.

3.2 Reuse of Software Modules in PLC and HMI with a Hardware-oriented Modularization Strategy

This subsection targets the definition and reuse of mechanical components on variable hierarchy levels in both PLC and HMI software. The focus lies on the hardware control and challenges arising during the reuse of the defined modules due to hardware variability. Different operation modes are not targeted. With this simple setting, the differences in the reuse of PLC and HMI software modules are highlighted.

The applied modularization strategy is hardware-oriented in the PLC and the HMI software, i.e., for the control of a conveyor (starting and stopping the transportation movement with a defined speed), a module in the PLC software is developed, and for its visualization a corresponding HMI software module is designed and available. Both software modules have the same interfaces, which means that both types of modules access the same actuators and sensors. Further, the software is modularized according to ISA 88, which enables the reuse of control modules, e.g., a pneumatic cylinder, in different equipment modules, e.g., the xPPU's stamp or PickAlpha.

Two different scenarios are focused to illustrate the different effects on the PLC and the HMI modules. These scenarios are depicted in Fig. 5.

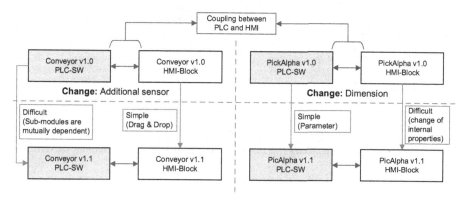

Fig. 5. Two evolution scenarios (sensor added to a conveyor, length of PickAlpha's linear actuator changed) and the effects of implementing them in PLC and HMI software

The two scenarios target the large sorting conveyor and the PickAlpha, which are considered composite elements in the PLC and HMI software. The composition of different control modules to equipment modules in the PLC software is performed by call dependencies, sometimes requiring instantiations of software units or parameterization. The composition of HMI modules is illustrated in the following before introducing the two scenarios' details.

Every visualization in CODESYS consists of basic geometric shapes (rectangles, circles…) to compose new objects such as a pneumatic cylinder. Their position, rotation, colors and other attributes can be configured with built-in functions. These functions are not only applicable to basic shapes but also composed objects. This configurability is the key for reusability and flexibility in CODESYS's visualization.

Clustering objects with the same or similar function in one sub-visualization saves time when reusing them. On this level, it is possible to implement the required functionality and I/O capability (controlled actuators and linked sensors) via the visualization element's VAR_IN_OUT section, i.e., to first compose the pneumatic cylinder out of basic shapes and then control the function (retraction and extending) via variables in the I/O section (cf. Fig. 6). This sub-visualization can be placed and reused with its whole functionality multiple times, only requiring the defined variables.

Assemblies out of these sub-visualizations to a composite HMI module can be created by placing them into the visualization of the whole system or the next bigger assembly. This way of placing existing visualizations into existing ones can be repeated multiple

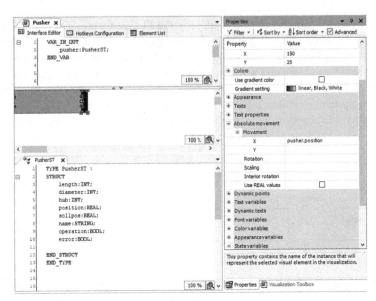

Fig. 6. Visualization element *pusher* (pneumatic cylinder), including data handling via variables and properties

times. The possibility of flexible sizing and placing the objects in the visualization eliminates the need for different sized or rotated elements unless the desired arrangement and proportion of the basic elements in the object differs from the proportion in the sub-visualization. Figure 7 depicts two variants of the PickAlpha.

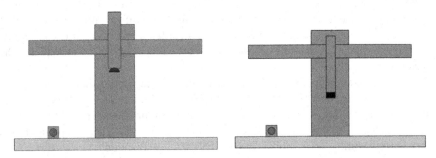

Fig. 7. PickAlpha with a suction cup (left) and a pneumatic cylinder (right)

In *Scenario 1*, a conveyor such as the xPPU's large sorting conveyor with different sensors for WP identification and various adjacent elements such as slides is considered. Due to a customer requirement or process optimization, an additional sensor is added to the conveyor modules. Via drag&drop of the corresponding sensor visualization element to the composed conveyor HMI module, this change can easily be handled in the HMI software by reusing the available visualization elements on two levels (sensor and composed conveyor element). In contrast, the addition of the sensor in the PLC software is not as simple since the added sensor provides additional information on the WP position or type, which must be included in the control of the conveyor's actuator. For example, the sensor might indicate a newly added WP type that needs to be distinguished when sorting the WPs into the slides. Consequently, depending on the changed sorting logic, the control of the respective pneumatic cylinder has to be modified. Since the control of a sub-module (e.g., control module) inside a composite module (e.g., equipment module) depends on other control modules with the composite module such as the additional sensor, reuse of the PLC conveyor module is not as trivial as reusing the HMI conveyor module.

In *Scenario 2*, a customer requests a variant of the PickAlpha with different dimensions since the underlying conveyor is longer. Consequently, the linear movement of a gripped WP for the sequence change of WPs on the conveyor needs to be enlarged as well. In the PLC software, variability of individual control modules is fairly easily possible, and existing composite modules can be reused with low effort. The reuse of composite HMI modules is not as simple if the dimensions of single sub-modules must be adapted. The proportional placing of a visualization element can produce a new variant without the need for any additional modification for simple basic elements on control module level (cf. pneumatic cylinder in Fig. 8, left). For bigger assemblies such as the depicted PickAlpha composite module, this placing does not produce a possible variant.

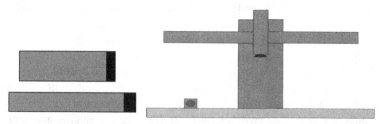

Fig. 8. Proportionally placed visualizations applied to the basic element pneumatic cylinder (left) and the composite module PickAlpha (right)

In the case of composite HMI modules, the reuse effort significantly increases. The PickAlpha consists of several basic elements and is modified due to updates or new customer requirements. Small additions like adding a new sensor to the gripper or replacing the suction cup with a pneumatic cylinder (cf. Fig. 7) are feasible since the new element can be placed at its new location and animated, as seen in Fig. 10. However, changes of the internal proportions as requested in Scenario 2 feature the challenges mentioned above. As it is unlikely and not economical to create and animate every axis by itself and compose the PickAlpha out of them, the entire PickAlpha is not reusable in Scenario 2 and needs to be changed, thus limiting the variability of the composite HMI module.

Overall, the two scenarios illustrate that even when considering hardware control only, the same variability in the controlled mechanical hardware has a different effect on the reuse of PLC and HMI modules, especially when targeting composite modules. Nevertheless, this example highlights a prerequisite for a holistic reuse approach of PLC and HMI software. If the design and reuse of so-called mechatronic modules, covering PLC and HMI software, is targeted, they must cover the same sensors and actuators.

With the same modularization strategy applied, the mechatronic module's status can be visualized in the HMI completely. Furthermore, the control of the mechatronic module via an operating panel is also possible, which is mandatory to implement extra-functional aspects such as error handling.

3.3 Manual Operation Mode in PLC and HMI – Control of CPPS Hardware Modules via Operating Panel

Apart from functional hardware control, PLC and HMI include extra-functional software parts such as operation modes. These are crosscutting to the functional hardware control. As illustrated in Fig. 2, error handling and the manual operation mode require a close link of PLC and HMI software since a human operator controls the CPPS via the HMI control panel or a decentral operator panel. In manual mode, single actuators can be individually controlled, for example to return from an erroneous situation to a stable CPPS status from which the automatic mode can be started.

In the PLC software, operation modes require interfaces to the HMI to receive control commands and parameters and forward them to the respective actuators. Furthermore, a manual mode needs to be defined for each actuator. For safety and security reasons, it must be ensured that interlocking conditions are kept even in case of manual operation of the CPPS. For example, extracting two pneumatic cylinders, which share a common working space, might damage the handled WP or the CPPS. In automatic mode, interlocking conditions are implemented to prevent erroneous situations. However, if the CPPS is controlled in manual mode and individual actuators are started and stopped by the human operator, not all interlocking conditions are automatically checked and operator knowledge is required, including knowledge about the control parameters.

In the HMI, the control side of the visualization requires a different view with different visualization elements. The view for manual mode control consists of control elements such as buttons and switches for controlling the automation hardware and is developed similar to the hardware HMI modules introduced in Sect. 3.2. Pre-defined visualization elements like buttons and lights can be configured to perform certain actions and control an element or visualization via the same VAR_IN_OUT variables (interfaces to the PLC and linked actuators and sensors) as the element itself. Rearranging and placing these control elements creates a control panel with the same functionality. An example of the control panel of a pneumatic cylinder is depicted in Fig. 9. Fields of the panel can be linked to selected variables to display the actual values, i.e., the CPPS status, during runtime. Depending on the variability of the hardware module, respective control elements are required. For example, a conveyor belt that can operate at different speeds requires an option to set the desired speed in the HMI when controlled in manual mode. The availability of pre-defined standard elements is an advantage in HMI software development.

Another limitation for the reuse of HMI software modules is the need for different views. Due to safety reasons, an operator is only allowed to manually control the part of the CPPS, which is visible from the position of the operating panel. This requires different views of the same mechanical module from different angles in the HMI, depending on the position of the HMI control panel. For example, when starting a conveyor belt, depending on the position of the operating panel, its running direction must be displayed from left

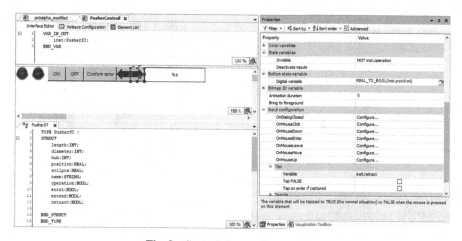

Fig. 9. Control element for a pusher

to right or from right to left. This causes additional variability in the HMI software, posing an additional challenge to reusing HMI modules. Often, even a visualization of the CPPS from a bird's eye view is required.

CODESYS was built to offer on-site visualization for operators and, hence, does not offer full 3D capability in its free versions. Because of the static point of view, new visualizations must be created for each different view. If an element is symmetrical, its visualization can be reused fully. For example, a pneumatic cylinder can be reused as long as it is only shown from the side (perpendicular to the rotational axis).

The HMI module of the picking unit PickAlpha is depicted in Fig. 10 (left), including control elements for manual mode. The HMI module of the PickAlpha is composed of sub-elements (cf. Fig, 10. right), such as a pneumatic cylinder, which is reusable only with a fixed width-to-height ratio (cp. red circle). Moreover, the elements of the HMI for manual control are reusable as well. For example, the manual control elements of a pneumatic cylinder are embedded in the PickAlpha (Fig, 10, left interface) and in different parts of the xPPU (cf. Fig. 10, top-right interface).

In summary, the extra-functional operation mode causes additional variability in the HMI software modules. Further, it highlights the close link between PLC and HMI software. An approach to link the PLC and HMI software despite their differences concerning hardware variability and modularization strategies for extra-functional software is the use of a pre-defined interface: a global variable list (GVL) in the PLC, via which all manually controllable actuators can be controlled and in which all current sensor values are stored. The preparation of this PLC-HMI-interface requires implementing all actuators' manual mode in reference to the GVL in both PLC and HMI software modules. Consequently, the GVL is part of the applied reuse strategy and links the two software types despite their differences and current challenges. However, this approach bears the risk that the GVL contains dead variables, which are not required in the present variant. In addition, the interface is entirely freely definable, meaning that variables can easily be forgotten. To avoid this, it is possible to define a 150% interface (similar to the family model approach from the software engineering domain).

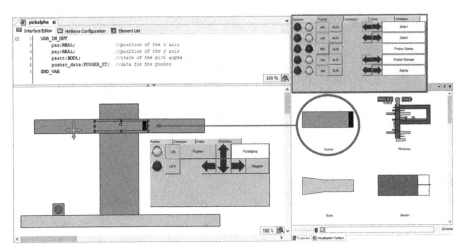

Fig. 10. HMI of the picking unit PickAlpha with embedded elements for manual control of the contained pneumatic cylinder (left). The HMI comprises sub-elements (right), including a pneumatic cylinder reusable only with a fixed width-to-height ratio (cp. red circle). (Color figure online)

4 Conclusion

Utilizing a lab-sized demonstrator, this paper showed the different modularization strategies of PLC and HMI software in CPPS. More precisely, it was highlighted that the reuse of PLC and HMI modules on a basic level is similar in both software types. However, the same variation point of a controlled hardware module has a varying effect on the difficulty of reusing the respective PLC or HMI module. Moreover, the manual operating mode illustrated the close link between PLC and HMI software. In case of error handling or manual operation of a CPPS, it has to be ensured that interlocking conditions are fulfilled, which is often implemented in the PLC software itself but also requires operator knowledge.

Furthermore, some causes for variability only concern the HMI software and lead to additional HMI module variants not affecting the respective PLC software modules. These include variants due to the view, meaning the position of the operating panel.

For designing a combined reuse concept considering HMI and PLC software, challenges and prerequisites have been shown and derived. A modular approach in both software types similar to the ISA 88 is required to enable the reuse of elementary basic elements and composite modules. Moreover, the design of PLC and HMI modules needs to be mechatronic, i.e., the modules in both PLC and HMI need to monitor and control the same sensors and actuators.

As a first step towards a holistic, mechatronic reuse concept, analyzing and improving the link between the PLC and the HMI is essential. As a first, simple means to link PLC and HMI, the definition of a 150%- GVL-interface was proposed.

References

1. Maga, C.R., Jazdi, N., Göhner, P.: Requirements on engineering tools for increasing reuse in industrial automation. In: IEEE International Conference on Emerging Technologies and Factory Automation, pp. 1–7 (2011)
2. Schröck, S., Fay, A., Jäger, T.: Systematic interdisciplinary reuse within the engineering of automated plants. In: Annual IEEE International Systems Conference, pp. 508–515 (2015)
3. Fischer, J., Vogel-Heuser, B., Wilch, J., Loch, F., Land, K., Schaefer, I.: Variability visualization of IEC 61131-3 legacy software for planned reuse. In: IEEE International Conference on Systems, Man, and Cybernetics, pp. 3760–3767 (2020)
4. Vogel-Heuser, B., Rösch, S., Fischer, J., Simon, T., Ulewicz, S., Folmer, J.: Fault handling in PLC-based Industry 4.0 automated production systems as a basis for restart and self-configuration and its evaluation. J. Softw. Eng. Appl. 9(1), 1–43 (2016)
5. CODESYS: CODESYS GmbH. Accessed 5 October 5 2021. https://www.codesys.com/
6. Lucas, M.R., Tilbury, D.M.: A study of current logic design practices in the automotive manufacturing industry. Int. J. Hum Comput Stud. 59(5), 725–753 (2003)
7. Neumann, E., Vogel-Heuser, B., Fischer, J., Ocker, F., Diehm, S., Schwarz, M.: Formalization of design patterns and their automatic identification in plc software for architecture assessment. IFAC-PapersOnLine 53(2), 7819–7826 (2020)
8. Vogel-Heuser, B., Fischer, J., Hess, D., Neumann, E., Würr, M.: Managing variability and reuse of extra-functional control software in CPPS. In: Design, Automation and Test in Europe Conference, pp. 755–760. Toronto (2021)
9. Pohl, K., Böckle, G., van der Linden, F.: Software Product Line Engineering. Springer, Berlin, Heidelberg (2005)
10. Rosiak, K., Schlie, A., Linsbauer, L., Vogel-Heuser, B., Schaefer, I.: Custom-tailored clone detection for IEC 61131-3 programming languages. J. Syst. Softw. 182(12) (2021)
11. Wimmer, M., Novák, P., Šindelár, R., Berardinelli, L., Mayerhofer, T., Mazak, A.: Cardinality-based variability modeling with AutomationML. In: IEEE International Conference on Emerging Technologies and Factory Automation, pp. 1–4 (2017)
12. Güttel, K., Weber, P., Fay, A.: Automatic generation of PLC code beyond the nominal sequence. In: IEEE International Conference on Emerging Technologies and Factory Automation, pp. 1277–1284 (2008)
13. Salihbegovic, A., Cico, Z., Marinkovi, V., Karavdi, E.: Software Engineering Approach in the Design and Development of the Industrial Automation Systems. ACM ICSE, pp. 15–22 (2008)
14. Urbas, L., Doherr, F.: AutoHMI: a model driven software engineering approach for HMIs in process industries. IEEE CSAE, pp. 627–631 (2011)
15. Sierla, S., O'Halloran, B.M., Karhela, T., Papakonstantinou, N., Tumer, I.Y.: Common cause failure analysis of cyber–physical systems situated in constructed environments. Res. Eng. Design 24(4), 375–394 (2013). https://doi.org/10.1007/s00163-013-0156-2
16. Papkonstantinou, N., Proper, S., O'Halloran, B., Tumer, I.: Simulation based machine learning for fault detection in complex systems using the functional failure identification and propagation framework. In: Computers and Information in Engineering Conference, pp. 1–10 (2014)
17. Ladiges, J., et al.: Integration of modular process units into process control systems. IEEE Trans. Ind. Appl. 54(2), 1870–1880 (2018)

18. Prähofer, H., Hurnaus, D., Schatz, R., Wirth, C., Mössenböck, H.: Software support for building end-user programming environments in the automation domain. ACM WEUSE, pp. 76–80 (2008)

19. Zinn, J., Vogel-Heuser, B., Schuhmann, F., and Cruz S., L.: Hierarchical reinforcement learning for waypoint-based exploration in robotic devices. In: IEEE International Conference on Industrial Informatics, pp. 1–7 (2021)

Research and Development of Botnet Defense System

Shingo Yamaguchi[(✉)]

Yamaguchi University, Ube, Yamaguchi Prefecture 755-8611, Japan
shingo@yamaguchi-u.ac.jp

Abstract. Six years have passed since the appearance of the malicious botnet *Mirai* targeting IoT devices, but Mirai and its variants still bring about damage worldwide. This paper proposes a new type of cyber security system, called Botnet Defense System (BDS), which uses a self-built botnet to disinfect a malicious botnet. The BDS repeats four steps: 1) Monitor the IoT network and detect a malicious botnet; 2) Plan a strategy for disinfecting the malicious botnet; 3) Build its own botnet according to the strategy; 4) Command and control the self-built botnet that autonomously spreads for disinfection. The heterogeneity of the IoT network may become an obstacle to cyber security. The BDS attempts to overcome the obstacle by utilizing the botnet that spreads autonomously even to unobservable and uncontrollable nodes. The effect was confirmed through modeling and simulation using extended Petri nets. Finally, the future challenges on the BDS were provided.

Keywords: IoT · Botnet · Cyber security · Multi-agent · Malware

1 Introduction

The IoT creates new value by interconnecting all kinds of things and humans, sharing information. The number of IoT devices is growing exponentially and is forecasted to rise to 50 billion by 2030. While the remarkable development of the IoT has benefited our lives, it has brought a new threat: cyber attacks. IoT devices are known to be vulnerable because their security may have been sacrificed in the rush to market or for the sake of price competition.

In September 2016, the threat turned into a reality. The IoT was hijacked by a malware called Mirai [1] and performed huge distributed denial of service (DDoS) attacks to major sites including Amazon and Twitter. Mirai is self-propagated and infects IoT devices one after another to turn them into remotely controlled bots. DDoS attacks generated from the IoT tend to be large and destructive due to the characteristics [2]. Mirai quickly spread around the world and infected more than 300,000 IoT devices in the following month [3]. Six years after its appearance, Mirai and its variants still cause damage in the world.

Supported by JSPS KAKENHI Grant Number JP19K11965.

© The Author(s), under exclusive license to Springer Nature Switzerland AG 2022
S. Yamamoto and H. Mori (Eds.): HCII 2022, LNCS 13306, pp. 433–445, 2022.
https://doi.org/10.1007/978-3-031-06509-5_30

There are several techniques to counter the threat of botnet, which are broadly categorized as detection, mitigation, and spread prevention. These techniques are useful for detecting botnets and mitigating their threats. However, they are not something to disinfect the botnet already spread. The US-CERT [4] has shown that since Mirai exists only in volatile memory, its bots can be removed by rebooting the infected devices. Mirai, however, is known to reinfect in minutes unless the devices are patched [5]. In addition, with the rapid spread of IoT devices, manually rebooting and applying patches is not practical. Therefore, we require innovative approaches to tremendously heighten the ability for defending against malicious botnets.

In this paper, we propose a new kind of cyber security system called Botnet Defense System (BDS) [6]. It embraces the concept of "Fight Fire with Fire" and uses a self-built botnet to disinfect a malicious botnet. Since the botnet can spread autonomously on the IoT system, their defense capability is expected to increase dramatically.

The rest of this paper is organized as follows. Section 2 introduces botnets and their countermeasure techniques, and a mathematical modeling tool, called Petri Nets in a Petri Net (PN^2) [7], which is available to the simulation of botnets. Section 3 describes the system configuration and operation of the BDS, self-built botnets and their operational strategies. Section 4 describes the modeling and simulation evaluation of the BDS with PN^2. Section 5 concludes this paper by summarizing the key points and shows the future challenges and perspectives.

2   Preliminary

2.1   Botnet

A botnet is a collection of remotely controlled computers (bots) that have been hijacked by cyber criminals, and is used to carry out various illegitimate activities such as sending spam messages, spreading computer viruses, and performing DDoS attacks. A self-propagated malware is used to build a botnet. It searches for vulnerable devices and turns them into bots. The resultant bots are taken in its botnet. As a result, the botnet will grow autonomously. Since the IoT includes lots of vulnerable devices, the threat of botnet becomes severe.

There are various types of IoT botnets, but Mirai is the most famous due to the magnitude of damage. Readers who are interested in the details of Mirai can refer to the literature [1,8,9]. Another reason why Mirai is famous is that its source code was released. This has given rise to dozens of Mirai variants. Many of them are still raging today. Notably, Mēris appeared in 2021 is called "a resurgence of Mirai", whose traffic reached more than three times that of Mirai as the previous largest DDoS attack [10].

2.2   Countermeasure

Several techniques have been proposed to deal with the threat of IoT botnets. They can be categorized as detection, mitigation, and spread prevention.

Detection techniques determine if a botnet is present in the target IoT system. This is an important first step in dealing with this threat. Bezerra et al. [11] proposed a host-based method for detecting botnets with one-class classifiers. It monitors a single device and determines the presence of botnet based on the monitoring data such as the CPU usage and memory consumption. Meidan et al. [12] proposed a network-based method for detecting attacks launched from botnets. It extracts behavior snapshots of a network and detects attacks by applying autoencoders to the snapshots.

Mitigation techniques prevent or mitigate the impact of the botnet on the IoT system itself or on the victim system. It is often used in combination with detection techniques to respond to detected botnets. Ceron et al. [13] proposed an adaptive network layer for mitigating the attack launched from botnets. It can block or rewrite the instructions sent from a botnet controller to bots to make them invalid. Hadi et al. [14] proposed a system called BoDMitM for detection and mitigation of botnets based on Manufacture Usage Description (MUD). It finds suspicious traces by comparing network traffic with MUD rules, and provides packet filtering as a mitigation mechanism.

Spread prevention techniques include hardening vulnerable devices for protecting them from botnets. The US-CERT [4] recommends the users of IoT devices to take steps such as changing default passwords to stronger ones, applying the latest security patches, monitoring or closing ports that botnets may use. Gopal et al. [15] proposed a solution to prevent botnets from spreading on the basis of whitelisting. It checks if the list includes an application just before running it and allows it to run only if included.

These existing techniques are effective in detecting botnets and mitigating their threats. However, they do not disinfect botnets that have already spread. With the explosion of IoT devices, it is not practical to manually reboot them for disinfection. Therefore, we need an innovative approach to drastically improve defenses against botnets.

2.3   Petri Nets in a Petri Net (PN²)

Petri Nets in a Petri Net (PN²) is a mathematical and graphical tool for modeling and analyzing multi-agent systems [7] and is one of extended Petri nets [16]. As its name suggests, intuitively, a PN² is a Petri net (called *environment net*), each of whose tokens represents a Petri net (called *agent net*). Each agent net represents the state transition of an agent. The environment net represents the state transition of the environment that the agents act. Each transition in the environment net fires in synchronization with the transitions in one or more agent nets. This synchronization represents the interaction among the corresponding agents. The condition for the firing is described by label rather than transition identifier. Therefore, the agent nets involved in the firing are determined by the dynamic binding by label. A firing may transfer, increase, or decrease tokens in the environment net. It indicates the migration, creation, or deletion of the agents. Nakahori et al. [17] have built a tool developed a tool called

PN2Simulator capable of editing, simulating, and analyzing PN^2. It enables to interactively study the behavior of multi-agent systems.

3   Botnet Defense System (BDS)

3.1   Concept

Since the Mirai source code came out, botnet technology has evolved at an accelerated pace and has turned out a variety of variants. Some of the variants no longer aim not for DDoS attacks but for cryptocurrency mining and proxying.

The most notable is a botnet called *Hajime*. Like Mirai, Hajime is a worm that infects IoT devices and builds a botnet [18]. However, Hajime does not have any function to do malicious activities like DDoS attacks. Instead, it protects the device from Mirai by blocking the ports that Mirai accesses for infection. Although Hajime is not ethical, it can be regarded as a way to defend IoT devices against Mirai. This precedent suggests a new possibility for botnet technology. Molesky et al. [19] stated that botnets can be used legally by explicitly stating them in the terms of use. In other words, botnet technology has the potential to become a solution for defending IoT systems against malicious botnets.

The author of this paper has researched and developed a cybersecurity system called *Botnet Defense System* (BDS) since 2017 [20]. The concept of the BDS is "Fight Fire with Fire." To fight malicious botnets, the BDS uses the same way, i.e. botnet technology. It builds a botnet itself and uses it to disinfect the malicious botnets. The botnet used by the BDS acts with good intentions and thus is called "white-hat botnet". Since the white-hat botnet can spread autonomously on the IoT system, we expect their defense capability to increase drastically.

White-hat botnets are not novel. There already exists some kinds. Typical examples are Linux.Wifatch [21] and Hajime. They protect the IoT system from malicious botnets. However, white-hat botnets are a so-called double-edged sword. This is because they waste the system's resources if staying there even after mitigating the malicious botnets' threat. Since the existing botnets are basically let go free, they may bring about a new risk. In contrast, the BDS systematically manages the white-hat botnet and pulls out its organizational power.

3.2   System Configuration

We illustrate the configuration of the BDS in Fig. 1. The rectangles on the left and right respectively represent the BDS and the IoT system that the BDS defends.

The BDS repeats four steps for defending the IoT system against malicious botnets: monitoring, strategy planning, botnet building, and botnet command and control (C&C). The detail of each step is as follows.

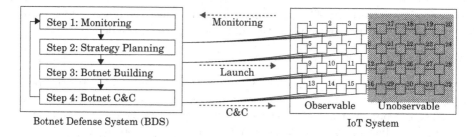

Fig. 1. Botnet Defense System (BDS).

Step 1 (Monitoring): Monitor the IoT system and check if the system is infected by a malicious botnet. The BDS performs the monitoring not only directly but also indirectly through the white-hat botnet.

Step 2 (Strategy Planning): Plan a strategy for exterminating the malicious botnet based on the information obtained in the monitoring.

Step 3 (Botnet Building): Send white-hat worms [22] to the IoT system to build a white-hat botnet according to the strategy.

Step 4 (Botnet C&C): Command and control the white-hat botnet that autonomously spreads for disinfection.

In Fig. 1, the inner graph of the right rectangle represents the network of the IoT system. This network consists of 32 nodes $n_1, n_2, \cdots, n_{32}$ and has the square-lattice topology. The topology is defined to reflect the physical and logical structure of the network. We incorporate the concepts of observability and controllability between the BDS and the network nodes [23]. A network node is said to be *observable* and *controllable* if the node is directly connected with the BDS. The BDS can check whether there is a bot in an observable node, or can add/remove a white-hat bot to/from a controllable node. In Fig. 1, the solid arc connecting the BDS to a network node represents that the node is directly connected with the BDS. In this example, the BDS is directly connected to $n_1, n_2, \cdots, n_{16}$. These nodes are observable and controllable. In contrast, $n_{17}, n_{18}, \cdots, n_{32}$ are not directly connected to the BDS. These nodes are unobservable and uncontrollable. For simplicity, we assume in this paper that the observable nodes are controllable and vice versa. We will apply a black diagonal lines pattern meshing to unobservable nodes. The concepts of observability and controllability enable us to model public and private networks.

3.3 White-Hat Botnet and Strategy

The white-hat worm and botnet of the BDS are ones proposed in References [22] and [23], respectively. The white-hat worm infects and turns a device into a white-hat bot. In addition, it has the following capabilities:

- Lifespan: The white-hat worm will destroy itself at the end of its lifespan. Even if it self-destructs, the device remains a white-hat bot and is immune until rebooted.

- Secondary infectivity: The white-hat worm can infect the devices infected by a malicious botnet and remove the malicious bot from the device.

The white-hat botnet has the following capabilities:

- Reconnaissance: Each white-hat bot can observe or control network nodes that the BDS cannot directly observe or control, instead of the BDS. The white-hat bot w at a node n can check whether there is a bot at a node n' which is adjacent to n, or can add/remove a white-hat bot to/from n'.
- Link: Like OMG, one of the variants of Mirai, the white-hat bot can relay messages. For the white-hat bot w at a node n, if there is a white-hat bot w' at a node n' adjacent to n, w can exchange messages with w'. They are said to be in a link relation. If n is observable, the BDS can indirectly observe and control n' and its adjacent nodes through the link relation. The link relation has the property of being transitive.

The white-hat botnet defends an IoT system but wastes its resources. Therefore, the BDS should use as small number of white-hat bots as possible and leave no white-hat bots after disinfecting the malicious botnet. We need strategies for bringing the white-hat botnet's organizational potential. A good strategy will lead to the success, and vice versa.

The strategy can be divided into two categories.

- Botnet building strategy: Define how to build the botnet by using the white-hat worms. Typical examples are the all-out, the few-elite, the environment-adaptive strategies [22].
- Botnet C&C strategy: Define how to operate the built white-hat botnet. The withdrawal strategy has been proposed [23].

3.4   System Operation

Let us illustrate how the BDS works. Figure 2 shows a state transition of the BDS and the IoT system. Figure 2a shows the initial state. This IoT system is infected by a malicious botnet which consists of ten bots, depicted as ●. As the result of monitoring in Step 1, the BDS detected the botnet because it found five bots which are at observable nodes $n_1, n_2, n_9, n_{14}, n_{15}$. On the other hand, the BDS has not discovered the other five bots yet because they are at unobservable nodes $n_{18}, n_{22}, n_{28}, n_{29}, n_{31}$.

Next, as a result of the strategy planning in Step 2, the BDS decided on the few-elite strategy. This is because it possessed a white-hat worm with excellent capabilities. Figure 2b shows the state of botnet building in Step 3. According to the strategy, the BDS launched white-hat worms at two observable nodes n_{10}, n_{16} and built a white-hat botnet which consists of two bots, depicted as ○. The BDS cannot directly access unobservable node n_{29} but it can indirectly observe it through the white-hat bot at observable node n_{16}. We will apply a yellow dotted pattern meshing to indirectly observable nodes.

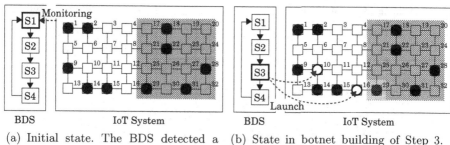

(a) Initial state. The BDS detected a malicious botnet by finding five bots (●) at the observable nodes.

(b) State in botnet building of Step 3. The BDS sent two white-hat worms (○) to build a white-hat botnet.

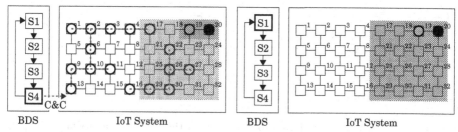

(c) State in which the white-hat botnet spread and drove out the malicious one. The BDS ordered a withdrawal.

(d) State after all the white-hat bots receiving the withdrawal command self-destroyed. Two bots remained.

Fig. 2. A state transition of the BDS and the IoT system.

The white-hat botnet autonomously spread throughout the system while disinfecting the malicious botnet. Figure 2c shows a state in which the white-hat botnet drove out almost all the malicious bots except for one at node n_{20}. Then, as botnet C&C in Step 4, the BDS checked the IoT system directly or indirectly through the white-hat botnet's links, depicted as ---, and decided the disinfection is enough. As a result, the BDS adopted the withdrawal strategy and commanded a withdrawal to the white-hat botnet. The command is conveyed to all the white-hat bots connected by the links.

Figure 2d shows the state after all the white-hat bots receiving the withdrawal command self-destroyed. One white-hat bot and one malicious bot remained at unobservable nodes n_{19}, n_{20}.

4   PN² Modeling and Simulation Evaluation

4.1   PN² Modeling

Since the BDS is a complex system, we take a mathematical approach to its research and development. We consider the battle between malicious and white-hat botnets as a multi-agent system, and build a mathematical model describing

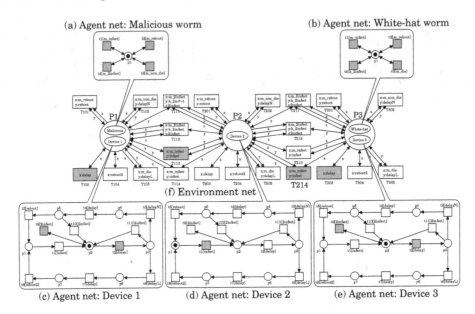

(a) Agent net: Malicious worm   (b) Agent net: White-hat worm

(f) Environment net

(c) Agent net: Device 1   (d) Agent net: Device 2   (e) Agent net: Device 3

Fig. 3. PN^2 model representing the battle between the malicious and white-hat botnets. In the initial state, the malicious and white-hat botnets respectively dominate Device 1 and Device 3.

its behavior in terms of PN^2. We study the BDS through the model. For the detail of modeling, please refer to Reference [22].

Figure 3 shows a BDS model with PN^2. Figures 3a–3e and 3f respectively show the agent nets and the environment net. A place, depicted as $\bigcirc$, represents a network node. A token within the place, depicted as $\bigcirc$, represents an agent such as IoT devices, a malicious worm, and a white-hat worm present at the node. Each token corresponds to an agent net which represents the state transition of the corresponding agent. In this state, the device d_1 in the left place P1 is infected by the malicious worm and has become a malicious bot. The device d_2 in the middle place P2 is normal. The device d_3 in the right place P3 is infected with the white-hat worm and has become a white-hat bot. A transition, depicted as $\square$, represents an action such as infection and reboot.

The PN^2 model is runnable with PN2Simulator. PN2Simulator highlights firable transitions in orange. Transition T113 indicates that the malicious worm of P1 is attempting to infect d_2 of P2. Meanwhile, transition T214 indicates that the white-hat worm of P3 is also attempting to infect the same device d_2. Assume T214 fired. The state after the firing is shown in Fig. 4. The white-hat worm makes a copy in P2 and the copy gets infected to d_2. In this state, the malicious worm can no longer infect d_2. It means that the white-hat botnet prevents the malicious botnet from spreading. In addition, since the white-hat worm possesses the secondary infection capability, it can infect d_1 that the malicious

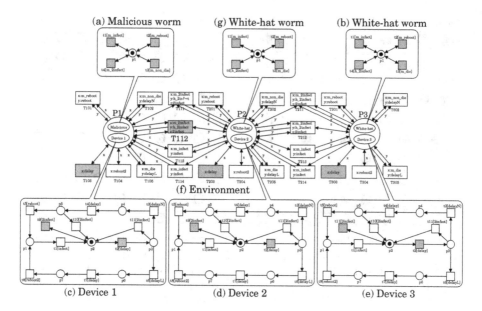

Fig. 4. State after a firing of T214. The white-hat botnet spreads to Device 2 and prevents the malicious botnet from spreading.

worm already infected. This is represented by transition T112. As a result of the secondary infection, the malicious botnet will wipe out.

4.2 Simulation Evaluation

We conducted an experiment to evaluate the effect of the BDS. We modeled the BDS including an IoT system as a PN^2 using the above-mentioned method and simulated its behavior with PN2Simulator.

The evaluation measures are the number of malicious bots and that of white-hat bots.

- $\#_{mal}(t)$: Number of malicious bots at Step t. This breaks down into:
  - $\#_{mal}^{obs}(t)$: Number that BDS can directly observe;
  - $\#_{mal}^{in-obs}(t)$: Number that BDS can indirectly observe; and
  - $\#_{mal}^{unobs}(t)$: Number that BDS cannot observe
- $\#_{wh}(t)$: Number of white-hat bots at step t. $\#_{wh}^{obs}(t)$, $\#_{wh}^{in-obs}(t)$ and $\#_{wh}^{unobs}(t)$ are defined in the same way as malicious bots.

The specification of the IoT system is as follows.

- The system consists of one observable network and four unobservable networks (See Fig. 5a).
- The observable network consists of 36 nodes and each unobservable network consists of 16 nodes.

Unobservable network 1   Unobservable network 2   Unobservable network 1   Unobservable network 2

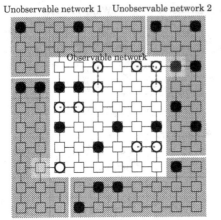 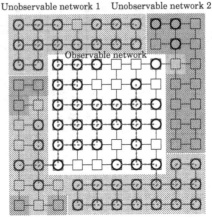

Unobservable network 3   Unobservable network 4   Unobservable network 3   Unobservable network 4

(a) At Step 0, the BDS detects a malicious botnet and builds a white-hat
botnet.

(b) At Step 10,000, the BDS drives out
the malicious botnet and commands
a withdrawal to the white-hat botnet.

Fig. 5. Scenario of the experiment.

- Each unobservable network is connected to the observable network by a single communication channel. This restricts the communication between those
networks and enhances network security against the spread of malicious botnets.

The capabilities of the white-hat worms are as follows.

- Lifespan ℓ is 3, 4, or 5 steps
- Probability of secondary infection ρ is 50%

The scenario of the experiment is as follows. It is illustrated in Fig. 5.

1. Let when the BDS discovered a malicious botnet Step 0 (See Fig. 5a). Let the
botnet consist of 20 bots, i.e. $\#_{mal}(0) = 20$, where they were placed randomly
without distinguishing between observable and unobservable nodes.
2. Following the few-elite strategy, the BDS sent white-hat worms to 10 observable nodes at random and built a white-hat botnet, i.e. $\#_{wh}(0) = 10$.
3. At Step 10,000, the BDS commanded a withdrawal to the white-hat botnet
based on the withdrawal strategy (See Fig. 5b).

Figure 6 shows the result. The horizontal axis is the lifespan ℓ of the white-
hat worm, and the vertical axis is the number of bots at Step 10,000. A
stacked bar shows the mean of $\#_{mal}^{obs}(10k)$, $\#_{mal}^{in\text{-}obs}(10k)$, $\#_{mal}^{unobs}(10k)$, $\#_{wh}^{obs}(10k)$,
$\#_{wh}^{in\text{-}obs}(10k)$, and $\#_{wh}^{unobs}(10k)$ for 100 trials. The lower red part is for the malicious bots and the upper blue part is for the white-hat bots.

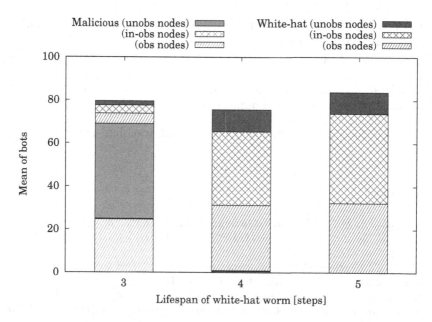

Fig. 6. Simulation result.

When $\ell = 3$, the mean of the malicious bots $\overline{\#_{mal}(10k)}$ reached to 70 and significantly increased over the initial value of $\#_{mal}(0)$ ($= 20$). This implies that the white-hat worm with a short lifespan is useless.

On the other hand, when $\ell \geq 4$, $\overline{\#_{mal}(10k)}$ was almost 0. In other words, the BDS was able to disinfect the malicious botnet. Instead, the mean of the white-hat bots $\overline{\#_{wh}(10k)}$ reached to 80. This breaks down into: $\overline{\#_{wh}^{obs}(10k)} \approx 30$, $\overline{\#_{wh}^{in\text{-}obs}(10k)} \approx 40$, and $\overline{\#_{wh}^{unobs}(10k)} \approx 10$.

Immediately after this, the BDS commanded a withdrawal to the white-hat botnet. As a result, the BDS was able to remove about 90% of the remaining white-hat bots, including those in unobservable nodes.

5   Conclusion

We presented the concept and configuration of the BDS, the white-hat botnet and its operational strategies. We also described the modeling and simulation evaluation of the BDS with PN^2.

The research and development of BDS have just begun. The following is a list of issues or open problems that the authors are currently working on.

- Development of techniques to make a small number of the white-hat bots stay permanently so as to protect the IoT system [24]
- Development of techniques for building and operating a heterogeneous white-hat botnet with synergistic effects [25]

- Development of techniques to build and operate a more effective white-hat botnets with AI and machine learning [26]
- Development of operational techniques for tactical-level white-hat botnets [27]
- Consideration of not only technical but also ethical, legal, and social issues, empirical testing, and system implementation

We hope the above-mentioned challenges will stimulate new and exciting research.

References

1. Antonakakis, M., et al.: Understanding the Mirai Botnet. In: Proceedings of 26th USENIX Security Symposium (SEC), Vancouver, BC, Canada, pp. 1093–1110 (2017)
2. Kolias, C., Kambourakis, G., Stavrou, A., Voas, J.: DDoS in the IoT: Mirai and other botnets. IEEE Comput. **50**(7), 80–84 (2017)
3. Nakao, K.: Proactive cyber security response by utilizing passive monitoring technologies. In: 2018 IEEE International Conference on Consumer Electronics (ICCE), Las Vegas, NV, US, p. 1 (2018)
4. Heightened DDoS threat posed by Mirai and other botnets. https://www.us-cert.gov/ncas/alerts/TA16-288A. Accessed 29 Oct 2019
5. Moffitt, T.: Source Code for Mirai IoT Malware Released. https://www.webroot.com/blog/2016/10/10/source-code-Mirai-iot-malware-released/. Accessed 4 Nov 2019
6. Yamaguchi, S.: Botnet defense system: concept, design, and basic strategy. Information **11**, 516 (2020)
7. Hiraishi, K.: A Petri-net-based model for the mathematical analysis of multi-agent systems. IEICE Trans. Fund. Electron. Commun. Comput. Sci. **E84-A**(11), 2829–2837 (2001)
8. Sinaovi, H., Mrdovic, S.: Analysis of Mirai malicious software. In: Proceedings of the of SoftCOM 2017, Split, Croatia, pp. 1–5 (2017)
9. Yamaguchi, S., Gupta, B.: Malware threat in internet of things and its mitigation analysis. In: Association, I.R.M. (ed.) Research Anthology on Combating Denial-of-Service Attacks, pp. 371–387. IGI Publishing, Hershey (2021)
10. A Brief History of the Meris Botnet. https://blog.cloudflare.com/meris-botnet/. Accessed 29 Oct 2021
11. Bezerra, V.H., da Costa, V.G.T., Barbon, J., Miani, R.S., Zarpelão, B.B.: IoTDS: a one-class classification approach to detect botnets in internet of things devices. Sensors **19**(14), 3188 (2019)
12. Meidan, Y., et al.: N-BaIoT: network-based detection of IoT botnet attacks using deep autoencoders. IEEE Pervasive Comput. **17**(3), 12–22 (2018)
13. Ceron, J.M., Steding-Jessen, K., Hoepers, C., Granville, L.Z., Margi, C.B.: Improving IoT botnet investigation using an adaptive network layer. Sensors **19**(3), 727 (2019)
14. Hadi, H.J., Sajjad, S.M., Nisa, K.U.: BoDMitM: botnet detection and mitigation system for home router base on MUD. In: 2019 International Conference on Frontiers of Information Technology (FIT), Islamabad, Pakistan, pp. 139–1394 (2019)

15. Gopal, T.S., Meerolla, M., Jyostna, G., Eswari, P.R.L., Magesh, E.: Mitigating mirai malware spreading in IoT environment. In: Proceedings of 2018 International Conference on Advances in Computing, Communications and Informatics (ICACCI), Bangalore, India, pp. 2226–2230 (2018)

16. Yamaguchi, S., Bin Ahmadon, M.A., Ge, Q.W.: Introduction of petri nets: its applications and security challenges. In: Gupta, B.B., Agrawal, D.P., Yamaguchi, S. (eds.) Handbook of Research on Modern Cryptographic Solutions for Computer and Cyber Security, pp. 145–179. IGI Publishing, Hershey, PA, US (2016)

17. Nakahori, K., Yamaguchi, S.: A support tool to design IoT services with NuSMV. In: Proceedings of 2017 IEEE International Conference on Consumer Electronics (ICCE), Las Vegas, NV, US , pp. 84–87 (2017)

18. Edwards S., Profetis, I.: Hajime: analysis of a decentralized internet worm for IoT Devices. https://security.rapiditynetworks.com/publications/2016-10-16/hajime.pdf. Accessed 10 Feb 2019

19. Molesky, M.J., Cameron, E.A.: Internet of Things: an analysis and proposal of white worm technology. In: Proceedings of 2019 IEEE International Conference on Consumer Electronics (ICCE), Las Vegas, NV, US (2019). 5 pages

20. Tanaka, H., Yamaguchi, S.: On modeling and simulation of the behavior of IoT devices Malwares Mirai and Hajime. In: Proceedings of 2017 IEEE International Symposium on Consumer Electronics (ISCE), Seri Kembangan, Malaysia, pp. 56–60 (2017)

21. Linux.Wifatch. https://gitlab.com/rav7teif/linux.wifatch. Accessed 30 Jan 2022

22. Yamaguchi, S.: White-Hat Worm to Fight Malware and Its Evaluation by Agent-Oriented Petri Nets. Sensors **20**, 556 (2020)

23. Yamaguchi, S.: Botnet defense system: concept and basic strategy. In: Proceedings of 2021 IEEE International Conference on Consumer Electronics (ICCE), Las Vegas, NV, US (2021). 5 pages

24. Makihara, D., Yamaguchi, S.: A proposal of patrol function by white-hat worm in botnet defense system. In: Proceedings of IEEE International Conference on Consumer Electronics Asia 2021, Gangwon, South Korea, pp. 165–169 (2021)

25. Ohsaki, K., Yamaguchi, S.: A proposal of heterogeneous white-hat botnet in botnet defense system. In: Proceedings of IEEE International Conference on Consumer Electronics Asia 2021, Gangwon, South Korea, pp. 175–178 (2021)

26. Pan, X., Yamaguchi, S.: Machine-learning-based white-hat worm launcher in botnet defense system. Int. J. Softw. Sci. Comput. Intell. (in press)

27. Kageyama, T., Yamaguchi, S.: On tactics to deploy white-hat worms in botnet defense system. In: Proceedings of IEEE Global Conference on Consumer Electronics 2021, Kyoto, Japan, pp. 320–323 (2021)

Author Index

Printed in the United States
by Baker & Taylor Publisher Services